················Edge of Crisis

Barbara H. Stein and Stanley J. Stein

Edge of Crisis

War and Trade in the

Spanish Atlantic, 1789–1808

The Johns Hopkins University Press · Baltimore

This book has been brought to publication with the generous assistance of the Program for Cultural Cooperation between Spain's Ministry of Culture and United States Universities.

The Johns Hopkins University Press
2715 North Charles Street
Baltimore, Maryland 21218-4363
www.press.jhu.edu

Library of Congress Cataloging-in-Publication Data

Stein, Barbara H.
  Edge of crisis : war and trade in the Spanish Atlantic, 1789–1808 / Barbara H. Stein,
Stanley J. Stein.
      p. cm.
  Includes bibliographical references and index.
  ISBN-13: 978-0-8018-9046-8 (hardcover : alk. paper)
  ISBN-10: 0-8018-9046-2 (hardcover : alk. paper)
  1. Spain—Commerce—New Spain. 2. New Spain—Commerce—Spain.
3. Spain—History—Charles IV, 1788–1808. 4. Spain—Commercial policy—History.
I. Stein, Stanley J. II. Title.
  HF3685.S736 2008
  382.0946′08—dc22   2008022425

A catalog record for this book is available from the British Library.

Special discounts are available for bulk purchases of this book. For more information, please contact Special Sales at 410-516-6936 or specialsales@press.jhu.edu.

Revolutions . . . are the result of an accumulation of causes and circumstances, "some appearing at the last moment," and none alike in time, place, or caudillo. Lemoine Villacañe

One thought alone preoccupies the submerged mind of Empire. How not to end, how not to die, how to prolong its era. By day it pursues its enemies. . . . By night it feeds on images of disaster. J. M. Coetzee

Contents

· ·

Preface

· ·

A microstudy is best introduced with a macrovision, however sketchy, before the reader gets lost in details. The last quarter of the eighteenth century in the Spanish Atlantic—those maritime highways tying Cadiz in Spain to Spain's colonies in and around the Caribbean as well as the South Atlantic—was a period of marked demographic and economic expansion and a marked political sensibility. The Spanish Atlantic was changing rapidly; the interests of the long-established silver-mining colonies of Peru and New Spain now competed with those of the developing economies of Cuba, Venezuela, and the Rio de la Plata. In the aggregate, the colonial exportables and consumers attracted English and French merchants competing for legal entry into Spain's "regulated" system of colonial trade that *formally* prohibited foreign direct participation. Spain's maritime highways came under pressure, especially in the decade after 1797.

Growth could not be tension-free. To widen the participation of native peoples in a commercializing colonial economy, Madrid introduced the intendancy as a basic administrative element; this, however, disturbed networks tying merchants, colonial district officers, and Amerindian peoples. At the same time, Madrid's policy of broadening trade between colonial and metropolitan ports had a comparably upsetting effect, exacerbated by extensive smuggling. Madrid's transatlantic trading system was caught between pressures to change or to maintain the status quo; further, after 1797 that system had to contend with the power and reach of England's blockading navy in Anglo-Spanish conflicts.

This systemic crisis had an overarching political dimension: revolution. First came the anticolonial insurgency in North America, then the revolutionary French Republic, and then England's paramount role in financing counterrevolutionary Continental monarchies. At the beginning of the eighteenth century the Spanish Atlantic had been the scene of the War of Succession. Over the "long" eighteenth century growth led to divisions between the elites of metropole and colonies, inspiring anxiety, then insecurity, and ultimately fear that the structures of the Spanish Atlantic might collapse. War, again, concluded the century.

This book opens with developments in the Spanish metropole, turns to those overseas in New Spain, and closes with the consequences of fissures between the political classes of Spain and New Spain in late 1807 and early 1808. It attempts a conspectus of an old empire overly dependent on its American colonies and seeks to conjoin the wealthiest colony and metropole—New Spain and Spain—in order to provide broad context of the Spanish Atlantic and to identify and understand how institutions, structures, interests, and ideology resisted pressure for change (or even adaptation) at the end of what has been felicitously termed the "first" Spanish empire. Empires, our data indicate, do not collapse; they crack, crumble at the edges, and erode as they fade away.

We focus on the Spanish empire in the western Atlantic in the unsettling period 1789 to 1808, a period of fluctuating international relationships of national power, trade, and wealth in the Atlantic. On the one hand, an integrated coalition of the political elite at Madrid and in the colonies realized that the foundation of their mature empire rested to an impressive degree on the silver *pesos,* on consumers of New Spain who preferred European wares, and on maintenance of "managed" oligopolistic colonial trade, a policy supported by French interests. On the other hand, England's commercial and industrializing economy was in a phase of rapid expansion and competition on a transatlantic and global scale, in wartime probing the Spanish Caribbean for consumers overseas when buyers on the European continent were cut off and for *pesos* to underwrite England's war effort at home and on the Continent.

This is a complex story parsing the factors leading to the crisis in metropole and colony in the spring of 1808. No historical reconstruction can flawlessly capture a world in rapid transition. This said, the parsing has a metanarrative that starts with Spain's response to the French Revolution and closes in early 1808 with the occupation of Spain by French armed forces and a French design for changing Spain's regime. This, to quote John Keane, "involves immersing readers in the detailed circumstances of a distant era . . . to understand that world . . . as it was experienced" by those who lived in it.[1]

In part the metanarrative describes the resilience of structures of property, wealth, and influence evolving over three centuries under the Hapsburgs and superficially modified under Bourbon monarchs in the eighteenth century. To be precise, at home these structures were a landholding ecclesiastical establishment, a landed aristocracy, a small commercial bourgeoisie, and a loyal, well-structured civil service—all supported by commercial, landed, and ecclesiastical elites as well as by the civil service in the colonies, especially in the major viceroyalties, Peru and New Spain, now three centuries old.

We open with Prime Minister Floridablanca's 1789 decision to isolate Spain and its empire from the contagion of French radicalism. Over the ensuing two decades the empire's "gothic" structures would gradually devour the well-intentioned, open-eyed progressive nationalists hoping to preserve both monarchy and Atlantic empire. By early 1808 two ideological and political factions had crystallized: the *fernandistas,* who were supportive of Charles IV's heir, Fernando, Prince of Asturias, and nostalgic for the old regime; and the *afrancesados,* who were prepared to craft a liberal authoritarian regime along the lines of the Napoleonic model. In fact, there were three factions separated by conflictive views of the future of Spain and its empire in America: the *afrancesados* would opt for a Spanish-crafted adaptation of the French model; the *fernandinos* would resurrect the past; and those behind Prime Minister Godoy, enjoying the confidence of Charles IV and María Luisa, ultimately would try to remove the royal family temporarily to New Spain, repeating the Portuguese royal family's removal to Brazil at the end of 1807 to avoid French occupation.

At bottom, this is a narrative about how an external factor, the catalyst of international warfare, once again forced change in Spain and its American empire. "It's the ending that gives shape and meaning to the otherwise random events that precede it."[2]

In prior volumes of our study we expressed appreciation for the assistance generously given by librarians and archivists in Mexico, Spain, and France. Here I would like to thank the librarians of Princeton University's Firestone Library, members of the staffs of Reference, Circulation, Inter-Library Loan, and Special Collections; without exception they have provided invaluable assistance and shown extraordinary patience. Trudy Jacoby, director of the Visual Resources Collection of the Department of Art and Archaeology, and Joëlle Hadley Stein tenaciously tracked down Robert Cleveley's painting *The Battle of Cape St. Vincent* (1797), at London's National Maritime Museum, reproduced on the cover of this volume. The meticulous copyediting of Joanne Allen is deeply appreciated as are the bibliographical expertise of Francisco Fonseca of Firestone Library's Special Collections and the unfailing technical support of Carla Zimowsk. And we have been blessed with the encouragement of family members and such loyal friends as Peter Johnson and Lois Dowey on innumerable occasions and in many ways.

Most important, this volume is dedicated to Barbara Hadley Stein, who died in December 2005, having completed her contribution to this volume and one to follow. Her insight, the research and organizational skills of a dedicated historian, and her consistently fierce critical eye suffuse this volume, as they did all my previous work.

Part One

Autumn of

Proyectismo

1. Continuity and Crisis, 1789–1797

Rest assured that this matter [*comercio colonial*] is the most important to confront the Nation.
Pedro Rodríguez de Campomanes, August 1788

Our trade with America is immensely useful to us, and we are therefore obliged to spare no effort to prevent its loss and to make it more and more and more exclusive.
Diego de Gardoqui, 16 May 1794

For three decades the administration of Charles III had benefited from the ongoing tension between French and English mercantile and manufacturing interests competing for hegemony in the Atlantic. Spain's entry into the Seven Years' War was delayed until 1761. The loss of two major overseas ports, Manila and Havana, to English forces was a profound shock, but those ports were returned to Spain quickly at war's end. The balance of Charles III's reign was relatively peaceful, except for financial assistance to French forces operating in North America, the Franco-Spanish siege of Gibraltar during the American War of Independence, and the ill-fated attack on Algiers in 1775 under Alejandro O'Reilly. On the whole, Spain enjoyed a period of halting, intermittently sustained initiatives to renovate structures by a small elite core of long-tenured government functionaries, conspicuously moderate "reformers" like Floridablanca, Pedro Rodríguez Campomanes, and Pedro Lerena, respectively prime minister, governor of the Consejo de Castilla, and secretary of the Hacienda (Treasury).

One should not be overwhelmed by the volume of analyses, some published and others pigeonholed, dedicated to the need for structural changes in key economic areas, such as land tenure, tax policy, tariffs, commercial treaties, and protectionism. Nothing better illustrates the wealth of analysis and the poverty of execution than the handling of the sensitive issue of agrarian reform, which surfaced in the 1760s, first entrusted to Campomanes and still unresolved twenty-five years later. Gaspar de Jovellanos, a strikingly facile writer, showed comparable skill as a politically sensitive procrastinator; hence his *Informe de la Sociedad Económica de esta Corte al Real y Supremo Consejo de Castilla en el expediente de la ley agraria* did not come off the press until 1795, and only after the startling agrarian revolution during the initial years of upheaval in France. Career bureaucrats approached change *(reforma)* cautiously; they had to be sensitive to the entrenched, entangled interests of their country's "gothic" structures, and they remained accommodatingly slow in enforcing even mildly reformist policy directives.

Another aspect of continuity in bureaucracy and immobility was striking in the first years of the reign of Charles III's son, namely, a perception evolving over decades that *the* area of realizable economic potential was not the imperial metropole but rather Spain's colonial world in the western Atlantic, especially the Caribbean and circum-Caribbean possessions—New Spain (Mexico), northern New Granada (Colombia), Caracas (Venezuela), and Cuba. While responses to government initiatives in the metropole proved disheartening, they had a more promising reception overseas in the mining colony of New Spain, the late-developing plantations of Cuba and Venezuela, and the cattle-ranching hinterland around Montevideo and Buenos Aires. As a result, Spain's colonial policy developed complementary objectives: to increase contact with newly developing colonial areas while providing stimulus to the long-established ones; to expand the participation of ports in Spain in colonial exchanges at the risk of antagonizing vested commercial interests in the traditional commercial centers, Cadiz, Lima, and Mexico City; and to make available to those seeking to expand exchanges with the American colonies reliable commercial intelligence on shipping, exports and imports, prices current, inventories, and, perhaps essential, an annual merchandise balance of trade. The government proceeded to disseminate these commercial data via an innovative publication aptly titled *Correo Mercantil de España y sus Indias.* Then it still seemed possible that with time and sustained prodding the Spanish metropole might at last become an effective colonial power fulfilling eighteenth-century requirements of a colonial compact. So thought the regime's bureaucrat-intellectuals. They were vectors of public and private interests in Spain's peripheral provinces, their ports and immediate hinterland, who remained relatively effaced. Policy seems to have emanated from Spain's middle- and high-level state civil service, which had informal links to private sectors. Issues of public policy and its implementation were confined to ministerial bodies like the Consejo de Estado and the Consejo de Indias, along with the Hacienda.

Bureaucratic stability and economic expansion in the Spanish transatlantic commercial system, that legacy of the era of Charles III, began to crumble in the four years following his death. The first shock came from revolution in France and the tepid support that a weakened, divided French government could offer Spain in its controversy with English interests over Nootka Sound. The second was the radicalizing phase of the French Revolution, the execution of the French Bourbons, and the third was the influx of counterrevolutionary clerical and other royalist émigrés from France who were resolved to find support and rapport in neighboring Spain for overthrowing the revolutionary government. It was only one step further to abandon the decades-old Franco-Spanish alliance—the "family pact"—originally directed against their common threat, England, and, as England's new ally, invade southeastern France (Roussillon) and cooperate with English naval forces against the French naval base at Toulon—both operations with disastrous results. In 1795 Madrid sought peace with republican France (whose navy it had just helped shatter), renewed its French alliance with the postrevolutionary Directoire, and had to finance outlays for national defense of a magnitude never contemplated. Continuity and crisis, colonies and metropole, America and Spain were now interlocked as never before.

Spain and Its Colonies in the Atlantic Complex

One bright spot, the Spanish Atlantic economy in the late 1780s, sparked exaggerated expectations. It was Prime Minister Floridablanca's memorial of 1788, a justification of his eleven years of leadership, that publicized the single most promising economic achievement of Charles III's reign, the "happy revolution in the commerce of Spain and the Indies,"[1] the surge of colonial trade between metropole and colonies over the decade 1778–88. Aggregate figures for the years 1783–85 show impressive growth, although there is reason to question the percentage of so-called domestic, or "national," goods shipped from peninsular ports to the colonies; certainly the "Spanish" textiles, which were effectively foreign-made, cast doubt on the pace of early industrialization in the most developing region of Spain, Barcelona and its environs. Nonetheless, Floridablanca's *feliz revolución* was one of the few bright spots in the otherwise colorless, not to say disappointing, economic performance of Spain under the ministers of Charles III.

Encouraging signs of trade growth were the result of Madrid's cautious adjustments of imperial trade policy to the economic potential of the American colonies. They had begun in 1765 with the limited opening of the principal metropolitan ports to direct contact with colonial ports in the Caribbean—Havana, San Juan, and Santo Domingo—triggered by the upsurge of shipping, merchandise, and slaves during the English occupation of Havana in 1762–63. In a real sense, Cuba by chance or design became the pilot plant of two administrative innovations in the colonies: the intendancy system and what the government later termed *comercio libre*. It was thirteen years before the imperial trade zone was widened to link peninsular to colonial ports in South America, to Buenos Aires and Montevideo, Santiago de Chile and Callao-Lima, in 1778. Joining France in 1779 in support of the revolt of England's North American colonies delayed the impact of the Reglamento del Comercio Libre of 1778 until 1783. In the meantime the central Andes became the scene of the most extensive violence of America's native peoples before 1810, the uprising of native people under the Native American cacique Tupac Amarú, directed against the exploitative distribution of goods and credit *(repartimiento de mercancías)* by colonial district officers and their immediate subordinates, *corregidores* and *tenientes de corregidores*. From 1782 to 1786 Madrid, basing its actions on the Cuban experiment, installed intendants and *subdelegados* first in Peru and then in New Spain, ineffectually prohibiting *subdelegados* from participating in commercial enterprise. Finally, in 1789, two years after the death of Colonial Secretary José de Gálvez, his replacement, Antonio Valdés, found backing for extending *comercio libre* to two closely linked colonial economies, those of New Spain and Venezuela. Among other initiatives probably designed to undercut the opposition of merchants at Cadiz and Mexico City to the expansion of the imperial trading area, Valdés insisted that the chief colonial officer of New Spain, Viceroy II conde de Revillagigedo, file a report on the local effects of *comercio libre* in 1789. Valdés also dispatched a naval expedition under Alejandro Malaspina to survey colonial economic conditions, much as José Patiño had ordered the naval officers Antonio de Ulloa and Jorge Juan to do fifty years earlier. In addition, Valdés advanced what Gálvez had deftly pigeonholed, the creation of new merchant guilds *(consulados)* in the colonial cities of Veracruz, Havana, Caracas, Buenos Aires, and Santiago de Chile, contracting the jurisdictions of the *consulados* of Mexico City and Lima.

Tangible results of increased trade flows between Spain and its colonies, the prospect of greater exports of Spanish products, and imports of New Spain's silver induced a kind of euphoria among Spain's civil servants, merchants, and manufacturers. In the early years of Charles IV's reign, under

Prime Minister Floridablanca, it seemed feasible to dream that the still-sluggish metropolitan economy might became an effective, rather than cosmetic, imperial power in the Atlantic. Euphoria was another facet of the expectation that the metropole would benefit from colonial expansion. Indeed, some contemporaries speculated that the country's economic buoyancy was a result of the retention of French commercial earnings in Spain and its colonies in 1789–92. French merchants and merchant-bankers were invested in exportables, in discounting letters of credit and IOUs, or, after 1781, in the Banco de España's treasury notes *(vales)* "to protect part of their fortune in case of frightening personal misfortunes." But once Spain joined the First Coalition in the war to suppress the French Republic, those funds, estimated at more than 64 million *pesos,* were transferred to Genoa, London, and Amsterdam.[2]

In the early 1790s what in retrospect seems the challenge of colonial growth and development was somehow matched by competent personnel at the colonial office at Madrid (Antonio Valdés) and overseas at major posts in New Spain (Viceroy Revillagigedo) and Cuba (Captain General Luís de las Casas y Aragorri). Revillagigedo and Las Casas were born in the 1740s, made their careers in the armed forces under Charles III, and were selected for key colonial posts between 1787 and 1790. Valdés y Bazán's family was Asturian and prominent: his father had been *asistente,* then *intendente* in the important province of Seville. Valdés entered the royal navy and was a very junior officer at Havana when English forces besieged that port in 1762.[3] Naval secretary at age thirty-nine in 1783, for a brief period (1787–90) he held jointly the portfolios of navy and colonies ("such a desirable and coveted ministry at that time").[4] As secretary of the navy he pressed the modernization of naval installations at Cadiz, its dry docks, ropewalks, and sail manufacture. As colonial secretary he backed an even wider range of initiatives, breaking with existing practices and irritating merchants entrenched at Cadiz, Lima, and Mexico City.[5] From colonial bureaucrats he insisted on detailed annual financial reports on income, expenditures, and net balances, along with their salaries and pensions.[6] Critical of the inefficient accumulation of formalities imposed on shipping between Cadiz and ports in the colonies, he adopted Diego Gardoqui's suggestions for reducing ship inspections, shifting their administration from the Cadiz *consulado* to naval authorities at that port. From the Casa de Contratación, at Cadiz, he insisted on quarterly reports on stocks of merchandise and their sources (Spanish, European, or colonial), prices current, and interest and exchange rates.[7] To symbolize his independence of Cadiz's commercial interests, he turned down the annual ritual gift of four boxes of chocolate from the *con-*

sulado presented by its Madrid agent.[8] In the same critical vein he aimed to limit the Lima *consulado*'s "delirios de monopolio" by insisting that it stop seeking influence through repeated "hospitality and tidbits" and accept certified imports arriving via the port of Buenos Aires or introduced by Madrid's Cinco Gremios Mayores.[9] Recognizing the need to support the expansion of silver mining in New Spain, he attempted to halt viceregal favoritism in the all-important allocation of mercury, which was fundamental in refining the colony's low-grade ores.[10] It was Valdés who dispatched the naval officer Alejandro Malaspina ostensibly to examine colonial economic conditions while hiding the "real purpose" of Malaspina's commission under the rubric of hydrographic surveys. His meticulously planned and executed three-ship expedition lasted six years; in 1795 he returned to Spain, receiving a warm reception at Madrid.[11] His initial reception and ultimate fate foreshadow the tragic trajectory of events over the decade following his return.

Malaspina returned from his six-year expedition a successful and applauded naval commander and rapidly became absorbed in the Madrid political scene, which was characterized by sharp divisions over policy directions. There was disagreement, for example, about the problem of revolution in neighboring France, until 1789 a model of "reform" from the top, with France effectively exploiting the most valuable plantation economy in the world, the Caribbean island of Saint-Domingue. And discontent surfaced among sectors of the aristocracy suspicious of the appointment of a possible *proyectista*-minded first minister. Floridablanca had been replaced briefly in the early 1790s by the conde de Aranda, a grandee-aristocrat, an independent-minded nationalist, a former ambassador to Paris and pragmatically Francophile. Unlike Floridablanca, Aranda believed that alliance with any French government, monarchy or republic, overrode other considerations in protecting Spain overseas from English military or economic aggression. The opposition to Aranda's policy seemed personified by Manuel de Godoy, whom Charles IV and Maria Luisa had chosen in the hope that he would continue the war against regicide France, as well as Floridablanca's counterrevolutionary position vis-à-vis France's Convention.

The second divisive factor, which was not negligible, was the quiet opposition to counterrevolution among those who hoped for a more responsive, less authoritarian ("despotic") government, containment of the influence of religious institutions over thought and property, and peace with France. Godoy, in brief, took high office when two powerful currents divided the political class. Besides, always in the background were the American colonies, especially New Spain and Cuba, which was undergoing a remarkable economic transformation, and the problem of how to mesh colonial and metropolitan interests harmoniously after the bitter rebellion in Peru under Tupac Amarú, which none discussed publicly.

Malaspina, for reasons that are unclear, thrust himself immediately into these crosscurrents at Madrid. He, along with others, could foresee England's intention to dominate the seas from India to the Pacific Northwest, hence the Nootka incident. Malaspina's public objective was to gather up-to-date hydrographic data; unpublicized and more important an objective was to draft a report on general conditions in Spain's colonies—as one analyst has phrased it, "estudiar la situación de las Indias, como objetivo primordial expedicionario"[12]—after the successful insurrection, financed in part by Madrid, of Britain's North American colonies. It is tenable to presume that he recognized the intimate relationship between the colonies, especially New Spain and Cuba, and their Spanish metropole and the necessity of maintaining the allegiance of powerful *criollo* and *peninsular* elites—all the more so because he had kept abreast of political developments in the new republic of the United States. He found the Madrid of 1794 disturbingly different from what he had left in 1789, and he made no bones about his revulsion. To his brother he wrote, "I find it impossible to describe this country . . . not only the pensions . . . but also the honors showered in that way upon people of that stamp."[13] He criticized Godoy and his administration on several grounds: for failing to gain support from either the traditionalists or the reformers and relying instead on clientelism by generous pensions, unmerited military promotion, and tolerating, if not abetting, the unprincipled pursuit of money, rank, and position. More to the point, he was convinced that the royal household's support for a losing war against Spain's former ally in confronting English expansion had to change. To this he added the judgment that the excesses of the revolution under the Convention were responses to the aggressive tactics of Europe's counterrevolutionary monarchies, with England of course in the lead.

An ingenuous but headstrong Malaspina committed his views to two documents that he circulated. The first hinted at the removal of Godoy, his replacement with the duque de Alba, and the recommendation of new ministerial appointments, including those of the second conde de Revillagigedo, just back from Mexico, and Gaspar de Jovellanos to head the Consejo de Castilla, and the continuation of Malaspina's mentor in the Colonial Office and the navy, Antonio Valdés. The second document openly criticized the government's anti-French policy, recommending a quick peace and a convention of representatives *(diputados)* of Spain's local governments to formulate their position on the ongoing conflict; this was addressed to Charles and María Luisa, both active in foreign policy, for presentation by Malaspina's mentor, Valdés. Appropriately, Valdés sent the document on 14 November 1794 to an insecure Godoy, who condemned the substance of Malaspina's text—it was filled with "seditious ideas" based on "the maxims of revolution and anarchy"[14]—and thus Valdés as well. One week later Godoy, with royal approval and the agreement of the Consejo de Estado, ordered the detention of Malaspina, seizure of his papers, and his imprisonment at the naval base at La Coruña.

To be sure, Godoy had other reasons to silence Malaspina. Many must have known of Malaspina's freeethinking and his interest in U.S. political institutions; he had aboard his ship copies of the *Journal of the United States* and the *Journal of the House of Representatives of the United States,* and even earlier, in the 1780s, agents of the Inquisition had charged him with reading prohibited French and English publications, heretical comments, and irreligious behavior. Small wonder that Godoy might be anxious about Malaspina's depiction of the colonial situation, which Malaspina once hoped might be reviewed by Aranda, Revillagigedo, and Valdés. It might well go beyond the by now canonical *proyectismo,*[15] from which Malaspina separated himself: "I flee from being a *proyectista* who concerns himself with small reforms or uprooting minor shortcomings in government." A situation report on the colonial situation that might be leaked to the public probably motivated the political economist and civil servant Bernabé Portillo, a confidant of Godoy, to suggest that Padre Manuel Gil, an acquaintance, work closely with Malaspina in preparing a draft. Appointed Malaspina's "collaborator and compiler" in July 1795, Gil two months later warned Godoy that Malaspina's manuscript might contain "certain highly circumstantial information" that would require "prudent and discreet silence." At the same time a troubled Valdés told Gil to delete from Malaspina's draft "what the public ought not know about the administration of the Provinces in America," which should be circulated "by separate, secret Memoires."[16] Two months later Malaspina was incarcerated at La Coruña.

The Malaspina episode of 1795 foreshadowed the Escorial affair of 1807 and its sequel at Aranjuez the next spring. There were the close identification of Godoy with his royal patrons, an enduring mutual loyalty; schisms in the political class that threatened high-profile civil servants and their associates, Godoy and soon his finance advisers Miguel Cayetano Soler and Manuel Sixto Espinosa; and the fragility of Spain and its empire in the culmination of the long eighteenth-century conflict between France and England over Atlantic hegemony and, specifically, access to the resources of Spain's American colonies.

Valdés also backed the appointment of Las Casas as Cuba's captain general in 1790. Born in Vizcaya in 1745, Las Casas, through the intervention of the conde de Aranda, became a page at court. In the 1760s he was an army officer in the Caribbean, first at Pensacola, then in Cuba under his brother-in-law Alejandro O'Reilly; also under O'Reilly he participated in the amphibious operation at Algiers in 1775 and in the siege of Gibraltar by Franco-Spanish forces in 1782.[17] On his mother's side he was related to Simón de Aragorri y Olavide, whom the marqués de Esquilache had commissioned to buy grain abroad during Madrid's subsistence crisis of 1765 and who later achieved prominence as an influential Madrid banker and financial adviser to the Spanish government in the 1790s.[18] During the administration of Las Casas, 1790–96, Cuba's sugar economy boomed. Las Casas supported Arango y Parreño's lobbying at Madrid to permit Cuban interests to contact foreign slave traders in the Caribbean, welcomed Valdés's authorization of a *consulado* at Havana, and tolerated trade between Havana and ports in the United States and in the English Caribbean during the war with France, 1793–95. Appropriately enough, along with other residents of Cuba such as Nicolás Calvo, Arango y Parreño, and the second conde de O'Reilly, Las Casas bought land (using O'Reilly as intermediary) and built a sugar mill, "Alejandria," in Güines, near Havana. His fellow army officer Francisco Xavier de Elío praised Las Casas when he was governor of Cadiz in 1799–1800 as "a very enlightened person, truthful, and I have full confidence in his judgment and impartiality."[19]

For the most important post in Spain's colonial service in the colonies, the viceroyalty of New Spain, Valdés picked another military officer, Juan Vicente Güemes y Pacheco, second conde de Revillagigedo. His father had been captain general of Cuba, then viceroy of New Spain, and then, after returning to the metropole, a member of the emergency junta convened by Charles III during anti-Esquilache rioting at Madrid in 1766. His son was born in Havana, entered military service in Spain, and briefly held a post in Panama that he insisted on abandoning, to the lasting annoyance of Charles III, who was not amused by his playboy antics in the company of Charles's brother Luis. Bright, observant, self-confident, and hardworking, a heavy investor in the new Banco Nacional de San Carlos, and, like many military men, a confirmed nationalist, young Revillagigedo was a realist when it came to Spain and its problems. As a nationalist he resented Spain's dependence upon France, convinced that the two nations' economic interests and objectives were incompatible in the long run; he was not, however, an Anglophile. In the 1770s he felt that the metropole had to encourage colonial exports of staples and discourage colonial manufactures that competed with metropolitan re-exports. Not surprisingly, he had a low opinion of the innate capacities of colonial peoples.

Imperial trade, he found, was hampered by counterproductive tax policies and monopolies in the metropole and the colonies. Worse, colonial officers at the district level, the *corregidores* and *alcaldes mayores* that the intendancy system had replaced, still fostered exploitation for the personal profit of underpaid administrators. Hence in 1787 Gálvez's replacement as colonial secretary, Valdés, turned to Revillagigedo for a critical examination of the impact of intendants recently appointed in New Spain. No doubt Revillagigedo's intellectual acuity and knowledge of colonial administration, its current state, and points requiring adjustment led Valdés to appoint him viceroy of New Spain, where he proved to be the colony's most distinguished colonial officer since the sixteenth century. His *instrucción,* or summary report, to his successor was immediately hailed as a classic document when he returned to Spain in 1795, the year Malaspina completed his tour of Spain's colonies in America and the Philippines.[20]

Considered together, Revillagigedo and Las Casas, to whom could be added José Espeleta y Galdiano, viceroy of Nueva Granada from 1790 to 1797, epitomize the flowering of Spain's late eighteenth-century colonial civil service. They shared characteristics: a gentry rather than a noble background; upward mobility; training in the armed forces and discipline that instilled dedication to the "nation" or "state" above loyalty to regional or local interests; and nationalism, which led them to question long-established elements of the "gothic" edifice of empire. This group typified elements within the *militares,* the corps of enlightened officers of Spain's armed forces at the end of the century, who were sometimes at odds with the more traditional state civil servants (*golillas*). They believed that the new American colonies, if managed rationally, could generate wealth and income to finance the expansion of the metropolitan and colonial administrative apparatus, expenditures for the defense of the metropole, and the troublesome public debt. This vision no doubt inspired them to look beyond the classic colonial pattern of importing American silver to pay for European (mostly non-Spanish) manufactures; it meant that inevitably they had to confront government-sanctioned monopolies in the major colonial emporia at Cadiz, Mexico City, Havana, and Lima, as well as in the colonies' webs of distribution.

Seeking a Statistical Base of Colonial Trade

Spain's elites' belief that the colonies were *the* motor of growth for the metropole, in the forefront of policymakers' considerations since the collapse of Esquilache's comprehensive effort in 1766, seemed confirmed by trade summaries available in the late 1780s and early 1790s. By 1783 *comercio libre* showed positive results in peninsular customs returns prepared for the Hacienda's division of Rentas Generales. Exports to the colonies rose reassuringly by a factor of 4.5 on average from 1778 to 1791; and although Cadiz's share of exports (already at 67.4 percent in the base year, 1778) continued to rise despite, or perhaps because of, *comercio libre*, three other Spanish ports previously barred from direct trade with the colonies garnered 17–23 percent.[21] Although Cadiz's closest peninsular competitor, Barcelona, still lagged appreciably, it *seemed* to export a far higher proportion of domestic than of imported goods: Catalan wines and brandies predominated along with textiles.[22] How much of the latter consisted of re-exports is moot. Catalans, it was well known, bought English cottons *(elefantes),* "which they proceed to print, with the result that the highly prized manufactories of Catalonia are really foreign but called national."[23] However, the low cargo value per ship clearing Barcelona for colonial ports suggests that wine and spirits predominated. The reassuring increase in colonial trade and derived government revenue prompted Hacienda secretary Diego de Gardoqui, who had been a diplomat at the busy port of Philadelphia from 1777 to 1790, to counsel fellow members of the Consejo de Estado in 1794 that "our trade with America is immensely useful to us, and we are therefore obliged to spare no effort to prevent its loss and to make it more and more exclusive."[24] For Gardoqui and like-minded members of Spain's political and commercial elites, *comercio libre* was never intended as free trade; it merely expanded the peninsular oligopoly embedded in a widening imperial trade complex.

Spain's mildly interventionist late mercantilism required statistics for policy planning and for informing would-be entrepreneurs in Spain who were entering the colonial trade outside of the major port at Cadiz. "In Europe's current condition, mercantile expertise is so very essential and necessary," a bureaucrat at Cadiz reported to Madrid, "because of its close ties to politics and the government."[25] Exporters at Barcelona and other Spanish outports scrambled to obtain information about consumer preferences, inventories, prices, and shipping facilities at the principal colonial ports of Veracruz, Havana, La Guaira, Cartagena, Montevideo/Buenos Aires and Callao/Lima. In a phase of economic growth when a major component of government income everywhere was customs duties, comprehensive (and comprehensible) port records formed "el Barómetro del Comercio" for calculating government financial resources, as well as the sectoral performance of the economy: "The state of our national manufactories, of our export Agriculture, the rise or fall of foreign industry with our colonies, and finally the Balance of Trade should orient every operation of the Real Hacienda."[26] Small wonder that government finance, degree of government intervention, and the national interest of Spain's old regime were transforming the Hacienda into a commanding state bureau that challenged the more competent civil servants.

The *Correo Mercantil de España y sus Indias*

Preparation of an annual trade balance *(balanza del comercio)* was an innovation Spanish officials borrowed from other European mercantilist states, or so it would seem.[27] The notion of a national annual trade balance had spread from England to France when in 1713 a French civil servant, realizing that recent English trade surveys had revealed France's trade deficits with England, recommended the formation of a Bureau de la Balance du Commerce, which was administered by the private sector, the *fermiers-généraux,* until 1781.[28] In the 1790s, as Madrid focused on domestic manufacture, those annual trade balances provided the basis of industrial protectionism by pinpointing "the profit or loss caused by the nation whose wares we intend to prohibit, to avoid greater loss in the course of avoiding a lesser one."[29] Fundamental to trade data was the availability and reliability of records to be sent to a central collection bureau in Madrid. Yet in the last decades of the eighteenth century such data were neither systematically gathered, uniformly categorized, nor promptly forwarded in Spain, in many instances by pure design rather than because of sheer incompetence.

Efforts to formalize the collection of trade data were initiated as a by-product of the Reglamento del Comercio Libre of 1778. In 1779 Madrid directed colonial officials to gather data on local production, imports, and consumption. These orders were renewed vigorously in 1787, when the newly installed colonial secretary, Valdés, required Contratación at Cadiz to report quarterly on local stocks of "national" and "foreign" goods, staples received from the colonies, prices current, maritime freights, exchange and interest rates, as well as commissions and factors' charges, in order to have an "idea de la Balanza del Comercio" with the American colonies at the metropole's major port, Cadiz.[30] Cognizant of the innate capability of that port's mercantile community to connive with local state servants to postpone inquiries into the colonial trades there, Valdés pointedly requested details about specific data sources. He ordered the president of Contratación, Manuel González Guiral, to request "reports from the consulate, from credit-worthy merchants, and recourse to public data," and, if necessary, even to take depositions from shipmasters returning from colonial ports. Valdés acted on the perception, perhaps somewhat exaggerated, that "in all of Europe there is no commercial center bringing together people of experience and knowledge of what is available and happening anywhere in the universe, because all are joined at Cadiz." Despite such hyperbole, Guiral got no cooperation from officials of the Cadiz *consulado* nor from the local merchant community; some suggested that he approach the local brokers, Spanish and foreign, because "Merchants in general conceal their operations and almost always avoid baring the motives for doing so."[31]

Stonewalling by Spain's most important merchant community was symptomatic of the difficulties the government faced in data collection, leading the *proyectista* (projector) Eugenio Larruga, the activist secretary of the state planning board, the Junta de Comercio, to express amazement that as late as 1789 Madrid "has not been able to obtain a separate and specific report of the goods leaving the kingdom, and those entering."[32] Ultimately a special division responsible for an annual balance of trade materialized six years later, in 1795, but with indifferent success. Government personnel found the data supplied by customs officers at Cadiz unreliable, flawed by "the incoherence and monstrous diversity in the way the Customs operate and set their rates," which produced official accounts "defective and hardly worthy of the name, causing many prejudicial errors." Without reliable data it would be impossible, revenue bureaucrats had to conclude, to improve the nation's trade "to its hoped-for prosperity."[33] What did emerge was the *Balanza del comercio de España con las potencias extrangeras en el año de 1792,* a publication postponed, as was typical, until 1803.[34] This was a meager result despite orders issued in 1800 for biweekly reports of trade with the colonies and Europe and in 1802 for the formation of a combined development and data-collection agency, the Departamento del Fomento Nacional y de la Balanza del Comercio.[35]

Data collection for an annual trade balance made feasible a further government initiative, dissemination of economic information through a periodical for the advancement of national and imperial, rather than provincial, interests. There had been encouraging precedents: Pedro Rodríguez Campomanes's popular publications on economic policy, such as his *Apéndice a la educación popular* (1775), and the recent and widely read *Semanario Erudito de Valladares* (later suspended by Floridablanca because of its dissemination of international, especially revolutionary, events), not to mention the useful articles in the *memorias* of the many regional *sociedades económicas,* which Campomanes had inspired, especially that of Madrid. These informed a small, influential elite prepared to profit from an economic journal. Behind government sponsorship of the properly titled *Correo Mercantil de España y sus Indias* was optimism about colonial economic growth and the metropole's intervention in colonial and foreign trade.

The *Correo* received strong backing from one of three newly created directors of colonial trade (1791), Diego Gardoqui, back from his post at Philadelphia and initially supervising a division of "comercio y consulados" covering metropolitan Spain and the colonies. The *Correo,* it was envisaged, would weekly disseminate commercial information, accompanied by commentary on the general economic scene at home and abroad. Every issue, the prospectus promised, would have a section on the colonies with data on trade volume, shipping, and harvest projections and prices of "American" sugar, cocoa, and cochineal. Like the trade balance, the *Correo Mercantil* would rely on customs officials and the metropolitan and colonial *consulados* for data; and for general economic comment, the periodical's editors planned to reprint articles culled from the *sociedades económicas* as well as from foreign periodicals. *Consulados* in Spain and the colonies were expected to contribute by subscribing to the *Correo,* forwarding data along with other relevant material; and to ensure compliance by the *consulados,* they were directed to send their data to the Hacienda for transmission to the *Correo*'s editors. The editors, Eugenio Larruga and Diego María Gallard, conferred in the planning stages with members of the Junta de Comercio, Moneda y Minas; government oversight and presumably censorship were performed by two assessors, Vicente Alcalá Galiano and Tomás González Carbajal. Months prior to the initial issue of October 1792, Gallard and Larruga circulated a twenty-four-point checklist of data needed from merchant subscribers and then the *Correo*'s prospectus; in late September Madrid ordered the *consulados* to comply.[36] Obviously Madrid stood behind the enterprise confided to the two nationalist, economically oriented editors; the Junta de Comercio alone paid for eighteen subscriptions.[37]

Nonetheless, the responses of the *consulados* varied. In Spain those of Seville, Málaga, La Coruña, and Burgos approved the concept of the *Correo Mercantil* and subscribed immediately. Responses from Lima and Manila were much delayed; eventually Mexico City's merchant guild ordered six subscriptions.[38] An exasperated Gallard complained that the colonial *consulados* not only delayed their subscriptions but then failed to remit "noticias y papeles" mandated by the government. Eventually subscriptions totaled 641 (198 in Madrid and its surrounding area alone), with an unrecorded number of public sales; significantly, among Madrid's subscribers merchants and civil servants predominated.[39] Santander's *consulado* complained that the data it supplied had not been used and expressed outrage that the *Correo Mercantil* had on the contrary printed data that were "barely accurate, and in no way favorable to the country."[40] Cadiz, which had consistently withheld cooperation from the bureau gathering data for an annual trade balance—it had forwarded no breakdown of its exports by provenance, whether "national" or "foreign"—responded in characteristic fashion. A special twelve-man junta selected two of its members (José Antonio Gutiérrez de la Huerta and Miguel de Iribarren) to opine on the nature of the data to be supplied to the *Correo*'s editors, who had been assigned exclusive rights to the periodical's publication.[41] Ever fearful of the government's surveillance of Cadiz's lifeblood, the colonial trades, the *consulado*'s officers offered to publicize commercial information in their own projected periodical and questioned Larruga and Gallard's motives.

Under Spain's old regime the Cadiz merchant community's ethics and strategy of resistance to policies threatening its dominant role mandated raising suspicions about the editors' personal financial stake in the new periodical. Gutiérrez de la Huerta and Iribarren admitted the need for accuracy and reliability. However, could procurement of basic data of high standard be entrusted to one who "has a purely personal interest in its publication"? Their experience proved that in "mercenary hands" standards could deteriorate. Private editors interested "only in their profit" and under the pressure of publication deadlines would not hesitate to skim "original sources" and unavoidably "exaggerate or distort matters, sometimes to make them agreeable and other times for different ends." A discerning but disillusioned public would quickly reject such a publication.[42] How much these merchants drew upon their own business strategies is matter for speculation.

Having questioned obliquely the integrity of the *Correo*'s editors, the two *consulado* members advanced a solution. For so essential a periodical to garner "appropriate reliability," the project should be entrusted to a respected corporate body, to the "care, charge, and name of the *consulado*, whose authority and zeal could supply all the information required and inspire the public confidence needed for acceptance." It would assign an employee to gather data from appropriate offices of the government; then either the employee or a member of the *consulado* would "coordinate and organize clearly, simply, and perceptibly" the materials gathered. It was all quite simple: "the whole operation could be reduced to these simple, hardly annoying operations" for publishing a weekly periodical, to be titled *Semanario de*

Comercio de la Plaza de Cádiz, on sale every Tuesday ("mail day") at the offices of the Cadiz *consulado* or in a public place. A copy would, of course, be made available to the editors of the *Correo Mercantil.* What they termed their "pensamiento," following the approval of the twelve-man junta, was mailed to Gardoqui at Madrid.[43]

Gardoqui (or one of his assessors) recognized the competitive drive *(emulación)* behind the Cadiz merchants' response to the government directive to provide specific kinds of data to the editors of the *Correo Mercantil* and, more important, the *consulado*'s real objective. "The folks at Cadiz" ran the marginal note appended to the *consulado*'s counterproposal, "refuse to allow others to obtain information, and until now no such material has been sent to the *Correo Mercantil.*" Still, the proposed *Semanario de Comercio* was praiseworthy, "muy útil," and an enterprise to be encouraged.[44] Madrid's assessment was clairvoyant: the Cadiz group continued to withhold categorization of exports by provenance, and the *consulado*'s *Semanario de Comercio* never materialized.

The *Correo Mercantil,* the joint brainchild of the Hacienda and the Junta de Comercio, lasted sixteen years, during which it was plagued by administrative turnover, data shortcomings, and what may be labeled a deliberate lack of cooperation from *consulados* at home and abroad. Larruga, simultaneously secretary of the Junta de Comercio and personally committed to editing two multivolume series based on the junta's archives, soon ceded his share in the enterprise to Gallard. After three years Gallard petitioned for another appointment in the metropole or overseas; later he managed the government-subsidized cotton manufacture at Avila. The Departamento del Fomento Nacional y de la Balanza del Comercio ran the *Correo* for the next four years, until Gallard reassumed editorial responsibility in 1799.[45] Yet in mid-1798 a government commission turned in a pessimistic prognosis: it doubted that any appreciable improvement was possible, especially in view of reservations on the part of Gallard, his collaborators, and the Hacienda's Dirección General de Rentas about shortcomings in the economic data forwarded by customs houses in Spain: inaccuracies, unreliability, and lack of homogeneity.[46]

There was another, equally critical factor. The *Correo*'s major sources of data, the *consulados* at home and abroad, cooperated reluctantly, probably antagonized by the explicit economic philosophy of the editors. In advertising the hope of engaging contributors, Larruga and Gallard had appended their candid reflections on trade, whose general thrust would discomfit a body that in fact enjoyed a virtual oligopoly of Spain's transatlantic exchanges with its colonies. Mirroring a sense of realism current among a small group of high public servants, their reflections on economic policy stressed commercial liberty over customary and government constraints—a scarcely veiled critique of managed colonial trade—and the overriding importance of exchanging nationally made or processed goods for imported colonial staples, while stressing the inherent dangers of long-term dependence upon the metropole's specie re-exports to cover imported manufactures.[47] These principles hardly endeared the *Correo Mercantil* to Cadiz, whose profits came mainly from the re-export of European imports in exchange for New Spain's and Peru's precious metals. For that matter, Gaditano merchants would not tolerate the *Correo*'s warnings about disregarding prohibitions on certain imports or failing to favor domestic manufactures.[48] To be sure, the Cadiz m·rchant community did have some legitimate grounds for withholding collaboration. In 1798 the *Correo Mercantil* inadvertently printed an article reporting that a ship belonging to the Cadiz firms of Guerra y Sobrino and F. Bustamante y Cia, carrying fake papers to elude English blockaders, was in fact Spanish-owned and bound for Veracruz in wartime with a Spanish cargo. As a result, an English blockader took the ship as a prize to Gibraltar, and the *Correo Mercantil* suspended publication of notices of departing vessels for as long as Spain remained at war with England.[49]

On balance, the periodical's appearance manifested the optimism in a few circles of the Spanish government during a brief opening before 1795. It also served as a medium for communicating in manuscript the government's developmental propensities to a small audience made up largely of well-intentioned civil servants and inspired preparation of the *Balanza del comercio de España con los dominios de SM en America en . . . 1792*, not published until 1805. The *Correo Mercantil* did fulfill one of its promises by making available commercial intelligence, albeit of varying reliability—nothing comparable had appeared before in Spain—along with a selection of annual reports issued by the newly created *consulados* at Buenos Aires, Veracruz, and Guatemala and the colonial official press.[50] Its shortcomings, and there were many, were evident in the generally disparate nature of articles drawn from European publications and in its strikingly small subscription lists.[51]

The Civil Service: Vanguard of Change

The relatively large number of subscribers in and around Madrid and the disproportionate number (16) purchased by the Hacienda alone underscore the role of ministerial groups in initiating change in the Spanish imperial trading system. In an old regime of few bourgeois or few bourgeois institutions imbedded in an essentially agrarian economy and a correspondingly circumscribed space for bourgeois aspirations, civil servants experimenting with a few mercantilist initiatives had to serve as the vanguard of economic experimentation. For instance, the Hacienda played a paramount role as the Spanish state tried to mobilize fiscal resources for national defense; the number of the Hacienda's personnel alone, Francisco Cabarrús, the French-born merchant-banker at Madrid, once estimated, may have increased by almost nine thousand over the twenty-year period from 1775 to 1795.[52] In general the civil service attracted intellectuals (far more than did the eighteenth-century religious establishment), many of them economists (*proyectistas*), political commentators, critics (usually safely anonymous), and literary figures. An expanding civil service afforded a ladder of upward mobility, steady (usually underpaid) employment, retirement benefits, perquisites and status, and especially entry into the prestigious Orden de Carlos III. State service assured the orderly functioning of government, continuity along with some social mobility to a growing professional middle class, and the incorporation of very competent adherents into an old regime based upon the principle of privilege—in no way contradictory.

Stability and continuity of state service, on the other hand, perpetuated local fiefdoms held by the "caciques of this Kingdom," as Intendant Eusebio Ventura Caro once complained to Prime Minister Floridablanca, who could hamstring change because "customarily one solicits comment on abuses in the bureaucracy from employees who are anxious about or unable to admit the abuses, and from others usually with an interest in preserving the abuses that should be eliminated."[53] Between the hesitant and the sly bureaucrats "it is easier to sideline any decree or law than to distract an animal in a bullring."[54] A fresh breed of optimistic civil servants occupied influential posts for a few years after 1787; prominent functionaries like Antonio Valdés at Indias and Gardoqui, Mariano Luis Urquijo, conde de Casa Valencia, Pedro Aparici, Soler, and Sixto Espinosa in the Hacienda were determined not only to propose but also to execute policy in a consistent fashion. After four years of service in the Hacienda, in 1794 Gardoqui could boast that his ministry had stimulated colonial trade "as a consequence of measures recently applied according to a constant, uniform system."[55]

This was consistent with the sentiment prevailing ever since the coup that had removed the "reforming" minister Esquilache in 1766. Thereafter, policymakers in Madrid understood that improved trade with the colonies in America could originate only outside (i.e., despite) the public and private networks centered on Cadiz. Together the persistent informal connections between government personnel in the Casa de Contratación and the *con-*

sulado at Cadiz "managed" colonial trade and shipping, forming a bottle-neck that the Esquilache regime attempted to break at the customs house and through the Reglamento de Barlovento and the *comercio libre* of 1765. The death of Colonial Secretary Julián de Arriaga permitted his replacement, José de Gálvez, to restructure the ministry and complete another phase of *comercio libre* despite Cadiz's opposition. Ultimately, however, Gálvez had to accommodate his ministry to the Cadiz commercial-bureaucratic complex. On his death, however, Antonio Valdés supervised the division of the ministry into two sections, Gracia y Justicia (Ecclesiastical Affairs and Justice) and Guerra, Comercio y Navegación (Defense, Trade and Navigation). And more reorganization was to come. To Colonial Secretary Valdés and Hacienda Minister Lerena it was obvious that Lower Andalusian networks, the collusion between Contratación and *consulado* at Cadiz, between public and private sectors, remained intact, capable of resisting Madrid's intention to push ahead with modifications in the transatlantic trading system by extending *comercio libre* to New Spain and Venezuela, creating new merchant guilds in the peninsula and the colonies, and collecting and disseminating trade and shipping information.

In May 1790 Madrid again resorted to policy modification by further administrative restructuring of colonial affairs. As part of the redistribution of colonial authority to other ministries, the Hacienda section of the Colonial Office, was placed in a joint ministry, Hacienda de España e Indias supervised by three directors: one covering North America (Pedro Aparici), another for South America (Casa Valencia), and a third for a very new division covering the peninsula, Negocios de Comercio y Consulados (Gardoqui).[56] The change in the handling of colonial economic affairs was for its time radical, evident in the broad authority now vested in Gardoqui's directorship. His office took jurisdiction over *comercio libre* in metropole and colonies, current and planned *consulados* (Hacienda's intentions were signaled), the revitalized trade in African slaves in response to pressure from Cuba's planters, and, not least, the Casa de Contratación at Cadiz. When the Cadiz *consulado* lodged a complaint about being moved from the jurisdiction of the Consejo de Indias to that of the Hacienda de España e Indias, it was rejected; and Contratación, hitherto controlled nominally by Madrid but in fact by Andalusian merchant groups, was abruptly eliminated in June.[57] Aware of Cadiz's inveterate lobbying techniques using its own funds and those remitted from the *consulados* at Mexico City and other colonial centers, the *consulado* was cautioned against holding juntas without government approval or subsidizing writings *(escritos)* on economic matters, even those approved by its *junta general*. More specifically, the legacies of Spaniards who died overseas, formerly deposited with the Colonial Office, were now assigned to the main Hacienda office at Madrid. The reasons were poor recordkeeping and failure to forward the funds to relatives in the peninsula.[58] Lerena, Valdés, and Gardoqui had decided effectively to circumscribe the influence of Spain's major commercial establishment, which had been unbending in resisting changing national and international trends.

Expansion of the Merchant Marine

By merging Contratación and Consulados under Gardoqui's administrative writ, Madrid signaled its intention to address a major bottleneck in colonial shipping, namely, the formalities at Cadiz for checking ships' seaworthiness before departing for colonial ports. These were particularly vexing at a moment when an increasing volume of traffic with the colonies required more ships sailing more frequently. Cadiz shipowners *(dueños de navios)* had enjoyed a virtual monopoly of shipping to selected colonial ports as long as New Spain and Peru remained excluded from *comercio libre*. As Gálvez was notified explicitly in 1786, "Cadiz has invested 3 million *pesos* in ships of four hundred to six hundred tons designed for the Indies trade that are fitted out only for Veracruz and Lima . . . consequently its freight charges are larger than those of the Kingdom's other ports."[59] Crews at Cadiz were larger than average, and ships' turnabout times there were longer. Yet according to one estimate, by concentrating on the high-value carrying trade with Veracruz and Lima, Cadiz earned on average about 44,000 *pesos* per round trip of sixteen months.[60] This situation enabled Gaditanos to insist on traditional ship inspections by Contratación employees, "examination and approval of hulls, fitting out, and licenses," which required proof of Spanish registry, Madrid-issued license to sail to colonial ports, nominal capacity and actual cargo loaded (including its composition by national or foreign origin), crew size, and provisioning, and a passenger list.[61] Shipowners also insisted that ships sail directly to their listed colonial port of destination and return to their peninsular port of departure. Such requirements inspired a report of 1790 to the effect that "navigation at Cadiz is the world's most expensive because of useless and costly careening, which causes so much delay. No other nation has them, nor their large crews, messes, and other expenses incompatible with a commercial economy; these . . . retard the advance of liberty while raising prices that prejudice consumers at home and overseas." Complacency was no preparation for competition. Once *comercio libre* included Veracruz, the commercial community of Cadiz had at last to confront aggressive, cost-conscious shipowners of other peninsular ports, such as Barcelona, who were now competing for the profitable trade with New Spain.[62]

Two factors drew Catalan and other merchants in Spain's peripheral provinces into colonial shipping in the initial decade of the reign of Charles IV. There was a "push" factor as ships from Italy, France, England, Holland, Sweden, and Denmark continued to compete with Spaniards in Spain's coastal and Mediterranean carrying trade, depressing freight rates and profit margins.[63] A second factor was promulgation of *comercio libre* in 1765 and again in 1778, which "opened the ocean to all Spaniards who, absent duties and expenses, may sail to the Windward Islands," eliminating multiple ship inspections, reducing the cost of others, and eroding Cadiz's century-old hold over traffic to the Caribbean and South American possessions. In addition, *comercio libre* in the early 1770s, by incorporating Louisiana, Yucatan, and the port of Santa Marta, stimulated other merchants to enter the colonial trades and expand the Spanish merchant marine for overseas trade. "Profits in overseas shipping were immeasurably greater and more advantageous than those in coastal shipping."[64] Shipmasters had no problem recruiting seamen, who migrated from the interior to peninsular ports in order to sign on, many intending to jump ship in colonial ports to take advantage of the opportunity to "better their fortune." Perhaps 12–16 percent of outbound crews never returned; shipowners blamed desertions on "wasteful spending at sea . . . on gambling, because of subordination and the fact that no sooner on land, they abandon ship at the first or another port."[65] Meanwhile, farmers and artisans invested in the construction of efficient and fast vessels of 100–200 tons, a valuable addition to the limited pool of commercial capital available.[66] Barks and *polacras* required smaller crews (downsizing from 500- to 250-ton vessels allowed for a 60% reduction in crew size); and once in colonial waters, they usually participated in the growing intercolonial carrying trade. Spain's transatlantic shipping may have increased by 16 percent in the years 1779–88.[67]

Since profit margins on small vessels were low, earnings depended upon operational efficiencies, small crews of low-wage seamen, short layovers, and bypassing wherever possible traditional peninsular shipping formalities. "Freedom from exit fees and the end of the old trammels" still persisting under *comercio libre* indicated to shipowners that "profits and advantages in their operations should consist in multiplying them at low cost, something impossible with large Vessels." It became common for small ocean-going ships either to find cargo or to abandon port without extended layover since freight rates alone "do not compensate long layovers."[68]

Expectation of profits generated by the colonial trades stirred speculative fever among Spain's petty bourgeois, who bought shares *(porciones)* in shipping. It infected as well shipmasters and supercargos, who enriched themselves licitly and illicitly and made no effort to conceal their new prosperity, or so it seemed to the envious among the custom-bound. "The old simple attire of shipowners and ship officers," it was commented, "became showy, and outfitting costs ballooned." *Patrones* undertook voyages without prior notice to shareholders *(porcionistas),* stayed overseas for extended periods without corresponding, or on returning to the peninsula neither filed an accounting of operations nor presented falsified ones.[69] They would ask shareholders in the enterprise to provide maintenance funds, which they then used to speculate in export goods; without informing shareholders, they raised additional capital by mortgaging their ships and future freight income, applying these funds to "covert speculation . . . entirely profitable only to the shipowner." This thirst to become rich overnight and risk free often terminated in drawn-out litigation, while the ships in question remained in port, a loss to all concerned.[70]

At this point the inability of *consulados* in Spain to perform their judicial functions impartially became a source of conflict. They tended to overlook legislation (prescribed in the *Ordenanzas generales de la Armada*) mandating that mortgagees be informed of any prior financial obligations of *patrones,* and they insisted on trying such cases in their courts, although adjudication was the "particular and exclusive attribution of the Marine courts."[71] The problem was the "espíritu de cuerpo," widespread in *consulado* courts, which favored "the corporation's members to the prejudice" of outsiders. By implication, the rights of merchants who had speculated in ship mortgages were favored over the rights of shareholders. Favoritism often took the form of "the sluggish procedures of our courts and insistence on reports that only the Lord knows how and when they will be finished" or by hewing to the "rigorous *consulado* method, 'Truth be known and good faith kept.'"[72]

No purpose is served in exaggerating the expansion of Spanish-registry shipping after 1783. While the number of low-tonnage vessels increased between 1779 and 1788, this growth must be viewed in comparative perspective: in 1788 England's merchant marine (with 13,827 ships) was roughly four times the size of Spain's (2,835).[73] Nonetheless, even the small increase in merchant shipping in the colonial trades troubled the small number of shipowners at Cadiz, who were struggling to preserve the virtual monopoly of their port against competitors at home and in the colonies. The perquisites of long-shared oligopoly are not readily relinquished. Despite a decade or more of *comercio libre* after 1778, and despite new policies advocated by influential Madrid ministries during the transition from Charles III to Charles IV, shipowners at Cadiz demonstrated their unwillingness—or was it sheer inability?—to value national and imperial over local and regional priorities.

For example, they complained that *consulados* in Spain's other ports failed to require formal inspection of ships sailing to colonial ports; they insisted on reenforcing "regulations that formerly were not observed" covering formal "careening and fitting out of ships in the Indies trade."[74] It was still the practice at Cadiz that large vessels undergo inspection prior to departure, in no small measure to ensure the safe arrival of their high-value cargo; for low-tonnage vessels, now common, such inspections were an unnecessary expense. We know that more than 45 percent of ships registered at Cadiz were *fragata*-class vessels, those of 251 tons or more.[75]

Then in 1791 fifteen Cadiz shipowners laid before the Madrid authorities a litany of complaints summarizing their dissatisfaction with the government's policy of broadening national participation in colonial shipping and trade. They charged that in colonial ports competition among ships from many peninsular ports was lowering freight rates to "ridiculously low levels," as cargo carriers from unnamed ports (Barcelona?) deprived other ports (Cadiz?) of "cargo they could handle legitimately." Equity in a "well-managed trade" required, first, that peninsular ports "certify only their own ships and exclude those from other ports from their trade" and, second, that ships clearing peninsular ports for the colonies must stick to the "single port listed in their exit papers and none other." Third, the shipowners considered it an abuse that ships from the colonial ports carry precious metals and staples to Spain and immediately return, undercutting shipowners in the metropole, whose vessels bore the additional expense of "careening and fitting out" before setting sail. Instead, they insisted, colonial-registry ships should be confined to their intercolonial trade. The litany ended on a traditional note of imminent disaster: "Ships are ruining their owners, evident in such poor returns that . . . Owners prefer to get rid of them."[76]

The director of Negocio y Consulados, Gardoqui, made clear, however, that Cadiz's effort to hamstring competition in colonial trade was unacceptable. Supervision of ship inspection was then shifted to the naval office at Cadiz.[77] Next, in 1791 the Junta de Estado suspended formalities "now or formerly observed" on ships loading for the colonies and rejected outright Cadiz's insistence that the ships return only to their peninsular port of departure. In fact, Gardoqui ensured that peninsular shipping could call at multiple colonial ports to deliver or collect cargo on the inbound voyage;

and to better integrate colonial economies, he authorized peninsular ships to carry New Spain's silver *pesos* to Venezuela for purchasing and loading cocoa, coffee, indigo, and sugar. At the same time, Gardoqui pressured foreign merchant firms at Cadiz to keep their accounts in Spanish, authorizing the *consulado* to enforce the order.[78] There was more. In Lerena's reorganized Hacienda, Gardoqui, presumably along with Casa Valencia and Aparici, pressed civil servants at Cadiz to loosen the cozy relationship between agents of the Colonial Office there and the *consulado*. It was obvious to the Cadiz merchant community that aggressive Hacienda functionaries were unsympathetic and convinced that the merchants evaded payment of duties and in general bypassed legal formalities.[79]

The Fate of a National *Consulado*

Lerena and Gardoqui also pursued another tack to minimize the obstructionist tactics of Cadiz and peninsular and colonial *consulados,* grafting new functions onto old structures. Typical of the mentality and praxis of the civil service in Spain's old regime, rather than eliminating an outmoded practice, Hacienda officials tried to gather all the *consulados* under an umbrella organization, a national *consulado* at Madrid variously labeled a "consulado general," "consulado y junta general de comercio," or "consejo supremo de comercio."

This initiative was not without precedent. As part of the seventeenth-century nostalgia of the *arbitristas*—their hope of reviving "Spain's former era of plenty"—the Habsburg government in 1632 had projected a *consulado* at Madrid with four consuls drawn from the Spanish empire in Europe— from Aragon, Portugal, Italy, and the Low Countries; its *prior,* however, had to be "one born in the kingdom of Castile." Nothing materialized, the reasons for which historian Eugenio Larruga sidestepped by saying, "I don't aim to examine."[80] The idea resurfaced in 1705 under the first Spanish Bourbon and was revived in 1766 under the marqués de Esquilache, advanced in 1775 by the prominent merchant Juan Antonio de Los Heros in the form of a "Supremo Consejo de Estado y Comercio, de Extrangería, Fábricas, Minas y Moneda" and supported by the naval officer and royal tutor Thomás Southwell. Southwell would include representatives from Spain *and* the American colonies, "the infallible, subsidiary help and primary resource."[81] In the 1780s Francisco Cabarrús, whose meteoric career as a Frenchman in Spanish finance gave him grounds for assessing the overall performance of Spanish merchants, recommended a "Supremo Consejo de Comercio" modeled on France's Conseil du Commerce as a way to enlighten peninsular merchants on trade and related matters. He believed that merchants serving on both a local and a national *consulado* might welcome the opportunity to "inform themselves, practice speaking in public, accept concepts of the public good they completely lack, and, above all, better educate their children." The lure of such service might also better the overall quality of *consulado* officials, whom Cabarrús deprecated as "lesser-known merchants" seeking in *consulado* officeholding "compensation for what they fail to earn in their profession."[82] The repeated revival after the 1760s of the notion of a national trade council underscored the necessity at the end of the century to coordinate colonial development with the needs of the metropole. Larruga lamented in the 1790s that no national economic council had yet been formed because, as he observed diplomatically, "other concerns prevented it" and because matters of trade and navigation fell under at least eight uncoordinated agencies. Policy remained plagued by "perplexity and sluggishness," as one Veracruz *consulado* official would later comment.[83]

The growth of colonial trade, pressure for regional *consulados* in Spain and overseas, and the unrealized aspiration of some ministers under Charles IV to "crown their labors with the desirable establishment of the Consulado and Junta General" ideated in his father's reign induced Lerena, probably abetted by Gardoqui and Valdés, to revive in 1791 the idea of a bureau of national development combining oversight of all *consulado* affairs with the economic-planning function of the Junta General de Comercio.[84] While this review was under way, the newly appointed prime minister, Manuel de Godoy, received in 1793 a "Plan del Consulado y Consejo de Comercio" under a cabinet-level minister ideated by a Barcelona merchant, Josef Francisco Vila, responding to Godoy's innovative appeal to the general public for advice.

Spain, Vila argued, needed a "cuerpo director" (planning agency) to block, among other things, the expansionism of an unnamed power, obviously England—"a Nation that, employing the arrogant power of its Navy, hopes, to the detriment of all and especially of us, to take command of the trade of the four quarters of the world." Vila's view of Spain's relative economic "backwardness and the gap between us and foreigners" motivated his proposal to coordinate consular jurisdiction and formulate guidelines covering trade, industry, and agriculture. His project criticized what later critics would classify as classic dependency: Spain sold abroad, Vila noted, "our wools, cotton, silk, barilla, and other primary materials, only to buy their woolens, bays, muslins, brocades, glassware and other wares," while foreigners distributed in Europe Spain's colonial staples of "cochineal, indigo, sugar, hides." At last, he pointed out, Spain had an opportunity to shed "this shameless dependence" and reduce its annual "appalling" trade deficits. Hence his project for a new government body fusing the functions of a national *consulado* and a junta general de comercio, directed by the prime minister, with broad authority over trade and industry, *consulados* and large, publicly held companies, and responsible for formulating a commercial code, for uniform customs regulations and rates, for setting import quotas on grains, salt fish, linens, and hardware, for preparing trade balances, and for setting up schools and libraries of commerce. The personnel of his proposed agency could be recruited from public and private sectors, from civil servants and wholesale merchants; explicitly excluded were retail traders— merchants, storekeepers, remainderers, traffickers, or retailers.[85]

Circulated by the Junta de Comercio, Moneda y Minas to all *consulados* in Spain, Vila's project drew responses from those of Valencia, Bilbao, Barcelona, and Cadiz. Barcelona's preferred simply to broaden the authority of the already constituted Junta de Comercio. Others agreed on a new cabinet-level ministry entirely separate from the proposed general *consulado* at Madrid or the current Junta de Comercio. However, no *consulado* questioned the proposed ministry's wide developmental authority, quoting Cadiz, "to inspire, stimulate, and undertake matters and obligations inaccessible to individual merchants"; to organize schools of commerce and language instruction in English, French, and Italian; and to draft a uniform national commercial code for regulating large mercantile firms and handling commercial litigation. Support was widespread for a high court of appeal within the proposed body to review all commercial litigation in order to eliminate the multiple overlapping jurisdictions that merchants faced in appealing to higher bodies—"consejos, direcciones y secretarías." Cadiz's *consulado* welcomed a new "Junta o Consejo del Comercio General" with jurisdiction over *consulados* in the peninsula and overseas; understandably it was troubled, however, by the recent reorganization shifting peninsular *consulados* from the oversight of the Consejo de Indias to that of the more demanding Hacienda de España.[86]

On two major issues agreement was notable. The four *consulados* insisted on the exclusion of all petty tradesmen from representation in the contemplated national junta because, to quote Cadiz merchants, they lacked "leading, universal concepts." Second, all expected the national *consulado* to limit the operations of large companies whose capital resources and "special privileges" bestowed by the government permitted them to dominate smaller enterprises, the individual companies. Here the Cadiz group followed its customary resistance to competition from large, corporate bodies, whether Madrid's Cinco Gremios Mayores, the Compañia de Filipinas, or the Banco Nacional de San Carlos. So the *consulado* requested that such enterprises have no direct representation on the forthcoming national economic council.

Last, the Cadiz *consulado,* which had drafted by far the most comprehensive *informe,* seized the opening to criticize the unsympathetic, adversarial style of Hacienda employees toward members of its commercial community. Gardoqui had just split the central accounting section *(contaduría general)* into two, one with oversight of *consulados* in the metropole.[87] The proposed economic ministry should not, *consulado* officials felt, continue the preoccupation of Hacienda personnel with revenue collection by enforcing "the obstacles, ridiculous formalities, vague mistrust, and improper trivialities," disregarding the fact that "Commerce is declining" and thus men of business needed "reasonable . . . profits." The ministry should not assume that a merchant's main goal was to "evade legitimate payment of duties, or avoid formalities." Under the current conditions of *comercio libre* Cadiz was "very distressed and harassed . . . more enslaved than ever." This lament hardly squared with what was already known about the upsurge of Cadiz commercial activity after about 1784.[88]

Apparent unanimity on most points raised by Vila's project for a national board of trade and development did not guarantee adoption by authorities at Madrid. An initial obstacle may have been the reservations of two civil servants who were holdovers from the reign of Charles III, Pedro Rodríguez Campomanes, *gobernador* of the Consejo de Castilla, and Josef Ibarra, a *fiscal* of the Consejo de Hacienda. They preferred that the government representatives on the proposed body be drawn from personnel in the Colonial Office and the Treasury and that each *consulado* appoint a representative; overseas, however, selection of *consulado* representatives would devolve on colonial officials—a significant difference. Campomanes and Ibarra, like Cabarrús, had grave reservations about the quality of representatives that might be chosen by *consulados,* because "our *Consulados* have many members whose election to office would be improper because they lack education and commercial know-how"; hence their reluctance to accept Vila's provision for a separate ministry.[89] Instead, they wanted the proposed body to adapt English and French models, in which representative of business and government were purely consultative; policy would still be decided by ministers of state. Their most important caveat concerned Vila's inclusion of a judicial function for the contemplated national *consulado.* The mountain of criticism directed at the delaying tactics of *consulado* courts motivated the categorical opinion of Campomanes and Ibarra: "It is inappropriate for this Tribunal to decide lawsuits," an interminable source of contention and "very destructive of the institution."[90] For a high civil servant like Campomanes, experienced in matters concerning trade, the presence of *consulado* representatives on what Cadiz was already calling a *consejo del comercio* was an unacceptable suggestion.

A second, perhaps greater obstacle may have been members of the Junta de Comercio who delayed moving ahead with Vila's project, or so Vila insinuated in May 1797. By then Godoy's initial *appertura* was fast vanishing. Writing to Prime Minister Godoy four years after submitting his plan, Vila complained that although he had responded to the critique of his initiative by the Junta de Comercio, no action had been taken nor word provided of the status of his dossier. He confessed that he did not know how "to grasp the reasons for the Junta General to withhold for a long time reports in its possession including the Fiscal's name, an incomprehensible silence on such an important matter." That *fiscal* was José Cistúe y Coll, whose fifteen-year career in the colonial bureaucracy—at Quito, New Spain, Guatemala, then *fiscal* of the Consejo de Indias at Madrid—must have suggested a cozy relationship with Cadiz commercial groups.[91] In addition, there was a note of urgency in Vila's letter. He recalled that the French government under the Directoire—again Spain's main ally in a war against England—had assembled a representative body of merchants to draft an economic program in an effort to revitalize the French economy. It behooved Spain to form a similar planning body, a "consulado o consejo de comercio," for calculating "convincingly how to counteract the large goals and ambitious projects of another Nation, which, relying on the arrogant power of its navy, seeks to take over the whole trade of the four quarters of the globe, prejudicing every other nation and especially ours." To counter English threats to Spain's transatlantic trade was, Vila emphasized to the prime minister, "the indispensable formation of a system," precisely what Vila had advanced four years earlier.[92]

The last item in Vila's dossier is a report of 1799 from the Junta de Comercio's Manuel Ximénez Bretón to the Hacienda minister, Mariano Luis Urquijo. Discussion of the dossier, Bretón advised, had been suspended pending a minority opinion *(voto particular)* from *fiscal* Cistúe, delayed by overwork and sickness.[93] Was this another example of a late eighteenth-century initiative pigeonholed by special interests colluding with "civil servants who will keep it for an eternity," just as nothing came of a much-applauded but never realized effort to form a uniform, national commercial code?[94]

2. War and the Colonies: Aranda and Godoy

Without the support of one of the two, we risk everything we have overseas.
Consejo de Estado, 24 August 1792

The interests of the Spanish nation are naturally opposed to those of England.
Bernardo Iriarte

Repercussions of the revolution in France upon Spain's empire in America had much to do with Spanish authorities accepting Rafael Antúnez y Acevedo's implicit argument. We must remember that returns on colonial trade from 1789 to 1792 had inspired optimism in the metropole. Trade reform seemed to correlate positively with expanding silver exports from New Spain, the world's silver-mining center, complemented by income from nonmetallic exportables like sugars from Cuba and Venezuela and hides, tallow, and salt beef from Rio de la Plata ports.

There was a downside, of course. A rising tide of government expenditures on a large royal household and patronage (the civil list), the defense establishment, and interest and amortization of the public debt (now the *vales*) produced annual peacetime deficits. Unsettling was fear that any involvement in international conflict would put already stretched finances at peril, leading to the state of affairs that had obliged the neighboring Bourbon monarchy to convene in desperation its Estates General, which had been followed by revolution, a defensive war, and the insolvency that the Directoire confronted after 1795.[1] More comforting, a buoyant colonial economy generating government revenues and profits to the business sector was a major factor in policy planning; more than ever the colonies were an irreplaceable source of silver and staples, a promising market for the exports and re-exports of the metropole. Yet colonial prosperity was imperiled by Anglo-French trade competition, by uncontrollable smuggling, and by the wide-ranging operations of England's navy in wartime.

Now more than ever, preservation of the colonies in America was *the* critical factor in Spain's international relations during the recurrent conflicts after 1792 between English and French commercial interests and, for that matter, in domestic politics. Directly and indirectly, colonial interests figured prominently in the last phase of Floridablanca's ministry, in the strikingly short-lived Aranda ministry, and in the subsequent decade and more of Manuel Godoy's administration. For policymakers at Madrid, as Bernardo Iriarte had stressed, the guiding principle remained neutrality. If that proved impossible, they had a difficult choice: either the most reliable supporter of an intact empire in America, France, or England. Realistically, neither the French navy, the French merchant marine, nor smugglers could threaten the Spanish colonies in the immediate future.

Floridablanca stayed on as prime minister in the first four years of Charles IV's reign. Since 1776 he had been the dominant figure in Madrid, gradually controlling the work of ministerial colleagues, often bypassing or overruling the Hapsburg legacy of *consejos* and deference to the aristocracy.[2] Floridablanca and associates in the various ministries, Francisco Cabarrús reflected at one point, "aimed to rectify, according to their own lights, the reports and sentences of the courts exercising in the name of the King the formation and application of the laws."[3] Young Charles, when Prince of Asturias in 1781, had complained of Floridablanca's administrative style to Aranda, then ambassador at Paris: "Ministers are absolute rulers in their domain; just look at Moñino [Floridablanca]."[4] Floridablanca's long tenure, judgment, and conservatism earned broad respect, but resentment from the more engaged *ilustrado* elements in the civil service, in society, and among bypassed aristocrats. Inevitably he became the target of anonymous widely circulated pamphlets *(libelos),* often drafted by a younger generation of bureaucrat-intellectuals hankering for innovative leadership and approaches to perennially postponed problems, chaffing at "abusos de autoridad," "poder arbitrario," or "despotismo ministerial"—even before Godoy's regime.[5]

The *libelos* were symptomatic of an intergenerational conflict and a logical response to decades of bureaucratic continuity and complacent rigidity. By the early 1790s both Floridablanca (the archetypical *golilla*) and his successor in the ministry, Aranda *(militar),* were sixty-five years or older and had been politically prominent since the 1760s. Floridablanca had kept France at a distance, wary of the contagion of concepts popularized or published there and quickly taken up by literary circles in Spain (as French fashions had been among the elite).[6] To complaints about tight-reined administrative tactics, Floridablanca's critics added his knee-jerk reaction to the first signs of radicalization in France in 1789. He directed the Inquisitor General to confiscate publications reporting on politics in France; he had university rectors eliminate courses on natural law; and he authorized only three official newspapers to circulate—the brief moment of relative opening had now closed.[7] At the same time Madrid opened its arms to counterrevolutionary émigrés from France, pensioning some.[8] Floridablanca's security measures dismayed the generation that had welcomed relaxation of press censorship in the late 1780s, and his readiness to cooperate with other anxious European monarchies in 1791 and 1792 to block the process of revolution in France undermined neutralists in Spain and the country's principal ally, France, in their efforts to restrain English naval and commercial activity in the vital Caribbean. In what many interpreted as a move to regain a neutral stance and lower the antagonism of aggrieved Frenchmen, the conde de Aranda—nationalist, anticlerical, aristocratic *militar* and a leader of the so-called Aragonese faction in the Spanish political class—was abruptly chosen to replace Floridablanca as prime minister at the end of February 1792.

Aranda as Prime Minister

Charles IV knew and continued to respect Aranda's views about Spanish government and society, at least at the outset. A *grande*, founder of the elite artillery school of the armed forces, Aranda as prime minister had stabilized Madrid in the wake of the 1766 riots that forced Charles III to abandon his leading minister, Esquilache. Later he was Spain's ambassador to Paris, whence he urged Floridablanca to join France in supporting the colonial insurgency in England's North American colonies. At the request in 1781 of young Charles, Prince of Asturias, who, incidentally, never forgot the trauma of rioting Madrid in 1766, Aranda advanced his ideas for improving what Charles himself realistically called "the messed up . . . machine of the Monarchy."[9] Aranda symbolized the antibureaucratic (anti-*golilla*), sometimes "renovating" faction of Aragonese *militares*, eager to occupy high government office.

Other factors also influenced Aranda's appointment as prime minister. In the 1760s he had authorized the project of internal colonization in northern Andalusia (the Sierra Morena), in part designed to protect the line of silver shipments between the port of Cadiz and Madrid, since Cadiz "constitutue le coffre de toutes richesses venant des Indes." He was credited with the appointment of the Peruvian *criollo* Pablo de Olavide to administer the project; Olavide had soon earned the plaudit of "the man who populated the wastelands of the Sierra Morena." The Sierra Morena project was a minimal effort at agrarian reform in an inhospitable region of Andalusia, but it was tracked in France and elsewhere in western Europe, as were Olavide's subsequent trial by the Inquisition and his escape to refuge in France—the inglorious end to this experiment.[10] Next, under Aranda's premiership and in the aftermath of the coup against the government in 1766, Madrid had ordered the expulsion of the Jesuits from Spain and its colonies (where a high proportion of the order was concentrated), executed with remarkable efficiency, stirring considerable local resentment. With these reformist credentials Aranda went to Paris as ambassador in 1772; four years later Floridablanca was appointed *secretario de estado,* in effect prime minister.

Ambassador Aranda mixed with luminaries of the Enlightenment, who valued him as anti-Jesuitical and anticlerical, a rare species of enlightened Spanish aristocrat and, moreover, a confirmed advocate of close collaboration between Spain and France. Within days of the announcement of Aranda's diplomatic appointment, Condorcet sent his congratulations, calling Aranda the "destructeur des Jésuits," opponent of "every kind of tyranny," and describing him as prepared to "shatter the scepter of despotism" and support a "wise constitution" turning kings into "the first servants of the people."[11] To Condorcet and other Spain-watchers, most significant for the immediate future was the promise that his appointment augured a lowering of tension in Franco-Spanish relations at a time when a surge of antimonarchical radicalism in France jeopardized the Bourbons' Family Pact.

A further factor behind Aranda's appointment was his oft-expressed sensitivity to conditions in the colonies and, as an aristocrat, to the sensibilities of *criollo* elites overseas. Writing to young Charles in 1781, he had reminded him baldly that the metropole had always foisted incompetents upon the colonial administration: "The Indies have been the destination of the useless, the wastebasket of Spain." In addition, peninsular Spaniards systematically alienated visiting *criollo* elites; to quote Aranda again, "They only know how to treat them as returnees from the colonies, suck what they have brought back, disparage them . . . which sows alienation . . . they will start a revolution."[12] This perception he never lost. Years later, in a letter to Floridablanca, he returned to his uneasiness about colonial exploitation, graphically voicing the average Spaniard's view of the colonies as "a piece of bacon for the soup pot."[13] He feared what he observed in England's North American colonies, rejection of English imperialism by aroused colonial elites. Aranda was understandably worried by colonial repercussions of the metropole's participation in a Pan-European intervention directed against France and its populist radical ideology; he was aware that in the colonies "nothing can be hidden from them, they have books that instruct them in the maxims of liberty," and he predicted that "there will be no lack of propagandists to persuade them at the proper occasion."[14] Aranda often showed arrogance, never ignorance. On taking over as the virtual prime minister in February 1792—a brief tenure of eight months—he understood that upon his government's skill in hewing to neutrality between revolutionary France and the English-dominated First Coalition of Europe's monarchical states might hang Spain's precarious hegemony in America.

Aranda's initial domestic measures were planned to temper the work of security-conscious Floridablanca. The Inquisition's investigation of Mariano Luis Urquijo and others was ordered suspended, censorship of the nonofficial press was relaxed, backing was provided for the *Correo Mercantil de España y sus Indias,* and even the pensions distributed by Floridablanca to émigrés from France were suppressed. He continued to focus on the colonies; during his brief tenure as prime minister the Consejo de Estado pushed ahead with creating new *consulados* there. Further, under Aranda the "destructeur des Jésuits" the government opened an inquest into the legality of the grossly undervalued sales of Jesuit properties to savvy *criollo* and peninsular Spanish buyers of those *temporalidades,* many of which were in the strategic colony of New Spain.

However, the critical issue for Aranda's administration remained Spain's policy toward France and its American repercussions. For six months, from March through August 1792, he held to neutrality, rejecting Floridablanca's policy of unrelenting opposition to the revolutionary government in France. Aranda's efforts were reflected in the minutes of the interministerial Consejo de Estado (he was its *decano*), whose influence he hoped might offset opposition to neutrality in the high civil service.[15] During those critical six months pressure on Madrid was relentless as the Consejo's members considered the issue of war or peace and its impact upon government financial and fiscal policy, national defense, and the security and integrity of the colonies.

In April a catalyst materialized: the former secretary of the French embassy at Madrid, Jean-François Bourgoing, returned from Paris as ambassador with broad powers *(ministro plenipotenciario)*. Knowledgeable in Spanish affairs since his first appointment to Madrid in 1777 and author of the recently published, impressive three-volume *Tableau de l'Espagne moderne,* Bourgoing was a dedicated *fonctionnaire* of the French state and private interests, monarchical or revolutionary.[16] His aim was to get the Spanish government to formally accept his ambassadorial credentials and thus recognize the new constitutional monarchy in France.[17] More pressing in his eyes was an unambiguous declaration of the Spanish government's position vis-à-vis France: friendship, opposition, or neutrality when Austria and Prussia were preparing for armed intervention to restore the *ancien régime* in France. If Spain remained friendly or neutral vis-à-vis France, then withdrawal of Spanish forces positioned along the Pyrenees during the Floridablanca administration would be feasible.[18]

Aranda was ready to accept Bourgoing's credentials, since rejection by Madrid could be interpreted as a sign of support for the interventionist forces threatening France. Not that Aranda was unduly sympathetic to the new regime in France, to its dedication to equality and liberty, to constitutional curbs on arbitrary royal power. Rather, he was pragmatic, avoiding war with France because his government needed a powerful ally to preserve its empire in America.[19] He put it succinctly in a letter to the Consejo de Estado on 30 April: "Without the support of one of the two, we risk everything we have overseas," a position he called "prudente indiferencia."[20]

Two weeks later the Consejo de Estado examined a report from Hacienda secretary Gardoqui on relations with France, government finance, and the defense of the colonies. Diego Gardoqui exemplifies the progressive merchant tapped for Spain's civil and diplomatic service in the last decades of the eighteenth century. Born into the Basque gentry of Bilbao in 1736, he managed a family firm ("fuerte Casa de Comercio") for decades, trading mainly with England, where he was educated and mastered English. He supported *comercio libre* in 1778, then argued for loosening regulations that constrained trade at New Orleans and Pensacola. The Cadiz commercial community held him at arm's length; as one of Aranda's Cadiz correspondents noted, "Here they say thousands of stupid things about the Hacienda minister." Floridablanca employed the firm of Gardoqui e Hijos to transfer 4 million *reales* to North American insurgents for munitions for their anti-colonial struggle for independence. Gardoqui was posted to London as consul in 1783 and to Philadelphia as chargé d'affaires in 1784; in 1790 he was back in the metropole as director of Comercio y Consulados, and in 1792, under Aranda, he became secretary of the Hacienda.[21] He blocked the attempt of the Cadiz *consulado* to recover control over inspection of ships outbound for the colonies and recommended expanding trade with the United States. He also turned for a second time to the merchant-bankers Hope & Company, of Amsterdam, who provided a loan of 6 million guilders at 5 percent repayable over the period 1798–1807. Under the Godoy ministry, following Aranda's ouster, he was shipped off first to the Spanish embassy at Turin, then to Turkey. In 1805 he declined oversight of Hacienda contracts with the French banker Ouvrard for the transfer of silver from Mexico City.[22]

In Gardoqui's view, the "perniciosa revolución" and the frailty of French finance—"we cannot rely on assistance from France at this time"—rendered an alliance with that former ally unwise. Spain now had to defend its "immensas" possessions in America from the "envy" of those nations that "hunger to acquire them for their openings for trade, facilitating the Metropole's exports of its production and wares, increasing enormously with the help of the colonies." Gardoqui broached the need to adopt "a system to economize on expenditures," coupled with government stimulus to domestic manufacturers, all the while avoiding the complaints of foreign governments about new regulations (novedades) limiting the volume of imported manufactures. He recalled that lack of foresight had plagued past "proyectos útiles y ventajosos." International tension, he emphasized, heightened the government's need of revenues and access to credit "to make us respected" if attacked, and he posed the dilemma for his audience of policymakers, how best to increase the flow of revenue: either reduce expenditure or, to be avoided except in extremis, raise taxes. Taxpayers, he warned, always preferred "old practices" even though the new taxes were more equitable. This meeting of the Consejo de Estado ended with a request that all five consejeros indicate where budgetary reductions could be made.[23]

At the end of May the Consejo returned to the situation in the colonies in a report to Colonial Secretary Valdés that concentrated on the Caribbean island possessions, "our Islands in the Mexican Archipelago." It proposed a strike force based on Guantanamo Bay, four sailing days from the mainland colonies and a mere twenty-four hours from Jamaica. Guantanamo was chosen based on Spain's hope of interdicting smugglers who were using Jamaica and operating along Cuba's southern coast and based on Spain's fear that London might attack the Caribbean ports preemptively if Spain reaffirmed its alliance with France.[24] Months later, in mid-October, Cuba's importance as a sugar exporter surfaced when Gardoqui laid before the Consejo a petition from Havana's planters for gracias (permits) to improve the competitive position of the island's export staples, transmitted by their aggressive agent at Madrid, Francisco Arango y Parreño. They asked for duty-free exports of cotton, indigo, and coffee by "Españoles" and non-Spanish slave traders directly to any foreign port, rebates on Cuban sugars re-exported from the metropole, and the lifting of duties on Havana's re-exports of silver shipped from Veracruz. The three points underscored the Veracruz-Havana link and the growing trade between Havana and Baltimore.[25]

The Consejo de Estado responded with limited concessions. It would allow both Cubans and non-Cubans to deliver the exportables to any foreign port in the Western Hemisphere (an opening for U.S. traders) in exchange for imports of slaves, money, and milling equipment. "Españoles" (presumably Cubans and *peninsulares*) would be able to export directly to any port in Europe, provided they returned to Havana after putting in at a peninsular port.[26] These proposed *gracias* were sent on to the Consejo de Indias for review; they were hardly minor concessions and were symptomatic of Cuba's expanding economy and Madrid's willingness to compromise longstanding policy to satisfy the island's agricultural and commercial blocs. The careful review of the Cuban petition of 1792 foreshadowed the island's political leverage more than a decade later, at the critical conjuncture of Spain's empire in America in 1808–10.

While the colonial situation formed the leitmotif of the Consejo de Estado's deliberations in 1792, the situation of Spain in Europe was paramount. In June of that year the duque de Almodóvar—*consejero,* ex-ambassador to London and St. Petersburg, translator (under the pseudonym of Malo de Luque) of a carefully abridged version of Abbé Raynal's multivolume *Histoire philosophique*—brought up the sensitive issue of Spain's "neutralidad o indecisión" toward "las revoluciones de Francia." Almodóvar, an unabashed admirer of Catherine's despotism in Russia, questioned Aranda's cautious policy. He was probably typical of many aristocratic figures in the higher reaches of Spanish administration who were profoundly antagonistic to the revolution in France, such as the *oficial mayor* (permanent undersecretary) José de Anduaga, whom Aranda inherited with his premiership, Francophobes whom Bourgoing circumspectly referred to as "the weight of the administration." Almodóvar feared that a radicalized France could spread the contagion of equality and civil and religious liberty, which in his judgment had destroyed the Bourbons in France. Anarchy was now endemic there, and sovereignty somehow dangerously diffused among king, ministers, and the new national assembly. Intimate linkage to France at this time was undesirable, and "its alliance [worth] nothing"; now Spain had to devise a strategy that did not rely upon "this powerful, natural, and neighboring ally."[27]

Was England a substitute, Almodóvar asked? It certainly was not a "reliable ally," and for pragmatic reasons. "The interests of the Spanish nation are naturally opposed to those of England," he said, a shorthand description of the decades of pressure by England's public and private sectors for direct access to the colonial ports in Spain's American empire. It was Bernardo Iriarte, an Anglophobe to be sure, who spelled out in a letter to his brother, the diplomat Domingo, how Spain's political elites felt about those opportunists in England who hoped that a war between Spain and France would offer a chance "to use this war to favor its navigation, trade, and industry." The English objective was "to keep open and at its disposition the commerce of our Americas that apparently we possess. . . . This has been and will remain the goal of the English."[28] Spain, Iriarte admitted, could not support a position of armed neutrality without revenues, credit, adequate armed forces, and "the public opinion any government must hope for." In addition, looking ahead to a postrevolutionary France defeated by the European coalition, he predicted that if Spain chose neutrality it would be judged a pariah.

Notwithstanding the sentiments of Anglophobic Spaniards, *consejero* Almodóvar recommended sending feelers to England (perhaps to forestall aggression against Spain's colonies) and a posture of armed neutrality while supplying secret subsidies to the Austrian forces attacking France and, in the ultimate case, to Spanish troops for invading France, since "defense is not as difficult as some disconsolate people imagine"—a jibe at Aranda, who remained convinced that his country was unprepared for a campaign in southwestern France. Almodóvar was moving the Consejo toward a declaration of war, his viable alternative to neutrality.[29]

Aranda's "prudente indiferencia" became untenable in late August, when joint Austro-Prussian troops challenged France, pushing the revolution into its second, more radical phase, imprisonment of the royal family and ultimately regicide. He was now becoming resigned to a risky war against Spain's long-term ally. Seventy-three-year-old Aranda was headstrong, often inflexible, a "character indifferent to others' opinions; self-esteem; way of thinking; his phrasing and expressions uncommon," as his fellow *consejero* Antonio Porlier y Asteguieta painted him.[30] He understood that the alliance with France was necessary to defend the American colonies against English aggression; he had reliable information from Las Casas and O'Reilly about Cuba and from Saavedra (Venezuela); and he probably worried about the influence of anti-Gallican traditionalists like José Antonio Caballero and others in the ministry who shared Floridablanca's post-1789 views. He was also realistic and foresighted, as his memorial of 1782 to young Charles on the implications of the North American revolution proved.[31] Now he put to the Consejo de Estado a number of questions in the debate over a wrenching policy change with multiple imperial ramifications.

Assuming that France, brought to "la razón" by the European coalition, had recovered its prewar "dominación," could Spain once more count upon France as "a support against the Britannic Crown" or—the worst-case scenario—could the Spaniards "once again manage to remain as we are without support"? Second, what about the possibility that during a war against France, England might "take advantage of the moment to attack Spain in the distant Americas"? Could the Spanish navy protect the colonies? To settle this question, he proposed that before joining the coalition against France, the government discuss with London its attitude toward the American colonies. In any event, he urged that before breaking relations with France, Spain make military preparations disguised as "preventivas y precaucionales," positioning troops and supplies close to the Pyrenees. Without such preparatory activities, war would interrupt Spain's overseas trade and communications. Although at this juncture Aranda probably envisioned further radicalization in France, he still preferred that Spain move cautiously toward war by joining the coalition against its powerful neighbor north of the Pyrenees.[32]

In truth, there were currents bearing Spain toward an inevitable conflict with France. Bernardo Iriarte noted at this time that Madrid's security forces were suspiciously lax in controlling anti-French mobs. "You can believe that because of the license and barely tolerated freedom given the Madrid populace," he wrote his brother in the foreign office, "I suggest to you that the government will yield too much to the masses and one day they may turn on the French." In the same vein France's envoy at Madrid, Bourgoing, reported that the anti-French cabal made Aranda hesitant to declare Spain's neutrality in the war against France.[33]

At the close of a meeting on 24 August 1792 the Consejo de Estado agreed (no record of votes cast is available) that France posed the "threat of general upheaval" and that those opting for Spain's neutrality only encouraged those who "seek to break up and destroy the Monarchy" by substituting "Democracias federativas." The Spanish government had no other choice but to support the "Monarch and Monarchy in France . . . the authority of Her Very Christian Majesty, Religion, and the Nobility of France."[34] Aranda and his supporters had lost the battle for neutrality, or as a later generation might say, for nonintervention.[35]

Of course Aranda feared the consequences of joining the anti-French coalition, and he continued, probably without authorization, to explore ways to maintain a neutral position. His great fear must have been the long-term loss of French support in America once hostilities ended. Three months later, nine months after becoming prime minister, Aranda received at his residence from his fellow *consejero* and colonial secretary, Antonio Valdés, a formal order removing him from his post as prime minister; however, he was allowed to remain on the Consejo de Estado. The septuagenarian Aragonese *grande* learned that his replacement was the twenty-five-year-old Manuel Godoy, who recently had joined the Consejo. Effectively, the era of Charles III was ending in what to some observers seemed a "capricious" ministerial appointment.[36]

Aranda's dismissal and the choice of Godoy as successor, followed in March 1793 by the declaration of war against France, would have enduring international and domestic repercussions. At the international level, the century-old collaboration between Spain and France that had served Spanish interests since 1700 was shattered, and although it was renewed in 1796, thereafter French government officials remained dubious about Spain's intentions, an attitude that without doubt contributed to the armed intervention by France slightly over a decade later. Domestically, the war raised tension between traditionalists and reformers that Godoy could not control. That tension led ultimately to the coup d'état that overthrew him along with Charles IV in the spring of 1808, and to the bitter divide between partisans of Fernando VII and those of José Bonaparte, between *fernandistas* and *josefinos/afrancesados*. In a broader context, revolution and counterrevolution in Europe after 1789 crystallized positions in Spain and its American colonies. Caught in a whirlwind, Godoy would seem contradictory and inept, to some a *poseur* cultivating inoffensive elements of the late Enlightenment, to others another "ministerial despot," as his administration attempted the impossible: to placate the two hegemons in western Europe.[37] Yet otherwise antagonistic factions in the Spanish metropole were linked by their shared devotion to maintaining Spain's imperial system at all costs.[38]

Godoy's promotion to prime minister probably came as no surprise to the *consejeros de Estado*. Only a few months earlier he had been seated as a *consejero*—Aranda had made no formal objection—although obviously lacking administrative, diplomatic, and military experience. The son of mid-level hidalgos of Extremadura, he had been brought to Madrid and placed in a regiment of the Guardias de Corps by his brother, a Guards officer. Young Godoy frequented the *tertulias* of Pedro Estala, a politicized priest with literary inclinations, where he mingled with writers critical of the status quo but not radically so—Juan Pablo Forner, Juan Meléndez Valdés, Leandro de Moratín, and Virio.[39] When he learned of Godoy's appointment, Forner bubbled with enthusiasm for "a Minister of talent, who chooses those who have it; who is honored . . . has a good grasp of the science of government." Meléndez Valdés's *Oda contra el fanatismo* expressed hopes for reform that Godoy's appointment inspired among civil servants and intellectuals.[40] Among Estala's coterie he must also have absorbed Estala's Anglophobia and interest in colonial conditions, two themes that would surface in Estala's *Viagero universal* and, later, his *Carta de un español a un anglómano*. The sudden appearance of Godoy revived hope for innovation; in fact, one of his first initiatives was to welcome publicly write-in suggestions for reform. At first he encountered no visible opposition. Aranda was aged, cantankerous, opinionated, intolerant; *grandes* had been notably absent from prominent administrative positions under Floridablanca. Nor could Spain's reform-minded forget that for all his aristocratic weight and anticlericalism, Aranda had not been able to protect Pablo de Olavide from the Inquisition in 1775.

Behind Godoy's promotion lay another consideration. He quieted such influential tradition-minded civil servants as Almodóvar, Caballero, and Anduaga, whom he inherited and kept in office. While he accepted the initial praise of reformers in the state civil service such as Meléndez Valdés, Godoy also approved Juan Josef Heydeck, Joaquín Lorenzo Villanueva, and others critical of the French Revolution and the concepts it popularized. In a real sense, in Spain in the 1790s political and intellectual agility and ambiguity were survival assets.[41]

Once the French Bourbons were imprisoned and it was probable that they would be publicly tried and condemned, Spain's policy of neutrality came under fire, and with it the removal of its prominent sponsor, Aranda, from the Consejo de Estado. In January 1793 Godoy aired his view of the instability caused by "the advance of the fanaticism for liberty . . . that could spread to other Kingdoms," and Ambassador Bourgoing countered that Spain's neutrality was "the only way to improve the fate of that Royal Family."[42] However, the execution of the French royal family triggered a declaration of war that no high Spanish official dared oppose openly and enhanced Godoy's popularity in those cities of Spain where French merchants large and small were prominent and resented—Valencia, Cadiz, and Madrid—and by those whom Godoy termed the "upper classes and influenced by the clergy" (some Spaniards termed it "une guerre de religion").[43] During the next year Spanish military operations in southwestern France (Roussillon) and joint operations against the naval base at Toulon alongside elements of the English navy reinforced the sense of a popular "cruzada" against France, while colonial trade flows remained unaffected.

Popular support for the war began to fade in early 1794 with news of military reverses, the threat of penetration by French troops moving toward Vitoria and Burgos, rumors that the Basque provinces might even collaborate with French troops, and rumors of skyrocketing defense expenditures — deficit spending, ever the critical factor.[44] Already by December 1793 the financial drain was taking its toll. Research ordered by Hacienda Minister Gardoqui revealed that in recent peacetime years, 1782–90, government income had barely covered outlays; two-thirds of total expenditures had been absorbed by the defense establishment. War, Gardoqui had predicted in August 1792, would necessitate borrowing abroad at Amsterdam or recourse to new taxes. On news of the execution of France's royal family, he took precautions to order all surplus revenues in colonial treasuries shipped immediately to Spain; as a result, of a total extraordinary expenditure of 500 million *reales de vellón* on the army and navy in 1793, 150 million were covered by funds from America, and in May 1794 he proceeded again to order "every bit of silver possible to come from America."[45] As never before, control over colonial trade and the availability of colonial revenues formed the bedrock of Spain's position in Europe.

At this conjuncture of war and finance in March 1794, the Consejo de Estado was the scene of tension and confrontation between the main ideological currents at loggerheads in eighteenth-century Spain. The *golilla*, or civil-service, faction supported the traditional approach to policy; the *militar* favored some adjustments to control pressures of change in Europe and America. The former may be classified as the Anglophile party, the other the Francophile, but both were profoundly nationalistic. Neither proposed to activate popular political participation or democratize the political process in Spain, much less permit colonial elites a voice in imperial policymaking. To both factions the empire in America was sacrosanct and subaltern. Perhaps a distinguishing feature was that the party of "reform" believed an enlightened elite bore responsibility for guiding change along lines enabling the old regime *en bloc* to survive. Preference for some unavoidable adaptation accounts for the reformers' affinity for prerevolutionary France and, later, the "liberal" authoritarianism of Bonaparte in France as a way to ram policy through the old regime. We can understand why many in Spain's political class would later back the government of the *josefinos* over the heirs of the *golillas,* the *fernandistas* in the juntas of Seville and Cadiz.

Aranda remained on the Consejo de Estado for more than a year after his removal from the post of prime minister, continuing to track the course of the war with France. In late February 1794 Generals Ricardos and O'Reilly (both former Aranda protégés) and Ventura Caro met at Madrid to plan the spring campaign; Aranda appeared at one session, perhaps more.[46] Two months later the situation of Spanish forces deteriorated along the Pyrenees, in Catalonia, Navarre, and the Basque country, and Aranda could contain his criticism no longer. He drafted a biting critique of his government's participation in the European coalition to restore the monarchy in France. His exasperated, indeed intemperate frontal attack was probably representative of a faction in the political elite dreading the consequences of abandoning Spain's major anti-English ally. Godoy was no doubt correct in defining Aranda's *militar* faction as "a small coterie," recruited among the "clase media" of young lawyers, teachers of "science," students, job-seekers—the "literary folk"—supported by some prominent figures in the "upper classes."[47] The tone of Aranda's criticism was predictably aggressive (he was, after all, "a person who did not welcome others' views"), even insulting; when Godoy examined it on 3 March at Aranda's request, he immediately perceived that he could use it to humiliate the Aranda faction by ousting Aranda from the Consejo and cement his ties to the traditionalist bloc in Spanish politics.[48]

Eleven days later Godoy had the secretary of the Consejo, Anduaga, read Aranda's freewheeling critique aloud to the full Consejo in the presence of Charles IV. It made short shrift of the government's motives for declaring war and its unpreparedness to wage it and pointed to the overwhelming ideological and material strength of French resistance, predicting eventual victory for the French. First, the ideology of revolutionary France: how could Spaniards resist French troops fired up by concepts of liberty and "fanatismo democrático" with the counterpropaganda of defending religion, a "passing vapor fed by the clergy" and "by old notions of submission and servitude"? Then Aranda moved on to denounce intervention in a neighboring country's internal policies to obstruct its rights of sovereignty and independence: "Between nations . . . there is no right to intervene in their respective domestic policies."[49] The decision to go to war, he insinuated, had been made by Charles IV not on the basis of *raison d'état* but to restore royal relatives to power. National interest, he made clear, was never synonymous with the rights of royalty. Above all, Aranda considered impolitic Spain's participation in the anti-French coalition: it destroyed the European balance of power, undermined the Franco-Spanish alliance fundamental to maintaining Spain's overseas empire against England's navy, and opened the way to the occupation of the Spanish colonies in America and the transfer of their trade to the English. Without the support of France, those colonies were at risk; England, "our eternal natural foe by virtue of her maritime interests and naval superiority," could and would seize the first chance to support future insurgents in the colonies.[50] Ominously and graphically he warned that if Spain did not withdraw promptly from conflict with France, one day French cavalry units would water their horses in the fountains of the Palacio del Prado.[51] Characteristically carried away by his convictions, Aranda was clashing with the ritual reserve of Consejo discussion, standing up before Charles IV, shouting and banging the table. Godoy and his supporters on the Consejo could have hoped for nothing more.[52]

The minutes of the Consejo de Estado as currently available do not record Godoy's preplanned rebuttal, crafted to justify Charles's reaction. Observing Charles's and his fellow *consejeros'* approval of Godoy's rejoinder, Aranda chose to reject the invitation to refute Godoy's presentation. *Consejeros* offered Aranda no verbal support: one, the conservative Caballero, wanted the incident hushed up; Campomanes's reaction was inconsequential; and Colonial Secretary Antonio Valdés (who was also a naval officer) would pragmatically stick by England "because of its superiority at sea over all others."[53] Charles stormed out of the meeting abruptly, commenting bitterly that Aranda (to whom he had once written, "I know your love for me, your integrity, and the good Patriot that you are") had never insulted his father, Charles III, before *his* ministers. One hour after the meeting adjourned, Aranda was ordered into internal exile at Granada, where he would be prohibited from communicating his "ideas and thoughts in writing or verbally" to anyone, and his private papers were to be sequestered. Later granted permission to return to his home province of Aragon, he died there in 1798.[54]

Godoy's political career began inauspiciously and would end in disaster. His appointment probably surprised many of Spain's political class. Unlike preceding prime ministers, he did not have a track record of note in the high civil service or the legal establishment, nothing analogous to that of Esquilache (whom Charles III had brought to Madrid from Naples), Aranda, or Floridablanca. In short, he was a rank outsider. Recent studies suggest that he was primarily the choice of the royal household: Charles and María Luisa wanted a chief minister beholden to them rather than the factions of *militares/aragoneses* and *golillas*, a figure with whom they could discuss policy issues frankly and from whom they could expect loyalty, respect, and accountability. These qualities he would return in spades.[55]

Initially Godoy seemed to adhere to the cautious, Floridablanca policy on domestic and international issues and critical of revolutionary France; his appointment would not threaten the traditionalists, although many aristocrats would consider him an unworthy upstart. On the other hand, reform-leaning elements in the political class seemed optimistic, hoping that a new influential figure might finally ram policy adjustments through a calcified system. Godoy would be bedeviled over the next decade and more by issues tied directly and indirectly to the Spanish Atlantic, in particular its Caribbean sector with its dynamic zones of New Spain, Cuba, and Venezuela—Mexico City/Veracruz, Havana, and Caracas. Spain had an inverted colonial compact; it was dependent on colonial revenues and re-exports, on colonial treasuries, on corporate and private donors/lenders (*españoles europeos* and *americanos* alike). New Spain's silver output was soaring spectacularly, and Cuba's agricultural base was shifting from tobacco and coffee to sugar and the incessant demand for access to imports of African slave laborers. The Spanish Caribbean had become more than a highway for introducing European wares and exiting with precious metals.

In point of fact, a looming policy issue centered on western Cuba and had been a preoccupation since the English (and North American) occupation of Havana in 1762–63. Then amphibious forces contained sizeable New England contingents, and thereafter Cuban trade with Philadelphia, New York, and latterly Baltimore brought shipments of flour, salted provisions, and wood products and exited with Cuban sugars and molasses, while contact with English slavers operating out of their Jamaican entrepôt facilitated the inflow of African labor. Havana was becoming a major exporter and a major entrepôt as well but was constrained by the restrictions of the Spanish transatlantic system, notably Veracruz's secular role as the Caribbean distribution center for re-exports shipped from the metropole.

Cuba's growth brought massive transfers of New Spain's colonial revenues for fortifications, shipyards, and a military garrison at Havana; in addition, it pressured the metropole to build up its navy to confront England's impressive, wide-ranging naval units, contested only by cooperating Franco-Spanish naval forces. More than ever, the Spanish Atlantic required a navy capable of defending the American colonies from Havana to Buenos Aires. It meant that Madrid had to formulate a fresh policy toward France, now alienated by Spain's thrust into southwestern France during the counterrevolutionary operations of the First Coalition; France could no longer be considered the dependable ally it had been since the settlement at Utrecht of the War of the Spanish Succession and the Bourbon Family Pact. After the Convention, France would be under new and unpredictable "management," whether Directoire, Consulat, or Empire responding to an aggressive, liberal, and imperialist-minded bourgeoisie.

Defense in Europe and especially defense of the colonies in America required financing, with liquidity in the public sector made possible only by the infusion of silver *pesos* from the mining colonies of New Spain and Peru and now supplemented by imports of staple exports—sugar, tobacco, coffee, dyestuffs and hides—from other, hitherto peripheral colonies. How might a reformulated policy for the Atlantic reconcile divergent and diverging interests during warfare at sea and in the face of English blockaders off Spain's metropolitan and colonial entrepôts, where warehoused staples deteriorated, unlike silver at Veracruz, for example? If staple exporters at the ports of Havana, La Guayra, and Buenos Aires insisted upon relaxation of the constraints of the Spanish Atlantic system, how were powerful trading groups at Cadiz, supported in the Caribbean area at Veracruz, Mexico City, and Havana, to be mollified? Even the most experienced figures in the Spanish political class would find it difficult to confront this avalanche of issues and, behind them, well-financed interest groups. The circumstances would require quick, ad hoc, pragmatic responses and frequent backtracking, which would appear poorly thought out. And if unforeseen Continental developments threatened the survival of the *monarquía* in the peninsula, could the royal family, along with high civil servants, abandon the *patria* for self-imposed exile in colonial America—which the Portuguese Braganzas would choose in late 1807 under the protection of the English navy?

The Labyrinth of Spanish Factionalism: Toward San Ildefonso

Aranda's *militar* faction held a view of metropolitan and colonial interests that emphasized reducing corruption and administrative inefficiency and the integration or bonding of metropolitan and colonial elites. Its members leaned toward federation on two levels: within the empire to solidify it and with France as a bulwark against England. At the international level, federation would not depend upon dynastic networks, and morality was pushed to the periphery. The principle was upholding the interests of Spain and, where necessary, France.

The policy demanded changes in the administration and exploitation of the empire, even structural changes that might tear the traditional fabric of colonial rule established piecemeal over more than two centuries. More precisely, patterns of colonial trade might have to undergo serious modification to curb smuggling, to open the colonies to all the peripheral provinces of Spain, to foment manufactures, agriculture, and commercial banking, to curb forced sales (*repartimiento*) to native peoples by district colonial officers, even to tolerate the re-export of a significant volume of French goods where Spain's industrial shortcomings were obvious. In sum, the combination of imperial defense and growth in the metropole required a kind of federation with France and implementation of Franco-Spanish unity.

Opposing the *militares* were traditional, often unrealistic conservatives. Their policy would minimize change at home and in the colonies, but they could be reconciled to some accommodation with England's commercial classes provided that England posed no threat of territorial aggression in America. They would now tolerate England's economic hegemony because it was unavoidable, and they would tolerate Spain and the colonies as its economic satellites rather than as co-equals with French interests as the principle of federation implied.

The events of 1792 injected dynastic factors into the equation. Traditionalists seized upon radicalization of French politics and then regicide—a package threatening the structure of Spain's old regime—as grounds for rejecting a Franco-Spanish federation. The classic ritual disgrace *(escarmiento)* of Aranda, manipulated by Godoy and Anduaga, now signaled to Spain's political class a significant policy change. In 1794 Aranda was clear sighted and arrogant when he reminded the Consejo de Estado that the survival of imperial Spain meant realignment with its powerful neighbor, whether republic or monarchy. Charles IV naturally felt "insulted"—as Godoy planned—when Aranda reminded him that regicide in France had to be tolerated in order to preserve imperial interests.

Despite the artfully engineered *escarmiento* of the prominent leader of an important political faction critical of war with France, at the end of July 1794 Madrid had to open informal negotiations for armistice and a peace settlement. These lasted until the peace treaty of Basel in July 1795, when reality caught up with the Spanish ideologues of counterrevolution, so much so that in August 1796, precisely as England's ambassador to Madrid had predicted ("the Treaty of Peace will be shortly followed by a treaty of alliance"),[56] Madrid renewed cooperation with France of the Directoire at the Treaty of San Ildefonso, which also returned Louisiana to French control (briefly, as it turned out). It was another sign that the Godoy government was coming to terms with reality at home and in the colonies.

Military reverses along the Pyrenees, resentment of the uncooperative attitude of English naval commanders during joint operations against France's naval base at Toulon, and unprecedented outlays for defense ultimately moved Madrid to welcome the Basel settlement. To be sure, the state of government finance—a frequent item on the Consejo de Estado's agenda—should not be construed as mirroring the private sector. Public penury and private prosperity are not always incompatible. Private earnings in the colonial trades during the early 1790s, coupled with stimuli to the domestic economy through outlays on national defense, created a buoyant economy and confidence in the government's capacity to amortize on schedule its outstanding treasury notes *(vales),* even to contemplate new issues of them.

Colonial revenues—not to neglect peninsular customs income from imports and re-exports, inflows of colonial staples, and the "patriotic" loans of peninsular merchants at Cadiz and their counterparts at Mexico City—kept the Spanish government afloat. In June 1794, when the government was considering a new *vale* issue of 22 million *reales de vellón,* the Hacienda's Gardoqui wanted to delay until the safe "arrival of some millions from America" could inspire confidence in potential investors.[57] At the same moment, prospering colonial trade and the demand for merchant vessels at all peninsular ports affected personnel at the naval base at Cadiz. Valdés, also navy secretary, recommended shifting that base north to Vigo in order to limit massive desertion to the merchant marine "by reason of the attraction to voyages to the Indies and the lure of higher pay."[58] At Cadiz, Madrid, and other peninsular cities wartime prosperity fueled speculation, with fortunes made overnight and prominent displays of new wealth in dress, carriages, townhouses, and living styles. To a naval officer of the old school like Alejandro Malaspina, who had just completed with distinction five years of duty in the Atlantic and the Pacific, the Madrid he returned to in 1795 seemed somehow coarsened and tawdry, flooded with the new rich buying offices and status.[59] This was the context of the decision to realign Spain with France at San Ildefonso in mid-1796.

Godoy claimed that in the aftermath of Basel, his office was flooded by rumors to the effect that Spain would be unable to maintain neutrality in future confrontations between Europe's superpowers. From Paris, Spain's ambassador reported the comforting news that the Directoire hoped to cooperate with the Spanish navy in order "to watch fully over the dominions in the Indies." From the *criollo* archbishop of Granada, Moscoso y Peralta, preoccupied with reports from churchmen of tension in the American colonies, came doubts of the wisdom of banking upon any English support for maintaining Spain's empire in America. "Will Spain," he asked rhetorically, "trust the English to preserve and guard its Indies, trusting the wolf to care for the tempting flock?" In proceeding with its realignment, the Consejo de Estado needed little encouragement in 1796.[60]

To newly rejoined Spain and France, reviving the Family Pact satisfied paramount colonial considerations. Both had overseas possessions to which they were closely linked; their combined naval forces, still formidable in 1796, might protect against English aggression. The Directoire trusted that with Spain's cooperation a French expeditionary force might repossess Saint-Domingue and that once France was again in control of Louisiana, a reconstituted French empire in America would be possible.[61] In French hands Louisiana might turn into an effective barrier to Anglo-America's infiltration of Spain's wealthiest colony, New Spain. In addition, part of the Directoire's grand design, really an aspiration pursued since the beginning of the eighteenth century and continued in the next, was to help French exporters obtain through a commercial treaty "liberté du commerce direct avec les possessions espagnoles." To this end, the initial step was to guarantee support for Madrid's policy of "commerce colonial exclusif," then via a commercial treaty to infiltrate Spain's transatlantic system of managed trade, and finally "to take over again Spain's principal markets," what became the Spanish policy of the empire under Napoleon.[62] This was a policy of boring from within, in contrast to what Spain's government and commercial interests feared most, English pressure from without.

To some Spaniards realignment with France promised assistance in containing English commercial expansion in America. Many Madrid officials remained convinced that London would never forgive the financial assistance their government had provided the revolution for independence in North America and that the English aimed to detach key portions of the American empire—a strategic Caribbean island, a port on the mainland such as Veracruz, which was the key to that colony's hinterland. Even during their joint war against France in 1793–95, England's island of Jamaica had been a base for extensive smuggling to Cuba's south coast and to Yucatan, Tabasco, and Veracruz. When Madrid authorities referred to England's maritime supremacy and the chance of contesting it with the joint naval forces of France, Holland, and Spain, uppermost in their planning were the Spanish colonies in America and their transatlantic lines of communication.[63]

Support for the colonial status quo was what Spain's negotiators obtained at San Ildefonso. Madrid elaborated a treaty of defense and offense with France aimed at England, as well as protection for its "Estados, territorios, islas y plazas." Article 15 of the treaty bundled many Spanish concerns: the promise of a commercial treaty of equality and reciprocity, respect for neutral shipping (critical for Spain's maritime communications in wartime), and the cooperation of France "to restore and set in place Spain's colonial system." Article 12 contained a hidden price: if Spain maintained its neutrality when France was at war in Europe, it would have to compensate by providing a financial subsidy.[64] San Ildefonso and the subsidy obligation if Spain elected not to participate in a French conflict would lead to the

Franco-Spanish treaty of 1803 specifying a subsidy, which would trigger in 1804 England's decision prior to a declaration of war to intercept a Spanish convoy bearing a cargo mainly of silver from the Rio de la Plata.

A Sea Change

A sea change of extraordinary proportion came between Aranda's dismissal in March 1794 and the treaty with the Directoire at San Ildefonso in August 1796. Revolution and counterrevolution, the nagging fear of the repercussions of revolutionary sloganeering in the American colonies, and the dependence of many interests in the metropole on income from those colonies dampened the influence of late eighteenth-century *proyectistas* in Spain's state service, Valdés, Gardoqui, and other, like-minded civil servants between 1787 and 1794. Although Godoy's administration continued to support innocuous elements of the Catholic Enlightenment in Spain, on more substantive issues Godoy had to maintain a conservative, traditionalist stance to placate ecclesiastical and commercial groups whose financial backing was essential. Once again Madrid was relying upon loans and gifts from the commercial interest groups at Cadiz and Mexico City. Nothing better illustrates the depth of change than the receptions given in 1795 to the returning ex-viceroy of New Spain, the second conde de Revillagigedo, and the distinguished naval commander Alejandro Malaspina.

Revillagigedo's replacement, the marqués de Branciforte (Godoy's brother-in-law, connected with commercial groups at both Cadiz and Veracruz), was critical of the humane way Revillagigedo had handled French nationals expelled from New Spain in 1794. Revillagigedo, Branciforte reported form Mexico City, had displayed "excessive, even tactless confidence or indolence" in executing their expulsion and in reacting to secret agents' reports of "freewheeling conversation at various . . . gatherings of French."[65] Godoy tried to make little of Revillagigedo at Cadiz rather than provide public honors for one already considered one of the most effective proconsuls ever sent to colonial Spanish America. His action was probably in response to the Consulado de México's vehement opposition to Revillagigedo's support of *comercio libre* legislated in 1789 and to parts of the intendancy system applied in New Spain in 1786. That colonial capital's *peninsular*-dominated *consulado,* an interest group whose lobbying and financial clout had to be heeded, helped float an impressive loan to the metropole during the war with France.[66] Another indicator of change was Godoy's drastic handling of Malaspina, which revealed his government's intolerance of knowledgeable, loyal, independent-minded, outspoken, but impolitic dissidents. When Malaspina returned after years of monitoring the situation in the colonies in America and the Philippines, he felt that he had returned to a society for sale, corrupt, immoderate, and immoral.[67]

In the aftermath of Malaspina's discrete "disappearance" into a prison cell at La Coruña, Colonial Secretary Valdés, who had been responsible for Malaspina's expedition in 1789, resigned his post as colonial secretary (though as stated above, he retained his post on the Consejo de Estado), and Hacienda Minister Gardoqui resigned the following year.[68] Their departure from these posts was one of many signs that the era of neo-*proyectistas* was drawing to a close. Simply put, the Godoy administration's economic policy lacked Gardoqui's vision. Godoy's policy recommendations included the ineffectual revival of sumptuary legislation to lower the level of luxury imports and the return to by-now traditional hyperbole: Spain could dispense with most of its imports since "everything [foreigners] bring is harmful to us."[69]

Pedro Varela, who replaced Gardoqui at the Hacienda, toyed with equally unrealistic, not to say bizarre, expedients for expanding government revenues and issuing treasury bills *(vales)*. He proposed to invite Jews from the Netherlands, who he was convinced managed "the greatest wealth in Europe or Asia," to return to Cadiz and other peninsular areas, provided they established a redemption fund for the *vales* secured on specific government revenues. He hoped the "Nación Hebrea" would somehow energize trade with the American colonies.[70] Varela had other suggestions for raising government income. One was to increase the sale of titles of nobility to wealthy residents in the colonies, though he warned colonial officials not to publicize "the sale of titles or favors for money"—as if the sale of titles, always coveted acquisitions of the status-conscious, could be concealed from an acquisitive society. But the most startling revelation of the shallowness of the new ministerial appointments, the sheer incapacity to ideate fresh solutions to longstanding issues, was Varela's drastic proposal to farm the monopoly of Spain's transatlantic imperial trade with the ports of Veracruz and Callao out to the merchants of Andalusia at Cadiz, Seville, and Málaga. In compensation the new oligopolists would advance to Madrid 50 percent of the estimated value of import duties collectible per annum.[71] This was tax farming on a scale unprecedented in three centuries of Spain's management of its Atlantic trade with the American colonies.

It was at this moment of a rightward shift in Madrid's political ambient, a time when a disillusioned Goya was etching his satirical *caprichos* to illustrate the chasm between the hopes and illusions of Spain's enlightened and the incapacity to realize them, that as one of his departing measures Gardoqui finally authorized the publication of Antúnez y Acevedo's implicit support for a return to Hapsburg-era management of the trades to America. Antúnez's backward-looking study of 1797 supported a policy completely at variance with the reality of English warships and corsairs simultaneously blockading Cadiz and ports in and around the Spanish Caribbean. Spain's support of France against England under the terms of San Ildefonso would lead inexorably and predictably to financial crisis and emergency measures contemplated but postponed: the forced sale of categories of ecclesiastical properties (the *Consolidación de Vales*) first in the metropole and then extended to the colonies and, for a brief period, the granting of *comercio neutro* between Europe and those colonies.

3. The Late *Proyectistas*

A society that was collapsing—the Old Regime—and another that apparently had failed in its effort to replace it, the French Revolution.   Antonio Menchaca

Among us Anglomania is widespread, and those who do not suffer from it are labeled, not good Spaniards, but French.   Bernardo Iriarte, 20 March 1806

Regardless of outcomes, it is instructive to look behind economic-policy initiatives in the transitional years between the administration of Florida-blanca and that of Godoy, roughly 1789–96, to a group of political econo-mists—they might be termed latter-day *proyectistas*—in the key Estado, Hacienda, and Indias ministries who continued the theorizing of those early eighteenth-century *proyectistas,* Jerónimo de Uztáriz and José del Campillo. Late *proyectistas* included prominent civil servants, Diego de Gar-doqui and Bernardo Iriarte, and less prominent, equally motivated indi-viduals like Bernabé Portillo, the collector of the tobacco excise at Cadiz, and Consul General Juan Bautista Virio, at Hamburg, commercial cross-roads of northern Europe. What they shared was direct contact with leading government officials; for example, Gardoqui and Iriarte met often with Floridablanca, while lower-ranked civil servants and autodidacts in political economy like Portillo and Virio seemed to enjoy the confidence of Florida-blanca's successor, Godoy. In a certain sense they epitomized the afterglow of eighteenth-century optimism about the efficacy of state intervention in the economy, optimism that would shortly fade in the course of the general crisis of merchant capitalism after 1796 and hostilities between Spain and England.

Analyzing the projects of late *proyectistas* illuminates the process of policy formulation by Spain's highest civil servants. Their propositions were far from revolutionary, hardly radical, and their criticism of current policy was offered in a spirit that was constructive rather than confrontational, never despairing. The context is important: these civil servants inhabited a backward and underdeveloped metropole of western Europe that was rooted in an agrarian economy controlled by less than 5 percent of the population, perennially and precariously dependent upon the trade and taxes of a large and equally underdeveloped overseas empire in the Western Hemisphere.[1] Other constraints on their formulae for change were developments after 1789 in neighboring France, where reformism nourished a startling harvest of economic and social radicalism tinctured with bitter anticlericalism that disconcerted many onlookers in Spain—"the broad negative reaction during the nineties when confronting the revolution in France."[2] Unlike in France, class conflict remained surprisingly muted despite the shocking chasms between the wealthy and the impoverished. At the same time, scattered among the owning classes—noble landlords, bourgeois renters of land, the clerical establishment, and the small urban bourgeoisie—were enthusiasts about the developmental potential of metropole and colonies, especially the *reino* (kingdom) of New Spain and the island of Cuba.

The Latter-Day *Proyectistas:* Gardoqui, Portillo, Iriarte

The economic writings of Gardoqui, Iriarte, Portillo, and Virio range from how to handle the foreign trade of Louisiana to the basics of a commercial treaty with republican France. These manuscripts reveal a common perspective in varying proportions. All were patriots who kept paramount the interest of nation and state, yet they were not superpatriots incapable of looking to other nations for useful models. They understood, of course, that national and imperial interests were imperiled by the currents loosed in western Europe in the 1790s; with good reason they were convinced that growth at home and in the colonies was throttled by what they called the English "coloso" of manufacturers, merchants, merchant marine, and royal navy. Understandably they chafed at the enduring constraints on national economic policy still imbedded, maliciously they believed, in the unequal treaties with England and France signed by ignorant or insouciant representatives of Spain between 1645 and 1713, between Muenster and Utrecht; these were seven decades of diplomatic incompetence under Spain's "Austrian" dynasty. Nonetheless, much could be learned from English protectionism for trade and navigation since the 1650s, which contradicted the offer of equity by English negotiators in dialogue over bilateral commercial treaties. London, the political economists of Spain were convinced, was interested in economic hegemony rather than international cooperation. Of course, the late *proyectistas* also perceived other models of reform under interventionist governments: France under Colbert, Russia under Peter the Great, Prussia under Frederick.

To confront an ever-expansionist England in the eighteenth century Spain had found an ally in Bourbon France. Under the first Bourbon in Spain the country experienced a wave of "revival" or "regeneration" rich in hopes and meager in outcomes that nonetheless contrasted with weakness, subservience, and sheer incompetence under the Hapsburgs. Many among Spain's political class in the 1790s still admired the recent French republican governments and believed that they would renew old international commitments on a basis of real rather than feigned equality. No doubt Francisco Cabarrús expressed a current of admiration in Spain when he observed of the French constituent assembly that it was "the greatest, most celebrated collection of talent and knowledge to honor humankind" in the process of attacking "every error and abuse."[3] They were not blind to the realities of social revolution in France, the prominence of aggressive French merchant-bankers and businessmen, many of whom they did not consider embodiments of the new France. By 1795, we must also recall, Spain's leading officials could not afford to minimize the fact that Spain's armed forces had collaborated in the coalition patched together by the English monarchy in 1793 to remove the republic in France and had briefly occupied Roussillon, in southwest France. Nor could they overlook that retreat from Roussillon and the penetration of French republican forces into northern Spain had forced the peace with Paris. Spain's abandonment of the alliance with France that had endured over most of the eighteenth century would color Franco-Spanish relations under the Consulat and the Empire.

Reaffirming the French alliance had decided advantages in 1795. Consider the preservation of French investment in Spain's Banco Nacional de San Carlos (which used its Paris agency for its financial settlements in Europe), raw-silk exports to Lyon and French silk manufactories at Valencia, and French credits and goods in Spain's colonial trades. In addition, there was a substratum of ingenuous faith in the good intentions of French governments formed after 1789—the Directoire, for example. Of course Spain's intellectuals later made much of the ravages of the Terror when they chose to reject revolution as a model for improving on their old regime, yet there remained an undercurrent of hope in the French as cooperative partners that would vanish in the disillusion fostered by ruthless economic imperialism under the Empire, by Napoleon, his finance ministers, and French merchant-bankers.

A major theme of *proyectista* analysis during the 1790s was finance, specifically the reduction of budgetary deficits in order to improve the government's credit standing at home and at Amsterdam, Europe's financial center. This preoccupation was understandable. Expenditures on defense had begun to rise after Spain joined France in 1779 to support the insurgents in North America, and they had continued to rise into the interwar decade after 1783. Spanish economists reviewed the French government's practices before the Revolution to conclude that poor fiscal and financial management had contributed to France's fiscal crisis in 1788 and 1789. This they proceeded to contrast with the English government's capacity to support its *consols* and consequently shore up its borrowing capacity. The combination of expenditures on defense and discretionary outlays on the royal household's elastic civil list forced Hacienda officials to contemplate new sources of income, but they were reluctant to adopt the easiest resolution, simply raising the rates of existing taxation, the multiple consumption excises that provided the bulk of *rentas generales* and *provinciales*. As Gardoqui put it candidly in 1792, "We are unable to resort to new taxes."[4] In 1790, a year of poor harvests and rising food prices, the Junta de Estado avoided raising rates or creating new taxes lest they "undermine the small towns and elicit dangerous protests, the more so with the unfortunate example of France."[5] There followed recourse to innovation in the form of treasury notes (the *vales reales*), interest-bearing obligations offering attractive rates, and the promise of amortization—all inducing an inflow of local and foreign investment funds in the 1780s and 1790s.

Fresh approaches to the unending problem of deficits heightened state functionaries' confidence in "principios económicos," a rational approach based upon forthcoming statistical materials, an appraisal of natural and human resources, and the balanced integration of economic sectors, all in a coherent "sistema." In the home economy they emphasized agricultural development to produce grain surpluses and lower otherwise appreciable outlays on food imports. They linked low productivity to absentee ownership, maladministration of rural estates, immiserization of landless peasants, and massive outmigration to large urban nuclei such as Madrid. The *proyectista* Bernabé Portillo, in Lower Andalucía, was convinced that some form of land redistribution, offering ownership to direct producers, was unavoidable, a sensitive matter in an agrarian economy bedeviled by property concentration, underutilization, poor management, and rack-renting.

An obvious target was ecclesiastical landholdings, which, when the government faced financial straits in wartime, might be expropriated in return for guaranteed 3 percent annual interest. Here would be the origin of the *consolidación* of the late 1790s first in the metropole, then extended to the colonies.

However, no matter how dismal the short-term economic prognosis, *proyectistas* retained one major perennial asset: the American colonies. They realized that the metropolitan economy had been dependent upon the colonial surplus for decades, if not longer. Some surplus had literally fed the metropole, draining funds abroad every year to cover food imports; the port of Cadiz alone had sent abroad about 15 million *pesos* for grain imports between 1785 and 1790. And this figure does not include the millions that had to be budgeted for the armed forces at home and overseas at Havana and other heavily fortified Caribbean ports.

Silver, staples, and consumers figured prominently in *proyectistas'* policy configurations. The objective was to establish effective control over imports in order to curb illegal trade flows into the peninsula and impede commercial penetration of the penetrable Caribbean colonies by English smugglers. Achieving this objective required expanded participation in colonial trade by the peninsular ports at Barcelona, Málaga, and Santander and—a kind of backward linkage—the development of import-substitute manufactures in the metropole to replace European goods re-exported to America. By supporting manufactures and building a merchant marine, Spain might reduce the visible and invisible items in its balance of accounts—freight, insurance, commissions.

Analysis and policy recommendations by Gardoqui, who was initially responsible for Comercio y Consulados and then promoted to Hacienda minister in 1792, mark the approach of a key state functionary shaped by experience in business, diplomatic exposure to the United States during the 1780s, and equipped with a capacity to integrate colonial and metropolitan policy. Charged with reorganizing government finance to meet defense needs, Gardoqui decided that the Hacienda could be most effective in the area of foreign and colonial trade. He fully backed Valdés's "constant and uniform measures adopted for a few years" to widen the Spanish transatlantic trade system, measures promising to loosen the oligopolistic control of the Cadiz merchant community. His activity bothered members of that group, one of whom observed unambiguously, "Hereabouts the Hacienda Minister is the object of thousands of absurd charges."[6]

In mid-1792 Gardoqui drafted a position paper for the interministerial Consejo de Estado in which he set out a perception of the national emergency along with a set of rational responses. In his view an abrupt, profound rupture had occurred that demanded "reformas y economías" as part of "a steady system of economy and order." The rupture was the "perniciosa revolución de la Francia," so that "for the moment we cannot rely upon French aid" to protect Atlantic sea lanes and defend the colonies overseas. Those possessions were "inmensas" and envied "for the large opportunities they gave to trade"; he envisioned domestic manufacture "augmenting extraordinarily with the assistance of the colonies." In Gardoqui's view, protected domestic manufactures could produce satisfactory substitutes for French and other products imported from Europe and usually re-exported to the colonies.

Protectionism had to be applied with discretion, however, "to avoid stirring the envy of foreigners and providing any reason for complaint about innovations adopted to reduce imports of foreign manufactures and raise the level of consumption and exports of ours." In other words, the constraints of the web of commercial treaties could be weakened only with "circunspección." Meanwhile, the costs of defense at home and overseas—the Consejo de Estado was at the moment preoccupied with deciding on whether to have a naval base at Guantánamo or Trinidad to protect the area between Guyana and East Florida, the Caribbean islands, and the "Archipélago Méxicano"—gave a high priority to fiscal responsibility, formation of "funds and credits to render us respectable," and sizeable revenue growth.[7] Here Gardoqui shared the government's reluctance to create new taxes, since "people accustomed to established practice are content to follow old practice and pay more rather than pay less according to a New method." Overall, Gardoqui foresaw in mid-1792 the unexpected consequences of upheaval in France on Spain—on its finances, on its economy, and especially on its colonies in America.[8]

Trade with the colonies, balance-of-trade deficits with trading partners in Europe, and government stimuli for developing a textile manufacture remained Gardoqui's preoccupation in his four years as Hacienda secretary. In his concurrent post as director of colonial trade he had to review the special status of Louisiana and, for that matter, the Florida enclave. The choice was obvious: either renew the legislation of 1782 authorizing New Orleans to trade directly with France, the United States, foreign ports in the Caribbean, and Havana or simply incorporate Louisiana into Spain's Atlantic system, which meant excluding direct contact with French ports. Up to this point commercial exchanges between New Orleans and Spain had been minimal; more disheartening in 1792, there were few indicators that merchants, manufacturers, and shippers in Spain could manage more than minimal trade exchanges with New Orleans, a condition Valdés had already questioned in 1788.[9] Gardoqui's data indicated that New Orleans imported virtually no Spanish products, since Spain "is in no condition to trade" with Louisiana, and it followed that a realistic policy simply could not impose upon New Orleans a "direct, monopoly trade." Still, Gardoqui shared Valdés's view that "meanwhile [we should] continue to acquire resources currently lacking in order to trade there directly and exclusively." New Orleans's status of exception would serve to affirm the reality of Spain's "imperial" monopoly of trade with its colonies in the Atlantic system.[10]

In two respects, however, Gardoqui as Hacienda secretary and political economist tried to move beyond mere renewal of the special status conferred upon New Orleans. First, he revived a recommendation forwarded in 1788 by the governor of Louisiana (at the time rejected by the Consejo de Estado) to grant Louisiana and Florida "total liberty to trade in Europe and America with any foreign nation with which we have a commercial treaty." This, he argued, merely confirmed reality. Next, to encourage the participation of cautious merchants in Spain, he proposed to lift all prohibitions on re-export of any "foreign product consumed in Louisiana" from peninsular ports to New Orleans. In addition, Madrid would issue Spanish merchants drawbacks on foreign merchandise imported into Spain for re-export to the colonies. Gardoqui insisted to the interministerial Consejo de Estado that this was the appropriate strategy to aid Spain's merchants to compete both in overseas Louisiana and in Europe; it was "the sole way to expand a commerce that, although it is lawfully ours, we cannot participate in for lack of natural resources." There are always euphemisms for underdevelopment.

In the long run, Gardoqui was convinced, economic growth in the colonies would have a metropolitan feedback as Spain's manufacturers imitated foreign wares and Spanish exporters packed them along with the re-exports "until we take control fully of the items that can best stimulate our industry." Also, manufacturers in the metropole could easily imitate items of wide colonial consumption—"mantas de Indios," which Palencia and Burgos could fabricate; the Bordeaux-like wines of La Rioja; and French-model muskets, which ateliers at Plasencia and Barcelona could reproduce. Despite reference to "total liberty," Gardoqui would keep Louisiana in a trade enclave: Madrid would prohibit New Orleans "forcefully from any commercial exchanges with our Possessions and Islands," especially with Havana, "a colony with a penchant for smuggling." If necessary, he would draw on New Spain's treasury to subsidize the administrative costs of Louisiana. Clearly, his long-range objective for New Orleans remained "the establishment of our exclusive trade there."

In drafting legislation covering the trade of New Orleans at the request of the Consejo, Gardoqui eschewed the use of "absoluta libertad" for the more muted "active and passive commerce." The effort to isolate New Orleans within Spain's Atlantic system persisted in his draft: Spanish-registry vessels—he added those from the Basque ports of Bilbao and San Sebastián, hitherto excluded—would be encouraged to carry exports, including some normally excluded from Spain's Atlantic trades, from New Orleans directly to ports in Europe "without coming to Spain."[11]

Gardoqui's sharpest critic on the Consejo was the aging civil servant and political economist Campomanes. Campomanes questioned what he termed "absoluta libertad" already enjoyed by New Orleans merchants to trade directly with Europe bypassing peninsular ports, and he was backed by a majority of the Consejo membership. It was their view, the recording secretary noted, that granting "total liberty" for that port's trading community would invite invidious comparison in those colonies of Spain that were "far more important and infinitely more useful," doubtless a reference to Veracruz and Havana, to Cuba and New Spain. It would be better to tone down the phrase, refer to "libertad" as only a somewhat amplified version of the 1782 *cédula* covering Louisiana, and imply conformity with the Spanish transatlantic trading system by stipulating that Spanish vessels bound for New Orleans obtain a *pase* at any port in Galicia.[12] The final version of the Consejo's *cédula* of 9 June 1793 incorporated the phrasing and intent of the majority: it proclaimed a renewal of the 1782 *cédula*, with only those adjustments necessary to "promote national commerce." Obfuscation can be the weapon of choice for the weak. In point of fact, however, there *were* innovative elements: shippers in Spain could import for re-export to New Orleans "goods, produce, effects" normally excluded from importation, and the two Basque ports could enjoy access to the special zone that was now Louisiana.[13] These concessions notwithstanding, Gardoqui remained a late mercantilist seeking to maintain the empire's transatlantic system, the eventual full absorption of Louisiana into that system, and government inducement to manufacturers in Spain to export future products to the closed colonial market in America.

International conflict invariably leads a state bureaucracy to clarify economic policy, to pinpoint inefficiencies and neglected economic sectors in the interest of maximizing resources to preserve state and society.[14] At such conjunctures—in 1794, "immense outlays caused by the current war"—the state may tolerate otherwise impermissible critique of the fundamental structures of the established order. Such times are moments of truth, when the pathology and etiology of society may be diagnosed even if therapy is not applied. It was the crucible of war that elicited Gardoqui's plan to protect Spain's infant industry as the main instrument for expanding foreign and colonial trade, his emphasis on the American colonies' importance to the metropolitan economy and the necessity of a certain elasticity in preserving Spain's monopoly of its transatlantic trade. Gardoqui's presentation brought a clash of opinions, of theory against praxis, and of flexibility versus rigidity within the Consejo de Estado, in the process revealing how old structures and mentalities of underdevelopment and dependence could undercut aspirations for development.

The immediate circumstances of Gardoqui's "Condition of our active and passive commerce" are not clear. One clue is the preceding meeting of the Consejo, on 9 May, at which Gardoqui, forecasting an upcoming and unexpected defense allocation of 20 million *pesos* for the next year (virtually equivalent to New Spain's silver coinage at that moment), had urged strengthening the government's major credit instrument, the Banco de San Carlos's *vales reales,* by directing all the colonial treasuries in America to forward "all possible silver."[15] His situation report on 16 May opened with an analysis of Spain's external trade and underscored increases in value since 1787, contrasted with an annual trade deficit with Spain's European suppliers of an estimated 20 million *pesos.* More specifically, his data disclosed that half the deficit on current account consisted of goods re-exported to the colonies. National policy, he concluded, should be designed to lower the deficit with Europe and "apply every imaginable effort to do so."[16]

Key to Spain's external trade growth was the American colonies, with their import capacity and exports of silver and other staples. It was clear that earnings on colonial sales could cover Spain's trade deficits with Europe and still provide an annual surplus of more than 9 million *pesos.* The colonies figured large in another context: Madrid, Gardoqui was convinced, could count on remittances from colonial treasuries to cover about 30 percent of the supplementary expenditures of 500 million *reales* projected for 1793–94.[17] He mentioned and deliberately excluded from his income estimates possible monetary grants or gifts from the overseas *consulados.* One conclusion in his introduction was predictable: "Our trade with America is immensely useful to us, and we are therefore obliged to spare no effort to prevent its loss and to make it more and more exclusive."

Gardoqui felt that to handle three issues—eliminating trade deficits with Europe, producing domestic products to substitute re-exports to the colonies, exercising an effective monopoly of colonial trade—a comprehensive and consistent policy of government intervention in the private sector through tax exemptions, outright subsidies, and calibrated protection, was indispensable. He had in mind two models of development: England's Navigation Act of 1660, which, he concluded, had led to an enviable merchant marine, and Colbert's protectionism, which had brought about an "aumento prodigioso" in French manufactures. What had gravely disadvantaged France's economy was the Anglo-French commercial treaty of 1786, an abandonment of Colbertian policy. As for Spain, under the Hapsburgs in the seventeenth century tariffs had been misused, although the Bourbons in the eighteenth century—here Gardoqui used hyperbole—by correcting tariff policy had registered "un grande aumento" in manufactures. The models proved that the proper posture for Spain was "to engage such nations in a trade war following the same system, prohibiting or raising duties regardless of whether we manufacture or can manufacture them." At the moment of commercial capitalism's apogee and the age of democratic revolution in western Europe, there was no room for international cooperation.

Since a large volume of textiles remained warehoused in Spain and effective government policy required protectionism, Gardoqui named three basic categories warranting recourse to tariffs. Comprehensive protection should be afforded textiles of mass consumption produced with domestic raw materials. Other products—woolens and narrow-width silks already manufactured in Spain with local materials and competitively priced—also deserved protection if the trade of the country producing a similar product "is not otherwise advantageous to us." And turning to fabrics that were highly desirable "for style or luxury," such as blends of silk, wool and cotton, along with embroidery that domestic manufacturers could reproduce with local materials, he said that imports of such manufacture "must be totally prohibited if we hope to promote their manufacture." Protection was a tool that should be applied with discrimination, he warned, since the Spanish government always had to be aware of the possibility of commercial retaliation. Tariff schedules needed fine tuning and unambiguous instructions to customs officers who processed imports of new fabrics not yet included in tariff schedules. In any case, decision making required accurate statistics on trade with all trading partners. Gardoqui's carefully elaborated position paper earned warm support from the dean of the Consejo de Castilla and also from a member of the Consejo de Estado, Campomanes. To the role of tariff protection he would add a prohibition on the sale or use of certain luxury fabrics and, more significant, "establishing cotton manufactories in Spain."[18]

It would seem reasonable to expect that Gardoqui's case for the development of manufacture and trade growth based upon textiles, especially the already popular cottons, with backing from an economic nationalist and state functionary of Campomanes's stature, would win the Consejo's unanimous approval. Instead, it produced unexpected opposition from the recently appointed Prime Minister Godoy. Why? Perhaps it was sensitivity to international reality as Spain's powerful Coalition allies tried to smother the French Revolution; or the intention of an inexperienced prime minister who had just staged the ouster of his elderly, distinguished, often uncontrollably outspoken predecessor, the conde de Aranda, to impart his own policy goals; or simply that Godoy seemed to represent the cautious, traditional approach to "the operations of our factories, and thereby to advance national industry and commerce."

In any event, Godoy took issue with Gardoqui's proposal to promote cotton mills, since they might undermine the state-subsidized woolen manufactures, causing sheepmen to reduce the size of their flocks (Godoy's family estates in Extremadura were devoted to sheep ranching), ultimately lowering the supply of mutton, "whose shortage would be highly disturbing in Spain." Only manufactures using an ample supply of domestic raw materials justified protection, "as is happening," for example, "with woolens and other textiles." Godoy claimed that the time was inappropriate for Gardoqui's developmental strategy, given the repercussions of the current war upon the country's "critical and sensitive" diplomatic relations with allies England, Holland, and Prussia, among others; it was risking much to antagonize them by moving against their influential businessmen, "their commercial and manufacturing interests, in which they are both zealous and tenacious." His strategy embodied a different tactic: the country could develop manufactures and trade by indirection rather than confrontation. The minutes of the Consejo de Estado record that Godoy's position received the unqualified support of Charles IV as well as the Consejo. In effect, Godoy and vested interests at the close of a century of mercantilist theory and practice accepted prescriptions for breaking out of the syndrome of economic backwardness but postponed their application to a more propitious time. A mentality formed by decades of economic backwardness does not easily abandon traditional patterns; it prefers attention-grabbing, low-cost, risk-free solutions.

There is perhaps a further explanation for Godoy's decisive intervention to head off the Hacienda minister's project for strong state backing for industrial development, which entailed breaking commercial treaties and providing subsidies when they were least affordable. Only one month earlier, in May 1794, Godoy had received a short, elegantly written communication from a self-styled political economist in the state tobacco monopoly at

Cadiz, Bernabé Portillo, who offered analysis and solutions for problems of government finance in an agrarian economy of low productivity and low-income taxpayers. His analysis had the attraction of intimating that the state could at last address the long-postponed issues of land reform, a single tax *(única contribución)*, flaws in the intendancy system, artisan guilds, and a commercial code—all issues "constantly discussed by People in Provincial Capitals, in Commercial Centers, even in small Towns."[19] Portillo's "Discurso político sobre la agricultura, la industria y el comercio" was a response to Godoy's announcement on assuming the position of prime minister inviting the public to write him about national needs with propositions for solutions. Godoy's initiative was part of the climate of change that it was hoped might follow his unexpected appointment in the spring of 1794; the much-talked-about "reforma de abusos" might, it seemed, move beyond salon talk and bureaucratic review groups to action.

Portillo had cultivated his "predilección irresistible" for the field of political economy (his "ciencia económica") in a number of unpublished papers during a career of government service in posts in the provinces, commercial centers, and the capital. The demands of government finance during war with England in the early 1780s had, he recalled, led him to discussions at the Escorial royal residence with a friend who was "very enthusiastic about Political Economy," on how to find revenues for defense.[20] Portillo had a complementary interest: as a Cadiz resident commuting often between the port and the capital of Andalusia at Seville, he had developed a preoccupation with agrarian issues, with the apparent paradox of large estates in the countryside coexisting with thousands of landless, half-starved day laborers *(jornaleros)* and their families, whose marginal existence had provoked a clerical acquaintance to lament one day, "Who has disinherited these people? What kind of society is this in which a blameless worker dies of hunger?" In the fall of 1793 this cleric had witnessed widespread starvation in Lower Andalusia, at Écija, Fuentes, Carmona, and Lora, where he had found "almost all residents reduced to begging and others working for three *reales* without food provided, in short, for a daily wage that cannot buy their daily bread." Portillo was reminded of the observations of the French social critic Simon Linguet, that mankind had lost much in ending the age of "dominio feudal" and that "esclavitud personal" existing under paternalism was preferable to the current conditions of a wage worker.[21] Government finance in Spain, Portillo argued, suffered from agrarian structures marked by religious and secular entailment leading to land concentration, landless peasants, and immobilism in government policy.[22] While Portillo empathized and commiserated, he was perhaps more meliorist than Gaspar de Jovellanos but certainly not as radical as Leon de Arroyal.[23] To the problems of deficits and a miserable rural proletariat, Portillo brought the expertise of a tax collector, contact with Cadiz's commercial world (he claimed friendship with two *consulado priores*), a directorship on a Cadiz maritime insurance company, and many drafts of economic analysis.[24] Portillo's "Discurso" offered Godoy a bourgeois functionary's analysis of his nation's economic situation. He had creditable credentials for forwarding to the new prime minister a brief memoir whose title belied its argument.[25]

In his introduction Portillo shared the classic conspectus of the decline of Hapsburg Spain gradually reversed under the Bourbons over the eighteenth century. Oddly, he omitted reference to the decades of Charles III that were marked by many economic initiatives, an omission also made by a conservative contemporary on the Consejo de Indias, Rafael Antúnez y Acevedo. Spain, despite soil that is "the most fertile and productive in all Europe" and possessor of "America's most wealthy and fertile Dominions, able to offer an immense exclusive Commerce," had not advanced enough over the Bourbon century to dispel "our current, lamentable great backwardness." It was still impossible to "promote industrial Establishments," because of an inefficient system of agriculture, an inequitable taxation system that bore heavily on the rural population, and an impoverished internal market. The overriding issue was how to improve the national economy to produce revenues for current and future needs, the perennial *proyectistas'* dilemma, now accentuated by intermittent years of warfare after 1779.

Despite analytical clarity, the solutions presented in the "Discurso" turned out to be conventional, which is perhaps not surprising given his citation of Simon Linguet on the charms of feudalism and the "personal slavery" of the rural working poor.[26] Instead of aiming at structural change, Portillo presented a standard solution relatively free of friction that emphasized people rather than the system: a reorganized bureaucracy. This solution had the advantage of leaving intact "the current Constitution of [our] State," rapid execution of policy, and, what was close to *proyectista* thought, "almost without Hacienda expense."[27] He believed that it would be wrong to disperse agricultural, industrial, and commercial affairs among several ministries, giving the Hacienda responsibility for broad economic oversight. A career revenue officer, Portillo understood the Hacienda's prime responsibility to be revenue enhancement, not "to meditate about and manage a system of Economy." It was precisely dispersed authority and preoccupation with revenue collection that accounted for the state's inability to handle major economic issues—overall economic backwardness, absence of a commercial code, failure to produce an agrarian law since 1766, the short-comings of the state-encouraged *sociedades económicas.*[28]

To correct *abusos,* Portillo proposed enlarging the state's role in the economy through a new cabinet post for agriculture, industry, and trade, its *consejo* to be drawn from the public and the private sector, from among intendants, embassy personnel, *consulado* members, hands-on property owners *(labradores)*—a kind of corporate representation *(consulado* litigation could be appealed to the new *consejo).*[29] And one of the immediate goals assigned to the proposed ministry of development would be implementing land reform in order to transform the landless into small holders ("without prejudice to any property"—*mirabile dictu*) by a general provision authorizing the sale of church-owned rural properties—*capellanías,* pious foundations and convents—and investing receipts in interest-bearing government obligations secured on specific tax receipts.[30]

There remains the question, why should the conventional, lucidly presented propositions of an obscure Cadiz tax collector, however intelligent and observant, be read by Godoy to the Consejo de Estado within weeks of receipt? Godoy had learned of Portillo's economic studies through an informal civil-service network: Francisco Saavedra had read Portillo's proposal for raising government resources in wartime by expropriating 400 million *pesos* of church-owned rural properties—"Brotherhoods, Trusts, Pious Works, and Chaplaincies"—and he had recommended it to Gardoqui, who mentioned Portillo's writings to Godoy. Here is the antecedent of Portillo's "Discurso político." In fact, after receiving a complimentary note from Godoy, Portillo added content footnotes to his "Discurso" in his "Suplemento por Notas," completed by 1 May. Someone on the Consejo then prepared a summary, attaching commentary in the form of "reflexiones." Every "inovación política," ran the summary, should be judged according to two prime criteria: absence of friction (the desideratum of all bureaucracy) and ease of implementation, which should be "the simplest and least expensive"—this last was underlined to emphasize its importance. The "Discurso" and notes offered a quick fix: through administrative reorganization the state could improve the national economy by concentrating on agriculture, strengthening the state's creditworthiness, and advertising through its new ministry a readiness at last to tackle major economic problems.

Behind Portillo's preoccupation with agrarian reform were his generation's impatience with former prime minister Floridablanca's "timid and irresolute policy" and his own retro-vision of the fictive "opulencia e es-

plandor" of the time of the Catholic Kings and Charles V, which he fanta-
sized had been based on "lands . . . worked by the hands of Owners." Carried by such rosy-hued retrospection, he imagined a halcyon condition that,
if it ever existed, certainly had evaporated with Castile's overseas expansion
as "active hands" were swallowed up by the "Western wealth obtained by
conquests"—an odd Gongorism for the torrent of America's precious metals. The investment of these funds in civil and particularly religious entailments led to "the complete lack of property in the hands of those dedicated
to cultivating it" Was Portillo rethinking the agrarian history of Andalusia?[31] He joins a line of eighteenth-century critics, *proyectistas* of the clerical
establishment's rural properties—Francisco Carrasco, Campomanes, and
Jovellanos. Like other late *proyectistas* in state service in the 1790s, he knew
of mistakes in the Sierra Morena of northern Andalusia, the flawed scheme
of internal colonization initiated by Madrid in the 1760s under Prime Minister Aranda and managed by Pablo de Olavide.[32] We know of Portillo's
interest in agrarian issues; sometime in March 1795 he had submitted to
Madrid's Real Sociedad Económica a manuscript on agriculture that
included a detailed "Plan de Nuevas Poblaciones," along with a cost-benefit
analysis.[33] Property owned by *capellanías* and *fondos píos* of the church generally deteriorated due to the "descuidada y a veces fraudulenta administración" that beggared the trust funds while lining the pockets of unscrupu-
lous managers of religious funds and properties; he estimated that the *fondos
píos* were receiving barely half of their potential annual income. In what in
retrospect was a vision of the process of *consolidación* in Spain and the American colonies shortly to come, Portillo proposed carefully planned sales of
the charitable properties of the church, spread over six to ten years, the capital formed to be invested in government securities, guaranteeing the church
stable returns.[34]

Portillo, whose critical eye saw the effects of incoming colonial silver on
metropolitan land tenure—it fueled the growth of large private and clerical
estates—also recognized that expanded trade with the colonies after the
comercio libre of 1778 had inspired Madrid to create new *consulados,* resulting
in increased litigation ("an infinity of Claims and Counterclaims"), handled
by often partial *consulado* courts. Hence another objective of Portillo's proposed ministry of development was a commercial code that would prevent
"fraudulent bankruptcies" and lack of public confidence in the merchants of
Spain. One of the purposes of *consulados,* which he saw as very useful institutions, was to streamline the settlement of commercial litigation by relying
on the simplicity of "truth be known and good faith kept" and avoiding
complicated and complicating legal briefs. He declared that Cadiz had more

than seventy lawyers responsible for "all the lawsuits tying up the Parties, confounding the Judges . . . because they do not sign anything, take no responsibility for what they promote and counsel, and enjoy an open field for sophism and arbitrariness."[35]

For this memoir to Godoy and subsequent essays on agricultural and financial themes, Godoy saw to Portillo's appointment in 1797 as co-director of a section of "Fomento General" for commercial and industrial oversight and for maintaining contact with Spain's consuls general. The senior co-director was the consul general at Hamburg, Juan Bautista Virio. Eleven years later, in 1808, Portillo would be the victim of political assassination— or was it a form of state terrorism at the hands of *fernandistas?* — at Granada, after making a reputation as the government agent responsible for expanding cotton cultivation there.[36]

Virio, Iriarte, and the Basel Negotiations

The appointments of Portillo and Virio were no bureaucratic accident, for both shared an interest and expertise in political economy. They were useful to young Prime Minister Godoy and to advisers and supporters in his first years in office who were nationalists sensitive to the relative backwardness of Spain and its empire, hopeful of selecting elements of European models of development, and ready to ideate informed changes in policy.

Just as financial issues inspired Gardoqui's and Portillo's position papers, the need to prepare fresh guidelines for treaty making became imperative in late 1796, when commercial arrangements with the Directoire were about to be hammered out. Juan Bautista Virio, a veteran consular officer positioned at a key European commercial synapse linking the trade of central Germany, Russia, England, Holland, and France, was also part of the small, influential group of progressive high civil servants / intellectuals that included Saavedra, Jovellanos, Portillo, and Iriarte. From Hamburg, a major center of German and international trade, he reported to Madrid on imports of primary materials smuggled from Spain's colonies in and around the Caribbean.[37] As Virio wrote to Bernardo Iriarte optimistically from Lyon in 1792, following his inspection of cotton and silk mills there, "We would have a striking advantage in everything compared with other countries if only we were properly organized to benefit."[38] Virio's good friend, Iriarte, frequent correspondent and fellow Anglophobe, also warmed to Godoy's pursuit of new approaches to old problems; his brother Domingo, at the time *oficial mayor* in Aranda's Secretaría de Estado, headed a group of Spaniards, including the financiers Simón de Aragorri y Las Casas and Francisco Cabarrús, who were responsible for negotiations with French representatives at Basel.[39] In September 1795 Iriarte, who had begun his diplomatic career as a secretary in Spain's London embassy, alerted Godoy that London might undertake a preemptive attack at Veracruz and occupy New Spain as compensation for the loss of its North American colonies and for Spain's financial support of the insurgents there; his motivation was to help Spain avoid "finding itself in serious difficulties with those arrogant and unfair Englishmen."[40]

In 1796 Virio was back at Madrid along with another experienced consular officer who had served in the Spanish embassy at St. Petersburg, Antonio Colombí. Godoy asked Virio and Colombí for "an outline of the commercial treaty that would be stipulated between Spain and the French Republic." Virio complied with two papers: a short statement of guidelines (the "Reflexiones") and a paper elaborating those guidelines by drawing upon studies of inexpert, not to say incompetent, prior Spanish trade negotiators, along with his policy recommendations.[41]

In sketching Spain's objectives in a commercial treaty, Virio advised Spain's negotiators in his "Reflexiones" to know precisely which products to protect and why. Key to protectionism were the necessary facts about a product's capability of having a domestic and a foreign market; otherwise protection would simply waste government monies. Underlying commercial agreements, Virio felt, should be the principle of reciprocity, and under no circumstance should potential advantages need to be abandoned to another nation "however close an ally and however lasting its friendship appears"— obviously he meant France. No country, Virio went on to explain, should abandon a product that gave employment to those in its domestic labor force who could not readily be shifted to other employments; in such a case, a Spanish treaty negotiator must be alerted to "sophisms and false flattery, or the power of its land and naval forces, seeking pretexts for insult and argument," an observation drawn from Spain's experience in treaty making from the mid-seventeenth century to the Treaty of Utrecht and beyond. High in his estimation were the *proyectistas* Bernardo Ward, Antonio de Ulloa, Nicolás de Arriquibar, and Pedro Rodríguez Campomanes, who had aimed to counter the policies of "the enemies of the Common Good, or ignorance of matters of political economy." Among this core of Spanish nationalists he counted the anonymous author of a tract published in 1762 at Madrid, *Profecía política verificada en lo que está sucediendo a los Portugueses por su ciega afición a los Ingleses.*[42] Virio did not elaborate, although he most certainly knew that the anonymous author was his longtime friend Bernardo Iriarte, who had returned in 1762 from his post as secretary at the London embassy. Iriarte's *Profecia,* published with the approval of Prime Minister Ricardo Wall (Spain's recent ambassador to London), elaborated an earlier Anglophobic French critique that had dramatized the impact of Portugal's "dependencia de Inglaterra," a fate that Spain had managed to avoid at Utrecht.[43] The moral of the Portuguese case study was self-evident: a metropole that chose to open its economy to a more economically developed nation on the principle of the international division of labor would become another Portugal and its colony in America, Brazil. This relationship was one that the English economist Ricardo would bend to his own purposes.

Virio elaborated the argument of his "Reflexiones" in a second memoir, an odd blend of a hardheaded review of the history of Spain's commercial accords with England (but not France) and an unalloyed, even ingenuous faith that the Directoire was dedicated to the new principle of impartiality and equity in international relations. "Reflexiones" was wrapped in a nationalist vision of a reenergized Spain becoming a major trading nation by drawing upon its colonial resources and functioning as a commercial hub linking Europe, the Mediterranean, and the American possessions. Spain, long victimized by "tricks . . . it had decided to tolerate," now had "the best moment to end." For the late *proyectistas* among Spain's civil servants/intellectuals there was still room for a reformed—not radicalized—old regime.[44]

Virio surveyed the history of Spain's commercial treaties and found none based on "common interest and mutual advantages truly equal." All had clauses permitting foreign businessmen to assume "certain ascendancy" over Spanish interests (fol. 1). Of course, he had to concede realistically, foreign powers invariably pressed their advantages, yet he attached no small blame to Spain's "wretched Negotiators" yielding pliantly to the pressures of "the bias and passions of incompetent and reckless ministers who have paid attention to and supported the avarice of a handful of merchants or smugglers, who have used their skill to distort facts and wrap their official capacity with a false zeal, misunderstood." It took no great stretch of the imagination to divine that his target was the pressure-group tactics of the Cadiz commercial community. He singled out English negotiators as especially skilled in appealing to Spain's diplomats by "the frailty of their philosophical principles" (fol. 2). Ever the colonialist, Virio turned to Spain's colonial experience to compare English tactics with those "frequently used by dirty Indians and Christians where governments tolerate those destructive people." Treaty concessions had eased England's intervention in Spain's domestic politics, producing "a precarious dependency" (fols. 2, 6).

To be sure, the counterpoise to England had to be France. Not an impractical diplomat, Virio understood that French businessmen who came to Madrid were driven by "the all-consuming commercial spirit" and viewed Spain as a "country of Hottentots," producer of primary materials for other countries to utilize in their manufactures (fol. 7). Politically sensitive, Virio skirted the revolution in France, its ideology and practice; instead, he expected the Directoire, issued from the revolution, to operate on principles far different from those of the English by adopting a "fair conduct" that he spelled out as "equality in the independence of nations and liberty in the free discussion of the interests" of each nation (fol. 3). Moreover, he felt confident that Paris valued Spain's friendship as essential to the security of both France and Europe. As allies, Spain and France could prevent any European power from exploiting another power's inferiority, ensuring the "general tranquility for centuries to come" (fol. 8). At this moment in his career, Virio was an optimistic Francophile. The goal of international policy for Spain, he advanced, was the elimination of the roots of inferiority, the constraints imposed upon Spain's manufactures, trade, and navigation "for so long" by unequal treaties, the better to develop the domestic and colonial economies (fols. 7–8).

Virio devoted the final third of his "Apuntamiento" for Godoy to the "valuable colonies" in America, more specifically to the possessions in and around the gateway to the Spanish empire, the Caribbean. His colonialist perspective was filtered through the prism of a consular career that required daily checking of Hamburg's large volume of commercial activities, the shipping, cargoes, merchants involved with English, Dutch, French, Swedish, and Danish vessels entering Hamburg freighted with staples and silver smuggled from Spain's colonies to foreign ports in the Caribbean. He considered Saint Thomas and other non-Spanish islands virtual warehouses, bulging with European manufactures and raw materials from Spain's nearby colonies. In 1795 alone he recorded thirty ships leaving Hamburg and nearby Altona with cargoes of German goods, not to mention hundreds of merchantmen outbound from English ports each year for Jamaica and other English colonies in the Caribbean (fol. 11). Such foreign commercial penetration Virio traced to Madrid's misguided fiscal policy—"measures . . . badly thought out, whose science to date has consisted of a few arithmetic rules"—which disadvantaged Spain's ships and cargoes, rendering them uncompetitive. Trade policy fashioned by Hacienda officials had focused exclusively on national revenue, he concluded, testifying to their ignorance of the "spirit of economic laws" evolved elsewhere in Europe (fol. 11).

At this juncture England's policy might serve as an attractive model. So that cargoes could be priced competitively, London provided exporters with drawbacks on re-exports, turning England's home and colonial ports into entrepôts and affording opportunities for speculators. By contrast, Virio found that Spain's policy, which placed equal duties on national and foreign goods, deterred shippers from competing in freight rates or type of cargo (fol. 12). Virio, however, shared with Portillo an exaggerated estimation of Spain's resources in land and manpower; properly calibrated state intervention, Virio felt, could transform the metropole into an important trade crossroads with an expanded merchant marine moving cargoes between the colonies in America, Europe, and the Mediterranean (fol. 12). This transformation depended also on the human factor. Virio understood that implementing his vision meant reorienting merchants in Spain to welcome "an education and training not limited to the counter, only to buy cheap and then destroy their fellow subjects." Reeducation demanded "great spirits" rather than "the limited, low level of talent, instruction, and experience" of the average Gaditano or Catalan businessman. Unlike Portillo's, Virio's judgment was unaffected by close contact with the commercial community at Cadiz.

The end product of his eonomic policy would be a self-contained, almost autarchic system linking metropole and colonies based on a tightened transatlantic trading system, lowered export duties, and government support for manufactures that utilized domestic and/or colonial raw materials. These, not fiscal policy alone, would settle the problem of government revenues. If not, then "the Gaditano, the Catalan, etc., will compete in vain," while the typical Spanish merchant would continue to stagnate as "a wretched straw man, for I know that the real owners of many ships leaving our ports for the Indies belong, along with cargo, to firms . . . that in this fashion have become influential at Hamburg and in other countries" (fol. 13).

The transformation Virio envisioned would have a transitional phase. Given the metropole's industrial shortcomings and the need to satisfy colonial import needs, temporarily there had to be sizeable quotas on re-exports to the colonies. This would remove the competitive edge of non-Spanish ports in the Caribbean islands that thrived on the smuggling trade with Spain's colonies. Virio advanced another innovation: Madrid could open a Caribbean port "near those very Islands" whence Spanish-registry ships could carry colonial products directly to a European port; on the return leg they would freight European products first to a port in Spain for temporary warehousing and ultimately re-export to the colonies, aided by drawbacks (fols. 13–14). By gradually terminating quotas and substituting Spanish goods, his policy would diminish smuggling in the Caribbean and trans-form ports in Spain into "towns of energetic speculators like those seen elsewhere" and Spain itself into "the great warehouse of what its colonies require, of its own and foreign goods" (fol. 14). And there would be exter-nal support: the Directoire in France, "being a real friend and ally," would surely collaborate by signing a commercial agreement based on the new international principle, endorsed by the French Revolution, of "impartial-ity and humanity" (fol. 15). As a response, Madrid would open channels for French businessmen to participate in the colonial trades; Virio would even cede to an unnamed "ambitious nation" a small colonial zone in compensa-tion for assisting Spain to attain "the implied independence and advance its own development" (fol. 4). In the view of Virio, Bernardo Iriarte, and mili-tary men like General Francisco Solano (who had been attached to the staff of the French general Moreau's Army of the Rhine), France's Directoire had metamorphosed into a coveted counterfoil to England.

On closer inspection, Virio's analysis and recommendations turn out to be less than visionary. His was a vision of hindsight; like other colonialists in Spain, he could not envision the world of free trade just beyond the hori-zon. He remained locked into the growth model of eighteenth-century Spain, where growth meant relentless beggaring of competitors. Mesmer-ized by the models he had examined, he believed that imperial Spain might replicate successfully the English experience, becoming a manufacturing and maritime superpower. Even in the choice of major ally, France, he re-mained within the structures of Spain's eighteenth-century international system.[45] Above all, like Portillo, Virio offered Godoy's ministry a kind of quick fix that sidestepped structural reforms: the colonies in America re-mained fixtures of the metropole, suppliers of silver and staples, and the metropole's principal trading partner.[46]

Were the approaches to national and colonial issues of prominent civil servants like Gardoqui and middle-level figures like Virio and Portillo rep-resentative of the mentalities of other high officials in the period of political transition between 1788 and 1795? Here the attitude of Bernardo Iriarte when he was a member of the Consejo de Indias and of the Junta de Co-mercio, Moneda y Minas, Spain's economic-development council, is illus-trative. At this point in a career initiated in the 1750s as secretary to Spain's ambassador to London, the conde de Fuentes, Iriarte was withdrawing from active government service to devote himself to study, reflection, cor-respondence, and analysis of the events of the day. Writing his diplomat brother Domingo in 1793 about his systematic "quality of existence . . . scribbling day and night" and avoiding "as much as possible the people who rub shoulders with Diplomats whose jargon, tricks, and dreams bore me," he filled his time with "my lucubrations," trusting that "the fatherland" could be insulated from "the contagion and troubles afflicting all Europe."[47] His approach to the English and French governments, the ramification of international agreements, and the role of the colonies in America reveal the nationalism shared by many in the upper levels of the Spanish civil service: deep-seated Anglophobia combined with grudging partiality to France. This complex of nationalism and necessary cooperation with the interests of France against those of England would ultimately draw seventy-three-year-old Iriarte in the awesome hour of decision fifteen years later to reenter government service, first under Napoleon's *lugarteniente* Joachim Murat, then under José Bonaparte. In the spring of 1808 he was asked to return to government service, and in a starkly pessimistic phrase he would jot in his journal: "What events am I going to witness?" He died at Bordeaux in 1814, an exile, and his wife died later at Bremen.[48]

Iriarte was born in the Canaries at Tenerife, where his grandfather had migrated from Navarre and married into a local family. His father's brother Juan was the source of Iriarte's link to France. Young Juan Iriarte accompanied the French consul in the Canaries on his return to France, where he enrolled first in a school at Rouen and then in a school at Paris, where one of his schoolmates at the elite Louis-le-Grand was Voltaire. Ultimately Juan Iriarte went to Madrid as tutor to the ducal families of Béjar and Alba. It was Juan who called his brother's son Bernardo to Madrid and facilitated his entry into the Spanish diplomatic corps, which posted him as embassy secretary to London, where he served from 1758 to 1761 or 1762—an unforgettable experience. There he served the conde de Fuentes, a *grande*, titular leader of the *aragonés* faction at court and related to another Aragonese aristocrat, the conde de Aranda. A confirmed nationalist like Aranda, Fuentes viewed the spread of English commercial interests and naval forces as a clear threat to the Spanish Atlantic. Fuentes, Aranda, and the *aragonés/militar* faction in general *(militares)* held fast to the principle that "unity with the house of France" was "indispensably necessary" if Spain was "to maintain its glory and power."[49]

England's Navigation Acts and their application impressed Bernardo Iriarte as the origin of the English government's protection for infant industry and the construction of a large merchant marine, so much so that he prepared for Spain's foreign office a lengthy report on their role. The long-term effects of English protectionism on relations with Portugal, in particular the Treaty of Methuen (1703), impressed young Iriarte and inspired his Anglophobic tract of 1762, the *Profecía política,* printed anonymously at Madrid shortly after he left London.[50] He was then twenty-seven. In the course of his diplomatic career he met frequently with Spain's Vatican envoy, José Moñino, later the conde de Floridablanca, whose Francophobia would surface in his reaction to the extremism of the revolution in neighboring France.[51] Perhaps Floridablanca's Francophobia fed Iriarte's Anglophobia; there is no doubt that Iriarte cultivated what some might call a typically French freethinking approach to the Inquisition ("a great nastiness and abomination . . . in every foreign nation") and to its thought-control tactics ("the darkness of its tyrannical prejudice") applied to publications imported from France.[52] During war with England in 1780 he transferred from the diplomatic corps (foreign affairs—Estado—fell directly under the new prime minister, Floridablanca) to the Consejo de Indias and a position on the ministry's economic-policy planning board, the Junta de Comercio, Moneda y Minas.[53] In addition, Iriarte had links to the Cadiz commercial community; he married into the prominent Gaditano merchant family of Sáez de Texada. By the early 1790s he was no neophyte to the world of diplomacy, to Madrid, the administrative center of Spain's empire in America, or to the trading world at Spain's major entrepôt, Cadiz.

Iriarte's orientation toward France and French interests was nuanced, at times even jaundiced. As a *consejero de Indias* he was involved in a plan in the early eighties to expand direct trade with Manila, which, like Havana, had been occupied by English amphibious forces in 1762, to the shock of Spain's political classes. The project for what became the Compañía de Filipinas— he hoped it would begin "to shake off . . . the yoke . . . of foreign industry"—drew the interest of the energetic, enterprising, profit-oriented Francisco Cabarrús and a coterie of French investors. Iriarte never concealed from Floridablanca his distrust of Cabarrús's self-interest, his readiness to manipulate political connections for his business enterprises, for example, the transport of silver *pesos* from Cadiz for illegal export to Bayonne. On the other hand, Iriarte had no illusions about the commercial value to Spain of the Bourbon alliance, which he believed provided merely "imaginary and empty reciprocity."[54]

Like Virio, Iriarte expected from the French government, monarchy and then republic, full support against the English, whose navy and commercial expansion posed a common threat to colonies in America. Iriarte's strategy was pragmatic rather then ideological, always driven by a nationalist's resentment toward "these powers that have put their foot on our neck."[55] He strove for an equilibrium for Spain between the two hegemonic powers of the time, revealed in a self-analytical letter to Antonio Ximénez Navarro in which, disclaiming any "personal antipathy," he justified his attitude toward France. "Although I am a Spaniard who seeks the good of my country . . . I am impartial, I am cosmopolitan," he wrote, adding that "among us Anglomania is widespread, and those who do not suffer from it are labeled, not good Spaniards, but French." Although distancing himself from Gallicanism, he had to accept the reality of geographical determinism: "I . . . cannot ignore the fact that Spain, by geography, needs to be allied with France."[56]

The shocking radical turn of the Estates General in France in mid-1789 inspired Iriarte to urge Prime Minister Floridablanca to welcome workers and artisans emigrating from France, invoking what he knew England had done with Protestant refugees after France revoked the Edict of Nantes. Skilled workers would raise the level of manufactures in Spain, sharing "their skills in promoting those manufactures." In fact, Iriarte was quite specific about which artisans were most desirable; he wrote Hacienda secretary Gardoqui that the skilled silk weavers of Lyon, "who would hope to come to Spain," should be targeted. His anticlericalism surfaced in his fear of the effect on Franco-Spanish relations if instead thousands of embittered counterrevolutionaries sought asylum in Spain. Floridablanca, however, preferred fanatics to French workers.[57] Iriarte shared with Gardoqui and Virio a preoccupation with the chasm between Spain's glowing future of "mills, industry, and commerce" and the disappointing reality of national manufactures incapable of meeting the needs of consumers in the metropole and the colonies.[58]

Indeed, the leitmotif of his thinking was the interrelationship between diplomacy in Europe and its overseas impact. Spain's economy, Iriarte understood, depended heavily upon its colonies, and the government's major concern, he felt, should be "to preserve that Dominion . . . and enjoy its riches in metals and other types, to increase its opulence and power."[59] Settlement of the Nootka Sound incident, whose terms he disapproved, seemed to grant English merchants an outpost for penetrating the Spanish colonies along the eastern Pacific from New Spain southward. The terms led him to urge modifying the tax structure of colonial trade: "If duties are not lowered . . . our trade and navigation will disappear, and they will be the suppliers."[60] Trade barriers between the "Metropole and those vast possessions," including Madrid's restrictions on trade between colonial ports, had to be lowered; most important, Madrid had to remove discriminatory statutes affecting colonials and, following Aranda, grant them equality "as true Spaniards living in the peninsula, even bestowing upon them special favors and exemptions." His nightmare was, clearly, the possibility that otherwise quiescent colonials might follow the recent example of the former North American colonies of England.[61]

When the violence of the revolution in France escalated into the execution of the Bourbons, Iriarte found Spain's delicate position between two superpowers undermined by its ensuing conflict with France. It stripped his country of its main ally in containing England's pressure on the Spanish colonies. English merchants, he predicted, would soon dominate Spain's shipping and commerce, and London would try to occupy the Windward Islands, in the Caribbean, in order to monitor "places on the American continent." An added anxiety was the possibility that France, backed by the United States, would retaliate by cutting Spain's transatlantic communications and ultimately "harass . . . New Spain."[62] From the *Gaceta de Madrid* of 15 April 1794 he learned that the Earl of Landsdown had predicted in the House of Lords that Spain's loss of France's support *"draw along with it all it possesses in Mexico."* Yet the prospect of a mésalliance with England disheartened Iriarte, who called up his earlier analysis of the fate of Portugal after Methuen. English interests would make Spain a dependent state, thus ending hope for economic development and an adequate merchant marine and leaving his country "stripped of trade and navigation with those dominions." England's long-term goals were unchanged: "to keep open and subject to its will the trade of all our Americas," which, he had to add ruefully and realistically, "we seem to possess."[63]

Such preoccupations—economic backwardness, a navy incapable of maintaining communications with the American colonies, an inadequate merchant marine, and the constraints of past treaties—motivated Iriarte's response to Prime Minister Godoy's request that he "advise and write him personally on foreign and domestic matters, sharing frankly my ideas." A dedicated civil servant who sensed "the fate of the Monarchy in the imminent crisis," he could do no less than cooperate. In effect, he offered to Prime Minister Godoy and his brother, Domingo Iriarte, *oficial mayor* of the Secretaría de Estado, who was about to leave for Basel and peace negotiations with France's representatives, the insight of a veteran diplomat and career civil functionary. His analysis of the history of Spain's international agreements matched Virio's: countrywide weakness and incompetent personnel representing Spain. At the level of general principle, he concurred that international treaties had often been made between unequals; inept Spanish negotiators had repeatedly locked the country into the inequality of backwardness; and Spain's commercial policy had been circumscribed by the Hacienda's objectives as defined by "Administradores y Dirección General de Rentas" focused on the "composition and duty level of the Customs." His recommendation was to avoid unequal commercial accords, "especially with any powerful nation."[64]

Unfortunately, we lack information about Bernardo Iriarte's response to the decision to go to war with the French Republic in 1793. Yet earlier he had predicted to Domingo Iriarte that London would press for a commercial treaty once Spain joined the coalition to suppress the revolutionary French Republic, and he hoped negotiators would know how to evaluate the factors "that are to decide our future, and leave and form Spain in a state of dependence or independence, with respect to England above all." Bernardo's realism came through when hostilities ended and Domingo was ordered to Basel to negotiate the peace. He counseled his brother to return to "union" with France as "natural, necessary, indispensable to both nations, and I am sick of talking to you about it." A treaty of mutual defense was in order, but under no circumstance, he cautioned prophetically, should Spain's negotiators consent to a joint declaration of unity against England. Paramount was his underlying sense of Spain's overriding importance as a neutral balance between the superpowers. After all the "waste and setbacks" of government finance during the war in 1793–95, he could not imagine Spain sustaining another conflict with England. The royal navy "is worthless," and the colonies were undefended: "There is much in America to frighten us." Only a neutral stance in future conflicts between England and France would keep open contact with the overseas colonies. To France he would offer concessions: its merchants could continue to export to Spain "its own manufactures and"—a major concession—"even making use of our ports."[65]

Bernardo Iriarte continued to serve successive cabinets formally and informally dominated by Godoy, in the colonial office and in the Junta de Comercio, Moneda y Minas until 1804. We may speculate that he remained in government service in the hope that the government might still undertake the basic adjustments that many in and out of government believed necessary to preserve the imperial establishment in the metropole and its colonies. In brief, Iriarte's long-term strategy was that Madrid must avoid the vortex of international conflict and the loss of the colonies, which were fundamental to the process of economic development in the metropole. He would like to put the hegemons, England and France, in a bag "together and shaken up, to bury them in the deepest place in the sea . . . the only way to stop them from harming us."[66] This was more easily said than done; the hegemons were millstones that would grind down Godoy's regime. For Iriarte there was also the general dilemma of Spain's Catholic reformers:

whether to work for change within the system or withdraw from official life to anguished contemplation from the sidelines. A radical alternative was unacceptable: the French model, the road of revolutionary change, promised mob violence, civil war, then international wars of containment, ultimately a military coup d'état and what Iriarte later labeled derisively "Sa Majesté Consulaire," General Bonaparte. The other option, an alliance with England, was the road to inevitable dependence.

The civil servant who had welcomed Godoy's promising *appertura* in the early 1790s, calling him "protector" and confessing "how much I love and admire him, for the gratitude and empathy I have for him," grew disillusioned with Madrid's inability to isolate Spain from the European superpowers' competition for hegemony in Europe and America. Godoy's administration joined the Directoire in a second war with England, from 1796 to 1801; nevertheless, Iriarte still hoped Spain might return to neutrality and the preservation of its colonies after the Peace of Amiens. Disillusionment withered to despair in February 1804, when he learned of another of the government's "extraordinary, incomprehensible, and contradictory actions": Spain's gambit to preserve neutrality by promising to pay Paris a large monthly subsidy, much of it to be drawn from colonial revenues. In his notes he opined that it was far preferable to allocate them "to overhaul our unfortunate, our imaginary Navy." In addition, he recognized that the subsidy would rule out the opportunity to lower the government's domestic and foreign debt and hasten "imminent bankruptcy."[67] His decades of analyzing English policy led him to conclude with customary prescience that London would judge the subsidy really indirect support for France. Cassandra-like, Iriarte confided to his notebooks that sooner or later England "will force us to go to War and to begin . . . will seize some of our ships returning from the Indies with funds," to which he appended, "they will occupy one of our Islands."[68] Iriarte was prophetic.

Probably an increasingly critical stance led to Iriarte's removal from office and official "exile" to Andalusia in 1804. There, inveterate *proyectista,* he drafted memorials on how to keep the American colonies from imitating the example of "the Anglo-American colonies," an ominous possibility after the disaster at Trafalgar, "a decisive and total victory . . . our whole fleet has been destroyed, all of it."[69] Iriarte stayed in Andalusia until 1808, when the government recalled him to Madrid to serve under Murat and then José Bonaparte, joining other distinguished nationalists such as Azanza, Gonzalo O'Farrill, Soler, Sixto Espinosa, Meléndez Valdéz, and Goya, who viewed alliance with an authoritarian France as the only way to correct Spain's "mistakes and mishaps" and avoid falling under English hegemony.[70]

Negociantes' Spokesmen at Veracruz and Cadiz:
Basadre and Antúnez y Acevedo

In the manuscripts of the neo-*proyectistas* Gardoqui and Virio the colonies, their trade, and the commercial bourgeoisie of the metropole were recurrent themes. In Spain's late mercantilist phase of trade expansion merchants were bound to become *the* focus of attention. Trade rather than agriculture seemed the primary stimulus for economic development, and the commercial bourgeoisie merited the close attention of state and society. Earlier, in the 1770s and 1780s, civil servants such as Valentín de Foronda and financial entrepreneurs such as Francisco Cabarrús had argued for greater social recognition of the merchant class. When Floridablanca sought recommendations for improving Spain's foreign trade in 1783, unabashedly Cabarrús pointed out that the country still lacked a "middle class of honored citizens" and that the commercial profession needed to be given honorable status.[71] Four years later, when Foronda drafted an essay (read to Veracruz merchants in 1796) on "lo honroso" of being a merchant, the upsurge in trade with the colonies had already reinforced the perception that merchants should be moved from social penumbra to broad daylight.[72]

The emphasis of Gardoqui, Virio, and other political economists on trade, trade-related issues, and merchants had a strong echo across the Atlantic, for example, at Veracruz in 1796. There the Spanish secretary of Veracruz's recently established *consulado*, Vicente Basadre, had to prepare annual reports *(memorias de instituto)*, as prescribed by the guild's charter; these were read every January to a *junta general* of the membership on a theme relevant to the *consulado's* purposes. Promising subsequent essays on the state of local agriculture, population, shipping, and manufacture, he concentrated his initial report on "the benefits of the condition of the honored profession of commerce."[73] His credentials were respectable: by 1796 he had already spent two decades in the colony of New Spain, where he had evaluated the potential of trading California otter skins for mercury from China, in the process visiting Manila and Canton. He had returned to New Spain critical of the Manila *consulado's* antagonism to the operation of the recently chartered Compañia de Filipinas. Apparently he enjoyed good relations with a leading merchant house of Veracruz, the Casa de Cosío; in 1794 Francisco Saavedra recommended Basadre's appointment as secretary of the new *consulado* there, citing his "personal knowledge of New Spain's trade."[74]

In Basadre's view, commerce formed what "Chancellor Bacon" had described as the "base fundamental" of human happiness, because exchange provided an indispensable spectrum of goods that individuals alone could not produce.[75] It furnished "a most vigorous momentum to the father-land's prosperity," augmented population, uprooted laziness, lightened mankind's labor, and "spreads opulence . . . the fountain of prosperity."[76] Trade as the dynamic factor in a national economy affected population through job creation in manufacture and a range of crafts. The magnet of trade alone drew risktakers to the "very deadly climate" of Veracruz and Acapulco, the Dutch East Indies, the Persian Gulf, and the caravans between Arabia and Suez; commerce, Basadre believed, had transformed London, Amsterdam, and the United States into entrepôts. Now every government understood that trade as measured by a national "Balanza Mercantil" was the "sole and reliable Balance of Power" and—using a metaphor comprehensible to Spanish merchants residing in New Spain—a "Mine that is always profitable."[77] Notwithstanding the obvious importance of the merchant's profession, Spaniards held that the status of nobility was the result of birth or membership in the profession of the sword or toga; crafts *(exercícios)* were incompatible with social distinction.[78] Of course, Basadre's perception of the merchant's role had to do more with its social utility than with its possible status conferral; once "they came to value and distinguish the honorable profession of Commerce," Spaniards might no longer "close their ears to the Voices of Truth" and might choose instead "to awaken from the Mercantile Lethargy that gripped us for two centuries."[79]

Basadre's "Mercantile Lethargy" was an oblique critique of the Spanish empire's obvious nucleus of resistance to commercial innovation, Cadiz, the critical point of the Spanish transatlantic system. Civil servants tend to minimize overt friction between government and powerful domestic interest groups, which makes understandable Basadre's approach, Virio's emphasis upon ineffective bureaucrats, and the focus of both Virio and Gardoqui on asymmetrical international relations as a major factor accounting for Spain's economic lag. However, the influence of the tradition-bound Cadiz commercial community did not deter prominent civil servants from venting criticism in anonymous pamphlets. In an era of growing public awareness of national problems and state censorship, pamphlet literature offered a medium of expression to the muzzled loyal opposition.

In late 1788 there had circulated at Madrid a satirical pamphlet with the title *Carta de un vecino de Fuencarral a un abogado de Madrid, sobre el libre comercio de los huevos,* which criticized the attitude of the Cadiz commercial community toward changes in Spain's transatlantic system after 1765. This was already well known; what was novel was the bald details about collusion between businessmen and bureaucrats to impede modifications in their shared monopoly of the colonial trades. The merchants of Cadiz (Fuencarral) preferred to earn "much with little" rather than "little with much" and guaranteed their oligopoly ("their . . . farm") by "showing generosity." In 1788 they were quite satisfied with the results of the Reglamento of 1778— "our cause has never had a better aspect." They remained "very devoted to custom," ever resistant to "novelty" and ever hopeful of reviving the *flota* system stabilized in 1720, so that "the system becomes managed as earlier"— sunk in what Basadre had termed their "letargo mercantil." Raising the *Carta de un vecino de Fuencarral* above the run of underground literature of the time was its brash satirizing of the Cadiz merchant community and its Madrid lobbyists. It was astutely crafted, reverential toward the Spanish Bourbons, knowledgeable about the details of Spain's transatlantic system. The satirist showed an insider's savvy about policymaking and policymakers. Last, that the circulation of the pamphlet was not impeded by the state security apparatus was an indicator of a degree of official toleration of loyal dissent by the late 1780s. Most worrisome to the Cadiz community was the author's evident praise for those who had tried to modify the structures of colonial trade, the foundation of Cadiz's commercial dominance.[80]

It is not surprising, then, that by the 1790s, when Valdés, Gardoqui, and Campomanes held high government office, Cadiz turned pessimistic: the policy made in Madrid after 1789 might ultimately erode its economic hegemony. Now Gaditanos had to revisit the recent past: the modifications in the transatlantic trade system to incorporate the wealthy colony of New Spain in *comercio libre* in 1789; elimination of the centuries-old Casa de Contratación; implantation of the intendancy system in Peru and New Spain to curtail the exploitation of native American peoples, and last, Madrid's intention to charter more *consulados* in the principal ports in its American colonies. The well-circulated broadside *Carta de un vecino de Fuencarral* rankled the merchant community of Cadiz, heightening its sense of being an embattled species, and led it to enlist a public defender to counter the ascendance of the late *proyectistas* and voice to Spain's political class the fear of innovations threatening their interests, which they had always identified with *Monarquía, Estado,* and *Nación.* A defender was found in government circles, in the influential Consejo de Indias, where in the 1790s, the Consulado de Cádiz counted on a veteran *consejero,* Rafael Antúnez y Acevedo.

Circumstantial evidence clarifies why Antúnez composed an indirect defense of the historical role of the port complex of Spain's transatlantic system, Seville-Cadiz, in Lower Andalusia. Born at Puerto Santa María in 1736, Antúnez was an *andaluz* whose family and career made Andalusia "his native region" and "his Fatherland." His father, educated in a Jesuit school at Córdoba, had earned law degrees at Osuna and Seville, and after serving as *alcalde* of Puerto Santa María, San Lúcar, and Cadiz, he had been appointed *juez asesor* in 1741 and later *oidor* of the Casa de Contratación. His mother was a *gaditana*. When his father retired in 1765, Antúnez followed him into the Casa de Contratación as a *fiscal* and then *oidor,* and in 1770 he became a *ministro togado* on the Consejo de Indias at Madrid. There he would serve for thirty years, conscientious, diligent, and knowledgeable like his much admired seventeenth-century predecessor, José de Veytia y Linaje. A civil servant and the son of one, emblematic of the typical functionary *(covachuelo)* of Spain's old regime, Antúnez petitioned the government toward the end of his career for a pension drawn on the treasury of the wealthiest colony, New Spain, to support a daughter and the career of his son.[81]

A veteran of the Consejo de Indias and a specialist in colonial mercantile law, Antúnez came to know Gardoqui and his fellow *andaluz* Tomás González Carbajal, in the Hacienda; Campomanes, the dean of the Consejo de Castilla; and Francisco Leandro de Viana, conde de Tepa, a fellow *consejero* of the Consejo de Indias who had served in the colonies at Manila and Mexico City. Since he habitually vacationed at Cadiz, "where there is the house I can call my own (it's the house belonging to my children's maternal grandparents)," Antúnez had occasion to discuss relevant issues with members of the Cadiz merchant community, who valued him as a sympathetic representative of their interests on the Consejo.[82] Critics, on the other hand, felt that he espoused views antagonistic to "sound principles and the current system" and partisan to "the system of the Reglamentos and Cadiz's monarchy."[83] In 1797, in the introduction to his *Memorias históricas sobre la legislación y gobierno del comercio de los españoles con sus colonias en las Indias occidentales,* Antúnez voiced the complaint of the Cadiz community that in recent decades Madrid had failed to consult it on vital colonial issues and the community's conviction that it was "necessary that the government not proceed to mandate . . . changes, especially in the difficult and sensitive area of commerce, without asking for statements from those engaged in it."[84]

Antúnez drafted most of his *Memorias históricas* between October 1791 and January 1792 (when Revillagigedo, in New Spain, was receiving local merchants' views of *comercio libre*), finishing the last section a year later. He disclaimed any intention of publishing a compilation that "at another time could be valued," hoping modestly that his free time would be used "honestly." Despite the humility, he circulated his manuscript among many "knowledgeable in trade matters," including his fellow *consejero* Viana, who, when serving in New Spain, had married the heiress to one of the largest pulque *haciendas* of the colony and on returning to the metropole had bought an estate in Andalusia. Antúnez probably also showed his manuscript to Tomás González Carbajal.[85]

Antúnez never stated explicitly that his publication was an apologia for the commercial system that had privileged (and enriched) the port of Seville in the sixteenth and seventeenth centuries and Cadiz in the eighteenth. Even references to the "Carta de un vecino" that originally appeared in the introduction to the *Memorias históricas* were excised to avoid offending the anonymous "distinguished" functionary who had authored that "comic allegory."[86] Also left implicit was his justification for limiting further modification of colonial commercial policy and for returning to the abandoned practice of convoyed shipping. Antúnez camouflaged his study as simply memoirs, its material culled from legislation covering the Spanish transatlantic system from its origins to his time; he confessed to having drawn heavily upon Veytia y Linage's classic *Norte de la contratación*, of 1672.[87] In fact, his coverage of the legislation that had significantly modified a two-hundred-year-old system of trade and navigation—the three major *reglamentos del comercio libre* from 1765 to 1789—is noticeably minimal. The memoirs are confined mainly to materials of the sixteenth and seventeenth centuries, precisely the years of Lower Andalusia's legal hegemony over all colonial trade flows. Praise for the pre-1765 system verging on the explicit surfaces first in his justification of the halcyon times of Lower Andalusia's trade monopoly. There he elaborates excessively on a *cédula* of 1529, signed by Charles V, opening ports in Galicia, Asturias, the *montañas* of Santander, Vizcaya, Guipuzcoa, Murcia, and Granada to direct trade with the American colonies, pointing out that the *cédula* was utilized only for a brief period. His explanation was designed to enhance the natural viability of the Seville-Cadiz complex over other ports in the peninsula, which had to contend with French and English corsairs and shortages of shipping and related facilities, exportables, and long-term financing.[88] His argument is also made explicit in the course of a discussion of the *flota* system before 1740. Consistent with the leitmotif of his *Memorias,* Antúnez ended by recommending that all those enjoying "influence at the higher level of our government" take a fresh look at a publication of 1740, Bernardo Ulloa's *Restablecimiento del comercio y fábricas de España,* chapters 14–20, where Ulloa urged maintaining the Spanish Atlantic's *flota* system (he reinserted a *flota* for Buenos Aires).[89]

In other ways, too, Antúnez advanced Cadiz's preference for the *flota* system centered on a single Andalusian harbor. First, although he emphasized pre-1700 legislation in detail, he did not review the system's short-comings, which were devastatingly apparent after about 1670, starkly so later during the War of the Spanish Succession. Second, it is striking that in a publication ostensibly highlighting the most relevant colonial trade regulations covering more than two centuries and designed to guide the merchant and shipping communities in Spain, Antúnez managed virtually to skip the three major *reglamentos,* from 1765 to 1789, which the Cadiz community had opposed vociferously and fruitlessly.[90]

Antúnez circulated his manuscript among friends and colleagues for about two years; one may speculate that only when he sensed a clear shift in the official attitude away from the neo-*proyectistas* of the early nineties did he resolve to obtain an official placet. Early in 1794 he received a note from Gardoqui, possibly prompted by one of Hacienda's *fiscales,* Tomás González Carbajal, inviting him to submit his manuscript to official censorship. Antúnez complied with a formal petition for a license to publish, to which he added a request for an "especial favor," authorization to dedicate his work to the crown.[91] After five months, in August 1794, Gardoqui forwarded the manuscript for critical evaluation to Gardoqui's friend and Antúnez's fellow *consejero de Indias,* Francisco Viana. Eight months later Viana—who it should be recalled had crossed swords with the merchants in the Manila *consulado* and had a good grasp of the conditions of recent growth in New Spain—finally had to release his critique, in which he charged Antúnez with partiality for "the system of the Reglamentos and the monopoly of Cadiz" and deliberate omission of the remarkable growth in colonial trade flows resulting from the three Reglamentos del Comercio Libre of the late eighteenth century. Partiality, Viana noted, was discernible in Antúnez's handling of the long-overlooked 1529 *cédula,* and he made a point of clarifying that other ports in the metropole had been deterred from citing the *cédula* by the tactics of Seville's merchant community, the "intrigues and tricks practiced by a Corps of rich Merchants, who hoped for exclusive trade." This critique clearly referred as much to the Cadiz of his time as to the Seville of the Hapsburgs. In what was a roundabout way of explaining the delay in submitting his critique, Viana confessed that he would not recommend rejection of the manuscript of an "Amigo" and much respected "magistrado," preferring to leave that to the enlightened readers after its publication.[92] Antúnez readily identified the unnamed reviewer. In a note to his "former venerable Compañero" Gardoqui, he suggested that a second evaluation be obtained from Tomás González Carbajal, who had initially handled the matter when still in the Hacienda.[93]

Another six months passed before González Carbajal presented his critique. He considered Viana's reservations unfair, a personal attack that understated the merits of Antúnez's manuscript. In contrast to Viana, he judged the memoir a dispassionate compilation, "a simple review of facts and measures . . . on Commerce to the Indies." As for Antúnez's reliance upon Veytia's *Norte de la contratación,* he admired Veytia's virtues as "hardworking, accurate as befitting a high authority, and creditable in his writing." Behind Viana's criticism, González Carbajal postulated, was not the compilation itself but Antúnez's failure to explain that the "old measures" cited were the product of the "ignorance" and "obscurity" of their time and place.

Although González Carbajal found no connection between the interests of the Seville-Cadiz merchant communities and Veytia or Antúnez (both of whom he considered models of dispassionate scholarship), he did advance an ideological explanation for Viana's acerbic critique. Viana had a long record of support for "the liberty of the colonial trade," and his unrelenting pressure for enlarging the Spanish colonial trading system was, González Carbajal judged, primarily responsible for Madrid's movement in that direction despite the opposition, what González Carbajal labeled "persistent contradictions." Nevertheless, he went on, Viana had not objected to publication of the *Memorias históricas,* which in the long run would have brought him "discredit." In sum, readers should make up their own minds about Antúnez's work. He offered one editorial revision: Antúnez should excise from his introduction his impolitic criticism of the anonymous author of the "comic allegory," the *Carta de un vecino de Fuencarral*—which implied that González Carbajal knew the author was no ordinary pen for hire.[94]

With the endorsement of González Carbajal in June 1796 and possibly pressure from other sources, Gardoqui at last authorized publication of Antúnez's *Memorias históricas,* minus, however, royal permission to dedicate the work to the crown.[95] When Antúnez later sought permission for exclusive rights to a reprint, Gardoqui's successor as Hacienda minister, Pedro Varela, turned for advice to the aging neo-*proyectista* and dean of the Consejo de Castilla, Campomanes. Like Viana, he found in the *Memorias* what he elegantly called "A support for the old system of *flota* and *galeones*"; just as one might predict, most of his critique expatiated elegantly on Antúnez's "excessive brevity" of the commercial legislation covering colonial trade gradually adopted under Charles III.[96] Under the Bourbons, Campomanes observed, colonial trade had recovered from the widespread stagnation under the last of the Hapsburgs that the much-admired Veytia had soft-pedaled. Yet Campomanes concurred in a second printing, provided Antúnez appended to his legislative compendium a selection of imperial trade regulations after 1765. Antúnez died three years later, before any reprint of his work; it is not known whether he intended to incorporate Campomanes's recommendations.[97]

Antúnez's *Memorias,* an implicit critique (as Viana and Campomanes sensed) of reformist commercial policies activated by neo-*proyectistas* under Charles III and extended by Valdés and Gardoqui under Charles IV, was virtually completed by January 1792, when the undercurrent of Catholic enlightenment and flexible economic policy still ran strong. Immediately after Charles III's death, Floridablanca's tightly run "despotismo ministerial" in 1789 issued the last of the epoch-making Reglamentos del Comercio Libre, opened the American colonies to foreign slave traders in response to pressure from Cuba's planters, and in 1792 was set to weaken the Cadiz–Lima–Mexico City network of oligopoly by chartering new *consulados* in the colonies. Antúnez had wisely chosen to await a sea change in official policy before seeking approval of his manuscript; that change began in 1794, after a year of war with France had sharpened debate over Spain's international policies and their colonial repercussions. Another two years would pass before Antúnez received the delayed official approval; by 1796 the political climate—only two years earlier less tolerant of Cadiz's oligopolists—had yielded to a countercurrent surprisingly supportive of Andalusia's hegemony over the transatlantic trade. In 1796 state finance was in disarray as a result of unprecedented war expenditures; now Madrid had to reconsider the special interests of a major source of financial aid, the Cadiz commercial community. The pendulum was now swinging away from even moderate *inovación.*

Part Two

·····························Fissioning of
New Spain

4. Reorganizing New Spain's External Trade: The Effects of *Comercio Libre*, 1789–1796

Merchants of sound judgment are sure that *comercio libre* has not given earnings for distribution, rather heavy losses and delays bemoaned.   Manuel García Herreros

Monopoly . . . is finished, one cannot give another name to a commerce in which those in this Kingdom with money, as a group, invested in buying up everything brought by *flota*.
                                                                                               Tomás Murphy

Only the class of merchants prospers and enriches itself, and those who establish commercial houses there are leeches who swell with the sweat of native peoples.
                                                                                               II conde de Revillagigedo, 1794

Over a three-year period the colonial administration of New Spain, under the direction of the recently arrived viceroy, II conde de Revillagigedo, undertook an examination of the performance of the colony's economy on a scale and precision rarely, if ever, before seen there. Revillagigedo executed the survey successfully; its inspiration had come earlier, in the administration of his viceregal predecessor. It is not far-fetched to speculate that the colonial office, under new management, hoped to validate Floridablanca's "feliz revolución" and—an outside chance—to stimulate metropolitan entrepreneurs. Noteworthy, however, is the effort to marshal quantitative rather than purely qualitative or descriptive data in order to refute the virtually unanimous position of Mexico City's Spanish-born merchant enclave, probably New Spain's most influential interest group.[1] Stimulus to the inquiry came from Antonio Valdés's colonial office in 1787, hard on the death of the Consulado de México's patron at Madrid, José de Gálvez, who, as we have seen, had stalled the extension of *comercio libre* to New Spain since 1781.[2] With his death, the Consulado de México lost its most influential defender at Madrid.

Valdés's initiative reflected two governmental goals: to furnish advance warning to Mexico City wholesale merchants, the *almaceneros,* of the intention to extend *comercio libre* to the empire's wealthiest colony; and to obtain on a regular basis trade information about colonial demand, supply, and population growth and hence to permit estimates of per capita consumption of imports, prices, and variation in colonial consumers' luxury-goods preferences. Motivating this initiative may also have been Valdés's need for data to support Madrid's intention to curb the coercion of native peoples under the *repartimiento* system, specifically prohibited in the *Ordenanza de intendentes,* extended to New Spain in 1786. In the late 1780s the colonial office and interested merchant houses knew that the volume and value of the colonial trades was rising, although the magnitude and composition were debatable. Such information disseminated in the metropole via the newly established government-supported commercial periodical, the *Correo Mercantil de España y sus Indias,* would make available to peninsular merchants outside the close-mouthed Cadiz mercantile enclave quantitative rather than impressionistic commercial intelligence indispensable for business decision making. Up-to-date, reliable data could be an incentive to merchant houses to commit their and other investors' funds to sustained involvement in colonial markets. For the function of commercial intelligence had been imperfectly executed by government-financed packet boats *(avisos)* inaugurated in 1765 after research and recommendation by Pedro Rodríguez Campomanes, then *fiscal* of the Consejo de Castilla. In two separate orders of 1787 Madrid directed the Consulado de México and then Viceroy Flores to prepare and forward such quantitative information.[3] In light of Flores's close ties to the Mexico City merchant community and its connections with major colonial civil servants, his administration characteristically ignored the government's request despite the evident impatience of Madrid.

The accession of a monarch in Spain usually opened the way to some changes, and in colonial affairs at this time matters were pushed along by the death of the colonial officeholder, Gálvez, who knew New Spain well and had followed developments with information from merchants and civil servants there, as well as from civil servants in retirement at Madrid. In 1786 Gálvez put the intendancy system into effect in New Spain and gradually advanced the possibility of including New Spain in the wider system of imperial trade inaugurated in 1765. In fact Gálvez had postponed including New Spain, aware of the resistance to inclusion in *comercio libre* of the wealthy, influential merchant elites dominating the external and internal trade of the colony. These elites were equally opposed to the intendancy system, particularly article 12 of the *ordenanza* designed to curb the volume of credit advanced to native people to coerce them to produce cotton yarn, cotton cloth *(manta),* and a valuable red dyestuff, cochineal. Both the intendancy and *comercio libre* threatened the dominant role of Mexico City's warehousemen *(almaceneros)* in the external and internal trades of the world's largest producer of silver *pesos.* Between the death of Charles III in 1789 and the appearance of Manuel Godoy in 1794 an *appertura* appeared, perhaps comparable to the early years of Charles III and Esquilache. In some respects Valdés, Malaspina, and Revillagigedo were among the last of the *proyectistas* the French Revolution would discourage.

Floridablanca and Valdés grasped the value of posting Revillagigedo, then fifty years old, to New Spain as viceroy at this juncture. Since the late 1760s he had lived at Madrid in the palatial town house—"one of Madrid's most elegant"—his father had bought, probably with funds amassed in America, on retiring from his viceregal post at Mexico City.[4] Apparently Revillagigedo *père* and the conde de Aranda, a fellow *militar,* became close friends after their collaboration in the immediate aftermath of the *motín* of Esquilache at Madrid in 1766. Young Revillagigedo became a *protégé* of Aranda's and came to share his mentor's pragmatism, nationalism, and uncompromising impetuousness.

Benefiting from his father's prestige and wealth, Revillagigedo passed his early years first in Havana and then in Mexico City. When the family returned to Madrid, he followed his grandfather and father into the army. During the Seven Years' War he distinguished himself in the campaign in Portugal, first under the command of the marqués de Sarriá, then under Aranda; at twenty-two he was a colonel in the Regimiento de la Reina at Ceuta. As part of Aranda's strategy for tightening the Spanish army's discipline and training on Prussian lines, Revillagigedo and his unit were transferred after 1765 to Panama, where his unit rebelled against his rigid discipline. Rejecting the local commander's request to modify his methods, Revillagigedo resigned and left for Madrid; Charles III froze his military career in retaliation.

Freed of official duties in the 1770s, Revillagigedo (like the civil servant Bernardo Iriarte) used his leisure to inform himself at Madrid's *tertulias,* talk to his father's friends in retirement from colonial service, reflect on his own colonial experience, and form a conspectus of Spain and its empire in the aftermath of the disasters of the Seven Years' War—something akin to Aranda's pessimistic analysis prepared for Charles III's son in 1782.[5] In managing the considerable estate of his father, accumulated over years of colonial service at Havana and then Mexico City, Revillagigedo developed antagonism toward monopoly aggressively manipulated for private gain, for example, Madrid's sole formal banking institution, the Cinco Gremios Mayores. In return for functioning as the *monarquía*'s principal lender, its investment strategies favored neither the metropolitan economy nor trade with the American colonies, much less domestic manufactures.[6] Perhaps this led him to become a shareholder in the publicly owned Compañía de Filipinas and the Banco Nacional de San Carlos. Francisco Cabarrús, perceiving his business skills, recommended him as one of the five directors of the bank.[7]

By his forties Revillagigedo had crafted his conspectus of the Atlantic world and the position of Spain and its American possessions. England and France were competing for "the possessions and . . . interests of the New World, maritime supremacy, and the commercial benefits of the New World."[8] He did not question the alliance with France to protect those possessions. There was, however, a downside: French influence upon Spain's government and society had been smothering national structures and identity ever since the early years of Charles III's reign under Esquilache and his successor, Grimaldi. Although mutual defense in the Atlantic was imperative, in order to use its colonies efficiently Spain had to break out of its dependence, for "Spain . . . will pursue its own path and destiny . . . as reason advises."[9]

The core problematic was construction of a respectable Spanish naval force to protect sea lanes and the colonial trades from inevitable English aggression. In linear fashion Revillagigedo linked a revived navy to a merchant marine, a consequent enlarged reserve of seamen, and the revenues to construct and maintain it. Spain's colonial trades should not be shared with France, whose commercial interests "especially in Trade, are and will remain incompatible with Spain's." In what could only be a reference to France, he pointed out that Spain's raw wools and silk were exported, when the country's real interest was in "drawing upon its own resources for most of the goods and wares needed in America, and exporting from those dominions an equal amount of raw materials, produce, and precious metals." Meanwhile, what was manufactured at home for export to the colonies found few consumers there because of poor quality and uncompetitive pricing. What was needed was a government policy oriented less to revenue enhancement and more to growth: Mexico's "much silver" (incidentally, he found this no real good fortune) reflected government policy for cheapening inputs. The stellar performer in the American colonies was "the island of Havana" because since 1765 it had enjoyed "un libre comercio." This was the true goal for the colonies; unfortunately, "real liberty of trade . . . is unknown in Spain."[10]

We can now appreciate why recently appointed Prime Minister Florida-blanca in the late 1770s brought Revillagigedo out of official penumbra and why he responded with a plan for the siege of Gibraltar, which seemed to restore him to royal favor. His father had cooperated with the French at Havana during the War of the Austrian Succession, and the son served under France's duc de Crillon at Gibraltar; Revillagigedo recognized the importance of the French alliance and—ever the nationalist—the policies shaped by divergent national interests. His view of the interrelated problems of metropole and American colonies was crystallized in the seventies in correspondence with friends who were prominent in Madrid's political class.[11] At the time of his appointment to the viceroyalty of New Spain in 1789 neither his mentor, Floridablanca, nor Colonial Secretary Valdés could doubt his commitment to support both the *Ordenanza de intendentes* (1786) and the third *reglamento del comercio libre* (1789); this approach, the influential *almaceneros* of Mexico City's *consulado* were convinced, would inevitably undermine their hegemony over the economy of New Spain and Spain's Caribbean possessions.

Before Revillagigedo left Madrid for New Spain, civil servants in the colonial office probably recommended Mexico City residents who might share his interest in pursuing the still controversial goals of the Valdés colonial office. For example, there were the well-respected Basque merchant Francisco Ignacio de Yraeta, incidentally the Mexico City agent (and a shareholder) of the Compañía de Filipinas, and Eusebio Buenaventura Beleña, a veteran colonial officer who had begun his career as *subdelegado* accompanying Gálvez on his *visita* to Guadalajara in the late 1760s. Yraeta and Beleña were respected and knowledgeable and might entertain a broader conspectus of imperial issues than their peers in the colony. So when Revilla-gigedo advised Diego de Gardoqui in September 1790 of what his predecessor, Viceroy Flores, had prepared for reporting on the economy of New Spain, with particular attention to trade with the metropole, he could rely upon data, advice, and support from reliable informants in commercial circles and civil administration.

Gálvez's replacement, Antonio Valdés, was one of the new administrative cadres who hoped for progressive rather than radical improvements, a group that included Jovellanos, Meléndez Valdés, Bernardo Iriarte, Gardoqui, Aragorri, and Cabarrús. Probably Valdés's initiatives terminated the Casa de Contratación (1790) and its influence on colonial economic policy;

promulgated the decree incorporating New Spain and Venezuela into the system of *comercio libre* (1789); posted nationalist, competent high colonial officers like Las Casas y Aragorri to Havana; and picked the Italian naval officer Alejandro Malaspina to head an exploratory hydrographic expedition to the Pacific and, "primary objective of his expedition," gather data for a report on general conditions in the American colonies.[12]

It is testimony to the power and inflexibility of New Spain's bureaucratic and mercantile structures that even so dynamic, inquisitive, and often ruthless a viceroy as Revillagigedo II—a remarkable example of Spain's efforts to refurbish its much criticized colonial civil service—could not (or did not) forward a definitive report in less than three years. On 26 September 1790 he promised Madrid to provide data requested and a report *(informe)* on economic conditions resulting from the modification of colonial trade structures under the *comercio libre* of 1778 and its supplement in 1789.[13] Nine months later, on 16 June 1791, he initiated his inquiry by requiring the local Hacienda agencies in the colony to search their files for statistical materials; he also formulated a questionnaire for distribution to both the state sector and members of the private sector, some of whom he had already consulted on other matters. Between late June and late August 1791 almost all the merchants' replies were received, with two exceptions, Yraeta's and Diego de Ágreda's, all of which were uniformly negative about current economic conditions and pessimistic about the implementation of *comercio libre*.[14] On the other hand, Revillagigedo also received an unexpectedly vigorous rebuttal of the merchants' position by the experienced bureaucrat Beleña. At the end of the year, on 2 December 1791, 115 of Mexico City's most important merchants, probably reacting to Beleña's persuasive support for the government's commercial modifications, complained that such fiscal charges as customs duties and sales taxes dampened business activity and, by indirection, the effectiveness of *comercio libre*. Early in January 1792 the Mexico City *consulado* itself came out in support of the individual reports.[15] Now it was the turn of a veteran, the prolific colonial functionary Ramón de Posada, to refute Mexico City's merchant guild; in turn a few guild members seem to have enlisted the collaboration of a key colonial fiscal agent, superintendent of Mexico City's customs, Páez de la Cadena, one of the viceroy's important respondents, who had delayed his response. Predictably Páez's posthumous report, dated 27 May 1792, vigorously upheld the negative view of the capital's merchant community. When in March 1792 Madrid officials expressed impatience at the absence of Revillagigedo's final report, forcing the viceroy at the end of June to detail the obstacles to his executing the requested survey, he had to pressure colonial officers in the capital, in the major intendancies, and in particular those at Veracruz for data requested initially by Flores in 1787.[16]

It was probably in late 1792, once necessary and long-awaited statistical data had finally materialized, that a refutation of Mexico City's leading merchants and their unofficial spokesman in the colonial civil service, Páez de la Cadena, came from the pen of an anonymous, extremely well informed functionary, the comprehensive "Ensayo apologético por el comercio libre, con reflexiones imparciales sobre las pretensione de negociantes."[17] It took another six months for there to appear an equally comprehensive rejection of the merchants' negativism, this time by a merchant from the Caribbean port of Veracruz, a relative newcomer to Spain's and New Spain's Atlantic trade, Tomás Murphy y Porro.[18] These vicissitudes in the case of what opened as an apparently innocuous government request for commercial information on the economy of New Spain in order to create a database for policy formulation and execution account for the delayed completion, on 31 August 1793, of Revillagigedo's model, classic analysis of the effects of *comercio libre* on the trade of Spain's principal colonial possession at the end of the eighteenth century, replete with statistics initially utilized by the anonymous author of the "Ensayo apologético." Since the publication of Revillagigedo's *informe* in 1930, other documents have surfaced, notably those of other colonial functionaries and one from a merchant respondent. What is evident is that *comercio libre* had few supporters among Mexico City's wholesale merchants—only two of twelve merchant respondents— and that support for the new economic policy came principally from the elite of New Spain's colonial civil service, notably Eusebio Buenaventura Beleña.

Revillagigedo's questionnaire revealed a classic standoff between civil servants seeking modest change and wealthy wholesale importers overseas who were experienced in merchandising and uncommonly effective lobbyists for the status quo. Change seemed to be a responsibility lodged mainly in the colonial administrative mind, or perhaps a wealthy colonial commercial enclave cradled in a long-term monopoly was psychologically ill-prepared to accept change, notwithstanding data to the contrary?

In retrospect, the overwhelmingly negative responses by the capital's Spanish merchants to the recent modifications of Atlantic trade policy—the slow extension after 1778 of so-called *comercio libre* to New Spain in 1789— should have come as no surprise to a pragmatic, opinionated administrator like Revillagigedo. In his first colonial post, in Panama in the 1760s, he had been rattled by local administrative and commercial interests, who simply outmaneuvered him. This experience, along with even a scanning of the merchants whom he had handpicked to respond to his questionnaire about *comercio libre*'s repercussions in New Spain—their provenances, careers, kin, and business networks—should have readied him for their negativism.

Of the twelve merchants selected, five (Yermo, Vidal, Basoco, Vicario, and García Herreros) had served in 1788 on a committee of the *consulado* charged with surveying the economic situation under the former *flota* system; their report had recommended maintaining limited annual shipping, along with tonnage maxima, basically supporting the *flota* system. In 1791 Yermo and Vidal refrained from further comment in light of their earlier report. Of the ten remaining respondents, the geographical provenance of eight is verifiable: six (Basoco, Angulo Guardamino, Meoqui, Yraeta, Ágreda, and García Herreros) came from northern Spain, one (Vicario) was from Valencia, and one (Icaza) was from Panama. Basoco and Angulo Guardamino hailed from the Cantabrian *encartaciones,* Yraeta from Guipuzcoa, while from Cameros, in the province of Logroño, came García Herreros and Ágreda. There were neither Aragonese, Andalusians, nor Catalans, suggesting the importance of the Cantabrian periphery as a recruiting ground for Mexico City's *peninsular*-dominated merchant community (or at least its most successful members) in the second half of the eighteenth century. With one exception (Icaza), the respondents were Spanish immigrants who had prospered in New Spain's commercial world and by 1791 were prominent in Mexico City's business community after decades of activity there.

Of course, all were part of the colony's economic elite. Basoco and Vicario were close friends; García Herreros and Ágreda, cousins from San Román de Cameros (Logroño), had taken passage together to Veracruz in 1784; Basoco had been succeeded by Icaza as collector of the principal and interest (4 *al millar*) on all goods entering Mexico City, applied to liquidate the *consulado*'s wartime loan of 1 million *pesos* to Madrid in 1782–83.[19] By birth or marriage some were also tied to the merchant community of the colonial capital. Invited to Mexico City by his uncle (Castañiza) to learn the merchant's trade, Basoco, typically, married a cousin, Castañiza's daughter; for his part Icaza married a daughter of Yraeta's. Basoco, Meoqui, and García Herreros were heavy investors in mining enterprises at Guanajuato and Zacatecas, and across the Atlantic were relatives at Cadiz (brothers of Ágreda and García Herreros).

Thus Revillagigedo tapped into the commercial elite of New Spain, many linked both to *criollo* mining families and to Cadiz commercial firms. Ágreda's brother was a prominent Cadiz merchant, and both were allied by marriage to a Cadiz merchant with agents at Veracruz, Francisco Bustamante y Guerra. In sum, these resident *peninsular* respondents were fully integrated into the apex of Mexico City's economic elite; many worked with leading *criollo* mining families and with merchants of Cadiz and other areas of the Spanish Atlantic's periphery. In selecting respondents among Mexico City's merchants, Revillagigedo knowingly sought the viewpoint of one of the Hispanic world's most powerful, intermarried, and otherwise interconnected interest groups.

Established, secure, eminently successful in their métier, the merchant respondents whose replies arrived in the remarkably short time of two weeks were respectfully frank. Most replies, such as those of Basoco, Puyade, and Icaza, were brief; a few, notably that of García Herreros, were extensive and wide-ranging. Rather than a repetitive summary of each respondent's opinion, what follows is essentially a composite picture of the negative views of *comercio libre* put forth by García Herreros and Vicario, supplemented by the observations of Basoco, Puyade, and Icaza.[20]

The Debate

The principal respondents recognized the opposition to Spanish transatlantic structures they favored from before 1778, the time of the *comercio de flotas*. This term they avoided, preferring the less negatively charged neologism *comercio arreglado*. The use of *arreglado* suggested a conscious choice of a more acceptable term than *flota* or *galeón*, which might immediately trigger the notion of past *decadencia*. Similarly there was no reference to that other feature of the pre-1778 commercial structure, the Jalapa fair. Coupled with praise for pre-1778 structures was support for the reprivatization of *alcabala* (sales tax) collections, administered until 1754 by the Mexico City *consulado*, and even for re-farming the customs office at Veracruz. While it was conceded that the trade patterns created after 1778 and 1789 had reduced shipping costs, insurance premiums, and the turnaround time of ships at Veracruz, these improvements, they felt, had been nullified by higher import duties and more complicated sales-tax zoning and collections. *Comercio arreglado,* as the *almacenero* García Herreros took pains to point out with obvious bias, had not been a monopoly as many insisted, for prices then had been lower, profit margins moderate, standards of business ethics higher, and men of business more satisfied.[21]

The respondents' perspective on the previous six decades, coupled with their grasp of detail, was impressive. They (or an amanuensis) distinguished between the trade policies of Ensenada, prime minister in the 1750s, and those of Colonial Secretary Julián de Arriaga (which they strongly approved) in the 1760s. But when dealing with events and patterns of the brief period following 1778, their evenhandedness disappeared as short-run interest predominated. *Comercio libre,* Manuel García Herreros quipped, "was really *libre* only in name"; "one could say that it was really costly" because of higher export and import duties, repeated *alcabala* collections, and discretionary evaluation of goods by arbitrary customs-house functionaries.[22] The respondents insisted that sales volume had fallen off and that knowledgeable merchants now stocked their warehouses cautiously, since the unregulated and unscheduled arrival of shipping at Veracruz to unload a range of consumer items, largely textiles ("called clothing packed in Bags and wrapped Chests containing Linens, Woolens, and Silks"),[23] made it difficult to calculate either the composition of effective demand or the proper level of inventory and appropriate pricing, not to mention forecasting long-term market conditions. Profits remained low, unpredictable, and discouraging to seasoned traders, who as a consequence, Basoco confessed in his response, were shifting capital from merchandising into the currently more profitable activities of mining, agriculture, and, in his case, banking. With excessive reticence Basoco, probably the wealthiest businessman in the colony, explained, "I've had no luck . . . with my purchases . . . , and the poor results have led me to give up my commercial affairs and . . . earn interest on investments, living in this fashion, along with some business separate from trading."[24]

The Spanish-born *(peninsular)* merchants resident at Mexico City had no illusions about the immediate possibilities of *comercio libre* as a stimulus to manufacture in the metropole. In fact, they felt that the metropolitan government should crack down on the collusion between Spanish and European manufacturers, "taking the most appropriate measures . . . right now."[25] Spain's manufacturers, they knew, produced a narrow range of goods for a luxury market, and as García Herreros put it candidly, no infant manufacture could expand without a large volume of sustained demand at home or abroad. In the pragmatic terms of Ángel Puyade, "A trade that avoids the poor consumer can be neither large nor profitable."[26] In addition, Spanish products had limited sales in New Spain because they were shoddy in quality and finish.[27] Far from creating a colonial market for such products, *comercio libre* had opened the colony to an overwhelming volume of European and Asian products, squeezing out imports from Spain. However, a wholesale prohibition on imports of non-Spanish origin would prove ineffective. Still, the Valencia-born Vicario pointed out that selective product exclusion, on the other hand, might protect some Spanish manufactures, such as Valencia's silks. Otherwise, massive smuggling would continue to grow, a phenomenon the respondents claimed New Spain had avoided to date ("no need for us to wipe our hands").

This pragmatism did not avoid contradiction. While recognizing that only a mass colonial market might in the long run provide sustained demand for manufacture in the metropole, Revillagigedo's tough-minded *almacenero* respondents held a dim view of the potential market in New Spain's Native American masses, whom they judged to be at best apathetic consumers. "The average Indian never hopes to rise above his level, he feels at home in his depressed state and natural laziness . . . he never changes his humble, coarse clothing, which does not increase consumption of European goods and wares."[28] Most crucial were the predictable effects of stagnating or contracting commercial operations upon the colony's main economic sector, mining, in which merchants were investors. In the long run, depressed commercial conditions and the consequent reduction in merchants' earnings and savings would limit mining operations and affect adversely the public and private sectors.

The responses to Revillagigedo's questionnaire, if not prepared by merchants themselves, were probably dictated and certainly carefully edited, for the style is direct rather than baroque, unambiguous, even earthy and quite un-bureaucratese, perhaps reflecting the *almaceneros*' European peasant origins. Both García Herreros and Vicario employed virtually the same graphic imagery when comparing trade before and after 1778 to the human body. Vicario saw New Spain as "a man's body." Before 1778 he would consume one sheep at one sitting daily and endure two annual bloodlettings; after 1778 he would consume pigeons hourly and suffer three to four bleedings monthly, with the result that "he must sicken visibly." To García Herreros, trade was a stomach that, when constantly stuffed, produced "violent . . . convulsions" such that "by continuing to overload the stomach, the machine falls apart because it retains nothing."[29]

From the logic of the *almaceneros*' argument—praise for a revived *flota* system as of 1720 (their *comercio arreglado*) interrupted by the legislation of 1778 and 1789—it followed that they believed that proponents of recent transatlantic policy had been inspired by un-Spanish, i.e., foreign, models: "at the court many opposed managed trade because they shared the views of Frenchmen, Englishmen, and others with far fewer colonies than we." Moreover, Spain's political economists formulated policies for New Spain "without keeping this Kingdom apart from the others in America."[30] Long experience with New Spain's unique colonial reality, the Mexico City merchants insisted, motivated their recommendations: that New Spain be supplied "by shipping . . . at specific times . . . every two or three years" (Vicario), that "a managed trade carrying cargoes to match consumption" (García Herreros) was most appropriate, that the colony be allowed to re-export imports from Europe to Lima and Guayaquil (Icaza), that customs schedules and internal imposts be both reduced and simplified, and that silver remissions be limited to one annual shipment.[31] Last, there was the desire to curb the development of Veracruz as commercial center in competition with Mexico City, because, among other reasons, it was notorious "for its bad weather and lack of everything necessary, because it imports everything—what abounds there is only inconvenience."[32] More critical, according to Ángel Puyade, was the necessity of hindering the entry of Catalan merchants into the trade of New Spain, because "no Valenciano, Vizcayno, Castellano nor Andaluz can compete with them," since the average Catalan "eats and dresses meanly, he bathes and feeds himself, doesn't need servants." Mexico City's wholesalers feared that if Catalans were to insert themselves into trade with New Spain, "the other people from Spain cannot improve themselves." In addition to their "excessive frugality," *almaceneros* like Puyade were convinced that Catalan *fábricas* were "generally . . . cruder than those of other provinces . . . causing the ruin of the other vassals of the Peninsula."[33] While there was competition between *vizcaínos* and *montañeses,* clearly they were united against the Catalans.

Given the interconnections between the colonial civil service and merchant oligarchs in Mexico City, leading *almaceneros* must have immediately learned of the extended rebuttal of their claims of local economic recession and its presumed causes that the *oidor* Beleña submitted to Revillagigedo on 24 August, after all but two merchants had responded. Beleña's vigorous support of the changes in imperial commercial policy must have given the merchant community pause. Now came frequent formal meetings of merchants in their *consulado,* which produced *acuerdos y consultas,* in which a majority voiced opposition to the whole policy of *comercio libre.* On 2 December 1791 those merchants residing in the capital who were registered *(matriculados)* in the *consulado* proposed that their corporative body support this position.[34] One month later to the day, the guild's three top officials, the prior and two consuls, wrote Revillagigedo that the organization had endorsed the merchants' pessimistic assessment of the local economic situation, its causes, and its remedies.[35]

Again it is appropriate to offer a composite presentation of the analyses of the *almaceneros* and their *consulado.* Their focus was not the whole colony but its capital, and they were convinced that for about a decade Mexico City's trade had displayed "stagnation and deterioration"; trade was now in a "decadente situación," indicated by two indices. First, while the population had grown, there had been an anomalous contraction in demand; and second, the *alcabala* records of the Superintendencia de Real Hacienda confirmed this: "a reduction in consumption is noticeable." The general illiquidity of the merchant community was such that they could no longer respond on short notice to the state's needs with voluntary, interest-free "extraordinarily pecuniary assistance," as they had during wartime in 1782.[36] As for the underlying causes of the commercial recession, these were pinpointed: oversupply of imports as a result of *comercio libre* ("continual flow of imports"); the capital's high level of municipal taxation of basic consumer items and its well-known high cost of living, both of which were reflected in local prices; the disproportionately high sales tax (9%) on goods sold in Mexico City, as compared with Veracruz's rate (3%), which induced merchants of the interior to purchase imports at Veracruz ("a merchant of the interior gains more by buying at Veracruz than by supplying himself from Mexico City"); and the uncontrolled outflow of silver to the metropole ("the steady export of money from this Kingdom to Spain"). Since the sole recent policy innovation of magnitude was *comercio libre,* Madrid's policymakers, adhering to the concepts of the "filósofos modernos," were responsible for the current conditions, according to "published documents that have recently come to us."[37]

The recommendations of the capital's merchant elite were predictable. Imports purchased at Veracruz should pay the same 6 percent *alcabala* that was collected on sales at Mexico City; unsold goods exiting the port for interior provinces should pay the normal *alcabalas* in transit and at the point of final sale.[38] The merchants reminded Revillagigedo of the real possibility that Veracruz might be attacked from the sea, as well as its unsuitability as a major entry point and warehouse and distribution hub. Silver exports, it was felt, should be limited to one annual shipment, contrary to the recommendation of the "filósofos modernos." On the main issue, the unscheduled arrival of imports, the *almaceneros'* complaint was clear: the government should abandon *comercio libre,* because all "intelligent and impartial people" would agree that "the main damage to commerce stems from the continued imports without method or order." Instead, Spain's manufactures and other products should enter only in "expediciones anuales," and non-Spanish imports every two to three years, a general policy dictated by "the wisdom of nature." Nature, after all, provides man with the example of one annual harvest; similarly, an annual outflow of silver would follow nature's pattern, since a mulberry bush, if stripped repeatedly in any one year, would soon perish (here one suspects the intervention of Vicario, from raw-silk-producing Valencia). Once again agrarian cycles and practices surfaced in the concrete imagery of Spanish peasants turned overseas merchants.[39]

No sooner had Revillagigedo received the *consulado*'s recommendations than he turned over the merchants' petition and the *consulado*'s endorsement to the *fiscal* Ramón de Posada for his assessment *(dictamen)*. Only six months earlier Posada had bowed out of the controversy over *comercio libre,* pleading lack of expertise, but the viceroy's evident involvement and his pressure now convinced Posada to accept the charge, which he completed in a few weeks; by 27 January 1792 Revillagigedo had his *dictamen.*[40] The next day Revillagigedo requested the views of another major figure in the capital's fiscal system, the superintendent of customs, Miguel Páez de la Cadena.[41] A colonial official of Revillagigedo's stature, cognizant of the background and sensitive to the local networking of a high civil servant integrated into Mexico City's economic and social milieu, must surely have requested Páez's opinion because he was motivated by a political consideration: to demonstrate that in his inquiry into the local repercussions of Madrid's commercial policy he had contacted all the major interest groups and their representatives. He exhibited a politically correct deference to the broad and influential opposition.

By turning pro forma to Páez, Revillagigedo was making his bow to the unofficial bureaucratic spokesman of Mexico City's *peninsular* merchant elite. By birthplace and career pattern, the extended Andalusian family of Páez de la Cadena belonged to the bureaucratic and mercantile networks of Lower Andalusia, of Cadiz and its principal overseas nucleus of the time, Mexico City. At least three of four identifiable family members were born at San Lúcar de Barrameda, at the mouth of the Guadalquivir: Sebastián, Juan Miguel, and Miguel. Sebastián Páez de la Cadena entered the colonial office at the lowest rung of the bureaucratic scale *(oficial sexto)* in 1769, thereafter ascended the administrative ladder, and in 1776 was *veedor* in the Casa de Contratación at Cadiz. The Cadiz *consulado* appointed Francisco Páez to a *maestría de plata,* in which position he supervised the registry, shipment, and delivery of silver from Veracruz to Cadiz aboard two outbound *flotas* whose silver cargo was uncommonly large, one (Antonio de Ulloa's) in 1778, just before Spain's entry into the Anglo-French conflict, and another in 1783; the appointment was a measure of the Cadiz commercial community's judgment of Francisco's trustworthiness. A nephew, Juan Miguel, entered the royal navy in 1788 (he already had brothers in both the army and the navy), then switched to the army upon graduating from Granada's Colegio Imperial de San Miguel. He served in the 1790s on the boundary commission for the Pyrenees under Ventura Caro and later in the expeditionary corps under the marqués de la Romana in Italy and then in Denmark. He would support the Junta Central (1808) and the Regency (1810), and he was the chief security officer checking on "subversive" (anti-*fernandista*) elements at Cadiz, then the temporary capital of Spain and its empire, in 1810, during the French occupation of the rest of the peninsula.

Miguel Páez de la Cadena Ponce de León y Pavón del Carral, Lopez de Moreda y Castaño, probably the brother of Sebastián and Francisco, arrived in Mexico City in 1750. Nearly twenty-five years later he had risen to the post of *superintendente administrador* of *alcabala* collections; he was honored with the designation *ministro honorario* of the Tribunal Mayor de Cuentas in 1773, and six years later, in 1779, he was admitted to the Orden de Carlos III. That he served steadily in *alcabala* administration in the years following the end of the *alcabala* tax farm managed for decades by the Consulado de México suggests a capacity for accommodation with Mexico City's merchants, a judgment strengthened by his subsequent joint appointment as *superintendente* of Mexico City's customs and *director-general* of the colony's *alcabala* collections.[42] Revillagigedo, no stranger to ethnic politics in bureaucracy and business among Andaluz families at home and abroad, would not have been surprised by Páez de la Cadena's support for the colonial capital's *almaceneros*.

It is symptomatic of Páez's links to the capital's merchant community that he repeatedly neglected requests for statistical data directed to him in 1791 from Acapulco by the naval officer Alejandro Malaspina, who was also collecting data on colonial economic and political conditions.[43] Equally revealing is the fact that in his *dictamen* supporting the merchants and the *consulado* and refuting the *fiscal* Posada, Páez both sought advice from and submitted a draft of his manuscript to four prominent Mexico City merchants who did not figure in Revillagigedo's selection of respondents, two of whom are identifiable—Pedro Alonso de Alles Díaz Inguanzo and Antonio Barroso. Páez's overt and long-term identification with Mexico City's influential Spanish merchant establishment undoubtedly motivated uncomplimentary observations about him as a poor administrator ("distracted by other, less important or essential obligations"), an employer of incompetent subordinates ("inexperienced and ignorant"), a defender of the merchants' position based on "reflections and arguments weak or based on false data," and as the inspirer of the 115 merchants' recommendations for reduction of Mexico City's *alcabala* rate.[44] Yet for all his backing of tradition-bound Mexico City *almaceneros,* Páez remained a well-informed colonial customs administrator who could cite political economists like the Spaniard Miguel Zavala y Auñón, along with Jacques Necker and Adam Smith (he tagged Smith as "customs officer in Scottish Customs in [17]88"), on the advantages of removing restraints on the "facility to find supplies and to traffick."[45]

Páez confined his *dictamen* to the stalking horse manipulated by the Mexico City merchants, the unduly heavy tax burden ("recargo de derechos") of the capital's commerce.[46] Aware of Revillagigedo's impressive effort to prepare a statistical base for demonstrating the advantages of modifying economic policy with data on receipts of Native American tribute, tithes, sales taxes, customs revenue, and the volume of silver coined and exported, Páez studiously skirted *comercio libre* in order to hew to the situation of the capital's merchant establishment. Only in his closing paragraphs did he confess reluctance to comment on what obviously were the fundamental issues — the euphemistically termed "introduction of goods not limited to specific times" and its counterpart, the "unlimited extraction of money." Three of the four points to which he limited his exposition concerned factors affecting the capital's competitive position as the major distribution hub for the whole colony. He found that the level of municipal taxation ("this city bears . . . greater taxes than others on subsistence"), food and clothing costs, and high rents had depressed sales for more than a decade; consequently, he claimed, foresighted merchants had been pushed out of trade toward investment in sugar- and wheat-growing estates. As for the sugar boom in New Spain, it was primarily a reflexive phenomenon of short duration produced by "the Negro uprising in Haiti, Martinique, and other [islands], destroying millworks, rebellious and disobedient to the Whites, unwilling to work."[47] Here Páez was voicing the sentiments of merchant friends like Alles. What was needed, he claimed, was reduction of the city's tax levels, notably the turnover *(alcabala)* rate, the merchants' main contention. In the long run, a reduced sales tax would stimulate sales and revenues overall.

Páez's last point elaborated a theme only tangentially mentioned, one that in a real sense posed more of a threat to Mexico City's commercial hegemony than did *comercio libre:* the evolving competition from Veracruz in the distribution of imports to provincial centers, what Páez described as "the establishment and development of commerce at Veracruz." He prefaced his description of the theme by stressing how Mexico City merchants wanted the metropolitan government to view their role in state and society. Their liquidity *(recursos)* had always been available for local emergencies ("scarcity of maize and seeds that so troubled [the colony] in '85"), for local charities ("convento de San Hipólito . . . for the care of the demented"), and for the metropole's financial crises ("large quantities at times of . . . grave needs").[48] On the other hand, he claimed that the Veracruz merchant community, despite its commercial and tax advantages, had neglected to contribute proportionately to social needs. To be sure, he also indicted "wealthy persons outside the capital," including the "opulent" Guanajuato mine owners (a majority *criollo*) who had not contributed proportionately.[49] He reinforced his criticism by asserting that Veracruz, unlike Mexico City, provided more latitude for defrauding government sales-tax collectors: "There is more petty corruption, neglect, or possibility for fraud . . . at Veracruz laxity and negligence are the rule."[50]

Particularly striking, given the sugar boom in the Cuautla-Cuernavaca area, is Páez's pessimism about investment in sugar exports. Local merchants had turned to plantation agriculture, not because of their liquidity ("abundance of money"), but simply because of poor earnings in the wholesale trades ("the decadent state of commerce"). Over the long haul, however, because of local cost structures the colony's sugar exports, like prior exports of wool, cotton, timber, or grains, would not be sustained unless sugar was produced along the Caribbean coast.[51]

Páez's presentation at least had the merit of limited focus and brevity: we can only speculate about how he would have responded to his critics, since he died in May 1792, two months before the comprehensive, statistically supported counterattack of the anonymous "Ensayo apologético por el comercio libre."

Earlier it was noted that of the twelve merchant respondents initially contacted by Revillagigedo in the spring of 1791, only two—Yraeta and Ágreda—backed the colonial government's position on the recent changes in imperial trade policy. These two men were belatedly joined by a third, Tomás Murphy, at Veracruz. Together they shared few characteristics to suggest why Viceroy Revillagigedo had singled them out, except that none was a *montañés:* Yraeta y Azcárate was a Guipuzcoan from the town of Anzuola, Ágreda was a Riojano from Cameros, while Murphy came from an Anglo-Irish-Malagan family of Málaga in Andalusia. Yraeta's family had deep roots in Anzuola; once in Mexico City, he prospered: he was appointed treasurer of the well-endowed Archicofradía del Santíssimo Sacramento of Mexico City's cathedral, and by 1783 he was listed as a major contributor to the massive loan (1 million *pesos*) to the metropole sponsored by the Consulado de México. First consul of that body in 1790, he entered the Orden de Carlos III the following year, and somewhat later he was a large stockholder in, and then the Mexico City agent for, the Compañía de Filipinas (Revillagigedo was also a large shareholder). When Revillagigedo returned to Madrid in 1794, he designated Yraeta as one of his *apoderados.* Yraeta married one daughter to an *oidor* of the Audiencia de México (Cosme de Mier y Trespalacios), another to a Mexico City *almacenero* who was a nephew he had invited from Anzuola (Yturbe e Yraeta), a third to Icaza, a Panama-born merchant and a respondent opposed to *comercio libre.*[52]

Revillagigedo's second supporter in Mexico City's merchant establishment was Diego de Ágreda y Martínez de Cabezón, from San Román de Cameros, who emigrated to New Spain in 1784. His godfather, Antonio García Herreros, was a Cameros resident; a cousin, Manuel García Herreros, was a prominent *almacenero* critical of *comercio libre;* and his maternal grandfather, Francisco Martínez de Cabezón, had held the office of consul in the *consulado* at Mexico City in 1782 and, along with Manuel García Herreros, had been a correspondent of the same Manila interests that Ágreda represented. Early in his commercial career Diego became *diputado mayor* of the Archicofradía de Nuestra Señora del Rosario of the Convento de Santo Domingo. Diego de Ágreda enjoyed a distinct commercial advantage through his merchant brother at Cadiz, Simón, who in the 1770s had bitterly criticized the powerful stevedores' guild *(palanquinado),* controlled by *montañeses.* A perennially generous benefactor of his birthplace in Spain, Ágreda continued to fund Cameros's municipal needs. Nevertheless, it was difficult to prove his family's claim to *hidalguía,* for which Diego had to marshal an impressive group of Mexico City's ecclesiastical, bureaucratic, and mercantile elites.[53]

The third supportive respondent whom Revillagigedo consulted, curiously, was Tomás Murphy y Porro, whom he contacted belatedly, in 1793, just before he summarized the repercussions of Madrid's changing transatlantic trade policy. Murphy was a *malagueño* born in 1766 to Juan Murphy y Eliot, presumably a wine exporter to England. Young Murphy, a shareholder in Málaga's recently chartered Compañía de Navieros, had been briefly a correspondent of Colonial Secretary José de Gálvez; in the late 1780s he had left Málaga for Veracruz to set up the firm of Murphy y Cotarro. In 1801 he had rented office space to José Benito de Aústria, a Riojano and perhaps brother of the energetic secretary of the recently created Consulado de Veracruz, José Donato de Austria y Achútegui. At Veracruz Murphy built on his knowledge of Málaga's English trade and established contact with merchants at Kingston, Jamaica, with the prominent Havana merchant Pedro Juan de Erice, and with the Hamburg export house of Brentano, Bovera y Urbieta. In the late 1790s Murphy married a daughter of a long-term colonial functionary, Martín José de Alegría y Egues, whom José de Gálvez had shifted from Havana to serve as the Hacienda administrator at Veracruz. Alegría married a second daughter to a nephew, the viceroy Miguel José de Azanza, in the late 1790s. Within the ambience of commercial growth at Veracruz then contesting the hegemony of Mexico City's merchant oligarchy, Tomás Murphy had caught the attention of Viceroy Revillagigedo, and with good reason.[54]

These disparate biographical elements merit observations but hardly generalizations. By the time of Revillagigedo's viceregal administration Yraeta and Ágreda had achieved respectable status in the capital's merchant community. Yet it should be noted that both Ágreda and Murphy were recent immigrants, relative newcomers to the colony's mercantile establishment, so that Revillagigedo could not have considered them veteran *almaceneros*. Moreover, Murphy was the sole respondent from Veracruz, Mexico City's burgeoning competitor, where pressure was building to establish a *consulado* independent of the jurisdiction and intervention of the Consulado de México. Furthermore, whereas only a minority of the merchant oligarchy (three of the twelve respondents) backed *comercio libre,* three of the four colonial civil servants consulted were in favor, and unlike the merchant minority, all three civil servants were seasoned career bureaucrats.

Posada and Lorenzo Hernández de Alba had been in America since the 1770s, while Beleña, the most senior, had arrived in 1765 in the entourage of the *visitador* José de Gálvez. A Castillian from Alcárria, Beleña was commissioned by the high commissioner Gálvez to oversee the expulsion of the Jesuits from the Audiencia de Guadalajara (1767); he then spent a brief period in the 1770s on the Audiencia de Guatemala. Returning to Mexico City in 1777 as the *fiscal del crimen* of that *audiencia* and in contact with Posada, he spent most of the next fifteen years in or near the colonial capital. *Oidor* there in 1784, he also served as *asesor* of the mining guild (1786) and a member of its *junta de arreglo* (1790) along with Antonio Barroso, a merchant consulted by Páez de la Cadena. In recognition of Beleña's proven competence he was reposted to Guadalajara at the end of 1792, this time as *regente* of its *audiencia,* no doubt a measure of justified respect for his *Recopilación sumaria de todos los autos acordados por la Real Audiencia y Sala del Crimen de esta Nueva México* (1787), dedicated to Gálvez's nephew Miguel de Gálvez y Saint Maxent (whose mother was a French *criolla* of New Orleans).[55]

For his part, Posada, from Cangas de Onís in Asturias, joined the extended Gálvez family by marrying a niece of Viceroy Matías de Gálvez's wife. By this marriage he also became a brother-in-law of the superintendent of Mexico City's prestigious mint, Francisco Fernández de Córdoba; and through his grandmother, a Cienfuegos, Posada was also related to

Gaspar de Jovellanos, who corresponded with Posada about issues when he was drafting his *Informe de la Sociedad Económica de esta Corte al Real y Supremo Consejo de Castilla en el expediente de ley agraria* (1795). It is not surprising that the well-read political economist and secretary of the Vera-cruz *consulado,* José María Quirós, later noted that Posada had favored land reform in New Spain, along with Spanish immigration and colonization. Among some of New Spain's *criollos,* such as Mier y Terán, Posada was esteemed as a civil servant of rectitude; to the Cadiz *consulado* in a moment of desperation he stood out as the archtypical, meticulous public servant ("Once an issue is assigned to Sr. Posada, there will be a prolonged exami-nation"), a judgment substantiated by detailed self-accounting of his civil-service dossier over a seven-year period, during which he claimed to have processed 29,290 briefs, 20,000 while serving as a *fiscal* of Mexico City's Real Hacienda.[56]

But Posada had more to his credit than his assiduousness as a quill pusher. Self-confident and ambitious, he applied for membership in and was ac-cepted into the Orden de Carlos III in 1785; one of his sponsors was José de Gálvez's one-time collaborator, Areche. More essential to Revillagigedo's purpose, Posada supported innovation in economic policy. For instance, he opined against Veracruz shippers who tried to fix prices on shipments to Havana in wartime (1781–83); he pressured Native American communities to divert funds retained in their *cajas de comunidad* to investment in shares in the Banco de San Carlos (1783); he condemned the illegal practice by *alcaldes mayores* of selling the posts of their assistants *(tenientazgos)* and pocketing the proceeds; and in 1785 he went on record in support of govern-ment efforts to stimulate the cultivation for export of new colonial staples such as flax and hemp for manufactories in the metropole. Appointed to the Consejo de Indias in 1798, Posada returned to Madrid, where he became a vice president of the Compañía de Filipinas. In 1808 he showed great pre-science in rejecting an invitation to attend the Congress of Bayonne, con-vened by Napoleon.[57]

The *Comercilibrista* Merchants: Yraeta, Ágreda, and Murphy

Of the three *almacenero* respondents favoring *comercio libre,* the two from Mexico City, Diego de Ágreda and Francisco Ignacio de Yraeta, offered at best tepid approval and cautious recommendations.[58] At the outset Ágreda confessed his disagreement with those who "claim . . . commerce has in-creased and invigorated by good earnings." Both had reservations: Ágreda, noting the complaints of Mexico City's "corporate body" and the current wave of bankruptcies at Cadiz ("the many losses and numerous bankrupt-cies") presumably reported by his brother there, confessed that he did not find either trade growth or exceptional profitability; Yraeta felt that merchants had failed to manage "shipments with necessary volume and knowledge," and he indicted Cadiz as an example of traders' "setbacks." The two men concurred that the fundamental problem was an oversupply of imports—described by Ágreda as "excessive competition and supply of goods"—at worst merely a predictable, temporary phenomenon.[59] As Yraeta expressed it, "It is understood that new institutions always bring trouble, although the passage of time and events correct the faults," and that cost-cutting would expand sales. More unsettling was the fact that the recent reduction in the number of *alcabala* zones (to three) through which goods moved from the port of Veracruz into interior sales areas had discouraged hundreds of small-scale *mercaderes viandantes* who formerly had made purchases on credit at Mexico City.[60] So both recommended using only one *guía* for more than three zones and that no *alcabala* be levied on goods purchased by Mexico City *almaceneros* for resale outside the capital, thereby making the capital competitive with Veracruz. Yraeta, joined by Ágreda, also objected to duties on both foreign and Spanish articles shipped from Cadiz—35 percent on foreign and 27 percent on Spanish items—and eventually sold in Mexico City, to which, they noted, one had to add commissions, freight, and insurance.[61]

Reductions in duties and sales taxes, Yraeta suggested, could be passed along to consumers, and he recalled the recent success of *factores* representing Madrid's Cinco Gremios Mayores at Mexico City liquidating quickly by large price reductions a large inventory of imported Spanish silks, which, he complained, "consisted largely of goods in little demand . . . hard to sell."[62] Ágreda was more precise in arguing that while "Libre Comercio is absolutely appropriate, but modified," oversupply and lowered prices left him a slight profit margin of 5.5 percent, barely above the current lending rate in New Spain, despite his advantages "in having made his purchases cash in hand and in having a brother at Cadiz who knows the trade there and in this Kingdom."[63] Yet despite his apparent commitment to the principle of *comercio libre*, Ágreda's recommendations were curiously close to the position of merchants openly opposed to recent changes in commercial policy. Rejecting quotas on imports of Spanish goods and wares, he urged that non-Spanish goods be re-exported from Spain on special vessels and at specified times, that is, "limiting to a specific time and cargo volume all licenses for Foreign goods," no vessel to carry foreign goods valued at more than 50 percent of the total value of its cargo, and that silver outflows be confined to one annual shipment on warships.[64] Surely he knew that these recommendations would never be entertained.

Yraeta's and in particular Ágreda's tepid, not to say equivocal, attitude stands in contrast to the unequivocal backing for *comercio libre* by the recently arrived immigrant Tomás Murphy, who forwarded his extended opinion to Revillagigedo from Veracruz two years to the month after Yraeta and Ágreda filed theirs. With the exuberance of a neophyte and a maverick, he declared to Revillegigedo that "monopoly is over" and proceeded to indict "the moneybags of this kingdom who [used to invest] in almost everything the *flotas* brought," along with the Tribunal de la Contratación at Cadiz and that port's *consulado.* If a few self-interested merchants had gained little from *comercio libre,* he wrote, "on the whole the nation" had profited measurably, and he quoted approvingly the criticism of "un famoso Político moderno" (perhaps Adam Smith) to the effect that "the interest of merchants has little in common with the common interest of society,"[65] already an insoluble issue in capitalism.

Murphy's commitment to *comercio libre* ("liberty is the soul of Commerce, and the only way to raise it to the highest level"), while tying the development of Málaga, one of Spain's peripheral provinces, to national development, displays a regionalist's satisfaction in attacking Cadiz's eighteenth-century hegemony ("the special privilege the Port enjoys") over Spain's transatlantic trade system. The crucial element in the success of *comercio libre* was what Murphy variously termed "convenience in shipping," "fairness in transportation," or, more specifically, "moderate cargo costs." As a prime mover behind Málaga's shipping company in the 1780s, the *malagueño* Murphy contrasted Cadiz's shippers, who complained about unprofitable freight rates, with the "industriosos" Catalans, who had "done away with superfluous costs that are ridiculous to foreign observers." Lowered maritime freight rates had, Murphy argued, raised New Spain's consumption of Catalan, Malagan, and Valencian brandies and wines—annual imports of Malagan wines had jumped from 300–400 barrels to 10,000— along with Catalan cotton prints *(angaripolas),* paper, hats, stockings, and velvets, not to mention imports of ironware and beer from Santander. In the same fashion, lower freight rates had stimulated New Spain's exports of cotton, sarsaparilla, vanilla, and hides. Murphy the economic nationalist was convinced that Madrid's economic policy since 1789, when "the method of allocating specific tonnage to each authorized Port was abolished," had been the source of "so much development in our Peninsula's commerce."[66]

Murphy's "nuestra Peninsula" was more than a figure of speech; it substantiated his imperialist point of view. The expansion of Spain's manufacture of "woolens, bays, hats, ribbons, and paints" required increased consumption in New Spain and the other colonies in America. To the question whether colonial policy should tolerate "the development of workshops in this kingdom [New Spain]," he answered emphatically that "in no way should it be allowed." Unequivocally he shared colonialist views aired by the Consulado de Barcelona in 1787.[67] Instead, New Spain should be steered toward production of agricultural exportables—cotton, sugars, dyestuffs—especially in Caribbean coastal zones, since European demand remained strong and their cultivation could draw labor away from colonial manufacture, thereby improving the otherwise "perverse, effeminate [style] adopted by almost all in manufacture in this kingdom, since they have a disposition for every vice."[68] Notable is the deliberate omission by Murphy and other *almaceneros* of any reference to the good to high quality of locally produced cottons and woolens in *obrajes* in Mexico City, its environs, and large provincial centers.

It is hardly surprising that Murphy concurred with Ágreda and Yraeta that duties, along with innumerable *alcabalas,* should be reduced on Spanish products at Veracruz. What *is* surprising, however, and superficially contradictory is the readiness of Murphy—a partisan of *comercio libre* at the wholesalers' level—to curb competition from peddlers *(viandantes)* distributing imports in the interior of the colony. He traced the growth in their numbers to *comercio libre,* to the availability of imports and to storekeepers able to draw on capital reserves to offer long-term credit to "men of little capital and who in general offer no guarantee other than their dubious integrity and honesty." Their competition cut into the sales of Mexico City and Veracruz merchants and, in particular, "dealers in small towns who use peddlers to supply their shops at the price and period for payment they demand."[69] By law these low-level *traficantes* were privileged to move their merchandise through five different sales-tax zones but paying only one *alcabala* at the point of sale, a privilege other vendors did not enjoy. *Comercilibrista* Murphy was convinced that "liberty of Commerce is compatible with the elimination of these traders," and he urged that their waybills *(guías)* be issued for just "un solo destino."[70]

Equally vehement and unrestrained was Murphy's critique of the practices of the Consulado de México, whose processing of commercial litigation was perennially flawed by "indifference, inactivity, and injustice . . . because of superfluous assessors and agents." Hence, merchants in the colony were generally reluctant to seek justice from "those who . . . delay payment or fail to do so, arbitrarily using outside interests, and eluding with imaginary laws those that commerce has wisely drafted." Predictably Murphy wrapped up his *informe* to Revillagigedo by recommending the establishment of a *consulado* at Veracruz, independent of the Consulado de México. Consistent with his bias for metropolitan over colonial interests, Murphy argued that "nothing is more needed for the Commerce of Spain" than his proposed *consulado,* where merchants from the peninsula would encounter "men with extensive knowledge of Commerce," presumably a quality absent at the colonial capital. In sum, although Murphy confessed to Revillagigedo that at the moment he lacked reliably accurate data on Veracruz's trade with its metropole, he had no doubt that "never before has commerce flourished as now."[71]

The *Comercilibrista* Colonial Service

Revillagigedo had called upon five civil servants to express their opinions on the policy of expanding *comercio libre,* but only Páez de la Cadena supported the Mexico City merchant oligarchy. Among the four supporters of the policy, the briefest opinions were basically qualitative and matched those of Posada, *fiscal de Real Hacienda* (27 January 1792), and Hernández de Alba, *fiscal de lo civil* (21 May), and both are quickly summarized. Hernández de Alba brought to his testimony personal observations ("I am an experienced observer") of the trade gains of Spain's islands in the Greater Antilles, Puerto Rico, Santo Domingo, and Cuba after 1765; according to Alba, the Reglamento of 1778 was "valuable fruit of the experience and knowledge of the benefits both trades began to enjoy . . . in the growth of Population, agriculture, exports, and sales."[72] The commercial changes of 1765, 1778, and 1789 had increased shipping to Veracruz, exports of New Spain's precious metals and agricultural staples ("valuable return cargo in silver and staples"), and perhaps most symptomatic of change, the number of *tiendas* in the capital and large provincial towns, as well as the number of merchants from the interior who "go down directly to Veracruz and purchase without intermediaries," precisely what Murphy had complained about.[73]

Both Hernández de Alba and Posada disparaged the arguments of Mexico City's 115 merchants and their *consulado* ("all began their careers in this capital"), whose complaints about the capital's municipal taxes, *alcabala* rates, and unregulated transfers of silver to the metropole were, in their opinion, to be expected from monopoly-minded businessmen ("wealthy merchants, accustomed to buying up all the supply, to monopolize everything in the age of the *flotas*").[74] If such propositions were accepted, Posada argued, prices would rise inexorably because "when a few sell the same good, it's never priced properly." Resorting to the analogy with the human body, Posada was convinced that if the Mexico City *almaceneros'* recommendations were accepted, "their limbs would soon lack blood or money to send to the head," while the common good of "this immensely opulent Empire" would be sacrificed for the benefit of "a handful of wealthy merchants." It was hardly a "measure of equality" that two hundred merchants "are rich and can make large loans," while all the others "are consumptive, dragged along and miserable."[75]

While Posada displayed unqualified optimism about the "feliz revolución" (echoing Prime Minister Floridablanca's memorial of 1788) brought about by the *comercio libre* of 1778 ("just imagine the benefits to Spain and New Spain that will come . . . from liberty!"),[76] Hernández de Alba felt that further modifications were in order, and he singled out the *repartimiento* system of distributing credit, goods, and services in predominantly indigenous localities, particularly in Oaxaca's most productive cochineal zones, Villalta, Xicayán, and Nexapa.[77] Since many officials in the metropole did not understand how *repartimiento* functioned, he gilded it as a kind of domestic trade hitherto controlled by what he termed "professional merchants" at Mexico City, who used local officials as their selling agents. The *repartimiento de mercancías,* it will be recalled, was a major target of criticism in the intendancy system set up in New Spain in 1786, and in the 1790s it was still under critical review by Madrid. Hernández de Alba recommended instead local distribution of goods by *verdaderos negociantes,* presumably small-scale tradesmen, rather than by *interpósitas personas,* who were in effect agents of "the richest and most powerful persons in the kingdom, who are also the guarantors of the Alcaldes Mayores," Mexico City's *almaceneros.* Presumably *repartimiento* would continue, but open to competition among less capitalized and less politically influential merchants.[78]

Two other public servants who supported *comercio libre,* and in particular the *reglamentos* of 1778 and 1789, were Eusebio Buenaventura Beleña and the anonymous author of the "Ensayo apologetico," probably drafted in the last six months of 1792.[79] Beleña's position paper of August 1791, as well as the "Ensayo," are distinguished by length, reference to statistical data, and last but not least, the "Ensayo"'s frontal attack upon the Mexico City merchant oligarchs and their virtual spokesman, Páez de la Cadena, who "declares his preferences for the merchants of Mexico [City]."[80] In point of fact Beleña had reported to Viceroy Flores in 1788 arguing that New Spain's overall economic performance had improved markedly since 1778. This may explain why Revillagigedo's request for Beleña's current view of the local economy referred to his "experience of many years, his knowledge of the Kingdom and zeal for the King's service."[81]

In Beleña, Revillagigedo found a veteran civil servant willing to question the hegemony of Mexico City's *almaceneros* over their external trade with the metropole and, equally significant, their distribution networks within the colony, from Durango in the north to Oaxaca in the south, and from Veracruz to Acapulco.[82] Three factors must have drawn Revillagigedo to Beleña. First, his long tenure as a colonial officer; and second, his grasp of the colony's economy, buttressed with data assembled in 1784, updated in 1788 for Viceroy Flores, and then pigeonholed. Revillagigedo must have known of Beleña's distance from Mexico City's merchant princes—"how lacking substantiation is the assertion that the main commercial sectors of trade are rapidly declining, when they are demonstrably more prosperous than ever."[83] A third factor is a matter of speculation: Revillagigedo must have reckoned with ethnic identities and politics, guessed that Páez de la Cadena's Andalusian connections would flavor his report, and banked on a broader, Castilian stance from Beleña. This careful colonial officer updated his database to 1790 and—key to his critique—addressed the source of the *almaceneros'* opposition, their emphasis on the benefits of the system of *flotas* and *ferias* (fairs) over the current *comercio libre*.

To this end, in thirty-four paragraphs Beleña carefully reviewed the history of *flotas* and their compulsory Jalapa *ferias* since 1728. He made a point of emphasizing the lobbying of Mexico City's merchants to have *flotas* renewed in 1757—there had been a two-decade lapse, 1738–57—on the questionable grounds of "avoiding the increasing number of bankruptcies and arrears, leading to the recourse of individual Registers," to which he appended the words "I've no idea what will be the outcome of the present difficulties."[84] Detailed coverage of that abandoned system was designed to substantiate his conclusion that its renewal would give grounds to "consider the many obstacles that the *flota* system created for both trades" and permit him to ask rhetorically, "How come the wealthy merchants of Mexico [City] clamor for the return of the *flotas*?" In his judgment, Mexico City's *almaceneros* hankered after the old system in order to renew their control over 250–300 factors arriving with merchandise on an average *flota* and at the same time to exploit "medium or small capitalized merchants in Mexico City, along with all those in the rest of the kingdom."[85]

Obviously Viceroy Revillagigedo was hunting for those who might justify *comercio libre* on a firmer basis than "purely theoretical principles or less accurate accounts." Now Revillagigedo wanted opinions stiffened by quantitative data.

A number of factors—the "Ensayo"'s statistical appendix, its historical perspective, its evident awareness of English and French economists of the eighteenth century, its exploration of the motives of Mexico City *almace-neros* ("who revived old and forgotten claims and covered their rejection of *comercio libre* by emphasizing their current depressed state"), and its recommendations for improvement—rendered it a major source for Revillagigedo's final report to Madrid on the repercussions in New Spain of changing imperial trade policy.[86] More important, it exemplifies both the perception of the colony's economic importance and an illusion of the metropole's growth and ability to fulfill the mercantilists' conception of a colonial compact at the close of the eighteenth century.

The "Ensayo" opens with the intention of disproving the merchants' conviction that termination of the *flota* system, followed by *comercio libre*, had depressed New Spain's economy. First, therefore, comes an analysis of statistical tables reflecting the priorities of eighteenth-century political economists—population, agriculture, mining, and domestic and overseas trade. Population growth is derived from mail-service revenue, in order to arrive at the growth of the upper class (*gente culta*, defined as "directors, magistrates, prelates . . . royal functionaries, military officers, and commercial people"), and from tribute collected from the lower orders of society (*gente vulgar*, the *plebeya*), indicating a total increment of 1,201,686 *pesos* (139,567 plus 1,062,119). Next the "striking increments" in agriculture are calculated from the most reliable data, the gross tithe income of New Spain's principal bishoprics (Mexico, Puebla, Valladolid, Oaxaca, Guadalajara, and Durango). Gross tithe receipts over the period 1780–89 (18,353,821 *pesos*) were up by 37.4 percent over those of the preceding decade. The value of coinage (here, a surrogate for mining output) for the thirteen-year period 1779–91 was 23.7 percent higher than in 1766–78. The rising production of New Spain's mines induces the anonymous author to observe that they constituted "the richest revenue source of the Crown" and, underscoring their impact in Europe and Asia, that they stimulated "not just . . . all the nations of Europe but the major nations of the globe."[87]

Clearly, according to contemporaneous indices of trade volume—sales taxes, customs duties on merchandise entering Mexico City, the outflow of silver from Veracruz to Spain and to Spain's Caribbean possessions, mainly Cuba—the colony's most impressive surge in economic growth occurred after 1788. Comparing thirteen years (1778–90) with the preceding period (1765–77), one sees that sales taxes rose by 72 percent, Mexico City's customs rose by 42 percent, and exports of precious metals jumped 44 percent. Reflecting overall growth in New Spain's economy, the colonial government's gross revenues were up by 77.1 percent (1778–90). We have no reason to question that bureaucrats and merchants alike recognized that some changes reflected inflationary pressure; nonetheless, the growth indices were still impressive.

Having effectively disproved with statistical data the *error* of economic depression, the "Ensayo" in its second section probes for the motives behind the "clamors and petitions" of Mexico City merchants, in particular Páez de la Cadena, in advancing their case "with such poor supporting data." Here the anonymous author refers to private "understandings and consultations" among the merchants and their confabulations with Páez, who "clearly favored the merchants of Mexico [City]," neglecting the interests of the colony as a whole.[88] And those interests were the preservation of control over transatlantic trade between New Spain and Spain and the elimination of Veracruz as an expanding competitive commercial entrepôt where shippers from Spain might readily sell their cargoes to merchants from New Spain's interior provinces, minimizing the role of Mexico City's *almaceneros,* a major outcome of the revised commercial system. In the view of the author of the "Ensayo," Mexico City's merchants were attempting to resuscitate an aspiration (temporarily blocked in 1735) of a time when they could remit funds to buy on their own account at Cadiz, becoming in effect their own shippers and avoiding Veracruz sales taxes, since there would be no need to haggle with Spanish *cargadores* or their factors.[89] This revived commercial position, which he terms "comercio activo," by re-concentrating in the colony's capital the distribution of imports, would inevitably negate the "foundations of the system of *comercio libre*" to the prejudice of "Spain's shipowners," who "will delay their sales and return shipments or sell cheap without any benefit to the domestic trading of these possessions."[90]

As a confirmed colonialist, the author of the "Ensayo" argues, citing the "best economists of Europe," that New Spain's overseas trade should be "passive totally, leaving active trading in the hands of merchants from the Metropole." Here he elaborates the *proyectista* mirage, the illusion of Spain's economic growth in the eighteenth century based upon trade with the colonies as the principal instrument of expansion and development in the metropole. Spain's *cargadores,* he insists, no longer had to depend upon the capital of merchants overseas in the colonies; indeed, "the Metropole is flourishing in all the major sectors, agriculture, industry, and commerce, which form the wealth of any state," and metropolitan producers could now readily supply "these colonies with [Spanish] and foreign goods, without the help and availability of American funds." Mexico City's *almaceneros* "must remain sidelined, reduced to a passive trade."[91]

In its third and final section the "Ensayo" shifts from rebuttal of Mexico City's *almaceneros* and their spokesman Páez to recommendations for trade improvement also advanced by other partisans of *comercio libre*. Two pieces of imperial legislation are singled out as obstacles to the expansion of commercial transactions and consequently government revenues, curbing "liberty . . . the obvious source of the people's growing prosperity."[92] The first was the article in the Real Cédula of 1774, which finally lifted prohibitions on intercolonial exchanges between New Spain and the colonies of Guatemala, New Granada, and Peru but specifically excluded from such exchanges "merchandise" imported from the metropole in *flotas* or *registros*.

As for the second obstacle, the anonymous author is concerned, not with traditional trade constraints, but with the recent legislation on *repartimiento*. He questions article 12 of the *Ordenanza de intendentes* (1786), which prohibited *alcaldes mayores* and *subdelegados* from engaging in forced sales *(repartimiento)* to Native American tribute payers through the mechanism of either credit or goods or both; he intimates that as a result tribute payments by indigenous peoples were lower than predicted, and sales and tax revenues down. In his view, New Spain's agriculture, industry, and commerce were sustainable mainly by *repartimiento*, which is why Native Americans "eat, dress, and earn wages to pay their church fees and tribute as vassals." Not that Native Americans were dissatisfied with current conditions; rather, re-legitimization of *repartimiento* would make native peoples "happier and the wealth of the state much more" and permit *alcaldes mayores* to continue to remit "to the Metropole funds that benefited their towns or homes and promoted the economy and wealth." Immigrants' remissions were not a negligible contribution to the metropolitan economy, especially at the local, community level. In the colonialist mentality of the anonymous author, no incompatibility existed between providing economic opportunity to more merchants from the metropole ("it is more beneficial to the State that the large incomes of a few are shared by many") and pressuring Native Americans to participate in colonial capitalism. In this way, the "Ensayo apologético" concludes abruptly, "the Kingdom will achieve the opulence whose main support is the continuation of *comercio libre*."[93] This position was satisfactory to Spain's eighteenth-century political economists from Gerónimo de Uztáriz on.

Revillagigedo's *Informe*

Nearly three years after Viceroy Revillagigedo assured Madrid that he would expedite economic data on New Spain, he completed his *informe* to minister Diego de Gardoqui. The report in fact fulfilled what had begun with the Valdés-inspired Real Orden of 30 October 1787, asking Viceroy

Flores to supply "calculations and information," ostensibly so that Madrid, to continue Gálvez's protective policy for New Spain's *almaceneros,* might estimate the colony's current import capacity and allocate quotas to major ports in the metropole now qualified for colonial trade as *puertos habilitados.* This was a plausible explanation, for it responded to complaints from the colony of an oversupply of imports and depressed price levels, part of the postwar cycle of boom and bust. Flores had sat on the request, not because of his "precarious health," but because he had foreseen that it was prelimi- nary to opening Veracruz to *comercio libre,* which his Mexico City merchant acquaintances firmly opposed. But Valdés was not another Gálvez, and Revillagigedo was not a carbon copy of Flores. It was left to Gálvez's re- placement, Antonio Valdés, to post Revillagigedo to New Spain at a time when the fresh wind that was customary at the initiation of a new reign blew through Madrid's ministries. On 26 September 1790 Revillagigedo, newly installed at Mexico City, promised to provide the data ordered three years earlier and again in 1788. Yet not until 17 June 1791 did Revillagigedo issue a formal questionnaire to respondents in the government and private sectors; and not until the following June (1792) did he pressure government agencies in the capital, in the major provinces, and at Veracruz for the long- awaited statistical data. These data were collated in mid-September 1792 and mined by both the anonymous author of the "Ensayo apologético" and Beleña. Meanwhile, the viceroy delayed completing his *informe* for yet an- other year.[94]

At this point one may speculate on the three-year delay: one suspects that the lack of bureaucratic compliance by some agencies at the colonial capital and Veracruz was the result of complicity between colonial civil servants and businessmen. Revillagigedo himself alluded indirectly in June 1792 to the tactics of obstruction: "Not everyone knows about [the complicated, ex- haustive, and original details], few judge them, some continue errors based upon misunderstood experiences, while others favor personal interest."[95] By then Revillagigedo had to handle what he must have long been aware of: the magnitude of the opposition of the capital's *almaceneros* to *comercio libre.*

On this note he opened his *informe,* underscoring to Gardoqui that his commercial respondents were hardly impartial. Accordingly, he had to separate himself "from those who had expressed their views," find "means more sure and exact," and collect data of "certainty, precision, and accuracy" not readily accessible.[96] In outline, the report summarizes data and conclu- sions presented by the "Ensayo" and Beleña, followed by an analysis of trade bottlenecks accompanied by recommendations. In this last, extended section the report goes beyond the numbers to become a wide-ranging critique by a perceptive and pragmatic colonial officer for whom the colony of New Spain was an instrument solely for the benefit and improvement of its metropole. Revillagigedo, an outstanding exemplar of the eighteenth-century rationalist civil servant, could not transcend his colonialist function.

With refreshing candor Revillagigedo began his critique with the flat-out declaration that "far from decline, there are obvious improvements in trade . . . if one compares the 13 years of Comercio Libre with the last [13] of the *flota* period" (14). He condensed the data presented in the "Ensayo" and Beleña's report: imports were up, reflecting increases in "consumers or buyers," while agricultural and ranching production had expanded "considerably"; mining output, measured by coinage at the Mexico City mint, had been increased without technological improvement, simply by larger factor inputs—labor, supplies, and animals (17).[97] Further proof of the vitality of trade was a "new kind of merchant" who did not pursue superprofits; these he categorized as "new, small-capitalized speculators better trained in the new commercial practices and less accustomed to profits." *Tiendas* of the "nueva clase de comerciantes" were proliferating everywhere, in the capital as well as in major provincial centers (15). And one further indicator of commercial activity was that merchants in provincial cities and towns no longer had to confine their purchasing to Mexico City *almaceneros;* instead they could travel directly to Veracruz, avoiding sales taxes on merchandise entering the capital and merchants' commission fees, a saving of at least 6 percent (17).[98] In brief, while the economic picture was much improved compared with the period prior to 1778, there remained much room for growth as measured by Revillagigedo's rough calculation of New Spain's per capita import capacity. Using the population of the major intendancy of the colony, Mexico, as a crude proxy, and estimating a population of 3.5 million and an average annual import value of 13–14 million *pesos,* he derived a per capita figure of four *pesos,* which to him seemed "ridiculously low" given the wide range of available imports, such as "wines and fruits . . . textiles made of silk, hemp, and linen or wool . . . iron, steel, and other prime necessities, and almost any luxury items" (22). New Spain's per capita import capacity was underserved. It was precisely this conclusion that led him to turn to the main focus of his report, the bottlenecks to further trade expansion.[99]

Two categories of constraints emerge from Revillagigedo's critique. In the first fall general factors: infrequent and unreliable maritime communications between Veracruz and metropolitan ports, impeding the flow of commercial intelligence between colony and metropole (Revillagigedo understood the effect of changes in Europe's trendsetting styles and fabrics);

the absence of well-constructed and maintained roads in New Spain; and the high cost of borrowing (5%) compared with that in Spain (3%) (27–30). An even greater constraint upon local sales was the pyramiding of *alcabalas* on merchandise sold or unsold that was moved from the port of entry through sales-tax zones *(alcabalatorios);* these imposts pushed the final cost of basic imports of great weight, such as ironware, to excessively high levels and, more important, reduced the sales of a critical, growing group of provincial distributors, traveling merchants *(comerciantes viandantes)* (43). Revillagigedo had in mind more than augmenting the inflow of Spanish and European imports, however; echoing one of his few supportive respondents, Yraeta, he questioned prohibitions on re-export of such imports from New Spain to nearby colonies in the Spanish Caribbean and beyond, to Central and South America via Pacific ports (39–40). Here one detects Revillagigedo's vision of New Spain as a major colonial entrepôt or point of transshipment. Yet he supported the prohibition on re-exports of similar goods from Havana to Veracruz—a bow or sop to Mexico City's *almaceneros*—on the ground that in the islands of the Caribbean "it is impossible to cut smuggling off completely" (41).

Important as a colonial entrepôt, New Spain considered far more critical the "progress and extension" of its consumption of local products and in particular its ability to absorb Spanish and European goods. This constituted Revillagigedo's second major category of interest, raising the income of the Native American masses and nurturing their desire to acquire Spanish products. As a nobleman, a high public functionary, and a colonialist, Revillagigedo was not impressed by New Spain's "ignorantes" Native Americans; even wage workers, including relatively well paid miners, "keep up an unbecoming nakedness and idleness, working only a few days to eat and drink on all the other days" (50). These he hoped to transform into consumers, an aspect of merchandising that "old-time merchants" (the pre-1789 years) had overlooked. Under "managed" import scarcities during *flota* times, merchants in the colonies had had few sales problems, since they could operate on the comforting principle that "in America no article is rejected, even if it is tarnished or lacking color, workmanship, or design" (23). As for the current crop of "comerciantes modernos," he found them appropriately concerned with assessing consumer preferences ("consumers' tastes . . . their real or imagined needs"), although many traders had yet to realize that "not everything is adapted to the temper, character, education, climate, and funds of these kingdoms" (23). However, before Native Americans could become consumers, their incomes had to increase; this was feasible only if the colonial economy remained focused on agriculture, more specifically the cultivation of cotton and silk and their transformation into yarn exportable to Spain's manufactories (46). The reduction or even elimination of export duties on New Spain's agricultural products, including flours shipped to Havana and other Caribbean ports, might also furnish a suitable stimulus, all the more necessary since yarn exports could hobble the colony's domestic textile industry.

In light of what the colonial bureaucrats Beleña and the anonymous author of the "Ensayo apologético" had observed about the colony's manufactures, it is no surprise that Revillagigedo did not recommend expansion of New Spain's *obrajes* to absorb unemployment and expand income and demand. While he recognized the quality and durability of locally produced goods, the presence of colonial manufactories—a sector notably omitted in the observations of Revillagigedo's merchant respondents—was explicable "because no comparable item comes from Europe, or merchants give up on a remnant or spoiled article" (45). He perceived that New Spain's cotton and woolen *obrajes* had benefited from indirect protection: textiles produced by Native Americans were *alcabala*-exempt, while textiles from Spain were subject to export duties, import duties at Veracruz, *alcabalas,* commissions, and last but not least, high freight costs within the colony. This accounted for the "woolen workshops at Querétaro and . . . those producing cotton cloth at San Miguel el Grande," along with the *obrajes* of Puebla, Sultepec, and Temascaltepec. Were Spanish merchants responsive to New Spain's consumer preferences, for example, in commonly used rebozos of cotton and cotton-silk mixtures, they could readily be reproduced in Catalan towns such as Manresa and exported to New Spain. Revillagigedo left no doubt of his sentiments about the basic direction for the most important colony of Spain: "Only Agriculture and Mining have the possibility of expansion." This categorically expressed colonial policy meant no import substitution in the colonies of Spanish, or for that matter European, manufactures. "Workshops should not survive, nor does sound policy tolerate them, even articles neither made in Spain nor shipped from there" (45).

To Revillagigedo's recognition of the low purchasing power of New Spain's *indios* must be added his accurate observation that "custom influences people, especially the ignorant . . . *indios,*" who preferred "to use credit or borrow" and hoard their few savings (33). In this sense article 12 of the 1786 ordinances for intendents prohibiting local colonial officials *(subdelegados* or *justicias)* from providing credit, goods, or draft animals *(repartimiento)* to native peoples in their jurisdictions, had the effect of curtailing consumption (33). Having just (in June 1792) analyzed the effects of article 12, Revillagigedo commented wearily on the *repartimiento* debate, about which "much has been written and time has passed with no results and no decision about anything" (34). As for tradesmen residing in Native American jurisdictions, two factors made them reluctant to provide advances in the manner of the former *alcaldes mayores.* First, there were "rich residents or merchants in the pueblos" who believed that their advances and sales were legal only in cash, and second, those new local officials *(subdelegados)*—who considered the traders' profits "taken from them"—were spreading the rumor that the intendancy system would shortly be eliminated and their resort to *repartimiento* relegitimized. Local traders concluded that they might never recoup their advances, since "in general *indios* are bad debtors" (33–34).

Revillagigedo's solution offered a balance between Madrid's reliance upon Native Americans' natural acquisitiveness when exposed to a capitalistic economy and the pragmatism of merchants in the colonies. Colonial policy toward native peoples in the eighteenth century was designed to break down the close relationship between the local district officers (whether *corregidores, alcaldes mayores,* or their *tenientes*) and their merchant backers *(fiadores),* many of whom were in Mexico City. For Revillagigedo the elimination of the privilege of such officials to force *repartimiento* upon native peoples, which was expressly prohibited in the ordinance, had to be maintained, for he found it incompatible that a colonial official be both creditor and judge simultaneously.[100] On the other hand, he fully supported the local traders' practice of advancing goods and credits to Native Americans, since thereby they could avoid the "harsh terms of the payment and . . . the repeated use of force" by the colonial authorities. While the viceroy appeared to tolerate the performance of local tradesmen, his attitude toward the merchant oligarchs, the *almaceneros,* was quite the opposite (34).

The revision of trade policy in the Spanish transatlantic system over the last third of the eighteenth century had at least two prongs: increasing the number of consumers in the colonies and their consumption of imports sent from the metropole; and no less critical, chipping away at the commercial hegemony of merchant oligarchs at centers of distribution in the American colonies. Identified with Madrid's shifting commercial policy, pursued vigorously under recently appointed Antonio Valdés, Revillagigedo privileged his "new type of merchants," while barely repressing animosity for Mexico City's merchant oligarchy—the wealthy, visibly influential merchants represented by the 115 *almaceneros* who had signed their petition of December 1791—and its "old-time" mentality. Aristocrat, army officer, and investor, Revillagigedo was uncompromisingly critical of their resistance to policy change and an unequivocal supporter of Valdés's policy of drawing more Spanish merchants into the competition for Native Americans' *pesos*.

No doubt he had been stung by Mexico City *almaceneros'* manipulation of their corporate body to impede implementation of fundamental changes in commercial policy, including efforts to undercut the chief colonial officer of New Spain, himself. He considered the Mexico City *consulado* to have been designed in principle for the "protection and development" of Spain's transatlantic trade; in fact, he found that it inhibited growth.[101] The colonial capital's mercantile community, via its *consulado*, exerted disproportionate influence through the funds generated by its sustained administration of the *avería*, currently a tax on all goods entering the jurisdiction of the capital that, he emphasized, was borne by local consumers rather than merchants. The *avería* surplus funded the salaries of the *consulado*'s chief elected officers, a prior and two consuls, the *consulado*'s personnel, and its Madrid lobbyists, all working toward making "the merchant guild of the city of Mexico more frightening and respected." That corporate body's primary interest, Revillagigedo concluded, was mainly "to advance its interests and advantages to the prejudice of merchants in other cities." In its role as a commercial court it was not expeditious, its legal counselors resorting unabashedly to a variety of procedural delays. Merchants in other commercial centers of New Spain, such as Guadalajara and Veracruz, had to litigate in person or hire Mexico City attorneys—in any event, costly procedures. Obviously, tradesmen in distant provinces or cities felt handicapped when litigating in the capital against a Mexico City counterpart (35).

Revillagigedo found the most visible proof of *almacenero* influence in the "irrational" petition by the 115 backed by their *consulado* and Páez dela Cadena's resort to "reflections and arguments that were weak or based on false information" (36). Here was evidence of their narrowly defined interests: the *consulado* petitioned for only Mexico City to enjoy a 3 percent *alcabala* reduction and for sales at Veracruz to be subject to an additional 3 percent. This would channel trade from Veracruz back to the capital, undermining Veracruz's status as a new entrepôt for tradesmen from the interior, not to mention its impact on *cargadores* from Spain or their factors. He put it succinctly: "Everything would flow into the hands of the merchants who financed their purchases in Spain, consigning their shipments directly to themselves" (36). In addition, in urging that silver remissions to the metropole be restricted to one annual shipment from Veracruz, Mexico City merchants were hamstringing the revival of the metropole's manufactures, whose survival depended on the "steady inflow of investment as well as demand for their manufactures in order to operate" (38). Nationalist and colonialist, Revillagigedo recognized that metropolitan economic growth and colonial trade were intimately linked.

The viceroy's harsh judgment of the *consulado*'s role was matched by his unambiguous recommendation: either "terminate this *consulado,* which would not be missed" or create others "according to better rules and principles," particularly at Veracruz, "where all of the merchandise arrives and where prompt and expeditious settlements of its lawsuits would be very welcome" (38–39). No doubt Revillagigedo was already privy to Madrid's imminent decision to expand the number of *consulados* throughout the empire in America and broaden membership to incorporate *hacendados* and merchants, as well as to the repeated petitions of Veracruz merchants for one of their own. This explains the selection of Tomás Murphy as a respondent.

Although Revillagigedo's *informe* ranged over administrative and economic aspects of Spain's most important colony in the New World, its main focus was the impact of *comercio libre,* that critical element of Spain's transatlantic trade policy hesitatingly and haltingly applied after 1765 despite resistance by interest groups at Cadiz and in the colonies. Given the cohesion of the Mexico City merchant community—their common Cantabrian provenance, their high incomes, and their ability to lobby effectively and cohesively—*almaceneros'* influence was indeed disproportionate to their numbers. This had long been a political reality and accounts for the careful preparation behind Revillagigedo's report.

That the viceroy submitted a report supported vigorously by a few colonial civil servants rather than a majority of prominent overseas merchants did not weaken the Madrid authorities' commitment to *comercio libre.* Madrid pushed ahead with its policy despite the virtually unanimous opposition of those dominating the corporate commercial bodies in the major distribution centers of the Spanish world, Cadiz and Mexico City. Their influence had many roots, not least that Mexico City's *almaceneros* were now the major source of financial support for exchanges between Mexico City and Cadiz and, since the 1780s, clearly the major source of funds at the metropole's critical moments. To be sure, the Madrid authorities and their high colonial officials did receive some support from the private sector: in the metropole, some merchants at Cadiz, Barcelona, Málaga, and Santander did benefit from the changes in commercial policy, and there were supporters among Spanish immigrants at Veracruz and in the interior of New Spain. In that colony, Revillagigedo's "nueva clase de comerciantes" could look to Veracruz as point of contact with merchants in the metropole rather than solely to *almaceneros* in the colony's capital city, just as they doubtless schemed to broaden their operations by penetrating the Native American *partidos* of the recently formed intendancies.

This extended analysis of how merchants and colonial officers in Spain's wealthiest colony reacted to the third, and last, *reglamento del comercio libre* merits a tentative synthesis. We begin by asking the obvious: why did Colonial Secretary Valdés formulate and forward his questionnaire soon after taking office, and was the appointment of Viceroy Revillagigedo integral to Valdés's plan of operations?

Let us look first at the context of the late 1780s in Spain's wealthiest American colony. There was a short-term commercial crisis in the middle of that decade, the downside of the postwar boom after the peace of 1784. In New Spain it was attributable partly to oversupply and partly to falling demand owing to devastating drought and consequent harvest failures and to epidemic disease. On the other hand, the population of the Western Hemisphere's largest urban center, Mexico City, was expanding, which by the end of that decade promised a greater concentration of consumers and greater consumption of imports; it was already a major magnet for smugglers from New Orleans via Tampico and from Jamaica and Saint-Domingue to the Veracruz and Yucatec coasts.

Now we can understand the drive of metropolitan authorities to engage more emigrant Spaniards in overseas opportunities by authorizing the participation of the peninsula's peripheral ports and their hinterland in Spain's transatlantic system. This remained a priority of Madrid's policymakers in the late eighteenth century: to maximize the colonies' resources in staples and silver in order to undergird the formation of viable manufactories in the metropole. New Spain's consumers and silver exports had to be harnessed; for the moment, there could be no backpedaling from the principle of *comercio libre* in Spain's transatlantic system.

In view of the customarily effective lobbying at Madrid of the Consulado de México, the selection of the second conde de Revillagigedo to replace Viceroy Flores was hardly serendipitous. Revillagigedo's father's Cuban investments had given his son a grasp of colonial issues, in particular the vexing one of trade relations between Havana and Veracruz. As a respectable shareholder in the recently chartered Compañía de Filipinas, Revillagigedo knew that the *almacenero* Francisco Ignacio de Yraeta was its Mexico City agent, although we do not know who at Mexico City helped him select respondents to Valdés's questionnaire. Long residence at court had made him a prominent, cosmopolitan member of Madrid's political class, well connected and visible in high administrative policymaking circles. Valdés must have sized him up as a tough-minded nationalist who understood the priority of developmental policy for the metropole, a proconsul needing no manual on the importance of commercial exchanges with New Spain and the extent of that colony's private and ecclesiastical wealth. He would insist on supporting the metropole's colonial objectives and could be counted on to share the vision of Valdés and his administrative personnel and to stand up to predictable opposition from influential private and public sectors clustered in Mexico City, whether the colonial capital's merchant oligarchs or elements of the high colonial civil service there, or both. Not to be overlooked, moreover, were those colonial civil servants—Posada, Beleña, the "anonymous author"—who shared Revillagigedo's *proyectista* vision of Spain's development of an effective colonial compact.

Revillagigedo's *informe* to Valdés can also be read as the swan song of an extraordinary proconsul, an archtypical authoritarian "reformer" in the autumn of *proyectismo*. Its brief initial section refutes the pessimism of those dominating the Consulado de México by underscoring the statistical base Revillagigedo had ordered prepared from reliable and convincing sources: tithe and *alcabala* collections, coinage at the Mexico City mint, the value of external trade recorded by the Veracruz customs, silver exports. All this, he asserted, had been undertaken *against* the opposition of all but two of Mexico City's influential *almacenero* respondents. Far more wide-ranging, the following section lays out a developmental strategy for the wealthiest possession of Spain overseas, a metropolitan design for exploiting the colony's raw materials, precious metals, and consumers while unambiguously suppressing the colony's manufactories. At the core of his analysis is the growth in trade between colony and metropole within the confines of the Spanish Atlantic, along with the elimination or minimization of twelve bottlenecks, all framed by his conspectus of the axis of New Spain's colonial economy—agriculture, mining, and consumption.

In agriculture Revillagigedo predicted realistically that New Spain's sugar exports could not compete even in the short term with Cuba's and that its flours could not compete with those shipped from the East Coast ports of the United States to Havana. Instead, he would focus on local production of raw silk and cotton for spinning yarns for export to infant textile enterprises in the metropole. Yet barely mentioned is the fundamental problem of land concentration in the colony, much less agrarian reform. As for mine owners, he found them unnecessarily overprotected by many mechanisms; he explicitly criticized the mining tribunal for misuse of its investment funds *(avío)* by privileging a few large operators. Instead, he favored smaller mining enterprises, since their multiplication would increase the employment of wage earners and thereby consumption.

Accepting the gains of *comercio libre,* Revillagigedo remained convinced that trade between metropole and colony required expanding New Spain's consumption of imports. Hence the emphasis on mineworkers (and of course farmhands). Mineworkers and their households, in particular, should be induced to abandon their habitual, ragged dress for cheap imported cottons and silk rebozos woven in metropolitan manufactories with yarns exported from New Spain. In addition, according to Revillagigedo, success in tapping colonial demand required eliminating *obrajes* clustered at Querétaro and Puebla, which had survived behind the unintended protection of multiple sales taxes, high transport costs, and poor infrastructure. Revillagigedo's preoccupation with consumption framed his final recommendation, the relegalization, with "proper" controls, of the *repartimiento de mercancías,* outlawed in the *Ordenanza de intendentes* of 1786. Here, once again, Revillagigedo revealed his grasp of certain retailing mechanisms in the colony: without easy credit, mass consumption by Native Americans would stagnate, because they preferred to save cash and rely on credit arrangements. As we will see, this was their self-protective mechanism against exploitation.

In sum, Revillagigedo ideated what was still a *proyectista* vision of economic development: access to colonial raw materials, yarns, and labor, along with a growing pool of consumers could and should undergird industrialization in the Spanish metropole. As he concluded with satisfaction, he had crafted an economic overview of New Spain that pinpointed and aimed to correct twelve major bottlenecks to trade growth in Spain's Atlantic economy at the risk of antagonizing "a certain class of people and corporations that were legal and well backed" (57). Put another way, fault lines were surfacing—between merchants at Mexico City and Veracruz, between the capital's merchant community and elements of the colonial administration, between a commercial oligarchy overseas and policymakers in the metropole (despite Madrid's evident dependence on the colony's wealthy lenders and donors). Was this the beginning of what John Brewer has termed in the North American context a "new view of imperial-colonial relations as asymmetrical and exploitative rather than reciprocal and mutually beneficial?"[102] The *comercio libre* of 1789, however, constituted but one of a series of economic issues fissioning the commercial oligarchy and civil service of both colony and metropole in the reign of Charles IV.[103]

5. A Hegemony Threatened: Mexico City and Veracruz

Indeed the *reglamento* of . . . 1778 can be considered by the people of Veracruz as the *cédula* creating its Pueblo.   Tomás Murphy, 6 December 1802

The Consulado de México hasn't even the vaguest notion of Veracruz's commerce, its economy . . . its products, or the other benefits that tie it to its *consulado*.
                                        Pedro Pablo Vélez to Consulado de Veracruz, 15 June 1808

[Veracruz], the sole key to the large, rich, and opulent Kingdom of New Spain . . . one of the most active trading ports of the dominions.   AGN, Consulado

The establishment of a merchants' corporation, or *consulado,* at Veracruz in 1794 was far more than a generous and unsolicited stimulus by the Spanish imperial government to a neglected port on New Spain's Gulf coast. It was formal if belated recognition of Veracruz's emergence as an aggressive competitor of Mexico City's for New Spain's internal commercial circuits and for hegemony over the burgeoning economy of Spain's principal Caribbean possession, the island of Cuba. One major thread running through the evolution of the colony of New Spain, what the Spanish colonial administration often called "América Septentrional" after 1763, was the counterpoint between Havana interests and those of Mexico City and Veracruz, as well as between Mexico City and Veracruz. Analysis of the factors leading to the establishment of Veracruz's *consulado* and the schisms it generated offers further evidence of colonial growth and the unavoidable tensions between commercial interests within the Spanish Atlantic system of the late eighteenth century.

Of course the dynamic growth factor of "America Septrional" remained what it had been for more than two hundred years, its mining economy, which to onlookers mushroomed in the closing decades of the century. Growth in silver output and in population heightened New Spain's importance in the New World and, as will be seen, further tied the colony to another expanding source of growth, agriculture around Cuba's main port, Havana. Again, a broad conspectus is appropriate, since the Cuban phenomenon was part of the general phenomenon of agricultural expansion in both the Caribbean and circum-Caribbean areas. Veracruz shipped to Europe not only Guatemala's major exportable, indigo *(añil)* but also cochineal *(grana)* from New Spain's province of Oaxaca and vanilla from Veracruz, while Havana exported sugar and molasses, tobacco, and coffee.

Unlike in New Spain, with its reserves of indigenous labor, in Cuba the diversification and expansion of its exports required imported labor, African slaves, along with food and clothing, cattle and lumber. To obtain these inputs Cuban interests expanded old links to nearby areas and crafted new ones. For African slaves they turned to dealers at Port-au-Prince (Saint-Domingue) and Kingston (Jamaica), who also provided cottons and a variety of other goods. From North American ports, mainly Philadelphia and later Baltimore, planters obtained cattle and lumber; for basic commodities like corn and wheat flour they relied largely on North American ports, to a lesser degree upon Puebla through Veracruz. Important as Cuba's relations with English, French, and "Anglo American" (U.S., that is) suppliers were after 1783, Cuba's major lifeline led to New Spain and its silver. New Spain financed Cuba's colonial bureaucracy with annual subsidies *(situados),* which steeply increased after the English occupation of 1762–63, for military fortifications, shipyards, troop support, including food and salaries, and the purchase on government account of Cuban leaf tobacco, shipped overseas to the metropole's tobacco factory at Seville for the manufacture of snuff, cigars, and cigarettes.[1] From the late 1780s on, New Spain's merchants, joined by the resident factors of merchants in Spain, transferred silver to Havana for investment in sugar exports to the metropole.

Cuba's labor force in sugar, tobacco, and coffee production required large flour imports. At most a trickle came from Santander millers, who received supplies from the metropole's Tierra de Campos; but over the forty years after the English occupation of Havana a growing percentage of flours came from Philadelphia and Baltimore, particularly after Madrid loosened constraints on slave trading with nearby foreign colonies in 1789. Then demand for flours soared, and New Spain's *haciendas* in the Puebla area could not meet the challenge. For a brief period in the 1780s and early 1790s Veracruz exported flours, but the volume gradually dropped in the face of U.S. competition. Whatever the constraints on Puebla production, there is no lack of evidence of Puebla's *hacendados* and Veracruz shippers railing against the high costs of shipping by muleback over the poorly maintained road between Mexico City and Veracruz, whose neglect they charged to the traditional insouciance of the well-financed Consulado de México. Exports of maize flour mark, however, the appearance of a staple export-oriented mentality on the part of Puebla's *hacendados* and Veracruz's merchants, who also shipped cochineal, indigo, vanilla, and sugar and envisioned growth in raw-cotton exports, even the export of hand-spun cotton yarn to Catalan manufactories.

In brief, the expansion of Veracruz's external trade after 1765 subtly began to transform that major port into a busy colonial entrepôt. The suspension of *flotas* in 1778 had ended that cycle of bustle and boredom, with frequent, unscheduled shipping now entering from ports in Spain and the Caribbean colonies, shifting the locus of exchanges between Cadiz and Mexico City from the old *feria* site at Jalapa to Veracruz. Veracruz, rather than upcountry Jalapa, now became the point where factors representing the merchants of Cadiz and other Spanish ports set up circuits with traders in New Spain's provinces, trying to bypass Mexico City's trade hegemony. Yet, from the perspective of the expanding Veracruz community of the 1780s, Mexico City's *consulado* was equipped only to process its own litigation; it was ill-equipped and even incompetent to judge Veracruz's diverse litigation growing out of its role as a shipping center in contact with Havana, New Orleans, and peninsular ports.

The blossoming of Veracruz as an entrepôt was an unplanned yet inevitable complement to Madrid's trade policy for the Spanish Atlantic. It provided a magnet of opportunity to entrepreneurs from the metropole and its American colonies, initially to Cadiz's factors or correspondents formerly resident at Jalapa. After 1778, when shipping increased and Cadiz's licensing of emigrants finally ended with the extinction of the Casa de Contratación (1790), Veracruz drew aspiring merchants from the *montañas* of Burgos and from the Basque provinces, from Galicia and Catalonia, Málaga and Valencia, as well as a handful of *criollos* of New Spain.[2] The port's activity also swelled with the entry of *arrieros* handling thousands of pack mules and with the opening of many small stores *(pulperías)* catering to sailors, muleteers, and a pool of stevedores, their families, and of course new small-goods traders *(viandantes)*. By incorporating *peninsulares* and *criollos,* providing an entry point for shipping from Cadiz and peninsular ports such as Santander, Barcelona, and Málaga, at last authorized for direct trade with New Spain, an expanding Veracruz business community promised to realize Madrid's design for an effective "colonial compact."[3] Formal recognition of Veracruz's new importance might, moreover, facilitate policy planners' goal of developing within the colony networks of exchange hitherto dominated by a small coterie of Mexico City *monopolistas*.

Founding the Consulado de Veracruz, 1781–1794

There was always hesitancy about putting into effect the policy of *comercio libre,* and it is not surprising that full implementation of the *reglamento* of 1778 was delayed too. In 1778 the formation of new *consulados* in the metropole and the colonies was promised,[4] yet only in March 1781 did a group of twenty-five "comerciantes españoles de la ciudad de Veracruz" gather at the invitation of Pedro de Cos, Eligio de Uztáriz, and Miguel Ignacio de Miranda to petition Madrid formally for a merchant guild independent of Mexico City.[5] In 1781 Veracruz's leading merchant house, that of the *montañés* Pedro de Cosío, was still a prime provider to Colonial Secretary Gálvez of situation reports on New Spain, which may account for the Casa de Cosío's figuring at the head of the petitioners; the list included prominent traders such as Andrés Gil de la Torre, Pedro de Cos, Juan Manual Muñóz, Remigio Fernández, Juan José de Echeverría, Francisco Antonio de la Torre, and Adrián Felix Troncoso. Basque names were notably absent.[6]

Given the importance of curbing the hegemony of Mexico City's *consulado* over Veracruz, the petition's explanatory preamble was surprisingly short, indeed laconic: "The reason of nature without dialectical support convinces us of the indispensable necessity and extreme importance of this Veracruz *consulado*." The petition then tied the proposal to the economic policies of "civil servants at Estado, Yndias, and Hacienda" and to stimulating agriculture and manufactories in the metropole by expanding "by every possible means navigation to these American dominions." Next, noting that article 53 of the *reglamento* of 1778 had promised new *consulados* precisely to develop the transatlantic trade, the petitioners then introduced the port of Veracruz unabashedly as "the single key to the large, rich, and opulent Kingdom of New Spain, the destination and resting place of all the *flotas,* mercury and other vessels from Spain and other overseas ports of America, . . . one of the most active trading ports of the dominions . . . and consequently the best place for business." The prominence of Veracruz made continued subordination to the commercial court of Mexico City's *consulado* intolerable: Mexico City was more than one hundred leagues distant in the interior, and the costs of traveling and residence there were expensive; in addition, on the whole agents in the colonial capital were to be distrusted for "indolence . . . confusion, disinterest." Worse, the judges of that *consulado* were incompetent in questions of maritime law.[7] Perhaps the petition's brevity was a measure of the local merchants' confidence in the colonial experience and their expectation of the cooperation of Colonial Secretary Gálvez, to whom the petition was addressed for appropriate handling. To ensure that their petition would not be pigeonholed, the petitioners designated two of their number, the *criollos* Andrés Gil de la Torre and Miguel Ignacio de Miranda, as their general agents (i.e., lobbyists) at Madrid. In point of fact, Andrés Gil de la Torre's brother, José, would move the petition through Madrid's bureaucratic labyrinth over the following decade.[8]

Ingenuous or mere victims of changing policies at Madrid, Veracruzanos found their confidence in Gálvez misplaced. For one thing, he turned against his former Veracruz confidant, Cosío, in 1782; for another, Mexico City's *consulado* officials learned immediately of the petition, which probably contributed to their readiness to lend the Madrid government 1 million *pesos* in 1782 and covertly forward via Gálvez a gift of thousands of *pesos* to Charles III's heirs, the Prince and Princess of Asturias (the future Charles IV and María Luisa).[9] Evidently the *consulado*'s Madrid agent, Fernando José Mangino, manipulated effectively the slush fund at his disposal, for there were reports of "the large sums [Mangino] has wasted, spent, and offered, [which] prove that he had much money at his disposition."[10] Gálvez informed Veracruz's agent, José Gil de la Torre, that the government had approved the petition of 1781, although a *cédula* was not officially issued until six years later; in January 1787, shortly before Gálvez died, the agent again petitioned him for the *cédula,* with no success. The agent's explanation of his failure to his Veracruz sponsors was at best politic, as he blamed "first . . . the pressing needs of the Crown during the last War, followed by the Minister's demise." In fact, Gálvez had simply pigeonholed the file *(expediente)* of Veracruz materials and, one suspects, the whole issue of new *consulados* in the American colonies. But no sooner had Valdés replaced the deceased Gálvez than Gil de la Torre reopened the matter; Valdés had to confess that the ministry's archives held no relevant materials.[11] When further searching for the *expediente* proved fruitless, Gil de la Torre guardedly advised Veracruz, "I think . . . the case got lost in the process and perhaps was filed along with cases, dossiers, and many personal papers in the office of the Deceased Marqués de la Sonora."[12]

Gálvez's death in no way diminished the influence of the colonial and metropolitan interests he had carefully cultivated for years. Structural continuities are made of interests more than of personalities, and an influential and well-financed group like the Consulado de México could be contained, as a civil servant uncommonly skilled in compromising policy and implementation put it in 1788, only "by using slow, indirect means that most people in our country use unobtrusively to their advantage."[13]

Now Valdés, joined by merchant and bureaucratic supporters, revived the long-sidetracked extension of *comercio libre* to New Spain and Venezuela, and indeed had to rely upon "slow, indirect means" to create new *consulados* in New Spain. Buoyed by a fresh bureaucratic emphasis upon implementing contemplated but usually suspended policy changes, the group of Veracruz merchants drafted its version of *consulado* ordinances, obtained the approval of their intendant, Pedro Corvalán, and submitted it to the newly arrived viceroy, the second conde de Revillagigedo, one of Valdés's judicious colonial appointments.[14] An eminently modern and secular spirit, Revillagigedo fully supported the rationale for a Veracruz *consulado*—the necessity of a local court to process commercial and maritime litigation— but was characteristically uninhibited in a caustic commentary on the mentality of Veracruz's merchant community. He saw no point, he wrote Valdés, in placing the proposed *consulado* under the protection of San José and La Virgen María; he recommended that instead of "the attributes of virginity and purity they hope to inscribe on their coat of arms, . . . they employ others alluding to liberty of commerce, which is the real source of their petition." He found similarly objectionable that the *ordenanzas* would admit to the new organization *only* peninsular Spaniards or their sons, thereby excluding "*criollos* and the sons of foreigners resident there," along with those who practiced "degrading occupations or crafts," restrictions he found inconsistent with a "reglamento moderno."[15] His was an oddly modern mentality.

Despite repeated initiatives by Veracruz merchants backed by the intendant Corvalán, by the aggressive and outspoken Viceroy Revillagigedo, by Madrid bureaucrats like Tomás González Carbajal, involved in similar issues, and by Minister Valdés himself, all were contained from 1788 to 1794 by the Consulado de México, its political fund, agents, and bureaucratic contacts at Madrid.[16] Moreover, there is evidence that the Consulado de Cadiz, which once hoped Veracruz merchants might protect their interests by providing that one of their two proposed consuls would always represent the "comercio de España," withdrew support on discovering that the proposed ordinance made no such commitment.[17] Individual Mexico City merchants in December 1791, the Consulado de México in January 1792, and then their contact in the colonial civil service, Páez de la Cadena, in May 1792 warned repeatedly of Veracruz's vulnerability to invasion from the sea.[18] In addition, the Consulado de México, ever incapable of "giving up ideas of hoarding and monopoly," ever prone to oppose "the system of *comercio libre* . . . the abolition of *flotas,* and other helpful government measures,"[19] found in Fernando José Mangino an effective lobbyist at Madrid. The Consejo de Estado, at Madrid, reviewed each proposal for a *consulado* in America individually. Havana's petitioners received approval in October 1792, and four months later the Consejo, with Charles IV and its newly designated *decano,* the conde de Aranda, present, agreed in principle to charter overseas *consulados* at Veracruz, Cartagena de Indias, and Chile "the same as what was ordered for the Havana *consulado.*"[20]

Yet eleven more months would pass without publication of a royal decision, and on 2 January 1794 it still seemed possible that the Consulado de México might sidetrack Veracruz's petition indefinitely. Late eighteenth-century Madrid, capital of an Atlantic empire, was the residence of many formally registered *agentes* representing colonial interests; it was also the preferred residence (for many, *the* retirement center) of civil servants and military and naval personnel with colonial service. One or more of such formal and informal Mexico City lobbyists managed to contact a functionary in the Colonial Office, through whose hands Veracruz's petition had to pass. On 2 January the functionary proposed to seek an opinion about elements of the Veracruz proposal, urging that none of the initiators of the Veracruz petition of 1781 be consulted. Instead, he suggested an informal opinion from a former resident of New Spain with excellent "conexiones" at Veracruz currently residing in Madrid, Fernando José Mangino. Mangino's friends knew when and how to return favors.[21]

Mangino's recommendation illustrates how an alert lobbyist manipulated both personnel and procedures of the state bureaucracy to kill legislation while appearing to improve its chances. Of course, Mangino was carrying out policy ideated by his overseas employer, the Mexico City *consulado,* and reflecting its needs and ideology.[22] Fundamental to that ideology, which Mangino reiterated, was the public utility of a chartered corporation of merchant entrepreneurs. Their corporate activities in pursuit of the commonweal, Mangino argued, including financial support of institutions ranging from Madrid's colonial office to Mexico City's insane asylum,[23] were "so many that they needed reams of paper to list them, although striving for brevity." Comfortable in baroque hyperbole, he (and they) believed that "in this capital there is no work dedicated to the service of the Lord, the King, or the Public that does not owe its origin or maintenance to the Consulado de México." Indeed, every stratum of New Spain's society, "from those of the highest to those of the lowest sphere," could find in the *consulado* a "ready, zealous, and charitable protector." The critical factor in its public role, in its "magnificencia," was its administration of the *avería* tax (.006, or 6 *al millar*) on goods entering Veracruz, which netted about 60,000 *pesos* annually (the proximate equivalent of the viceroy's salary). Not only would *consulados* at Veracruz and Guadalajara reduce Mexico City's *avería* receipts, forcing it into "an unseemly indigence . . . [and] mendicity," but they would stimulate neither the colony's valuable indigo and cochineal exports nor local manufactures ("common woolen and cotton textiles, of poor quality, only used by *indios* and other people reduced to the utmost misery").[24]

Mangino skillfully exploited his opening by assaulting the idea of more *consulados* in New Spain, employing the rationale and ideology of the Mexico City *consulado*.[25] He portrayed the *consulado* in a fashion presumably most attractive to a metropolitan government that was inadequately financed and struggling with a rapidly mounting public debt after warring with revolutionary France of the Convention. The reply was also cast in the traditional format employed by the trinity of mercantile corporations of Spain's empire at Cadiz, Lima, and Mexico City: the extent to which private interest in a state-sanctioned corporation utilized its maintenance impost *(avería)* for presumably disinterested ends such as public works, military security, and government finance. The Consulado de México had committed about 900,000 *pesos* to the Huehuetoca drainage system to reduce the inundation of the capital, to construction of Mexico City's new customs house *(aduana),* and to renovation of the Inquisition's prison, the insane asylum, and the welfare shelter *(hospicio).* Moreover, the *consulado* had allocated another 100,000 *pesos* to what were really government operations—to support Gálvez's survey of the colony's northern provinces and to maintain the *consulado*'s own Regimiento del Comercio and a regiment of dragoons for Veracruz's defense. Thus it had allocated in all more than 1 million *pesos*. Finally, to help the metropole finance the war with England, it had given Madrid a grant of another 1 million *pesos*.

Mangino insisted that the two *consulados* contemplated would curtail the Mexico City *consulado*'s current and future activities, especially when New Spain's external trade—here he reiterated Mexico City's stance on *comercio libre*—"is so depressed that it doesn't need these tribunals."[26] His closing observations represented no more than standard bureaucratese. Indeed, his proposal that the whole *expediente* of position papers be passed to the Consejo de Indias "along with the comments of the Consulado de México for its appropriate judgment" was potentially destructive of the whole process of forming new *consulados*. His was a classic manipulation of the bureaucratic process whereby the Consejo de Indias, a key instrument of vested interests in metropole and colonies, could and usually did bottle up major policy modifications.[27] Mangino and the *consulado*'s stratagem for exaggerating a mercantile corporation's involvement in public finance was more suitably directed to the bureaucracy of the seventeenth-century Hapsburg state than to the more critical policymakers of late eighteenth-century Bourbon Spain and many newcomers to colonial trade.

Mangino's request for delay until the Consulado de México could be heard elicited a deft riposte. Mangino, commented an anonymous public functionary knowledgeable in the ways of Madrid's administrative labyrinth, was a lobbyist troubled by the possibility of salary reduction if his employers' income shrank; he did find perplexing, however, that Mangino had waited to present his instance until after publication of the decrees establishing *consulados* at Caracas and Guatemala and the promise of more such corporations.[28] As for the financial role of the Consulado de México, some of whose funds had been committed to the colonial capital's needs, it was perhaps commendable but hardly gratifying to New Spain's ultimate *avería* payers, the colony's consumers. Although the *consulado,* said the anonymous commentator, "builds customs houses, sumptuous prisons, and insane asylums, . . . forms and supports regiments and even makes considerable pecuniary favors when the State needs them" to justify its "air of majesty and opulence in assisting the state," it did not finance agriculture and trade, which were, after all, the "real and perennial sources of the wealth that should avoid such state demands." Worse, there was its record of neglecting "this kingdom's sole Port," Veracruz, where incoming ships had to navigate past dangerous, unmarked shoals as well as warships at anchor; shipmasters found the mooring zone *(canal)* undredged and mooring facilities inadequate, wharves few and lighterage boats *(barcos)* unseaworthy; and outbound ships found water supplies and ballast in short supply and expensive. And there was the road from Veracruz to the capital, more than 60 percent of which, he asserted, was over level terrain but poorly maintained.

Impatience with the stratagems of interest groups surfaced in the anonymous bureaucrat's dismissal of the lobbyist Mangino's proposal that the *expediente* on new *consulados* be routed to the Consejo de Indias and also reviewed by the Consulado de México as "a well-known tactic to postpone the outcome." That stratagem was, he recalled, precisely what the Madrid lobbyist of Lima's *consulado* had done to delay the decree setting up a *consulado* in Chile. The Consejo de Indias, he predicted, would delay "as long as possible" until, under pressure, it would request input—*instrucciones*—from Mexico City's *consulado*. And if these subterfuges did not prevail, the capital's *consulado* "will order with no more knowledge than it now enjoys precisely what has already been mandated by the Crown in consultation with the Consejo de Estado." The anonymous bureaucrat concluded tartly that Mangino's request was "unworthy of consideration" and "unfair" and that he should "without further delay" conform to what had been submitted.[29] Later Mangino conceded that the Veracruz *consulado* might incorporate within its territorial jurisdiction the former *feria* town of Jalapa, given its "dependence, connection, and shared interests" with Veracruz, excluding, however, pueblos administered from Jalapa. Then, drawing on his personal assessment of Veracruz's merchant community, he proposed as "those most suitable for the jobs of prior and consuls . . . Andrés Gil de la Torre, Sebastián Pérez, and Eligio de Uztáriz as individuals who have so many personal qualities."[30]

Reactivation of Veracruz's petition of 1788 peaked in early 1795 thanks to the activity of the Consejo de Estado and Hacienda Minister Gardoqui. Once again, however, the *expediente* was held up, perhaps because of pressure from Mexico City;[31] only in December was an initial list of officers selected, leading in 1795 to the formal decree establishing the Veracruz *consulado*. Fourteen years had passed since the original petition.

In one sense Madrid's decisions did counter recommendations by Mexico City's *almaceneros,* for of the three principal officeholders recommended by Mangino, only Gil de la Torre was kept, and even Mangino's list of suggested *consiliarios* was modified.[32] True, the Consulado de México's opinion was respected: Veracruz's territorial jurisdiction was far smaller than those of the new *consulados* of Guadalajara, Havana, Guatemala, Caracas, Buenos Aires, and Chile.[33] More than a setback for Veracruz interests, Veracruz's limited jurisdiction affected towns in the intendancy of Veracruz such as Acayucán, which was dissatisfied and unhappy with the Mexico City *consulado* as "guardian of those areas in mercantile matters" and embittered enough to advance the "scandalous proposition" that the Mexico City *consulado* "has not even the most general sense of the trade of Veracruz, its economy, extent, products, or other advantages of such an institution."[34] The Veracruz corporation shared one characteristic with all new *consulados,* one reflecting both the intentions of metropolitan policymakers and pressure from Spain's peripheral provinces. Unlike the electoral procedures mandated decades earlier (1742) for the faction-ridden Mexico City *consulado,* those of Veracruz contained no provision for alternation in office of regional groups *(partidos)* of *vizcaínos* and *montañeses.* Perhaps Mangino's perception of the heterogeneous origins of the Veracruz merchant community—*vizcaínos, encartados,* and *montañeses,* along with *gallegos, malagueños, valencianos,* and *catalanes*—inspired his observation to Gardoqui that "I have no fear that *partidos* that might compromise the high aims of a *consulado* at Veracruz exist."[35]

Whether his perception reflected reality or hope, there is no question that at its creation and over the next decade and more, Veracruz's *consulado* separated into *partidos* mirroring new directions and interests, as well as the rapidly changing conditions of Spain's Caribbean and circum-Caribbean colonies and their metropolitan links. Growth in the late eighteenth-century Atlantic economy had led to the Veracruz proposal for a *consulado* in the first place. Madrid's modest solution—near replication both in metropole and colonies of the early capitalistic merchant guild—could hardly contain pressures unleashed by industrializing, export-oriented, expansionist England.

Interest Groups and Factionalism: Veracruz

Corporate associations in the Spanish and Spanish-American economies and societies survived because they aggregated a variety of interests to further mutual goals. Overall unity for the commonweal was balanced, however, by competition among the interests aggregated; hence the intense factionalism within the Consulado de México in the eighteenth century formalized (or bridled) in the viceroy's mandated alternation of office *(alternativa)* between *montañeses* and *vizcaínos*. Mercantile corporate bodies, the *consulados,* remained leading elements of the Spanish matrix of commercial capitalism; Spain's eighteenth-century political economists *(proyectistas)* envisioned corporate bodies like *consulados* and *sociedades económicas* as economic stimuli in their models of growth. Replication of *consulados* in the colonies and metropole was, obviously, no symptom of innovation, for dominant in the mentality of *consulados,* whether metropolitan or colonial, remained the goals of shared monopoly; of constraint rather than liberty; of immuring Spain's transatlantic commercial structures from the profound changes in the Atlantic system induced by England's precocious industrialization, by the commercial projection of England's former North American colonies, and in particular by Havana's role in the Spanish Caribbean. While the charter of the Veracruz *consulado* contained no provision for the alternation of factions, that guild could not avoid factional conflict over policy. At best, Mangino's statement about the absence of factionalism, which he defined accurately as "parties based upon friendship, birthplace, or others of which we have many examples," was a pious, if not downright misleading, expression of hope.[36]

The definition of interest groups is fallible since interests and individuals defy sharp analytical categorization. We can compare an interest group to a constellation or mosaic, the approach followed here in composing a profile of Veracruz's two principal factions. Probably the most influential faction consisted of traditionalists often self-styled as commission agents, employees, or correspondents of merchants in Spain, many of *montañés* provenance and, in the 1780s, agents of Cadiz merchants (in *flota* times, the "comercio de España").[37] Ultimately the traditionalists' orientation fused with the interests of most members of the Mexico City *consulado*. They shared with the capital's merchant community an economic viewpoint shaped by two centuries of Hapsburg (Austrian) rule, which in New Spain had emphasized managed supply via *flotas* and *ferias*, silver exports to the metropole and investment in mining enterprises, and, latterly, government finance rather than export agriculture or ranching. Yet traditionalists tolerated artisanal production in the colony, provided no comparable European products were available. For them Spain constituted the exclusive supplier of Europe's products except when, under extraordinary circumstances, Cadiz's merchants were privileged to procure and ship them from non-peninsular ports. Sustained profit margins resulted from scarcity rather than from sales volume, as long experience proved; in wartime, when English warships could block shipments from Spain's ports, traditionalists opted for sales of their stocks of basic imports *(abarrotes)* such as paper, mercury, bar iron and steel, olive oil, wine, and brandy at inflated prices.[38] Covertly they did handle, albeit through third parties, European goods introduced clandestinely along the Gulf coast north and south of Veracruz; *in extremis* imports from the recently formed United States were tolerated provided Cadiz's merchants could legally order them shipped directly to Veracruz from U.S. ports.

Veracruz's traditionalists envisioned *consulados* in America as ever subordinated to Cadiz and other peninsular ports "to keep the close ties joining merchants here to those in the Motherland."[39] We must recall that traditionalists' business practices, formed in an earlier, less competitive phase of commercial capitalism, had usually produced substantial earnings, and they remained convinced that by accepting recent policy innovations such as *comercio neutro* and *gracias* "they render useless or confuse the calculations and suppositions forming the basis of merchants' enterprises and trades."[40] Procurement of imports outside the Spanish transatlantic system conjured up for Cadiz merchants the trauma of eventual colonial (local) over metropolitan trade hegemony.[41] In a similar vein they shared with the Mexico City merchants a view of New Spain as a submetropole with hegemonic jurisdiction over Spain's Caribbean colonies. Just as New Spain's silver *pesos* generated government income to subsidize Cuba's civil service and defense establishment, New Spain rather than the United States should, they felt, provision Cuba's planters with flour and beef. Cuba's merchants should not export aguardiente to New Spain to compete with local producers, much less re-export European goods received from Spain or, under special conditions, from U.S. ports.[42] This Cuban enterprise threatened to shift from New Spain to Cuba the hegemonic role of entrepôt, or *emporio,* for the Caribbean and in the long run to transfer from Cadiz and the metropole to England and its "Anglo-American" merchant collaborators hegemony over New Spain's external trade.[43]

Traditionalists appear to have been tepid supporters at best of a Veracruz *consulado* and antagonistic—aggressively, as will be seen—toward one of the truly innovative features of the new *consulado*'s charter, its secretaries, chosen by Madrid, Vicente Basadre and his successor, José Donato de Austria y Achútegui. Veracruz's traditionalists were uncomfortable with commercial data and statistics gathered by the *consulado*'s secretaries and circulated in their annual economic surveys—surveys never prepared (and never required), for example, by Mexico City's *consulado.* Secretary Austria recognized that their "personal contempt for the truths I hope to affirm" defined the group ("because among us there is a lineage of those for whom politics, ingenuity, diligence, and new undertakings are irritating, reinforcing their ideas and transmitting from generation to generation the evils of ignorance"), and he concluded that they invariably decided that "the most sensible and creditable documents in favor of happiness . . . fail to produce the outcomes promised when they were printed."[44] The traditionalists identified the secretaries, and rightly so, with the policies of the opposing *partido,* the Veracruz "independents" behind the *consulado*'s creation, who controlled its policies until 1799, when the traditionalists José Ignacio de la Torre, Juan Antonio Reyes, and Tomás de Aguirre were elected chief officers.

The initial predominance of so-called independents in the Veracruz merchant community for nearly two decades (1781–99) reflected the interaction between, on the one hand, metropolitan expansion on the periphery at Santander and Barcelona, Valencia and Málaga, and, on the other, colonial growth in the Caribbean at LaGuayra and Maracaibo, Cartagena, Veracruz, and Havana, as well as in the southern cone at Buenos Aires and Valparaiso. Thirty years earlier the prospect of greater exchanges in the Spanish Atlantic had inspired Esquilache's policy of opening ports in the metropole and colonies to direct mutual trade and the creation of *consulados* in *puertos habilitados* on the peninsula's periphery. In the metropolitan outports of colonial trade, the initial phase of that policy increased exchanges with French and English suppliers at Barcelona and, at Málaga, growing participation of Irish-Spanish merchant families. One outcome of this reciprocal interplay was that New Spain after 1795—unique in Spain's American colonies—contained *three consulados.*

Independents at Veracruz shared with traditionalists recognition of the critical role of silver in their colonial economy and proved eager and effective in cementing commercial contacts with New Spain's mining zones and those *criollo* mine owners who were embittered by Mexico City merchants' manipulation of the supply and price of basic inputs of imported bar iron, steel, blasting powder, and of course mercury. Like Veracruz's traditionalists, they hastened to purchase shares in one of the two competing silver-freighting firms *(compañías de plata)* that appeared after the bankruptcy of the long-functioning firm of Vértiz y Oteyza. Veracruz's independents also challenged the capital's merchants by seeking to penetrate and compete in export-oriented zones of Oaxaca hitherto monopolized by Oaxaca–Mexico City networks of *habilitadores, alcaldes mayores,* or, latterly, *subdelegados* and their *tenientes.* Not content with handling commodity exports like silver and dyestuffs, the independents as developmentalist offspring of the metropole's *proyectistas* promoted new exportables such as flour and sugar, along with items needed by Barcelona's late-developing textile industry, raw cotton and yarn, silk and flax. The major thrust of Veracruz's independents, however, was their design to capitalize on their port's geographical position so as to transform it into a coastal entrepôt attracting merchants of the interior seeking to bypass the added freight costs, warehousing, commission fees, and customs and sales taxes of Mexico City wholesalers and their *consulado.* Small wonder that Veracruz independents sponsored improvements in portworks, accommodations for muleteers and their *recuas,* road and bridge construction and maintenance, public infrastructure studiously neglected by the capital's merchant body.

In circumventing what first surfaced as temporary supply shortages resulting from war at sea after 1797, independents displayed adaptability. Emigrants from the peninsula's peripheral ports only recently liberated from Cadiz's total hegemony over colonial trade, Veracruz independents privileged products from regions of their provenance, eliminating the intermediation of Cadiz merchants: wines, brandies, papers, and cotton prints from Barcelona, silks from Valencia, wines from Málaga. It is also reasonable to hypothesize that contact between Irish-Malagan and English wholesalers strengthened the London connections of the Murphy-Porro network at Málaga and later facilitated arrangements engineered by Tomás Murphy (after settling at Veracruz) with suppliers at Kingston (Jamaica) and with "Anglo-American" exporters at Baltimore, Philadelphia, New York, and Boston. Veracruz independents' ties to Cadiz interests were therefore attenuated, and unlike Mexico City's *almaceneros,* they leapt at the chance to counter local import shortages by establishing direct contact with neutral ports, merchants, and shipowners in Europe (Hamburg) and North America (Baltimore, Philadelphia) to stock their port and thus their colony.[45] In another respect they proved more enterprising than the traditionalists at Veracruz or Mexico City: at Kingston they purchased prize goods seized by English warships and privateers in order to restock their warehouses,[46] and they formed commercial networks with Havana merchants already in contact with exporters along the eastern seaboard of the United States.[47] They had no illusions, hence few inhibitions, about New Spain's hegemonic role in the Caribbean, particularly their port's role as re-exporter of European imports to the nearby Spanish Caribbean.

In brief, the heterogeneity of independents entering the Veracruz entrepôt from Spain's peripheral provinces and from the ports of nearby Spanish colonies, their financial autonomy from Cadiz, and their readiness to expand operations within their own colony and, when Atlantic imperatives were overwhelming, permitted by Madrid with neutral Europe, North America, and the port of Havana were factors that shaped their developmental preferences and supported their development-minded secretaries Basadre and Austria. Basadre once neatly defined the independents' goals as "to avoid closing our ears to the voices of truth, to awaken from the mercantile lethargy that gripped us two centuries ago."[48]

Among Veracruz's independents, few embodied their qualities as did Tomás Murphy. Born to Anglo-Irish and Spanish parents (Juan Murphy y Elliot and Barbara Porro), this *malagueño* invested in Málaga's initial Compañía de Navieros; in the early 1790s he surfaced at Veracruz, called there by his uncle Pedro Porro, as Viceroy Revillagigedo's sole Veracruz merchant respondent on the issue of *comercio libre,* one of its few supporters in the mercantile communities of Veracruz and Mexico City. Elected to a succession of posts in the Veracruz *consulado,* engaged in commercial speculation created by *comercio neutro* and its sequel, individual *gracias,* an investor in Veracruz's Compañía de Seguros and in one of New Spain's two new *compañías de plata,* and subsequently associated with *criollo* mine owners at Guanajuato, Tomás Murphy in 1805–10 would be the main intermediary for transferring New Spain's silver through Baltimore, Kingston, and London to Spain and France on royal and private account.[49]

To be sure, categorizing interest groups as independent or traditionalist runs the risk of oversimplification, for over the period 1781–1810 the nature of the divisions shifted. In the first fourteen years (1781–95) came fission over formation of a *consulado* independent of Mexico City. In the next, briefer period, roughly 1796–99, divisions followed different cleavage lines: on the one hand were those primarily engaged in New Spain's long-term external trade, based upon silver supplemented by selected agricultural exports exchanged for a few basic and luxury imports; on the other were those aiming to diversify the export orientation of the colony's economy by expanding agriculture to supply inputs to hoped-for manufactories in the metropole. In a third phase, after 1799 and the formal termination of *comercio neutro,* the grounds of cleavage shifted once more, splitting the Veracruz commercial community: one bloc was committed to complementarity of the economies of New Spain and Spain on the basis of mutual exchanges *limited* to the imperial transatlantic trading zone; another perceived the shortcomings of the imperial commercial system and, to preserve its essence, would engage in *direct* maritime contacts with Havana, with U.S. Atlantic ports, and, after 1808, with Spain's powerful and unexpected ally, England. One may associate with advocacy of the closed imperial system many late-coming immigrants to New Spain's trade who imagined the immediate profitability of an effective colonial compact, *montañeses* from the *montañas de Burgos* and Catalans. They and counterparts at Mexico City and Cadiz would constitute the nucleus of those favoring preemptive action in the summer of 1808 and later counterrevolutionary activity to retain New Spain's colonial status.

Veracruz's Secretaries

The secretaries of the new colonial *consulados* were incorporated by statute, since Madrid policymakers of the 1790s conceived of the new merchant guilds as more than commercial courts of litigation, which had been their function when they were first created at Burgos and Seville, Lima and Mexico City, in the sixteenth century. Sensitive to the mercantile communities' profit-making ends, functionaries at Madrid handpicked secretaries in the hope that they might provide perspective and leadership for their corporations and, in particular, search out areas of potential economic growth in their territorial jurisdictions. Such expectations would be amply filled by appointment of personnel of the caliber of Francisco Arango y Parreño at Havana, Manuel Belgrano at Buenos Aires, and the succession of Vicente Basadre, José Donato de Austria y Achútegui, and José María Quirós at Veracruz.

The Veracruz trio filled multiple roles, first meeting the needs of their commercial community, then situating local issues in the broader economic context of New Spain, the Caribbean, and the metropole, supplying statistics and (when required) analysis and interpretation to assist both their merchant community and the imperial trading system as a whole in forecasting, planning, and profit calculation. In their activities the secretaries of the Veracruz *consulado* typified the last phase of economic-policy planning of the eighteenth century, haltingly implemented under Esquilache and later Gálvez, then selectively reinvigorated under Valdés, Gardoqui, and Urquijo. In this phase, and especially in the American colonial context, the metropole's policies crystallized in a form of colonial physiocracy embedded in the framework of a colonial compact.

As generators and ultimately as publicists and disseminators of commercial data, the secretaries fulfilled what had once been the purpose of the *avisos,* or packet boats, and the subsequent government administration of maritime mail retrieved from private interests under Esquilache in 1764. Now, annual reports from the new American *consulados* flowed to the empire's capital at Madrid for analysis by the civil service, which was preparing an imperial trade balance, the *balanza del comercio,* and by a bureaucratic innovation devoted to economic development, the Departamento del Fomento General del Reyno, financed by the commercial levy *(avería)* collected by all *consulados.* The metropole's Hacienda supported the empire's first periodical devoted to economic intelligence covering Spain and the colonies, the *Correo Mercantil de España y sus Indias,* "because of how useful to Spain's commerce is the process of calculating and speculating and an idea of Cadiz's trade with our Americas."[50] Fittingly, Veracruz's first, detailed annual report, drafted by Vicente Basadre in 1796, was published in the *Correo Mercantil* as a model *consulado* report; subsequent annual reports of the Veracruz *consulado* were frequently cited in Mexico City's *Gazeta* and its short-lived competitor, the *Diario.* Such was the impact of the *Correo Mercantil,* and so regionalistic was the appreciation of New Spain's real and potential economic importance, that in 1803 Veracruz's agent at Mexico City, Francisco Maniau y Torquemada, proposed that the colony publish its own *Correo Mercantil* under the editorship of Juan López Cancelada, a publicist of sorts and in all probability already a covert government agent.

From 1795 to 1805 first Basadre and then his successor, Austria, prepared the Veracruz *memorias de instituto,* which were read annually to the *consulado's* general assembly. In fact, while over the period 1796–1802 they were signed by Basadre, it was Austria, then treasurer, who really compiled the data and—although this remains unclear—apparently prepared first drafts.

This detail is perhaps irrelevant, since they shared a mutual orientation; in turn, Austria's replacement, José María Quirós (1806–21), continued his predecessors' approach until well into the third decade of the nineteenth century. Such continuity in the annual *memorias* is remarkable, since events often profoundly divided the Veracruz community—over the long-sustained attempt by the Mexico City *consulado* (and for a time even the colonial government) to eliminate New Spain's new *consulados* at Veracruz and Guadalajara; over the effect of expanded commercial contacts under *comercio neutro* (1797–99) and continued as *gracias* (1804–5) and their role in the transfer of governmental and private silver to Europe via the Gordon & Murphy contracts (1805–8); and over the episode in which Viceroy Iturrigaray's administration virtually shut down the port of Veracruz and attempted to shift Veracruz's commercial operations in wartime back to the former *feria* site at Jalapa (1805–7).

The persistence of the Veracruz secretaries' economic outlook, at least until 1810, permits a conspectus that minimizes minor divergences. This should not imply that the secretaries were repetitive; rather, there was complementarity in their views. It is not surprising that as personnel serving a "new model" merchant corporation in New Spain's major Atlantic port, they shared Madrid's preoccupation with the colony's economic development or that they considered trade *the* critical sector in which the colony's production intersected with the requirements of the metropole's agriculture and manufacture. They accorded high priority to the collection of statistical materials on Veracruz's trade with Spain and nearby Spanish colonies as well as on New Spain's aggregate output—in its fashion an estimate of gross domestic product; such data informed merchants throughout Spain's transatlantic empire and furnished public servants with a factual basis for analysis and projection, for "economía política." The secretaries, as had Revillagigedo before them, soon discovered that only a statistical base offered a suitable rebuttal of what they considered unfounded criticism of their analyses and recommendations by Veracruz's traditionalist merchants, criticism that Basadre and Austria found rooted in an overriding preoccupation with personal over national interest.[51]

Basadre and Austria served at a critical historical juncture, in the decade 1795–1805, when a spurt in both the volume and the value of Spain's transatlantic trade created a mirage of economic revival—what a later Spanish generation would term *regeneration*—shattering the "mercantile lethargy that gripped us about two centuries ago."[52] The history-minded secretaries traced "letargo," or stagnation, back to historic policy decisions, to sixteenth-century precedents and their legacy of enduring structural constraints. By allowing immigrants from the corners of Hapsburg Spain's European empire—Flemings, for example—to occupy a commanding position in peninsular trade, Spanish policy had advanced the economic growth of the Low Countries; for their part, Spaniards had overlooked the justified criticism of Flemish privileges by seventeenth-century *arbitristas* like Damián de Olivares and Sancho de Moncada. Second, by shifting a monopoly of trade *(comercio exclusivo)* with the Spanish Atlantic's colonial ports from Seville to the port of Cadiz at the end of the seventeenth century, the government had inhibited economic growth in the metropole, since Cadiz merchants, "the most respected and privileged of the Nation," failed to stimulate domestic production of common textiles and clothing, the merchandise most in demand in the colonies. Without government intervention, merchants in the privileged Cadiz and Mexico City *consulados* followed the accepted axiom, preferring the quick returns to be had from re-exporting Europe's products, favoring their own over the national interest. A case in point: the Consulado de México's secular neglect of Veracruz's infrastructure, water supply, sewage disposal, ballast availability, portworks and warehousing facilities, not to mention a well-maintained road between capital and port.

Comercio libre of 1778 had reversed Spain's long-term stagnation, the secretaries argued, and even advantaged those Cadiz merchants who had fought that commercial innovation. Now, they felt, economic policy mandated that the national had to predominate over the particular interest; in principle, *comercio libre* opened Spain's transatlantic trade to all citizens *(vasallos),* whether peninsular or colonial, whether registered shippers *(cargadores de Indias)* or matriculated in the *comercio de España.* They now proposed setting up special academies for commerce, to be organized and maintained by *consulados* as part of their developmental functions, in order to train merchant entrepreneurs entering Spain's transatlantic trade for what some "model" countries had come to recognize as the "onrrosa profesión de comerciante."[53]

In the secretaries' view, Bourbon-administered intervention through *comercio libre* had at the century's end designed a wide imperial trading area geared to the requirements of the metropole, whose interests were paramount. Within this area the volume and value of New Spain's trade, data for which were collated and presented annually to the Veracruz merchant community and then disseminated in Spain and Europe, unavoidably inspired in Veracruz's merchant community a sense, perhaps overblown, of their colony's performance in the Spanish transatlantic system and its importance to the metropolitan economy. The system would be framed on a colonial pact, an imperial division of labor in which New Spain and the American colonies accepted subordination to Spain as the "exclusive right of the Metropole." Put another way, this division of labor aggregated strata of hierarchy: metropolitan manufacture and trade would dominate colonial production, while among the subordinate colonies certain were more strategic than others. New Spain (therefore Veracruz) was privileged to re-export its surplus of imports of European goods to nearby Spanish colonies, but the reverse was prohibited: flours from Puebla would supply Cuba's needs without having to compete with a supplier external to the system, such as the United States, just as New Spain's *chinguirito* should not have to compete with imports of Cuban rum.

Hierarchy in this colonial pact and the presumption of New Spain's hegemonic role as submetropole in the Caribbean zone of the Spanish Atlantic was a late projection of New Spain's once uncontested economic dominance and the interest groups it had fostered. This vision of the colonial pact attracted long-established Mexico City merchant houses, as well as the recent *montañés* immigrants surging into the interior provinces of the colony, its capital, and the port of Veracruz at the end of the eighteenth century. Threats to New Spain's role as submetropole after 1805 would, however, fuse otherwise antagonistic merchants of the capital and port, Mexico City and Veracruz. If in wartime no imports from the metropole could seep through English blockaders, should Havana merchants be permitted to re-export to Veracruz *their* surplus of European imports? Necessity, some claimed, would destabilize New Spain as submetropole, temporarily forcing a barely tolerable accommodation.

But might one distinguish a real surplus at Havana from one contrived, and how could one be sure that Havana merchants would not be mere fronts for "Anglo-American" and English merchants scheming to lay hands on silver rather than colonial staples, even contemplating penetrating networks of internal distribution? Might deviation from the colonial pact ultimately undermine the lifeline of the transatlantic system, that long-maintained link between Cadiz and Mexico City in which Veracruz served as a junior, if growing, partner? The decade of shifting pressures after 1797 finally induced Secretary Quirós early in 1808 to propose a reformulation of the imperial trading system in what he envisioned as an *acta de navegación* in order to invigorate the colony's long-neglected but potentially fastest-growing sector, agriculture. He believed that increasing primary exports was the only way to raise the colony's import capacity while functioning as the dynamic pole of the metropole's economy. In his view, the fundamental flaw of the Veracruz commercial community, the gap in its perception of reality, was the absence of a developed agricultural interest in New Spain pressing its claims.

The three secretaries over the three decades of the life of the Veracruz *consulado* (1795–1824)—Basadre, Austria, and Quirós—furnished both the Veracruz commercial community and Madrid information about economic conditions at the port and the surrounding areas, along with equally essential perspectives and opinions about the major issues Veracruz traders confronted. Indeed, sections of Alexander von Humboldt's informative *Essai politique* on New Spain's external trade, which he completed at Paris in 1808, apparently incorporated the reporting of Basadre and Austria.

It would be a mistake to treat these men and the annual *memorias de instituto* they submitted to the junta of the Veracruz *consulado* as just another expression of enlightenment, of *luces* in the Hispanic world, this time on a distant colonial frontier. This would minimize their significance. Basadre and Austria were, in effect, instruments of the political class at Madrid that was trying to force developmentalist policy on the tradition-minded interests overseas in the colonies. They were in the mold of Antonio Valdés, Alejandro Malaspina, Mariano Luis Urquijo, and Francisco Saavedra, maneuvering to adapt the Spanish empire to the tectonic shifts in the Atlantic economy.

After 1796, for the first time in almost three centuries of colonial rule, the colony of New Spain had personnel who were not wholly within the formal colonial bureaucracy, collectors and analysts of economic data appointed to submit annual reports on topics of their choice, and a trade balance substantiated with notes and reflections if they so desired. Their *memorias* were read each January, at the first general assembly of the year, which was open to all *consulado* members; the reports, balances, and reflections were quickly publicized locally and forwarded to the Madrid authorities responsible for oversight of commerce in the empire. The secretaries' responsibilities were considerable—Veracruz was the sole major colonial port on the Caribbean of the most populous and wealthy colony of Spain in America—and they proved remarkably equal to them. Biographical details, uneven and spotty, put their writings in some perspective.

Of the three secretaries, the first, Vicente Basadre y Varela, was perhaps the most traveled, most cosmopolitan, and most well connected in Spain and New Spain. Probably a *gallego,* he entered New Spain in the 1780s, perhaps as an agent of the recently chartered Compañía de Filipinas, although this is conjecture. Over the next decade he was involved with Gálvez's scheme to increase New Spain's mercury supplies by trading otter and nutria skins for the Chinese product. The deal was contracted out to the

Compañia de Filipinas, which then turned to the services of one of Vera-cruz's largest trading houses, the Casa de Cosío — Pedro Cosío was a former collaborator of Gálvez's — which hired Basadre to purchase otter pelts. He went north to the California coast to obtain them, framed a plan for the exchange of furs for mercury, then sailed to Manila and on to Canton to implement it.[54] English fur traders at Canton crushed this plan, and Basa-dre returned via Manila to New Spain, where he drafted on behalf of the Compañía an attack on the Consulado de Manila's monopoly of that colony's external trade. Not unexpectedly, in 1792 he was *vocal* of one of the company's committees.

Basadre's responsibilities in New Spain and the Far East suggest that authorities in Madrid trusted him.[55] Family connections — on his maternal side he was related to Pedro Varela y Ulloa, a minister of Marine and later of Hacienda in the 1790s — along with what Basadre once called his proper ful-fillment of "the strong obligations man contracts as part of Society, with respect to King, Fatherland, and fellow Citizens" and contact with one of the prime initiators of the Veracruz *consulado,* the Casa de Cosío, suffice to explain Madrid's decision to appoint him the first secretary of the newly cre-ated mercantile body of Veracruz. There is a cryptic indication of the reasons for his selection — "a recommendation of the Consejo [de Indias] to appoint him," as an anonymous recommendation phrased it, on the ground that he "has fulfilled important trade commissions at royal order in Mexico [City], the Californias, the Philippines, and China," that he had acquired "personal knowledge of New Spain's commerce," and because he was a talented per-son "disposed to work who would carry out well the duties of secretary."[56]

Over the years 1796–1802, as mentioned above, Basadre's collaborator and the *consulado*'s *tesorero,* Austria, assembled trade balances and made in-formed comments *(reflexiones)* where necessary. And there is reason to be-lieve that much of the research and even drafting of the *memorias* presented to the *consulado* that were signed by Basadre were in fact done by Austria.[57] Basadre was ill in 1797, and at the end of 1799 he asked to be relieved of his post and put on half-pay pending reassignment. His decision to leave — he hoped for a "quiet and peaceful" post — may have been strengthened by the stiffening opposition of the traditionalist faction in the Veracruz merchant community and their victories in the elections of prior and first consul.[58] Basadre proposed that until he was reassigned he simply exchange functions with Austria, whom he recommended as a "person with the qualities that the post requires." The Consejo quickly approved the switch.[59]

Over the next five years Basadre muted his voice in the *consulado*. His critical view of the *consulados* of Cadiz and Mexico City was, of course, already a matter of record. The faction of independent merchants had nothing but praise for him and his successor ("if something good has been accomplished at this time, we owe it only to the excellent talents of . . . Austria . . . and . . . Basadre");[60] in 1802 he appeared as director of the newly established Compañía de Seguros Marítimos at Veracruz, whose councilors included Pedro Miguel de Echeverría, whose background, social networks, and business interests placed him among the independents.[61] The maritime insurance company was obviously competing with Cadiz firms. At the end of 1805, referring to his wife's poor health and his years of service at Veracruz, Basadre petitioned for transfer to Spain, where in mid-1807, characteristically, he presented Godoy with an unsolicited report on Spain's overseas trade "in its current state." In that report he detailed the minutiae of smuggling operations at Veracruz, highlighted the large and growing volume of smuggled English cottons there, and urged a program of stimulating Catalan textile production with imports of raw cotton from the American colonies. In fact, modesty ill-suited him, for he suggested that Godoy appoint him *intendente* of Catalonia so that his "direction, intelligence, knowledge, and patriotism" might energize the manufacture of Catalan cotton textiles, which could compete with English goods.[62] Later, in the critical months of 1808, he would surface as the secretary of Seville's Junta Suprema's Comisión de España e Indias, which renders plausible the possibility that he might have advised the junta's representatives sent on a mission to New Spain in mid-1808, Juan Jabat and Manuel Francisco Jaúregui, about whom to contact immediately at Veracruz and then at Mexico City.[63] Doubtless Basadre knew that these representatives also carried authorization to sanction the removal of Viceroy José de Iturrigaray if necessary.

It was Basadre's partner, José Donato de Austria y Achútegui, Veracruz's most vigorous exponent of fresh approaches to the port's problems, who ultimately drew the heaviest fire from the commercial community's traditionalist, Cadiz-linked members.[64] Appointed treasurer in September 1795, Austria served the *consulado* for just over a decade, until his death in early 1806. The biographical information on Austria is limited. It is not stretching evidence unduly to assume that he was the brother of José Benito de Austria y Achútegui, who is listed in the Veracruz census of 1801 as occupying a lawyer's office in the building that housed the firm of "Cotarro & Murfi." José Benito was the legal representative (*apoderado*) of that firm, which was one of the enterprising merchant houses that established contact under *comercio neutro* with the then neutral port of Hamburg; he was possibly linked to the independent network bitterly opposed by the traditionalists, headed by José Ignacio de la Torre.[65]

Presumably José Donato, like his brother José Benito, came from the Spanish province of La Rioja; José Donato outspokenly supported Veracruz's wartime trade with neutral ports and in neutral shipping to maintain adequate flour imports, stabilize prices, and thereby undercut smugglers.[66] This stance fueled even further the ire of the traditionalist faction, some of whom Austria once identified as "individuos preponderantes," pinpointing Antonio de la Sierra, José Ignacio de Uriarte, Francisco Guerra y Ágreda, Felipe Vivanco, José Gil de Partearroyo, and Juan Bautista Lobo. They tolerated his presence at the *consulado*'s general juntas with their "inattention" and led him to confide bitterly to Hacienda Minister Miguel Cayetano Soler, at Madrid, that "speaking in all candor, I must state that there has been no serious matter that I have carried out, or that is still pendant, in which I have not encountered obstacles created by a spirit always contrary to my ideas and writings." Even more galling to his sense of accomplishment and pride was the opposition of tradition-bound traders to the "reflections I have appended to the annual reports forwarded to Your Excellencies, which have caused me days of thought and synthesis and which they customarily attacked at the annual Junta with the most trivial objections their heads use to deprecate what is strange to them." Austria's request for reassignment was ignored, as was a subsequent recommendation from the *consulado* in 1804 that his salary be raised from 2,600 to 4,000 *pesos*.[67] Fortunately, the paucity of biographical data on Austria is made up for by the quantity and quality of his *memorias, balanzas,* and footnotes first as treasurer, then as secretary until his sudden death in 1806, when he was immediately replaced by José María Quirós.

Fifty years old in 1806, Quirós, an *andaluz,* had come to Veracruz in the 1780s and was listed in the Veracruz census of 1801 as "vecino y del comercio," married, and the employer of two clerks.[68] He owned property in Cotaxla (Veracruz), where he raised cotton. This time it was the turn of the Consulado de Veracruz to nominate him to fill Austria's position. His selection from the members of the local merchant community must have represented an unexpected degree of unanimity. His *memorias* were generally well received locally and in Spain as well, and his orientation was such that even in the difficult years of revolution and counterrevolution in New Spain after 1810 he managed to defend Veracruz's interests while earning the praise of so vociferous a proselytizer in Spain for the tradition-bound *consulados* of Mexico and Cadiz as Juan López Cancelada.[69] Moreover, factionalism in the *consulado* abated once both groups joined forces in opposing Viceroy Iturrigaray's handling of their port's traffic in wartime, executing Madrid's contradictory orders between 1805 and 1808, and it is a reliable measure of

Quirós's competence that he continued as secretary over the next two decades, gradually adapting his orientation to profoundly changing circumstances, which earned him praise in 1818 as "the sole impartial person in said corporation . . . best equipped with economic principles."[70]

The *Memorias:* Physiocracy on the Colonial Frontier

Curiously, of the *memorias* prepared annually for the Veracruz merchant guild in the period 1796–1809, two were devoted to the lack of local infrastructure (poor roads and port facilities, inadequate provisions, water, and ballast), three dealt with trade, and the balance (six) concentrated primarily upon agriculture, which was, to be sure, linked to commerce.[71] An aggregate approach is misleading, however, since the first annual reports (1796–1802) in general treated the overall significance of merchants and commerce, the shortcomings of the Veracruz port complex, and the short-sightedness or even purposeful neglect of New Spain's major port by the Mexico City *consulado*. There were references to agricultural themes—the potential of flax cultivation to supply Galicia's infant linen industry (1799) and the constraints of New Spain's land-tenure patterns, which favored the formation and preservation of large rural estates (1801). However, in the *memorias* from 1804 to 1809 there surged a preoccupation with specific aspects of colonial agriculture, along with methods to augment the production of established crops or introduce new ones. In fact, the first three annual reports of the *consulado*'s third secretary, Quirós, drafted during the years of New Spain's acute commercial instability (1807–9), emphasized not so much trade as the interrelationship of the colony's agriculture *and* trade. Over most of the first decade of the nineteenth century, before the bitter colonial insurgency in New Spain, the in-house political economists of the Veracruz merchant organization were articulate exponents of colonial physiocracy and, implicitly, an effective colonial compact.

Basadre, Austria, and Quirós viewed the colony of New Spain through the lens of an imperial economic system that put the colonies at center stage in the potential development of the metropolitan economy. They viewed colonial demand as key to the metropole's economic growth. And while the private sector, the *interés individual,* was the centerpiece of their growth model, implicit most of the time was the need for some central coordination by a metropolitan agency. The secretaries could not afford to minimize the colony's mining sector but underscored what later analysts would label its enclave function. The increased volume of silver exported at the end of the eighteenth century had not inflated proportionately the price of imports, they concluded from available data, because whatever income from mining was retained in the colony flowed not only to relatively few mine owners, workers, and dependents but also to *hacendados* and civil servants in the capital. On the other hand, the availability of silver to finance imports did inhibit self-sufficiency. More to the point, the development of colonial agriculture in the form of exports of raw silk and raw cotton to Spanish *fábricas* would, they claimed, tend to reduce silver outflows from the metropole to foreign manufacturers.

Superficially there was nothing novel in the secretaries' emphasis on export agriculture, on the production of raw materials and foodstuffs as a way to augment trade between colony and metropole. Their physiocracy, however, had special, colonial facets. Since they accepted unreservedly the principles of a colonial compact, agriculture in their colony was tied not to local but to metropolitan manufacturers. And since estate agriculture in New Spain was grossly inefficient, with low productivity, unused resources, rural unemployment and underemployment, the fundamental remedy might be the formation and cultivation of small landholdings, beginning, of course, with property around the port of Veracruz. Smallholders could be recruited not just among Canary Island immigrants or residents of Spain's former colony Louisiana who were unwilling to accept U.S. sovereignty. Farmland could be distributed to *colono* families through the sale of government (crown) land or purchased from cooperative large estate owners. Financing could include initial annual outlays from joint contributions by the Veracruz town council and the *consulado* or by temporarily drawing on income from church tithes.

The progression of the secretaries' physiocratic thought is best illustrated by reviewing five relevant *memorias* issued between 1801 and 1809, all concerned with the condition of agriculture in New Spain and how to improve it. Basadre's first memoir (1801) presented an initial critique of land use in the vicinity of Veracruz, explaining shortages of fresh produce in terms of the absence of "agricultural workers, gardeners" such as the Canary Islanders, whose enterprise in Cuba had turned the city of Havana into "one of the best supplied of America."[72] By contrast, Veracruz had no Canary Islanders in farming. Basadre rejected the facile and widely held belief that everywhere in "lands of conquest Agriculture is commonly abandoned." It is no small credit to his grasp of metropolitan (probably Andalusian) and colonial (New Spain's) landholding patterns that he ascribed the agrarian situation in these areas to "proprietors of great *haciendas* in Spain and America . . . profoundly egoistic" and invariably supported by civil and judicial authorities ("administrators and magistrates"). Surviving *proyectistas* in the metropole would applaud this. Basadre's next (and last) memoir (1802) addressed a nagging issue, the annual transpacific outflows of about 1 million *pesos* from New Spain to China via Manila for purchasing raw and finished silk ("raw, loose, thread, *pelo*"), to which he appended a specific remedy: stimulate "in the pueblos of the jurisdiction of Veracruz the cultivation of silkworms." From the context of his observations it is evident that he conceived of New Spain's silk raising as a colonial complement to a revived metropolitan silk manufacture.[73]

Basadre's successor as Veracruz's in-house political economist, Austria, touched on colonial agricultural development in his second report (1804) in order to expatiate on its role in Spain's transatlantic system. Nominally addressing the condition of agriculture in Spain's American colonies, the memoir is in fact preoccupied with how to expand New Spain's exportables of sugar, cocoa and coffee, indigo, cochineal and other dyestuffs, cotton, sarsaparilla, *purga de Jalapa,* quinine, and vanilla. Once again the Cuban model of agricultural growth is cited, with a warning of the unexpected consequences that model might encourage. While Caribbean sugar plantations over the previous century had produced an impressive volume of exports drawing upon African slave laborers ("robust African arms"), it was disquietingly evident that "slaves participating in revolution and violent liberation" had ravaged Saint-Domingue's plantations. Nonetheless, Cuban planters were now pursuing a similar policy of large-scale imports of slaves to expand production. To achieve comparably impressive production growth, however, New Spain might avoid "violent measures" in a different fashion: through judicious land redistribution *(repartimiento)* favoring "society's active classes" by "tearing from large landowners their fields left uncultivated." Ever present remained the connection between colonial and metropolitan economies: an increase in the volume and variety of colonial exportables competently planned by a "central body pulling together politico-economic insights drawn from the key parts of the Monarchy" could bring an upsurge of Spain's colonial trade.[74]

The *consulado*'s third and last secretary, Quirós, pursued the same themes in his first three annual reports, 1806–8. The *memoria* of 1807 opened by contrasting New Spain's agricultural potential with its depressing reality: the colony was "soil poor, very uncultivated, underpopulated," and the fertile coastal strips north and south of Veracruz, capable of producing cotton, agave, cocoa, and vanilla, remained "largely abandoned and depopulated . . . useful only to pasture wild and domesticated animals." Quirós's explanation of such conditions was reminiscent of that of his predecessors: first, the practice of distributing and confirming injudicious land grants at the time of conquest; next, the irresponsible attitude of possessors of entailed estates and their typical colonialist racism vis-à-vis the native born, which Quirós shared, referring to "the natural laziness and negligence of local people" ever prone to follow "their vices and appetites."[75]

Like his predecessors, Quirós was reluctant to endorse massive imports of African slaves for agricultural labor, preferring to link the prosperity of Cuba and Puerto Rico to the presence of emigrants from the Spanish possessions of the Canaries, Florida, and Santo Domingo. New Spain, he urged, should encourage family-sized and family-operated holdings for such settlers, guaranteeing security of property title and uncontestable inheritance. Land could be made available through grants of government holdings or even by pressuring owners of uncultivated estates to offer emphyteutic leases at an annual rent of 5 percent of current value; for funding he would mobilize the capital of the *consulado* and the Veracruz *ayuntamiento* to finance jointly the rents of the first ten years.[76] This was the first time that a secretary of the Veracruz merchants' guild moved beyond generalizations about equitable agrarian reform to specific details. Indeed, Quirós was even more innovative when he proposed that the exportables produced by settlers (omitting cochineal, whose profitable re-export from Spain might be prejudiced) be shipped by local merchants directly to European ports in Spanish as well as non-Spanish ships, as had been legislated for the island of Cuba in 1792.[77]

In his annual reports Quirós reiterated his view of agriculture as a vital sector of the colony's economy. In by now familiar fashion the basic points developed were agriculture's contributions to trade (pointing to the benefits of *comercio libre* and implicitly to the underlying principle of "libertad del comercio") and the disadvantages of depending upon silver mining while perennially neglecting what was truly "the first, noblest, and most indispensable occupation of mankind," farming. These observations were buttressed with citation to recently prepared and publicized statistical data, as if Quirós wanted to call attention to the expertise of the *consulado*'s political economists.[78] Yet behind a balanced sector-by-sector examination of New Spain's economy fleshed out with statistics, however, Quirós highlighted the fundamental role of agriculture ("it sustains, nourishes, and enhances the State . . . furnishes materials for crafts, without which neither republic nor nation can flourish or survive").[79] Downplaying the centuries of silver mining's central importance in New Spain, while enhancing the role of agriculture, was bold but risky.

A novel, cosmopolitan, physiocratic conspectus surfaces in Quirós's handling of what he perceived to be the state's role in executing agricultural policy in a number of nations. He cited England's subsidization of grain exports; the conviction of France's Colbert that without a prosperous agriculture and related techniques "no Kingdom can prosper"; Prussia's policy of providing "the major support for its rural establishments"; the expansion of farming in the United States, to which Quirós (who had obviously studied its policies) attributed "the original source of its rapid growth"; and last, but by no means least, efforts under Charles III to "stir our decadent agriculture," which had failed the hopes of many ("the first remedies do not cure long-term illness").

Probably external pressure after 1805 in the form of England's blockade of New Spain's Caribbean coast and English propaganda in the form of small printed cards *(tarjetas)* affixed to boxes of imported yarn promising the people of New Spain "paz, libertad y comercio" led Quirós to recommend resettlement of the colony's urban and generally unemployed poor ("the poor, homeless families all the large cities of the Kingdom have")[80] on small holdings to produce both subsistence and export crops. Among the poor he identified 1.3 million native people, whose "gloomy and indolent" characteristics could be modified by new government policy offering "the hope that by increasing his goods, fields, and sowings, he might rise from his humble state and dejection."[81] Was Quirós sensitized to rural poverty in the colony by what had happened in France in the early stages of the revolution there or by the recent publication of Gaspar de Jovellanos's *Informe de la Sociedad Económica . . . en el expediente de ley agraria*?

In this unpredictable fashion there intersected in the first decade of the nineteenth century public servants planning to raise New Spain's per capita import capacity by terminating *repartimiento de mercancías* to native peoples and physiocrats in the colony hoping to increase exports to Spain, other European nations, and Spanish islands in the Caribbean. For Quirós envisioned a "nueva agricultura" in the colony of New Spain capable of supplying Cuba's flour imports, which had already doubled from 78,756 *quintales* in 1789 to 154,000 in 1805, most of which came mainly from the United States (Quirós' "provincias Anglo-Americanas"). Ever the pragmatist, Quirós conceded in 1808, as he had the year before, that financing his rural resettlement program was "a difficult and prickly affair." He abandoned the financial stratagem sketched in the *memoria* of 1807, relying instead upon church funds, "the gross receipts from tithes" collected in the colony's bishoprics. The two-ninths customarily allocated to salaries of curates, to benefices, and to maintenance of *cabildos eclesiásticos* might be diverted, or, more directly, the state might simply claim two-ninths as part of its *real patrimonio*.[82] In this instance Quirós was no doubt moved by

Madrid's recent appropriation of church property of public utility, actually a forced loan under the much debated *consolidación*.

In closing what was essentially a reformulated program for colonial agricultural development, Quirós repeatedly emphasized that commerce throve on liberty, that "it is the widely accepted maxim of all statesmen and politicians that liberty is the soul of commerce." Shorn of further qualification, such precepts could be misunderstood by the tradition-bound among the Veracruz merchant community; hence he carefully explained that commercial "liberty" in a colonial setting necessitated subordination to the "progress of agriculture and industry in the Metropole" and to Spain's international commercial relations—considerations fundamental to an "acta de navegación" that only the metropole, he hastened to note, was empowered to formulate in order to effect a favorable trade balance.

Quirós's *memorias* drafted in January 1809, a few months after the merchants of Mexico City engineered the preemptive coup against Viceroy Iturrigaray with the overt, full approval of Veracruz's merchants and the sanction of Seville's representatives Jabat and Jauregui, is oddly repetitive of prior analyses. Once again the reciprocity of agriculture and commerce is elaborated, eloquently but unrefreshingly; once again it is recommended that poor farmers, along with impoverished families in urban areas, receive parcels of land taken from unoccupied land on the principle that property and "personal interest will produce wonders"—once again supported by references to agriculture in the United States but also to the advice of the "wise, patriotic" Gaspar de Jovellanos, lifted from his proposals for agrarian reform in Spain: "Turn uncultivated land into private property, and the state will enjoy an incalculable benefit." In point of fact, the sole reference to the tumultuous last six months of 1808 in colony and metropole, to the policies of Godoy and to the hapless Iturrigaray, who had tried to execute them faithfully, surfaced when Quirós commiserated with the "farmers" (there is no mention of *hacendados*) squeezed by those executing *consolidación* legislation in New Spain. By January 1809 Veracruz's colonial physiocrats seem to have abandoned conflict for accommodation with New Spain's most powerful vested interests, those of Mexico City's *almaceneros*.

In the fifty years after 1759, as Veracruz's economic role expanded, it witnessed exponential growth in the external trade of Spain's most important colonial possession, by then the largest contributor to its colonial trade and income. In the *memorias* of its *consulado*'s secretaries one essentially views Veracruz, New Spain, Spain, and the world of the Atlantic economy through the eyes of cosmopolitan political economists (late *proyectistas*) of vision.

Basadre was the most widely traveled, but all three were well informed, and Quirós was eager to disseminate news of developments in Europe and the rapidly developing "provincias Anglo-Americanas" to the north.

Why agriculture and small-scale farming rather than the mining sector dominated their annual reports precisely when the volume and direction of trade preoccupied the port's mercantile community is unclear, which is not to say that one cannot attempt educated hypotheses. Early on, most of Veracruz's merchants probably concluded that they could not directly infiltrate the mining enterprises of central and northern New Spain; this helps to explain the secretaries' reiterated critique of the fixation on silver mining and the *consulado* of the capital on the one hand and their interest in export agriculture on the other. After all, from the 1790s on, Veracruz's merchants forged a foothold in the export trade in southern New Spain's cochineal and Guatemala's indigo, which augured agricultural development. In effect the three secretaries ideated an agricultural growth model by stages, shifting from the problem of local food shortages seemingly endemic in a port town whose resident and transient populations were expanding to a vision of exporting local flour and other subsistence crops to provision Cuba's slave laborers. In the third stage, New Spain would supply primary and semifinished products such as raw cotton and silk and even cotton yarn to Spanish manufacturers in Catalonia and Valencia. Expansion of yeoman farming *(labranza)* in a colony heavily dependent for 250 years on the production and export of silver might create the complementarity that a colonial compact required and Spain's *proyectistas* and other political economists belatedly espoused.

There was, furthermore, that wider context of physiocratic thought and praxis, the demand for agricultural products that sparked the physiocratic impulse in the Atlantic world of the eighteenth century. Increased output required access to a major resource, land, inadequately exploited by those "proprietors of large estates in Spain and America" viewed critically by Basadre and, for that matter, by Portillo and Virio in Spain. Hence the secretaries' acerbic observations about the ineptitude of rural estate owners in New Spain. It was but a short step to advocate the entry of new proprietors capable of working an abundant and underutilized resource like those coastal lands surrounding the port of Veracruz at a relatively low cost, since *colonos,* whether local residents or immigrants from the Canaries, could mobilize family members as cheap labor. All the more so after the terrifying consequences of chattel slavery had flared at Saint-Domingue and frightened slave owners throughout plantation America, from Brazil to the United States.

Veracruz's physiocrats, like their counterparts in Spain throughout the eighteenth century, were studiedly temperate in skirting the agrarian question, advisedly so. Only unique historical conjunctures offer an ambient for attacking successfully the inherited structures of privilege and possession. The secretaries of Veracruz's *consulado* criticized *criollo hacendados,* recommended pressing them to grant smallholders emphyteutic leaseholds, and proposed renting uncultivated crown lands and even diverting tithe income to finance the initial payments of *colono* settlers. Yet they rejected one major technique of land redistribution under the market system, the sale of land mortgaged to religious corporations, even ecclesiastical properties. This is the only way to interpret their strictures apropos *consolidación*. On the other hand, they did accept the concept that private enterprise *(interés individual)* and rent-taking constituted major driving forces behind innovation and agricultural growth.

Finally, there is the possibility that the three Veracruz secretaries focused upon agrarian issues to unify otherwise conflictive groups in the Veracruz community. Thereby one might dampen smoldering friction over the critical issue of trading with Cadiz, with nearby Havana, and with the "neutral" United States, now perceived as fronting for aggressive English trading interests. It was their mode of enhancing the role of Veracruz merchants in the crisis of the colonial order in the Spanish Atlantic. Veracruz, however, was not Boston, and its merchant community was not bubbling with would-be bourgeois revolutionaries.

6. Mining and Its Fissures

The Zacatecas–Mexico City axis symbolized in good measure the spinal column of New Spain.
Laura Pérez Rosales

The operating costs [of the "Valenciana" mine] have risen at an astonishing rate.
Alexander von Humboldt

The men and women [of Guanajuato] who were exiled, imprisoned, mutilated, or hanged and quartered at the order of José de Gálvez.	Felipe Castro Gutiérrez

The war for independence [was] situated in the Bajío . . . precisely in those very regions affected by forced recruitment for the mines.	Brígida von Mentz

New Spain's economy in 1800 — its population close to that of England and Wales, its wealth measurable in high per capita silver output and consequently its demand for imports and remittances of silver — made that colony across the Atlantic *the* major pole of the Spanish empire's economic growth at the end of the eighteenth century, as the late *proyectistas* recognized. It was the mainstay of Spain's metropolitan economy as well.[1]

New Spain's mining operations and the annual coinage reports of Mexico City's mint were swiftly communicated to would-be speculators in Spain, France, and England, which explains the immediate utility and widespread popularity of Alexander von Humboldt's *Essai politique,* his handbook on New Spain, which quickly became a bestseller. His data, generously provided by statistically-minded colonial civil servants, soon would become the basis of analyses in the *Edinburgh Review* and later in the two-volume *Mexico,* written by England's minister to Mexico in the 1820s, H. G. Ward. Mexico's silver production in coin and bullion dominated world production, as Humboldt reiterated, and he put it tellingly, noting that all French minting could at best occupy Mexico City's Casa de Moneda for about fifteen working days per annum.[2]

Silver and Trade

New Spain's silver production was *the* barometer of its external trade, *the* regulator of its exchanges with the metropole and its busiest port, Cadiz. Its silver *pesos* and *reales* flowed out of about five hundred mining camps and thirty-five hundred mines, large and small, through wages paid to thirty thousand workers, purchases of locally produced foodstuffs, forage for mules and horses, leather, and inputs from Europe of iron, steel, and mercury.[3] Silver was the vehicle by which consumer demand in the colony's principal monetized zones—Mexico City, Puebla, Guanajuato, Zacatecas, and Oaxaca—for imports of linens, woolens, and cottons, along with wines and brandies from Spain, was satisfied. Silver was the foundation of the peninsular merchant community concentrated at Mexico City, with links of interest and kinship to Cadiz and Manila and to Spain's other peripheral urban centers.[4] The colonial civil servant Beleña encapsulated the importance of New Spain's mines when he once noted that silver constituted "the most important item of the Crown and foments not only all the Nations of Europe but also the principal nations of the rest of the globe."[5]

There was a factual basis for Beleña's observation. For 234 years, from 1537 to 1771, New Spain's average annual output had been 1.9 million *pesos*. In the next half-century, from 1772 to 1821, the total output was virtually double that of the previous centuries, reaching an average annual output of at least 17.4 million, a ninefold increase.[6] And in the twenty-two years before the outbreak of civil war in New Spain, from 1789 to the year of crisis, 1810, the average annual output of coined silver and gold of Mexico City's mint was at least 22.6 million; this does not include unregistered silver in coin or bullion.[7] The peak occurred in 1805 with the astounding official figure of slightly more than 27.1 million *pesos* in silver and gold coined, immediately recognized as "the largest coinage since the Crown took over the Mint."[8] Silver enjoyed decided advantages over other colonial exports: meteorological fluctuations had minimal impact on output, and silver could be warehoused indefinitely. In this connection, at least 50 percent of total silver production in 1796–1810, about 190 million *pesos,* may have been retained in New Spain to avoid maritime risks after 1805, when war between England and France broke out again.[9] What did affect output was the supply of bar iron and steel for mining equipment and especially imports of mercury, a government monopoly. Mercury shortages account for the wartime trough in silver and gold coined in 1800–1802; nor can one overlook the impact of local fluctuations in the supply of maize and fodder, mules and horses, on mining operations.[10]

A convergence of factors accounts for the extraordinary performance of New Spain's mining sector in the final four decades of the colonial period, when the colony was responsible for two-thirds of world production. On the one hand, improvements occurred in existing production methods: mine shafts were deepened, massive drainage operations undertaken, blasting power widely utilized, and greater reliance placed upon refining with mercury using the amalgamation process rather than smelting. As Humboldt pointed out, just three mining districts, Guanajuato, Zacatecas, and Catorce, accounted for more than half of the colony's silver production. On the other hand, government policy modifications were equally relevant, if not more so.[11] However, at Zacatecas and elsewhere, as Richard Garner has noted, the overall level of technological change in New Spain's mining sector remained unchanged; the decisive factor was the increase in "human labor."[12]

Most relevant was the 50 percent reduction in the price of mercury provided through government monopoly in the years 1767–76. The coinage increase may also reflect the government's decision to empower its bureaus in mining zones to purchase *(rescatar)* silver that small producers offered in the form of *pasta* (unrefined silver), which they customarily and illegally offered at discount for cash to *mercaderes* and *rescatadores* operating locally. What is obvious is that the increase in the scale of mining operations demanded large-scale capital investment; here the industry benefited indirectly from changes in imperial policy induced by the trade *reglamentos* of 1778 and 1789. In addition, growth in the volume of shipping, and consequently of imports, briefly lowered the price of iron and steel, at least in the 1790s, while the expansion of trade and earnings favored merchants, the well-established along with the surge of recent immigrants, mainly *montañeses,* to continue to speculate by provisioning and investing in mines, the wealthiest *almaceneros* financing large mining companies in Guanajuato and Zacatecas.[13] This speculative fever was caught by Humboldt: "New Spain, better administered and populated by industrious people, will one day be able, alone, to provide in gold and silver the 173 million francs that all America produces now."[14]

The Mines

In the twenty years after 1789 New Spain's most productive mining zones were Guanajuato and Zacatecas, together supplying about 30 percent of the colony's total output over the five years from 1785 to 1789. The leading producer was, of course, Guanajuato, which alone averaged 23.3 percent of the colony's total output. Its major mines were the older "Rayas," whose output rose after the 1720s, and the more recently expanded "Valenciana," whose rose after 1766, both working the same lode or vein. From 1795 to 1810 Valenciana produced on average 6.5 percent of New Spain's silver annually; it was the single most productive silver mine in the world.[15] Quite expectedly data on population and labor indicate that of Guanajuato's work force of 10,679 in 1792, fully 55 percent was employed directly in mining and refining, and if one adds the ancillary activities of food, cattle production, and transport, the figure rises to 65 percent.[16] Both mines were controlled by *criollo* mining families interlocked with Basque merchant houses of Mexico City, known for their *criollo* links. Cases in point are the Sardaneta of Rayas, and Valenciana's Obregón.[17]

As for Zacatecas, in the sixteenth and seventeenth centuries it had been the colony's most productive zone, while in the eighteenth it was surpassed only by Guanajuato. Its richest lode was the "Vetagrande." Overshadowed by Guanajuato's Valenciana in the eighteenth century, Vetagrande matched and even overmatched the output of Valenciana in the years 1804–8.[18] About 1800, mines in Zacatecas accounted for roughly 16–20 percent of New Spain's total silver output, slightly behind Guanajuato's 24 percent; 1802 and 1803 were the "most spectacularly productive years" for mining in Zacatecas, with more than thirty-five hundred workers employed in mine and refinery operations.[19]

In Zacatecas mining after the 1780s, two separate, often antagonistic family consortia competing for dominance are discernible, one group representing the *criollo* and Basque elements, the other composed of what appear to be peninsular latecomers to commerce and mining. A number of factors exacerbated differences dividing the consortia, some of a general nature affecting all mining operations in the colony in the twenty years after 1790, others more specific. Consortia of miners, refiners, and *almaceneros* proved the most efficient means for mobilizing labor, while interconsortia competition was driven by the large capital demands of expanding mining operations,[20] the costs of so-called dead works: construction of drainage adits and especially mine shafts and the rising cost of iron and steel, not to mention access to an adequate supply of a rationed commodity, mercury imports. It was Humboldt who publicized the impact of rising operating costs in his analysis of the imposing operations of the most productive mining complex in the world, the Valenciana, which was probably representative of New Spain's mining situation.[21] He calculated the construction costs of a fourth vertical shaft, deeper than three preceding ones: the first had cost 1,744 *pesos* per meter; the second, 633; the third, 2,029; and the cost of the fourth, when pushed below the 500-meter line, to become "the deepest point then known in the entire world," would be much higher. Average annual expenditure on the operating costs of Valenciana for two periods, 1787–91 and 1794–1802, had risen about 8.5 percent.[22]

There is reason to believe that such costs rose even higher as a result of price inflation in iron, steel, leather sacking, candle wax, mules, and forage after 1802. As the volume of these inputs rose, so did unit prices, especially after the renewal of war at sea in the closing months of 1804. In fact, from 1802 to 1806 the price per *quintal* of imported iron rose 167 percent, steel 60 percent, and both continued to rise thereafter; Valenciana alone consumed about 48 percent of all of the colony's imported steel in 1804. To be sure, the mounting cost structure and declining net return as a percentage of the value of output of Valenciana may perhaps exaggerate the general mining crisis at the end of New Spain's colonial regime. This said, however, Valenciana's profit performance must have seemed disheartening. Expenses in current *pesos* had virtually tripled, and since the value of output remained roughly constant, net return fell. In other terms, earnings of the most productive silver mine fell precipitately from a high of 1,249,650 *pesos* in 1797 to 181,278 three years later, a collapse of 85.5 percent. Small wonder that Humboldt would observe of Valenciana that "operating costs have risen at an astonishing rate."[23]

Mercury Distribution

Transforming ores into refined silver most efficiently required amalgamation with mercury—"this vast and delicate subject," the patio process—rather than by the more expensive process of smelting.[24] Hence, mercury imports at Cadiz, from Almaden in Andalusia and the Idrian region of Austria for shipment to New Spain, as well as the pattern of distribution to the colony's refiners (proprietors of *haciendas de beneficio* for processing *pasta*), were a further, perhaps major source of division among mine consortia. "There is so much rivality [*sic*] in mining matters in Mexico," Ward had to conclude in the 1820s.[25] In this respect, decolonization had changed little.

Like his predecessors, the newly arrived Viceroy José de Iturrigaray understood immediately that the prosperity of Spain's imperial enterprise depended upon silver mining, that "the most appropriate way . . . to increase the prosperity of these dominions and the whole monarchy is to supply large quantities of mercury to this Kingdom."[26] New Spain's mining economy required a high level of mercury imports, and to quote a prominent *criollo* rhetorically addressing New Spain's elites in 1810: "If your mines lack mercury and production falls, Good-bye to silver, Good-bye to wealth, Good-bye to commerce. How will you now pay the person from Veracruz who brings goods?"[27] Mercury imports made increases in ore production feasible. From 1761 to 1782 such imports almost doubled, from 5,000–6,000 *quintales* per annum to almost 12,000;[28] the need to compensate for mercury shortages during years of warfare, 1797–1801 and again after 1805, accounts for the large volume—from 20,000 to 50,000 *quintales* annually, 50,000 in 1803 alone.[29]

The demand for mercury in New Spain led the metropolitan government to augment production in its Andalusian mines at Almaden and to supplement these with supplies from another of Europe's major producers, the mines of Idria, on the Adriatic. Idrian output furnished one-third of New Spain's annual needs, Almaden the balance; Idrian mercury was contracted with the Italian firm of Greppi y Cia, of Cadiz, in 1790, at a price roughly 50 percent above that of Almaden mercury. Cadiz shipments to colonial mining centers were expedited during the years 1776–1803 by Manuel Albuerne, a civil servant whose experience in colonial matters would make him a critical figure at Cadiz in 1810.[30]

Typical of the metropolitan civil service's readiness to utilize any expedient to generate colonial income was the effort in 1783 to raise the price of mercury sold through the state monopoly to New Spain's mine owners. The intervention of the then newly established Tribunal de Minería blocked this, but with strong backing from Guanajuato's mine owners it induced the guild to subscribe to two loans of 1 million *pesos* each to the Spanish government by drawing from its development fund *(avío)*.[31] No doubt Spain's two European sources matched mercury demand in the silver-mining colonies up to 1797; thereafter, however, English warships and corsairs interrupted wartime shipments to Veracruz and pushed mine owners and refiners to procure supplies at England's principal West Indian entrepôt, Kingston (Jamaica).

Despite orders to the contrary issued during war at sea in 1800–1802, vessels in Yucatán's ports received authorization to sail to Kingston to recover Spanish ships and cargoes taken as prizes, provided that repossessed mercury was sold at cost. Following the Peace of Amiens, government shipments brought what Viceroy Iturrigaray called "the expected prosperity . . . and the amazing amount of coinage . . . at the Mint . . . not only is the supply of mercury available, it is abundant." At the same time, he warned that during the recent shortage the mine owners' guild had proposed to arrange for shipments by neutral vessels and that should shortages recur, the tribunal would appeal "for assistance to avoid its ruin," a warning to go over the head of the viceroy to Madrid.[32] The renewal of war at sea in 1805 opened the way for mercury shipments from the neutral port of Lisbon to Veracruz in vessels charted by the London firm of Gordon & Murphy, an arrangement approved by Madrid, perhaps marking the beginning of close ties between Mexico's mine owners and British investors in the early years of the nineteenth century.[33] While there was a possibility of mercury shortages when war began again in the Atlantic, it failed to materialize, and when England became Spain's ally against Napoleonic France in the spring of 1808, New Spain managed to import about forty-four thousand *quintales* over the following year, one of the highest annual import levels to that date.[34]

The involvement of Iturrigaray and, for that matter, all viceroys in mercury distribution reflected their recognition of the pervasive effect of mining on the colony's whole economy, the viceroy's prestige as chief colonial officer, and his chances of personal gain. Mercury allocation to New Spain's mine owners had always been considered a perquisite of viceroys and Hacienda officials in the mining centers' *cajas reales;* it provided an unauthorized yet tolerated form of income to colonial officials, who were in effect bribed *(gratificado)* by mine proprietors and refiners or their agents in Mexico City. In the first flush of housecleaning under Charles IV, Colonial Secretary Antonio Valdés attempted to shift mercury allocations from the viceroy to Madrid. Requests for data on output per mine and ore samples were disregarded, however, still leaving mercury distribution "abandoned to the viceroy of New Spain." The marqués de Rayas (Sardaneta), a wealthy Guanajuato mine owner and a friend of Iturrigaray's, explained the tipping practice as follows: "These gratuities were begun years ago, by various of your predecessors, just as they were common and current among Ministers of the Real Hacienda." With disarming candor Iturrigaray's wife, whose father had been a viceroy of Peru, once described tips this way: "in the Peninsula harvests consist of grain, wine, olive oil, etc.; here the mine owners harvest gold and silver, which by custom they use as gifts." Yet it cannot be overlooked that when Iturrigaray was first offered *gratificaciones* for "an allocation of mercury," he sought advice from Ciriaco González Carbajal, an *oidor* of Mexico's Audiencia, about the propriety of accepting them, he was told that "they were the perquisites of office, and all previous viceroys had received them."[35] When some mine owners later charged Iturrigaray with accepting the bribes, his defense retorted that "those same mine owners have taken the initiative in offering such rewards."[36]

Viceregal jurisdiction over mercury formally began at Veracruz, where a viceregal *comisionado*—Iturrigaray chose José Mariano de Almanza, one of the colony's few important *criollo* merchants and a resident of that port—would notify Mexico City of imminent and actual arrivals and then inspect the shipments.[37] The colonial government accepted bids for five-year contracts for freighting mercury flasks and goatskins from Veracruz (at times from Acapulco as well) to the capital; in 1803 the contract went to the mine owners' guild, which underbid by 41 percent the nearest competitor for handling 23,000 mule loads *(cargas)* over the contract period. Bunching of mercury arrivals at Veracruz often led to virtual mobilization of all local muleteers and their *requas,* which tended to drive up freight rates in general. This system of mixed government and private enterprise brought mercury to Mexico City, where it was allocated to mine centers and ultimately to individual proprietors of *haciendas de beneficio.*[38]

Purchase and shipment of mercury was centralized in the capital, the hub of commercial distribution and the center of merchant capital. Mine owners and refiners (the *principales*) bought mercury through agents or bondsmen *(fiadores),* almost invariably "merchants resident in this capital." In Iturrigaray's time, some Mexico City merchants apparently serviced particular mining areas; for example, Miguel Ángel Michaus, Antonio Uzcola, and Antonio Morán were tied to Zacatecas ore refiners.[39] No doubt small quantities were bought for distribution by less capitalized merchants to supply small refiners despite prohibitions against "monopoly by merchants and lenders, who bought mercury in large lots only to retail it at very high prices." Both small and large-scale Mexico City *fiadores* waited for reports of the arrival of mercury imports, which they intended to sell through their regional firms *(dependencias).* No doubt officials in local *cajas reales* moonlighted, supplying credit to local merchants and mine owners for supplies such as mercury despite official admonitions like that of 1789 that "prohibit employees in Royal Rents from such commercial activities."[40]

Inevitably viceroys became entangled in factional conflict generated by the indispensable mercury allocations. Since silver mining was the key sector of the colony's economy, tension over access to mercury was bound to rise between major and minor production and refining areas, between refiners, and ultimately between the well established and the latecomers to mining. Not for nothing was it observed in Iturrigaray's time in office—

which coincided with the peak in New Spain's silver production, when Humboldt estimated that New Spain's annual consumption averaged sixteen thousand *quintales*—that "buying and selling mercury is a delicate matter" when "the poor miners are generally sacrificed to the influence of the richer." The large production areas seem to have had first claim on allocations, namely Guanajuato and Zacatecas, leaving lesser mine owners such as those of Taxco, Temascaltepec, and Copala to scramble for the remainder. It was logical, Humboldt concluded, "to favor the richest and most influential individuals."[41] The tendency to favor a group of refiners within a given area was evident at Guanajuato in 1780–82 and again in 1798. Of 3,867 *quintales* allocated to Guanajuato in 1780–81, two mines (Valenciana and Rayas) received 46 percent; in the first half of 1798 the Guanajuato mining area as a whole obtained 32 percent of all mercury allocations, with Valenciana alone garnering 64 percent of the area's allocation.[42]

Given pressures on Iturrigaray from the metropole to maximize silver production to assure large exports of coined and bar silver to Spain and the Caribbean colonies, it is no wonder that he privileged the major producing area, Guanajuato, and the two leading mine owner–refiner consortia there, those of Obregón and Sardaneta. Both had entertained the viceroy on one of his earliest excursions to Guanajuato. As Sardaneta (marqués de Rayas) recognized, immediately following Iturrigaray's visit "it was rumored that he sought payment in the form of gratuities from the mine owners to whom he allocated extraordinarily large quantities of mercury."[43] Indeed, following his visit Iturrigaray advised Hacienda secretary Soler, at Madrid, that the Valenciana absorbed fifty-six hundred *quintales* of mercury annually; the figure was somewhat exaggerated yet symptomatic of the viceroy's perception of that mine's importance. At about this time he also began to invest his *gratificaciones* in funds of the Tribunal de Minería "so that with interest of 5 percent his wife and children could live comfortably." By early association with the mine owners Obregón, Rul, Sardaneta, and Fagoaga of the Valenciana-Rayas group and its principal Mexico City merchant-banker, Antonio Basoco, the colony's chief executive appeared to fraternize with a well-connected and established *criollo* mining consortium allied with an equally prestigious *peninsular* (but "creolized") merchant firm.[44] Thereby Iturrigaray was enmeshed in the competition between this interest group and one of mainly recent immigrants from Spain engaged in the colony's trade and mining, competition evident in the Tribunal de Minería, in the formation of rival *conductores de plata,* and in Zacatecas's Vetagrande mines. By policy and perhaps personal inclination Iturrigaray would find himself at the epicenter of factional crosscurrents in the colony's leading economic sectors, mining and commerce.

Factionalism

In the first half of the eighteenth century a group of silver merchants (*mercaderes de plata, banqueros de plata*) still farmed the separation of silver from gold ores and coinage at the Mexico City mint. These operated as, or were connected with, *almaceneros,* many of whom were also prominent in Mexico City's *consulado. Mercaderes de plata* included the firms of Fagoaga and Valdivielso, Rodríguez de la Madrid and Landa. By marriage to a Sánchez de Tagle, Valdevielso was involved in minting operations, while Fagoaga farmed the process of separating silver from gold *(apartado).* Predominantly although not exclusively Basque *(vizcaíno)* by peninsular provenance, another primary characteristic of the Fagoaga-Valdivielso group was affiliation with predominately *criollo* mine owners. About 1750, however, only one *banco de plata* survived, that of Fagoaga and associates; two decades later this *banco* too disappeared, on the death of Francisco de Fagoaga's son-in-law and nephew whom he had invited to join him, Manuel Aldaco, who subsequently managed Fagoaga interests in trade, mining, and agriculture.[45] It spurred Fagoaga heirs, led by Fagoaga's widow, Josefina Aldz-queta, to concentrate capital and expertise on the family's mining enterprises in the north at Sombrerete and Zacatecas.[46]

After midcentury the colony's mines entered a remarkably expansionist phase, particularly in Zacatecas and Guanjuato. The attraction of profit-taking in mines and trade of these zones drew two immigrant currents, one essentially Basque *(vizcaíno)*, the other from Spain north of Burgos *(montañés).* The consortia can be categorized as *criollo* mine owners and Basque *almaceneros,* in competition with many recent immigrant *montañeses* comprising *flotistas,* merchants, and new mine owners.[47]

An upsurge of contending factions in mine operations was visible at Guanajuato from 1779 to 1793. In the 1779 elections for Guanajuato's representatives on the Tribunal de Minería, the *criollo* mine owners Antonio Obregón and Pedro Luciano de Otero, along with Basque merchant associates, dominated; a decade later a new group exerted itself, made up of the recent *montañés* immigrants Francisco Septien de Arce, Manuel García Quintana, and José Hernández Chico.[48] The electoral outcome of 1793 revealed a kind of ethnic division: one deputy was *criollo* (Obregón), the other *montañés* (Septien y Arce).

Control over Guanajuato's regional *diputación* conferred judicial authority upon *diputados* and their factions, which is perhaps why the problem of local jurisdiction resurfaced in the two years after 1790.[49] There were two instances of conflict, typically over mine boundaries; one never came to a head, the other did. In the first instance the *montañés* group of Septien y Arce, García de Zeballos, and Andrés Sagaz y Herrera took control of Guanajuato's "Tepeyac" mine, bordering on the Valenciana of the *criollo*-Basque group of Obregón and Otero. One source insinuated that the *montañeses* aimed to steal Valenciana ores through Tepeyac's underground galleries. In any event, this remained only an insinuation; it never became subject to judicial proceedings by the Guanajuato *diputación*.[50] The second case, also over boundaries, opened with a dispute in Guanajuato between the *montañés* Hernández Chico and the *criollo* Otero. When Hernández Chico (a deputy in 1791) used his judicial power to jail an Otero supporter, Otero appealed for the intervention of Viceroy Revillagigedo. Forthwith the viceroy, on advice from the *criollo* Francisco Xavier Gamboa, *regente* of the Audiencia de Mexico and believer in a tribunal of centralized rather than decentralized jurisdiction, commissioned an *oidor* of the Audiencia, Juan Francisco Anda, to resolve the dispute.

Fearing a precedent for reduction of the authority of regional deputations, Guanajuato's *montañés* group turned to a Mexico City lawyer, Francisco Primo Verdad y Ramos, while the Otero-Obregón interest hired another, equally prominent *criollo* lawyer there, Miguel Domínguez. Once again Madrid authorities, notably Gardoqui and possibly Valdés, reprimanded viceregal intervention in a dispute subject to a regional mining jurisdiction. That the *montañeses* had gone over the viceroy's head directly to Madrid may reflect their anxiety over the possible revival of Gamboa's hope of a mining tribunal controlled by the *almaceneros* of Mexico City's *consulado*.[51] Meanwhile, Guanajuato's *montañeses* carried their case for the authority of regional deputations into the general elections for the highest offices in the Tribunal de Minería, those of administrator-general and deputies general. And to augment their voting strength, the *montañeses* Septien y Arce and García de Zeballos joined forces with the *diputación* elected at Zacatecas, the group of the recent immigrants Fermín de Apecechea and Bernardo Iriarte.[52]

Open confrontation in the early 1790s between an aggressive group of mainly *montañés* traders, merchant *aviadores,* and *ex-rescatadores*—relative newcomers to full-scale involvement in mining in New Spain—and what they perceived as their competitors—established, essentially *criollo* mine owners of Guanajuato and Zacatecas, their associates among Mexico City's most influential merchants, certain members of the Audiencia, and vice-roys—had many roots, general and specific, metropolitan and colonial. At Zacatecas, according to David Brading, "a new wave of Basque immigrants began to enter the industry active as merchant bankers and independent refiners."[53] Clearly, the conjuncture of the 1770s, when Madrid had chartered the Tribunal de Minería, had changed. The international situation of the metropole forced Madrid to ask (or pressure) wealthy groups in the American colonies for monetary gifts, interest-free or interest-paying loans during and after war with England in 1780–83.[54] Authorities in the metropole seesawed regarding tactics, in the 1770s helping new peninsular mining and merchant groups to try to penetrate old colonial networks, then, as international conditions worsened, shifting to the most assured sources of funds, the established, wealthy, influence-wielding mine owners and, of course, *almaceneros*. While the tribunal between 1777 and 1786–87 emphasized loans *(avíos)* to often unqualified mine owners and the judicial authority or semiautonomy of mine owners' *diputaciones,* the decade-long financial incompetence of the tribunal's chief administrators led Gálvez and his successors to change tactics.[55]

This seems to have been why Madrid suspended elections by the tribunal's *junta general* in 1786 and appointed the prominent Mexico City *almaceneros* Antonio Basoco and Antonio Barroso as two of the three *diputados generales* on the tribunal, followed later by the appointment of other Mexico City merchants to the tribunal's *junta de arreglo.*[56] The possibility of merchant control of the tribunal's high-level administrators, which the creators of the tribunal had carefully rejected in the 1770s, surfaced in the second general assembly for the election of officers in 1789. Most of the twenty-eight regional deputies present were not mine owners. The implications of this situation appeared when one deputy proposed that the tribunal eliminate the requirement that officeholders prove ten years' mining experience—a motion Viceroy Revillagigedo rejected. At about the same time, one of the two prominent *almaceneros* appointed in 1786 as *diputados generales,* Barroso, moved that two *diputados generales* always be drawn from merchants; it was obvious that the Mexico City merchant community would provide the pool of candidates.[57]

There were other indications that *montañeses* and other newcomers to the mining sector might interpret as constraints on their growth. The *Ordenanza de Intendentes* of 1786 set up Hacienda agencies in mining towns that were prepared to offer cash *(rescatar)* to small mine owners for their silver in the form of *pasta,* which would eliminate competition by recent immigrants among *montañés* and *encartado rescatadores*—such as Apecechea and other newcomers—who used this route to accumulate capital and expertise for larger mining and refining enterprises.[58] In 1790, when the first of such Hacienda offices opened in San Luis Potosí, Viceroy Revillagigedo, influenced by the aging *criollo* regent of the Audiencia, Gamboa, revived the latter's proposal, earlier rejected by Gálvez and Velásquez de León, for a consortium of the Consulado de México and the Tribunal de Minería to finance and operate mines.[59] Decisive in Madrid's rejection of Revillagigedo's proposal was the unfavorable report of a member of the Consejo de Indias, the marqués de Herrera, a career colonial administrator who had served in Guatemala and New Spain, where he had married a daughter of the mining magnate and proprietor of Pachuca's "Real del Monte," Romero de Terreros (conde de Regla).[60]

Spokesman for the insurgent *montañés* mining faction as well as a deputy of Guanajuato to the tribunal's general assembly of 1793, Septien y Arce acted predictably. First, he attacked what few would seriously overlook, the mismanagement of the tribunal's *avíos;* next, he insisted that the tribunal's officers demonstrate ten years' involvement in mining; and then he stated that he would assert the authority of regional deputies over that of the guild's major officers. In the election that followed, the votes mustered by Septien y Arce (Guanajuato) and Apecechea (Zacatecas) plus the votes of the deputies from Catorce led to the elimination of Barroso as a general deputy and his replacement by Manuel García de Zevallos, Septien y Arce's associate, as a *diputado administrador general*. More to the point, the general assembly of 1793 brought the confrontation of fairly well defined groups over control of the tribunal, the consortium of the newcomers Septien y Arce and Apecechea at Guanajuato and Zacatecas versus the long-established mine owners in both mining zones, the Obregón-Otero-Sardaneta-Fagoaga group.[61]

The unity of the *diputaciones* from Guanajuato and Zacatecas at the general assembly of 1794 emerged from shared interests and tactics. Just as Guanajuato's *montañés* newcomers to mining operations like Hernández Chico, Septien y Arce, and García de Zeballos tried to dominate their *diputación territorial* and the principal tribunal offices while they were also litigating the boundaries of their mine properties with the *criollo* group of Obregón, Rayas, and Fagoaga, so to the north at Zacatecas the newcomers Apecechea and his associates Bernardo Iriarte, Pemartín, and Manuel de Rétegui were litigating the boundaries of the most profitable vein of the Vetagrande, controlled by the *criollos* Fagoaga, Ramón de Goya, Antonio Vivanco, and their Mexico City merchant associate, the *vizcaíno* Basoco.[62] Brading, who analyzed carefully this intra-elite conflict, summarized it as "an open struggle for power between a group of Guanajuato Montañeses acting in collaboration with the Basques of Zacatecas against the almaceneros and the Fagoagas of Mexico City."[63] To extend this vision, perhaps there had emerged, following the *comercio libre* of 1778, a division within both the commercial and mining elites of the colony—broadly speaking, new versus "old" capital, *vizcaínos* versus *encartados/montañeses?*

At both Guanajuato and Zacatecas, litigation flared between the major groups over the possibility of working underground silver veins that formerly had been highly productive and that, with skill, tenacity, large capital inputs, and much patience, might return to profitability. In the 1780s the earlier experience of the *peninsular* entrepreneur José de la Borda, who for a period had revived Zacatecas mining with his Vetagrande and "Quebradilla" operations, was still fresh; after all, until the eighteenth century, indeed until after 1766 and the extraordinary earnings of Guanajuato's Valenciana and Rayas mines, Zacatecas had remained the colony's leading area of silver production.

Borda died in 1779, leaving as a kind of legacy a group of mine owners and/or refiners at Zacatecas inspired by his tenacity and, above all, his good luck: Roque Ventura de Arteaga, the miner and refiner Marcelo de Anza, and Borda's nephews Francisco Xavier and Julián Pemartín, these last two, like Borda, immigrants from the French Basque countryside.[64] In 1783 the leading mining consortium operating the Vetagrande mines included Arteaga, Anza and his Mexico City *almacenero* backer, the *aviador* Goya, and the mine owner Vivanco. Within three years this and another group of investors had fused into the United Company, whose director-manager was Arteaga, and whose shareholders included the established *criollo* mining family of Juan Bautista and Francisco Fagoaga, Vivanco, and the prominent Mexico City merchant-bankers Basoco, Gaspar Martín Vicario, and Vicente Olloqui. Arteaga managed competently, for over the five years after 1795 the Vetagrande mine of the United Company produced about 951,000 *pesos* and in the next five years, 2,157,274, peaking in the following five-year period at more than 7 million and constituting "a vast integrated enterprise . . . among the greatest in Mexico."[65] Such remarkable returns to investors after decades of low profit margins galvanized other mining consortia, such as that of Anza, his merchant-banker Goya, and a Guipuzcoan newcomer, Manuel de Rétegui. However, by 1791 Anza's operations had bankrupted Goya, who had drawn partly on funds deposited with his firm by the Obregón family of Guanajuato's Valenciana. This left Rétegui and a recent Navarrese investor in Zacatecas mines, Apecechea, along with Bernardo Iriarte, as the surviving major consortium.

In a pattern similar to that followed by Septien y Arce at Guanajuato, Apecechea, Iriarte, and Rétegui proceeded to win control over the *diputación territorial* of Zacatecas. Apecechea—in 1794 *diputado* to the general assembly of the mining tribunal—then joined with Septien y Arce to elect their partisans to the tribunal's high offices, part of the "wave of Basque immigrants [who] controlled the local *diputación*."[66] Next, armed with the authority of Zacatecas's *diputación territorial,* Apecechea, Iriarte, and Rétegui contested ownership of certain Vetagrande mines, desisting only when the Fagoaga family appealed for the intervention of Viceroy Revillagigedo. In addition, Apecechea obtained control of another Zacatecas mine owned by José de la Borda's heirs, Quebradilla, a process legalized in 1794 by the "machinations" of the Zacatecas *diputación.* And once again, Madrid overruled an intervention by Revillagigedo in response to a request by Borda's heirs. In 1810 Quebradilla produced 60 percent of the production of Zacatecas's *minería,* and its profits were "enormous."[67]

It is valid to presume that capital for rehabilitating and expanding the Zacatecas mines of the two principal mining consortia in the first decade of the nineteenth century came from outside the area. Fagoagas could draw upon profits from their Sombrerete mines, and they could procure funds through their kinsman and associate, Mexico City's wealthiest merchant and *aviador,* Antonio Basoco, and his circle of associates. Fagoagas's patience and deep pockets contributed to the startling success of Vetagrande after 1800 and particularly five years later. Their operations were probably eased by the ability of Basoco, the Mexico City merchants Miguel Ángel Michaus and Antonio Uzcola, and the mine owners Moran and Fagoaga to garner above-quota mercury allocations under Viceroy Iturrigaray. On the other hand, the smaller consortium at Zacatecas of Apecechea, Iriarte, the Pemartins, and others felt cheated in their mercury allotments, and in the 1790s they encroached upon mines controlled by the Vetagrande group. At Guanajuato another group allied with Apecechea and his associates opened shafts close to the mines of Valenciana "and then stole the best ore underground."[68] In any event, the Zacatecas group may have run into financial problems. In this context we note that they borrowed illegally large sums (one estimate ranges as high as 200,000 *pesos*) from the Hacienda office *(caja real)* at Sombrerete, administered by Pablo Agudo. When Agudo later turned down a higher appointment by Viceroy Iturrigaray as administrator of the Veracruz Hacienda office, an investigation revealed that Agudo, a colonial civil servant, had manipulated government funds unofficially and illegally to benefit "varios mineros de dicho real de Zacatecas."[69]

Is it more than pure coincidence that the proprietors of Zacatecas's Quebradilla who approved the coup against Viceroy Iturrigaray in the fall of 1808 were Apecechea, Rétegui, the Pemartíns, and Septien y Arce?[70] And may more than partisanship clarify why one historian of the coup d'état against Iturrigaray noted that the conspirators "confiaban en los mineros ricos de Zacatecas," another that the *golpistas* could count on the "acaudalados mineros europeos" (here, *montañeses?*), and a third that the "Zacatecanos europeos" had joined with merchants at Veracruz to recommend the viceroy's deposition.[71]

Perhaps a synthesis of the complex interconsortia rivalry is in order. Framing the overall problematic is complicated, for all the elements do not fit neatly, but an argument may be presented. Fissions before 1808 within powerful interest groups of the colony, the mine owners of Guanajuato and Zacatecas, appear to have prefigured divisions leading to the overthrow of Viceroy Iturrigaray in that year. They had surfaced in the course of elections in the Tribunal de Minería in the early 1790s, and they had resurfaced in competition for mercury during the English wartime blockades and consequent shortages in 1800 and again in 1806.

First, there was the competition between, on the one hand, the long-predominant, old *vizcaíno* mine-owning oligopolists of Guanajuato and, on the other, their counterparts among a *montañés navarro* group at Zacatecas, one vaguely *criollo* and the other *gachupín/europeo*. At Zacatecas the two competed for access to the Vetagrande mining complex, pitting an older generation of proprietors—the Fagoagas and their partners—against recent immigrant entrepreneurs from southwestern France and Navarre, men like Apecechea, the Pemartins, and Iriarte. Appropriate to this context is the observation that "every twenty years a new generation of owners would emerge with seemingly few ties with the [mining group] it was replacing."[72] Second, the tight English blockade in the Caribbean in 1806 induced *criollos* like Rayas, of Guanajuato, to propose that Viceroy Iturrigaray explore the possibility of obtaining mercury from neutral ports in neutral ships, a proposal that Iturrigaray rejected out of hand. Two years later, however, with Veracruz still blockaded, Rayas and associates would be behind Iturrigaray's apparent support for the formation of a local, "national," junta of representatives of the colony's principal cities empowered to exercise autonomy as long as civil war and political instability ravaged Spain. That junta might help them contract with neutral nations for mercury, a proposition vigorously criticized by certain Zacatecas mine owners, led by the *navarro* Apecechea and his associates. Iturrigaray's removal would temporarily paper over the fissions separating autonomy-tending mine owners from the loyalists *(patriotas)* among Mexico City's *almaceneros* who were responsible for removing the viceroy.[73] Apecechea, one of Zacatecas's wealthiest mine owners, would be one of the prominent endorsers of the *almaceneros'* unprecedented action.

Mine Owners and Merchants: *Compañías Conductoras de Plata*

Further indications of fission in New Spain's economic elites of mine owners and merchants surfaced in another sector of the economy after the unexpected bankruptcy *(quiebra)* in 1802—"the most shocking and complicated Bankruptcy that the Nation has seen"—of the colony's long-established, trusted, and sole officially designated silver transport firm *(conductora de plata),* the Casa de Vértiz y Oteyza, "esteemed as a highly reliable bank offering many benefits to the public."[74] This freighting enterprise was essential to the trading and mining operations of the colony, linking New Spain's commercial and financial hub at Mexico City to the colony's major Gulf coast port, Veracruz. Into Mexico City flowed bullion from mines and provincial distribution centers, while from its public and private holdings flowed out bullion and specie via the *conductora de plata* to Veracruz and on to Cadiz to settle the colony's balance of trade, remit private charitable and other funds, and provide the metropole with the colony's surplus on government account and, on occasion, with impressively large loans and gifts from individuals as well as lay and clerical corporate bodies. Mexico City's merchant community depended upon a secure relationship between the colony's external trade and its *conductora de plata*. As the Veracruz *consulado* once elaborated, "The job of shipping to Veracruz merchants' funds to carry on trading is so tied up with, and dependent upon, that very trade that without this help it is impossible to find or purchase merchandise, pay overseas merchants, remit funds that promote commerce in the Peninsula, or pay for this Kingdom's imports."[75] This structure of trade, explained the *consulado*'s officials, "has made indispensable the dependence of Commerce on the firm of a conductor at Mexico [City] for receiving funds for shipment" to Veracruz. By 1802 the Casa de Vértiz had functioned for nearly a century as "the sole Bank of the Public Treasury," maintaining in the business community such a sense of *confianza* by virtue of its "careful operations and correspondence, the profits of this large enterprise, its many properties, and the honesty, conduct, and moderation of the proprietors" that many trading houses kept deposits with the Casa de Vértiz for domestic and overseas payments and receipts. Its certificates of deposit *(conocimientos)* circulated among Veracruz and Mexico City merchants with the same security as specie or bills of exchange.[76]

The firm's role was heightened, furthermore, by surging silver production and the consequent growing demand in the colony for imports and by the general expansion of the volume of business transactions following termination of the system of *flota* and *ferias* after 1778.[77] Under the *flota*, silver shipments by muleback *(conductas)* had occurred mainly during the period of *ferias*, but beginning in the early 1780s, shipments exited Mexico City on a monthly schedule to meet the now frequent shipping leaving Veracruz for Caribbean and metropolitan ports.

The Vértiz family had maintained extensive networks in the colony's mining and mercantile communities. In 1736 Francisco Vértiz appeared as a large creditor of the prestigious Francisco de Fagoaga (first marqués del Apartado), merchant, mine owner, and farmer of the mint; in the 1770s and 1780s Pedro Vértiz owned three *haciendas* near Durango (later valued at 300,000 *pesos*), ran a *tienda* in that city (the *almacenero* Antonio Basoco was his partner), was a prominent Mexico City *almacenero,* and, of course, managed the silver-shipping enterprise that, in the 1790s under his immigrant nephew and then son-in-law from Navarre, Juan Joseph de Oteyza y Vértiz, held the *asiento de cargas reales* for freighting government merchandise such as stamped paper, mercury, and tobacco, along with silver.[78] Through generations of entrepreneurs, its scope of operations ranging from managing stock ranches, mule teams *(recuas),* and *arrieros* to banking manipulating millions of *pesos,* the Casa de Vértiz forged connections with *criollo* mine owners and their often Basque *almacenero* associates—Obregón, Fagoaga, Basoco, Puyade, and Meoqui. The firm's sole competition appeared after 1796, when, responding to the growing volume of financial transactions, the *montañés* immigrant merchant Diego Fernández Peredo, after two decades of trading in the colony, formed a competitive *casa de conducta* in association with his cousin, a Mexico City *almacenero,* Juan Manuel Fernández Peredo. For a brief period Juan Manuel had been an investor along with other wealthy *almaceneros* in one of the enterprises exploiting Zacatecas's Vetagrande.[79] The Peredo firm, however, was far overshadowed by that of Vértiz y Oteyza.

There was, to be sure, nothing extraordinary in the history of New Spain's economy in the collapse of a trusted, prestigious family firm as a result of entrepreneurial incompetence despite a generally buoyant economic situation. So fundamental, however, was the *conducción de plata* from Mexico City to Veracruz and Acapulco after the Peace of Amiens in 1802, with the resumption of shipping in the Atlantic and the truly enormous outflows of silver and imports of European goods, that it was only a matter of time before the vacuum created by the bankruptcy was filled. For the perennial optimist there was the solace expressed by a *socio* of Oteyza's: "Just one fortunate moment when War is declared, of shortages of seeds, etc., more than compensates for many years of losses."[80]

Now, however, instead of one major and one minor firm, there functioned two equally matched, formally registered *compañías* rather than family firms, listing not only the organizers but also shareholder associates (*fiadores* and *socios*) acting as guarantors of funds entrusted to the firms. By publicizing both their financial resources and their shareholders, both enterprises assured prospective clients of reliability, security, and, perhaps more important, the factional bond, that is, ethnic affiliation.

The first company to advertise was chartered by two *almaceneros* of the capital, Miguel Ángel Michaus and Antonio Uzcola, who jointly put up 100,000 *pesos* backed by a 200,000-*peso fianza* of eight shareholders—two from Mexico City (Juan Bautista Fagoaga and Juan Fernando Meoqui), one from Guanajuato (Obregón), one from Zacatecas (Manuel de Rétegui), and four from Veracruz, "all highly distinguished and of well-known credit" (Pedro Miguel de Echeverría, Tomás Murphy, Ángel González, and José Gutierrez de Cuba); the firm's Acapulco agent was another merchant, Juan Sánchez de Movellán. Conspicuously, all eight *fiadores* formally renounced the protection of their "special rights, homes, and neighborhoods" against judicial authority. Mexico City's merchant and mining elites must have immediately connected these shareholders with the bankrupt Vértiz y Oteyza *conductora de plata:* Fagoagas (Juan Felipe, Juan, and José Mariano), Ignacio Obregón, "whose mines were then booming," the Murphy brothers (Tomás, Matías Lorenzo), and Meoqui would surface among their supporters in the course of the Vértiz y Oteyza bankruptcy proceedings. Coincident with official approval of their charter, the firm of Michaus y Uzcola was awarded the government contract for freighting government silver and goods.[81]

Michaus y Uzcola was quickly matched by a company organized by Peredos, really an expansion of the firm founded in 1796, because the "Comercio de este Reyno" had been unsettled by "a saddening event undermining confidence in good faith, pure and simple." Reporting that his current freighting business over the previous eight years had drawn clients by "my credit, honesty, and skill," Diego Fernández Peredo addressed "the public interest, the real treasure of the State," announcing that he and his cousin had mortgaged as security for their *casa conductora* 100,000 *pesos* of their real estate backed by a 200,000-*peso* guarantee of twelve supporters "of well-known credit," ten from the capital's *almaceneros* (Sebastián de Heras Soto, Francisco de Chavarri, Diego de Ágreda, Pedro González de Noriega, Francisco Alonso de Terán, Manuel García Herreros, Juan Marcos de Rada, the conde de la Cortina, José Martín de Chaves, and Manuel Ordóñez) and two from Veracruz (Francisco López del Diestro and Ignacio García Saenz).[82] Notably, there were no representatives of mining centers among these shareholders, and only two came from Veracruz. On the other hand, this consortium included relatively recent immigrants tied to merchant houses at Cadiz *and* Manila. For example, Diego Fernández Peredo was a cousin of Manuel García Herreros; he and Diego de Ágreda were brothers-in-law *(cuñados políticos)* of the Cadiz merchant magnate Francisco Bustamante y Guerra; Diego de Ágreda was the brother of another Cadiz magnate, Simón de Ágreda; and Francisco López del Diestro was presumably a relative of Cadiz's José López del Diestro. As for the Manila connections of this group, Francisco Alonso de Terán, Diego de Ágreda, and Juan Marcos de Rada formed a consortium customarily making large-scale purchases of Manila shipments arriving at Acapulco on the annual *nao de Filipinas*. Incidentally, the sharcholder Francisco de Chavarri was also the Mexico City *factor* (agent) of Madrid's Cinco Gremios Mayores. It is relevant to note that five of the twelve mainly *montañés* shareholders would be among those whom the insurgents wanted deported to Spain in 1811.[83]

To view the unexpected demise of the major firm for the *conducción de plata* and the rapid chartering of two substitute companies as normal and inevitable consequences of New Spain's economic expansion risks minimizing the significance of the conflictive currents splintering the colony's mining and merchant elites in the closing decades of the colonial era. Two *compañías* marshaling twenty guarantors had replaced Vértiz y Oteyza, just as two factions vaguely marked by ethnic or regional differences now competed for dominance of the colony's mining and commerce, one definable as *criollo-vasco*, the other as *montañés*. The *criollo-vasco* consortium of Michaus y Uzcola drew its eight backers from longtime merchant houses of the capital and Veracruz; through its Obregón and Fagoaga *fiadores* it was tied to groups at Guanajuato and Zacatecas; two of its Veracruz merchant representatives—Echeverría and Murphy—were in the process (as we shall see) of diversifying their Spanish commercial connections to Hamburg and London, the English West Indies, the United States, and Cuba. For its part, the competing *montañés* consortium of the Peredos collected its twelve backers almost exclusively from *montañés* immigrants among Mexico City *almaceneros*. Direct links to New Spain's mine owners are not evident; however, this group was connected essentially to the port of Santander and its *montaña* hinterland by recent emigration and to *montañés* figures at Cadiz and Manila.

This is not to argue that the two consortia were hermetically sealed, for there were points of personal and interest connection. Every elite, whatever its differences, contains cohesive elements. One group, *criollo-vasco,* was associated with elements of New Spain's "traditional" elite establishment who owned and managed mining properties that produced the highest volume of silver and therefore had to bank on reliably large supplies of basic inputs, especially mercury—whether the supplier was from Spain, the English West Indies, or neutral European ports—at stable rather than inflationary prices. The other group, identifiably *montañés,* was more closely tied to Cadiz and the traditional structure of Spain's Atlantic and Pacific trading systems; because of its high percentage of recent immigrants, perhaps it remained relatively apart from the colonial mining elite. This brief catalog of differences suggests, then, the significance of two *compañías* that, by advertising their shareholder-guarantors, publicly appealed for the business and allegiance of two fairly distinct ethnic constituencies in the colony's economic and social elite. In fact, factionalism evident in the elections of the Tribunal de Minería during the 1790s sharpened after 1800; and the fact that the important *asiento* for freighting silver was awarded to Michaus y Uzcola in 1804 implied that the *criollo-vasco* mining interest was resurgent under Viceroy Iturrigaray.

Certainly this is a tenable interpretation of selected aspects of the tribunal's evolution over the two decades after 1790.[84] First, the judicial authority of the *diputaciones territoriales*—where newcomers to the industry might exert more influence—was reduced after 1793, while that of the tribunal's chief officers expanded. On the recommendation of the *junta de arreglo* established in 1787 by then director general Elhuyar, together with the Mexico City *almacenero* Antonio Barroso and Viceroy Revillagigedo, Madrid's Consejo de Estado, which then included Aranda, Valdés, Gardoqui, Campo Alange, Acuña, and a rising star, Godoy, introduced colonial functionaries such as intendants into the judicial proceedings of the *diputaciones territoriales,* then broadened the judicial jurisdiction of the tribunal's officers over all *diputaciones* by in fact making it a court of appeal.[85] Second, in 1802–11 three mine owners epitomizing the predominant *criollo-vasco* group were elected administrators-general of the tribunal—José Mariano Fagoaga (of the family of the marqués del Apartado) in 1800, Sardaneta (marqués de Rayas) six years later, and Fagoaga again in 1811. In this sense, the *montañés* faction seemed submerged, only to surface after the coup d'état against

Viceroy Iturrigaray in the form of the election of the immigrant Spanish mine owner–refiner Apecechea at Zacatecas as a *diputado general* in 1810. To be sure, analysis of the tribunal's formal body of four *consultores de México* reveals a persistent division between *vascos* and *montañeses,* since in 1794 there were Meoqui and Heras Soto, in 1809 José Mariano Fagoaga and Francisco Cortina Gonzalez, suggesting the balancing of representatives of the two competing *compañías conductoras de plata.*[86]

Third, the resurgence of the long-established proprietors of New Spain's most productive mines seems clearly evident in the election of administrators-general, with corresponding authority over allocation of the tribunal's *avío* (investment) funds. There is no reason to doubt, for example, that Sardaneta influenced allocation of tribunal funds once he took office, for by 1814 he and his fellow *criollos* Obregón and Romero de Terreros were responsible for 97 percent of the two hundred thousand *pesos* outstanding in or accounts receivable from mine owners. By 1808 Sardaneta's use of office had become a point of friction separating him and his *criollo* circle from the *peninsular* Elhuyar and his *peninsular* friends on the Audiencia de Mexico, notably Miguel Bataller. As we shall see, it was Sardaneta (marqués de Rayas) who, along with others of Guanajuato's *criollo-vasco* mining interests, like Ignacio Obregón, would openly approve Viceroy Iturrigaray's policies that led in the summer of 1808 to crisis and the September coup d'état. In the critical year of 1808, Guanjuato's predominantly *criollo-vasco* consortia depended upon inputs—iron and steel, mercury and blasting powder—that might conceivably be ordered directly from English suppliers, saving the commissions of Cadiz and Santander intermediaries. Autonomy, limited and temporary, seemed to lie behind their and Iturrigaray's position.

Family-client divisions splitting *vizcaínos* from *montañeses* were long a fact of life in the colony, and they probably were aggravated in the eighteenth century.[87] As mine owners and/or managers ("the dominant directing class"), however, the two groups tended to fuse when their workers confronted them at Guanajuato, Zacatecas, or Pachuca.[88] The industry employed from thirty thousand to forty thousand workers above and below ground, plus managers and other employees, making mining "una de las mayores negociaciones de Nueva España."[89] Skilled workers at the mineheads *(barreteros)* were relatively well paid, their assistants *(peones)* a lot less so.[90] *Barreteros* were customarily mobile, depending on wage inducements, daily production quotas *(tequío),* and share in above-quota output *(partido).*[91] Another source of worker-proprietor confrontation was labor procurement. At large mining enterprises owners still solved the problem of worker shortages by resorting to forced recruitment and the dragnet of vagrancy law in neighboring or distant native communities, authorized by the tribunal's *Ordenanza de Minería* (1783).[92] In fact, recent investigation has tended to contradict Humboldt's finding that he found no coerced miners.[93] Coercing a labor force was, as mine owners recognized, complicated by worker mobility, by the need to increase the number of workers to deepen and drain shafts, and by the cost of inputs, which reduced profit margins even as output grew.

Since labor costs were at least 60 percent or more of operating costs, many proprietors used a variety of techniques to depress wages. They demanded higher daily quotas from *barreteros,* increased the size of ore bags *(costales),* cut down or eliminated *partido,* lowered wages, and shifted certain costs (candles, tools) to workers. Inevitably, where immigrant mine owners, administrators, and shopkeepers predominated, anti-*gachupin/peninsular* feeling was rife: they owned and managed the workplace, reduced workers' income, herded them into deep mines, sold them not only food, drink, and clothing but candles and tools to boot. Since wage rates in the mines apparently had remained unchanged for two centuries, workers reacted. This was clear at Zacatecas, where the *peninsular* mine owners Apecechea, Iriarte, and Rétegui, recent immigrants of the second half of the century, were singled out.[94] As Mentz has noted incisively of violence at Guanajuato and surrounding areas in 1808, "What led to the outbreak of violence . . . was above all the refusal of owners of mines and refining mills to pay higher wages to workers coming from surrounding pueblos and to *barreteros* for their extra output, as well as their insistence on coercing via *repartimiento* peasants for temporary labor."[95] How many *tenateros* of Valenciana and Rayas would join the thousands of *indios, mestizos,* and *mulatos* who marched to Guanajuato behind Hidalgo in September 1808?

Ethnic Conflict or Generational Difference

The mine owners' community in New Spain had a problem that, certainly at the end of the eighteenth century, barely existed in the *almacenero* community of the capital: a keen sense of ethnic rivalry that would surface in the summer of 1808, when Iturrigaray, shortly to be removed by coup d'état, feared "disunity . . . or schism" among the colony's "European residents, partisans of the different regions of their birth."[96] To be sure, deep-seated ethnic solidarity was also evident in the emerging nation-states of western Europe, and inevitably interethnic friction would reproduce overseas among *criollo* and *peninsular* elites, the *europeos americanos,* and the *euro-peos peninsulares* in the colony.

At the beginning of the eighteenth century two dominant figures among the Zacatecas silver merchants were the *montañés* Luis Sánchez de Tagle and the *vasco* Francisco de Fagoaga Iragorri. Both were immigrants, both began careers in trade with Cadiz via Veracruz and the Jalapa *feria* and/or with Manila and China via Acapulco. Both supplied goods, credit, ironware, and mercury to mine proprietors, then bought their silver bars, which they shipped to the Mexico City mint. Francisco de Fagoaga and his merchant *socio,* Francisco de Valdivielso—both in their early careers trading with Manila—aided by the mercantile firm of the father of Fagoaga's wife, Josefa de Arozqueta, methodically worked their way up to the pinnacle of the mining community, becoming *banqueros de plata* and officeholders in the capital's *consulado.* Ultimately Fagoaga and his descendants farmed the process for separating silver from gold *(apartado)* at the Mexico City mint from 1706 to 1778; in the process Fagoaga acquired the appropriate title of marqués del Apartado.[97] The Fagoaga dynasty would maintain its mining and social preeminence until well into the postcolonial decades of the nineteenth century.[98] Typically, silver "bankers" like the *vasco* Fagoaga and the *montañés* Sanchez de Tagle kept close ties to *paisanos* in the *peninsular*-dominated Consulado de México and customarily invited from Cantabrian Spain— Asturias, Vizcaya, Guipúzcoa, Navarra—relatives, usually nephews, to help administer their extended holdings in mining, mercury distribution, cattle and grain estates supplying mining centers, and both domestic and external trade.[99]

Inevitably, interethnic rivalry among the colony's mining magnates, who then were also *almaceneros,* flared in the first half of the eighteenth century, with probable repercussions in the *peninsular*-dominated commercial corporation, the Consulado de México. For instance, we know that the conflict over control of high office and benefits derived in that corporation was such that Madrid had to intervene in 1742; thereafter two party lists of voters were formed to permit alternation in officeholding between the *montañés* and *vizcaíno* factions *(parcialidades).*[100] Later, rivalry surfaced in the elections of provincial deputies to the mine owners' tribunal in the closing decades of the century.

By the 1790s one major outcome of the two *reglamentos del comercio libre* was the upsurge in the colony's transatlantic trade and corresponding earnings, which induced many *almaceneros* to search for fresh investment opportunities and to form mining *compañías* rather than partnerships.[101]

The unexpected bankruptcy of the long-established *compañía conductora de platas* Vértiz y Oteyza, whose "bankruptcy affects every trader," provided an outlet for competing groups, *montañés* and *vizcaíno*.[102] Another outcome was capital concentration, the formation of well-capitalized companies for financing mining operations, especially the extensive renovation of adits and shafts, the associated *ranchos* and *haciendas* of the most profitable, vertically structured mine properties at Zacatecas, and, spectacularly, Valenciana and Rayas at Guanajuato ("the richest and most opulent mineral district of the kingdom") and Zacatecas's Quebradilla.[103] Complicating the issue of ethnic affiliation was the recent wave of immigrant *vizcaínos* and *montañeses* from Cantabrian Spain, repeating the pattern of earlier immigrant generations: *cajeros* in the tiendas of Mexico City and provincial capitals, peddlers *(viandantes)* and *rescatadores* buying silver from small-scale mines and from the *partidos* of mineworkers *(barrenadores)* and at last buying into mines, refining mills *(haciendas de beneficio)*, and nearby agricultural and ranching properties—immigration as an intended consequence of Gálvez's development policy, which Velázquez de León also favored. This late wave of newcomers, such as Fermín de Apecechea from Navarre and the brothers Pemartín from the French Basque country, were in the two decades before 1808 aggressively moving to dominate mining operations at Zacatecas and, more generally, challenging dynasties of the mining establishment like the Fagoaga and Obregón families originating in the Basque provinces or the *montañas de Burgos* and competing in the elections of the tribunal and for mercury allocations. In assigning large mercury allocations to Valenciana and Rayas, Viceroy Iturrigaray would seem to have been privileging establishmentarians over newcomers, *criollos* over *peninsulares*—in David Brading's striking phrase, "the two halves of the Spanish nation." And those two "halves" appear to have been geographically distributed between New Spain's two major mining cores after the 1770s, *peninsular* at Zacatecas and *criollo* at Guanajuato.[104]

The daily operations of the most productive mines, which involved thousands of workers, thousands of draft animals, and the overhang of diminishing profits as output peaked between 1800 and 1810, led mine owners to pressure Iturrigaray for *azogue* allocations. If English blockaders along the Veracruz coast temporarily throttled imports from the metropole, pragmatic *criollo* mining magnates had no qualms about tapping nearby Caribbean sources at England's West Indian port of Kingston. Unlike the predominantly *peninsular almacenero* community of the capital, they found no long-term damage to the metropole's transatlantic system by contacting Kingston's English merchants in wartime. In fact the mining tribunal itself suggested that Iturrigaray authorize contact with "some neutral Power" to procure mercury, which was expressly prohibited by Madrid in 1802; the tribunal accepted the viceroy's rejection "although it could readily be obtained."[105] Nor were mine owners averse to—they may even have inspired—the idea of temporary autonomy in certain decision making voiced by members of Mexico City's *ayuntamiento* in 1808, which the viceroy seemed to accept, if not welcome.[106]

Iturrigaray's desperate attempt to bridge the split in the mine-owning elite may be viewed in this light. In September he would seek advice on the controversial issue of calling a "national congress" to govern the colony until Fernando VII returned from enforced exile in France—an invitation for temporary autonomy. He would select a "junta" made up of Fausto de Elhuyar, the marqués de Rayas (*administrador-general* of the tribunal), Marcelo José de Anza, and José Antonio Terán *(diputados generales)*. Rayas emphatically supported a "congress"; Anza and Terán equally emphatically disagreed.[107] A division between Guanajuato and Zacatecas interests, between a stronghold of established families and those of recent immigrants from the metropole?

Iturrigaray now seemed to distance himself from the capital's powerful *almaceneros* and recent immigrants like Apecechea and the Pemartins at Zacatecas, where they "were igniting the fire of civil discord."[108] That outspoken mining magnate who supported autonomy, Sardaneta, the marqués de Rayas, would emerge untouched—or really untouchable.

7. Export Agriculture: Growth and Conflict

In fact the condition of our colonies' agriculture and trade is improving every day, to the mutual benefit of the colonies and their metropole.

Correo mercantil de España y sus Indias, 9 July 1795

Coercion . . . was the sin qua non of colonialism.   Robert Patch

The Bourbon reformers . . . failed to recognize that the *repartimiento* existed for rational economic reasons.   Jeremy Baskes

Emphasis on growth and change in New Spain's mining industry after 1789 in terms of silver's spectacular predominance in the value of aggregate exports and its dynamic effects on New Spain's interregional economy should not minimize the colony's commodity production for internal and external markets. To judge by data assembled for Revillagigedo's *informe* on the impact of *comercio libre* in the colony after 1778, agricultural production climbed steadily in the 1780s, and the growth trend continued over the following two decades partly in response to capital outlays by merchant groups noting the profits in agriculture and ranching, in corn, sugar and sugar brandy *(aguardiente)*, cochineal *(grana)*, in sheep and cattle.[1] In short, merchant investors drawing upon earnings from trade, mining, and finance now focused on the possibilities of both domestic and external markets for commodity production.[2]

The demographic growth of the colony from 1790 to 1810, when the population reached 6.1 million—recently calculated as roughly 1.3 percent annually—coupled with the expansion of the urban population, in particular at Mexico City, created a demand for foodstuffs, beverages and clothing, for maize and wheat, cacao and sugar, aguardiente and pulque, mutton and beef, raw wool and cotton.[3] Furthermore, export possibilities were also shaped by the growth of population in western Europe; economic expansion there; and demand for cotton, dyes such as New Spain's cochineal, cultivated in Oaxaca, and sugar. Expanding sugar consumption in Europe in the early eighteenth century had brought the extraordinary economic phenomenon of Jamaica and, spectacularly, Saint-Domingue, with its large-scale imports of African slave laborers and its output of sugar, indigo, and coffee. And European demand sparked the emergence of Spain's largest possession in the West Indies, and a world-class sugar producer, the island of Cuba.[4] In belatedly opening the Cuban slave trade to foreign and national slave traders and eliminating metropolitan export duties on milling equipment (copper utensils, iron presses) in 1789–91, Spain's imperial policy and the initiative of Cuban planters laid the basis for the island's agricultural expansion once the rebellion of Saint-Domingue's slaves awed plantation owners throughout the Western Hemisphere and curtailed Europe's sugar supply. The disruption of Saint-Domingue also revived the production of sugar in Brazil's *nordeste* and encouraged sugar planters and merchant investors in New Spain's plantations south of the Central Valley, between Cuernavaca and Cuautla.[5]

There were, in addition, agricultural commodities whose potential drew producers and their merchant associates: corn and wheat flours grown in Puebla for consumers in Tabasco and Campeche, especially Cuba. Indeed, the volume of Cuba's needs attracted Puebla's wheat *hacendados* and also the overpowering production of the United States in Baltimore's hinterland.[6] Yet for a brief moment New Spain's corn, wheat, and cattle *hacendados* enjoyed the mirage of a kind of continued economic hegemony over Spain's major Caribbean possession that went beyond the colony's annual silver subsidies and even promised to overcome long-recognized obstacles to New Spain's growth in exportables other than precious metals.

Since conquest, New Spain's commodity production for export had been centered in the Central Valley and its nearby northern extensions and in Oaxaca in the south. Sustained exports consisted mainly of silver and cochineal, whose low bulk and high value counterbalanced the prohibitive costs of transport by wagon or mule; mules rather than wagons provided the basic transport between Mexico City and the port of Veracruz. With reason, in the 1790s backers of a Veracruz *consulado* repeatedly criticized the Mexico City *consulado* for 250 years of neglect by allocating insignificant portions of its *avería* income for road construction and maintenance of the vital transport section linking the New World's largest capital to its Veracruz entrepôt. While a generation of recent immigrants among Veracruz's merchants wanted to access farmland, *criollo* landowners refused to sell or even rent to Veracruz entrepreneurs desiring to raise crops for local consumption or export, probably because such agricultural enterprise might draw down their reservoir of low-paid permanent and seasonal labor.[7]

Most analysts of New Spain's underutilized agricultural resources pointed to lack of capital as a prime obstacle. Both *criollo* and *peninsular* commentators explained this in terms reminiscent of what a later era would call decapitalization. They cited the constant specie outflows drained off to the metropole or to Spain's colonies of Puerto Rico, the Philippines, and after 1765 especially Cuba in annual financial subsidies for defensive works, garrisons, and administration, drawn on the colonial treasury at Mexico City, as well as payments before 1778 to *flotistas* and other intermediaries from Cadiz at Jalapa's *feria* for overpriced, overdutied, and overtaxed imports. They understood the tight relationship in their colony's unique economy between underdeveloped agriculture, trade, and government fiscal policy: "Through its metals America [here, New Spain] has helped to fill the large vacuum created by agriculture in Old Spain. . . . This remission is the root cause . . . of the backwardness of its Agriculture."[8] This was an obtuse reference to the metropole's use of silver from New Spain to finance grain imports from Italy, southern France, and North Africa. As a consequence of such silver outflows, they claimed, the colony's savings rate remained low, along with the pool of loan capital held by ecclesiastical institutions, which favored commercial firms (whose borrowers could generally offer the security of their urban and rural properties) and enterprises servicing the domestic market. On the whole, such capital was available for at most some ten thousand *hacendados,* and it was available in limited volume to small, high-risk renters or proprietors.[9]

Capital, both merchant and ecclesiastical, was shifting in the second half of the eighteenth century into export agriculture based upon sugar in the Cuernavaca-Cuautla region and to a lesser extent into what seemed until the mid-1780s perennially profitable cochineal *(grana cochinilla)* in Oaxaca.[10] Sugar was produced on large estates drawing upon the land and labor reserves of nearby Native American communities, while cochineal was produced on peasant holdings. Sugar production responded mainly to internal demand and, after the Saint-Domingue upheaval of the 1790s, to the possibility of tapping into European shortages. Cochineal's fate, however, was determined primarily by falling demand in Europe's textile industry.

In what was a secular pattern, Oaxaca's Native American peasants were financed by local colonial officials *(alcaldes mayores)* linked to merchants in Mexico City and, in the 1790s, in Veracruz. They made loans and advanced goods and draft animals in the system of *repartimiento de mercancías,* which was usually, if not invariably, imposed upon a subaltern population. In the 1790s and the first decade of the next century, it remained a matter of animated debate whether cochineal production by Native American farmers could be maintained if a near monopsony of loans and/or goods by local colonial officials were eliminated and replaced by the stimulus of market pricing and competition among traders.[11] Fundamentally it was a division between the school of rational choice and the believers in forcing subsistence farmers into market competition.

Execution of the metropole's *comercio libre* began to produce measurable results in the colony's agriculture after 1790 and inevitably generated factional divisions and conflict of the type discernible in the mine owners' community. *Comercio libre,* it will be recalled, was formulated in part to stimulate manufacture in Spain and in larger measure to expand the volume of colonial exportables, to broaden their composition, and, not to be overlooked, to introduce more northern peninsular immigrants—*montañeses, vizcaínos,* and *catalanes*—into circuits of production and distribution relatively closed to one or the other ethnic groups. In New Spain, where *montañés* networks had once predominated in the *grana* trade, Basques and other newcomers were now penetrating; in the sugar- and *aguardiente*-production areas of Cuernavaca/Cuautla, *montañeses* and *encartados* also were establishing footholds.

Growth in agricultural exportables through the port of Veracruz seems to have been a response more to external "pull"—a "vent for surplus"—than to internal or domestic "push" factors. For example, the urbanization of Veracruz, which became a year-round shipping center after the promulgation of *comercio libre* in 1778, translated, first, into demand for foodstuffs for its resident and large transient population and, second, into increased ship departures, requiring stores of flour, biscuit, beef, and *miniestras,* products marketable as well along the coast of Tabasco, Campeche, and for a time even Havana. Trade expansion at Veracruz also required forage for hundreds of mule teams—the backbone of the colony's transport network—and ultimately motivated the insistence of Veracruz merchants on road construction and maintenance to link the port to Mexico City via Jalapa, Perote, and Puebla. Moreover, the Veracruz *consulado*'s successive staff members in 1795–1810—Basadre, Austria, and Quirós—stressed modifying (it was hardly agrarian *reform*) patterns of land tenure to facilitate the entry of small and medium farmers in order to satisfy the needs of Veracruz's population, as well as the needs of other, nearby circum-Caribbean ports.

Growth and Factionalism
Grana *and the Mobilization of Peasant Labor*

It seems clear that the growth of Veracruz's merchant community after 1780 nourished divisions between merchants of the port and those of the capital at Mexico City and even within each community. One source of discord was control at Veracruz of exports of Oaxaca's high-value cochineal, which with Guatemala's indigo and Campeche's logwood formed a triad of natural dyes basic to the trade of Europe's drysalters and the industries they supplied. *Grana* production by Native American peasants in Oaxaca, who "borrowed" to cover production costs and its "sale" to local officials and through them ultimately transported it to merchants at Veracruz for export to Spain, had by the 1770s long been a major structure of Spain's colonial rule. Since Hapsburg times it had coupled the colonial administration of a financially anemic imperial state apparatus to private enterprise: *repartimiento*.[12] It was a structure of public office in the Spanish colonial system that was exploited for profit by a network of private interests and colonial officials and at bottom was based upon overt or covert coercion.[13]

Under this system before 1786 the metropolitan government had sold low-level district posts in the colonial civil service *(alcaldías mayores, corregimientos)* to bidders, who might consult manuscript manuals outlining the financial possibilities of the colonial civil service in the viceroyalties of New Spain and Peru.[14] For their purchase appointees received administrative and judicial jurisdiction over the tribute-liable Native American peoples of their districts. Since the office carried only a nominal salary—a percentage of gross tribute payments from the indigenous population—the colonial officers were empowered to introduce what in theory was a limited number of goods and/or services *(repartimiento* or *reparto de mercancías)*, whose profits constituted a salary supplement.[15]

This pragmatic system of low-cost colonial administration whereby an ethnically and phenotypically distinct subaltern people subsidized their imposed rulers/occupiers and business associates was congenitally prone to abuse. Would-be office seekers usually borrowed to purchase offices and to cover travel overseas and a security bond *(fianza)* on arrival, for example, in New Spain.[16] Newly arriving *alcaldes mayores/corregidores* would in general approach Mexico City merchants for credits to cover operations in their districts, as well as the value of goods *(habilitación* or *avío)* shipped to them for distribution to the native people they administered. Often even the colonial officials' subordinates *(tenientes)*, who maintained daily contact with the Native Americans were selected by the Mexico City business associates (*habilitadores* or *aviadores*).

Practitioners of coercive store-minding did not want for philosophical rationalization based on a pessimistic assessment of human motivation. They insisted that without credit to facilitate the sale of goods, impoverished native peoples would balk at participating in the evolving money economy and would instead confine themselves to subsistence farming, preferring to be "idle and tied to custom or example" and reverting to the "idleness and loafing . . . to which they are naturally inclined."[17] Emphasis on "laziness" was Spaniards' reluctant confession "that Spanish and native societies were of different cultures," that Native Americans had "a different value system."[18] The assessment of the psychology of Oaxacan native peoples by colonial business elites and civil administration was no different from their assessment of the psychology of subalterns elsewhere in New Spain. What they had to come to grips with was the reality that Oaxaca's peasant landholding communities, rather than the *haciendas* of central and northern Mexico, remained the base of the production pyramid of a valuable exportable.[19]

Although local merchants and wealthy families of Mexico City bought *haciendas* and *ranchos* in areas surrounding Oaxaca and in small towns like Ocotlán to cultivate *nopaleras*, from which cochineal was extracted for processing, Native American small farmers supplied the bulk of production—one of the colony's few examples of peasant production for domestic and export markets. While Native American peasants cultivated the agricultural base, at the apex of the *grana* production pyramid until the late 1780s were primarily resident *peninsular* merchants linked on the one hand to local colonial civil servants and on the other to their suppliers in Mexico City. Theirs was a predominantly *montañés* network, judging by such Mexico City *habilitadores* as Pedro Alonso de Alles, Diego de Ágreda, Manuel Ordóñez, and Pedro González de Noriega. How to account for *montañés* predominance by the 1780s is subject to investigation; it may be related to the surge of *montañés* immigration following resumption of *flotas* to New Spain in 1757, to immigrant *montañeses* who abandoned the Jalapa fairs after 1778 to become *mercaderes viandantes,* and to those who chose to participate as *cosecheros* in financing and marketing tobacco production in the Veracruz area until the government formed its monopoly.[20]

Three changes in colonial policy promised to weaken, if not eliminate, the predominance of *montañés* networks in cochineal exports; the introduction of new groups of Spanish merchants; the prohibition of *repartimiento,* that key element of cochineal production in Oaxaca; and the promulgation of the Reglamentos del Comercio Libre of 1778 and 1789 and the *Ordenanza de intendentes* of 1786. The ordinance terminating *repartimiento,* however, was immediately subjected to review. In law prohibited, in fact tenaciously surviving, *repartimiento* was still under review in 1803, when a revision of the ordinance prohibiting the practice and mandating adequate salaries to *subdelegados* and their *tenientes* was abruptly withdrawn.[21] Like much of Spain's legislation in the eighteenth century for "improvement" in both government and the private sector, the *ordenanza* legitimized a twilight zone that neither preserved intact the old nor fully sanctioned intended change.

Open to debate now as then is the nature of the relation between the administrator/seller/creditor and the Native American producer/buyer/debtor, whether equitable or inequitable, fair or unfair, or simply the best possible arrangement under colonial conditions of production for the market. In Yucatán, Patch has concluded, *repartimiento* was the "leading sector" of the local economy and "the only way to bring the Indians into the economy as producers and consumers."[22] Suffice it to say that in the second half of the eighteenth century a handful of civil servants in the colony (merchants are notably absent), along with some in the metropole, concluded that the relationship was fundamentally coercive and hence inequitable, limited Native Americans' participation in frontier capitalism, and required either serious oversight or outright elimination.

There are at least two modes of assessing *repartimiento* to produce *grana cochinilla* during the late eighteenth century, when overseas demand and Oaxaca's production peaked: the relations between the colonial state and native producers and that between local officials *(corregidores,* later *subdelegados)* and Native American farmers. The kernel of the issue, for commercial intermediaries in a profitable enterprise and colonial civil servants aiming at more revenue for the state, was energizing peasants to reduce subsistence crops to expand the output of a valuable commodity.[23] Early in Spain's occupation of New Spain, and clearly by the last quarter of the sixteenth century, the state had coerced native peoples to enter the marketplace, if only to obtain specie to pay tribute and religious fees. By the eighteenth century Oaxaca's peasant farmers were the main source of this exportable, and the intermediaries' problem—local officials networked with merchant suppliers of credit, goods, and cattle—was how to induce greater cochineal production.[24]

One way to stimulate production was to raise the cost of credit to peasant farmers, charging what appears to have been exorbitant interest while simultaneously underpricing the seroons of cochineal repaying credits advanced. Creditors exporting the finished product through Veracruz found this to be an effective mechanism because it was backed by the judicial (and punitive) power of local colonial civil servants over Native American debtors. Current economists rationalize what seems to have been usury and monopoly: while the rates and profits may seem high, in fact they represent a creditor's protective device in the form of a "risk premium."[25] On the other hand, late eighteenth-century critics of *repartimiento* among the metropolitan and colonial civil service and clergy believed that Oaxaca's native peoples required no coercive mechanisms, merely equitable financing made available by competition among lenders and buyers. This is why in 1765 José de Gálvez, on departing from Madrid for his *visita general* to New Spain, was instructed secretly "to remove the benefits of empire from the grasp of *alcaldes* and *corregidores*."[26] For such *proyectistas* and reformers, however, coercion by colonial officials and their business partners had two disadvantages: it generated subaltern resentment through monopsony of credit and monopoly of purchasing, and it was seen as restraining output and ultimately sales to Native American consumers.[27] In bald terms, one group believed that Oaxaca's native cochineal farmers/peasants had to be coerced to participate in the market; after all, Adam Smith and many contemporaries had tolerated coercion of the English peasantry.[28] As for the critics, they reflected the eighteenth-century belief in a moral economy, free of gross individual exploitation.

Aside from the issue of coercion, at stake in the Oaxaca *repartimiento* was maintaining cochineal production levels for export. This, along with government revenues, was ever the preoccupation of both supporters and critics. The prohibition of *repartimiento* credits coincided roughly with the peak of production in the 1780s, while European cochineal prices suffered only a slight decline, the terms of trade favoring producers. When output began to fall, merchants, their agents, and local officials blamed the *Ordenanza de intendentes*'s prohibition. In fact, it is arguable that peasant producers preferred to emphasize subsistence farming over the cochineal market, causing "noticeable drop in indigenous production for the market."[29] It is also evident, first, that more traders began to penetrate the circuits of production as Mexico City suppliers of credit shifted their investment strategy to mining and estate agriculture in the face of competition from "the agents of new commercial firms" at Veracruz and, second, evident even before 1786, that Europe's demand for *grana* was falling. Nonetheless, *repartimiento*'s supporters insisted that the *ordenanza*'s credit constraints were responsible for falling production, offering "overt resistance by vested interests in defense of their methods." Quite possibly, their pressure on Madrid may have been responsible for the otherwise inexplicable abandonment of the revised *ordenanza* in 1803. In fact, in 1810 merchants, joined by some colonial officials and clergymen, were demanding full-scale resumption of *repartimiento*.[30] One conclusion is incontrovertible: overseas demand was responsible for Oaxaca's cochineal boom and widespread use of *repartimiento* credits, "risk premiums," and coercion, and the decline in European demand ended the cycle. On the other hand, elsewhere in New Spain *repartimiento de mercancías* was gradually transformed into a form of forced labor by the expansion of estate agriculture. This was the pattern in Yucatán after about 1780, especially in the production of sugar, and in the tobacco-growing area of Orizaba and Córdoba.[31]

Weakening of the once relatively closed *avío-repartimiento* structure opened the way in the 1790s for a new network in the cochineal economy competing with the hitherto predominant *montañés* groups in Oaxaca, financed from Mexico City. One basic network still was made up of Mexico City *almaceneros* like Michaus and Meoqui plus the financial resources of the Basque *cofradía* of Nuestra Señora de Aránzazu; the other, new network included the Veracruz merchants Pedro Miguel de Echeverría, Francisco Guerra y Ágreda, Juan Manuel Muñóz, Pedro del Puerto Vicario, and Murphy y Cotarro operating through new Oaxacan traders like Antonio Sánchez, Juan de Siga, Antonio Rodríguez, Vicente Domínguez, and Murguía y Galardi.[32] The geographical provenance of this network is multiple: Anglo-Malagan (Murphy y Cotarro linked to London's Gordon, Reid & Co.), Valencian (Puerto Vicario), and Basque (Echeverría). Colonial treasury accounts covering silver transfers between Veracruz and Mexico City *principales* and their agents in Oaxaca indicate that in 1792 only one Veracruz house furnished *avío* to Oaxaca, while by the end of that decade most cochineal credit seems to have originated with Veracruz firms.[33] By then at least two factors were undermining cochineal production, which peaked between 1777 and 1783, thereafter sharply declining by almost 50 percent. Jeremy Baskes's careful monograph cites, first, the reduction in lending by local officials and their Mexico City merchant backers to Native American peasant cochineal producers once promulgation of the *Ordenanza de intendentes* (1786) prohibited such financing and, more important, the compression of profitability in the cochineal trade by a falloff in European demand and the cost of risk premiums for shipping in wartime.[34] Or is it plausible that Veracruz merchants intervened when the previous lending network of district officers and merchant backers withdrew?

The recent appearance of the Murphy y Cotarro firm as a major Veracruz competitive network is significant. By 1802 it had become prominent enough to have its investment advice solicited by the director of the state trading enterprise at Madrid, the Negociación del Real Giro, which was then weighing the merits of whether "to speculate in that Kingdom's staples on the account of the Real Negociación." Cochineal as an "object of trade," Murphy y Cotarro observed, was "always profitable, but demands outlay of money spread over a year," perhaps an oblique reference to *repartimiento*. Director Antonio Noriega should "forward funds to the Province of Oaxaca in order to arrange with collectors for their cochineal, advancing at good interest rates most of the final price"; on a thousand seroons of cochineal sold at the high prices current at Veracruz in 1802, the state could expect a profit of 90,000–100,000 *pesos,* more when it was shipped to Spain for re-export.[35] Murphy's recommendation was the straightforward commercial technique: monetary advances to peasant producers based upon low, pre-harvest prices, presumably without the juridical-administrative coercion formerly legitimized by *repartimiento.* In fact, this is substantiated by a contract between Murphy y Cotarro, of Veracruz, and the *mercader viandante* Manuel García Girón, operating in the *grana*-producing zone of Teposcolula, whereby Murphy y Cotarro advanced García Girón 22,813 *pesos* in merchandise, repayable within ten months, "on the condition that"—agreed to by García Girón—"the stipulated amount be invested in cochineal on the account of said merchants, and profits split."[36] The volume of Veracruz cochineal exports in 1802–4 was high because much had been retained during the wartime years, 1800–1801.[37] Clearly, Murphy's profit estimates for Madrid were accurate.

Prosperity real and promised, however, heightened rather than dampened network or factional conflict over shares in the Veracruz trade. This was evidenced by the demand of *montañés* merchants at Mexico City seeking to guarantee that Spanish naval vessels carry their high-value product, a demand that Murphy y Cotarro contested.[38] Madrid's approval of the request led to a bitter dispute between networks over loading priorities. After 1804 the slump in *grana* output reopened the debate over *repartimiento* and probably induced Viceroy Iturrigaray to support creation of a state purchasing monopoly *(estanco)* for cochineal like the one for tobacco, in effect a method of guaranteeing equitable prices for Native American producers by limiting the participation of local buyers. When the "representatives of the Oaxaca traders" petitioned in May 1807 for the right to review Iturrigaray's proposed monopoly, arguing "that they had many considerations to offer," within a week they received the curt decision of Viceroy Iturrigaray: "this communication is rejected."[39]

It is thus no surprise to find that the signers of the petition—Francisco Antonio Goytia, Antonio Sánchez, and other Oaxacan merchants like Vega and Juan de Berberena—approved the coup that removed Iturrigaray in September 1808. In September 1810 they petitioned for relegalization of *repartimiento* on the ground that merchants would not risk lending to Native American peasants, since "only *alcaldes mayores,* using their authority and in the interest of their trading, were able to risk financing *indios,* encouraging them to work and forcing them to do so if they refused to." In their post-preemptive-coup euphoria, "once the *alcaldes mayores* were financed by wealthy merchants in the capital of Mexico, Veracruz, and this city," the cochineal trade would operate smoothly "without bankruptcies, defaults, or any cost to the Real Hacienda."[40] Sentiments of a backward-looking commercial bourgeoisie?

Sugar

In another sector of agriculture, that of sugar and its by-product *aguardiente de caña,* expansion to meet domestic demand and an unexpected, potentially large overseas market produced—inevitably, one is tempted to observe—factions and factionalism among the elites of the colony of New Spain. New Spain's exports over the period 1796–1807 show that sugar and cochineal constituted roughly 10 percent of the aggregate value of Veracruz's exports; *grana*'s share was a low 6.6 percent, although still virtually double that of sugar (3.4%).[41] On a semi-logarithmic scale, which would clarify the rate of change, their export fluctuations would coincide. However, in 1799 and again in 1801–3 cochineal shipments by value overshadowed those of sugar, probably because in wartime Spanish naval ships preferred to load high-value *grana* and, of course, silver on their return voyage.[42] In 1792 New Spain furnished about 22 percent of all categories of sugars arriving at ports in Spain from its American colonies.[43] The colony's sugar exports rose markedly thereafter, for the annual average level of Veracruz's sugar exports for the quinquennium 1796–1800—145,043 *arrobas*—almost doubled over the following five-year period to reach an average annual level of 268,760. To be sure, New Spain's sugar exports were dwarfed by Cuba's, whose annual average in 1796–1800 was 2,179,248 *arrobas,* almost fifteen times that of New Spain. And while New Spain's exports fluctuated markedly over the fourteen-year period 1796–1808, Cuba's sugar exports, already high by 1796, rose steadily by 259 percent in the same period.[44]

The oscillation of Veracruz sugar exports, in contrast with those of Havana, underscores the fact that exports from Veracruz of sugar (and flour too) were determined by short-term conditions that produced a level of external prices temporarily offsetting New Spain's high transport costs from the interior to the port of Veracruz, estimated at roughly 400 percent higher than those of Cuba's planters.[45] Moreover, New Spain's sugar *hacendados* in the Cuernavaca-Cuautla area could not reduce costs by increased output and sale of *aguardiente de caña,* or *chinguirito,* since over most of the eighteenth century Madrid had prohibited *chinguirito* sales in order to privilege exports of Catalan wine brandies.[46] Oddly, however, over the last decade of the eighteenth century, when the prohibition was lifted, annual imports at Veracruz of Spanish *aguardiente* rose to an average of 50,000–55,000 barrels; Cadiz, along with other peninsular exporters, relied upon brandy as basic cargo *(pie de cargo)* to cover shipping costs and because they knew that in New Spain their brandies were usually diluted with cheaper local *aguardiente de caña.*[47] In fact, fully 80 percent of the brandy consumed in the colony was locally produced *aguardiente.* No wonder that in the late 1780s Mexico City *almaceneros* like the Bárcenas and their son-in-law Gabriel de Yermo, who foresaw the potentialities of sugar and *aguardiente* production near Cuernavaca, claimed that they could export sugar profitably to the metropole provided Madrid legalized *chinguirito* sales. Here they were backed by a high colonial fiscal agent, Silvestre Díaz de la Vega *(contador general* of the Renta del Tabaco), who recommended *chinguirito* sales to revive the colony's "decadent" agriculture.[48]

Recent studies indicate, however, that far from declining, the colony's sugar production had been expanding, slowly from 1700 to 1750 and more rapidly thereafter. The Cuernavaca-Cuautla region, south of Mexico City in what is today Morelos, reported thirty-two *ingenios* in 1708 and 42 in 1800, while annual production climbed from 1,619 metric tons in 1708 to 7,820 in 1800–1804.[49] From the early 1790s to 1809 exports fluctuated, depending on the rigor of English blockading of the port of Veracruz; after the Peace of Amiens they reached 4,966 tons, to peak in 1803 at 5,565 and then slip thereafter, though still reaching 2,771 tons in 1809.[50]

Behind this performance were a number of factors. For one, there was a shift in ownership and management, from ecclesiastical corporations and their managers to merchant investors, a shift well under way before 1778 and accelerating after *comercio libre.*[51] For another, earnings in domestic and external trade led Mexico City's wealthy merchants to invest in plantations—Gabriel de Yermo, for example, owned three inherited *haciendas*—as they did in mining and cochineal; many merchants also retailed sugar in the capital, and the acquisition of cane plantations provided a form of verticality, tying producer to consumer. In the sugar-growing zone of Cuernavaca and Cuautla de Amilpas in 1805–6, four *almaceneros*—Yermo, Meoqui, Michaus, and Velasco Torre—accounted for about 33 percent of the total output of 28,767 sugar loaves *(panes)*; ten *almaceneros* produced 60 percent of the region's output. Viewed in a wider context, that region's aggregate value of sugar and *aguardiente* production reached nearly 40 percent of the colony's total output.[52]

In the early 1790s the export potential of New Spain's established planters as well as newcomers to cane agriculture seemed promising. In 1792 metropolitan policy eliminated duties on exports from Spain of refining equipment, and in 1796 sales of *chinguirito* were legalized. At the same time, the unexpected liquidity of Mexico City's *almaceneros*—what Humboldt characterized as "the enormous pool of capital controlled by merchants"—led prominent *almaceneros* like Pedro Alonso de Alles Díaz, Francisco Ignacio de Iraeta, Gabriel de Iturbe, Domingo Ruíz de Tagle, and Antonio Basoco, some of whom, in their own words, were "dedicated to the cultivation and processing of Sugars, others to the business of sales and distribution, investing all their money in this valuable branch of agriculture and commerce," to petition for the elimination of *alcabala* duties on sugar exports at Veracruz. To buttress their case, they pointed to the slowly evolving state policy of "freeing [Spaniards] from the heavy yoke to which foreign trade subjected them," and they trusted that their current proposal would belie the widespread European misconception of Spain as "lazy, indolent, and incapable of prospering in agriculture, crafts, and commerce."[53] Interestingly, they envisioned shipping their sugars to *montañés* merchants in Spain, to Antonio Mier y Terán of Cadiz and to Nicolás Vial of Santander's expanding community of merchants in the colonial trades.

Their optimism was justified by sustained demand in the colony and in western Europe, open resources in land, and the incorporation of what they considered the underemployment of Native American labor, which made the purchase of imported African slaves unnecessary. These substantiated Humboldt's optimism, not to mention that of the Veracruz *consulado*'s secretary, Quirós, who in early January 1808 marveled at the "remarkable advance of sugar in this Kingdom, having exported in the past 12 years 2,245,258 *arrobas*, excluding exports to Gulf ports" to the value of more than 7 million *pesos*.[54] It was not long before there surfaced another constellation of *almaceneros* also interested in sugar exports—at Mexico City, Fernando de Meoqui, Juan Bautista Oteyza, and Sebastián Heras Soto; at Veracruz, Murphy y Cotarro, Pedro Miguel de Echeverría, Ángel González, Pedro del Puerto Vicario, Francisco Guerra y Ágreda, Juan Bautista Lobo, Felix de Aguirre, and Miguel de Lizardi.[55] Speculation in sugar, the relative inelasticity of local production, and perhaps what appeared as a *montañés-encartado* dominance in the Cuernavaca-Cuautla area may have led Tomás Murphy and other Veracruzanos to transfer some silver earnings from their local trading operations to Havana for the purchase of sugar for export. In this circuit, New Spain's payments in silver *pesos* for imports from the metropole ultimately went to Havana for its sugar exports.[56]

Yet trade between Veracruz and Havana proved a mixed blessing. Now Havana exporters made clear their intention to ship Cuban *aguardiente* to compete in New Spain's local markets and to turn to the cheapest suppliers of foodstuffs, even if this meant preference for U.S. flour over that of Puebla in New Spain. Most unsettling to traders at Veracruz and Mexico City, Havana's merchants aimed to re-export to New Spain merchandise imported in U.S. ships, then protected by that government's neutrality status.[57] What was evident to New Spain's merchant elites was that economic growth in Spain's Caribbean colonies might, and probably would, undermine New Spain's longtime economic hegemony over the Caribbean possessions. It might further divide the colony's mercantile elites.

In 1799 indications of tension surfaced between Cuba's *aguardiente* producers and those of New Spain. On receipt of a request to open New Spain to Cuban brandies, Viceroy Azanza ruled that its "introduction is not permitted in this Kingdom."[58] There the issue rested until Madrid in 1807 assigned to the Cadiz merchant firm of Mariano Malancó a license *(gracia)* to ship Cuban *aguardiente* to Veracruz. Now, however, another viceroy, Iturrigaray, authorized its import, to the dismay of producers in Cuernavaca-Cuautla; mitigating its local effects, Veracruz customs officers laid on a duty that Cuba's exporters claimed was as high as 154 percent. Worse, Iturrigaray distanced himself from Mexico City merchant-planters on two counts: he insisted that they pay a fee per barrel of *aguardiente,* and he persisted in executing the *consolidación,* which affected many planters who had borrowed from affected religious bodies. In sum, the viceroy satisfied the interests neither of producers in New Spain nor of those in Cuba.[59]

Flour

In yet another sector of New Spain's economy the drawing power of external demand brought growth and the unintended frustrations of growth, accentuating existing cleavages between and within New Spain's and Cuba's economic elites. In no small measure the friction flowed from the conviction of New Spain's bureaucratic and economic elites that territory, population, natural resources, and variety of products justified the colony's subimperial hegemony over the Caribbean and circum-Caribbean possessions.

At bottom the assertion of hegemony was the effect of centuries of silver subsidies annually drawn from New Spain's colonial treasury to subsidize relatively poor, undeveloped colonies, Cuba for example.[60] As a secretary of the Veracruz *consulado* put it, perhaps exaggerating New Spain's "flourishing state" in the 1790s, that was an era when "the products and manufactures of this kingdom supplied at reasonable prices Havana and places in and around the Mexican gulf."[61] To be sure, many in Campeche or Cuba, obliged to buy Puebla's wheat flour, may have thought otherwise of the prices demanded.[62] What changed Cuba's position was its large imports of African slave laborers after the English occupation of 1763–64 and consequent requirements of food imports, along with provisioning the naval and military garrisons at the port of Havana. The initial response was to carry Puebla's exports by mule teams down to the coast at Veracruz and then ship them to Havana. Military needs there were given priority "to invigorate the languishing and abandoned agriculture of New Spain."[63] One group of Veracruz merchants, those centered in the *montañés* firm of the Casa de Cosío, may have profited by heading a government purchasing program to supply Havana's garrisons in the 1770s and 1780s, a program criticized for curbing private initiative. By the late 1780s, however, supply and demand seem to have been the sole factors determining Havana's flour prices.[64]

Financing Puebla's flour production was also part of the more general movement of mercantile capital into agriculture, whether into Oaxaca's *grana* or Cuernavaca's sugar. Flour exports, it was widely held, were contingent upon Havana price levels high enough to neutralize New Spain's overland transport costs and—a critical factor—upon the exclusion from Havana of a high volume of competitive imports from grain-exporting ports such as Baltimore in the United States. Apparently, rising prices at Veracruz for flour exports, doubling between 1778–81 and 1809, Puebla's high yield ratios, and some limitations at Havana on flour imports from the United States briefly minimized local overland transport costs.[65] From 1789 to 1794 Veracruz managed to export to Havana on average 7,698 *tercios* annually, a figure that obscures marked annual oscillations; indeed, in 1808–9 such exports averaged 23,899 *tercios*.[66] In the mid-1790s, demand and prices at Havana brought Veracruz merchants already involved in handling cochineal and sugar—for example, Murphy y Cotarro, Pedro del Puerto Vicario, and Ángel González—to trade in flours. Even then, however, shipments from Veracruz filled only about 10 percent of Havana's flour requirements; the balance was met by Philadelphia and Baltimore exporters, who undersold Puebla by 30 percent because of lower transport costs, despite a wage rate in the United States that was, according to Abad y Queipo, more than double that of what he termed New Spain's *operarios del campo*.[67]

It is tenable that short-term conditions, not the least of which were New Spain's annual financial subsidies to Havana and military procurement, created an artificial demand for the production and export of Puebla flour despite admittedly high transport costs. Put another way, as long as the Spanish transatlantic trading system could afford to exclude or minimize external factors, New Spain's producers and exporters of flour could operate profitably in the Havana marketplace. On the other hand, after 1763, even in peacetime, ships from Philadelphia and then Baltimore managed to slip into Havana with cargoes of flour and other foodstuffs. And when Spain went to war against England in 1779, special licenses, or *permisos,* that authorized North American shippers to supply Havana signaled to New Spain's exporters that the threat might materialize again, as it did in the late 1790s.[68] In addition, New Spain's producers and exporters at that time already had to contend with two downward pressures on profitability: from freight rates that the colony's *arrieros* raised from 1.5–2.5 *pesos* per *tercio* (8 *arrobas*) to 8.5, bringing the price f.o.b. Veracruz of Puebla *harina* to 18 *pesos* per *tercio;* and from the sheer volume of U.S. flour exports to Havana. Still, even at 18 *pesos* per *tercio,* the secretary of Veracruz's *consulado* opined in 1796, local merchants "would be motivated . . . to ship considerable amounts if they were assured that the Anglo-American colonists would not export their flours to Havana."[69] The win-win situation of Havana's merchants was enviable: abundant imports from the United States lowered flour prices, while U.S. purchasers of return cargo drove up the price of sugar, "creating an advantageous situation for Havana in every marketable article."[70] In February 1797 there were reports of 18,000 *tercios* of flour stockpiled at the port of Veracruz subject to deterioration in six months; in 1798 Puebla's *ayuntamiento* complained about a Madrid order of June 1798 permitting Havana under *comercio neutro* to import foodstuffs from the United States, including flour. As a consequence Puebla's producers and Veracruz exporters had to contend with the fact that "either our flour would remain unsold at Havana and subject to spoilage or we would sacrifice it by selling" below cost.[71]

To be sure, businessmen tend to exaggerate real or potential loss and to view a temporary situation as long-term. For example, when Madrid in 1802, intending to promote "national Commerce" with Spanish grain exports, prohibited the entry of U.S. shipping at Havana, colonial officials at Mexico City quickly publicized Havana's flour shortfall, as well as the

204 • *Fissioning of New Spain*

price of up to 30 *pesos* per *tercio*.[72] According to reports of Puebla's intendant, Flon, flour and other agricultural exports had become critical for the
survival of Puebla's farmers *(labradores),* and as late as 1808 and 1809 they
supplied most of the 29,970 *tercios* Veracruz exported but still a fraction of
Havana's annual consumption.[73] Nonetheless, this did not deter hege-
monic-minded consortia of Mexico City and Veracruz merchants from
insisting in 1808 that Madrid prohibit all trade between Havana and U.S.
ports in order to facilitate the sale of New Spain's flours to supplement
those from the metropole. Meanwhile, planters and merchants in New
Spain insisted that no *aguardiente* from Cuba enter their colony and that
Havana, a new intermediary, not be permitted to re-export to Veracruz
manufactures imported on U.S. vessels.[74]

Inconsistencies and contradictions in the positions of New Spain's merchant elite were highlighted by Francisco de Arango y Parreño, able representative of agricultural interests in Havana's merchant guild and openly
contemptuous of the concept held by New Spain's merchants of their
"imperio mexicano." Those who keep reminding us, he observed acidly, that
"only New Spain can furnish all the flours we may order simultaneously and
with the same fervor support flour shipments from the Peninsula." If the
colony of New Spain could supply Cuba's requirements, he concluded
ironically, then "Good-bye to the privileges of Metropolitan shipping and
commission agents."[75] The logic of reality, however, often fails to deter interest, for as late as mid-1810 Puebla's instructions for the *diputado general*
of New Spain to the Cortes, soon to convene at Cadiz, included "the total
prohibition of the trade in flour by 'Yngleses americanos' with the Spanish
Islands."[76] Of course, among the merchant elites of Mexico City and Veracruz—those vaguely identifiable as *criollo* with *vizcaíno* associates—were
those who recognized that the era of New Spain's economic hegemony over
the Caribbean, and Havana in particular, was crumbling and that under
certain circumstances trade with neutral merchants from the nearby United
States was unavoidable, necessary, and tolerable. But in 1808 they were
overshadowed by many *montañeses* and *encartados* who would countenance
no fundamental change in Spain's transatlantic trading system.

Analysis of New Spain's mercantile elites invested both in mining and in
export agriculture suggests cleavages between traditional and recently established interest groups. In mining and sugar one detects a group of recent
Spanish immigrants seeking predominance over, even displacement of, *vizcaínos* and *criollos.* In the case of cochineal, the positions seem reversed, since
Basques, *criollos,* and their recent immigrant Anglo-Malagan and Valencian

associates were penetrating a sector hitherto preempted by *montañeses*. The phenomenon of flour exports is unique inasmuch as both factions seem to have entered this sector simultaneously, although, as we shall see, *montañeses* would adopt an equivocal position on trade with the United States. We need to recall that mining remained the fundamental sector of the colony, and here two factions, groups, or consortia were most visible in the distinct *compañías conductoras de plata* of Michaus y Uzcola versus the Peredos. Even a cursory examination of how their respective *fiadores* and *socios* operated in export agriculture reinforces the hypothesis of two competitive networks, although clearly there were crossovers, with some members seeming to be linked to an opposing faction. Nonetheless, important as factionalism was in mining and export agriculture dividing *criollos* and their associates from more recent arrivals from the peninsula, it was overshadowed by divisions within the essentially *peninsular* merchant community over a key factor in Spanish colonialism: trade relations within the empire, between New Spain and Spain, between New Spain and Cuba, and ultimately between New Spain and other trading economies in the Spanish Atlantic.

8. Comercio Neutro / Comercio Directo

Firm and enlightened leaders who refused to listen to the clamor of ignorance and sanctioned *comercio libre* with all neutrals.　　　　　　　　　　　　　Francisco Arango y Parreño

It's the view of Commerce that foreigners should know nothing about the route to America.
　　　　　　　　　　　　　　　　　　　Consulado de Cadiz, 3 December 1797

The irresistible laws of the most imperative and total necessity had obliged the Junta de Gobierno y Real Hacienda at Havana to depart from current orders covering the temporary opening of that Port.　　　　　　　　　　　　Amicus Plato, sed magis Amigo Veritas
　　　　　　　　　　　[Valentín de Foronda or Carlos Martínez de Irujo?]

The formation of the Consulado de Veracruz was a product of New Spain's overall expansion at the end of the eighteenth century matched by that of the island of Cuba and Havana's ultimate emergence as *the* major port in the Caribbean. Yet the growth of the two colonial economies and their principal ports, far from reinforcing Spain's transatlantic structures, generated schisms that transformed what might have been complementary systems into antagonistic ones. To many merchants the long-held hegemony of the port of Veracruz, and by extension of New Spain, over the Caribbean sector of the Spanish empire was abruptly questioned in the period 1797–1808 by Havana's trading operations. New Spain's political crisis in 1808 has a neglected Cuban and Caribbean counterpoint.

Viewed within the context of the Atlantic patterns of the time, there was a convergence of New Spain's expansion with that of England, of colonial demand and Europe's industrialization, of Mexican silver and English textiles.[1] The surge in New Spain's silver production, which in turn affected its agricultural output, no doubt induced a further concentration of income among the colony's elites, but growth also incorporated new consumers hitherto isolated from the colony's market economy. Demand increased for luxury goods from Europe and Asia and for low-priced cottons. Coincidentally, the rapid spread of Cuba's sugar plantations in response to rising international price levels transformed Havana and its near hinterland; the port became a point of convergence for Spanish, English, and U.S. commercial interests, not to mention those of New Spain's businessmen. More was involved than the export of Cuban sugar, for the inadequacy of Spain's manufacturing base and in wartime the virtual shutdown of maritime communication between the peninsula and its American colonies threatened to transform Havana into a distribution point for European products arriving from Kingston (Jamaica), Providence (Nassau), and Philadelphia and Baltimore. Havana now threatened the mercantile hegemony of Veracruz and Mexico City. These are background elements for what has become known as *comercio neutro* and its sequel, *comercio directo,* two developments contributing to the general crisis of the Spanish Atlantic system that would implode in New Spain under Viceroy Iturrigaray in the late summer of 1808.

Background to *Comercio Neutro,* 1797

The roots of Spain's economic policy allowing its American colonial possessions to accept in wartime neutral-flag carriers of Spanish-owned cargo, in effect from November 1797 to April 1799, can be traced to earlier wartime practices, to those of France in the Caribbean, to unexpected growth in the colonial demand for European goods, and to the outflows of New Spain's silver to its metropole on government (royal) and private account. Moreover, one of the major and unexpected consequences of *comercio neutro*—tension between commercial groups in Veracruz, Mexico City, and Havana—grew out of frequent contacts between New Spain and Cuba after Spanish forces reoccupied Havana in 1764.

Despite the rigidity of Spain's transatlantic system, which formally excluded the participation of foreigners, flexible responses to overriding necessity occurred repeatedly over the eighteenth century. During the War of Succession (1701–14) French warships and merchantmen repeatedly entered Havana and Veracruz, Valparaiso and Callao; and again during wartime in 1739–48, when Madrid had to suspend its *flotas* and *galeones,* French merchant vessels as *navíos de registro* helped supply the American colonies. Not surprisingly, the two decades after 1739 were years of peak French exports through Spain to its colonies. It was therefore logical that when Spain supported the insurgents in Britain's North American colonies, Madrid resorted to the vessels of neutral Portugal and Spain's ally, France, to trade with its colonies. No doubt, too, utilization of Portuguese vessels had inspired London to issue "the rule of the war of 1756," which claimed that "a neutral vessel had no right to carry on in war a trade prohibited to him in time of peace."[2] Fifty years later England's enforcement of this unilateral proclamation would induce a profound crisis in Spain's colonial system.

In 1784 French colonial legislation suggested the utility of the French Bourbon "model" for Spanish authorities. At that time French civil functionaries, recognizing the strategic and economic importance of England's ex-colonies in North America from Boston to Charleston, opened seven "free ports" in the Caribbean allowing exports of rum and molasses and re-exports of French merchandise in exchange for flours, salted provisions, lumber, and cattle on the hoof. Nine years later, during the first of the revolutionary wars with England, France opened to neutral U.S. shipping all its Caribbean ports along with those in the Indian Ocean.[3]

From 1779 to 1783 Madrid's response to war in the Atlantic was more restrained. Neutral vessels carrying Spanish-owned cargoes were required to recross the Atlantic directly to those Spanish ports whence they had departed; in addition, neutral shipping had to proceed directly from Spain to one Spanish colonial port—no movement from one colonial port to another was permitted. Atlantic crossings were not to be initiated from ports in the colonies, for trade in the Atlantic was still the initiative of merchants in Spain. Similarly, the hegemonic role of Mexico City and Veracruz merchants over Caribbean ports was sustained unmodified: Veracruz could re-export both Spanish and non-Spanish products to Havana and San Juan (Puerto Rico), to Campeche and Merida, but not the reverse.

To Havana interests after the reoccupation of Havana in 1764, such restrictions were tolerable. First, silver subsidies financed massive defense expenditures at Havana on fortifications, dockyards, garrisons, and provisions; in 1779–82 alone as much as 35 million *pesos* was drawn mainly from New Spain's colonial treasury.[4] And there were the proceeds of New Spain's tobacco excise tax, about 300,000 *pesos* annually, which Madrid employed to purchase Cuban tobaccos for shipment to the state-owned cigar and cigarette factory at Seville. Next, merchants in New Spain explored the possibilities of the growing Cuban plantation economy. They shipped flours from Puebla by mule to Veracruz for export to Havana despite competition from U.S. flour traders. At the same time, as the Cuban physiocrat and planter Arango y Parreño put it, "Veracruz's merchants made large remissions of funds for purchasing sugar" to avoid export duties on silver at Veracruz and import duties at Cadiz or other peninsular ports.[5] Before 1797

New Spain's commercial and agricultural interests found in Cuba a market for agricultural products and a place of investment; there was, of course, growing competition from Philadelphia, New York, and Boston exporters in food, cattle, and illegal European goods.

Cuba's requirements, often exaggerated, also provided a rationale to Spaniards and non-Spaniards alike for requesting from Madrid special licenses to trade with Spain's Caribbean ports at Veracruz, La Guayra, and Cartagena. Integral to licensing was the element of state intervention as dispensation, favor, and privilege. Crown beneficence reinforced the monarchy by promising reward for past or present service to the government, a structure imbricated in Spain's late-developing commercial capitalism. Under *comercio libre* at Cuba there still persisted the age-old practice of executive exception to the formally "closed" commercial system in the form of *permiso* or *gracia* bestowed upon individual merchant houses, privileging them to forward cargo, often duty-free, to specified colonial ports and to freight merchant vessels returning to the peninsula with colonial staples and silver.

It was an instrument frequently utilized in wartime. For example, to supply the Compañía Guipuzcoana, at Caracas, during wartime (1779–83), Francisco Cabarrús arranged to sell a Spanish vessel and cargo to an Ostend firm, for which, incidentally, he was the Spanish agent; the company also employed at Cadiz the Geneva-based firm of Cayla, Solier, Cabanes & Jugla to dispatch three neutral Danish vessels from Altona and Cadiz to La Guayra. Perhaps more illustrative of government practice was a "private royal permit" to forward a cargo to Omoa, in the Gulf of Honduras, and to return via Havana in order, in the words of Colonial Secretary Gálvez, "to stimulate trade and ship from Havana the huge sums of money in the Kingdoms of America." The goods were listed on the ship's manifest as property of Juan Roseti of Trieste, who provided the "appearance of a neutral person," and were to be handled by Roseti's Cadiz agent, Greppi y Cia, which, in turn, hired a ship of "Imperial" (Austrian) registry captained by an Austro-Hungarian. Ostensibly the vessel would return to Trieste laden with sugar and silver.[6]

Once Madrid opened Havana to full participation in the slave trade in 1789, there came an upsurge in special licenses (*gracias*) to import wheat and other staples from the United States. Cadiz firms took the lead in seeking them: in 1790 the firm of Bilbao y Arriete, associated with Medina, Arriete y Compañía, petitioned for "an exclusive privilege for 5 years to export 200,000 barrels of flour . . . from U.S. ports to our Islands."[7] The following year, Girón y Moctezuma sought recompense for services rendered in wartime during the early 1780s in order to ship to Veracruz "the goods of the Real Hacienda and 2,500 *quintales* of mercury," while Bustamante y Guerra de la Vega, also at Cadiz, received a *permiso* to export 1 million *pesos* of non-Spanish products to Veracruz plus another "million in silver [*pesos*] to foreign ports." Preoccupation with provisioning Cuban plantations surfaced once again in 1793, when the Spanish chargé d'affaires at Philadelphia was granted authorization to issue special licenses for sending foodstuffs, especially flours, to Havana; the authorization was withdrawn in peacetime, in 1796, "to permit the reestablishment of exclusive trade between Spain and America." In 1795 another Cadiz merchant house, Domingo Terry y Compañía, was licensed to send three neutral-flag ships with three hundred tons of "solely foreign goods" to Havana and Veracruz; in 1796 Ángel and Mariano Álvarez, of Cadiz, obtained a *gracia* "as on other occasions" to export from the United States to Havana and La Guayra forty thousand barrels of "desperately needed" flour. Lacking the required financing, the Álvarez brothers had to turn to another Cadiz house with Veracruz connections, Torre Hermanos, for financing. This led to a loss of almost 2 million *pesos fuertes* in a joint and hopelessly mismanaged operation. For their part, Cuban planters like the conde de Jaruco y Mopox, reluctant to have Cuba's flour trade handed over entirely to Cadiz firms, petitioned in 1796 for a license to export to the United States nine thousand *pipas* of rum in exchange for food ("flours in particular"). With the resumption of international conflict from November 1796 to the following June, Madrid had to license firms at Cadiz (and Madrid too) to utilize neutral ports in Europe to ship goods to Havana and Veracruz, La Guayra and Cartagena.[8]

Other signs indicate that Madrid foresaw drastically curtailed contact with the American colonies under blockade, and in 1796 Godoy's ministry lifted the centuries-old restraint on commercial initiatives by *criollo* merchants (*españoles americanos*), allowing them to dispatch their own vessels to trade with metropolitan ports. The ministry further irritated the *consulado* at Cadiz by urging its merchants to consider setting up "casas de comercio españolas" at Elsinore in Denmark, a proposition the *consulado* rejected as "very inopportune." That body had just turned down Cabarrús's invitation to buy shares in a shipment from Hamburg to Montevideo and Callao, reasoning in its narrow nationalist perspective that "el mayor bien del Comercio de Indias es la pribación de él a los extrangeros y la promoción del fomento de las fábricas nacionales por medio de prohibiciones y cohartaciones de los Géneros de aquellos." It countered by bargaining to advance the ministry one hundred thousand *reales de vellón* for every *gracia* of one thousand tons of non-Spanish goods sent to the colonies in neutral or Spanish bottoms.[9] As not only merchants but also major investors in the government's interest-bearing *vales reales,* they knew of Madrid's deepening financial difficulties and its propensity for choosing panaceas like special licenses over long-term, painful change.

Spain's policymakers resorted to licenses of exception to meet the needs of Cuba's economy in order to allow merchants in Spain and New Spain (in fact, those of Cadiz, Veracruz, and Mexico City) to maintain a commanding position in the island's external trade. For their part, Cuba's landed and mercantile groups found subordination tolerable if the supply inadequacies of the metropole and New Spain were compensated by tolerating Havana's foreign contacts with nearby Jamaica, Nassau, and Saint-Domingue as well as with the more distant "Anglo Americanos" in the United States. Havana's unauthorized commercial contacts with foreign ports had developed within the hegemony of the metropole and its major colonial submetropole, New Spain. One need only recall Havana's earlier trade with Saint-Domingue; with Jamaica's slave traders, represented at Havana by Philip Alwood, resident agent of the Liverpool slaving firm of Dawson, Baker & Company; and with the English "free ports" at Kingston and Providence.[10]

We can now understand why Havana interests, foreseeing in mid-1796 the real possibility of renewed warfare in the Atlantic between Spain and England, took the initiative. First, on 29 September a special junta of Havana's *consulado* petitioned Hacienda Minister Diego de Gardoqui to "admit neutral vessels to this Port" in case of war and to "protect convoys bearing staples to Spain" to be furnished by the royal navy. Then, on 26 November the *consulado*'s officers (José de Veitia y Castro, Juan Thomás de Jaúregui, and Lorenzo de Quintana) responded to publication of the long-expected declaration of war, reminding Gardoqui that the onset of hostilities "caught the commerce of [Havana] completely short of textiles, ironware, and the most basic articles" after five years of no trade contacts with France, "which used to supply mass-consumption goods," leaving Havana with the "most deplorable shortage of items of consumption." Within the next few days speculation in basic commodities drove up prices to "unheard-of levels," while export staples remained warehoused. Again the *consulado* officers urged that escort vessels be made available to protect their shipping and that Havana enjoy "the means customary in other conflicts with the English nation to seek supplies wherever available."[11] Such pressure from planters and merchants for extraordinary measures led the Cadiz *consulado*'s agent at Havana, Gabriel Raimundo de Azcárate (in communication with

Mexico City merchants like his kinsman Francisco Ignacio de Yraeta), to propose in early 1797 that Havana's importers turn to the textiles of nearby New Spain to reduce shortages "without leaving our national trade."

As the representative of the Cadiz *consulado,* which was the major beneficiary of Spain's "closed" transatlantic commercial system, Azcárate knew he was operating in an inhospitable environment dominated by informed and aggressive export interests spearheaded by the special junta of the Havana *consulado.* This body proposed in February 1797 that local officials be empowered to grant to "Anglo-Americans and other neutral powers permits to bring here all kinds of foodstuffs except Flours and Cod, and Textiles and Ironware." As Azcárate advised Cadiz in early March, he was wrangling with an impressive junta made up of the island's governor, the intendant and a Cuban-born syndic of Havana's *ayuntamiento* (the "aristocratic lawyer" Arango y Parreño), backed up by the officers of the Havana *consulado* and merchants registered in the *consulado* as either merchants or planters. Azcárate noted that two *consulado* officers were well over seventy and had been "*Hacendados* rather than Merchants, and since the most powerful *partido* in this City is of *Hacendados,* it has more influence than that of Merchants."[12] His breakdown of the major power bloc within the *consulado* was probably designed to justify the meager results of his intervention: postponing for one month the opening of Havana to neutral shipping and limiting it to three months. On 17 March the governor (conde de Santa Clara) and the intendant (José Pablo Valiente)—Arango described them as "firm and enlightened leaders who refused to listen to the clamor of ignorance and sanctioned *comercio libre* with all neutrals"—authorized opening the port to U.S. shippers and their vessels. Notice of this deference to Havana's town council and *consulado* was immediately dispatched to Pedro Varela y Ulloa at Madrid for approval, since "necessity justifies departure from the regular system."[13]

It was now the turn of business and bureaucracy in the metropole, Cadiz and Madrid, to handle the unilateral decision by Havana's economic and bureaucratic establishment. Criticism from the Cadiz merchants Manuel Ruíz and Pedro Martínez de Murguía, who had been informed privately by Azcárate, was formulated at three levels. First, the pragmatic: opening Havana even for three months would irreparably damage "comercio español" by permitting "Anglo-Americanos" to undersell merchants already stocked with high-priced imports and charged with "royal duties, very high insurance and cargo rates." Second, the economic: "privilegios exclusivos" prejudiced every sector of the metropole's economy, especially commerce, where "uniformity is absolutely indispensable, and resists deferring to anything but better information, activity, and well-founded calculations, which must guide enterprise and mercantile operations."[14] Their third, Spain's Atlantic structures: the major criticism was rooted in the presumed economic primacy of Cadiz merchants and, by extension, the metropole's hegemony over its transatlantic system. If other colonies were to duplicate Havana's actions, "which undermine the structure and regulations of trade and are destructive of that of the Metropole," the end product would oblige Cadiz and the metropole "to give up forever the trade with the Indies and accept in this area the pressures of the American *Consulados* and Merchants."[15]

Madrid authorities faced a dilemma whose solution could not long be postponed. Havana's most influential business group, supported by leading colonial officials there, had long argued for open and legitimized contact, albeit temporary, with U.S. and even English Caribbean ports. In opposition was the Cadiz establishment, which spoke for peninsular merchants operating at Veracruz, Mexico City, and elsewhere in the American colonies. For Madrid's civil servants, at the center of the empire, survival of the imperial trading system now required an acceptable, even if ambiguous, compromise: grudging acceptance of the colonies' potential for some autonomous decision making. There was, moreover, the danger of cumulative ad hoc decisions, such as granting a special license to Cabarrús and associates at Madrid seeking to freight neutral shipping to Montevideo and Callao or opening Cartagena or Havana (but no other colonial port) to neutral shipping.

At this juncture Madrid tapped experienced public functionaries like Hacienda Secretary Francisco de Saavedra, informed by colonial service as intendant of Venezuela.[16] Saavedra told Pedro Varela that only those "of limited information" counseled inaction ("the worst advice"), since no colony had stockpiled enough European imports to sustain suspension of trade with the metropole. Only a variety of measures might provide import needs: escorted convoys from peninsular ports, "neutralized" and neutral ships sailing from Spanish and foreign ports, and, "in cases of absolute necessity," recourse to nearby foreign Caribbean ports. Saavedra's experience in Venezuela had made him aware of Havana's unique capacity to supply itself in wartime. Spanish warships entering the Caribbean sooner or later touched there and could convoy merchant vessels; for that matter, Cuba was located near foreign islands, where supplies could be obtained, "as was done in the previous War against the British nation." Location, low costs, the availability of goods, and the possibility of high returns drew merchants in Spain's colonies to trade with foreign colonies. A perceptive and astute observer of Spain's Caribbean world, Saavedra conceded that foreign contacts, if handled prudently, could supplement Cuba's trade with the metropole. If they were not, he confessed, "as soon as the reins are loosened, constraints are no longer useful." In any event, postponing a decision would open the way to smuggling, which, "like an irresistible fluid, will flow everywhere and fill every vacuum."[17]

The order of Saavedra's recommendations reflected his sensitivity to Andalusia's dominant mercantile body, the Cadiz *consulado*. First of all, Madrid should advise Havana that measures were under way to supply imports and export its staples; second, warships would be assigned to convoy duty; and third, Spanish-owned merchandise could be shipped to Havana from peninsular and foreign ports in neutral ships—the germ of what became *comercio neutro*. But only in cases of "urgent need" were Havana officials to authorize ships to sail *from* Havana to foreign colonies for goods not supplied by merchants in the peninsula.[18] The logic and colonial experience of Saavedra and other former colonial officers probably persuaded Madrid in July 1797 to ratify the decision made in March by Cuba's Captain General Santa Clara and Intendant Valiente.

While Madrid had postponed a comprehensive ruling on the wartime trade of its American colonies in the hope that piecemeal concessions might palliate colonial interests, the government's financial situation worsened as colonial trade and general revenues fell after the declaration of war against England. The mid-1797 crisis and the subsequent decree of *comercio neutro* in November point up both the intersection of peninsular and colonial economies and the critical role of colonial revenues and trade flows to Spanish government finance. Historians of Spain and Spanish America have with few exceptions overlooked the interpenetration of imperial interests broadened and deepened by growth in the colonies at the end of the eighteenth century, a linkage dramatically highlighted by Madrid's budgetary deficits in the 1790s and by the perception of Madrid's officials that the colonies were fundamental to the survival of the metropole rather than appendages of Cadiz and its Andalusian hinterland.

Two currents flowed together to produce prosperity and even a sense of fiscal euphoria in peacetime but depressing penury in wartime. The first was colonial economic expansion, notably in New Spain's mining and Cuba's plantations, which, in turn, generated surplus revenues that were sent to the metropole. In two wars before 1797 (in 1779–83 and 1793–95) Mexico City's *consulado* had arranged "patriotic" loans netting the peninsula millions of *pesos fuertes*.[19] The second current consisted of New Spain's tax surpluses, derived from Indian head taxes, the tobacco excise, from mining and related activities (mercury sales, the 10 percent on refined silver, coinage fees), from sales taxes, and, most important, from customs duties. While a large percentage of the colony's average annual gross revenues were absorbed by salaries and other costs, the average annual net, or about 120 million to 200 million *reales de vellón,* sent to the peninsula represented by conservative estimate about 15–20 percent of total metropolitan revenues.[20] On balance, New Spain furnished two-thirds of all colonial silver sent to the metropole.[21] The flows of public and private income across the Atlantic from the American colonies had fortified Madrid's decision in 1781 to have the recently created Banco Nacional de San Carlos issue *vales reales,* interest-bearing, redeemable instruments negotiable in public and private operations in the metropole. Rising colonial revenues helped guarantee principal and interest payments on the public debt, while private income from America accruing to Cadiz and merchants in other peninsular ports could be tapped by the *vales.*[22]

Transatlantic income flows financed the two largest items of government budgetary allocations, outlays on the royal household and, rising steeply with the first "French" war, of 1793–95, defense allocations. Military expenditures pushed up the rate of annual deficits, so that over sixteen years, 1780–95, military outlays tripled the public debt.[23] To Charles IV's civil servants, the state of the treasury in 1797 was critical: international tension raised the level of defense expenditures, while government income depended upon reducing nonessential outlays and especially upon uninterrupted colonial trade and income flows. These factors help explain the formation of the Dirección del Fomento General within the Treasury in the 1790s, under whose direction an annual balance of trade was at last undertaken;[24] the state's involvement in publishing the trade journal *Correo Mercantil de España y sus Indias;* and the ability of the Hacienda to attract talent to posts vacated by such traditionalist personnel as Miguel de Múzquiz, Pedro López de Lerena, and Francisco Machado. Hence the appointment of capable men such as Gardoqui, Soler, Varela, Canga Argüelles, Saavedra, conde de Casa Valencia, and Pedro Aparici, as well as recourse to the advice of businessmen with government experience like Cabarrús and Aragorri. Deficits in wartime, the pursuit of cost-cutting, and fresh revenue sources sparked efforts to clarify with some precision the size and composition of the metropole's income. Financial reviews prepared from 1797 to 1808 provide some data (however incomplete and proximate) showing the Spanish government's total resource picture and the fundamental role of colonies in the decision on *comercio neutro* in November 1797.

One may gauge the importance of colonial remissions to imperial revenues by examining estimates of net colonial income registered on arrival in

Spain. There were boom years (1793–96), followed by a sharp contraction (1797), then another boom (1798–1804) and a second contraction (1805–6).[25] Another proximate gauge of the colonies' contribution to covering the metropolitan government's deficits from 1792 to 1808 indicates that of contributions from many sources of about 3,000 million *reales de vellón,* the colonies provided 28 percent.[26] How much colonial revenue actually entered Spain's Tesorería General demands further research, yet there is little doubt that colonial revenues remitted to Madrid's *caja principal* were siphoned off at Cadiz to meet a variety of pensioners' claims as well as interest due. The economist José Canga Argüelles once calculated that over the decade 1787–97, receipts from the fiscal category "Indias" in peacetime averaged 20 million *reales de vellón,* or less than 3 percent of total metropolitan revenues.[27] Curiously, Canga Argüelles's data elsewhere show larger shipments of precious metals to Spain in 1796–1806 from Veracruz alone.[28] Moreover, "Indias" funds registered at Madrid minimize the importance of colonial income, since all along the path from colonial treasuries (and even prior stages) to Madrid, deductions were made, legal and illegal. If the metropole appears to have profited minimally, one should not overlook people and interests perennially fattening at the colonial trough. There is no incompatibility between an underfinanced, anemic government and wealthy groups in society.

Fortunately, there is a careful preliminary analysis of the composition of the Madrid treasury's *(caja principal)* receipts at the end of the century that modifies the minimization of the role of colonial revenues and, more significant, measures the financial impact of the war with England that began in late 1796. Two categories of treasury receipts, "Indias" and remittances from the regional treasury of Cadiz, furnished at least 20 percent of total receipts over the period 1784–1805, the "single largest ultimate sources of Madrid income." Cadiz's revenues were generated mainly from customs duties and related taxes on colonial trade flows—a high proportion with Veracruz and Havana—and it is not surprising that over the same period Cadiz alone produced 61 percent of all remittances from Spain's regional treasuries.[29] War with England had an immediate impact. There followed a downward inflexion of Madrid's receipts precisely in categories based on colonial trade ("Cadiz," "Generales," and "Ejército"), contributing to the overall drop of 38 percent in the revenues of Madrid's *caja principal* from the thirteen-year peak of 1795 to 1797.[30] This shortfall exacerbated the cumulative deficit, substantiating the overview of government income and expenditures for 1783–90 assembled by Diego de Gardoqui in 1794, when he observed that in peacetime net government income barely covered ordinary expenditures; by 1797 war with England had cut off remissions from the colonies, leaving Spain "reduced to revenue from the peninsula . . . which made it impossible to satisfy the immense expenditures caused by war."[31] Once again Madrid had to find a solution to the problem of moving goods and revenue across the Atlantic between colonies and metropole despite ever more effective English blockaders.

The intersection of colonial trade and revenues with metropolitan government finance was obvious to Hacienda Secretary Saavedra[32] in late 1797, when he appointed a junta of businessmen (including the bankers Aragorri and Cabarrús) and public functionaries (Felipe Ignacio Canga Argüelles, Manuel Sixto Espinosa, and later Soler) with instructions to plan for financing "the defense . . . honor and . . . maintenance of the Monarchy" in order to meet the "unavoidable continuation of War." Cabarrús, raised at Bayonne, recalled to the junta recent policy failures in Bourbon France, where Louis XVI's timidity in demanding financial sacrifices from the public had provoked the "shocking revolution." Among the junta's range of proposals, a major recommendation was the imperative "bring funds from the Indies" by dispatching ships, especially to Veracruz. By conciliating merchants in the colonies, the government could tap the largest possible funds available, supplemented by issuing letters of credit *(libranzas)* on colonial treasuries to private individuals or privileged companies. Once again, to cite the astute secretary of the Veracruz *consulado,* Madrid was "blithely relying" on the silver mines of New Spain.[33]

Comercio Neutro: The Real Orden Circular of 1797

In April 1797 Saavedra had cautioned Pedro Varela that in handling the request of Havana's *consulado,* "not to permit cargo aboard neutral vessels coming from our ports and even foreign ones." Seven months later Madrid accepted the fact that continued special licensing was really a form of inaction, and drift the most dangerous policy. Now Saavedra had to countersign the Real Orden Circular of 17 November 1797, authorizing neutral ships to enter colonial ports. Appropriately, the circular's preamble cited peninsular and colonial demands as responsible for the decision: the petitions of merchants at Cadiz who were fearful of the long-term consequences of interrupted maritime trade with the colonies and Madrid's recognition that colonial exports of perishables were backing up, while the colonies lacked basic imports. These demands obliged the government to employ this "extraordinary resort," permitting shipments of nonprohibited goods in Spanish or foreign bottoms from neutral ports or from Spain as long as such vessels returned to Spanish ports *first;* temporarily suspended were the current requirements concerning the proportion of foreign to national goods carried. To lend the new policy a patina of precedent, the phrase "as was done in the War during 1779" was added.[34] To mollify shippers at peninsular ports, notably Barcelona, subsequent orders lowered export taxes along with colonial duties on their cargoes. Even the Vizcayan port of Bilbao was temporarily authorized to deal directly with the colonies.

Reference to 1779 camouflaged the innovative nature of the order of November 1797. The government, sensitive to resistance to innovations, had bypassed administrative procedures requiring the Consejo de Indias and the metropole's interest group most involved in colonial trade, Cadiz and its *consulado,* on the ground that royal authority in trade matters could be handled solely by the "crown" in secret consultation with the treasury— "personally by the King, who handles it through Hacienda," to cite the language of the Leyes de Indias—precisely as José de Gálvez had done with the Reglamento del Comercio Libre of 1778.[35]

Saavedra's ministry had accepted the petition of Havana's producer-exporters, who could now welcome neutral ships or proceed to the nearby English island of Jamaica to purchase ships and cargoes seized as prizes of war. Now the royal navy and merchant vessels, including those of neutrals, could carry back to Spain precious metals from its colonies to alleviate the government's liquidity problems. Yet the ministry still had to confront protest from the metropole's principal colonial interest group, the *consulado* at Cadiz, speaking for similar bodies overseas at Veracruz and Mexico City.

There was little delay. On 3 December the "consulado y comerciantes" of Cadiz formulated their protest *(representación)* to Hacienda Minister Saavedra requesting the revocation of *comercio neutro* and the discretionary powers of intendants overseas to allow imports of "the most needed goods" brought by neutral carriers. The petition skirted one rationale of the 17 November order, shortages in the colonies, but challenged another, petitions from dissident "varios Comerciantes" of Cadiz. These were "Españoles ingratos que sacrifiquen en sus . . . aras los derechos de su patria vendiendo sus nombres a nuestros implacables enemigos." It predicted that *comercio neutro* would benefit only the English, who would intercept neutral shipping and at the same time smuggle goods from their ports in the Caribbean.

Underlying the opposition of Cadiz was the mentality of its merchants and community, a blend of reality and mythmaking. The myth consisted of the imputed expenditures of the metropolitan government to protect the colonies, "enormous expenditures on its administration and defense"; the reality was that "a nation with colonies" could survive only by exercising "a monopoly trade." What it termed the "concesión" made on 17 November— really a step toward that "vague commercial liberty" popularized by a few political economists—was incompatible with the fundamental laws of the Spanish monarchy and the Spanish Atlantic system. The traditional mentality of Cadiz and indeed other metropolitan merchant bodies was made explicit: "It's the view of Commerce that foreigners should know nothing about the route to America" because a wartime concession would arouse foreigners' greed in peacetime. European maxims about "livertad mercantil" as the foundation of the "prosperity of trade" were rejected by "all good Spaniards" and should be kept from "the soil of America with great care."[36] Circumspectly, the Cadiz *consulado* did not criticize high officials at Madrid; rather it criticized the intendants of both Cuba and "Caracas."

Three weeks later Saavedra received the Cadiz protest and reaffirmed the government's position. Bowing to the inevitable, the *consulado* requested that cargo already ordered by Cadiz merchants and shipped from foreign ports to the colonies continue to pay the 1.5 percent duty assigned to the Cadiz *consulado* to reimburse a loan of 22 million *reales de vellón* advanced by merchants there for the war against France in 1793–95.[37]

Despite the government's effort to claim that the 17 November circular was merely following precedent, the Cadiz *consulado* had accurately perceived otherwise. A wartime expedient, and clearly incorporating elements of exception and privilege, it was now applied to the whole Spanish transatlantic system, not just one geographical sector. It was an overlay upon existing structures inevitably generating ambiguities that interest groups quickly exploited to their separate advantages and with contradictory outcomes—the fate of reform by expedient.

The preamble of the 17 November circular asserted that it was designed to help merchants of Spain. Did this mean Spaniards of the peninsula, Spaniards resident in the ports of western Europe, Spaniards domiciled in the American colonies *(españoles europeos),* or only Spaniards duly registered *(matriculado)* in Spain's *consulados*? Were neutral ports only those in Europe, or those in Europe *and* the Western Hemisphere, that is, in the United States and the Caribbean? Inviting ambiguity was the reference to goods shipped: did this cover *any* foreign merchandise, including goods normally prohibited to protect Spanish "manufacture"? Could Spanish-owned cargo seized at sea and recoverable by purchase as prize merchandise at England's Caribbean "free ports" of Kingston and Providence be imported into Spanish colonial ports? More critical was the possibility that ambiguities over what constituted legitimate cargo would attract smugglers in an already crowded field of commercial enterprise. Finally, since hostilities blocked European merchandise from moving directly from peninsular to colonial ports, could a colonial port holding a surplus of European imports introduced by neutral carriers re-export them to another colonial port? More specifically, could Havana, which had always imported European goods from peninsular ports and *from* Veracruz, now re-export them *to* Veracruz? Who would decide when a local "surplus" existed? Most critical, could Havana be permitted to become an entrepôt undermining the role of Cadiz and other peninsular ports as intermediaries in the Spanish transatlantic system?

To put the issue in another light, would the policy of *comercio libre,* transformed by wartime expedient into *comercio neutro,* inevitably become the much-resisted (and dreaded) *comercio directo* between foreign and colonial ports? And what would consequently be the lines of cleavage and aggregation as networks and alliances of commercial interests in Spain and the colonies formed, reformed, and crystallized? The range of fundamental issues generated by the 17 November circular is a measure of currents and countercurrents in colonial policy, which Madrid's officialdom would try to contain by compromise in the critical decade ending in 1808.

New Spain's Hegemony Challenged

Given the importance of New Spain's mining sector, the upsurge in production of Cuban sugar plantations, and the geopolitical importance of the Caribbean complex, inevitably the ambiguities, not to say contradictions, of *comercio neutro* surfaced at the ports of Havana and Veracruz and, by extension, pitted a cluster of interests in New Spain against those of Cuba. Yet not until midsummer of 1798, roughly nine months after promulgation of *comercio neutro,* did the repercussions of the modified economic policy seriously affect the interests of Veracruz.

Despite the inconclusive nature of statistical materials available and the viewpoints of bitterly antagonistic interest groups, it is possible to discern the economic situation of Veracruz during the first year of *comercio neutro.*[38] Two categories of factors shaped business conditions there and in the colony of New Spain as a whole. Among general factors was the mining of silver and gold, products that could be stored indefinitely for ultimate export.[39] Agricultural exportables such as cochineal, indigo, and jalap could tolerate extended storage time, while perishables such as flours and sugar could be redirected into the domestic market. In addition, two-thirds of the colony's consumers absorbed domestic woolen and cotton manufactures;

the remaining one-third was partly supplied with Asian silks, linens, and printed and unprinted cottons brought on the annual *nao de Filipinas,* in which Mexico City's *almaceneros* were heavily invested. As for alcoholic beverages, New Spain produced cane brandies *(chinguirito)* and, of course, pulque.

Equally essential for an understanding of the Veracruz situation are certain specific elements. Over the last quarter of the eighteenth century the colony's imports had soared impressively in iron and steel, beverages, olive oil, yard goods, and clothing. In 1792 Veracruz was the largest single destination of Spain's re-exports of European goods, including linens (33%), woolens (40%), and cottons (68%)—this, well before the great rage for East Indian and English printed cottons swept Latin America.⁴⁰ Once war with England began, shortages did occur in fine fabrics (muslins, *gazas, panas, cotonías,* silks and silk stockings), in wines and brandies, paper, cinnamon, almonds, and metallurgical products. Over the two-year period from 1797 to 1799, however, it was estimated that Veracruz's level of imports dropped roughly 60 percent, from 11–12 million *pesos fuertes* to 4 million; the decline in volume was probably greater. No doubt the shortage of metallurgical products (bar iron and steel) at the end of 1799 became critical, since supplies on hand were about two-thirds of annual consumption. As the secretary of the Veracruz *consulado* noted pessimistically, imports from Spain were "little more than zero" (about 500,000 *pesos fuertes*) but profitable for "those few with the good fortune to avoid the risks of navigation."⁴¹

On the other hand, the opportunity to invest earnings in low-tonnage vessels from Cadiz, the highly maneuverable *místicos,* which slipped through the net of English blockaders at Cadiz and Veracruz to unload insignificant amounts, made some *almaceneros* optimistic about future shipments from the peninsula in wartime. Merchants retained silver, awaiting what many hoped would be an immediate peace, and the general public refused to pay inflated prices lest peace lead to a flood of cheaper imports. Meanwhile, many merchants utilized their retained silver for short-term investment in local manufactures, in agricultural enterprises, and in internal trade. For many *almaceneros* it was a virtual return to *flota* times, when stocks of imports could be gradually liquidated over a two- to three-year period without the threat of unexpected cargo arrivals. It was, however, quite another matter for those disadvantaged by English blockaders and corsairs: Cadiz merchants with few or no contacts in Europe's neutral ports or in the United States and Veracruz *almaceneros,* whose stocks might be undercut by unpredictable shipments from neutral ports or, worse, by the inflow of re-exports from Havana's aggressive merchants.⁴²

In retrospect, it was inevitable that Havana's merchants would challenge Veracruz's hegemony over Spain's Caribbean ports in general and Havana in particular. The expansion of exchanges with Veracruz, and through that port to the market of New Spain's consumers, was fueled, first of all, by the influx of shipping from U.S. ports before and especially after 1793 and by exchanges with nearby English and French island ports. As we have seen, U.S. merchants habitually introduced European goods and flour barrels often packed with those manufactures. In any event, U.S. flours and corned beef consistently undersold comparable articles from Veracruz and Tampico, to the chagrin of New Spain's producers and exporters.

Far more important a stimulus to Cuba's growth were shipments of New Spain's silver from about 1765 on. Of the 159 million *pesos fuertes* dispatched after that date by Mexico City's treasury to Cuba and Spain, Cuba received more than 115 million, excluding a further 128 million that New Spain's merchants forwarded on their own account or those of clients. Some private funds represented payments to Cuba's exporters by Spaniards in the peninsula who were drawing upon their silver balances in New Spain to buy sugar for export to Cadiz and other Spanish ports. Havana's merchants induced the Madrid government to overrule Viceroy Branciforte, who in the 1790s had suspended silver exports on private account to Havana, and lower to 5.5 percent the export duty on silver destined for Havana consigned "to buy sugars for shipment to Europe." We must recall, on the other hand, that as late as the early 1790s Havana's merchants could not legally re-export European manufactures to New Spain, "lest they disadvantage *comercio directo* with Spain," while in 1799 Veracruz customs continued to reject imports of Cuban rum.[43]

By late 1798, however, it was virtually impossible for Veracruz to maintain intact its hegemony over the Spanish Caribbean. At Cadiz, a few firms, such as those of Domingo Terry, Torre Hermanos, Álvarez Campana, Guerra y Sobrino, and Bustamante y Compañía obtained special licenses *(gracias)* to ship to Havana and Caracas flour and other foods purchased at Baltimore and shipped in neutral vessels. Their access to capital, to influence at Madrid, and—the essential—to webs of international connections that small-scale Cadiz *cargadores* lacked enabled them to carry out Godoy's injunction to operate in wartime from neutral ports in Europe and North America. Even Madrid's Compañía de Seguros Marítimos y Terrestres petitioned Madrid for special licenses to ship cod to an agent at Mexico City, Joaquin de Quintana. Pressure to modify the Caribbean system also came from Veracruz firms—those of Lobo, González, Gutiérrez de Cubas, and Murphy y Porro—prepared to import from Baltimore via Havana. Murphy's

English contacts probably enabled him to obtain a special license authorizing his Havana agent, Santa Cruz, to proceed to Jamaica to buy prize ships and cargoes of such scarce items as mercury and stamped paper originally owned by the Spanish government; as part of the *gracia* Murphy would send one vessel monthly from Kingston to Veracruz with cargo and intelligence about English plans, blockaders, and related matters. Whether operations were controlled by Cadiz, Veracruz, or Havana, by late 1798 the port of Havana was emerging as a hub of commercial networks despite the stiffening opposition of merchants in their *consulados* at Cadiz, Veracruz, and Mexico City.

This is not to say that the Veracruz commercial community or its Cadiz counterpart unanimously opposed this development. One of the prominent traders emerging in Havana's commercial circles in the late 1790s was the merchant-banker Pedro Juan de Erice. Erice managed capital deposited with him for investment in Cuba's booming sugar economy; one may reasonably hypothesize that he also invested funds, his own as well as those from Veracruz, in sugar exports to Baltimore and elsewhere. His operations were multiple and complicated, and they typify the way Havana firms maximized opportunities in the Cuban sugar economy, in trade with New Spain, and in resorting to the United States as a neutral intermediary during the French revolutionary years and their Napoleonic sequel.[44]

In 1796, for example, Cuba's Captain General Santa Clara contracted with Diego Barri, of Baltimore, for 300,000 *pesos'* worth of provisions for an expected naval fleet at Puerto Rico. It is plausible that the initiative came from Erice, who had funds on deposit at Baltimore. Erice was asked to finance Barri's contract, so he used 40,000 *pesos* "that he had on deposit in others of those States" and an authorization to export from Havana 6,101 *bocoyes* (casks) of sugar payable in Spain "in silver specie." Thereafter the story becomes complicated. When Madrid rejected Santa Clara's contract, while authorizing *comercio neutro,* Erice countered by asking his Baltimore agent to use a local cover (ultimately, Diego Walker) to send an assortment of goods to Veracruz aboard the *Halcyon* on consignment to Pedro Miguel de Echeverría, Erice's correspondent there.

The assortment, carefully selected for the Mexican market and valued at 43,134 *pesos fuertes,* contained mainly woolens, linens, and cottons (49.5%) and Spanish wines and brandies (34%). Although Veracruz customs agents initially questioned its real ownership, the shipment was accepted because Erice, "as the result of services to the King . . . held in Baltimore 300,000 *pesos* when the circular of 17 November 1797 was issued." They dutied the shipment "as though it had left Spain, according to the tariff schedules of

1778 and 1782."[45] In effect, the arrangement substantiated a report from Madrid to Mexico City in April 1798 that Spanish-owned cargoes were leaving peninsular ports aboard neutral vessels destined for Veracruz "registered in a foreigner's name, outbound to neutral ports in America, to feign ownership." Clearly, Spanish-owned cargo was originating in neutral U.S. ports rather than in Spanish and neutral European ports, and Erice's example was repeated by other Havana traders, who ordered U.S. ships to come to Havana and transferred their cargoes (deliberately selected for Mexican consumers) to third parties, who then consigned them to the Veracruz merchants Echeverría, Felix de Aguirre, Murphy y Porro, González y Cubas, Francisco Antonio de la Sierra, and others.

The situation was sized up by the Havana merchant Pedro María Ramírez, who advised his Veracruz correspondent Felix de Aguirre in January 1799, "I have learned that several ships have been admitted at your Port with cargo from our possessions, such as Cartagena de Indias, La Guayra, and New Orleans, and also that an American frigate, a Danish schooner from Saint Thomas, and a brig from Hamburg, *La Providencia,* have departed from here and that recently there have arrived at Veracruz two brigs from Jamaica carrying valuable goods, including ironware, which have been unloaded. This development makes evident to me that [ports] have been opened up to every ship that arrives." Ramírez observed that despite the intentions of the 17 November order, "we have received no word of even one ship arriving under rules prescribed in the Reales Ordenes mentioned," since all vessels leaving Spain had been seized at sea. Logic and interest led him to conclude that since *comercio neutro* legislation permitted "any" Spanish vessel to proceed from foreign ports to Veracruz, "it seems reasonable to conclude that it is also without risk for a vessel to leave from here for Veracruz." Havana-based merchants were in fact seizing on legislative ambiguities ("all Spaniards" and "neutral ports") to manipulate the rules of the Spanish transatlantic system that proscribed shipments "unless direct from authorized ports of the Peninsula" and covered by *gracias,* that is, permitting shipments from Havana to Veracruz.[46]

Havana's trading interests were not alone in seizing upon advantages created by the metropolitan government's concession to expedience, nor could they hope to open a trade in European re-exports without the cooperation of Veracruz merchants. Erice's counterpart at Veracruz was Tomás Murphy, the active member of the Veracruz firm of Murphy y Porro. Tomás, it should be recalled, was one of the few merchants who had supported *comercio libre* extended to New Spain in 1789. Cadiz eyed such independent operators with suspicion; in early 1799 the official correspondence of the *consulado* there recorded the arrival from Málaga of "a Dn. Juan Murfi, brother of . . . the one resident at Veracruz," bound for Madrid and then Lisbon, there to board an American ship for "Nueva Inglaterra," where he planned to set up "a large trade" to Havana and Veracruz "jointly with his brother and others at Havana and elsewhere."[47]

The Murphys maximized their contacts, their grasp of the international commercial situation, and the gaps in the Spanish system opened by English blockade to arrange a network of correspondents at Hamburg, Baltimore, Havana, and the "free port" of Kingston in order to introduce European goods at Veracruz. There Tomás Murphy dealt with the like-minded merchants González y Cubas, Echeverría, and the *criollos* Juan Bautista Lobo and José Mariano Almanza, all members of the local *consulado*. At Havana Murphy called upon Erice and two *dependientes*, Clemente and Francisco Santa Cruz. Through Havana's captain general and intendant, Murphy managed to commission Clemente Santa Cruz to proceed to Kingston to buy prize ships and their cargoes, owned by Spain's Real Giro and originally shipped for sale to consumers in New Spain; in fact, Santa Cruz overfilled his quota of prize cargoes forwarded to Murphy at Veracruz. Appropriately, Santa Cruz employed letters of credit issued by the Murphys' prominent Hamburg correspondents (Brentano, Bovera y Urbieta) to cover the purchase of ships and cargoes at Kingston. Murphy and Erice shared optimism about the expanding colonial trade, they called upon each other's services, and with associates—contrary to a vociferous faction of merchants in the Veracruz *consulado*—they insisted upon the transfer of silver from Veracruz for investment at Havana.[48]

Havana versus Veracruz

Against this background of fissures in direct trade links between Cadiz and Veracruz, whose volume had expanded remarkably between 1789 and 1796, one may imagine the impact of a request to Viceroy Miguel de Azanza, at Mexico City, six months after the 17 November order, to legalize "direct trade, free and reciprocal," between Havana and Veracruz and open to "all Spaniards."[49] Ostensibly the initiative came from Joaquín de Quintana, then resident agent *(comisionado)* at Havana of a Madrid insurance group that had received a *gracia* to market cod in colonial ports and had arranged for neutral ships to carry goods from Hamburg to Havana and Veracruz under the terms of *comercio neutro*. Quintana was probably related to a prominent member of Havana's recently created *consulado*, Lorenzo de Quintana. On 3 July 1798 Joaquín de Quintana petitioned Mexico City authorities for special authorization for "all who might want to adopt this system" to re-export from Havana to Veracruz Spanish-made wines and brandies, as well as foreign-made cables, sailcloth, coarse cottons, brines, and sewing thread—goods permissible under the *comercio libre* of 1789.⁵⁰ He also wanted to export from Veracruz copper, lead, sugar, and duty-free coined silver.

Quintana's initiative was noteworthy in light of a publication then circulating at Havana, *Reflexiones sobre las nuevas relaciones de comercio que forzosamente se han de establecer entre la isla de Cuba y el reyno de Nueva España*. His initiative was further magnified by the unambiguous support of Francisco Arango y Parreño, the Havana-born lawyer well traveled in the Caribbean, the United States, and western Europe and a key figure in Havana's *ayuntamiento, consulado,* and political elite. He seconded Quintana's petition with a report issued under the auspices of Havana's *consulado* that articulated the economic vision of Havana's business classes. New Spain, ran his argument, lacked imports because of the interrupted shipping between Spain's ports and the American colonies, while Havana was overstocked. Havana, therefore, had more justification than foreigners to ship to Veracruz under such conditions. Arango urged New Spain's Viceroy Azanza to grant the petition, "so that once this Island has turned into the warehouse of the American empire and a channel to its riches, they will pour out over the states of the united provinces of the northern part, permitting *habaneros* to profit handsomely at the end of the day." In other words, acting in behalf of "brothers" in New Spain, Havana would have the satisfaction of protecting New Spain from contact with foreigners. To shocked officials of Veracruz's *consulado,* Arango and the Havana corporate body had presented "a petition novel in the annals of Spanish commerce in America" by applying "the pressure of commercial liberty." If Azanza granted Quintana's petition, Havana would become, to quote Veracruz's complaint, the "depository of America's riches: Mexico, Peru, and the whole mainland would consider it the central place for their enterprises; and the United States of North America, like a New Cadiz, formed for its prosperity, rising amid the ruins of Old Cadiz."⁵¹ Simply put, modifying the ongoing system spelled disaster.

This acrimonious observation by the Veracruz *consulado*'s secretary-treasurer José Donato de Austria mirrored the reaction of other members to the aggressiveness of Havana's planters and merchants in their phase of economic expansion.⁵² Arango's vision of his city as a "general warehouse" competing for Veracruz's commercial hegemony in the Caribbean was not taken lightly. He was no minor official, no hired propagandist; rather, he spoke for Cuba's *criollo* interests, who were committed to growth through agricultural rather than mining exports.

Arango's credentials as the *criollo* spokesman for Havana's business establishment were impeccable. In 1680 a grandfather had come to Havana from Navarre (Sangüesa) as a treasury officer and married a *criolla,* Josefa de Losa y Aparicio. One son (Miguel Ciriaco) had married a *criolla* (Juliana Margarieta Parreño y Espinosa), daughter of the Cadiz-born army officer Julián Parreño y Montalvo; their son, Francisco Arango y Parreño (b. 1765), was thereby related to a prestigious Cuban planter family of the late eighteenth century, the condes de Montalvo; from his uncle, Arango inherited an honorary *regiduría* of Havana's town council. In 1788, at the age of twenty-three, Arango was already the *ayuntamiento*'s agent at Madrid, and in 1789 he was admitted to the bar there.[53] He advised the government's Consejo de Estado about Cuban planters' aspiration for a "free trade in blacks," their interest in the expansion of their agricultural exports, and the establishment of a *consulado* (he was appointed its first *síndico*).

Like New Spain's Francisco Xavier Gamboa in the 1760s, Arango was a born representative of dominant Cuban interests as planter and publicist, lobbyist at court and bureaucrat. Where Gamboa had served New Spain's mine owners and the Mexico City merchant guild, Arango defended Cuba's planters, their merchant associates, export agriculture, and the slave trade. Like the Veracruz *consulado*'s Basadre and Austria, Arango was a physiocrat on Spain's colonial frontier; but where Basadre and Austria envisioned a future flourishing export agriculture, Arango was defending its Cuban reality. He accepted Raynal's concept of the maturing colonial world through the bowdlerized Spanish translation by Carlos Martinez de Irujo, chargé d'affaires at Philadelphia in the 1790s, who issued licenses to U.S. exporters of flours and European merchandise trading with Havana. In the early 1790s Arango planned a joint reconnaissance trip with a cousin, Montalvo, to England and France, to return via their Caribbean colonies in order to learn how to improve Cuba's sugar economy through new refining techniques and wider distribution of the processed product; no doubt it was with tongue in cheek that he proposed to visit Saint-Domingue as a *contrabandista.* One outcome of this reconnaissance was his recommendation that the Spanish government permit the full refining of sugar in Cuba.

In 1796, on behalf of Havana's *consulado,* which was pressuring Madrid to permit duty-free exports of silver from Veracruz to Havana for purchasing Cuban sugar, Arango questioned the government's long-held fixation on silver and gold mining in New Spain. He pointed out that silver passed through few hands and required little shipping, while "the products traded stimulate agriculture and industry, increase population, utilize much cargo space." Silver had no multiplier effect; his was the voice of late-developing colonies on the periphery of the Spanish empire, counterpoises to the mining colonies of New Spain and Peru. In fact, in 1796 probably Arango had written Hacienda Minister Gardoqui in a typically physiocratic vein that "the time has passed when the trade in silver was held to be the most profitable."[54] By contrast, he observed, industrial goods constituted the "real wealth of States," and Spain's misfortune was precisely the inability to settle its balance of trade with domestic production. A wide-eyed physiocrat recognizing the interrelation between agriculture and commerce, Arango warmly supported Joaquín de Quintana's proposal that *all* Spanish subjects participate in Havana's re-export trade to Veracruz. Because Veracruz officials followed a rigid interpretation of who could participate in *comercio neutro,* non-Spaniards leaving Havana or "unknown ports" could enter Veracruz without suspicion of fraud, while residents from Spain's colonial ports automatically came under suspicion. Such contradictions were shocking—"A foreigner can do what is prohibited to a Havanero"—and he insisted that the spirit, if not the letter, of *comercio neutro* of 1797 was designed to benefit Spain's citizens, "never foreigners." When the Cadiz *consulado*'s Havana agent, Azcárate, noted that "*Hacendados* form the most influential faction in [this] City," he was no doubt thinking of Arango y Parreño as their spokesman.[55]

Quintana's petition and the supporting material prepared by Arango for the Havana *consulado* were addressed to New Spain's recently appointed viceroy, Miguel de Azanza, an army officer and former diplomat who had served in New Spain and Cuba and was connected by birth and marriage to residents of Mexico City and Veracruz. Like an uncle, Martín de Alegría, a civil servant first at Havana and then Veracruz, Azanza was from Aoiz, in Navarre's Valle de Bastán, a traditional transport route from Béarn, in southwestern France, over the Pyrenees to Pamplona. At Havana were well-established Navarrese families like the Aróstegui, who by the 1740s were invested in the slave trade, tobacco, and sugar. Navarrese contacts with Béarn, which surfaced in the early development of Cuba's export economy, may have forged a cosmopolitan conspectus of Spain's colonial trade and an awareness of its physiocratic potential, in contrast to the mentality of *montañeses* and *encartados* flocking to New Spain in the second half of the eighteenth century to exploit mines and native peoples.

Azanza began his career as a young officer attached to José de Gálvez's expedition to California; he then continued in Cuba before returning to

Spain and service in Europe and Spain. As captain general of Valencia, he earned praise from that city's merchant guild for initiating a review of local trade regulations and convening a junta to oversee exports and related matters. Posted to the colony of New Spain in 1798 to replace Viceroy Branciforte, who was uncritically responsive to the interests of Mexico City businessmen, Azanza found there a number of distant as well as near relatives—the merchants Juan José Alegría and Ysidro de Lezaur, the widow of his uncle Martín de Alegría, Lorenza Yöldi, and her four children, who were Azanza's cross-cousins *(primos hermanos)*. He married one daughter, María Josefa (widow of the conde de la Contramina), through whose sister, Manuela, who married Tomás Murphy at Veracruz, Azanza was related as *concuñado* to that prime mover of Veracruz's trade with Havana and neutral ports in America and Europe. His viceregal staff included the bureaucrats Francisco Guillén, Manuel de la Bodega, and Miguel Bachiller, and one of his principal channels to the influential Mexico City merchant community was Diego de Ágreda.[56]

Prior colonial service, contacts with the commercial communities of Mexico City and Veracruz, and his enlightened perception of the role of foreign trade in the economies of New Spain, Cuba, and their metropole sensitized Azanza to the gravity of the controversy over *comercio neutro* and intercolonial trade between Havana and Veracruz.[57] In his words, "Since I arrived in this Kingdom it has been debated whether during the present War the prohibition on bringing to this country legally accepted European goods from other ports of Spanish America" to end shortages, to lower import prices, and "revive its sluggish economy." Before deciding, he had opted cautiously for sounding out "public opinion and the thoughts of corporate bodies and persons interested in this prohibitive measure." The flood of contradictory opinions—as he put it, "differing interests . . . absence of learning of some, while others pay no attention to the extraordinary events of the day"—explain his final dispositions about Quintana's request.[58]

The opposition of the Veracruz *consulado* was rapidly formulated by a commission of two men, Juan Felipe Laurnaga and Vicente Basadre, appointed by the *consulado*'s Junta Extraordinaria. Basadre's role suggests that he had the confidence of Veracruz supporters. At the root of Basadre and Laurnaga's reasoning lay the conviction that New Spain constituted a unique trading zone specifically isolated from an article of the *comercio libre* legislation of 1778 authorizing re-exports of European goods from one colonial port to another. Further, they recalled, Saavedra had admitted in December 1797, in the course of justifying *comercio neutro,* that he had found more hurdles in opening colonial ports to contact with foreign ports in America than in opening them to contact with ports in Europe. The fundamental consideration was how to assess the impact of New Spain's supply shortages, high price levels, smuggling, and the accumulation of sugar, indigo, and cochineal stocks. They noted that *místicos* could elude English patrols at Cadiz, they were optimistic about the imminent arrival of *místicos* from other Spanish ports, and they worried about the effects of the rapidly spread news of the 1797 circular on *comercio neutro*. "The rumors circulating were so many and so public that they could be overlooked only by those residing in some remote Indian hamlet, but it is incredible that some inhabitants of this and other large cities of the Kingdom ignore them, since this capital is so commerce-oriented and anxiously awaits news and ships arriving at Veracruz . . . announced by Proclamation and reported in the Gazettes."[59]

Laurnaga and Basadre found shortages of basic imports—iron, steel, paper, olive oil, almonds, cinnamon—much exaggerated. And shifting consumer preferences rather than real shortages were the main cause of price increases after the outbreak of hostilities. "Rarely does one favor what is scarce; instead one chooses items that are most accessible and profitable or offer the possibility of hope and progress." Yes, there was smuggling (they used the euphemism *clandestinidad*) but this occurred in muslins, woolens, *pañuelos, cotonías,* stockings, and other stylish cottons, which were smuggled regardless of stocks on hand. Smuggling was no real sign of shortage; rather, it indicated an entrepreneurial spirit. "A man, always eager to improve his luck, better his fate, and increase his fortune and wealth, encounters no danger he cannot overcome, no difficulty he cannot conquer . . . the greater the drive behind his interest, the more extraordinary and effective his efforts." Havana's merchants were not interested in exchanging textiles for New Spain's sugars; they would accept payment solely in silver, cochineal, tin, or copper. Were Havana permitted to re-export to Veracruz, the "English Americans," through Havana, would try to capture New Spain's trade, flood New Spain's markets, take away in exchange only the most valuable products, and undermine the metropole's manufacture and trade. From this analysis flowed their recommendation to Viceroy Azanza: since ships from the peninsula and Europe's neutral ports were already entering Veracruz, "we find no basis for opening free and reciprocal trade with Havana."[60] They were convinced that Veracruz merchants would forsake temporary advantages "for the general good of the nation, which ought and must take precedence in our esteem." Other documents from the Veracruz *consulado* expanded on the threat posed by Havana's petition, noting that since Havana's re-exports to Veracruz came from England on U.S. ships, England—"oppressor of liberty of trade"—would indirectly dominate the "powerful and wealthy Mexican empire."[61]

Additional and unsolicited support for Veracruz's position came from the resident agent of Cadiz's *consulado,* Francisco Antonio de la Torre, a relative of the influential Veracruz merchant José Ignacio de la Torre. Torre felt impelled, as an agent and a "patriot," to advise Azanza that the petition of Havana's merchants and planters would be disastrous for both the trade with Spain and "felicidad pública." It was more appropriate for loyal colonies to bear some financial loss to support their metropole, "which created and sustains them." In fact, Havana was ineligible for handling neutral shipping from the United States, since *comercio neutro* (1797–99) had legalized only "direct commerce via neutrals in Europe handling Spanish accounts," that is, of *peninsular* Spaniards. Through Torre's correspondence, Cadiz had learned of Havana's initiative and the resistance of the Veracruz and Mexico City *consulados,* and it complained to Madrid authorities that Havana's proposal would stimulate in New Spain "desires and appetites in those who have known how to lack luxuries or willingly pay current prices for them." In defense of self-interest, the Cadiz *consulado*'s prose could show brutal candor.[62]

Viceroy Azanza also sought an opinion from a key administrative body in the colonial capital, the Real Hacienda. Its *fiscal,* Lorenzo Hernández de Alba, fully shared the preoccupation of the *consulados* of Mexico and Cadiz that Havana might become "the general Warehouse, the emporium of these Americas . . . at the cost of ruining Spain's trade." Since peninsular shippers were more heavily involved in trade with Veracruz than in trade with any other colonial port, Alba emphasized, to permit Havana to re-export to Veracruz would dishearten the merchants of Cadiz, Barcelona, and other peninsular ports trading with New Spain and attracted by the "lure and attraction of [its] riches." It would be tantamount to "shutting the [ports] of Spain."[63]

The position of the influential *consulados* of Veracruz and Mexico City, formalized by Laurnaga and the Veracruz *consulado*'s secretary, Basadre, and fortified by the opinion of Mexico City's *fiscal* Hernández de Alba, would seem to furnish convincing ground for rejecting Havana's proposal. Oddly enough, however, supporting Havana were a Veracruz merchant and *consulado* officer (Miguel Ignacio de Miranda), the *consulado*'s *síndico* (Genaro Garza), the Oaxaca merchants' deputies to the Veracruz *consulado,* and two Hacienda officials at Veracruz.

Miranda, a resident of Veracruz since 1778, a supporter of a *consulado* there and an early *consul,* a friend of one of the few *criollo* merchants at Veracruz (José Mariano de Almansa), was the sole dissenting voice of support for Havana's position at a *junta extraordinaria.* In principle, Miranda wrote, there should be neither commercial exchanges with foreigners nor reexports of European imports between colonial ports. There were moments, however, when reality trumped principle, and this was why Madrid had authorized *comercio neutro* in November 1797 over the protests of both Cadiz and Barcelona, partly to facilitate New Spain's exports aboard neutral ships, few of which had yet come to Veracruz. It was imperative for New Spain to import textiles and clothing, to control smuggling and the illegal outflow of silver. Miranda recommended to Viceroy Azanza that he authorize exchanges between Veracruz and Havana with suitable controls: that 75 percent by value of all imports from Havana consist of agricultural products, the balance in silver, restraints also proposed by *síndico* Garza. It is plausible that Miranda spoke for more circumspect Veracruz merchants, for the *consulado's síndico,* Genaro Garza, for the deputies of Oaxaca's merchants, and for the two Hacienda officials at the port.

Garza shared with Miranda a physiocratic preoccupation with colonial stockpiles of sugar, cochineal, indigo, and hides in periods of war at sea; these were products that deteriorated, a major factor in the promulgation of *comercio neutro.* English squadrons blockading colonial ports had already forced the retention of "two or more harvests of all its products subject, unlike others, to wastage and spoilage." The greater the shortage of imports, the greater the smuggling, and Garza joined Arango in insisting on accepting imports from non-Spanish ports. He recommended accepting all categories of textiles up to the value of 2–3 million *pesos,* which was roughly equal to estimated value of annual smuggling. Convinced that only Havana "offers at this moment everything to alleviate these inhabitants," he recommended aggregate duties of 32 percent on all imports (actually, the level when processed through ports in Spain), including textiles from non-English sources, and on basic commodities such as iron, steel, and stamped and cigarette papers. His final recommendation seconded that of Miranda: 75 percent of the value of what Havana would export to Veracruz must consist of agricultural products.[64]

Divided views concerning Havana's desire for "reciprocal" exchanges with Veracruz were also mirrored in the annual reports and supplementary observations by the *consulado's* two appointed officials, Secretary Basadre and Treasurer Austria. Basadre's annual reports virtually ignored the issue, although his view appeared indirectly in the report he drafted with Laurnaga. More revealing of the aspirations of a large section of the Veracruz merchant community, and more pointed in discussing fissions within it, were the annual supplementary "noticias y reflexiones" sent by Austria to Hacienda Minister Soler in 1799 and 1800, where he elaborated on the statistical materials he had organized for Basadre's annual reports. There is no doubt that Viceroy Azanza, given his connections to the Veracruz merchant community, was aware of Austria's perceptions.

Austria's "Noticias y Reflexiones"

In commenting on Veracruz's external trade in 1799, Austria suspected that the Havana merchants' petition was driven mainly by the possibility of expanded exchanges with Veracruz and to a lesser extent by the arrival of neutral vessels from European ports. On the whole, ships from Europe had introduced an insignificant volume of imports; the overriding threat was that Havana might become the *almacén general* (general warehouse) of the American colonies and, especially during hostilities, the "depositary of American riches." Stating that Spain's American colonies were differentiated by economic function and diversity was his way of underscoring New Spain's unique role in the Caribbean. For that colony held a hegemonic position ("raises its noble and majestic head above the multitude of countries under Spanish dominion") and could be relied upon to remain "ever faithful, ever submissive and grateful to her Metropole." This was why it rejected the prospect of trading with foreigners ("makes no plans to develop trade with foreigners").[65]

Austria would impose limits on Havana's re-exports, since New Spain's mines and staples could support its role as submetropole for Spain's colonies in and around the Caribbean. In wartime its output of manufactures expanded, although its cottons and woolens could not compete in peacetime with imported European textiles. Production of agricultural exportables, namely, dyes, flour, and dried beef for Havana, was promising. While Europe, in his view, enjoyed virtually free trade in grain, Spanish producers monopolized markets in the colonies, avoiding, of course, "monopoly, oppression, or unjustified prohibition"; only under special wartime conditions should the colonies substitute grains from the metropole. New Spain could perform this role with respect to Cuba, Santo Domingo, Puerto Rico, Louisiana, Maracaibo, and Caracas, "which induce considerable annual consumption." The problem was that the expansion of New Spain's already "impressive grain harvests" required better roads between Perote and Veracruz.

As a colonialist civil servant, economic reporter, and physiocrat, Austria ranked agriculture ahead of manufacture in New Spain. Growth in manufacture drew upon large reserves of native peoples seeking employment in Mexico City and Puebla, but they were difficult to control. On the other hand, agriculture would continue to draw manpower and produce goods that, along with locally produced coarse woolens, could be traded with nearby Spanish colonies. Overall, New Spain as submetropole would advantage Spain, whose trade would expand wherever there existed "more people, agriculture, and wealth, precisely the role of New Spain."

Austria was more than an inflexible physiocrat on the colonial frontier at "the World's richest canal," Veracruz. He had an appreciation for both the pervasive structures of silver mining in the colonial economy and the imaginative way some merchants of Mexico City and Veracruz employed earnings from mercantile operations. For instance, he claimed that no longer did the colony's merchants consider silver "the only or principal item of exchange for the products in the trade with the Metropole"; because of current price levels of colonial staples, merchants often remitted their payments to peninsular creditors in that form. By locally investing silver that ultimately was remitted to Spain, merchants supported the price level of New Spain's staples and financed contracts between merchants and growers for future harvests. In the case of sugar destined for export, some had been converted into *aguardiente* to substitute the customary Catalan brandy imports. Speculators also forwarded silver to Havana and Venezuela to purchase staples for export once hostilities ended. This innovative employment of New Spain's silver explained why blockade and shortages stimulated the economy of some nearby colonies, while Cuba and Venezuela ("Caracas") "consider themselves ruined once their navigation and trade with the Metropole are cut."

These colonies were far less favored than New Spain. "Habana" and "Caracas" growers, despite cultivation of "the most fertile and fortunate lands of the New World," failed to profit by wartime trade with the French, Danish, Swedish, or "Anglo-American" traders entering their ports. Non-Spaniards arriving at the ports of Havana, La Guayra, and Maracaibo, Austria found, imposed unfavorable terms of trade by overpricing manufactures and underpricing exports, further proof that trading with non-Spaniards was "by its nature self-seeking and destructive to the Spanish countries . . . because since they have no control over them, they don't view them in the same way." Here Austria saw the unique role of silver-producing New Spain in the economy of Spain's Caribbean and circum-Caribbean possessions. Since at least 66 percent of New Spain's exports by value were silver, while other colonies provided only export staples, New Spain's merchants could invest *pesos* in purchasing their staples at equitable prices, finance their agricultural operations, even supply foodstuffs. The pattern of Veracruz's exchanges with Cuba and Venezuela supported Austria's statistics and argument: New Spain had imparted to "the agriculture, trade, and navigation of these important possessions an increase and energy quite visible in the nation's trade Balance." Havana, he pointedly observed, could not pay for its imports without New Spain's silver.

From this conspectus of New Spain's key function in the economic structure of the Spanish Caribbean flowed Austria's recommendations. First, he would accept Havana's re-exports to Veracruz provided that regulations under *comercio neutro* were rigorously enforced, particularly those concerning proof of Spanish ownership of cargo aboard neutral ships. Second, under no circumstances should metropolitan authorities allow a "foreign" nation—obviously the United States—to dominate the Caribbean flour trade; shortages should be met only by those Spanish colonies "able to substitute the Metropole in this trade," a clear allusion to New Spain. Most important, non-Spaniards should not participate in the reciprocal trade of Spanish America under Spain's "system of exclusion," whether by tolerating smuggling or by special licenses (here labeled "particulares concesiones").

In sum, informing Austria's analysis and recommendations was his interpretation of pre 1797 trade patterns and their future projection. At the core of his conception of New Spain's hegemonic role was the expectation that its merchants would repatriate a proportion of earnings in the form of exportables of Havana and other colonies. Commenting on operations in 1798, he observed that the English blockade had led many merchants to withhold silver shipments to Havana and Venezuela. In February 1800 he expressed disappointment that Veracruz's exchanges in the previous year had been dominated by residents of Havana generating a deficit on current account. As a result, silver exports to Havana had risen sharply despite the objection of the Veracruz *consulado*. In Austria's judgment, there were no grounds for opposition; otherwise, silver would be smuggled out, something he considered a "recourse unfortunately widely used."[66]

Austria's annual "noticias y reflexiones"—actually supplements to his annual statistical compilations—were prepared for Veracruz *consulado* officials and the membership. In 1799 his observations encountered criticism from many *consulado* members. In a personal note to Hacienda Minister Soler in February 1800, he alluded to the tension splitting the Veracruz merchant community, which was affecting his performance and his work satisfaction. Measures such as neutral trade, adopted to circumvent wartime dislocation of the Spanish commercial system, had set the colonial administration ("the political body") at Veracruz against the general body of merchants ("the commercial body"), generating "discussion . . . representations . . . complaints, projects, and discord." It was, he felt, a critical moment: implementation of changing colonial trade policy required "the collection of political and economic knowledge" to achieve well-considered decisions on how to preserve Spain's transatlantic system. Yet could there be balanced decisions, he asked almost rhetorically, when the Veracruz *consulado* lacked a strong agricultural interest-group representation? Besides, he ranked himself a mere employee of a mercantile body in a city "puramente mercantil" whose leading citizens talked only trade and used one standard of judgment: "All goes well when there is profit. All goes badly when there is loss." When he introduced a more nuanced view, he found himself arguing point by point with the *consulado*'s officers. Especially bitter was the review of Veracruz's trade performance for the year 1799, when he had to defend the outflow of silver to Havana. Henceforth, he confessed to Soler, he would avoid personal observations and confine himself to the data in order to avoid "arguments with people I must meet daily."[67]

Austria's revelation to Soler of policy divisions at Veracruz, which Tomás Murphy or other merchants of Veracruz or Mexico City probably passed along to Viceroy Azanza, helps account for Azanza's cautious pursuit of opinions held by colonial officials and merchants after August 1798. Azanza relied upon his *asesor general comisionado,* Manuel de la Bodega y La Cuadra y Mollinedo, to select informed opinions and evaluate them. Bodega was a sound choice: he knew well both the colonial and metropolitan worlds of business and bureaucracy. A *criollo* from Lima and son of a family of colonial officials, he had attended Lima's university and then the University of Alcalá in Spain, where he studied under Lizana y Beaumont (subsequently archbishop and viceroy of New Spain), then competed for a chair at the University of Toledo. In 1786 he was designated *oidor* on the Audiencia of Guatemala (he also managed the mint there), and six years later he moved to Mexico City, where he was *oidor, fiscal del crímen,* and then *asesor general* in Azanza's secretariat.[68] As Azanza noted, Bodega counseled him on resolving interrelated and nettlesome issues stemming from New Spain's unique role in the structure of the Spanish Atlantic's commercial system and the local impact of the ambiguous phrasing of *comercio neutro* of 1797, which had led to Havana's petition.

Azanza proceeded to settle the issue of neutral shipping from neutral ports entering Veracruz bearing cargo properly certified as Spanish-owned in late November 1798. Few neutral vessels from European ports had managed to slip past English blockaders after November 1797; only neutral U.S.

ships had made an appearance.[69] He reported shortages of essential imports, widespread commercial speculation, and smuggling "along the coasts . . . almost out of control, lured by big profits." Since the 1797 decree did not exclude neutral shipping from U.S. ports, he did not feel authorized to stop what seemed a legitimate trade as long as the ship's cargo contained normally permitted goods, its ownership was indisputably Spanish, and its manifest *(registro)* of cargo and carrier was in order. Azanza understood that this put him at odds with members of the Cadiz, Veracruz, and Mexico City merchant communities. Later, in defending his cautious acceptance of U.S. vessels at Veracruz from the heated criticism of local merchants, notably José Ignacio de la Torre, a *montañés* merchant closely related to the Cadiz community, Azanza recorded pointedly (as Austria had also recorded) the "grumbling of ordinary people and the affected complaints of those who could only express their feeling because they lacked needed opportunities to obtain the profits they hankered after."[70]

On the collateral and controversial issue of Havana's proposed re-export trade to Veracruz, Azanza sidestepped further confrontation, again following Bodega's counsel. Bodega had briefly referred to his prior support for Azanza's resolution accepting neutral U.S. vessels, intimating that Havana's petition ran counter to the "extraordinary, appropriate measures" from Madrid about Spain's overseas trade in wartime. Now, however, Bodega recommended that the dossier of contestatory opinions be shipped off to Madrid for review—in effect denying Havana's petition—because of the gravity of the issue and because of his realization that at Veracruz "it's not easy to fully convince respectable people and corporate bodies opposing the petition."[71] Azanza accepted this counsel without modification on 27 March 1799; he could hardly ignore the undercurrent of opposition within New Spain and elsewhere, which was too influential to antagonize. In a matter of weeks, however, the whole problem of *comercio neutro,* its ambiguities and the pressure from Havana to exploit them *seemed* settled when Madrid recalled the troublesome circular on *comercio neutro* on 20 April 1799.

Why *comercio neutro* was recalled is open to conjecture. In November 1797 the preamble to *comercio neutro* had rationalized Madrid's action by referring vaguely to pressure from unnamed Cadiz merchants seeking to minimize the effects of interrupted trade with the colonies in America. Seventeen months later, in April 1799, the rationalization for its recall stipulated that *comercio neutro*'s formalities had been circumvented by "Spaniards themselves" to the benefit of English manufacture and trade.[72] Was this an allusion to statutory ambiguities improperly exploited by the same Spanish interests that Madrid had intended to protect? One point is evident: Madrid avoided publicizing metropolitan and colonial pressure groups as principal factors in its reversal. Equally evident is the fact that recall was not the work of a new ministerial group bent on policy changes. Successive prime ministers in the years 1792–1800—Godoy, Saavedra, and Urquijo—had concurred on the vital role of colonial trade and how to handle it in wartime, as did treasury ministers Saavedra from November 1797 to September 1798 and Soler after that. Saavedra, a key figure who had doubled briefly as prime minister and Hacienda secretary, resigned both posts because of serious illness, not because his policies were rejected. Since the initiators of *comercio neutro,* Havana's export interests, never abandoned demands for trade with the United States, circumstantial evidence leads to the conclusion that the combined efforts of the merchant corporations of Mexico City, Veracruz, and Cadiz were principally responsible for the recall of *comercio neutro* in April 1799.[73]

There are no ambiguities about Cadiz's role as a metropolitan pressure group. Only days after news of the recall, officers of Cadiz's *consulado* wrote their Madrid agent, conde de Casa Rábago, that with the help of the former viceroy of New Spain, Branciforte, their lobbying had been so successful that "the wishes of commerce are fully satisfied."[74] Later, official correspondence referred unambiguously to the "shameful intriguing" of Cadiz in pressuring the ministry to reverse itself.[75] Other sources suggest that major commercial firms at Cadiz—those of Simón de Ágreda, Nicolás Badillo, Juan Francisco de Vea Murguía, and Bartolomé de Alzásua—may have conveniently provided short-term loans when the Madrid authorities badly needed them in 1798.[76] One may conclude that by early 1799 Hacienda Minister Soler had decided that a major concession had to be made to Cadiz merchants in view of their colonial interests, the "advances our trade, navigation, and agriculture in the colonies must make" once hostilities with England ceased, and Madrid's hope of tapping the silver balances of merchants in major colonial ports in the form of more loans, interest-free.[77]

On initial examination, the order of November 1797 authorizing neutral trade appears to have been another stage in the Bourbon policy of trade reform or adjustment characteristic of the previous thirty-year era of Charles III. In this view, opening the Caribbean to contact with many peninsular ports, rather than solely with Cadiz, in 1765 and then its extension to most of the South American colonies in 1778 and finally to New Spain and Venezuela in 1789 seem logical antecedents that the royal order of 1797 merely elaborated. On closer examination, however, that order was a marked innovation in response to the deepening crisis in the Spanish Atlantic.

First, for eighteen months it authorized neutral ships from Europe and

America to enter Spanish colonial ports from which those vessels had hitherto been barred; while Madrid continued to dispense special licenses, they were no longer the core of the new policy. Second, that so innovative a stratagem was adopted illustrates the desperate, unprecedented dependence of the metropolitan government's finances upon colonial trade and income. This is not to minimize Havana's initiative in 1796, yet one must recall the depth of Madrid's financial crisis in 1797, when the government of Charles IV confronted rising deficits and the falling value of its treasury notes *(vales reales)*. Support of the *vales* was a primary consideration, if not *the* primary consideration, in authorizing neutral trade. In this sense too the order of 1797 was indeed innovative, for it showed that as during the eighteenth century, henceforth in a war in the Atlantic against England some device would be needed to utilize neutrals as intermediaries between Spain and its American colonies. Here was a foretaste of the involved stratagems of public and private contracts employed by Godoy, Hacienda Minister Soler, and the director of the Caja de Consolidación, Manuel Sixto Espinosa, between 1804 and 1808, which, like the order of 1797, embittered traditional commercial interests in Spain's transatlantic trade system, with dramatic results in 1808.

Third, the order was de facto recognition that New Spain's hegemony over the Spanish Caribbean, based on silver, was now in question. A critical phase in colonial economic growth had begun, and somehow a degree of autonomy had to be granted to insistent planter interests in Cuba. Here too the innovative nature of the order becomes manifest: it confirmed Cuba's regular trade contacts with U.S. Atlantic ports, maintained despite the recall of neutral trade in 1799, since the port of Havana remained open to U.S. shipping through a variety of devices that continued to threaten New Spain's hegemony.[78] And finally, the success of the *consulados* of Cadiz,[79] Veracruz, and Mexico City in forcing Madrid to rescind its order of 1797 revealed a commercial bourgeoisie on the peninsula's periphery unwilling to adapt to the changing structures of the Atlantic economy.

Postscript to the Controversy: Foronda versus Cerdán

There are, in fact, reasons to believe that Havana's aggressive export interests had inspired publication of an anonymous pamphlet drafted "por un Español, en Philadelphia" in October 1799 and, significantly, printed simultaneously in Spanish and English (at Philadelphia) in 1799 and in English (at London) in 1800. Informed, skillfully presented, candid, the ably crafted pamphlet justified *comercio neutro,* sharply criticized the lobbyists of

Cadiz for misinforming Madrid's officials and demanding the recall of *comercio neutro,* and, perhaps more notable, offered an exposition of the importance of export agriculture in colonial economies. Appropriate to the Philadelphia context, the Spanish version stressed "comercio," while the English version, more revealing of the author's thesis, focused on agriculture and trade. Both editions were targeted at audiences in Europe and America: the *Reflexiones sobre el comercio . . . en tiempo de guerra,* enhanced by blending fact and opinion, quickly surfaced in the Caribbean area and was contested by the regent of Guatemala's *audiencia* in the same year.[80]

The pamphlet marked the ascendance of physiocracy on the colonial periphery, for the anonymous author introduced a wealth of details about agrarian conditions in both Cuba and Venezuela.[81] Publicizing a bitter internal debate over imperial policy might, however, endanger the career of even the most loyal Spanish civil servant, particularly when the critique targeted influential merchant corporations at the metropole's major ports, Cadiz, Barcelona, and Santander. Anonymity in this instance was more than a literary device; it was a technique of sheer survival. The anonymous author was probably the Spanish diplomat and political economist Valentín de Foronda y González de Echávarri, then serving at Philadelphia as consul general under Chargé d'affaires Carlos Martínez de Irujo, whose post Foronda subsequently filled from 1801 to 1809. One should not exclude Irujo as a possible author.

Foronda's family roots on both his maternal and paternal sides were in Álava, and he was born at Vitoria, where his mother's family had been established for at least two generations. His parents were Alavés gentry.[82] Early in his career he joined the Basque economic society—the Real Sociedad Vascongada de los Amigos del País—and devoted himself to economic issues, supporting the Compañía de Filipinas's use of silver earned in America to buy luxury goods in Asia for sale in the Spanish colonies and Europe; advertising the benefits of the Banco de San Carlos to the metropolitan and colonial trades and—a major issue—the primacy of agriculture and trade in economic development. "Without commerce there can be no thriving agriculture and industry; and without agriculture, industry, or commerce men will be idle," he wrote.[83] His warm support for the Banco Nacional de San Carlos probably led some to tab him as the "gran protegido" of Bayonne-born Francisco Cabarrús, ideator of the national bank.[84] In political economy his preferences were clear: he contrasted enlightened groups ("a few people endowed with insight, at the same time full of the majestic concept of the liberty of commerce . . . open enemies of any exclusive privileges, of anything smelling of monopoly") with traditionalists ("peasantlike mentalities horrified by every new project").[85] In 1787, to be sure, these beliefs found support at the highest levels at Madrid—from Floridablanca, Gálvez, and Campomanes.

Like many Basques of his generation, Foronda was drawn to French models, experience of economic growth, and physiocratic preoccupation, as confirmed by his residence in the United States in the late 1790s.[86] There and via reports from Cuba and Venezuela entering Philadelphia through its extensive Caribbean trade, he was aware of agricultural expansion in the colonies and the need to curb constraints maintained by governmental and private-sector interests in the metropole.[87] This is confirmed by an epigraph from Adam Smith, that "apóstol de la economía política," in the printed English version of the "Reflexiones"—*Observations*—on commercial profits "often impolitically obtained" to the detriment of agriculture, and by Foronda's cautionary conclusion that citizens of the United States "shook off at last the yoke of the Metropole because of innumerable restrictions imposed by the Government bowing to Great Britain's merchants and craftsmen."[88]

Foronda was stationed at Philadelphia, one must recall, in an era of rapid commercial expansion, when U.S. merchants were forming great fortunes on the basis of U.S. neutrality during war in the Atlantic between the world's two great naval powers and neutral U.S. cargo vessels could operate in what was one of the world's major economic (also war) zones, the Caribbean and the Gulf of Mexico.[89] Understandably, he was troubled by what he knew and what he continued to learn about Spain's merchants and their contrast with the high-risk propensities of U.S. merchants forwarding cargo everywhere despite the "risk of encountering well-stocked Markets"—smuggling everywhere "in our Americas." He was impressed by the absence of tight governmental controls over domestic trade in the United States, where he observed few customs personnel ever ready to intervene, Spanish style, with the words, "Hold on, gentlemen . . . I want to search you . . . I want to put my hands in your pockets—pay so much on departing—so much on entering—where are your waybills?" At Philadelphia he sensed, and perhaps exaggerated, a kind of implicit trust between importers and customs personnel, as well as swift execution of justice; sworn cargo manifests were generally accepted without question, but if fraud were suspected, inspection quickly followed, goods were confiscated, and the perjured merchant brought quickly to trial.[90]

Foronda's "Reflexiones" illuminate the transformation of a Basque political economist and public intellectual, from a protagonist of Spanish merchants clustered at Cadiz, Barcelona, and Santander and of Spain's imperial trading system to a confirmed physiocrat at a time when Spain's colonies in America producing agricultural exportables were seriously challenging the hegemony of colonial silver producers.[91] Whereas once, like Cabarrús, he had considered merchants a dynamic element, now he perceived them as inimical to the Spanish economy. He faulted those merchants receiving "privilegios" detrimental to the mercantile body as a whole because their "protección exclusiva" disadvantaged agricultural and manufacturing interests. In any case, neither category deserved government intervention when "comercio nacional" could not supply basic needs and in fact operated as a monopoly.[92] "I will only state in passing that eight or ten commercial houses at Cadiz were in fact the masters of Spanish trade from the Floridas to the Californias and that in loadings in Spain, sales in Americas, and remissions to the Peninsula, one discerned only one ruinous chain of a very scandalous monopoly." After all, those merchant houses had deliberately misinformed Madrid officials by insisting that *comercio neutro* was the source of "widespread harm." Were those merchants really pursuing the national interest, he asked rhetorically? "No; your God is gold, the goal of your efforts, proven by the fact that shortages satisfy you and abundance saddens." Merchants in Spain's colonial trades, he concluded, aim to amass in four to six years a fortune unattainable "by a commerce of moderate profits spread over 15 or 20 years." And when government officials, "full of good intentions," relied upon merchant guilds—he really meant the Cadiz *consulado*—for impartial advice on commercial policy, the *consulados* "through ignorance or the sordid designs of self-interest disfigure or alter truth." Cadiz's misleading advice had led Madrid to revoke *comercio neutro* on the ground that "since Spaniards themselves had taken particular advantage [of *comercio neutro*], it had turned into general harm . . . and the growth of their enemies' industry and commerce."[93]

Not that Foronda believed that the influence of Spain's merchants on civil servants' decision making was unique. Even where agricultural growth had been impressive, as in France or especially in England, whose agricultural and industrial production were even more impressive, commercial interests sought to perpetuate in the colonies countless government controls. In England this "blind favoritism toward merchants and craftsmen"— aggravated by tea duties, the absence of parliamentary representation, and other irritants inscribed in "la Declaración de la Independencia"—had led George III to lose "the best jewels in his Crown."[94] On the contrary, Louis XVI's ministers in 1784 had barely avoided a similar disaster by opening four free ports in the French West Indies to permit "neutral" shipping to bring provisions and lumber and to export staples. French merchants at the ports of Nantes, La Rochelle, Le Havre, Bordeaux, and Marseilles had prophesized disaster: "Prophets, who invariably surface at moments of calamity like mushrooms after rain, prognosticated the collapse of the trade of France." They resembled, Foronda cleverly inserted, those Spanish doctors "when Madrid was cleaned up" in the time of Esquilache or the Cadiz merchants when *comercio libre* appeared in 1778. The French government had settled the controversy skillfully by inviting public debate, leading to a "war of quill pushers" in which French planters in the colonies demonstrated convincingly the adverse effects of merchants' monopoly. The outcome: "Public opinion backed the colonists," persuading the government to open four Caribbean ports to neutral carriers introducing animals on the hoof, wood products, and many varieties of provisions in return for certain staples. As a result, France's plantation colonies, Foronda concluded accurately, were never as prosperous as in the years just before the Revolution.[95] Foronda's analogue with the Havana-Veracruz situation was a close fit.

By contrast, even in wartime Spanish merchants insisted that they could maintain contact with the colonial ports, reflecting the fact that "Merchants will promise everything." In fact, few if any Spanish ships managed to elude the English blockade in the western Atlantic, which was maintained by fourteen warships supplemented by corsairs based at Nova Scotia, Bermuda, Providence, Jamaica, and Trinidad—"an active swarm galvanized by greed"—patrolling a vast area from Trinidad to the Chesapeake. Consequently Havana, Veracruz, and La Guayra found their warehouses overstocked with exportables whose prices fell; their economies stagnant, they were desperate for imports of "clothing, linens, shoes, liquors," while everywhere there were signs of "hunger, nudity, depression, and neglect of valuable crops." Meanwhile, self-serving Spanish merchants insisted that the situation was otherwise, while Foronda's sources ("disinterested channels") reported that the "partial and passing liberty" provided by *comercio neutro* had briefly turned around the colonial trade situation. To cite cases, Foronda pointed out that Havana's harbor had quickly filled with neutral ships mostly from the United States, the volume of imports rose, and the prices of exports were bid up by competition among buyers. Since few neutral vessels managed to get through to Veracruz, smuggling flourished there. Meanwhile, responding to news of shortages in Spain's American colonies, the English government opened Jamaica and Providence to Spanish-registry vessels, even furnishing passports and convoy protection. A Philadelphia merchant mentioned to Foronda that on a single day he had seen seventeen Spanish ships leave the port of Providence under English naval escort and that on most Sundays one could see Spanish flags fluttering in the harbor.

This reality had been distorted by merchants (unnamed) who had "taken advantage of the Good Will of the ministry to obtain the latest Real Orden [April 1799]," closing colonial ports to neutrals on the excuse that foreign exporters of their colonial staples were detrimental to Spanish trade. Would it not be more appropriate, Foronda proposed, to remind them that "to follow the same principle, you ought to complain that foreigners carry away the wines and brandy of Catalonia, the fruits of Valencia, the linen, esparto, soda, and ash of Murcia, the raisins, almonds, and wines of Málaga, the oranges and fruits of Seville, the wines of Jerez, and other products in the vicinity of Cadiz"?[96]

In the same ironic tone, Foronda raised the issue vexing Havana's merchants in the 1790s: if Spanish merchants could ship goods from peninsular to colonial ports, why, then, were Havana's merchants prohibited from dispatching *their* vessels to peninsular ports or, for that matter, to Veracruz? This one-way monopoly in wartime ("a destructive monster"), he insinuated, could on occasion net peninsular merchants profits of 200 percent or more. Insurance on ship and cargo (including superprofits) covered full loss by capture at sea; if the cargo arrived safely, returns on sales at the import-starved harbors of Havana or Veracruz must be equally profitable. "So that whether or not his Ship arrives at a Port, the merchant earns in any case a secure, considerable profit."[97]

Foronda's "Reflexiones" concluded with predictable recommendations inspired by his appreciation of the unexpected and promising dynamism of export agriculture in Spain's American colonies, tempered by disasters foretold to "nuestras posecieones" as long as remnants of the "gothic edifice of our traditional colonial trade" survived: uncontrolled smuggling on a scale worse, Foronda recalled, than that once described by Bryan Edwards,[98] even the independence of the colonies. All major colonial ports, Foronda urged, should immediately be reopened to neutral shipping, with no English goods to be imported except "Negros" and English-made agricultural equipment—revealing exceptions. All major colonial ports should include a flat 33 percent duty on imports and a 10 percent duty on exports; however, Spanish merchants should be privileged, paying only 5 percent on imports and nothing on exports of colonial staples.[99]

Foronda signed his pamphlet "Amicus Plato, sed magis Amica Veritas," and the candid accuracy of his analysis, together with the repercussion of its distribution, touched off an immediate counteranalysis by the leading official *(regente)* of Guatemala's *audiencia,* Ambrosio Cerdán de Landa Simón Pontero.[100] The revocation in mid-1799 of *comercio neutro*—Madrid's unplanned response to an unexpected colonial crisis—had metamorphosed into a serious threat to Spain's Caribbean trade and by extension to its transatlantic system of exchange with its colonies.

By 1800 Cerdán was a veteran of a quarter-century of colonial service. Presumably a Gálvez appointee to a *fiscalía* on Chile's *audiencia* (1776), he had been posted next to Lima (1779), where he served as *alcalde del crimen* and then as *oidor* (1784) of its *audiencia*. His ability to conciliate interests (or get along with the influential ones) brought him a promotion to *regente* to the Audiencia of Guatemala and entry into the Orden de Carlos III (1794).[101] Cerdán's upward career mobility suggests a civil-service personality adroitly tuned to interest groups and accommodating to one of the best financed, most prestigious, and most politically powerful in the colonial world—merchant guilds, in Cerdán's case the *consulados* of Lima, Guatemala City, and Veracruz. There is no reason to question his sensitivity to the conservative stance of Guatemala's recently established *consulado* or to the views of the Veracruz commercial community, whose members handled Guatemala's external trade. Guatemala City's merchants barely tolerated a colleague, Juan Bautista Irisarri, who had secured from Madrid a special license to import shipments of food and textiles from Baltimore and Philadelphia via Veracruz under *comercio neutro*. By his own admission, Cerdán as chief officer of the *audiencia* had collaborated with local *consulado* members, the *alcabala* administration, and "a few Spanish consignees" to block Irisarri's operation; more to the point, in the cargo of neutral U.S. ships bearing Irisarri's shipments from Philadelphia were copies of Foronda's *folleto,* the *Reflexiones.* To Cerdán, Irisarri's activities epitomized the "abusos" by merchants "greedy to obtain an exclusive, fraudulent trade in this America," who were only too eager to exploit *comercio neutro* to import goods underselling those of peninsular exporters at Cadiz, which consequently had to be sold with "losses in the value of their cargo caused by the unavoidable competition of foreign goods." He backed this critique with a report about two low-tonnage vessels from Cadiz, a ketch and a bark, that had entered Guatemala's port of Omoa, where "they found to their disappointment . . . the schooner *Hannah* with a sizeable cargo from Baltimore: the schooner having returned later to the same port with another, similar cargo."[102]

Cerdán's "Apuntamientos en defensa de la Real Orden de 20 de Abril de 1799" reveals a high colonial civil servant conversant with eighteenth-century French publications on political economy who was nationalistic, anti-Gallican, and Hispanically xenophobic and whose immediate reaction was predictable: "I tried to carry out my duty by trying to recall it." Setting his tone were early asides claiming that the printed version, *Reflexiones . . . por un español en Filadelfia,* must have drawn inspiration from "suspect anti-Spanish sources, like General Huet [*sic*], Montesquieu, Voltaire, Coyer, and the Amis des Hommes," from the anonymous *Historia, o descripción general de los intereses del Comercio;* that they could hardly have been written by Spain's chargé d'affaires at Philadelphia [Carlos Martínez de Irujo].[103] Like most high-placed colonial officials, Cerdán was conversant with English and French analyses of flaws in Spain's transatlantic commercial system, which he detected in Foronda's references to "monopolio" and to his criticism of "the unjust pretensions of monopolistic merchants, or of a dozen greedy speculators in our ports."[104]

Six years of colonial service in a zone buffeted by new Caribbean commercial currents rendered *regente* Cerdán critical of Havana's mushrooming role in the area's trade, although he was by no means a sophisticated political economist. This is evident in his approach to Havana and Veracruz. References in the recall of *comercio neutro* in 1799 to trade *abusos* by Spaniards, Cerdán claimed, were really directed at Havana ("one of the Spanish possessions that have committed the most abuses"), which was becoming "a universal supplier of the Americas" because of cargo, mainly re-exports of English products, introduced by ships from the United States. Thanks, however, to the Veracruz *consulado*'s "zealous and repeated representations," New Spain's viceregal authorities had avoided Havana's "contagious" example by rejecting the "dangerous efforts" of Cuban exporters to re-export to Veracruz goods brought on U.S. merchant vessels. Here Cerdán followed the strict interpretation of *comercio neutro* voiced by the *montañés* faction of Veracruz merchants, led by José Ignacio de la Torre, to the effect that *comercio neutro* legislation had authorized Spanish and neutral shipping to depart *only* from ports in Spain or neutral Europe, since "it was never planned in the Americas to have *comercio directo* with foreigners," which, once permitted, could not be readily reversed. Left standing, "the most carefully guarded foundations of the government of the Spains" would be seriously eroded.[105]

Having shifted blame for the shortcomings of *comercio neutro* from peninsular to Havana merchants and to their unpatriotic rush to obtain goods from English sources, Cerdán questioned Foronda's evidence of economic crisis in the Spanish colonies after 1797. He sketched conditions in New Spain without introducing fresh data. In that colony as elsewhere in the New World, import substitution by "provisional workshops" had produced a broad range of European-style products acceptable to colonial consumers, who rejected, he asserted, expensive imports in favor of cheaper "varied, attractive, and in no way crude provincial manufactures." As for the role of shippers in neutral U.S. ports, whom Foronda had considered basic to the Spanish colonies at the time, Cerdán reasoned that their merchandise must consist of English-made goods (the United States lacked factories, he noted); they—not Spaniards—profited because U.S.-introduced goods undersold whatever shipments from the peninsula managed to elude the English blockade.[106]

The principles undergirding Cerdán's "Apuntamientos" illustrate his identification with supporters of the Spanish version of a colonial pact and foreshadow the ultraconservative rejection of subsequent efforts to adjust the metropole's trade monopoly to rapidly shifting patterns in the Atlantic. In his words, "One of the most important pieces of Public Law" among the nations of Europe was the right to fasten "exclusive trade" on their colonies "without . . . foreign exchanges." The colonial pact was integral to international law, and smugglers contravening it deserved the death penalty, "confiscation of property and loss of merchandise."[107] "Liberty of trade" in Cerdán's view meant abundant supplies of wares and goods produced in Europe and entering "our Indies" through legitimate channels, through multiple peninsular ports ("the trade of Spain"), which he viewed as a "general point for unloading the products of the industry of Europe, or as a public good in which the other nations can participate." Trade monopoly, however enshrined in law, was, he ruefully acknowledged, ignored in practice. Spain's transatlantic system could be undermined by Havana officials, who tolerated the export of the island's "valuable products" directly to non-Spanish ports, just as it had already been weakened under *comercio neutro* by their deliberate misinterpretation of Madrid's policy. The *Reflexiones* was evidently a "subversive" publication in that it endorsed "liberty and systems of commerce among foreign countries it characterized as more liberal." And by extension, Havana's policy was equally subversive, since it would separate the colonies from their metropole, sundering "that mysterious tie linking their brotherhood and dependence."[108]

Cerdán and Foronda hoped to sustain trade between metropole and colonies, but their commonalty ended there. Cerdán, a colonial civil servant of the old school, would prohibit in war as in peace trade by the colonies with carriers from neutral "Anglo-American" ports such as Philadelphia or Baltimore trafficking in goods of the English enemy or with merchants at the enemy ports of Providence and Kingston. In his view, inevitably such exchanges would put colonial elites on the road to independence. This reasoning clarifies the virulence of Cerdán's critique of Foronda's pragmatic toleration in wartime of English trade and sea power in the Caribbean and of his reference to "the example of the United States shaking off the yoke of their Metropole because of the innumerable restrictions imposed upon them by the English government," yielding to pressure from its merchants and craftsmen. Whether he knew it or not, Cerdán was convinced that Foronda was subverting the established order. Cerdán's references to England and the English in the Caribbean were legion: Foronda's *Reflexiones* was probably the handiwork of "sly English, or their close friends and brothers, the Anglo-Americans"; England manipulated *comercio neutro* "in order to redouble its maritime forces . . . and its attraction for some unhappy and greedy Spaniards to realize an exclusive and fraudulent commerce" and then advertised that trade between Jamaica and the Spanish colonies was "one of its richest and most valuable," protected by its royal navy. In fact, Cerdán denied that serious import shortages existed in the first case, but if they did, loyal colonials would tolerate them "with humble obedience." In the event, Madrid could not tolerate trade "by illegitimate channels, destructive of the State's basic laws, as well as open trade with foreigners."[109] This position was supported at Veracruz by its *consulado*'s secretary, Austria, who took a different tack: Havana's situation ("the main point of the Reflexiones") differed from that of the other colonies in America, since New Spain, Peru, Buenos Aires, and Chile "are resource-rich countries that hardly need anything from Europe."[110]

Were Cerdán and fellow traditionalists like Austria delusional? Did they believe in a "mysterious tie" of brotherhood and dependence binding the empire together in this major crisis of the Spanish Atlantic system? Cerdán put his faith in a short maritime conflict with England, after which Spain might return to its modified "old system" as of 1797. Colonial trade policy shaped by Floridablanca and Gálvez had by now been absorbed by Cadiz, Barcelona, and Santander; however, public discussion of the policy under somewhat relaxed censorship in the late 1780s was muffled by Floridablanca's reaction to terrorism in neighboring France after 1789. What public discussion there was of flexibility in economic policy was focused on the metropole, not the colonial world. The "gothic edifice," Cerdán would argue, was still sustainable if the advice of most metropolitan and colonial authorities were followed and the *comercio neutro* experiment under former colonial officers like Francisco Saavedra properly closed down.

Was Foronda's *Reflexiones* also delusional? Its merits suggest otherwise. First, he challenged publicly—albeit anonymously, probably with the tacit approval of his superior at Philadelphia, Carlos Martínez de Irujo, translator and editor of a studiedly sanitized *Wealth of Nations*—the consensus in the metropole. Second, he shifted the spotlight overseas to the Caribbean core of Spain's Atlantic system, to silver mines and sugar plantations, to

New Spain and its rising competitor, Cuba. He also forecast—his third point—that under a more flexible trade policy, revenues could rise to cover foreseeable metropolitan defense outlays that the "edificio gótico" could not. Fourth was his physiocratic orientation: he fused observation of the development of Philadelphia's agricultural near hinterland with the French government's support of Saint-Domingue's sugar planters, who opposed "merchants at the seaports" of France and opened the French islands to neutral traders bringing foodstuffs and carrying away a growing volume of colonial staples. Foronda saw agriculture and trade, physiocracy and commerce, as the fundament of the Spanish Caribbean's prosperity. The major threat to his vision of Spain's Caribbean development—Foronda's fifth and perhaps keenest analytical insight—was the increasing ability of the English navy and corsairs to sustain a blockade in a *long* war, severing Spain's transatlantic lifeline to its colonies. In reality he skirted a kind of Hobson's choice: return to the gothic edifice of transatlantic trade and irrepressible smuggling spearheaded by English and/or "Anglo-American" collaborators or resurrect *comercio neutro* with a few limitations.

Foronda's *folleto* in Spanish and English, printed at Philadelphia and London, and its rapid diffusion throughout the Caribbean had reopened a debate that would take decades, even bloodshed, to resolve.

After *Comercio Neutro:* Viceroy Azanza's Dilemma

Cerdán's unambiguous attempt to label Havana merchants' operations under *comercio neutro* as "a misuse" and "subversive" may have convinced some that its recall within two years was merited. This should not, however, obscure the fact that officials at Madrid and Havana continued to rely upon neutral U.S. intermediaries to supply Cuba and New Spain through special licenses to selected merchants; French ambassador Guillemardet commented that the licenses were a thin disguise for allowing the colonies to import English merchandise.[111] Necessity, in other words, forced the Spanish state to rely upon mechanisms of privilege inherent in an old regime and thereby subverted its commercial system, contributing to schisms at major ports like Cadiz, Havana, and Veracruz. From May to September 1798, precisely when *comercio neutro* equalized opportunity for all "Spaniards" to use neutral ships to supply the American colonies, Madrid was *secretly* issuing such licenses to Cadiz firms or individuals in their networks, to the conde de Casa Flores, Miguel López, and to Menéndez, Conde y Compañía.[112] The latter claimed that the war had caused them losses of 2 million *reales;* that further losses would undermine the firm's "reputación y crédito"; and that to stabilize its position, it needed a *permiso* to export to Veracruz "or any convenient port in America" twenty thousand *quintales* of cod shipped from U.S. ports in Spanish or neutral ships.[113] More special licenses materialized for the purchase of prize cargoes in neutral or English ports: a *permiso* issued to Juan Domingo de la Torre to buy "goods taken from prizes" at Lisbon for shipment to his brother at Veracruz, José Ignacio de la Torre; one to Tomás Murphy at Veracruz ("married to one of Azanza's cousins") authorizing him to send a representative to Kingston to purchase a prize cargo. The Cadiz *consulado* complained immediately that special licenses were responsible for an upsurge in direct trade with the English, that "all privileged are true monopolists," whose privilege undermined the equal protection of the law that covered those carrying "the most cargo and . . . commercial liberty."[114] As the Cadiz agent of the Veracruz merchant Antonio de la Torre pointed out, *permisos* undermined Spain's trade with the colonies, since "the English and American colonists will absorb all the trade of New Spain through Havana."[115]

Two *gracias* to the conde de Casa Flores (José Antonio Flores) in May 1798, which were renewed with modifications in 1799, illustrate graphically the symbiosis between colonial trade monopoly for all Spaniards ("livertad mercantil") and favoritism ("privilegio"), characteristic of the old regime. Equally characteristic was the government's resorting to traditional devices to counter threats to its Atlantic pipeline. Casa Flores's *gracias* also show how patronage and privilege connected monarchy to the upwardly mobile and newly titled nobility of military or mercantile background. Manuel Antonio Flores, José Antonio's father, served first in Pedro de Ceballos's military expedition to the Rio de la Plata in the 1770s later as New Spain's viceroy in the 1880s before retiring to Madrid. Young Casa Flores was born in Buenos Aires and married a *criolla* daughter of the wealthy and prominent *montañés* merchant Gabriel Gutiérrez de Terán in Mexico City. The marriage integrated Casa Flores into a geographically dispersed *montañés* network of merchants tying Mexico City and Manila (Gutiérrez de Terán and Alonso de Terán), Veracruz and Oaxaca (Torre, Muñóz), Cadiz and Santander (Bustamante y Compañía, Bustamante Parientes). Birth and marriage alliance, residence in Mexico City and, in the 1790s, a post in the Guards of the Royal Household—"Brigadier de los Reales Ejércitos y Mayordomo de Semana de la Real Casa de SM"—all singularly equipped Casa Flores to manipulate levers of patronage and friendship to exploit profit possibilities in the Spanish empire's wealthiest colony in America.[116]

In April 1798 Casa Flores, probably in concert with Francisco Bustamante y Guerra ("rich and reputable merchant"), who was lobbying for him at the royal *sitio* at Aranjuez, petitioned Prime Minister Saavedra (then also Hacienda minister) for a *permiso,* claiming that war with England was harming his trade operations and that he had helped finance the "American" unit of the Royal Guards. Implicit was his hope that the *permiso* would let him take advantage of shortages in New Spain. Specifically, he sought two licenses, one to export three hundred tons of staples from Veracruz aboard a neutral vessel to a neutral port, the other to ship from Acapulco to Manila and then on to the Far East three hundred thousand *pesos fuertes.* Both licenses would exempt cargo from all duties. Informal pressure was evident in a personal covering note to "my friend" Saavedra asking him to handle his petition promptly so that he might "use the Mail to America at the end of this month" to inform his associates at Veracruz and Mexico City and insinuating that Saavedra knew that the queen "has been the support and protector of my parents and me, as is well known." Saavedra handled the petition expeditiously, for in a matter of weeks the government authorized the *permiso,* specifying that the neutral vessel from Veracruz might sail only to "Santander or any other authorized Port of the Península." Kept from public notice, as Viceroy Azanza was alerted, was the fact that the cargo would in fact go directly to "the ports of neutral or allied Powers" and that the viceroy, "to avoid publicizing and stimulating others to petition for similar *gracias* currently conceded to an unprecedented degree," should send the ship's manifests directly to the Hacienda at Madrid "instead of addressing customs officers in the regular way."[117]

Such subterfuge could hardly escape the intelligence network of the Cadiz *consulado* and its overseas correspondents. On 19 April 1799 the U.S.-registered frigate *Ocean,* chartered by Casa Flores's partner at Cadiz, Francisco Bustamante y Guerra, departed Veracruz ostensibly for Santander but really for New York, with cargo valued at two hundred thousand *pesos* consisting of three hundred tons of cochineal and indigo, *purga de Jalapa,* Guayaquil cocoa, Tabasco pepper, raw cotton, hides, and Campeche wood. Casa Flores's share was sixty tons of cargo; the balance was in the account of other exporters. The *montañés* network was efficient: Azanza advised Madrid that the *Ocean*'s cargo would be transshipped by James Cramond, in New York, to Thomas Fleetwood, the London agent of Bustamante y Compañía of Cadiz, in association with the London firm of Thelluson Brothers.[118]

In early June 1799 Casa Flores went over the head of Saavedra's replacement at the Hacienda, Miguel Antonio Soler, directly to Charles IV to seek more *permisos.* He claimed that inadequate funds at his disposition at the port of Veracruz had reduced his first *gracia* to 60 instead of 300 tons of exports; worse, suspension of *comercio neutro* on 20 April (one day after the *Ocean* left Veracruz) nullified any further use of neutral shipping. He now petitioned Charles to order Viceroy Azanza, "as an extraordinary and special concession" despite the recent suspension of *comercio neutro,* to permit Casa Flores to ship from Veracruz the balance of 240 tons of staples duty free, in neutral ships to a neutral port. In addition, he appended a supplementary request to import at Veracruz, also free of duty, 240 tons of cargo aboard a neutral ship "from any port of a friendly or neutral power, as the case may be"; this request was quickly rejected.[119] Nonetheless, Casa Flores returned to Charles and Maria Luísa in July with a modified petition: duty-free exports of 200 tons consisting of "Spanish and foreign goods" valued at five hundred thousand *pesos fuertes* shipped from Spain to Veracruz in a Spanish-registry vessel.[120]

Shortly thereafter, Casa Flores had to decide whether he wanted the exemption from export duties at Cadiz or Veracruz. He delayed for time, "because he did not have the needed information to make an appropriate choice," in order to confer with his *apoderado* and "the head of the affair," Francisco Bustamante y Guerra, who advised him to choose duty-free exports from Cadiz and to insist that the Cadiz shipment be registered "on the invoices and manifests . . . in the name of someone else, but not his." The second *gracia,* with these clauses, was authorized on 5 November.[121] These concessions to royal favorites like Casa Flores who were really fronting for merchants like Bustamante y Guerra and associates at Cadiz amply justified the outrage of the Cadiz *consulado* at the duplicity of imperial policy. Casa Flores and Bustamante went to court subsequently to settle a quarrel over the disposition of the profits generated by the two licenses.[122]

Casa Flores and Bustamante y Guerra, working the levers of patronage at Madrid to bypass constraints imposed by Madrid's fluctuating trade policy, were matched by Havana-based groups.[123] The operations of the Havana merchants Luís Beltrán Gonet and Pedro María de Aguirre, the Baltimore commission agent *(consignatario)* John Hollins, and the Veracruz merchants Félix de Aguirre and Murphy y Porro exemplify efforts in the Caribbean to punch loopholes in that policy. A resident Spanish merchant of Havana, Beltrán had accumulated a balance of 40,000 *pesos* with Hollins, probably the return on sugar shipped by Murphy y Porro from Veracruz or purchased with their funds on deposit at Havana. Beltrán asked Hollins to send an assortment ("clothing, wines, crystal, goods appropriate for that Kingdom") aboard the U.S.-registry frigates *Felicity* and *Hen.* Meanwhile, it was reported at Havana that Spanish-registry vessels from Cartagena de Indias, La Guayra, New Orleans, and Jamaica, not to mention U.S. and

Danish ships from Saint Thomas, were unloading at Veracruz, where no ship from Spain or neutral European ports had arrived since November 1797. This information led another Havana merchant, Pedro Maria Ramírez, to buy Beltrán's shipment and forward it to his agent at Veracruz, his *paisano* Felix de Aguirre, since, Ramírez gloated, "they have opened [Veracruz] to whatever arrives." Ramírez offered his own interpretation of the *comercio neutro* of 1797 when he wrote Aguirre that since "any Spaniard is authorized to sail from Foreign Ports to [Veracruz], it would seem more reasonable and less risky to sail there from Havana too." Viceroy Azanza, over the objections of Hacienda employees at Veracruz and the *consulado* officials, allowed Aguirre, "representing . . . Ramírez at Veracruz," to dispose of the cargo but denied him the chance to export to Baltimore cochineal, indigo, and sugar "because this petition is completely contrary to the letter and spirit of the Real Orden of 17 November 1797."

A third category of deviation from Spain's transatlantic trade policy derived from the need to maintain official correspondence between Havana and Veracruz during wartime. In January 1800 Cuba's captain general notified Azanza of the safe arrival of a silver convoy, with its "valuable treasure," bound for Spain, along with an additional 800,000 *pesos* that Azanza had transferred from New Spain's treasury to cover outlays on Havana's defense works; simultaneously he alerted Veracruz authorities of an English squadron off Havana. Previously Cuban colonial officials had used the Havana firm of Casa de Santa María for official dispatches. Now a junta of Havana's military commanders ordered Intendant Luís de Viguri to utilize a U.S. ship for official mail to Veracruz. Several merchant-brokers approached Viguri, who found their bids too high—10,000–12,000 *pesos* of insurance plus "exorbitant freight rates." Besides, Viguri was suspicious of the motives of U.S. ship captains, since, as he put it in a note to Viceroy Azanza, "it occurred to me that these Americans will surrender their ships to the English, speculating on recovering in silver the value of their insured vessels." There was only one acceptable bid, from a local merchant, Sebastián de Lasa, who promised to charter a fast U.S. vessel, *Nimble,* just in from Charleston, South Carolina, with a shipment of provisions for "various Americans at . . . Havana." Lasa's bid was modest: neither freight nor insurance fees, only official license to ship to the merchant firm of Tomás Murphy at Veracruz forty-nine *tercios* of dutiable goods of European (i.e., non-Spanish) origin, such as *platillas, creas, ruanes contrahechos, Picardías, Olandas finas,* and *bretañas angostas.* Viguri accepted the bid even though *comercio neutro* had been suspended since April 1799.

Predictably, the wide international web of commercial operations established by Murphy was considered a possible abridgement of the Spanish transatlantic system during and after the months of *comercio neutro*, 1797–99, when cargo was presumably the property of Spaniards using neutral shipping. Murphy, the lone supporter of *comercio libre* at Veracruz in 1792, when he had responded to Revillagigedo's questionnaire, was among the first to explore the possibilities of *comercio neutro* in Europe (Hamburg), the West Indies (Havana, Kingston), and New Spain (Veracruz). At the neutral port of Hamburg,[124] for example, Murphy or his associates there contracted with the Spanish firm of Urbieta y Cia. to choose and ship aboard the *Amalia* an assortment of linen and woolen textiles made in Silesia, Saxony, France, and Brabant.[125] The *Amalia* was routed via Havana and the merchant firm of Pedro Juan de Erice to Veracruz, its cargo consigned to Tomás Murphy.[126] To disguise the Spanish ownership of the cargo, the *Amalia* carried false manifests; the real manifests, authenticated by Spain's consul general at Hamburg, the *proyectista* Juan Bautista Virio, were hidden in a bale of French linens along with business correspondence detailing "secret commercial directions for sales and remissions to the people involved and impressing in particular upon the consignee the wishes and desires of the owner." In Caribbean waters, however, English blockaders intercepted the *Amalia*, examined its false papers and cargo, and allowed it to continue on since the incriminating documents had been jettisoned. But when the *Amalia* prepared to unload at Veracruz, Murphy's operation was blocked by the prior and both consuls of the Veracruz *consulado* and a *fiscal* of the Audiencia of Mexico, Hernández de Alba.[127]

For his defense Murphy hired an attorney renting office space in the building housing Murphy's commercial firm, José Benito de Austria y Achútegui, brother of the *asesor-secretario* of the Veracruz *consulado*, José Donato de Austria y Achútegui. Benito de Austria's brief, which foreshadowed the position of Havana export interests after 1808, argued that Urbieta y Cia. had fulfilled all the requirements for participation in Spain's colonial trades under *comercio neutro*: it was a Spanish firm under the protection of a consul general of Spain at neutral Hamburg, then a "very apt and suitable European market for neutral expeditions." To the literal construction of the *fiscal* Hernández de Alba that *comercio neutro* "was limited to only national merchants shipping to the Indies" duly registered in *consulados* in Spain, whose trading operations were interrupted by war, Austria countered with a looser interpretation.[128] First, *comercio libre* of 1778 had sanctioned "los intereses de todos los Españoles de Europa *y America*" (emphasis added), whether matriculated or not in *consulados* in Spain and its colonies, registered or not as "shippers to the Indies," and the Spanish consul at Hamburg had properly certified Brentano and company for *comercio neutro*. Second, *comercio neutro* of 1797 addressed "all the merchants who were vassals, without limiting this *gracia* only to those residing in the King's dominions." In an aside obviously directed at Torre and others who asserted that there were few, if any, shortages of goods at Veracruz despite the war, Austria added that the *Amalia*'s textiles would remedy the "marked scarcity of cloth at the moment, substantiated by the eagerness to buy whatever cloth arrives and by the unprecedentedly high level of prices." His brief ended on an oddly aggressive note to the effect that, if necessary, Austria on behalf of Murphy would pursue his case despite opposition, which earned from Viceroy Azanza's *asesor* (Guillén) the reprimand that Murphy's legal adviser "had expressed himself without due moderation in his statements."[129] In the face of opposition from the *consulado* at Mexico City and the *audiencia*'s *fiscal* Alba, Azanza authorized Murphy to dispose of the *Amalia*'s cargo (subject, of course, to further resolution by authorities at Madrid) after he obtained a favorable opinion from an *oidor* of the *audiencia,* Manuel de Castillo y Negrete.[130]

New Spain's shortage of both stamped and cigarette paper, consumed by government offices and the profitable tobacco monopoly, the need of intelligence about English naval operations in the Gulf and the naval base at Kingston, and the right under international law to redeem by purchase prize cargoes put the Spanish commercial system under extraordinary pressure. It is difficult to decide whether Viceroy Azanza relied unduly upon the services of Tomás Murphy to ensure a flow of goods and information between Kingston and Veracruz; the relationship, of course, was seized upon by Veracruz merchants linked closely to Spain. Indeed, almost at the moment when he authorized discharge of the *Amalia*'s cargo from Hamburg, Azanza signed a *permiso* covering shipments from Kingston, thus exposing himself to charges by *fiscal* Alba at Mexico City and by former viceroy and now lobbyist at Madrid, Branciforte, who in a *papel confidencial* claimed that he was sponsoring "*comercio directo* with our friends" to favor his brother-in law Tomás Murphy.[131]

Azanza had concluded upon arriving at Mexico City that the colony lacked basic European imports, including mercury, especially cigarette paper, and data covering "English plans against our possessions . . . [our] forces on sea and land . . . convoy sailings." This assessment coincided with Murphy's business operations. Both knew that Madrid had authorized colonial officials at Havana to allow merchants to recover Spanish-owned prizes at Kingston; the firm of Santa María y Cuesta had done precisely this to recover five thousand reams of government paper, which it sold at Veracruz 29 percent cheaper than the local price current. With Azanza's approval, in mid-1798 Murphy dispatched an employee, Clemente (Francisco?) Santa Cruz, to Havana, where he received permission to proceed to Kingston to recover three ships belonging to Murphy y Porro and their cargo of *paños, sargas, rompecoches, Chalones,* and *resmas de papel*.[132] Under the terms of Azanza's license, Santa Cruz could remain at Kingston, whence he would forward to Murphy y Porro every two months one vessel bearing intelligence reports and up to twenty-five thousand *pesos* of cargo for sale to the colonial government at Mexico City and resale under its monopsony of "mercury, stamped and plain paper, and other goods of the Real Hacienda."[133] To continue what Murphy's opponents at Veracruz challenged as direct exchanges with the English at Kingston, Murphy y Porro could export New Spain's staples to Kingston but neither silver nor gold in coin or bar. Azanza's concessions to the firm of his relative by marriage incensed competitors at Veracruz and Mexico City.

They were understandably angered by what turned out to be Murphy's "very fortunate business affair" when Santa Cruz's first ships from Kingston arrived at Veracruz with passports *(pasavantes)* from English officials; worse, they were infuriated on observing that entering the port of Veracruz was "not a vessel with merchandise worth 25,000 *pesos,* but three ships with a cargo worth upwards of more than half a million." By their calculation, Murphy would be importing from an enemy port about 3 million *pesos'* worth of goods each year—twenty times the value of Azanza's license. The operations of Santa Cruz and by extension Murphy, in the sarcastic opinion of Mexico City's *fiscal de Real Hacienda* Hernández de Alba, would render "useless starting *comercio libre* between Havana and Veracruz, when trade has far greater security between Veracruz and Jamayca, no matter that it is a colony of the enemy," and when the English are "amassing funds to finance a war against us." For the traditionalist-minded Veracruz critics of Azanza's decision, Santa Cruz was engaged in the "serious fault of *comercio directo* with our enemies."[134]

These critics exaggerated the value of imports, which independent evaluators later recalculated at 365,987 *pesos.* Murphy did concede that he could not "applaud the conduct of my employees," while pointing out that the shipments would provide customs revenue and imports for "these dominions lacking what is needed for clothing," as well as 5,888 reams of paper ("a very scarce item") for sale by the royal tobacco factory at Mexico City. Confronting a divided official opinion, Azanza ordered the cargo unloaded, full customs duties assessed, and, pending final decision by Madrid, a bond posted for the cargo. This was rapidly supplied by Murphy's associates at

Veracruz—José Mariano de Almanza, Juan Bautista Lobo, Ángel Gónzalez, and Pedro de Echeverría.

These case studies of merchants at Cadiz, Havana, and Veracruz using and misusing the seventeen months of *comercio neutro* require an assessment. Madrid's decision in 1797 to legitimize supplying its colonies in America through neutral intermediaries in wartime had not been used for more than fifty years—to be precise, since the War of the Austrian Succession (1739–48). Now, however, earlier ad hoc deviations were on a magnified, riskier scale. At best short-term tactical responses to pressures—on the one hand, pressure to sustain a flow of silver from New Spain to its metropole, and on the other, pressure from traders at Havana—would resurface during the following decade. Intentional or otherwise, *comercio neutro*'s ambiguities had expanded the role of neutral ports in the western Atlantic—Philadelphia, Baltimore, and Charleston. At the same time, at Havana and Veracruz during war or peace, colonial governments and the private sector found trade with nearby Kingston indispensable. Profit-making opportunities in New Spain and Cuba in war and peace fostered an environment that was propitious for fresh commercial networks—what Murphy at Veracruz and Erice at Havana epitomized.

Meanwhile, traditionalist commercial networks, convinced that the pre-1797 trade system might be restored, overlooked the inability or unwillingness of officials at Madrid and Havana to cut off regular contacts with the Atlantic ports of the United States after 1799 and, more significant, after the Peace of Amiens in 1801. Perhaps misled by the departure of ships like the *Argonauta* from Veracruz in 1802 with a cargo of more than 2 million silver *pesos,* merchants at Mexico City, Veracruz, and Cadiz, joined by crisis managers at Madrid, assumed that they might somehow reestablish the Spanish transatlantic system of *comercio arreglado* and, on clear evidence of colonial growth rates, expand it more profitably. They failed to reckon with the force of the subterranean or parallel economy: the smuggling virus in the Gulf of Mexico.

9. "Informal" *Comercio Neutro,*
1804–1808

[The Spanish colonies] are quickly reaping the fruit of that fortunate revolution, the suspension of their prohibitory laws. . . . The gigantic infancy of agriculture in Cuba, far from being checked, is greatly aided in its portentous growth during the war, by the boundless liberty of trade and the perfect security of passage. . . . To the Spanish continental colonies, also, war has changed its nature; it has become the handmaid of commerce and the parent of plenty.

James Stephen

What dismayed many merchants in Veracruz, and not a few in Mexico [City], was the responsible and effective measures taken by Iturrigaray to avoid smuggling, so destructive to us in other wars with the same Power.   Conde de Casa Alta to Floridablanca, 25 November 1808

[A] neutral vessel had no right to carry on in war a trade prohibited to them in time of peace.

Alexander Baring

The marked upsurge of smuggling in the Caribbean sector of Spain's transatlantic system after 1797, on an even greater scale after the renewal of Anglo-Spanish conflict at the end of 1804, reflected the inability of the metropolitan economy to supply the American colonies with European and national goods despite Madrid's short-lived decision to rely upon neutral carriers of Spanish-owned cargoes leaving from the neutral ports of Europe and America in the years 1797–99. In this light, smuggling was both cause and effect of Madrid's commercial policy, which provided latitude for the many varieties of illegal trade. It was responsible for the vacillating and contradictory nature of post–*comercio neutro* policy.

The economic policy of Godoy and the upper-level Hacienda officials Soler and Sixto Espinosa, who were in his ministerial group after 1800, fluctuated because they had to juggle too many factors. First were the commercial interests of Spain's major ports, Cadiz and Barcelona, trading with the colonies in America. For six of the nine years from April 1799 to April 1808, Spain was at war with England, which proceeded to monitor imports at Cadiz and other peninsular ports, especially inflows of New Spain's silver for private and public sectors; specie was critical to Spanish government finance in meeting defense outlays and maintaining the value of the *vales nacionales.* Pressure from Cadiz forced Saavedra's ministry in 1798 (24 March, to be precise) to direct customs houses in America to apply a surcharge of 1.5 percent ad valorem on imports aboard neutral carriers to reimburse the merchants of Cadiz for loans totaling 3 million *pesos.* Pressure from the same interests led to revocation of *comercio neutro* the next year (April 1799).[1]

Second, Havana-based sugar planters insisted on importing general stores from the United States and slaves and agricultural equipment from nearby English islands, and in February 1798 they insisted on "liberty" to re-export precious metals from Havana to any neutral country. To outside observers, this smacked of turning Havana into the "general supplier of the Americas . . . with shipments of goods carried there by the Anglo-Americans."[2] More vexing, Havana interests managed to keep their port open to neutral shipping arriving from the United States despite the revocation of *comercio neutro* in 1799. As a result, in 1800 the *consulado* at Veracruz complained that "*comercio neutro* continues despite its categorical prohibition"; in 1801 Viceroy Marquina reported that "the scandalous introduction of all kinds of goods and wares of foreign trade continues in complete liberty"; and at the same time Madrid authorized colonial officials at Havana to accept imports of goods in short supply carried by foreign vessels.[3] Over the five-year period 1799–1804 Madrid seemed incapable of restoring the commercial status quo ante as of 1797 and fueled the fears of Veracruz and Mexico City traders, who, profiting in the short run from handling smuggled goods, foresaw permanent loosening of their ties to Cadiz and other peninsular ports and the emergence of Havana to challenge New Spain's economic hegemony in the Caribbean.

Last, there was pressure from English cotton manufacturers and exporters, whose calicoes and muslins provided about 84 percent of the growth in value of England's exports of manufactures over the decade after 1794. Cottons as a percentage of the value of all English exports rose from 15.6 percent to 42.3 percent over the decade 1794/96 to 1804/6; the dollar value of textile exports to "America and Australia" more than tripled, while the sterling value of cottons officially destined for the "West Indies" more than tripled, from £754,000 to £2.57 million, and that of cottons destined for "Latin America" increased astonishingly, from £7 million to £595 million.[4] One may speculate about the value of English cottons re-exported from Philadelphia and Baltimore to Havana and Veracruz in 1804–6. Contemporaries in England could refer only obliquely to such exports (e.g., "the manufactures of Great Britain were not scantily distributed to His Catholic Majesty's dominions"), while *consulado* officials at Veracruz lamented that English cottons aboard a U.S. vessel in the harbor "due to their fine quality and general use inspire a criminal dealer to speculate on them without respect for, or fear of, the law," all the while warming themselves in anticipation that banning all English manufactures from Spain's colonies as of 20 December 1806 would have English "infractors of the law of nations . . . raging over piles of bundles and goods rejected everywhere."[5] The imagery is a measure of the rapid, unpredictable shift of consumer preferences in New Spain and Cuba from traditional to new textiles, of English merchants' innovative probing of markets overseas, and of the inefficacy of Madrid's legislation to wall off the effects of England's industrialization and of war between the superpowers of the Atlantic basin, England and France.

Ad Hoc Legislation, 1804–1805

To *almaceneros* at Mexico City and Veracruz, Madrid's legislative vacillation (or incoherence) from 1797 to 1799 was tolerable only if it promised a return to the status quo ante once warfare ceased, maintaining the trade artery between Spain and Veracruz, as well as the subordination of Caribbean ports to Veracruz. Provided that legislative bulwarks of the system survived, smuggling and even the occasional formal contacts with English commercial centers at Kingston and Nassau and with the United States at Baltimore, Philadelphia, and New York could be tolerated as short-lived, if irritating, expedients. However, once the English navy shattered the Peace of Amiens in late 1804, crisis managers at Madrid were cornered by London's new, inflexible policy toward neutral shipping in wartime, the troubling shortages in the American colonies, particularly Cuba and New Spain, and the vested interests of merchants at Cadiz and Barcelona, Veracruz and Havana. Madrid may have hoped that its regulatory performance would be interpreted as a measure of system preservation; New Spain's mercantile elite, with few significant exceptions, interpreted the direction of intention as dismantling the imperial transatlantic system, including the hegemonic role of Veracruz (and Mexico City) in the Spanish Caribbean.

The year 1804 was critical, as officials at Madrid characteristically veered about. In June they declared that no further licenses of exception (*gracias, privilegios*) would be issued. This mollified Cadiz and Veracruz despite the decision two months later to allow Havana to re-export surplus imports from peninsular ports to other colonial ports.[6] Shocked in mid-December by England's interception off Cadiz of a convoy carrying millions of *pesos* from the Rio de la Plata, Madrid ordered all colonial ports in America immediately to terminate contact with English ships or nearby non-Spanish ports under any circumstance.[7] On 24 December Madrid modified drastically (the Veracruz *consulado* claimed that it "abandoned") the hermetic stance of June. Now it had to confront the reality of England's rejection of neutral shipping and the necessity of opening new channels to transfer colonial funds to the Spanish treasury in order to service the *vales nacionales,* now the major support of the government's creditworthiness.[8]

Addressed under the classification "secret" *(reservada)* to Viceroy Iturrigaray and countersigned by Finance Minister Soler, the royal order of 24 December legitimated a form of *comercio neutro* that in some senses was more specific and in others strikingly broader than the *comercio neutro* of 1797. It was justified, to be sure, not by explicit avowal of the metropole's incapacity to fulfill the colonial compact, but by implicit admission of financial necessity.[9] It was more specific in that it awarded licenses to commercial firms at specified neutral ports—Hamburg (Thornton & Power), Gothemborg (Hortelmann & Sons), Danzig (Johan Laber), Emden (P. Abegg), Konigsberg (Schwink & Koch), Stockholm (Romann, Hassel & Borges), Copenhagen (Duntzfelt & Co.), Philadelphia (Susserl & Brown, Eric & Louis Bollmann), New York (John H. Thompson), Boston (Thomas Amory & Co.), Baltimore (Luke Tiernan)—to supply specified colonial ports such as Veracruz.[10] It was broader in that the designated neutral firms could freight as many vessels as desired, depart from their home port or "qualquiera otros neutrales en Europa y América," and carry return cargo to ports in Spain *or* those of neutral countries in Europe or North America. Gone was the compulsion to return to peninsular ports first ("at liberty to send or not to send them to the ports of this Peninsula"). The broadest provision, a desperate departure from precedent and one certain to complicate the control of smuggling in New Spain, concerned the composition of cargo destined for Veracruz ("whatever fruits, goods, and wares traded, *without exception*"), as well as return cargo ("gold, silver, and fruits and products of that country").[11]

Unlike most royal orders, which customarily offered a justificatory preamble, that of 24 December had none. Yet those aware of the government's ever-growing burden of deficits and its current obligation to transfer to France's Trésor Public a monthly subsidy under the terms of the Treaty of San Ildefonso could detect the motives midway through the text, where it was specified that within two months of each ship's arrival at Veracruz the designated neutral firms would have to deposit in Spain's Tesorería General for the Real Caja de Consolidación duties that re-exports from peninsular ports normally incurred. A sop to Cadiz surfaced in the duty payable to its *consulado* ("the *consulado* fee levied in this Peninsula").[12] However, this could hardly lower the anxiety level of firms at Cadiz, Veracruz, and Mexico City as they pored over the precedent-breaking clauses covering the goods acceptable as imports and the unrestricted export of precious metals.

Notably absent were constraints listed in the *comercio neutro* of 1797 mandating a balance between "foreign" and "national" products in exports from peninsular ports to the colonies and banning outright foreign cotton goods, mercury, and paper; the obligatory return voyage to a peninsular port; and limited participation by foreign carriers in the flow of precious metals to Europe. By comparison, the decree represented much more of a break with Spain's transatlantic system; it was an unplanned, unwanted, and contradictory stumble from *comercio libre* to *comercio directo*. Catalan dealers in French and English cottons, which they printed or wholly manufactured locally, saw protection of their nascent industry evaporate.[13] For their part, Veracruz and Mexico City wholesalers, who had once rationalized the *comercio neutro* of 1797—which had later been revoked on the ground that it opened "a los negociantes de España un canal por el qual con menos peligro continuasen sus especulaciones con las Américas"—now insisted to Viceroy Iturrigaray that the 1804 order did not authorize neutral firms to ship to Veracruz blasting powder and mercury, which were "notoriously forbidden," or "cotton goods . . . mainly English," which "have been and are absolutely prohibited."[14] On the other hand, for English merchants, Madrid's response to the Atlantic's changing economic reality was an opportunity to trade directly with Veracruz and participate in the transfer of New Spain's precious metals to Europe via the intermediation of the United States and Jamaica. At London the Board of Trade obliged in 1806 by licensing ships from Jamaica, the neutral United States, and neutral ports in Europe for trade with Veracruz, permitting their passage through the English blockade.[15] This inspired the Englishman James Stephen in 1808 to applaud with some hyperbole "that fortunate revolution, the suspension of [Spanish] prohibitory laws . . . the boundless liberty of trade and the perfect security of passage."[16]

As England's naval forces tightened controls over shipping in the Atlantic and the Gulf of Mexico, and smuggling expanded in and around the Caribbean, Madrid's ad hoc responses deepened the anxieties of New Spain's merchants. Responding to a petition from the Cadiz *consulado* ("on behalf of national commerce"), Madrid modified another fundamental structure of its commercial system: an order of 16 June 1806 permitted Spanish shipping departing from peninsular ports for a specific colonial destination ("with only one destination overseas") to stop at other colonial ports en route and "divide and sell all or part of the cargo . . . ending discharge wherever most convenient."[17] This heightened the threat to the Veracruz merchants' commercial hegemony, long mandated by legislation that authorized Veracruz alone to re-export imports received from the metropole to nearby Spanish Caribbean ports, notably Campeche and Sisal, and to restrict Havana's exports to Cuban products.

The threat was also implicit in an unnoticed order of 1 August 1804 whereby merchants at colonial ports could re-export unsold European goods.[18] This was precisely the basis of the argument of Havana's intendant Rafael Gómez Roubaud in 1806. Havana, he informed Godoy, had suffered a trade deficit of more than 6 million *pesos* ("an enormous and harmful amount") in 1805 because "imports far exceeded our exports," stocks of European goods could not be re-exported under existing regulations, and local importers lacked the liquidity to settle customs duties and pay U.S. creditors. The statistical data that he presented marked the dominant role of U.S. shipping, freight, and creditors.[19] Gómez Roubaud blamed the cashflow problem on New Spain's Viceroy Iturrigaray, who, he charged, suspected without proof Havana's "clandestine trade" with Kingston and Nassau, eyed all Cubans with "distaste," and consequently forced the retention in Mexico City of more than 15 million *pesos* due to the Cuban colonial administration as subsidy, for purchases of leaf tobacco for Seville's tobacco factory, and for maintenance of Havana's naval arsenal and military garrison. Gómez Roubaud did not speculate about why U.S. merchants allowed their large balances to accumulate at Havana. Perhaps there was no need to.

More important was Gómez Roubaud's extraordinary recommendation that Godoy open Veracruz and Campeche to vessels from Spain and also allow them to sail on to other colonial ports from "this Island with produce, goods, and wares whether locally produced, national and foreign" after paying existing exit duties to local customs. Nine months later Madrid seemed to confirm Arango y Parreño's vision of Havana as a New World "emporio," as well as the apocalyptic vision of New Spain's *almaceneros*—dependence upon Havana—when on 10 May 1807 it authorized Veracruz, Campeche, and Puerto Rico to accept shipments from Havana of Cuban products, along with any national or foreign wares sent from the peninsula. In effect, this matched Gómez Roubaud's recommendation. He, moreover, did not improve his standing with Cadiz interests connected to Veracruz trading firms, namely, the Cadiz firms of Mariano Malancó and José Lorenzo de la Torre, which had just arranged with Madrid a *permiso* to ship five thousand *bocoyes* of Cuban rum to Veracruz and Campeche. He took the unprecedented step of permitting Cuban planters to export their rum to those ports under the 10 May order.[20]

These frantic efforts of Godoy's ministry to correct distortions induced by international economic warfare after 1804 stirred contradictory reactions in two fundamental segments of the Spanish transatlantic commercial system, the Cadiz–Veracruz–Mexico City and Havana-Cadiz axes. Capitalizing on lobbying funds and good official contacts, Havana's planter-merchants in February 1808 tried to expand their wedge in New Spain's domestic market. In the pattern of ritual reverence, Havana's *consulado* officers expressed gratitude for "the paternal and enlightened approval of the King," whose order of May 1807 establishing "proper reciprocity among sister colonies" had opened "completely a door always kept closed to us," a barrier that had been the source of years of "jealous enmity" fueling the Havana *consulado*'s obstinate insistence on *comercio neutro* in 1797.[21] Now, in view of the recently affirmed "perfecta reciprocidad" between Havana and Veracruz (for no longer did Veracruz have the right to ship to Havana whatever "cloths and other wares" it wished), there was no legal basis for Veracruz merchants to prevent the flow of "wares from one American port to another." Following the ritual of gratitude and the affirmation of principle, Havana's *consulado* officers got down to specifics: the Malancó-Torre exclusive privilege to ship five thousand *bocoyes* of *aguardiente* contradicted the 1807 order, as did the policy of Veracruz customs officers to levy upon goods re-exported from Havana to Veracruz an additional import duty, which rendered Havana's goods uncompetitive.[22] The officers of Havana's *consulado* did not believe that the 1807 order and their petition for its effective implementation could dissipate "divisions and jealousy" between the two competing commercial entrepôts.

On the other hand, the decisions of Godoy's ministry and their enforcement by colonial civil servants widened the chasm between the Cadiz–Veracruz–Mexico City commercial axis and Madrid. To the Cadiz commercial bodies, suspicious of Havana's expansionist commercial pretensions since 1797, the 1807 order seemed to transform Havana into a way station en route to Veracruz and Campeche, fulfilling the dreams of foreigners who "of all the places in America, have aspired to take over the commerce of New Spain." The order of 1807, affirmed Cadiz's businessmen, opened a field of smuggling operations at Havana into which poured goods from Jamaica and Saint Thomas, Martinique and Trinidad, with the connivance of the "venality of Hacienda employees," the customs officers. They charged that Havana's exporters, "who will prostitute themselves," were shipping to Veracruz and Campeche not just their *sobrantes* but also their "clandestine imports."[23]

The Veracruz merchants' corporate body now initiated a protracted, acrimonious two-year exchange with New Spain's chief colonial officer, Viceroy Iturrigaray, over his strict interpretation of the basic royal orders of 1804, those specifying neutral firms and the composition of their cargoes. In February 1806 the *consulado* there reported that the U.S. merchant vessel *Matchless,* from Baltimore, to the "widespread surprise and shock of this Port's traders," was unloading items expressly prohibited—English goods, to be precise. *Consulado* officers noted the contradiction between Godoy's order of 20 December 1804 banning from colonial ports all incoming English vessels and cargo whatsoever, and the order of 24 December 1805, under which the *Matchless* had arrived with cargo including *platilloes royals, brittanias, craies,* and *piezas de coletas de China.* In New Spain people would view with "horror patriótico" the sale of "those manufactures made by the hands of our cruel enemies, stained with the blood of fathers, Sons, Brothers, or Relatives of those to whom they sell textiles for clothing." Off-loading such wares would unavoidably prejudice the economy of Spain, "its industry and workshops, mainly in Catalonia."[24]

Within three days they had Iturrigaray's terse reply. Godoy's order of 24 December was, he was convinced, unambiguous; the firms listed were indeed authorized to ship merchandise "without exception," and he was ordering that the cargo of the *Matchless* be delivered without delay to its Veracruz consignee. Iturrigaray ended his reply on a threatening note, reminding the merchants of Veracruz that royal orders were not subject to discretionary interpretation and that the off-loading must occur "without the least impediment or limit to the wares, goods, and fruits brought from Baltimore." Veracruz now chose to exert its right of appeal over Iturrigaray to Madrid, but without success.[25]

The handling of the *Matchless* incident must be placed in context. By February 1806 two major issues involving Iturrigaray's inflexible execution of orders from Madrid had put him on a collision course with elements within the Veracruz trading community and colleagues at Mexico City and Cadiz: his determination to control large-scale smuggling at Veracruz and his unquestioning support for Godoy's *gracias* and *permisos.*[26]

Iturrigaray's Dilemma

A reaction to unavoidable pressure can bring boiling to the surface currents and countercurrents of unsuspected or, worse, underestimated power. A case in point is Madrid's decisions at the outbreak of hostilities with England in late 1804 and their unquestioned, strict execution by New Spain's viceroy, General José de Iturrigaray. Iturrigaray's disciplined response, conditioned by intelligence about the "informal" commercial economy in and around the colony's major port at Veracruz and by his field commander's assessment of the indefensibility of Veracruz in the face of an amphibious attack by English forces, widened the gap between influential local colonial trading interests and high colonial authority. In a real sense, the colonial situation mirrored metropolitan cleavages. Indeed, the two situations were not unrelated; Godoy's directives on controlling smuggling set off reactions simultaneously at Veracruz in the colony of New Spain and Bilbao in the metropole. As a *consulado* officer would later express it, Veracruz was really part of the "security and defense" of Cadiz.[27]

In January 1805, when Mexico City received copies of Godoy's orders covering shipping between the peninsula and the colonies in America, General Iturrigaray had been in the colony almost two years. The record indicates that he took his viceregal responsibilities seriously: He oversaw the transfers of war-delayed subsidies to Caribbean colonies and many large transfers to Madrid, a matter of no small satisfaction to him. He informed himself about the scope and ramifications of the subterranean economy at Veracruz, the exchanges between English smugglers and their collaborators off and on shore, and the organized inefficiency of Veracruz's naval and customs personnel in curtailing illicit trade.[28] This is evident in a letter Iturrigaray wrote to Godoy, referring to "the many, even outrageous smugglings" in and around the port of Veracruz between 1797 and 1801 involving "some of the residents of that city" and detailing that "the [boats] at the mouths of rivers . . . along the coasts . . . carry English goods, which those boats unload from the Ships that appear, alerted beforehand by the information one or another obtains to unload and send the goods upcountry."[29] A reading of the voluminous correspondence of a predecessor, Revillagigedo, would have alerted Iturrigaray to loopholes in customs operations at Veracruz, just as letters written by a more recent viceroy, Azanza, covered the shortcomings of coast guard operations against hovering English naval vessels. Indeed, in October 1803 a new *instrucción* tightening up the operations of coast guard stations in all the colonies had come from Madrid.[30] The recently arrived, activist naval commandant of Veracruz who had served under Malaspina, Ciriaco de Cevallos, immediately activated several provisions in the *instrucción* by posting patrol vessels to stations without Mexico City's approval, particularly to a preferred rendezvous of smugglers, the Campeche coast.[31] More relevant as precedents for Iturrigaray's subsequent activity were reports as far back as 1798 of limited use of escorted convoys between Havana, Campeche, and Veracruz and, in 1803, the recommendation that trading operations at Veracruz be withdrawn to highland Jalapa and its "benigno temperamento," where, insisted an infantry colonel then stationed at Veracruz, Pedro Garibay, both troops and newcomers at the port might be isolated from epidemics of yellow fever, an annual phenomenon since the early 1790s. The possibility of "transferring trading to the town of Jalapa" haunted officers of the Veracruz *consulado,* who predicted that the Mexico City merchant guild would use this move to strengthen the case for eliminating their *consulado.*[32]

The sudden, preemptive seizure of a convoy, four Spanish vessels inbound from Montevideo, by an English squadron patrolling off Cadiz (prior to England's formal declaration of war in late 1804) and Madrid's awareness of extensive English smuggling in Spanish and colonial waters brought the response of Godoy's ministry in the form of two orders, one "that ports be closed without permitting the sailing of any ships except mailboats," the other requiring that mailboats from the colonies have their seaworthiness evaluated by local naval commanders.[33] Appropriately enough, a small, swift *místico, La Valiente,* delivered these orders to Veracruz on 8 January 1805.[34] In the following weeks, officials at Mexico City learned that most of the shipping that had left Veracruz for Spain had been captured by English cruisers, resulting in a loss of more than 4.5 million *pesos.* Disturbed by reports of "the continued and well-advertised smuggling" at Veracruz, Iturrigaray on 9 March ordered the *comandante del Apostadero* at Veracruz, Cevallos, to suspend all coastal traffic between Veracruz and Tabasco, Laguna de Términos, and the Yucatecan coast, and on March 20 he ordered him to halt all maritime movement at Veracruz ("no type of ship, even including launches").[35] Meanwhile, on 14 March Iturrigaray advised authorities at Veracruz and *consulado* officers there that he had "decided absolutely that that Marketplace would not be defended if invaded" and that "all silver, gold, and other high-valued goods would be moved immediately" to Jalapa.[36] He had no reservations about carrying out the orders issued by Godoy as head of Spain's *almirantazgo:* curtailment of smuggling, or what Godoy had termed "prosecution of smugglers as the most detestable criminals," which required "vigorous measures" regardless of "the claims and humiliation voiced by the same people who find freedom to

268 • *Fissioning of New Spain*

engage in smuggling very convenient."[37] In addition, to provide material incentives to track down smugglers and their goods, Iturrigaray directed in specific and unambiguous language that the full value of goods confiscated be paid to anyone cooperating, "whatever his claim."[38] Unsolicited praise came from several sources—from Bishop San José Muro at Puebla, from *fiscal* Borbón of the Audiencia de México; and perhaps most gratifying, from Madrid.[39]

For all his military background and his experience as a field commander in Spain's Roussillon campaign of 1794, Iturrigaray displayed a typical civil servant's adroitness in covering his flanks. He foresaw that Veracruz merchants, who in wartime easily handled each month "a half-million *pesos* . . . excluding gold . . . which is more easily hidden and spirited away," would probably try to bypass him ("perhaps they will make every effort to carry their protests to higher Authorities") in order to have Madrid override his order closing Veracruz to all coastal traffic. They would use the pretext that their coastal craft "transport food, construction materials, and other things," all of which, he added, could be obtained in other ways or were simply not needed then. In this vein Iturrigaray wrote Godoy on 5 May 1805 to explain why Veracruz enjoyed "a large supply of English merchandise, far exceeding what has been seized," and, indirectly, pleading that Madrid disregard the arguments of the "many" hoping for "revocation of the mentioned order."[40] Two months later, probably to drive home the effectiveness of his countersmuggling measures, he reported to Godoy the seizure of 175 bolts of English chintzes slipped into Mexico City from Veracruz and the discovery at Veracruz of another 107 "packs of English goods."[41] Later he learned that Godoy had passed along to Charles IV news of his *providencias* and sent congratulations for his "care and skill." Only indirectly, however, was Iturrigaray assured that there would be no recall of his measures, since Godoy noted that "H.M. has approved all your orders."[42]

After vigorously applying antismuggling measures in the first six months of 1805, Iturrigaray was more flexible in the following months. Perhaps he sensed the undercurrent of opposition in the merchant communities of Mexico City and, of course, Veracruz as the full impact of his directives was felt. That fall, however, a few ships were permitted to leave for Spain in ballast alone, and later they were permitted to load sugars and "other heavy cargo." Much later, on receipt of instructions from Madrid, Iturrigaray authorized loading all peninsula-bound cargo except specie, provided that the ships' swift sailing characteristics were confirmed by the naval commandant at Veracruz. At Cevallos's insistence, when Iturrigaray inspected the defenses of Veracruz in October, he consented to permit coastal shipping under armed escort "as the only way to balance what Veracruz needed with the advantages of his measures."[43] Unperceptive or simply ingenuous, Iturrigaray then sent Cevallos to the wolves when he authorized him to arrange with Veracruz's *consulado* and *ayuntamiento* for joint financing of the construction and maintenance of six armed patrol craft *(lanchas cañoneras)* to patrol the Veracruz coast and thereby allow coastal shipping to sail without escort craft.[44] These merchant-dominated entities lost no time in telling Cevallos that they had no disposable funds, that the viceroy should seek to finance the craft from the colony's treasury or, what they really wanted, "that he allow free coastal navigation." The viceroy did not back down; in early 1806 he proceeded to revive the system of armed escorts for all coastal convoys, effectively utilizing limited personnel, two brigs, and *paillebotes*.[45]

Iturrigaray's antismuggling controls centered on and around Veracruz brought little immediate protest. If anything, reports from Veracruz on the growth of smuggling probably strengthened his resolve to control the large number of coastal vessels there, all the more so when reports intimated collusion on shore and at sea between Veracruz merchants (unnamed) and English naval vessels off the port and cruising along the coast.[46] In short, there was enough evidence to fire Iturrigaray's suspicions about direct contacts between English naval officers and members of the Veracruz merchant community. Veracruz merchants did not dissipate his suspicions when they claimed that no disposable funds were available for patrol craft, but they offered to pay for one soldier posted aboard each coasting vessel to prevent smuggling—their counterproposal to Iturrigaray's request. The viceroy noted acidly that they had responded "without considering the inadequacy of their proposal with respect to the soldiers' lack of authority and character and given the traffic obtained until now by the use of convoys."[47] Or perhaps they had considered too well?

Evidently Iturrigaray was undeterred by the negative assessment of his countersmuggling measures, which were publicized by José Donato de Austria, the usually well informed secretary of the Veracruz *consulado*. Austria found the surveillance systems of the Veracruz customs "inadequate," the patrols at sea and ashore "costly to the Hacienda," and legislation prohibiting the wearing of smuggled textiles "repugnant to civil liberty"; none of these measures, moreover, would contain "the spread of luxury and ambition." Years of exposure to commercial operations at Veracruz had taught Austria that regulations alone could not keep New Spain a preserve for Spaniards, as if it were, in his terms, "el Imperio de la China." One may assume that Iturrigaray must have read the annual report of January 1805, in which Austria vividly reminded his Veracruz audience of merchants that "from Wallix, on the Yucatán Peninsula, to the Mississippi are visible the Flags and establishments of foreigners, whose proximity to silver from the mines feeds and excites." Iturrigaray—a disciplined military officer or simply a careerist ready to please superiors—could not or would not absorb Austria's implicit message, that the vigor and extent of the underground economy based upon smuggling represented a qualitative change fueled by English merchants who, blocked by war from consumers on the European continent, chose instead to divert to New Spain the cheap, attractive cotton goods produced by East Indian workshops or English mills imitating them. He probably also underestimated the ability of Veracruz's coastwise shipping to distribute European goods to Spanish ports along the Caribbean coast and to import agricultural staples from nearby Tabasco and Yucatán and even far-off Maracaibo. By strict interpretation and execution of instructions from Madrid, Iturrigaray was reinforcing the pseudomercantilism of the Spanish transatlantic system and made more apparent the dichotomy between Godoy's prescriptions for the *país legal* and the *país real* of smugglers.

By late fall 1805, however, the Veracruz *consulado,* in conjunction with the *ayuntamiento* it dominated, broke its silence, and with good reason. The viceroy's measures, its officers complained, had induced a collapse of 89 percent in their port's total annual trade, falling from roughly 37.9 million *pesos* in 1804 to some 4.2 million in 1805; imports alone had dropped from about 16.5 million to about 3.3 million *pesos*.[48] There was a comparable decline in total ship movements; more irritating were Iturrigaray's controls over sailings to Spain, which they claimed had reduced the number of outbound vessels from seventy-eight to three.[49] Worse, there was a virtual collapse of the colony's exports, since Iturrigaray insisted that peninsula-bound vessels exit in ballast. Meanwhile, the total value of the trade of Veracruz's main competitor in the Spanish Caribbean, Havana, was five times that of Veracruz, virtually all carried in neutral U.S. bottoms.[50] Last, the merchants of Veracruz may have been emboldened by an order of September 1805 in which Godoy's ministry, back-pedaling, admonished "all the high-level colonial officers in America" that they had been too stringent in implementing his orders of 17 November 1804, and now urged them to facilitate ship departures for Spain, coastal trade, and intercolonial exchanges.[51] It was one more contradictory and confusing decision by an embattled administration in the metropole.

Over a five-month period, from mid-November 1805 to mid-April 1806, the Veracruz mercantile corporation first complained to Iturrigaray and then, finding his responses unacceptable, appealed for reversal of his policies to higher authority at Madrid, to Finance Minister Soler and then to "Su Magestad," relying upon their Madrid lobbyists.[52] Although their initial complaint, on 15 November, focused on their right to receive imports brought by neutral shipping under the *permisos* awarded to neutral firms the previous November, subsequent correspondence suggests that their real target was the viceroy's *providencias militares*—the obligatory withdrawal of merchants and their stocks from the port to the interior (Jalapa), prior inspection for seaworthiness by naval authorities of vessels outbound for Spain laden only with ballast and mail, and coastal sailings in convoy under armed escort.[53] When Iturrigaray appeared selective in executing Godoy's modifications in the September 1805 order, the Veracruz merchants took issue with his assertion that coastal shipping was largely responsible for smuggling activities.[54] Iturrigaray, however, remained adamant, and by late February officers of the *consulado* (Tomás Murphy, Juan Bautista Lobo, Domingo Lagoa de Miranda) had turned to the highest authority, Madrid, recalling their earlier reports about the viceroy's *providencias militares* and their "terrible, ruinous consequences" to merchants in Spain and New Spain.[55] Iturrigaray, they said, mistakenly believed that the apparent departure of English patrol craft off Veracruz and along its coasts was the result of his directives; in fact, they argued, his restrictions on coastal ship movements raised inordinately the price of imported Venezuelan cacao and Yucatecan salt at Veracruz, while depressing the prices of New Spain's agricultural exportables.[56] Bridling at Iturrigaray's suspicion that their complaints were made with the aim of protecting illegal activities, the *consulado*'s officers asserted that they wished only to minimize the impact of his measures, "with regard not so much to the trade, navigation, agriculture, and crafts of this America as to the Metropole's speculations, workshops, and industries," which sounded patriotic, but given the known situation of Spanish manufactures, it was hardly convincing.[57]

Whatever the strength of their argument, by May or June 1806 officials at Madrid, in particular Gil y Lemos, head of the naval ministry, an ex-viceroy of Peru, continued to distance themselves from Godoy's directives of November 1804. They explained that Godoy's controls on coastal shipping and sailings from Veracruz to the peninsula had been formulated to protect shippers in case of war, but once hostilities involving Spain had begun, they were "at liberty to speculate as they wished . . . and as to coastal navigation, it should be protected, not prohibited."[58] To be sure, Iturrigaray had to moderate his position gradually, justified, first, by the shipping records of the port of Veracruz from September 1805 to September 1806 (supplied by Ciriaco de Cevallos), which showed a total of 364 arrivals and departures: 53 from Spain, 82 from colonial ports, 165 from Caribbean ports ("from this Gulf"), and 64 from neutral harbors.[59] In addition, Iturrigaray argued, if the merchants of Veracruz turned down his proposal that their *consulado* help finance the construction of six small convoy escorts, then surely "once again they will find these coasts as lost as in previous wars." So Iturrigaray proceeded to insist on escorted coastal convoys, precisely what local merchants wanted to suspend. The fact remains that the exchanges between the colony's chief officer and the influential merchant communities of Veracruz and, in the background, Mexico City had generated bad blood. The maritime restrictions and the ensuing bitter exchanges with the "Supreme Officer of the Kingdom" brought the Veracruz trading community later to view Viceroy Iturrigary as "obsessed and convinced of the notion that we might be open enemies of the nation, beings of a species and constitution different from the rest of mankind."[60]

Accustomed to the accommodating stance of the former viceroys Branciforte and Marquina to pressure from New Spain's influential commercial interests, the merchants of Veracruz probably imagined that Iturrigaray was overreacting as a disciplined career military officer to orders from his superiors. This is perhaps a charitable view of the attitude of the Veracruz community. For his part, Iturrigaray was hardly charitable. Preformed or presensitized by his early months in the colony of New Spain, at the outset he had predicted that his "providencias vigorosas" might invite outcries from "some residents of that city" who aimed to preserve their "liberty to engage in [smuggling]" and that they might protest to "that higher authority," Godoy.[61] Early in 1806 he informed the Veracruz *consulado* that data covering port movements at Veracruz over the period when his stringent regulations were enforced did not substantiate their complaints about shortages of imports, which were purely a "necessary and inevitable consequence" of the war at sea. Hence, the Veracruzanos' case, he charged, was founded upon "ideas and suppositions hardly convincing"; the officers of the *consulado* should instead "stand behind the sensible precautions of the . . . Generalísimo [Godoy] promptly and correctly . . . without interpretation or discourse that might undermine them." As viceroy, he simply had no authority "to alter or improve upon what has been stipulated and ordered on those matters."[62]

Aware that Veracruz interests might attempt to misrepresent to Madrid his measures for the "protection of direct and coastal commerce" as solely responsible for the current low import levels at the port of Veracruz, Iturrigaray clarified to Godoy that his target was smuggling. As proof, he forwarded a translation of a Kingston publication reporting on the formal protest of forty-five of that port's merchants about an overzealous English naval officer whose vessel had intercepted Spanish craft arriving "to engage in clandestine commerce." Obviously Iturrigaray had some supporters in the colonial civil service and the trading community. He concluded that the "smugglers [Spaniards] proceed in collusion with the enemy."[63]

In March 1806 the major themes recurrent in Iturrigaray's exchanges with the Veracruz *consulado* and town council resurfaced. Again he insisted that his directives had been designed to attack smuggling and that local merchants' insistence upon "libertad" for their coastal shipping would only "open the door to smuggling." Second, the rest of the colony, he pointed out, had accepted his directives "with resignation, without encouraging complaints or inventing projects that could protect them." Third, as "Supreme Officer of the Kingdom" he had to follow through on orders "punctually and scrupulously," for to modify them would be "a real transgression of sovereign dispositions" transmitted by the "Generalísimo."[64] Last, stung by the successful joint campaign of the Veracruz merchant body and the town council to have Madrid direct him to modify directives on coastal shipping, he put in a parting shot. On receipt of the order of 7 June 1806, he forwarded it to the local *consulado,* at the same time accusing the Veracruz merchant community of misrepresenting his motives, concealing "the authentic and true basis of my measures . . . the indispensable order from the authority making these resolutions," and in unequivocal terms told them henceforth "to draft their representations with the necessary sincerity."[65] An anonymous civil servant in Madrid's naval ministry ably captured the undercurrent of mistrust in Iturrigaray's relations with the Veracruz merchant community. As he put it, the viceroy "infers . . . the lack of sincerity and good faith with which the *consulado* and *ayuntamiento* of Veracruz have exaggerated damages that do not exist."[66]

Ever suspicious of Veracruz's motives in questioning his efforts to root out smuggling, Iturrigaray delayed modifying his directives for almost one year, until August 1807, when a directive of 18 March 1807 from Madrid, countersigned by Finance Minister Soler, forced him to recall in toto his orders of 1805. As he had to write his opposition among Veracruz's merchants, "I issue today appropriate orders to permit . . . coastal vessels to enter and leave freely."[67] For a proud man, this was bitter medicine.

In sum, more than an oddity of personality was behind Iturrigaray's assessment of the operations of Veracruz's merchants. There was a matter of fact: while the private sector at the port insisted that coastal ship movements had dried up, the public sector in the person of the naval commandant Ciriaco Cevallos—dedicated, competent, and zealous in the performance of duty, as his former mentor, the distinguished naval commander Alejandro Malaspina, had been—produced statistical data disproving the private sector's allegations. Next, the viceroy found the Veracruz group consistently implying that his measures were idiosyncratic, while he remained convinced that they were only the proper execution of "the indispensable order from the authorities." Most important, Iturrigaray had come to conclude that those who questioned his measures to contain smuggling by prohibiting unescorted coastal shipping were the real beneficiaries of smuggling, and all were in the Veracruz private sector. Snared in his anti-smuggling *providencias* was a junior naval officer stationed at Veracruz, Juan Jabat, who would surface in mid-1808 under circumstances ominous for Viceroy Iturrigaray.

Iturrigaray may have been stubborn, perhaps ingenuous, but he was no coward. His insistence upon honoring all the *gracias* and *permisos* covered by Godoy's order of 24 December 1804 further distanced him from major, if not all, elements of the mercantile communities of Veracruz and Mexico City and furnished the Veracruz community with the substance of another charge against him: responsibility for "the fatal consequences of the transfer of pious funds to the Real Caja de Consolidación."[68]

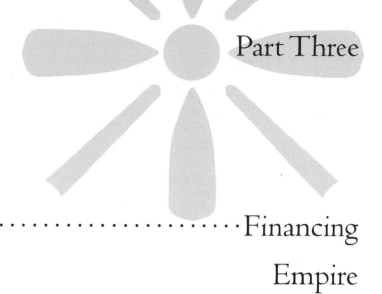

Part Three

Financing

Empire

10. *Consolidación:* Spain

[T]he pleasing, favorable feeling given the public by a Real Decreto for the sale of said properties and the deposit of its proceeds in the Caja de Amortización.
Miguel Cayetano Soler, "Memoria que el ministerio
de hacienda pasa al de Estado . . . 1801"

Especially in May 1803, on the reopening of hostilities between France and England, the commerce of Spain, along with the resources of the Caja de Consolidación, began to stagnate,
which had to lead to the uncertain neutrality of Spain.
"Résumé historique des opérations de la caisse royale de Consolidación"

Iturrigaray's meticulous remission of ecclesiastical funds *(fondos de obras
pías)* to the metropole simply conformed to a decree of December 1804
issued immediately after the renewal of hostilities between Spain and England. The decree extended to the colony of New Spain and other Spanish
colonies a financial device, the *consolidación,* initiated in the metropole after
1798 by Finance Minister Soler to encourage the investing public to continue to support government-issued treasury bills, paper *vales reales,* at a
critical moment when funds from America did not reach Spain.[1] It was
another indicator of the metropole's worsening financial situation. Unrav-
eling the long-term roots of insolvency over two decades after the war of
1779–82 bares again the relationship between the economy of colony and
metropole, New Spain and Spain, and the impact of Spain's French connection, first Bourbon and then Napoleonic, in the crisis of 1808.

The historiography of the *consolidación* in Spain and New Spain is intriguing. For long it was virtually neglected. Then decades ago, in a hardly
respectful, pioneer biography of Iturrigaray in New Spain, the Spanish art
historian Lafuente Ferrari highlighted the political impact of *consolidación* in

the colony, and there followed attention to both its economic and political repercussions. The contributions of Brian Hamnett, Asunción Lavrín, Romeo Flores Romero, H. Masae Sugawara, Margaret Chowning, and Gisela von Wobeser included quantification of New Spain's *consolidación* receipts, what Richard Herr and Francisco Tomás y Valiente have essayed for Spain.[2] There has been a predictable Atlantic compartmentalization: studies of the phase in the colony of New Spain have barely alluded to the metropolitan phase; in the case of *consolidación* in Spain, we have the metropolitan rationalization of 1804 that the operation was so successful at home that it was applied overseas.

In fact, New Spain's silver and the vicissitudes of the metropole's *vales* were interlocked from the initiation of the treasury bills after 1780, not to mention the preoccupation of French commercial and financial interests with silver exports from New Spain and with tapping them. As Richard Herr noted, the initiation of *consolidación* in Spain in 1798 occurred partly because "Spain could receive no funds from America" in wartime. Was it mere coincidence that in November 1804 — once again, in wartime — officials at Madrid contracted with Gabriel-Julien Ouvrard for the transfer of government specie from Veracruz, while simultaneously extending *consolidación* to New Spain because it had produced "such excellent results in Spain"?[3] As will be clarified, Viceroy Iturrigaray's execution of *consolidación,* although tending to separate landholding and mining interests from those of Mexico City's *almaceneros,* produced on an annual basis more funds per capita of *consolidación* than in the metropole. In this area as in others, New Spain overfilled its role in Spain's imperfect version of the colonial compact.

The Financial Crisis

Within months after Spain's declaration of war with England in 1779, Madrid officials confronted a financial crisis whose main elements resurfaced in the 1790s and, with greater intensity, in the first decade of the nineteenth century. It was a complex of chronic misallocation of government income on royal household patronage (after all, this was what the *monarquía* was all about), spiraling military and naval budgets, gaps between government income and uncontrollable expenditures, and a Cadiz mercantile community whose funds were temporarily retained in the colonies in wartime and pressured to pay the costs of borrowed capital.[4] Analysis of the response to these interwoven pressures brings to the fore the eroding foundations of Spain's transatlantic economy before the crisis of the old regime and the collapse of the first Spanish empire.

The government's conditioned response in 1780 had been to turn first to its traditional lenders, Madrid's Cinco Gremios Mayores, then to foreign and domestic merchant houses at Cadiz, to Madrid's merchant-bankers, and finally to Amsterdam, which was western Europe's financial center at the time. When loans from these lenders, as well as from Mexico City's wealthy *almaceneros* and religious corporations, proved inadequate, Madrid explored newer instruments—a national bank, followed by the innovative interest-bearing convertible treasury bills, the *vales reales.* For generations the metropolitan government had borrowed from Madrid's purveyors of luxury imports banded into a corporate body, the Cinco Gremios Mayores. When the government had to assist Cadiz's capital-short merchant houses, whose overseas receipts in wartime were retained in America, and at the same time cover its own revenue shortfalls, first it tapped the Cinco Gremios. Urged by the cautious finance minister, Múzquiz (conde de Gausa), Prime Minister Floridablanca called in representatives of the Cinco Gremios to request a loan of 70 million *reales* over the next six months.[5] Four months later, unable to meet the promised installments, the Cinco Gremios suggested that Floridablanca tap foreign capital; they excused themselves as intermediaries and possible guarantors, claiming that they lacked a sound credit standing with Dutch and Genoese bankers.[6] Again at the prodding of his finance minister, Floridablanca approached the Cadiz community of Spanish and non-Spanish merchants, that "wellspring of wealth . . . always the most reliable resource at moments of urgency," to quote a civil servant who had once been heavily involved in colonial trade at Jalapa (New Spain) and Cadiz, Tesorero General del Ejército Francisco Montes. In fact, well known at Cadiz was "the high opinion [of Montes] held by Commerce in general and especially at Cadiz."[7] Cadiz offered little and implied that in exchange it wanted revocation of the *comercio libre* of 1778, a price Madrid rejected.[8]

The government then took up the proposal of Francisco Cabarrús, whose Bayonne-based extended family, the Lalannes, dealt in silver. He had set up at Madrid the merchant-banking firm of Cabarrús & Lalanne, with warehouses in the French commercial enclave at Carabanchel de Arriba on Madrid's northern outskirts. Cabarrús offered to deliver at Paris 25 million *livres tournois* (100 million *reales*) in installments over 6 months, from March to August 1781. In return, he asked for a draft or bill of exchange *(libramiento)* of 5 million *pesos fuertes* drawn on the colonial treasury at Mexico City and signed by "the hand and letter of the King . . . and his Minister of the Indies [Gálvez]," to be sent *via reservada* to the viceroy of New Spain by the Consejo de Indias; this was to avoid any "doubt or dispute over the legitimacy of this enterprise." Cabarrús understood Spaniards' ingrained suspicion of foreign businessmen. Francisco Montes, Cabarrús insisted, was to have no oversight of his proposal "under any pretext at all." In addition, he wanted authorization to dispatch three vessels with up to a thousand tons of customary merchandise valued at 60 million *reales*, loaded at any French port, duty free at all stages. Since secrecy was the "very spirit" of his proposal lest it be leaked to the English, no civil servant was to know of the *libramiento*.

This leonine proposal was rejected, probably on the advice of Finance Minister Múzquiz. Yet here were antecedents of the later contract with Gabriel-Julien Ouvrard. Cabarrús was nothing if not persistent, and in 1782 he lent the government 1 million *pesos sencillos (pesos of 15 reales)*, repayable on the treasury at Havana in *pesos fuertes (pesos of 20 reales)* forwarded from Mexico City, a gross return of 33 percent.[9] At the same time, the government also turned to an international banking syndicate cobbled together by Cabarrús and France's Necker for a loan of 9 million *pesos sencillos* repayable with 9.9 million *pesos fuertes* in *vales* offering 4 percent interest. Two years later Cabarrús & Lalanne negotiated a loan of 3 million guilders at 5 percent with the Amsterdam bankers Hope & Fizeau Grand. In 1805, when Hope & Company agreed to collaborate with Ouvrard, the Dutch firm could record decades of profitable dealings with Madrid.[10] For his part, Cabarrús could reflect on years of experience in Spanish government finance when in 1808 he agreed to enter the cabinet of José Bonaparte, now José I of Spain, as finance minister.

Procurement of funds from Spanish and non-Spanish resident merchants at Madrid and Amsterdam's merchant-bankers induced Floridablanca's ministry to activate another measure, invariably postponed: the establishment of a government-sponsored national bank for an empire using paraformal credit and banking institutions.[11] At the end of the eighteenth century the Spanish imperial economy needed a multipurpose, creditworthy, and dependable financial institution that might transform Madrid into a financial center to attract deposits from "the influential" wealthy, to finance colonial trade, especially in wartime, to monitor for tax purposes outflows of silver bullion and specie in and around Cadiz, and, when necessary, to satisfy the government's short-term financial needs. Otherwise, as Peter Dickson has noted of England in the eighteenth century, "A badly organized system of borrowing . . . would deliver the state into the hands of financial cliques."[12]

In the 1750s and 1760s, when the Hacienda secretaries Ensenada and then Esquilache had contemplated a national bank, they circularized the Spanish diplomatic corps for European models, including data on the techniques of international exchanges, in order "to place all nations in the position of getting no silver from Spain's Indies except through its intermediation and at high cost."[13] A French innovation, a commercial bank of the late 1770s, the Caisse d'Escompte, one of whose directors was a LeCouteulx with Cadiz merchant-family connections, provided the long-sought model.[14] Confronting financial problems insoluble by traditional funding resources, Floridablanca in 1781 advanced the concept of a national bank patterned, he claimed, on English and Dutch models, capitalized at 300 million *reales* in 150,000 shares. To bypass internal opposition, notably from the Consejo de Castilla as well as the "money transferers and . . . usurious moneychangers" in Madrid's financial community, he turned to his protégé Cabarrús, who proved an effective lobbyist. The charter of the Banco Nacional de San Carlos was approved in late 1782, after an extraordinary effort to achieve consensus among "the different classes of nobility, deputies, government attorneys, ministers of councils, and competent merchants of Madrid and Cadiz, as well as aldermen and deputies of the *ayuntamiento* of this city [Madrid]."[15] Information about the Banco Nacional was circulated immediately to potential investors overseas in Mexico City, Lima, and other colonial capitals, whose official press informed the public of the bank's multiple functions: supporting government credit by redeeming the recently issued *vales reales;* paying the Hacienda's obligations abroad; provisioning the armed forces; and, generally overlooked, financing the Atlantic trades in wartime—"by helping commerce and the quick settlement of transactions between people in America and Spain." Specifically, the Banco Nacional, assisted by branch offices in Spain and colonial capitals, would offer merchants low discount rates on commercial paper; branch offices were established in peninsular and colonial capitals cities. Finance, like trade, linked the two geographical sectors, metropole and colonies, of the Spanish imperial system.[16]

The broad outlines of the operation of the Banco Nacional de San Carlos are clear, far more so than the geographical dimensions of its operations, colonial and European. Shares were bought by investors in both the metropole and the colonies; residents in the colonies could transfer their silver to Spain tax free.[17] In Spain and New Spain, respectively, for example, civil servants like Gaspar de Jovellanos and Ramón de Posada, irritated by the low-keyed response of those in the colonies with disposable incomes, diverted the savings of native peoples' *cajas de comunidad* into the purchase of bank shares.[18] There is reason to accept the criticism that the insiders Cabarrús and his father-in-law, Gelabert, directors of the bank, along with French merchant houses at the Cadiz branch, namely Magon & Lefer and

Le Normand, may have abused their position to favor French firms at Cadiz in discounting their paper or preference in loans.[19] In France, the comte de Mirabeau criticized the bank's preference for the Caisse d'Escompte in settling payments in silver to creditors in Paris, Amsterdam, and London, underscoring the "intimate" friendship between Cabarrús and the Parisian banker LeCouteulx.[20]

These and related charges apparently convinced skeptical Spaniards that the Banco Nacional was manipulated by French interests: "although not seeming so, in reality it is."[21] Perhaps Mirabeau's criticism stemmed from the Banco Nacional's control of silver flows from Cadiz to Lisbon and on to London, and to Madrid, Paris, Amsterdam, and Hamburg, in which Cabarrús seems to have been a participant. There is evidence that Cabarrús as director withdrew specie from the Cadiz branch that was secretly borne by packtrain to Madrid and on to Pamplona, San Sebastián, and Bayonne by a ring of smugglers self-styled "The Mint." Investigation did lead to his temporary imprisonment in the early 1790s.[22] Other international aspects of the bank's silver transfers and their effect upon France's silver imports require perspective. In early 1789, when the French government's financial impasse brought political instability, its receipts of New Spain's specie were dwindling because exports of French linens, silks, and cottons could not match English and German competition pricewise in the markets of Spain's major American colonies. Mirabeau, it would appear, attacked a symptom, not a cause, of the decline in France's silver imports.

Of the three resources on which Madrid fell back to cover financial commitments in wartime from 1779 to 1782—domestic and foreign borrowing, the Banco Nacional, and the *vales*—the interest-bearing treasury notes, or *vales,* proved in the short run to be the most productive and efficient but in the long run divisive of society in Spain and New Spain. Successive and apparently successful issues of *vales* in 1780–1800, along with measures adopted to sustain their par value once war broke out again in 1796, were the direct antecedents of the royal order of November 1804, which would oblige Viceroy Iturrigaray to expropriate selected ecclesiastical properties and capital funds in the colony.

There seems to be an inner logic to the pattern of Madrid's repeated recourse to paper money in the years 1780–1800, which may explain how the government managed to counter the pressures of wartime finance and deficit spending down to 1808 and even beyond. The investing public accepted the *vales* perhaps because of Spain's tradition of government-issued *juros* beginning in the late sixteenth century; we cannot overlook the fact that in the time of Charles III a prominent factor leading to the coup d'état against Hacienda secretary Esquilache was his aggressive inquiry into who was receiving annual interest payments on very ancient *juros,* and why. There were also reassuring international examples of the growth of the public debt; Madrid's *Gazeta,* for example, warmed to reports of England's national debt rising by 34 percent over the years 1775–80.[23] Then came the first issues of *vales* in 1780, followed by two more emissions in eighteen months. By July 1782 there were circulating 83,500 *vales* (in 300- and 600-*peso* denominations) totaling 452 million *reales,* offering 4 percent annually and redemption at par over twenty years.

Merchants found *vales* useful because they could be applied to "all types of transactions and commercial enterprise" and were accepted at all government bureaus "as if they were effective, common, and current money."[24] Merchants prized them at first because they regularly paid their holders interest and were convenient for international and domestic payments. Confidence in the first *vales* was sustained subsequently by peace with England in 1782, ending the "retention of our funds in America," bringing an inflow of colonial revenues for the government once Madrid ordered "that money come from . . . the Indies," and permitting redemption by Cabarrús & Lalanne and the Banco Nacional.[25] Success inspired further emissions for government financing of provincial waterways (Aragon's Azequía Imperial in 1785, in the amount of 99.3 million *reales*) and raising the capital of the recently chartered Compañía de Filipinas by another 59.8 million in 1791. Scheduled redemption lowered the outstanding *vales* to 35.6 million in 1793: they were often bought at a premium because of the "ample money supply" that was the result partly of silver inflows from trade expansion with the American colonies, especially with New Spain, and partly of international monetary movements as investors in France, discouraged by the economic dislocations of the Revolution, moved funds into reliable Spanish *vales.* "Foresighted Frenchmen with goods in Spain and its Indies, seeing the desolation threatening their Fatherland, warned their correspondents here not to send their earnings but to keep some, discount letters of payment and IOUs, or *vales reales,* to preserve some of their wealth as a safeguard in case of personal losses, which they feared."[26]

The long breather, so to speak, of Spanish finance ended with Spain's abandonment of its long-term ally to join England in war against France from 1793 to 1795. As government outlays skyrocketed by more than one-third in 1793–94 alone, Hacienda officials returned to the successful resource of the early 1780s, issuing over the next thirteen months almost 300,000 *vales,* more than double the volume of the initial *vale* issues in 1780–82. At such critical junctures, resorting to *vales* seemed "more expeditious and cheaper."[27] Merchants at Cadiz prized *vales* because they paid interest regularly and were convenient for large domestic and international payments, so that in 1796, just before war against England, "this paper was the principal and virtually the only currency hereabouts, using money only for small payments . . . with the result . . . that almost all of the wealth at Cadiz . . . consisted of *vales reales*."[28] Such was public investors' confidence in the government's financial responsibility that there seemed to be no "suspicion of losing capital or interest" among "those merchants holding four-fifths of the *vales,* accustomed to requiring no security other than credit on the basis of prompt payments." On the other hand, there was a large-scale sell-off of *vales* by French investors just before and during the war with England, shifting 90 percent of their funds from Cadiz and Madrid to Genoa, London, Amsterdam, and other banking centers.

Put another way, in 1795 the government's cumulative debt due to *vales* was three times that of July 1782, and interest payments alone absorbed annually 55.8 million *reales.*[29] To reassure investors, the government instituted a redemption fund, the Caja de Amortización, financed by a 10 percent tax on "the Kingdom's properties and taxes," on the product of the Banco Nacional's tax on silver exports, and on a one-time "extraordinary subsidy" conceded by the Vatican.[30] Because of the volume of outstanding *vales,* not to mention interest charges, over the next four years, 1795–98, no new *vales* were offered.[31] Instead, the government floated internal loans of 800 million *reales* secured on specific revenue sources: the sale of stamped paper, the customs revenues of the colonial trade center at Cadiz, and, to support borrowing 400 million *reales,* the lucrative "tobacco tax in the Indies."[32] Tapping into the colonial system at various levels remained metropolitan Spain's critical means of acquiring income. However, if England's navy temporarily choked off colonial revenue transfers despite *comercio neutro,* Madrid could continue to borrow against future colonial income; the resort to small denominations and a correspondingly large number of certificates per internal borrowing indicates the design of tapping a neglected pool of small domestic savers.[33]

Spain's finance ministers held back on further *vale* emissions because the government's financial situation and capacity to pay interest and redemption at par were badly undermined by the second conflict of the 1790s, the war with England starting in late 1796.[34] Early in 1798, after the shocking loss of Spanish warships at Cape Saint Vincent (1797) and eighteen months of the English blockade of Cadiz and the Caribbean ports, together with the disappointing results (to some, at least) of *comercio neutro,* Hacienda officials monitoring receipts and expenditures began to review options. In reality, the monitoring had begun earlier, when Diego de Gardoqui—prosperous Bilbao merchant, diplomat at Philadelphia and then London during the 1780s, supporter of *comercio libre,* and recently appointed Hacienda secretary by Prime Minister Aranda—on taking up his appointment in 1792 initiated a thoroughgoing review of government finances since 1783.[35] Like Antonio Valdés, who had replaced the deceased colonial secretary Gálvez, Gardoqui brought a fresh approach to colonial trade and fiscal policies. A preliminary report concluded that net revenue had covered the "usual obligations of the Crown if they remained stable" and went on to recommend that funds be reserved for unexpected contingencies; in a warning aside, the report underscored that sound fiscal administration required prompt satisfaction of all state obligations incurred in the course of past conflicts.[36] There were oblique references to past practices; to the constant diversion of colonial income ("sus preciosos metales") to maintain the royal household and the civil list and "satisfy the Monarchy's domestic and foreign expenditures, thereby augmenting the luster of the Royal Household and the Royal Family"; and to the anxiety of *vale* holders when interest was deferred. At the same time, the government "concentrated on unwarranted trifles, while overlooking more important matters."[37]

In making war against France as England's ally in 1793, the Spanish government, whose peacetime budget allocated two thirds of its income to the army and navy, broke the delicate balance between income and expenditures. One year of the conflict caused a deficit of 124 million *reales,* exceeding income by 21 percent, while the cumulative deficit over the years 1793–96 reached 1,269 million *reales.* The predicted outlay for 1797 was double that of 1793, although trade, "then the most flourishing," with the colonies and associated customs receipts remained mildly unaffected;[38] the projected 1797 overrun of 944.5 million seemed inevitable but still manageable as long as England would tolerate neutral shipping in wartime.[39]

A sense of urgency had pushed the recently appointed finance minister Francisco de Saavedra to permit *comercio neutro* at the end of 1797 in order to maintain communication with the colonies in America and to shore up confidence in *vales.* Drawing on funds that included *depósitos* of the military orders and a loan of 39.3 million *reales* put at the government's disposition by religious orders, Saavedra netted only 60.3 million, "nothing to cover the immense obligations of the crown." As the war continued into early 1798 he predicted another large deficit, of 800 million *reales;* meanwhile, the discount *(premio)* on *vales* rose to 18.3 percent between January and May, up 80 percent since 1795 and the highest discount rate since the initial issue of *vales.*[40]

Saavedra scrounged for funds to meet repayment schedules contracted with the three corporations that had met the Spanish government's financial needs in recent decades: the Banco Nacional, handling the government's international payments; the Cinco Gremios Mayores, responsible for provisioning the armed forces; and the stockholders of the Compañía de Filipinas. At this critical juncture it was probably the Basque elder statesman and prominent Madrid banker Simón de Aragorri (marqués de Yranda)—a director of the Compañía, a correspondent of banking establishments in Paris (LeCouteulx) and Amsterdam (Hope), a *consejero de estado* since 1795, and, incidentally, a collaborator of Esquilache's in the 1760s—who urged Saavedra to gather "people of recognized intelligence and capacity" to analyze the government's fiscal options. Or perhaps this recommendation came from the merchant-banker Francisco Cabarrús? Leaving nothing to chance, Saavedra obtained crown approval of a special junta to meet in Yranda's splendid Madrid town house. Its membership included Yranda, Cabarrús, Miguel Caetano Soler, Manuel Sixto Espinosa, Ignacio Felipe Canga Argüelles, and others—a select group including some seasoned under Charles III (Yranda, Cabarrús) and others (Soler, Sixto Espinosa, Canga Argüelles) who would shortly hold key policymaking posts under Manuel Godoy in the Hacienda, which could now boast of its tradition of attracting very competent civil servants. The junta's proceedings were to be secret ("at the highest level"). To the *junteros* Saavedra sent a copy of the royal commission's responsibilities, accompanied by a report on the current financial situation—a kind of position paper drafted, one suspects, by a *juntero*, probably Soler.

Saavedra's Special Junta

The quality of the junta's membership is a measure of the competence of Finance Minister Saavedra, soon promoted to prime minister. Fifty-two years old, Saavedra was an ex-seminarian who at age twenty had switched from theology to the army in 1766 and in 1778 had served at the Lisbon embassy under the conde de Fernán Núñez, confidant and biographer of the late Charles III and Saavedra's protector and patron. In 1780 Gálvez's Colonial Office had posted Saavedra to New Spain to supervise the transfer to Havana of New Spain's silver to finance the French admiral de Grasse's fleet during the Yorktown campaign, which ended England's effort to suppress its rebellious colonists in North America. In a real and overlooked sense, this was an unsolicited, unrecognized major contribution of New Spain's silver mineworkers to the independence of other colonial peoples.

From New Spain, Saavedra went on to become intendant of Caracas, a defender there of Venezuelan planters against the holdovers of the old, monopolistic Compañía Guipuzcoana, recently folded into the Compañía de Filipinas, and a protagonist of new *consulados* in the American colonies. Recalled to Madrid, he was appointed to the Consejo de Guerra. Appointed Hacienda secretary in 1797 on the death of Pedro Varela, Saavedra was now a cosmopolitan veteran of colonial service, attuned to the problems of export agriculture in America, skeptical—and understanding, too—of the issues troubling influential merchants in both Cadiz and Mexico City. It was probably Godoy who urged Saavedra to serve as finance minister, even to consider becoming prime minister. Perhaps too much of the seminarian remained to make him a decisive micromanager as a top civil servant, leading to the comment, "Under Saavedra matters loosened up and took on an air of familiarity." Some characterized him in his ministerial capacities as "relaxed" and "kind," which may have been another way to describe his permissive discretion with subordinates; others, like Juan de Escoiquiz, Fernando VII's *éminence grise,* cut him for his "excessively foolish kindness." A contemporary French assessment found him "learned" and supportive of the "close, open liaison" between France and Spain.[41] An enlightened *andaluz* colonialist in 1797, a decade later, when he would surface as a member of Seville's Junta Suprema, English and French observers were more caustic, describing him as "a man of little decision . . . easily influenced by others" and an "old man . . . tenaciously adhering to the gothic edifice of Spanish institutions."[42]

Saavedra's selection of Aragorri and Soler as *junteros* in 1798, however, intimates that he was not then an unreconstructed defender *(godo)* of the status quo. Simon de Aragorri y Olavide, from Guipuzcoa, near the porous Franco-Spanish zone of Hendaye-Irun, had a solid education before migrating to Madrid, when "he didn't have a penny, or anyone to lend him one." His career as a merchant and then a banker was meteoric—one thinks of his contemporary Cabarrús—and must have owed much to his management of grain imports for Madrid ordered by Esquilache in the early 1760s and then to oversight of the contracts with the Cinco Gremios Mayores for provisioning the navy. Esquilache had also put him on the junta that justified *comercio libre* in 1765 for the Caribbean, in particular Havana; Aragorri soon developed extended family links to the Cuban elite.[43]

Through the first marriage of his sister María to a member of the Las Casas y de la Cuadra family (from nearby Galdames, in the Encartaciones), he was an uncle of Luís de las Casas (captain general of Cuba in the early 1790s, one of Valdés's appointments, along with that of Revillagigedo to

New Spain), and his sister Rosa was married to General Alejandro O'Reilly, whose son became a Cuban planter and a good friend of Francisco Arango y Parreño. Through María's second marriage, Aragorri became an uncle of Francisco Xavier Castaños y Aragorri, an army officer who in 1810 would preside over the Regencia, the successor of the ill-fated Junta Central. In the early 1780s Aragorri channeled Spain's subsidies to the insurgents in England's North American colonies coincident with Saavedra's oversight of the financing of Admiral de Grasse's fleet at Yorktown. As a wealthy Madrid banker, Aragorri was a correspondent of France's Compagnie des Indes, for whose outbound Indiamen he arranged their supply of silver *pesos* at Cadiz. At his Madrid residence he entertained, among others, the distinguished French civil servants Bourgoing and Dupont de Nemours, the latter of whom was impressed by Aragorri's "great knowledge and liberal sentiments." On his way to New Spain and South America via Madrid, Alexander von Humboldt found Aragorri "a most distinguished person" and "endlessly patient" in arranging his funds in the colonies. Made a marquis in 1769, three decades later he was indisputably the logical host for Saavedra's junta of financial crisis managers.[44]

When in 1798 Saavedra appended Soler's position paper to his proposal for a junta, it indicated his appreciation of the young civil servant's proven capability. Like Gardoqui, who had backed proposals for more *consulados* in the colonies, a national *consulado* at Madrid representing all the *consulados,* and a periodical for disseminating commercial information that would later materialize as the *Correo Mercantil de España y sus Indias* (1792–1804), Soler embodied a new breed of finance personnel, who were willing, if necessary, to chip away at vested interests, including those of the church, if only to ensure the survival of the empire as a whole. A realist and nationalist, Soler survived at the Hacienda during a decade of intensifying crises only to be assassinated by one of the hit squads mobilized by ultratraditionalist *fernandistas* shortly after the overthrow of Charles IV and Godoy. Soler would not be the only civil servant so fingered in the sequel to the Aranjuez coup d'état in the spring of 1808.

Like Aragorri, Soler grew up on the peninsula's periphery, in Mahon, on the island of Mallorca. The family had commercial contacts with the eastern Mediterranean and North Africa, was "fecund in men of consular quality," and drew praise from Floridablanca for "his great zeal for the affairs of Spain."[45] Saavedra often reviewed financial and fiscal policy with Soler, whose analytical ability is substantiated by three *memorias* on the economy of Spain drafted between 1798 and 1801. The carefully researched, eighty-page *memoria* to orient Foreign Office personnel in peacemaking with English representatives in 1801 and another for developing the Spanish economy, as well as his sustained efforts after 1798 to mobilize the funds of church corporations first in the metropole and then in the colonies for wartime finance, inspired Godoy at one point to consider him "one of the most upright ministers that the Real Hacienda has ever had."[46] It is tenable that Soler's grand design, which included disentailing church properties and capital indirectly first in the metropole and then in the colonies and then creating the Caja de Consolidación to enhance the reliability of *vales* was a prime factor leading to his political assassination. Like Esquilache's career, Soler's offers a provocative—and disheartening—lesson on the limits of translating analysis into reality.

In late May or early June 1798 Saavedra's junta weighed the options laid out in Soler's *memoria,* along with proposals advanced by Cabarrús. In the discussion, the group predictably sidestepped the hard options for handling an estimated deficit of 800 million *reales.* No *juntero* proposed to increase the general taxes—wherever possible, eighteenth-century governments hewed to a policy of avoiding new taxes—imposed on an already restive population struggling with food shortages, commodity speculation, and inflation. At this moment the options laid out by Soler ranged from taxing bills of exchange *(letras)* and commercial IOUs *(pagarés),* an interest-free "patriotic" loan by residents of the metropole and colonies (lenders to be registered and honored when they petitioned for favors), to techniques for tapping the major resources of Spain's transatlantic system, its colonial revenues, "particularmente" those of "New Spain . . . as occurred in the last War with England," when Mexico City's treasury had subsidized military and naval operations, while transferring to Spain via France 4–6 million *pesos.*[47] Spanish warships, each authorized to freight up to 1.5 million *pesos,* could be dispatched to pick up silver; or colonial treasuries would lend to merchants, or to the Compañía de Filipinas to help finance its Asian operations, with repayment guaranteed by peninsular treasuries on the return of that company's ships via the Indian Ocean.[48] These "aids" from the colonies would support the *vales* and lower, if not eliminate, their discount *(agio).* Buried in the fourth option presented to Soler was the sale of crown properties such as the *encomiendas* of the military orders along with specific church holdings designated as being of "social utility"—the "properties of hospitals, fraternities, foundations, and pious works," whose proceeds would go into the *vales'* redemption fund, the Caja de Amortización, in exchange for 3 percent annual interest, 1 percent below the fixed rate for *vales.* This last option would turn out to be the most radical in many respects.[49]

Cabarrús offered his proposals, whose differences with Soler's were minor.[50] He would reject a patriotic loan repayable over twenty-five years, since even during the very "popular" war against revolutionary France in the early 1790s, which was sustained, he pointed out, by "an enthusiasm aroused and nourished by many factors" (he did not mention ecclesiastical enthusiasm for that anti-Jacobin crusade). The loan had yielded only 140 million *reales*. Similarly, he rejected Soler's proposed sale of titles of nobility on the ground that "to compensate the great value of distinction in politics with money would surely cheapen it, while the Monarchy would lose the immense treasure that is honor"—logical sentiments in an era of unprecedented inflation of titles in return for cash.[51] Moreover, mindful perhaps of the recent history of the Bourbon household in prerevolutionary France, Cabarrús objected to unregulated, usually disguised royal expenditures, which, "absorbed and confused in the category called 'hacienda,'" could not be calculated with precision but which he estimated at 120 million *reales* annually, roughly 30 percent of the government's gross annual income. On this score he recommended an equilibrium between—the contrasts are revealing—"dissipation and stinginess" and "splendor" and "economy," to be programmed by a small interministerial group that would follow a strict "overall domestic economic plan."[52]

These and minor differences aside, Cabarrús concurred with Soler's proposal for tapping into public and private wealth in the colonies, using warships as carriers—in his own words, "to order funds shipped from the Indies aboard merchant vessels and frigates . . . and procure them especially at Veracruz." Funds borrowed from merchants engaged in the colonial trades would receive interest, just as in the war with England two decades earlier. Moreover, drafts on colonial treasuries could repay major creditors of the government, the Banco Nacional de San Carlos and the Cinco Gremios Mayores.[53] Significantly, Cabarrús's last option, designed exclusively to fund the redemption of *vales,* referred only to the sale of crown, not church, property, including that of the military orders. No specific sums from these sources were estimated, since the junta "has a total lack of information of its existence and value."[54] Like his friend Gaspar de Jovellanos, Cabarrús avoided the possible expropriation of ecclesiastical holdings, confining himself solely to crown and municipal properties *(fincas de comunidad).* Still, implicit in one of his observations was the possibility that the state might have to pressure Spain's religious establishment for a large financial commitment. The *monarquía* was now exposed to "imminent risks" because of the "inevitable continuation of the war," and he had to remind fellow *junteros*—as if this were required—that a "frightening revolution" had unseated Louis XVI because of that government's "weakness . . . in not demanding at the appropriate moment from clergy, nobility, creditors of the State, and the wealthy classes" the funds necessary for its survival.[55]

If the ranking in which the *junteros* Soler and Cabarrús laid out their options is any clue to the junta's priorities, it is not surprising that they chose interest-free loans and gifts *(donativos)* and the dispatch of swift naval vessels to return with colonial funds, rejecting other proposals as "prejudicial and useless." Unpopular new consumption taxes were avoided. Instead, the government accepted the recommendations, supplementing them by borrowing 3 million florins from an Amsterdam banking house, Croeze & Company and another from "the Holy Churches."[56] As foreseen, the returns were disappointing, quickly so; the expected interest-free *donativo* of 200 million *reales* netted about one-tenth, 23,046,281 *reales,* and domestic borrowing yielded only 693,750; Croeze managed to place with European investors barely 1.5 million florins.[57] Then religious organizations came up with 35.7 million; worse, transfers of silver from the American colonies were delayed and unpredictable in wartime. In July and August 1798 the fiscal situation worsened because of pressure from the Cinco Gremios demanding payment for provisioning the armed forces, from the Banco Nacional de San Carlos, and from the impact of England's blockade of Cadiz, which cut contact with the colonies.[58] At this point a very ill Saavedra had to resign, replaced at the Hacienda by Soler and as prime minister by Mariano Luís de Urquijo.

Soler's Fourth Option

At this critical juncture Soler, confronting a deficit in 1797 of 944 million *reales,* or about double the government's expected income, 1.4 million in outstanding *vales,* and an unprecedented total indebtedness of 2.587 million *reales,* had to order his priorities: first, restoring confidence in the *vales,* and second, the search for new sources of revenue, "extraordinary measures to produce large sums."[59] Since the measures proposed by the Yranda junta had yielded little, and "unable to seek external arrangements"—floating a loan abroad secured on colonial silver transfers—Soler now reverted to what had been the drastic fourth option sketched in his *memoria* to the junta, one sidestepped by Cabarrús and with good reason: "sell the property of foundations, Brotherhoods, pious funds, Hospitals and Chaplaincies, as well as the lands of the Encomiendas of the Military orders, depositing their product at 3 percent in the Caja de Amortización in order to liquidate *vales reales* and shares in loans."[60]

In a patent disclaimer of originality, Soler felt driven to review how and why he had come to this decision. He cited recent government *memorias* of 1794 and 1796, which had recommended the sale of church property, but studiously overlooked Campomanes's *Tratado de la regalía de amortización* (1765), commissioned by Esquilache, Jovellanos's recent, government-circulated *Proyecto de Ley Agraria* (1795); and the economic manuscripts of Francisco Carrasco, Pablo de Olavide, and Bernabé Portillo.[61] Instead, he linked his proposal to his immediate predecessor at the Hacienda, Francisco Saavedra, to the "lengthy and respected conferences we have had on this issue" (high-level debates scrupulously unpublicized), all substantiating his claim that the sale of ecclesiastical holdings had long been entertained by "sound politicians" and "public opinion." Moreover, Soler's proposal, after due reflection, was "the most natural and in keeping with the best, soundest principles of politics and economics" for meeting the government's current and projected expenditures in an uncomplicated, acceptable fashion.[62]

In emphasizing the approach of "buenos políticos" and the opinion of the political class, Soler was taking into account the value and management of entailed properties distributed over the peninsula in every "city, town . . . place . . . even hamlets." His conservative estimate put their total market value at more than 200 million *pesos* (4,000 million *reales*) despite "poor management" and the inevitable "colusiones" leading to their "deterioration and abandonment" and low productivity. He foresaw no problems in mobilizing potential investors, those four hundred thousand "wealthy people" who Soler later calculated would prefer to convert their *vales* into real estate in order to guarantee their future "tranquilidad" rather than persist in investing in government tax returns.[63] Indeed, a close reading of Soler's *consulta* of late summer 1798, which he virtually devoted to the theme of disentailment, turns up overstatement and undiluted optimism, blind faith in the cooperation of corporate bodies and individuals receiving income from entailed properties and in a favorable public reaction to disentailment. "We can hardly calculate," insisted Soler, "the pleasing, favorable feeling given the public by a Real Decreto for the sale of said properties and the deposit of its proceeds in the Caja de Amortización." Perhaps Soler's hyperbole was mere salesmanship, based on the hope that termination of hostilities would permit the metropole to profit from "the remarkable progress that our trade, navigation, and colonial agriculture should make."[64]

The results of the Yranda junta crystallized in decrees signed on 19 October 1798 reflecting the influence of Soler's fourth option, designed to mobilize by indirect expropriation religious and lay entailed properties. These were to be sold at public auction, the proceeds deposited in a special fund, the Caja de Amortización, for systematic redemption of *vales;* the entailed properties included "the real-estate holdings of Hospitals, Hospices, Mercy institutions . . . brotherhoods . . . Pious Works and lay Trusts," along with the outstanding loan capital of such "establecimientos y fundaciones" when amortized. Also affected were yet unsold Jesuit properties (the *temporali- dades*), the buildings of the *colegios mayores* of the universities, and lay entail- ments *(mayorazgos, vínculos)*. In return, the affected ecclesiastical institutions were guaranteed 3 percent annual interest on their expropriated property and funds.

In one sense the decree, by not incorporating entirely Soler's program, showed an awareness of potential opposition from very influential groups. Only affected were the charitable and social functions of religious establish- ments ("public establishments"), not their strictly religious functions; left unaffected were the properties of parish churches, cathedral chapters, reli- gious orders, as well as the *fincas* (properties) of the military orders.[65] In another sense, however, the decrees revealed administrative haste. At first, Soler's ministry was directed to take charge, but four months later, in Janu- ary 1799, the Caja was put under an autonomous *junta suprema,* whose presiding officer was, appropriately, a prominent cleric, the archbishop of Seville, and among whose members was the Caja's director, Manuel Sixto Espinosa. Perhaps an autonomous junta would mollify the fears of *vales* holders that the Caja's receipts might otherwise be diverted to the Ha- cienda's general funds *(rentas generales)* — in January the *vales'* discount reached an average of 26 percent, up 73 percent over the 1798 rate. Further administrative modifications appeared in August 1800, sixteen months after the largest single emission of *vales* (800 million *reales*), again, we may pre- sume, to reassure investors, whose lack of confidence was recorded in the dismayingly high discount of *vales* in the first semester of that year.[66] Now the Caja de Amortización was renamed the Caja de Consolidación, admin- istered by a *comisión gubernativa* separate from the Tesorería General, and Sixto Espinosa was installed as its *contador,* the effective director. For the remainder of the reign of Charles IV the government's key financial bureau- cracies, Hacienda and Consolidación, would be run by two civil servants working in tandem for better or for worse.[67]

These were the immediate repercussions of going to war against Eng- land, whose naval strategy initiated in 1796 was choking off Spain's overseas commercial arteries at their Cadiz and Caribbean terminals, especially at Veracruz, and virtually drying up inflows of colonial revenues that normally covered wartime deficits caused by relatively inelastic metropolitan reve- nues and mounting expenditures. Proximate figures are better than none, even if lower-bound. One indication of the magnitude of colonial inflows on government account not remitted during the war against England is the average annual inflow in years of unobstructed traffic, 1793–96 — 178,276,460 *reales*—compared with the inflow in the first year of hostilities, 1797 — 12,360,128 — after a precipitous drop of 93 percent.[68] The Caja de Consolidación would evidently be Madrid's major instrument of credit and income for financing the war.

How effective was the expropriation in the metropole of ecclesiastical and lay entailments, as well as their capital at loan *(censos),* in terms of receipts deposited in the Caja from public auctions, from the redemption of *vales,* from a lower discount rate and, since the *vales* were acceptable at par in settling debts to the government, from reduced revenue losses? What was the disposition of receipts? And critical to the whole process, why was *consolidación* finally extended to the American colonies, in particular to New Spain, six years after the inception of the process in the metropole?

Estimates of receipts from the liquidation of "public establishments" and their *censos* are available thanks to the labor of Richard Herr and his associates. By the end of 1804, 53 percent (786.7 million *reales*) had been deposited in the Caja de Consolidación; over the whole period of *consolidación,* 1798–1808, receipts came to 1,487 million. Based on the census of 1797, which tallied a population of 10,541,221 in Spain, and on sales of 1,653,376,402 *reales,* returns on disentailment in the metropole over ten years work out to 156.8 *reales* (7.8 *pesos fuertes*) per capita.[69]

If one presumes that the sales volume of expropriated properties correlates positively with the geographical concentration of *vales* holders, then to the end of 1807 the provinces of Madrid, Cadiz, and Seville, where the largest volumes of sales were recorded — 14.8, 10.7, and 9.9 percent, respectively, or 35.4 percent of all such property sales — were home to a significant percentage of all owners of *vales.*[70] Equally notable is the fact that a high percentage of sales receipts — 65.7 percent, or 1,292 million *reales* — deposited in the Caja from September 1800 to April 1808 consisted of government paper, *vales.*[71] Nonetheless, despite a fourfold increase in receipts over two sales periods, 1798–99 and 1800–1804, the sums allocated to redemption rose by a factor of 2.5 in the latter period. In other words, only 25 percent of the sums deposited in the Caja by disentailment were allocated to the specific purpose of the *consolidación,* the redemption of *vales.*

What happened to the remaining 75 percent of Caja receipts is only too clear. Contrary to its presumed autonomy vis-à-vis the Tesorería General, the Caja had to transfer funds to support the government's crisis responses. First, under the Caja de Amortización in 1798–1800 there was a net transfer of at least 528.7 million *reales* to current expenses, roughly the equivalent of one year's receipts from peninsular sources.[72] Subsequently, in 1800–1808, the Caja de Consolidación siphoned away funds to cover the by-now perennial annual deficits, despite (or because of?) the spectacularly large inflows of colonial revenue transferred to Madrid on government account across the Atlantic in 1801–4, 37.5 million *pesos fuertes,* or 750 million *reales.* About 89 percent came from New Spain alone.[73] In 1803 and 1804 internal and external disbursements simply pushed the government's financial managers to greater withdrawals from Consolidación funds. In these years, we must recall, the peninsula suffered an epidemic, an earthquake and acute food shortages, whose effects on Madrid's floating population of the marginalized worried officials. Since the capital's food-storage system (its *pósito*) lacked "grains, d'argent and de crédit," the Caja de Consolidación had to furnish "prodigious sums" for meat, charcoal, and domestic and imported grains.[74] The sums probably were not exaggerated, since in an earlier period, 1785–90, when price levels were lower, the government's outlays on imported grains through Cadiz alone had totaled 300 million *reales* (about 15 million *pesos*).[75]

Yet these turned out to be minor disbursements compared with Caja transfers resulting from the country's dependent international position once France and England renewed hostilities, the English navy proceeded to sever Spain's colonial silver links in the Atlantic, and the French government demanded what was in effect a ransom for Spain's neutrality. "Clouds covered Europe's political horizon," Spanish finance experts later reported to French authorities, "especially in May 1807, on the reopening of hostilities between France and England, the commerce of Spain, along with the resources of the Caja de Consolidación, began to stagnate, which had to lead to the uncertain neutrality of Spain."[76] Under Bonaparte the French government had posted a high price for Spain's neutrality, a monthly subsidy of 16 million *reales* retroactive to May 1803; at 192 million each year, this alone absorbed about 35 percent of the government's peninsular receipts.[77] In despair Bernardo de Iriarte lamented in his diary how much more efficient it would be to apply these funds "to overhauling somewhat our unfortunate, our imaginary, Navy? At the least this money would stay in the Kingdom."[78] Iriarte would have more occasions for lamentation.

Worse followed. In late 1804 an English squadron patrolling off the port of Cadiz assaulted in peacetime four Spanish frigates from the Rio de la Plata "freighting treasures from Peru on royal and private account" to the tune of 4.7 million *pesos* (roughly 1.3 million of it on government account) as London made clear its naval forces would seize any vessel seeking entry to Spanish ports laden with colonial funds. English aggression raised to national policy forced reluctant Spanish officials to declare war, and "henceforth this country is dominated by events and burdened with new expenses." The English government confirmed what Iriarte had foreseen as a consequence of Spain's subsidy to France, that England "will oblige us to begin War, and as a preliminary will seize . . . a few of our ships arriving from the Indies with funds." On 12 November Iriarte had to add to his diary, "Already my earlier prediction that in the end we will have to enter the war has been verified . . . and as a preamble the English have seized 3 frigates with their cargo of money, sinking the other."[79] To pressure upon the Caja de Consolidación to meet subsidy payments to France were now added new financial commitments "that the irresistible force of necessity has accumulated with a rapidity that nothing could stop."[80] Soler and Espinosa had to divert more Caja receipts (declining in 1803–4 from the levels of 1801–2) to current expenditures on armed forces in Vizcaya, Mallorca, the Canaries, and Ceuta, as well as on the artillery corps, not to overlook other Caja outlays on Hacienda personnel and the royal household.[81] Beginning in 1805 comparable charges were made on the Caja de Consolidación to provision all the armed forces, to pay seamen and naval officers (19.2 million *reales* per month), and to cover the gap between projected and effective income from certain religious rents and from the *maestranzas* of the military orders (4.5 million monthly). On an annual basis these totaled 284.4 million *reales,* nearly four times what Madrid's finance experts had conservatively calculated as the annual income of the Caja in wartime.[82]

By late 1804 Soler and Sixto Espinosa perceived that income from alienating peninsular religious entailments was falling short of current and predicted outlays, redemption of *vales* aside. The ratio of sales to the total value of entailments was not encouraging, averaging 15 percent over a decade of amortization, 1798–1808, although in 1804 one might still expect this to increase.[83] The low rate reflected the toll of covert and overt sabotage (which was both "public and vigorous") by religious groups, prelates, administrators of church holdings, and parish priests.[84] The government acknowledged the clergy's opposition in a "letter written by a certain parish priest in which, to prevent the sale of the properties of a pious foundation managed by him, he explained his opposition in inappropriate terms to the royal authority." Meanwhile, there remained another tactic in the strategy of selective religious disentailment: revenues stripped from colonial treasuries ("her distant colonies . . . pay large direct contributions to the parent state") from Mexico City and other colonial capitals in 1801–4, years of peace, could be augmented by the technique already employed in the metropole: tapping the wealth of religious establishments overseas.[85] Obviously, the rise in the price of *vales* in 1802, after the discount rate had dropped to 18.6 percent, was related to heavy inflows of silver once hostilities ended; by 1804, however, that rate had begun to rise ominously as the colonial lifeline was threatened.[86]

It is perhaps pointless to ask whether Godoy's administration had more than the most general knowledge of the composition of church wealth in the colonies, for example, the relative proportion of capital at loan to real-estate holdings. Few doubted that the aggregate wealth of the colonial church was large and that the imperial state in a financial crisis might draw upon church wealth at home and abroad. If there were reservations about using such wealth, they receded when Spain entered the vortex of Anglo-French warfare in late 1804; on 26 November Madrid, advertising the government's "care and high regard" for the residents of the colonies in America, decreed that they too might share in the "beneficios" of disentailed properties and the capital of "pious funds," whose product would be deposited in the Caja de Consolidación in return for 3 percent annual interest. At the same time, Soler and Espinosa were contracting with neutral merchant houses in Europe and the United States, beginning with France's Gabriel-Julien Ouvrard, to withdraw the proceeds of ecclesiastical disentailment in New Spain by circumventing the already tight English blockade. Now, more clearly than at any other time since the end of the seventeenth century, New Spain's mines and commerce constituted the major support of the metropole and its transatlantic system.

Soler's Francophile Conspectus, 1801

Soler's role in the financial crisis of 1798 and the following two stages of disentailment, first in the metropole and then in the colonies, becomes clear if one analyzes his conspectus of Spain and its empire in the European matrix and its pivotal role in the Anglo-French struggle for mastery of the Atlantic. An influential Hacienda minister for ten critical years, Soler was the epicenter of correspondence with domestic and colonial treasury personnel, and his ministry was responsible for the oversight of the national and imperial economies and expanding the empire's tax base. A brutally candid position paper of fifty manuscript pages, footnoted and buttressed by statistical tables prepared under his direction in November 1801 to orient Spain's delegation to the peace negotiations at Amiens, brings together Soler's preference for disentailment, analysis of the Spanish economy, and the influence of Spain's international treaties.[87] It can serve as an epilogue to the breakdown of attempts to devise an Anglo-Spanish treaty of commerce. Here Soler displayed a broad historical perspective, colored by the writings of a generation of eighteenth-century Spanish economic nationalists—the *proyectistas*—troubled by a lagging or stagnating economy. Its particular novelty lies in the views of a major state official empowered to shape and execute policy, rather than a lesser civil servant pleading for policy change.

In Soler's view, discord in Europe had begun in the sixteenth century, when early political economists made trade ("the dependable source of power and conquests") a national monopoly rather than sharing with other nations. England, by formulating later a navigation act and concentrating on "its manufactures and trade," its merchant marine and royal navy, had achieved a virtual "tiranía de los mares." Although its national debt had reached 22.8 billion *reales* in 1793, it had managed to add another 11.6 billion over the years 1793–97, while western Europe was impoverished by comparison (fols. 214r, 224v–225r). By building on an expanding economy and extending its international projection, England's astute diplomats through one commercial treaty after another had come to dominate the European continent and, more specifically, Spain's economy and polity. Over more than a century of England's Navigation Acts, Spain, "from the peak of grandeur, slipped into the abyss of misery" because of "ruinous laws and measures . . . expenditures more damaging by their nature than by their quantity, forgetting the laws of economics" (fol. 214r). To Soler, clever manipulation of tariffs illustrated the skills of England's policymakers compared with those of Spain, a perennial theme of the publications and manuscripts of Spanish economist-*proyectistas* of the eighteenth century and still prominent in the 1790s in the manuscripts of Portillo and Virio. Where the English had adjusted their tariffs both to stimulate domestic manufacture and generate revenue, Spanish policy continued to privilege merchants, not commerce; its tariffs were marked by "obscuridad y versatilidad," by varying rates on the same category of good, measurements sometimes by piece, sometimes by yard, and by viewing tariffs solely as a source of government income. This tariff policy was engendered by the "fiscal spirit of those fatal times, of the maxims of the Hebrews, who controlled our government's customs," oblique references to the last Hapsburg and the long-term farmers of Andalusia's customs in the late seventeenth century, Eminente and his family (fol. 234r–v).

Spain's gradual subordination to English interests could be traced, Soler claimed, to the pattern of unequal commercial treaties between the two nations beginning in the seventeenth century and extending into the next. It had begun in 1645 and been reinforced by the treaties of Madrid in 1667 and 1660 ("monstrously favoring the English"), which were sequels to England's Navigation Act of 1660 ("the source of England's Maritime and commercial power") (fols. 238r, 240r). Parsing clause by clause the concessions yielded by Spain's representatives in treaty making from 1645 to 1783, Soler discerned two contrasting currents: "the good faith and cooperation of Spain . . . and the despotism" of England, ever ready to take advantage of "its power" and "our destiny." He recalled that as late as the Treaty of Versailles, in 1783, England's commercial advantages in the ports of peninsular Spain conceded in all prior treaties had simply been reconfirmed (fol. 243v). However, three years later, when London proposed a new commercial treaty—in the same year as the publicized Anglo-French commercial treaty—Madrid resisted English pressures. The pitfalls of those English proposals, Soler warned, should now be analyzed meticulously, for they would undoubtedly be revived at the forthcoming negotiations at Amiens.

Soler recalled pressures in 1786 to lower Spain's duties on English beers and ciders, which were usually re-exported to the American colonies, and he cautioned against automatically extending to English merchants benefits granted other nations. He would reject wholesale reconfirmation of all twelve Anglo-Spanish commercial treaties signed from 1645 to 1783. Elements of those treaties tolerated smuggling by English vessels in peninsular ports, raised the possible renewal of English participation in, and abuse of, the African slave trade to Spain's colonies (the *asiento*), and infringed upon the sovereign right of Spain "to sell, pledge . . . transfer to France or another Nation" any colony of Spain in America (fols. 243v–244r, 246r–v). There was in Soler's hardheaded analysis an undercurrent of admiration in references to the English tactic of scouring international treaties to find advantageous clauses that were later inserted in their treaties with Spain to augment "their privileges with our ruination." Through the "duplicity" of its proposals, London "has outwitted us . . . making us yield to its whims . . . and has subordinated us to its interests, while damaging ours."

Spain's negotiators were advised to beware of England's protestations of "good will and harmony to get Spain to affirm and ratify harmful trade agreements," which undermined "our industry and paralyze our commerce," and to deflect London's insistence on signing a commercial agreement by following the principle that "we will handle them just as they do us in commercial matters" (fols. 248r–250r). This, Soler confided elsewhere in his *memoria,* was part of a defensive strategy for buying time for implementing a policy of national recovery, "clever conduct in treating with the English . . . without disturbing their zeal and suspicion." His was an example of counterposing guile to power, the strategy of an underdeveloped state toward the hegemon, of an imperial system measuring the chasm widening between its economy and that of the most developed nation of the time (fol. 226v).

It should be evident by now that underlying Soler's policy recommendations for negotiating an Anglo-Spanish commercial treaty was a profoundly pessimistic assessment of Spain's economy in 1801. Despite what Soler judged a favorable resource base in metropole and colonies ("the most considerable"), Spain's agriculture, manufactures, and trade were "in a fatal State." Soler—like Vicente Basadre across the Atlantic at Veracruz—had a physiocratic fixation on land, the benefits from its efficient utilization, and Spaniards' misuse of this natural resource: the structural shortcomings of mortmain and entail ("the baneful spirit of entailments") with consequent concentration of tenures ("accumulation of property in a few hands") reinforced by the example of "the nonproductive classes," a guarded reference to absentee aristocratic landlords and the large clerical establishment. To these factors Soler added excessive government oversight that disregarded the real driving force behind man's "activity and vigor," the "powerful drive of his interest" (fol. 216r–v). These bottlenecks were the cause of low productivity, low output of beef and grains (consequently "dependent upon Foreign suppliers"), and shortages of industrial raw materials—silk, flax, and hemp. Other raw materials, such as wools, salt, and soda ash, were neither fully taken up by domestic manufacture nor profitably exportable, since transport costs and taxation made them uncompetitive in markets abroad.

The situation of Spain's manufacturing sector was no better, despite domestic and colonial demand for "great amounts of Manufactures." Using the Lorena census of 1791, Soler produced figures for domestic plant and output indicating that they were grossly inadequate in textiles, iron, paper, and crockery. Given the low output of agricultural commodities and manufactures, misdirected tax policy and inferior infrastructure, Soler asked rhetorically, "What commerce, domestic or foreign, can Spain have?" (fols. 217v–218r). The volume of the peninsula's internal traffic was low, it lacked transport facilities "to accelerate the circulation of its production," and goods were delayed at repeated checkpoints for government taxes and possible smuggling. In addition, Spain's foreign trade was hamstrung by customs regulations that provided no effective protection to domestic manufacture, by the absence of an adequate merchant marine, by too few ports authorized to engage in foreign trade, and by the *consulados'* "baneful corporate mentality," which "strengthen our ignorance and favor our misery" (fols. 218r–v, 236v). Soler's down-to-earth overview ended on a characteristically downbeat note reminiscent of a decades-old manuscript of José del

Campillo y Cosío: "Agriculture declining, Workshops either ruined or para-lyzed: foreign trade held back by the Fiscal system and by England's acquisi-tions . . . an enormous debt . . . after ruining our public credit . . . this is the condition of Spain in . . . 1801" (fols. 219v–220r). He estimated the pub-lic debt at 4.108 billion *reales.*[88]

Spain's recession in the seventeenth century and stagnation in the eigh-teenth were in awesome contrast to England's progress toward the "tyranny of the seas." Soler's *memoria* incorporated tables on England's navy and merchant marine, its annual foreign-trade surpluses contrasted with Spain's perennial deficits, which he traced back to the high percentage of European goods that Spain re-exported to its American colonies (fol. 219r–v). By care-fully breaking down exchanges between Spain and England in 1796, he made explicit the structure of classic unequal economic relations between exporters of raw materials and those of manufactures. In that year Spain had imported from England 192.3 million *reales* of goods and wares, of which 63.6 percent (122.4 million) were woolens, linens, and cottons, running up a trade deficit of 129.3 million. Of its exports to England, 63 percent had been raw wool and cotton (12.6 million) and dyestuffs (27.1 million). From these figures, Soler had to conclude that "the current situation of [Spanish] industry" revealed that Spain was dependent upon England "to supply us and the colonies" (fols. 227r–228r).

These long-term problems were now complicated and exacerbated by the five years of war against England's formidable naval forces. That navy in a very special sense represented to Soler the very projection of national power: in 1796 it had seized at sea "very valuable cargoes" en route from Spain's colonies to Cadiz. Now it was blockading metropolitan and colo-nial ports, stopping specie inflows from the colonies, reducing Spain to solely its domestic revenues, which were inadequate in peacetime and in wartime necessitated "expenditures as immense as they were useless" to defend Cadiz, Alicante, Ayamonte, Málaga, and Palma de Mallorca in Eu-rope and the ports of Havana, San Juan de Puerto Rico, Campeche, and Veracruz in the colonies. Such was the state of Spain on entering negotia-tions for peace—"poor, debt-ridden, having to tolerate . . . the insolence of England in American and Asian waters" (fols. 225v–226r).

Soler's review of the distant and immediate past of the Spanish economy and trade relations with England was designed mainly as the basis for both short- and long-term policy recommendations. In the short term Spain had to shore up its international position through an alliance with the French Republic, "natural friend who cannot offend her nor allow another power to trouble her," in order better to confront the English hegemon. Only

France had been able to curb England, having "secured its independence . . . and expanded its commercial relations" (fols. 225r–226r). Its government, "prudent and vigilant," had forged that nation's "military and federative power," silenced factionalism, instilled in all classes "vigor and activity," and lifted government revenues by 20 percent while pushing its frontiers to incorporate 8 million people; all this was muted admiration of France's military success since 1797. Yet the nature of the French state remained "federativo," while that of England was clearly "preponderante." Nor did Soler overlook the fact that in two years an "Outstanding Genius" had managed to restore France to the position where now she "dictates Laws to Europe and gives it a firm peace." Here surfaced an undercurrent among many of Spain's political elite, guarded admiration for the liberal and authoritarian figure of Bonaparte.

Soler's reliance upon France rejuvenated under Napoleon Bonaparte mirrored the support that many Spanish civil servants and intellectuals had found in Bourbon France, which they now hoped to revive despite the previous decade of revolution, regicide, severe inflation, and economic disorganization. Spain's monarchy and France's republic could continue a policy of realignment—a "Pacto Nacional," as Bernardo de Iriarte rephrased it, rather than a "Pacto de Familia"—whose objective was "to keep free and under our control the commerce of all our Americas," excluding England. In this vein, Soler saw in France at the critical juncture of 1801 a "respectable guarantor" of Spain's interests, one that "must help us counteract British power, which is more threatening to us than ever" (fols. 224v–226v, 249r). An equitable settlement with England based upon Franco-Spanish collaboration could give Madrid breathing space to put into play those "measures our present situation requires" and "pull us out of the fatal state in which we are sunk, assisting us in promoting our interests and removing obstacles that destroy us." Spain's government could then develop its agriculture, trade, and artisan crafts in order to contest England at last in "a War of industry" (fols. 249r, 252v).

For many in Spain's political class, this vision—rather, an aspiration formed earlier under Charles III—of a France fraternally collaborating with its natural ally to develop the economy of the Spanish metropole and colonies was still tenable in 1801. Thereafter it would erode rapidly, yet it remained an undercurrent in the internal war beginning in Spain in 1808 and explains the stance of so-called *afrancesados* like Azanza, Cabarrús, Goya, and others in the regime of José Bonaparte.

These reflections prefaced the long-term policy recommendations at the end of Soler's *memoria,* under the rubric "Measures that will have to be

taken to advance our political interests." Economy and national development were clearly interconnected in his thinking, baring the bedrock of a
developmental plan, its strength and weakness. Two initial observations are
in order. Soler had assessed past developmental policy and realized the dys-
utility of government intervention in behalf of certain categories of infant
industry, "basically useless projects although brilliant in appearance" that
had produced "fine manufactures from luxury workshops," typifying a policy of "commencing where one should end" (fols. 252v–253r and n. 1). Second, underlying his argument is the necessity of freeing up resources and
entrepreneurship in the vein of Adam Smith, or J.-B. Say, who recommended "allowing manufacture and export to be free . . . the sole fundament of a commercial code" (fol. 227r). In the physiocratic tradition of
many Spanish eighteenth-century political economists and/or civil servants,
such as Carrasco, Campomanes, Olavide, and Jovellanos, Soler's program
assigned high priority to farming. To increase the acreage under cultivation,
he advocated colonization projects on newly available land (reminiscent of
Olavide's Sierra Morena project), accelerated enclosures supplemented by
elimination of the pasture rights of sheepmen, and incentives for food and
industrial crops. To simplify land taxation and lower effective rates, he proposed to substitute for the multiple forms of *rentas provinciales* a broad land
tax *(contribución territorial)* and to tithe the net rather than the gross value
of farm production. Briefly mentioned were measures affecting the fundamental and hitherto virtually inviolable structures of land concentration:
prohibition of further entailments ("so often requested . . . so often agreed
upon in the Cortes, so often practiced and now unfortunately forgotten")
and further concentration *(agrupaciones de mayorazgos)* through primo-
geniture. Soler aimed his criticism especially at the ecclesiastical establishment when he discussed entailment and, later, charity dispensed to the
"clusters" of poor and vagabonds by convents, monasteries, and clergymen
out of a "false notion of piety"—the marginalized were a different species,
even a subspecies. This reflected Soler's commitment to disentailing the
wealth of "pious foundations" of public utility for transfer to the Caja de
Amortización.

The balance of Soler's *providencias* revolved around stimulating the flow
of agricultural commodities from producers to consumers at home and
abroad. To lower export prices, he would abolish internal customs, along
with most export duties, and lower transport costs through state-financed
construction of roads and canals. He would authorize more peninsular
ports to handle exports, which in turn would be augmented by an enlarged
merchant marine and the training of seamen. Despite references to prepara-

tion for a "guerra de industria," Soler opted for state support for artisanal crafts *(artes)* over *manufacturas* or *fábricas*. Consistent with physiocratic ideology, Soler judged the most efficient support for crafts and commerce was simply removal of those corporate regulatory bodies—the guilds—that manipulated apprenticeship (equated with slavery) and controlled output. His position foreshadowed the oncoming "liberal" economists' criticism of state intervention in support of outmoded institutions as obstructive to economic growth. Last, innovation in manufacture and chemistry for the improvement of production could be spread through the medium of publications such as an "Anales de Artes y Obras" (fol. 253r–v).

A number of conclusions flow from Soler's policy paper of 1801. First, there is the uncritical, even biased, faith in the willingness of the French bourgeoisie—businessmen, manufacturers, financiers—behind Directoire, then Consulat and its "Genio Singular," Bonaparte, to respect Spanish interests in a common front against England. After all, in the second half of the eighteenth century Madrid's nationalist high civil servants remained demonstrably reluctant to sign commercial treaties with England or France, a stance that evidently irritated French textile and related export interests, whose products were being displaced in Spain's colonial markets—the peninsular market remained secondary for them. Although Soler footnoted the size of England's trade surpluses, merchant marine, and external debt with data culled carefully from French publications such as the *Encyclopédie du commerce* and now the *Moniteur,* the omission of comparable data on the performance of the French economy after 1790 suggests deliberate avoidance of materials that might undermine confidence in France's economic capacity. That country's remarkable resurgence under General Bonaparte, its "vigor," military strategy, and consistent anti-English policies, made it a "natural" ally against ubiquitous English interests. This attitude of Soler and other high civil servants and military officers would lead later to their collaboration with prominent French figures imposed upon Spain, Murat and Joseph Bonaparte. We should also recall that in 1801 at least, Foreign Minister Cevallos seemed to share Soler's faith in France's businessmen and *fonctionnaires* as allies, a faith he would abandon in 1808.

Second, Soler could be critical of the past yet remain fundamentally uninnovative about current policy. As with *proyectistas* of the eighteenth century, his hindsight was sharper than his foresight. And poor foresight is evident in the priority assigned to land, a theme running through his *memorias* of 1798 and 1801. There is that physiocratic preoccupation with land tenures and their utilization, the efficient marketing of agricultural products along with liberating crafts and commerce from privileged oligopolistic constraints—"custom that dominates man" (fol. 255r). For a metropole favored by expanding colonial demand for imports of many categories of manufactures, a physiocratic emphasis on the economy of the metropole seems misguided, misdirected, or worse. Colonies like New Spain, with a population almost half that of the metropole, needed to import textiles and metallurgy, not merely Spanish wines, brandies, almonds, and cigarette paper. Yet Soler's *providencias* omit manufactures despite references to gearing up in peacetime for an oncoming "war of industry."[89]

Third, omission of the colonial world in the economic recovery Soler envisioned in peacetime revealed a dangerous insensitivity to the changing colonial situation, to ways in which colonial eonomic structures, especially the financial ones, differed from those of the metropole. Curiously, Soler's vision of Spain's trade expansion was focused, not on the colonies, but on potential trade with Russia, Sweden, Denmark, Holland, Prussia, and "the Republics that France has formed in Italy and the Levant" (fol. 226v), just what one might expect from this member of a well-connected Mallorcan commercial family scattered around the Mediterranean basin. In his conspectus, from the colonies in America came *caudales,* money.

Finally, Soler's conspectus of Spain's position within the western European economy after Westphalia, its current situation as of 1801, and future policy should be put in context. Forthcoming peacemaking, in the opinion of Soler and his French counterpart, Alexandre Maurice Blanc, comte de Hauterive, might lay the foundations of a new international order ten years after the onset of Europe's most unsettled period since the Thirty Years' War. Both argued that the Westphalian settlements had been weakened by England's expansion in the late seventeenth century and then undermined dangerously throughout the eighteenth. They concurred that England symbolized a larger phenomenon, commercial expansion with all its geographical and economic linkages. Its commercial dynamism and naval muscle had empowered its diplomats to negotiate with European nations ostensibly on a plane of equality; in reality, its economic and naval power had extracted concessions that, as Soler and later Pedro Estala made explicit, stifled Spain's economic development. England, not France, was the omnipresent hegemon to be confronted. The forthcoming diplomatic negotiations might eradicate the constraints of unequal treaties and permit arrangements to conform to the new reality. This would reflect the principle of real equality among contractants, one designed to curb England's virtual monopoly of power: it would be founded upon the military power and self-sufficient resources of France, which, in turn, had to have the support of other Continental powers, such as Spain, prepared to activate fresh economic policies. Both Soler and Hauterive lauded France's recent and surprising achievement of apparent internal class harmony, its military power, and its role as the sole effective core of anti-English opposition.[90]

Understandably, Soler and Hauterive parted company on the projection of these mutual principles, and this division would lead to the crisis of 1808. Soler, to put it charitably, misread sections of Hauterive's analysis that were rooted in French national interests, some barely discernible, others fully emergent. Implicit in acceptance of Napoleon Bonaparte's revolutionary settlement was the convergence of the interests of bourgeosified peasants and capitalistic noblemen of the *ancien régime:* LeCouteulx de la Noraye, Hauterive, Talleyrand, and the military and commercial *arrivistes* of Directoire and Consulat (Murat, Sièyes, Ouvrard). François Cabarrús (a blend of Bearnais and Castilian) successfully bridged the two cultures and two eras of Spain, those of Charles III and Charles IV. From this consensus came Soler's vision of a new international coprosperity sphere, to be shared among France and other collaborating nations of western Europe.

A careful reading of Hauterive could reveal, however, that while a nation's sovereignty would be respected, he would consider its economic frontiers limitless in a market sense, embracing all consumers of its exports regardless of national boundaries. As Hauterive put it, and perhaps even Adam Smith and J. B. Say would have concurred, "Consumers belong less to the nation they live in than to the one whose production they consume."[91] Hardly collaboration, this was decidedly hegemonic. Buried in Hauterive's exposition of 1800 was this muted warning of French economic imperialism rooted in bilateral and unequal commercial treaties, no more nor less than what would be evident in the commercial treaty of 1810 between England and the Portuguese government in its Brazilian refuge. To penetrate Spain's transatlantic trade structures, ultimately the French would look back to their mirage of privileged access to Spain's colonies in America, while the English would choose the imperialism of free trade. In Hauterive's view, some nations were not yet ready for immediate liberation from the oppression of custom, tradition, and imperial force. Hence, it was senseless, he remarked candidly at one point, "to free people who lack the necessary foresight to accept the price of liberty or enough resolve to support the efforts of their liberators."[92] (Perhaps the experience of the recent revolution in Saint-Domingue or the French occupation of Egypt motivated this observation). Bayonets would be useless in prodding liberty forward in Spain, but they might be needed to maintain the alliance.

But in 1801 Soler could envisage only a cooperative arrangement with

French interests, a viewpoint he shared with some in the Spanish political class under Charles IV and maintained at the Hacienda over the next seven years. It was left to Pedro Estala, in 1805, to elaborate Soler's position by assigning to England's economic domination full blame for Spain's "backwardness," a case of transference common in psychological warfare. In any event, Soler's extension of *consolidación* to the colony of New Spain and his contracts with Ouvrard and later Gordon & Murphy for the transfer of government funds from New Spain derived partly from Soler and Hauterive's vision of a collaborative European confederation. Across the Atlantic, however, Veracruz's merchants had a different view of that vision. They labeled *consolidación* an "error político" stemming from "the common conviction that in the Americas wealth abounds so generally and extraordinarily that there is neither inhabitant nor class that does not own and enjoy it."[93]

11. *Consolidación:* New Spain

 . . . .

The funds of pious foundations in the Kingdom [New Spain] should properly be called the universal refuge, first aid, and the spirit behind Agriculture, Mining, Commerce, and Industry.
"Representación de la Tribunal de Minería"

The Spanish government, no longer knowing how to avoid national bankruptcy, lured by an excess of paper money, attempted a very risky operation.   Alexander von Humboldt

Spain's Hacienda cannot make a move without arranging with [the Hacienda] of America.
Alejandro Malaspina

In the spring of 1805 the economic elites of the colony of New Spain were upset by receipt of the royal decree of 26 December 1804 countersigned by Hacienda Minister Miguel Caetano Soler. Affirming that the alienation of real estate and capital resources of certain charitable foundations *(obras pías)* initiated in Spain in 1798 had benefited the monarchy in general, those who had purchased and improved the state-auctioned properties, as well as those whom the pious works maintained, the decree extended the alienation program to Spain's overseas possessions.

Subsequently, the *consulado* of Veracruz accused Soler of an *error político,* and with reason. The error was Soler's failure to analyze the structure of the colonial economy, how it differed from that of the metropole, and consequently the economic and political repercussions of expropriating the capital and real estate of New Spain's wealthy religious corporations. Operating through differing mechanisms in metropole and colony—in Spain via real estate, in New Spain via loan capital—disentailment of the annuities and real estate of religious foundations upset links between philanthropy and economy and affected—and disaffected—many social groups. The effort to consolidate and support government treasury bills *(vales)* through disentailment by the process of *consolidación* would undermine a basic structure of the colonial economy. An example of "bold incrementalism gone awry"?

In Spain and New Spain tithes provided income for the principal churches and key religious personnel, and disentailment left such income intact. Philanthropy channeled into religious institutions *(capellanías, obras pías)* supported individual clerics and a large and varied assortment of eleemosynary corporations. These trust funds financed hospitals, poorhouses, orphanages, schools, convents, chaplaincies, and chantries, as well as the personnel associated with their operations. *Obras pías* touched all classes and status groups.

In Spain, income from *obras pías* came primarily from urban and rural liens either bestowed upon or bought by religious foundations. Disentailment of this property, deemed to be serving public rather than religious ends, and depositing the proceeds in a redemption fund (first the Caja de Ámortización, then the Caja de Consolidación) seemed a logical, beneficial policy to mitigate the financial crisis at the end of the century. In 1804 Soler and the director of Caja de Consolidación, Sixto Espinosa, no doubt had in mind the results of the Caja's operations from September 1800 to the end of 1804, when it had taken in 483.4 million *reales;* it was presumable that similar or better results might occur if *consolidación* were applied to the empire's wealthiest colony, New Spain, where what was really a form of expropriation and sale of *capellanías* and *obras pías* might produce much desired specie.[1] One must ask, however, whether Soler and Espinosa understood, or chose simply to overlook, that New Spain's *obras pías* were overwhelmingly in the form of capital at loan, almost the opposite of conditions in the peninsula, where real estate predominated.[2] The decision to include New Spain and other colonies was logical in light of an impressive, recent development, the inflows of specie from America on government and private account at Cadiz in the interregnum between wars, the peacetime years of 1801–4.

In the preamble of the *real decreto* of 26 December 1804, extending *consolidación* to the American and Philippine colonies, Madrid softened its intervention in the financial structure of the colonial economy. It claimed that at first it had not intended to include the colonies but that since the expedient had benefited the metropole, the government had resolved to allow its colonial "vassals" to share comparable benefits through "alienation and sale of properties of *obras pías* of whatever class and condition" to pay *subsidios,* debts to Amsterdam's merchant-bankers, and unexpected defense costs. Well toward the end of regulations for executing the alienation was a paragraph providing for rapid remission of funds to the metropole and specifying how to accomplish it. To guarantee annual interest on expropriated property and funds at the rate current in the colonies, Madrid committed "the returns on tobacco, turnover taxes and the rest of . . . Real Hacienda entering those treasuries."[3] Through their taxes, residents in the colony would have the opportunity to pay for the loss of their principal source of loan capital.

Derived from human impulses for general as well as specific philanthropy, that is, support for a religious community or specific family members via religious office *(capellanía)*, as in Spain, the pious funds of New Spain by the time they were affected by *consolidación* consisted virtually of capital at loan rather than real estate. By bestowing annuities *(censos)* produced by specific urban or rural properties upon religious foundations, individuals such as merchants, mine owners, and landowners contributed to the support of convents, chaplaincies, hospitals, and schools; the properties bearing the *censos,* however, remained in private hands and were transferable. A chaplaincy, a kind of trust fund established by the "wealthy . . . for the use of their descendants," was often held by a layman who was a descendant of the founder and would pay a priest to "fulfill the spiritual functions of the endowment while he used the rest of the income of the *capellanía* for his own support."[4] In this fashion, large-scale entails were limited, mobility of property was unimpaired, and there existed the possibility of insuring family members and their descendants against the ever-present vicissitude of downward mobility. By the end of the eighteenth century, the Juzgado de Testamentos, Capellanías y Obras Pías administered three types of religious funds: perpetual, redeemable over a fixed term, and *depósitos irregulares,* which were, in fact, usually rolled over. The colony's religious foundations of one sort or another had become "un verdadero Banco de avío," an investment bank for the whole colonial economy.[5] The economic upsurge in agriculture, ranching, and mining in the late eighteenth century increased the returns to many enterprises, and religious philanthropy took the form of annuities based on real estate. So the pious funds, rather than merchant banks, financed economic growth in the colony.

Mexico City's *almaceneros,* that key component of the colonial elite, enjoyed an unexpected capital surplus when English blockaders intercepted their remittances to Cadiz. In many cases their funds were invested locally, and, in fact, evidence indicates that they bought up properties auctioned by debtors liquidating debts to *obras pías*. Although *almaceneros* as a group did not protest *consolidación,* mine owners and *hacendados* did because they foresaw financial disaster.

The financial history of New Spain's nunneries in the eighteenth century records the expansion of their operations. They shifted from the purchase and management of rural to predominantly urban properties; in Mexico City, nunneries ended up possessing much of the city's real estate.[6] While additions to income continued to come from new annuities, the major source of income growth came from lending via the *depósitos irregulares.* Thus nunneries and pious funds became the major source of loan capital. The *depósito irregular* required no collateral, stipulated a time of amortization, was secured by cosigners or bondsmen *(fiadores),* and was usually rolled over. According to William Taylor, "Because monasteries, convents and priests generally considered interest payment as a desirable fixed annual income, they did not encourage estate owners to pay off the principal."[7] For example, Manila's trade with Mexico City drew upon the capital of Manila's Mesa de Misericordia, once described as a "spiritual and commercial bank" whose funds were accumulated through the collection of "alms for . . . masses for souls in purgatory" and earning on its commercial operations "excessive profits."[8] The pressure to select reliable borrowers probably accounts for the predominance of *peninsular* merchants as *mayordomos* and *tesoreros mayores* managing the lending of the colonial church's pious funds. Since borrowers often shopped for financing in a number of bishoprics, *mayordomos* with a network of correspondents able to uncover background credit information were indispensable. As the Tribunal de Minería observed, "Over here most of the pious funds are based upon liquid capital, in which Patrons or Administrators intervene only when they are loaned at interest and the interest is collected."[9] Whether peninsula-born *mayordomos* favored *peninsular* over *criollo* borrowers remains uncertain (they probably did); the judicious disbursement of gifts, tips, and gratuities could modify the judgments of *mayordomos, tesoreros,* and *jueces de capellanías.*[10] In response to strong demand, greater risk, or both, the interest rate on *depósitos irregulares* shifted upward from 3 percent to 5 percent over the eighteenth century.[11]

An indication of the volume of lending may be gleaned from reports of the operations of prestigious religious corporations such as the convents of La Concepción and La Encarnación, which received over several decades at the end of the eighteenth century repayments ranging between 185,000 and 400,000 *pesos.* By the first decades of the nineteenth century, philanthropy, religious finance, and private enterprise were interdependent to an unprecedented degree. Merchants viewed the funds of religious bodies—*obras pías, comunidades, capellanías*—as a "new mass of circulating capital . . . which could be considered like a family fund supporting many households." Gabriel de Yermo—*almacenero,* sugar planter, and supplier to Mexico City retail *azucareros*—compared these funds to a "wellspring of agriculture, mining, and commerce."[12] He was correct: estimates of *obras pías* wealth in New Spain as of 1805 vary from 24.5 million *pesos* to 47.5 million, of which the value of directly owned real estate was between 2.5 million and 3 million—at a maximum only 12 percent. One may detect here a major difference in the economic structures of metropole and colony.

Much of *obras pías* capital was invested in financing agriculture, ranching, and, to a limited degree, mining and commercial operations. Religious foundations tended to avoid the direct *habilitación* of mining enterprises, which were invariably speculative. Thus, owners of large mines tended to turn to their suppliers *(aviadores),* to silver merchants in Mexico City, and to the mining guild itself for capital or, like wealthy *almaceneros,* borrowed against their landed properties, urban or rural.[13] In times of warfare at sea, as in 1805 and subsequent years, *almaceneros* avoided inventories of luxury goods lest a sudden armistice open the way to a flood of lower-priced imports; indeed, some merchants turned to lending on a large scale, since "no one wants to keep money idle."[14] It is also evident that many small and medium-sized *peninsular* or *criollo* enterprises found financing in religious foundations. Not atypical could be the "merchant who, starting his career with a small capital, to increase and invest it with a reasonable expectation of gain, borrows at interest from pious foundations, which, combined with his own capital, gives him the chance to pursue his fortune."[15] These "small and medium-sized merchants" operated between, on the one hand, the large merchants of Mexico City and, on the other, the provincial centers and the mass of colonial consumers.

There was justification for *obras pías* capital to flow into rural properties.[16] Data on output, coinage, and overseas trade that Viceroy Revilla-gigedo had prepared in 1790 with regard to the repercussions of *comercio libre* had underscored the prosperity of the countryside. While the overall increase in tithe collections from 1771–80 to 1781–90 averaged 37.4 percent, those of the archbishopric of Mexico rose by 71.4 percent, Guadalajara's by 36.5 percent, and Puebla's by 18.3 percent.[17] The surge in land values provided leverage whereby large, medium-sized, and small rural proprietors could increase their borrowing from pious funds on the collateral of inflated real estate, "properties whose valuations were exaggerated in order to borrow." Demand for mortgage funds, especially those of pious funds in Mexico City, was "irrefutable proof" of thousands of *labradores* borrowing from six thousand to twenty thousand *pesos* from *juzgados, cofradías,* "and any willing lender," while "most principal, as soon as it was repaid, was sought by other *lavradores.*"[18] While some proprietors claimed that borrowing financed improvements in land and production, leveraging in the aggregate led to an overhang of interest obligations and limited amortization when mortgages were not rolled over. This was precisely the situation that Puebla's intendant reported in 1803 when he detected "that property was overburdened with mortgage and interest payments, most due to charitable foundations."[19]

By 1804 New Spain's rural enterprises had on the whole overborrowed, and while most rural properties carried a debt load, some could weather a financial squeeze better than others. Recall of outstanding mortgages on properties of small farmers, as Alexander von Humboldt found (probably echoing his informant Manuel Abad y Queipo), could push these *labradores* to the wall. Small farmers and *rancheros* owning from ten to twenty acres up to two hundred or five hundred were a "broad middle segment," but of this critical group we still know little.[20]

In the short span of nine months, from late December 1804 to early September 1805, Madrid advertised its intention to alienate the land and capital of New Spain's charitable foundations dedicated to social utility and appointed two officials in the colony to oversee operations.[21] By early September these civil servants had begun to receive not only lists of clerical benefices and foundation endowments but also the first deposits of the *consolidación.* Over the next two months, beginning with the prestigious and predominantly *criollo* Mexico City *ayuntamiento,* the colony's landholding and mining elites vehemently demanded suspension of the 16 December 1804 decree extending *consolidación* to New Spain. They were shortly joined by a supporting cast of regional interest groups. They relied upon prominent *criollo* lawyers to draft their protests: Francisco Primo de Verdad y Ramos for the capital's *ayuntamiento,* Waldo Indalecio Bernal for the *hacendados* of the province of Mexico, Miguel Domínguez for the mining tribunal, and Juan Francisco Azcárate y Ledesma for an unidentified area. The rapid concert of protest testified to the degree of intercommunication among the colony's economic elites and their perception of how essential *obras pías* were as investment banks.

As we have seen, *consolidación* came to New Spain without warning in April 1805 and was activated rapidly by Viceroy Iturrigaray, already pressured by Hacienda Minister Soler to divert as much specie as possible from colonial revenues for remittance to the metropole. Worse, Madrid's use of neutral cover firms and shipping to export specie through Veracruz by indirect channels from 1805 to 1808 would further sour Iturrigaray's relations with influential members of the merchant communities of Mexico City and

Veracruz, where *peninsulares* dominated. By tampering with the operations of a basic financial structure of the colonial economy, one firmly integrated with the economic welfare of innumerable residents, the Spanish state was intervening in the lives of colonial people to an unprecedented degree. This form of expropriation rippling through the colony's economy stripped many Indian parishes, religious orders, provincial convents and monasteries, church schools, and orphanages of virtually their only source of income.[22] Many perceived the metropole as arbitrary, unaware of or insensitive to colonial realities—"despotic" as contemporaries put it. The crisis of Spain in Europe now threatened the lifeline to its wealthiest colony in America, New Spain.

Who Bore the Burden of *Consolidación* in New Spain?

Consolidación's execution involved millions of silver *pesos* transferred from the colony to the metropole from 1805 to 1812. But upon which groups was the burden the heaviest?

Major mine operators were in general financed by suppliers *(aviadores)*, silver merchants or the mining guild. When borrowing from *obras pías,* they could use their landed estates as collateral. Small to medium-sized mine owners probably depended more on venture and working capital borrowed from charitable foundations. On the other hand, proprietors of large *haciendas, criollo* or *peninsular,* were pressured by officials of *consolidación,* which is not to argue that they lost their holdings on any major scale. To be sure, some did, but as Asunción Lavrín has found, liquidation of large estates was infrequent.[23] Such were the terms of *consolidación,* moreover, that debtors with *haciendas* whose appraised value was fifty thousand *pesos* or more could, through a settlement *(composición),* offer a down payment of 20 percent or less, the balance payable in installments over six to ten years, and often even the down payment could be delayed.[24] Lavrín is on solid ground when she concludes that there was no significant change in the pattern of ownership of large estates as *consolidación* was enforced. Moreover, not all *haciendas* were burdened with debts, despite the impression created by the protestations of 1805.[25]

As for the colony's economic elite of *almaceneros* in overseas trade with Cadiz, Barcelona, and Manila, as well as in domestic circuits of distribution, they held a capital reserve when English blockaders halted remittances to the metropole. Their funds were invested locally, and, in fact, evidence indicates that merchants—peninsula-born *almaceneros* like Heras Soto and the second conde de la Cortina—bought up urban and rural properties auctioned by religious communities in Mexico City, Puebla, and Veracruz to liquidate their *obras pías*. It is not surprising that much of such property was urban real estate.[26] Not only did the capital's predominantly peninsular *almaceneros* bid for real estate but they could empathize with Cadiz merchants eager to convert their sizeable holdings of paper *vales* into silver.[27] These factors may explain why the *consulado* of Mexico City failed to file a formal *representación* with Viceroy Iturrigaray in 1805, when the mining tribunal, the *ayuntamiento* of the capital, and the large *hacendados* of the intendancy of Mexico did, and why, as Iturrigaray wrote Finance Minister Soler, *consulado* officers had assured him—orally, to be sure—that "for their part, and speaking for their commercial corporation, . . . they will never take any action that might hinder" the execution of orders enforcing *consolidación*.[28]

Not so New Spain's small and medium-sized *labradores*. Doubtless they were among the 5,092 *rancheros* listed by Fernando Navarro y Noriega in 1810, especially those 3,001 (59 percent) clustered in the intendancies of Mexico, Puebla, Valladolid, and Guadalajara, who had to pay into *consolidación* 82 percent of the total collections.[29] For example, at Cholula (part of the intendancy of Puebla), small landowners had borrowed 70–100 percent of the value of their real-estate holdings; of fifty-eight properties surveyed, fifty-four were funded largely by *obras pías*.[30]

Most capital borrowed from *obras pías* was invested in rural properties, which would fit revised figures for the sectoral composition of New Spain's gross domestic output in 1810, when, according to Fernando Rosenzweig Hernández, such properties accounted for 47 percent.[31] Contemporary evidence supports this calculation: Antonio de San José Muro reported in 1805 that most small properties *(fincas)* were mortgaged to up to two-thirds of their value; Abad y Queipo warned Sixto Espinosa that most *obras pías* mortgages were placed on agricultural properties; and a Mexico City finance junta of 1815 claimed that New Spain's rural areas were divided into "innumerable small *haciendas* whose mortgage payments consume all of their profits."[32] For these, *consolidación* proved a disaster.

The small *haciendas* had been purchased (leveraged?) mainly on borrowed capital by those attracted by rising food prices, the possibility of growing income, and the status conferred upon property owners. They were at the margin; the debt ratio of their operations was high, of their savings, low. While large *hacendados* usually could arrange a *composición* with the local *junta de consolidación* for relatively small down payments and installments spread over many years, *labradores* and *rancheros* could barely satisfy their financial obligations. Hence the tentative conclusion of Lavrín ("the number of smaller rural properties exchanging hands was much larger") and Romeo Flores Caballero ("most affected were the large number of small or medium-sized proprietors").[33] When in 1808 Melchor Talamantes referred to the execution of *consolidación* "despite the outcry of the people" and in 1811 the insurgent leaders Ignacio Rayón and José María Liceaga denounced the "sacking and distress" of *consolidación,* they had in mind the mass of small rural landowners, not the *hacendado* elite. Significantly, a small *hacienda* and adjoining *rancho* belonging to Miguel Hidalgo y Costilla, valued at thirty-one thousand *pesos* and encumbered by overdue mortgages of seven thousand *pesos* owed to two *capellanías,* were seized in December 1807 and held by *consolidación* agents but released in February 1810.[34]

On the other hand, perhaps the impact of *consolidación* on small holders was exaggerated. None of the recent agrarian studies by Jan Bazant, David Brading, William Taylor, and Henrique Semo's associates on San Luís Potosí, León, Oaxaca, and parts of the Valley of Mexico covering the half-century before 1810 indicate more than minimal dislocation from *consolidación.* In fact, Bazant, after reviewing the cases of five Potosino *haciendas* and the level of their outstanding mortgage debt to religious bodies, concluded that "contrary to the impression produced by the complaints of 1805 about the *consolidación de vales reales,* not every *hacienda* was debt-burdened."[35]

Consolidación in New Spain and Spain

Lavrín's *consolidación* data permit an estimate of total receipts and their geographical distribution. Over the period 1805–8 about 11.1 million *pesos* were collected, or for comparison with the metropole's experience, roughly 222 million *reales de vellón.* Not unexpectedly, the distribution of returns between real-estate sales and loan capital recalled fits the chorus of assertions by New Spain's principal corporate bodies, as well as Bishop-elect Abad y Queipo, insisting on the critical financial role of charitable foundations' funds in the colony's economy. Fully 87 percent of New Spain's collections would consist of capital recovered from outstanding liens and loans. Furthermore, three ecclesiastical jurisdictions returned a disproportionate share—82 percent—of total collections: Mexico, with 51.3 percent Puebla, with 21.1 percent, and Valladolid, with 9.4 percent.[36] And the percentage of the presumed wealth of the colony's *obras pías* actually alienated? Relying upon the often used estimate of 47 million *pesos* claimed by Abad y Queipo in 1807, when he pleaded personally with Sixto Espinosa in Madrid to suspend *consolidación* in New Spain, we find that the amount secularized reached 24 percent.[37] This would match the conclusion of a recent study that found that of 44.5 million *pesos* of debt to pious funds, only one-quarter were affected. No massive property auctions occurred, and many debtors arranged to pay *consolidación* agents in installments via *composición*.[38]

Richard Herr's calculation of *consolidación* receipts in Spain leads to the conclusion that the metropole obtained from its *consolidación* more than 6.7 times the value of collections in New Spain, its richest colony, namely, 1,505 million *reales de vellón*. On an annual per capita basis this yields 15.4 *reales;* in other terms, New Spain, with a population equivalent to about 58 percent of its metropole's, generated on a per capita basis almost 79 percent of the peninsular collections.[39] More noteworthy, Spain's distribution between real estate and capital at loan was about the inverse of New Spain's, with 92.5 percent, as against 12.6 percent, consisting of receipts from sales of religious real estate.[40] The three peninsular zones closely tied to the empire's colonies—the cities and provinces of Cadiz, Seville, and Madrid—accounted for 33 percent of collections, of which Madrid furnished 14 percent.[41] In one respect there was an unexpected difference: the 24 percent of ecclesiastical capital expropriated in New Spain over three years of *consolidación* (1805–8) was appreciably higher than the percentage in Spain, where religious real estate lost 15 percent over ten years.[42]

One may debate the relative burden imposed by *consolidación* in metropole and colony, Spain and New Spain. Undoubtedly, the withdrawal of 24 percent of the value of charitable foundations from the general financing of the colonial economy was crucial. There are other considerations too. New Spain's returns from *consolidación* were withdrawn from the colony's economy and transferred abroad, amounting to nothing less than decapitalization of major proportions, or an "expropriation of national savings," particularly if the remissions are added to the capital exports from New Spain on government account alone in the previous surge of 1801–4—31.5–35 million *pesos* (630–730 million *reales*).[43] Second, the 11.1 million *pesos fuertes* transferred to Spain consisted of silver. Converted to *reales de vellón,* New Spain's silver represented 40 percent of all specie obtained by *consolidación* in Spain and New Spain combined between in 1800–1808.[44]

Finally, if Madrid accepted the risk of compromising the economy of its wealthiest colony in America by abruptly withdrawing critical investment funds despite the timely information provided to Sixto Espinosa by Abad y Queipo, did the funds reach the metropole? The transatlantic transfers by a variety of mechanisms that Madrid had to employ would lead one of the participants in this operation to describe it as commercial theater with many actors.

Certainly Godoy, Soler, Sixto Espinosa, and their associates did not expect their policy to draw France under Napoleon into Spain. True, the French political elite since the age of Philip V had cultivated the illusion that their administrative skills could transform Spain and its American empire. But when French troops began to occupy Spain, behind them were manufacturers, export merchants, and bankers who expected Napoleon Bonaparte to establish a long-coveted trade monopoly *(exclusif)* with Spain's colonies in America and to access the silver stored in the Mexico City mint earmarked for subsidy payments to France.

One issue is beyond debate: the French occupation would produce a crisis of legitimacy in Spain and its empire that justified the movement toward autonomy under local juntas. One can imagine the anxiety of *peninsular* merchants in the summer of 1808 when they realized that the most vocal exponents of a local junta in Mexico City were the *criollo* lawyers Verdad y Ramos and Azcárate, authors of two formal protests in 1805 against the execution of the *consolidación*. Such a junta promised the autonomy that would inhibit the kind of expedients epitomized by *consolidación*—"this infernal project . . . beyond question the first day of the disasters of America."[45]

12. Strange Saga: The Transfer of New Spain's Silver, 1804–1808

The Hacienda ministry, considering exclusively the largest revenue collection, ordered all available money to be dispatched to the Peninsula.   José Luyando, 6 December 1810

One of the largest enterprises of the epoch, the transfer of silver from Spanish America, with the connivance of the English government.   A. Raffalovich

Licenses, permits, or dissimulations . . . to carry on prohibited trade with Great Britain and its Islands.   Gabriel de Yermo to Junta Suprema de Sevilla, 1808

Viceroy Iturrigaray's dilemma after the outbreak of hostilities in late 1804 reflected the tactics of Madrid's harried crisis managers. They confronted the strands of the old regime in metropole and colonies, which, interwoven by war, would ultimately strangle Charles IV, Godoy, Soler, Sixto Espinosa, and others, including the viceroy of the colony of New Spain, Iturrigaray, in that year of imperial crisis, 1808. The scenario of 1804 seems comparable to that of 1797, but the closer one examines the events of the four years 1804–8, the more the adage should be modified to, "The more it *seems* the same, the more it *has* changed."

In late 1797 Francisco Saavedra's reaction to hostilities with England and Spain's naval disaster at Cape Saint Vincent had led to the stratagem of *comercio neutro,* whereby some Spanish merchants could rely upon neutral shipping to maintain trade between the metropole and its otherwise isolated American colonies. The policy could be sustained for only eighteen months, however, collapsing under pressure from disaffected merchants in Cadiz, Veracruz, and Mexico City. Thereafter, from 1804 to 1808, Madrid had to revert to its traditional policy of restricting trade to Spanish citizens and on occasion issuing special licenses (*gracias, permisos*) to firms in Cadiz and Havana in order to meet specific shortages, particularly the provisioning of Havana and Caracas. It is no accident that the two peaks in the performance of U.S. exports between 1790 and 1807 coincide, first, with the months of *comercio neutro* (1797–99) and, second, with the phase of Spain's policy of *gracias, permisos,* and *contratas* with specific neutral merchant houses (1804–7).[1] How to tolerate the predominantly North American shipmasters entering and then departing from Veracruz in 1805, 1806, and 1807 with silver and seroons of cochineal, all under legitimate royal contracts, was the dilemma facing Viceroy Iturrigaray, further poisoning his relations with members of New Spain's commercial elites.

If Saavedra's resort to *comercio neutro* in 1797 was a response to the Spanish colonies' import needs and to massive smuggling, Soler and Godoy's tactic of awarding contracts to neutral firms in 1804 was aimed at ensuring an uninterrupted inflow of colonial silver on government account—specifically, from New Spain—to peninsular ports. Of course, over three centuries the metropolitan government's liquidity had always been maintained by American specie and bullion imports on *galeones* and *flotas;* after the extension of *comercio libre* to New Spain in 1789, the flow of silver, mainly to the port of Cadiz, rose.[2] The metropole's dependence upon its colony of New Spain was heightened: that colony's rising net yields from turnover taxes *(alcabalas),* from customs receipts and Indian *tributo,* and from government monopolies of mercury, blasting powder, tobacco, and coinage fees, provided the metropolitan government with roughly 66 percent of all net colonial revenue from the colonies in America.[3] In addition, the *almaceneros* of Mexico City, together with the colony's estate owners and ecclesiastical corporations, furnished both interest-free and interest-bearing loans to finance the metropole's wartime expenditures from 1779 to 1781 and again from 1793 to 1795. The extraordinary burst of silver shipments from Veracruz to Cadiz from 1802 to 1804 would underscore New Spain's critical role in sustaining the liquidity of the metropolitan government, while sharpening the appetites of young Basque and Asturian emigrants who were outward and also upward bound to relatives in New Spain's commercial networks.

There was in addition the international context of New Spain's silver streams. A drying up of silver flows into France from Spanish sources just before the French Revolution was a factor in the financial instability of the French monarchy,[4] while in 1797 a similar shortage affected England's public and private sectors. Widespread smuggling in and around Cadiz of English goods purchased at Gibraltar after 1797 was possible only with American silver. In brief, upon New Spain's silver production and export at that moment depended Spain's social and bureaucratic elites, the maintenance of its military forces, the stationing of naval units at Brest for joint Franco-Spanish operations and, commencing in 1804, the Madrid government's commitment to monthly subsidies of 1.4 million *pesos* (about 6 million francs) to support the imperialist government of the Grand Empire under Napoleon Bonaparte. Recall, too, the importance of colonial silver, especially New Spain's, in supporting the metropolitan ecclesiastical establishment, its chaplaincies and *patronatos,* its universities' *colegios mayores,* and a broad spectrum of eleemosynary activities. Broadly speaking, the treasury departments of Spain, England, and France, along with their private bankers, had a vital interest in furnishing New Spain's mine owners' inputs of mercury, blasting powder, bar iron, and steel to ensure the return outflow across the Atlantic of millions of silver *pesos* annually.

Circumventing Blockade

The policy of opening colonial ports to neutral shipping in 1797 could not be replicated seven years later. For one thing, English policy no longer tolerated Spanish-owned cargo aboard neutral carriers; for another, few questioned the effectiveness of English blockades in European and Caribbean waters. Now, only with London's tolerance could neutrals move in and out of Spanish colonial ports in the Caribbean, at Veracruz, Havana, and La Guayra. Those officials directly involved in state finance and responsible for what were in effect forced loans from religious corporations under *consolidación*—Hacienda Minister Soler and his subordinate Sixto Espinosa—now devised a stratagem that ostensibly resembled the monarchy's traditional practice of rewarding "service" to the state with *privilegios, gracias, licencias,* or *permisos.* Once these were allocated to a handful of firms in neutral ports of Europe and the United States, the now "privileged" firms could make arrangements with presumably willing English authorities. Also, under cover of neutral firms and their shipping, the Spanish government's trading arm, known as the Real Giro or the Real Negociación del Giro, could ship to New Spain mercury, blasting powder, and cigarette paper. Under such conditions disentailment of church property in Spain's wealthiest colony, New Spain, and other colonies was put into effect with the expectation of success, as had occurred in the metropole.

The timing of the extension overseas is significant: *consolidación* was extended to the colonies in America on 28 November 1804, just one month prior to the awarding of contracts to neutral firms (24 December) for transferring across the Atlantic an extraordinary volume of funds by French,

English, and U.S. intermediaries. In another sense, moreover, the two-faceted operations marked a shift from the alliance with France toward a more nuanced stance in pursuit of greater autonomy for Spanish diplomacy.

These considerations explain why Madrid issued contracts to the French firm of Ouvrard & Vanlebergh (1804) and to the English firms of Gordon & Murphy and Reid, Irving & Company (1806). In a fashion that was byzantine in its apparent, if not real, complexity, Ouvrard's contracts, or *licencias,* were ultimately allocated to the brothers-in-law, merchants Robert and John Oliver (Baltimore) and John Craig (Philadelphia), via the mediation of Amsterdam's Hope & Company, which proceeded to use the young merchant-adventurer David Parish, formerly of Antwerp. Parish, in turn, would draw upon the funds and political connections of important merchant-bankers of Amsterdam (Hope & Company) and London (Baring Brothers). When neutral vessels from New Orleans, Baltimore, Philadelphia, and Kingston entered the port of Veracruz carrying English and European textiles and presented bills of exchange or drafts *(libranzas)* on New Spain's treasury (its Reales Cajas), on designated silver transport companies *(casas conductoras de plata),* or on individuals of Mexico City's merchant community (Lorenzo Angulo Guardamino), a perplexed Viceroy Iturrigaray had to choose between honoring royal orders and yielding to the opposition of militant elements among the commercial communities of Veracruz and Mexico City. A victim of Madrid's pragmatism, Iturrigaray was also victimized by ritual deviousness in the dispensing of privilege by crisis managers at Madrid and by attempts to circumvent the constraints imposed in wartime by the English government, its Board of Trade, and its armed branch, so to speak, the royal navy.

Certain considerations need recalling. The immediate goal of Madrid's policy was the transfer of colonial funds (including the earnings of the Real Giro) to the metropolitan government via the neutral United States or even the ostensible enemy, England. Next, despite the variegated lexicon of *gracias, permisos,* and *contratas,* all favored selected commercial houses that would pay customs duties into the Caja de Consolidación. Third, the legal basis of each license — a royal order — was not always made public. These were known only by the Hacienda minister who countersigned, by the benefited commercial firm, and by the chief colonial officer, whether viceroy or governor general of the colonial port of call. In this sense the *consulados* of Cadiz, Veracruz, and Mexico City, bitterly opposed to this expedient, correctly referred to the special licenses as *gracias* and to the firms so benefited as *agraciadas.*[5]

To Spain's high officials in 1804, after three years of uncertain peace in the Atlantic basin, the lessons of 1797–1801 were evident. The device of *comercio neutro,* by the toleration or connivance of London, had permitted the movement of some goods in wartime across the Atlantic, between the Spanish colonies and the peninsula, between the mines of New Spain and the bottomless budget of Spain.[6] The fact that *havaneros* tortuously maintained *comercio neutro* with Baltimore, Philadelphia, Boston, and New York after 1799 was incidental and tolerable, for the essential after 1801 was full-scale resumption of the heavy Cadiz-to-Veracruz traffic.

And full scale it was. After due consideration to the backlog of exports at Veracruz as a result of the English naval blockade, still the magnitude of silver transfers on royal and private account from 1802 to 1804 was nothing short of extraordinary. The total registered exports of New Spain's silver and gold in these three years varied between lower- and upper-bound limits, excluding precious metals sent to the Philippines, as well as the value of colonial staples. We can generate four estimates varying from 53.7 million to 71.5 million *pesos.*[7] The lower-bound estimates (53.7 million or 55.6 million) may be more accurate, since they include Havana, whose exports reflect Veracruz shipments to "Havana" or "America." The port registers of Cadiz indicate that Spain received from all ports in the colonies on both private and government account about 113 million *pesos,* of which New Spain's shipments accounted for an impressive 63.3 percent. Limiting our analysis to amounts listed specifically on royal or private account, we find that New Spain provided 57 percent of all private shipments and a very high 78 percent of all government shipments.[8] The Atlantic system, not to mention the Spanish Atlantic, had never had such extraordinary capital transfers.

Viceroy Iturrigary was responding loyally to Madrid's "shortages . . . and the necessity for us to help it meet its unavoidable obligations." In October 1803 he authorized a shipment to Madrid's state-owned Banco Nacional de San Carlos of 3.6 million *pesos* drawn on the treasuries of Mexico and Lima; and in the first six months of 1804 he managed to remit on government account alone more than 9.9 million *pesos,* promising another shipment of 3 million shortly. This was the product, he noted pridefully, of his "preoccupation with collecting and forwarding promptly a treasure so commendable, appreciable, and necessary in the current circumstances."[9] Few comparable three-year transfers to the metropolitan government and merchants had occurred in more than three hundred years of Spain's hegemony in the Western Hemisphere.

In the immediate post-Amiens years of apparent trade growth, Madrid policymakers judged that they could return to earlier practices of exception, to reissuing *permisos* and *privilegios*—the terms were interchangeable—to selected firms. Even in the months before Amiens, Godoy and Soler allocated *permisos* to domestic firms in return for sums "those involved had to pay in advance to the Treasury."[10] In mid-1802 Veracruz's *consulado,* supported by its counterpart at Cadiz, complained of the arrival of neutral carriers laden with textiles and wares, and Madrid had to reveal that they were the result of disguised loans, the "payment of the sums they paid into the Central Treasury to satisfy the urgent needs of the Crown"[11]—here the civil servant responding drove home his point—"when neither Merchants' loans nor royal tax receipts could satisfy the government's large obligations and interests."[12] Special licenses were also distributed to titled nobility, to the dukes of Osuna and Vezmar, and to others—to Godoy's relative by marriage Branciforte, the former viceroy of Mexico, who received a *privilegio* to supply Havana and Caracas with one hundred thousand barrels of flour, which were subsequently transferred to a third party.[13] Moreover, peacetime *gracias* to neutral merchants or shippers could provide the precedent, if worst came to worst, for using neutrals to transfer government funds by indirect parties across the Atlantic to Europe.

Nonetheless, such was the antagonism to the device of special licenses that Hacienda Minister Soler had to countersign a royal order on 21 June 1804 clarifying policy: the "gracias y privilegios" already issued would be honored, but henceforth no further petitions for licenses would be entertained. This was made explicit, according to the order, to facilitate planning by merchants at home and in the colonies; it was repeated in a second order of 13 July, and lest there be further doubt, it was published in toto in the official commercial gazette, the *Correo Mercantil de España y sus Indias.* Oddly, it was virtually paired with the insistence that peninsular exporters match the value of their re-exports with an equivalent in domestic products, surely an example of ungrounded optimism. And yet within five months Godoy and Soler had to abandon their self-denying ordinance and fall back upon "a labyrinth of contracts with foreigners for trade in all those dominions."[14] This would be the first of the prices Godoy's administration had to pay for weakness.

Behind the oscillation between a kind of euphoric nationalism in June and July of 1804 and a public confession of maritime weakness in December by publicizing government contracts with European and North American firms was the heightened perception at Madrid of the Spanish transatlantic system's dependence upon its American colonies. In 1804 the primary preoccupation of Godoy's ministry revolved about sustaining the eastbound inflow of New Spain's silver exports that Iturrigaray's careful oversight confirmed. If its flow directly from Veracruz or indirectly via Havana to Cadiz and Barcelona were interrupted, then other, neutral channels had to be devised, as had occurred during preceding times of hostilities, under a generalized form of *comercio neutro,* or *permisos.* Underscoring the importance of New Spain's resources was Madrid's decision in November to extend to New Spain and other American colonies the financial device that since 1798 had generated funds for the government: *consolidación.*

Neutral carriers would transfer *consolidación* receipts to the metropole, while delivering to New Spain inputs for major revenue-producing colonial enterprises—mercury for silver refining and cigarette paper for the large and profitable Mexico City tobacco factory. Neutrals would also carry provisions to Cuba for the slave labor force of sugar plantations, accepting in exchange perishable colonial staples such as sugar. The Madrid government could also profit by investing the income of colonial governments in the purchase of such staples as sugar, cochineal, tobacco, and cocoa for shipment to Europe, an operation that neutrals could execute for the state-owned Real Giro, whose revised statutes were published in 1802.[15] Finally, there was the possibility that ample neutral supplies of textiles might curb the predictable upsurge in smuggling in wartime. Small wonder, then, that once England renewed warfare against Spain in late 1804, the distribution of *permisos* and *contratas* "to bring mercury and other goods of the Real Hacienda, recover prizes, and export the funds there" was entrusted to the director of the Caja de Consolidación, Sixto Espinosa. To protect arrangements with neutral firms, Sixto Espinosa had to contract with Spanish, French, Dutch, English, and U.S. interests in so complicated a fashion that by 1814 one observer had to conclude that "it is impossible to form a complete picture of the outcome of these transactions."[16] This was no exaggeration.

The Spanish government's overall strategy had to be based on an understanding with English authorities, which was all the more necessary since English naval forces had quickly established full hegemony in the Atlantic basin as a consequence of victories at sea in the Caribbean and off the coasts of the Iberian Peninsula. At its peak that control covered the western Atlantic from Halifax to Port-of-Spain, Newfoundland to Trinidad. By 1800 Madrid's high officials understood that London's toleration was indispensable for the eastbound movement of New Spain's specie. A member of the firm of Thornton & Power, of Hamburg, a major distribution center for English cotton goods after 1792,[17] reported to English authorities in October 1800 that England's consul at Cadiz, Diego Duff, had advised that "there is a great disposition in the Spanish government to permit the Silver laying in their ports of South America to be brought to England, and that upon a proper understanding with the British government they would grant licenses for this purpose." Silver, Thornton added, was in short supply at London to cover the "[e]xchanges . . . to other parts of Europe" for grain imports, not to mention the East India Company's operations, which were "greatly distressed for silver to make their usual remittances to China" for tea. He proposed that London issue a safe conduct or passport to a director of Spain's Compañia de Filipinas, Bernardo de Lizaur, so that he might proceed to London for further discussions.[18] Lizaur went there, a draft agreement was drawn up, and the intentions of Madrid seemed substantiated by the licensing of sixteen neutral ships and cargo for colonial ports. However, sometime after May 1801 the negotiations terminated.[19]

Four years later, in 1805, the capture at sea of Finance Minister Soler's dispatches to the colonial government at Caracas revealed to English and ultimately U.S. authorities not only that the Spanish government had contracted with neutral firms listed in the public order of 24 December 1804 but also that, "instead of this permission being confined to the houses mentioned," runs the English translation transmitted to the U.S. president Madison from Kingston, "H.M. authorizes equally expeditions by any Neutral House on their shewing a Royal Permission signed by me."[20] Another captured letter intended for internal distribution (this bore the *reservado* classification) placed orders for *gracias* and *contratas* in their true light. Licenses awarded to such titled nobility as Spain's marquesses Branciforte and Osuna and to Cuba's conde de Jaruco y Mopox were also granted to firms listed earlier in the 14 December order, and—a key item—the director of the Caja de Consolidación, Sixto Espinosa, was not to be construed as manipulating public office for private deals in his operations. Quite the contrary, the "true person interested is His Majesty himself in his real caxa de Consolidación." Soler ended his communication to the colonies with the reminder, "I [so] advise you with the greatest of secrecy."[21]

Evidently, Prime Minister Godoy, along with his chief Hacienda officials, Soler and Sixto Espinosa, had settled upon a two-pronged scheme to maintain contact with the colonies in America during wartime. One, the older form, reverted to *gracias* to specific individuals or firms, but with the novel stratagem of enabling recipients to transfer the privilege to non-Spanish neutral merchant houses (Osuna's was ultimately reassigned to the Philadelphia firm of John Craig, brother-in-law of the Olivers of Baltimore). A new form was the publicized *contrata* with specific neutrals as evident in the 24 December order. There was an added novelty, moreover: unpublicized contracts with London-based firms.

Despite the absence of a complete listing of all *gracias* issued over Soler's signature, one may discern a pattern at least with respect to contact with the port and merchant community of Veracruz. At Cadiz certain firms—Francisco Bustamante y Guerra, Torre Hermanos, Mariano Malancó y Badia, Guillermo Barrón—were authorized to use neutral carriers. For instance, Barrón could dispatch from Cadiz, Málaga, or Ayamonte (close to the Portuguese border) "directly for Veracruz, under neutral flag" a four-hundred-ton vessel freighted with "any type of goods and wares normally traded," and he promptly sent to Veracruz Josef Lorenzo de la Torre to take charge of shipments on arrival. Barrón also chartered a U.S. frigate, *Sally,* to sail from Cadiz to Veracruz under, however, "an open and simulated register" for Lisbon.[22] Neutral Lisbon then offered advantages to belligerents, and hence a *permiso* went to the Lisbon merchant José Antonio Pereyra to export to Veracruz or La Guayra.[23] Meanwhile, the duque de Osuna's original *permiso* for flour imports, presumably designed to feed the starving residents of his Extremaduran and Andalusian estates, became at Veracruz a "rich cargo" carried aboard a U.S. ship out of New Orleans.[24] The utilization of *gracias* and *permisos* inspired Veracruz's *consulado* to complain that continuation of this policy by Madrid "would tie the trade of the Americas, either to foreign firms or to those few Spanish ones able to obtain some royal *Gracia,* leaving all others in noticeable inactivity."[25] There were grounds for such pessimism.

Clearly, Madrid's *gracias* after 1804 could not be reassigned without a prior understanding with London. Readiness to come to an agreement surfaced in early December 1804, immediately preceding the order of 24 December, when Spain's ambassador reminded Prime Minister Pitt of England's profitable trade with Spain's American colonies, claiming that Spain "had the right to be heeded in view of the great benefits she offered England with licit and illicit commerce."[26] London delayed its response for a month to assess England's export needs and silver shortages. In mid-June 1805 the Board of Trade, reflecting perhaps the experience of London merchants after 1797, who had begun to shift their trade from Cadiz to a "commerce in neutral vessels which went direct to the Spanish colonies,"[27] recommended licensing English nationals to charter intermediaries—neutral shipping—for trade with the Spanish colonies, "such licenses to . . . protect neutral as well as British property." On the return leg licensees could carry precious metals valued up to 200 percent of the value of outbound invoiced cargo.[28] Apparently the English cabinet delayed decision on these recommendations, perhaps reluctant to stimulate neutrals in competition with English shipping operating at the free ports of Kingston and Providence. However, between February and June 1806 London proceeded to issue permits to ten "principal houses engaged in the secret trade" to the Spanish American colonies, ranging in value from £1 million to £2 million, approximately 5 million to 10 million *pesos fuertes*. And while William Auckland and William Grenville authorized licenses with the proviso that only English goods could be exported, the extraordinary volume of the projected specie and bullion returns signaled that these were no ordinary licenses.

These arrangements constituted a massive maritime transfer of silver from the colony of New Spain to Europe via the United States; the indirect participation of important merchant banking firms at Amsterdam (Hope), Hamburg and Antwerp (Parish), and London (Baring), as well as the Paris-based firm of Ouvrard; and the direct participation of the London merchant houses of Fermín de Tastet, Gordon & Murphy, and Reid, Irving & Company and the firms of the Olivers and John Craig, at Baltimore and Philadelphia, respectively.[29] For a price, English authorities could now monitor the colonial operations of Madrid's Real Caja de Consolidación, which, for its part, permitted London merchant-bankers to purchase at Madrid from the Banco Nacional de San Carlos, the Compañía de Filipinas, the Treasury's Consolidación, and private firms drafts of exchange drawn upon Spain's colonial treasuries, mainly that of New Spain,[30] whose silver would be shipped directly to London or indirectly via Kingston and Baltimore. Concurrently, English authorities could also monitor the movement of Spain's subsidy to France's Trésor Public. At one of the most critical conjunctures in the history of the Spanish Atlantic, silver currents (some invisible) flowing out of New Spain to Spain and western Europe began to surface.

The Price of Neutrality: Madrid, Paris, London

Before dissecting the operations of the major merchant houses involved as "neutrals" from 1804 to 1808 under the stratagem of Spain's Hacienda and its subsection, the Caja de Consolidación, we must recall that what in historical perspective appears lineal was in fact a system of expedients, of trial and error, by Godoy and his finance specialists, Soler and Sixto Espinosa. First, the governments of Spain and England spread their operations among a few trading and banking firms to minimize risk, with three firms dominating the Veracruz zone: at first, David Parish ("general agent" of Hope and Baring) and his subsequent partners, Oliver and Craig, later supplemented by Gordon & Murphy, which would merge with Reid, Irving & Company. Second, the time frame was short, since none could predict the length of hostilities. The covert tactics of both Madrid and London were crafted by governments of unequal power: England was *the* hegemonic power, since its control over the Atlantic seaways channeled or blocked Spanish and neutral shipping bound for Spain's colonial ports. Last, England's naval and commercial dominance enhanced London's role as an international banking center, already eclipsing Amsterdam. Barings of London rather than Amsterdam's Hope & Company controlled the movement of New Spain's silver flows at the European terminus. Ultimately the funds flowed through an international network linking Hamburg, Amsterdam and Antwerp, Paris and London, Málaga, Lisbon, and Cadiz in Europe and New York, Philadelphia, Baltimore, New Orleans, Havana, Kingston, and Veracruz in the Western Hemisphere.

Spain's initiative indicates that both governments relied upon the private sector to transfer colonial silver. Madrid employed a variety of covers: *gracias* to titled figures were made public before 1804; they were left *un*publicized when shifted to third-party neutrals in 1805. Publicity accompanied the permissions issued by contract on 24 December 1804 to a dozen European and U.S. firms, apparently none of whom became significantly operational; on the other hand, the unpublicized contracts to Ouvrard (1804), Craig and Oliver (1805), and Gordon & Murphy (1806) allowed them to handle extraordinary sums. Soler issued packets of blank *permisos* signed by him, each indicating the aggregate value of goods exportable, along with the official sums authorized for withdrawal by drafts on colonial treasuries. These were delivered to Ouvrard at Paris, through him to Hope's agent David Parish (for Antwerp and Hamburg), to Craig (Philadelphia), to Oliver (Baltimore), and to Gordon & Murphy (Madrid and London). The publicized contracts omitted what the unpublicized specifically stipulated: that the contractants "assumed the obligation to obtain from the British Government extensive permits or passports to send out ships with [the consent of] . . . Manuel Sixto Espinosa."[31]

For its part, London tolerated, even abetted, Soler's stratagem to suit its purposes. Contractants had to place sums received at Veracruz at the immediate disposition of the English government in order to subsidize its war with France at a time when the liquidity of the English banking system was precariously inadequate. Via London's licensing, furthermore, English manufacturers whose exports to the Continent slackened after the outbreak of hostilities shipped cottons to Spain's American colonies, especially New Spain, where demand promised to be sustained, even growing. Most important, perhaps, was the way the Board of Trade could manipulate its licenses for economic and psychological warfare. The value of its passports was enhanced when in late 1806 it was bruited to have "granted licenses to a great many [North] American vessels to trade with Veracruz," while effecting a policy "now to capture every vessel [without proper passport] bound to or from Veracruz."[32] This was hardly perfidy; rather, it was skilful employment of sea power to discriminate among neutral carriers. At the same time, London, slowly throttling Spain's communication with its colonial world, brought to a crisis that government's relations with the Continental hegemon, France under the regime of Napoleon Bonaparte. What activated Soler was the desperate hope of maintaining contact with the colonies, in particular New Spain, when warfare renewed between England and France, which Spain was now obligated to join.

However, long before 1804, Godoy and his ministers were banking on an intelligently crafted policy of neutrality, in Godoy's words, that "Spain remain neutral in wartime, to preserve its commerce."[33] This required that Spain preserve nominal control over its American colonies and tolerate England's indirect commercial links to them while minimizing the predictable demands of Spain's ally, France, for tangible support in troops, warships, and less visible trade and financial assistance. Contingency policy planning in the event of hostilities between England and France was hardly novel after a century of repeated international trade and open warfare. A decade earlier, revolution in France and the international counterrevolutionary response had produced a wrenching Spanish cabinet crisis in 1793, the dismissal of the conde de Aranda and the entry into Spanish politics of Manuel Godoy. The expansionism of postrevolutionary France under Bonaparte only aggravated the long-term problem of Madrid's crisis managers, who were anxious to preserve a contracting "space" between Europe's hegemons. Preserving neutrality was as dangerous as going to war.

As Madrid officials labored to remind the representatives of France in 1803, a neutral Spain could supply their economy with products that were otherwise difficult to obtain in wartime. These included the raw materials normally exported to France—raw wool, silk, olive oil, soda ash—as well as, "above all this, our wonderful products from the two Americas." A neutral Spain, then, through its commercial intermediation could allow French merchants "to supply themselves at our marketplaces with colonial staples and other goods."[34] To make this proposition attractive, Spanish officials toyed with an "attempt at *comercio libre*" between France and Spain reminiscent of the commercial treaty of 1786 between France and England, including mutual tariff reductions and even the removal of articles from the prohibited list. This approach revived the concept of more equal economic relations between Bourbon Spain and Bourbon France that intellectual-bureaucrats of the 1790s, like Bernardo Iriarte and Juan Bautista Virio, had postulated as the proper framework of relations between the Spanish monarchy and the new French Republic. Godoy espoused this proposition partly because a prohibited list of imports had failed to stimulate domestic manufactures, partly in the hope that French internal demand might generate in peninsular ports greater trade with the American colonies, at the same time reducing the still preponderant role of Cadiz. As Godoy obliquely and pragmatically framed the dilemma decades later with the benefit of hindsight, "The monopoly system with respect to the Americas, in the state of civilization and progress of those inhabitants, could no longer be maintained without displeasing them and alienating their hearts."[35]

The proposal, vigorously analyzed by Godoy's ministers, generated opposition spearheaded by Foreign Secretary Pedro Cevallos and the head of Gracia y Justicia, José Antonio Caballero, who claimed that it might undermine existing domestic industry, notably Catalan manufacture and printing of cotton (indianillas). It was implicit, too, that mercantile interests at Cadiz, where Cevallos had connections, were also antagonistic. Instead, Cevallos counterproposed that the government respond to French insistence on open collaboration with Spanish troops and naval vessels with indirect, monetary assistance—the subsidy (contingente). To Godoy's pertinent query about London's doubtful toleration of Spain's subsidy to France, Foreign Minister Cevallos—since his Valladolid university years an admirer of the Dutch internationalist Grotius—responded that under international law "peace countenances subsidies to your ally, provided they are stipulated in prior agreements." Cevallos' position, less neutral than yielding trade concessions to France, received Charles IV's backing despite Godoy's reservations, and Cevallos went ahead "buying Spain's neutrality" with a monthly subsidy of 6 million francs, whose consequences were subsequently blamed upon Godoy. Charles's position reflected less the merits of Cevallos's point about international law than his prediction that French competition might eliminate workshops in Spain and, worse, generate "discontent and unrest among workers,"[36] a reminder to Charles of his family's scrambling over the roofs of the royal palace when fleeing from Madrid to Aranjuez during the 1766 uprising against Hacienda Minister Esquilache. His psychic fear of tumultos would profoundly upset him years later at Aranjuez. The Godoy-Cevallos tiff over the economic fundaments of neutrality, as we shall see, would climax in concessions to French merchants in the Treaty of Fontainebleau in 1807 and in London's decision later to back the foreign policy of Pedro Cevallos.

Implementing the subsidy and continuing it once warfare again erupted between France and England, complemented by London's decision to attack the inbound Spanish silver convoy in late 1804, prior to a declaration of war, motivated Soler's stratagems for maintaining specie and trade flows between metropole and colonies from late 1804 on. They began with the French contracts (November 1804) and were followed by the *publicized* contracts with twelve European and U.S. merchant houses (24 December 1804) and the *unpublicized* agreements with Craig (March 1805) and the London firms of Gordon & Murphy and Reid, Irving (1806). All were crafted primarily to transfer to the peninsula silver from colonial revenues, including New Spain's *consolidación* returns, under neutral cover and with English compliance. The complex and interlocked arrangements promised much: to supply colonial demand for basic imports and some luxuries; to finance the metropolitan government's defense expenditures, cover growing deficits on current operations, and shore up its public credit by redeeming *vales reales;* to fulfill its commitments to France's Trésor Public and French and Dutch bankers; and, not least, to pacify the English with the sales of its manufactures and earnings from financial intermediation.

On balance Soler and Godoy were trying to mesh strategy and tactics to shore up Spain's imperial regime. The strategy would fail less because it was overly complex (it was) than because it remained subordinate to the strategy and tactics of England and France. For his tactical ingenuity, which domestic opponents considered a threat to Spain's imperial transatlantic trading system, Soler would ultimately pay a high price: political assassination.

Enter Ouvrard

Soler's tactics seem devious, contradictory, to some downright deceiving and unconnected. Contrary to the impression of Gabriel-Julian Ouvrard, who viewed him as Spain's financial lifeline, Soler never concentrated on one instrument. Consistently it was the Spanish government's purpose to keep its options open, distribute licenses to many firms, and negotiate with many merchant banks rather than just one. If one pursues the French "connection" through the Breton financier Gabriel-Julien Ouvrard, the logic of Soler's complex web becomes intelligible.

Ouvrard, a Breton of bourgeois background, was born at Rennes in 1770. Educated at a private academy, he entered trade at Nantes, Brittany's economic capital and the center of France's African slave trade. After starting a paper manufactory, he was swept up by revolutionary currents and participated in contra-guerrilla operations in the Vendée. His bourgeois formation, business skills, politically correct credentials, and facility in making connections made Ouvrard, *munitionnaire* and *financier,* emblematic of upwardly mobile business types in revolutionary and Napoleonic France.[37] To some he was the archetypical *arriviste;* to others, the *bourgeois triomphant* who survived the Revolution's radical phase, throve under the Directoire, and blossomed under Napoleonic expansionism. In fact, his survival kit allowed him to live well beyond the Restoration.[38]

To each reign of Bourbon Spain in the eighteenth century, its symbolic French entrepreneur. Philip V's reign nourished at Cadiz the Norman merchant-family house of LeCouteulx of Saint-Malo, later merchants and prominent court bankers at Paris.[39] Charles III's three decades fostered the enterprise of Bayonne's François Cabarrús, later the leading partner in Madrid's banking house of Cabarrús & Lalanne, whose daughter, Teresa, would parlay beauty, body, and salon skills advantageously under the Directoire, the Consulat, and the Empire. And Charles IV and Napoleon shared Gabriel-Julien Ouvrard, international speculator. A LeCouteulx de Canteleu, whose family fortune flourished at Cadiz through the use of Spanish straw men *(prestanombres),* became a regent of Napoleon's Banque de France in 1804, when Ouvrard exploited his Spanish colonial connection. Between LeCouteulx and Ouvrard, regent and speculator, there is perhaps only the distinction between wealth laundered by banking and the raw stuff of unvarnished speculation. French economy and society made room for both.

Ouvrard's conspectus of Spain and its American empire was colored initially by meeting the conde de Cabarrús in 1795 during the preliminaries of the Treaty of Basel, which settled the conflict between republican France and monarchic Spain. Cabarrús, Ouvrard recounts, was already obsessed with transferring silver from colonial treasuries to Madrid.[40] His Spanish connection became firmer when Ouvrard, now a contractor *(munitionnaire)* for the French fleet, also advanced 4 million *pesos* (20 million francs) to cover the expenses of the Spanish fleet at Brest, under Admiral Mazarredo; in payment he received drafts *(libranzas* or *traites)* on the treasury of New Spain at Mexico City.[41] Ouvrard's operation at Brest—he has been called "one of the most successful contractors for the French navy"[42]—probably connected him to another inveterate speculator, Talleyrand, who was subsequently accused of dirty tricks *(friponnerie)* in handling supplies for French naval forces. Talleyrand's defender before an angry Napoleon was LeCouteulx de Canteleu.[43]

Over the eighteenth century, from Pontchartrain and Orry, Choiseul and Choiseul-Praslin, to Ouvrard, Talleyrand, and Napoleon—all were mesmerized by the mirage of silver in America, the road to which ran through Madrid. Ouvrard's vision of silver, which a banking acquaintance categorized as his overdeveloped "spirit of distrust and avarice," began to materialize with the drafts on Mexico City's Real Hacienda. Madrid supplied a passport for Ouvrard's brother to travel to New Spain; he had already established Ouvrard de Chailles & Cie at Philadelphia, a port favored by French *peso* hunters like Talleyrand and Parish. At Mexico City he made a point of touring the Hacienda storehouse, where he found his brother's minted silver neatly tagged amidst a mouth-watering store of 72 million *pesos* awaiting export, or so he reported.[44] On the basis of a tour of New Spain and other Spanish colonies, Ouvrard's brother compiled "accurate information about their commerce and resources," emphasizing, Ouvrard later confessed, "opportunities for the prosperity of Spain, as well as the inexhaustible treasures to be gained through well-planned exploitation."[45] Hyperbole and keen hindsight aside, we may trust Ouvrard's assertion that this information inspired him to suggest that Napoleon, by exploiting France's *ascendant* over Spain, "could find on this rich continent the resources he sought in vain among the conquered peoples."[46] Napoleon needed little persuasion.

Ouvrard stepped onto the high road of Spanish finance in 1804, when François Barbé-Marbois, France's treasurer, scrambled to finance Bonaparte's projected military and naval operations and Madrid was already in arrears on its subsidy, roughly in the amount of 3.6 million *pesos* (22 million francs). On behalf of the recently formed Compagnie des Négociants Réunis, funded by the ex-*munitionnaires* Ouvrard, Vanlerberghe, and Desprez, Ouvrard agreed in April 1804 to lend the Trésor Public 32 million francs (5.3 million *pesos,* roughly the value of eight monthly payments of Spain's subsidy) in return for *libranzas* (bills of exchange) on Mexico City's Real Hacienda signed by Soler and payable to the French treasury. Two months later, encouraged by the prospect of further access to New Spain's *pesos,* Ouvrard, representing the Négociants Réunis, offered a second loan, this time for 150 million francs, or 25 million *pesos.*[47] Within two months Ouvrard's banking firm had accumulated a claim of more than 30 million *pesos* on the Madrid treasury and its principal colonial resource, the Real Hacienda of Mexico City, initiating Ouvrard's meteoric career in Spanish finance, which burned out two years later in the bankruptcy of the Négociants Réunis, leaving claims of 142 million francs partially secured on Madrid's Caja de Consolidación and "Spanish America." Disgraced by Napoleon, Ouvrard—now happily integrated with Teresa Cabarrús, ex-comtesse de Fontenay, then "Our Lady of Thermidor," who as Mme Tallien had sponsored the Parisian salon frequented by the young Bonaparte—was not exactly poverty stricken.

Over two years, from 1804 to 1806, Ouvrard spread his financial operations from Paris to Madrid, to Amsterdam and London, to Philadelphia and Baltimore, to Havana and, of course, Veracruz. Enticed by the dual possibilities of hefty commissions on the transfer of New Spain's silver and earnings from supplying New Spain's imports, Ouvrard visited Madrid in 1804. A product of the French Revolution, alternating between culture shock and fascination as he encountered the musty, seventeenth-century flavor of Spanish institutions, ritual, and personalities, Ouvrard used his experience under the Directoire to maximize the profit-making potential of Spain's empire. Or perhaps Ouvrard personified that tradition of French entrepreneurs who were always hankering to draw from the Spanish empire primary products and precious metals in exchange for French manufactures, in effect to "colonialize" the Spanish metropole and its American possessions. Doubtless, unresolved issues of government finance whereby the Spanish government's credit fluctuated with its *vales reales*, which, in turn, fluctuated with inflows of New Spain's silver, brought to mind France's trauma early in the Revolution with the confiscation of church property and the issue of *assignats*.[48] Furthermore, at Madrid Ouvrard must have observed the operations of *consolidación* as it absorbed religious funds and real-estate holdings. Presumably fitting together the French and Spanish experience with church funds with his brother's reports from New Spain and the glint of a silver utopia in the western Spanish Atlantic, Ouvrard submitted to Hacienda Minister Soler (with whom he breakfasted frequently) a report that he claimed persuaded Soler to extend *consolidación* to the American colonies. Breakfasting with power led him to ask Soler to assign him "the monopoly trade of the Americas," along with the transfer of "all kinds of gold and silver belonging to the crown."[49]

Two months after his arrival in Madrid, Ouvrard's conversational skills, business acumen, and sheer bravado paid off. On 26 November 1804 he signed an agreement with the Hacienda minister to provision Spain's army and navy with 2 million *quintales* of grain and advance the Caja de Consolidación 10 million guilders on a bond issue to be floated in Holland; as security, Soler handed over silver drafts on Mexico City's treasury. Oddly enough, this financial coup contained elements of a proposal advanced to the Spanish government in 1780 by the father of Ouvrard's later mistress, Francisco Cabarrús.[50] In 1804 Ouvrard was either more persuasive or just lucky. To provide neutral cover for exports to the Spanish colonies and transfers of silver to Europe, Soler and Ouvrard formed a "cover" company, François Ouvrard & Cie of Bordeaux, in which Sixto Espinosa on behalf of *consolidación* held a *commandite;* each "partner" put up 4 million *livres tournois*.[51] Ouvrard & Cie would distribute five hundred blank licenses signed by Soler to firms in neutral ports of Europe and the United States;

normal duties levied on peninsular imports and their re-export plus colonial duties on the same goods were payable to Madrid's Caja de Consolidación. For his role, Ouvrard would earn a commission of 0.5 percent on all silver transfers, producing what Spain's ambassador at Paris, Eugenio Izquierdo, would denounce as "the outrageous profits businessmen seek."[52]

Two elements of Ouvrard's agreement merit close analysis. First, in the 26 November agreement, under article 6, François Ouvrard & Cie appeared as the Spanish government's sole, exclusive intermediary in trade with the American colonies during war with England. Thereby the company held the "exclusive privilege of importing under neutral flag, at the ports of Veracruz, Havana, Caracas, and Montevideo" all types of merchandise, along with the "privilege to export from said colonies, and under neutral flag, all kinds of commodities, products, and gold and silver objects they are able to produce." Here are overtones of the rejected proposal of an "attempt at *comercio libre*" between Spain and France that Godoy had once supported. Second, slightly later, on 4 December, further provisions were added to the November "treaty," notably article 1, which assigned to Ouvrard & Cie management of exports from the colonies by the Spanish government's Real Giro enterprise, an arrangement prefiguring a similar charge on the twelve neutral firms listed in the royal order of 24 December 1804.[53]

The agreements with Ouvrard (what he termed a *traité*) and the royal order of 24 December can be interpreted in two ways. Either the listing of twelve neutral firms in Europe and the United States was designed to camouflage the licenses to be distributed by Ouvrard & Cie, or it illustrates Soler's intention to keep open a variety of policy instruments. Soler did issue licenses independent of those to Ouvrard, for example, to Craig of Philadelphia in March 1805. Clearly, by the contract signed with Gabriel-Julien Ouvrard and the licensing of neutral firms, the Spanish government accepted in 1804 what it had denied Cabarrús during the war with England in 1780, offering a "poor example of permitting *comercio directo* . . . in the richest and most important part of the Indies."[54]

The critical element of Ouvrard's agreement was receipt of silver from Veracruz, the "only solution to the shortage of funds" in Spain and France.[55] Since the English could monitor shipping in the Atlantic, Ouvrard asked Prime Mister Pitt to allow his operation, which Pitt promptly refused to do. Ouvrard, with the backing of the speculator-diplomat Talleyrand, then turned to the U.S. minister Robert Livingston and Livingston's speculator friend Daniel Parker; tentatively, Livingston and Parker agreed to make available 57 million francs at Hamburg, Amsterdam, and Paris in return for 15 million *pesos* payable at Veracruz, Havana, and Montevideo.[56] Godoy, however, rejected this proposal. At this point, in March 1805, Madrid dispatched Francisco Cabarrús to the Amsterdam merchant-bankers Hope & Company to facilitate (or monitor?) Ouvrard's operations. The goal was to capitalize on the Hope family's connection with Barings of London in order to secure London's approval of the Spanish government's recourse to neutral firms.[57]

Enter Hope & Company and David Parish

Cabarrús's business dealings with Hope went back more than two decades, to 1781, when the Spanish government had commissioned the Madrid banking firm of Cabarrús & Lalanne to place a loan with the Amsterdam merchant-bankers Hope & Fizeaux for 3 million guilders at 5 percent, repayable in annual installments from 1789 to 1792.[58] This, liquidated promptly, led in 1801 to a second placement, this time of 18 million guilders at 4.5–5 percent, to be liquidated in 1809. The interest level and the longer repayment schedule suggest the Amsterdam firm's confidence in the solvency of the Spanish government or, pragmatically, in its access to the output of New Spain's silver mines.

In 1804, foreseeing a resumption of warfare, Madrid turned to a French banking house at Madrid, the firm of the marqués de la Colonilla, to arrange with Hope for 5 million *pesos* at 6 percent payable in francs to France's Trésor Public.[59] And when Spain joined France in war with England, Hope's Amsterdam director, Pierre Labouchère, recommended that silver transfers henceforth be routed from Veracruz and other Spanish colonial ports to Amsterdam via the United States. Labouchère even proposed that the Spanish government close Veracruz to all ships except those exporting silver.[60] Now he counted on his father-in-law, Francis Baring, to procure English licenses for neutral shipping, "above all to secure to your Country the Quantity of Dollars which it constantly wants."[61] At the same time, Labouchère signed an agreement with Ouvrard (6 May 1805) whereby Hope & Company would act as the commission agent of Ouvrard & Cie, in effect the executor of Ouvrard's Spanish contracts. Hope brought to the deal Barings of London, their "closest business associates." Presumably satisfied that London authorities would permit the use of neutral ships and cargoes, in September 1805 Hope & Company loaned the Spanish government 10 million guilders at 5.5 percent repayable over ten years.[62]

Labouchère had driven a hard bargain with Ouvrard. In the combined agreements of May and September 1805 there were fifty licenses for neutral "expeditions" to Spain's colonial ports, 4 percent commission on cargoes, plus drafts totaling 10.4 million *pesos* on Mexico City's Hacienda at a 7 percent commission, of which Ouvrard was guaranteed 2 percent.[63] This turned out to be Barings's "most extraordinary operation" and the "most lucrative trade [the firm of Robert Oliver] ever pursued."[64] But there was an underside. When the French government investigated the operations of Ouvrard and the Compagnie des Négociants Réunis in 1806, it discovered a huge debt owed to the Trésor Public.[65] In May 1806 the Spanish government agreed to cover 60 million francs of the French company's total debt of 142 million with drafts of another 10 million *pesos* on funds in colonial treasuries.[66] As late as January 1808 Soler and Sixto Espinosa were still signing drafts on Mexico City's treasury for a total of 2 million *pesos* payable to Hope & Company, through whose hands the funds would go to the French treasury.[67]

With the agreements of May to September 1805, Hope, in tandem with Barings, took over effective management of Ouvrard's contracts. It now fell to Hope's Amsterdam director, the Nantais Labouchère, to select personnel to handle the export licenses assigned to neutrals, oversee Veracruz's silver shipments, and keep accounts and correspondence at the critical commercial synapses of the not so secret operations. International financial operations invariably depend upon trustworthy personnel, all the more so in wartime; it was especially true when sailing vessels were the quickest vehicles of communication. For the synapse at Veracruz, Labouchère picked Armand Pierre Lestapis, a native of the French Basque country (Béarn), formerly a clerk in the Santander firm of Juan Plante, where a fellow clerk was José Gabriel Villanueva. Lestapis had been in charge of Spanish correspondence in Hope's Amsterdam establishment. Now, as a Spanish "cover" agent Lestapis surfaced at Veracruz as "Villanueva," having adopted the name of his recently deceased fellow clerk from Santander, and was instructed to conduct business operations through the Veracruz merchants Pedro Miguel de Echeverría and Francisco Luís Septién.[68] Labouchère appointed Vincent Nolte, like Labouchère a native of Nantes, to go to the Caribbean port of New Orleans to establish contact with Havana and Veracruz, and he put his trust in David Parish as his main agent in the United States ("America").

Parish's credentials were solid. At a time when an individual's competence was presumed to reflect the qualities of one's ascendants, young Parish must have impressed Labouchère. His commercial lineage was impeccable: his father was a Scottish merchant at Hamburg who over a period of fifty years had accumulated fortune and prestige. David Parish left his father's firm for Antwerp after the Peace of Amiens and traveled to Paris, where, unsurprisingly, he struck up an acquaintance—a French connection, as it were—with Talleyrand. Apparently, Francis Baring, Hope's London correspondent, formed an equally high appreciation of Parish's competence and responsibility. Like Ouvrard, David Parish was quick, brash, and not above dipping into the considerable funds of the trinity of Hope-Baring-Ouvrard passing through his hands to speculate in cotton during his residence at Philadelphia. After earning a fortune at Philadelphia as Hope & Company's principal agent in the transfer of Spanish government funds, Parish returned to Europe. Years later, when his large investment in the Viennese banking house of Fries disappeared in its bankruptcy, Parish's meteoric career ended not in burnout but in splashdown: in 1826 he drowned in the Danube.[69] Still, the Parish family's link to Latin America survived in Argentina, in John Parish's grandson John Parish Robertson and in Woodbine Parish, diplomat, speculator, publicist.

Hope and Barings dispatched David Parish to the United States, where he peddled to justifiably suspicious merchants the blank licenses of the Ouvrard-Hope syndicate for trade to Spanish colonial ports.[70] "Passports were indispensable for Mr. Parish's operations," Robert Oliver once wrote to Tomás Murphy at Veracruz, "as he intended to sell them and could not say who would use them."[71] He managed to get New York's Archibald Gracie to take three and distributed a few through his New Orleans agent, Nolte, and in Baltimore. There and at Philadelphia, his headquarters, he found his claim to exclusive distribution of the Spanish treasury's blank neutral licenses energetically contested: he learned that Soler and Sixto Espinosa had never intended to make Ouvrard the sole instrument of Madrid's international financial strategy.

Enter Oliver of Baltimore

By 5 March 1806, when the Baltimore merchant Robert Oliver wrote his agent at Veracruz that "Mr. Parish of Antwerp arrived lately from Europe with a Royal Order to trade to Veracruz . . . Mr. Parish says his Royal Order is the only one now in force," for months Oliver had been sending ships to Veracruz (as well as Havana and Caracas) under neutral licenses assigned to his brother-in-law John Craig in the royal order of 5 March 1805.[72] Understandably, Oliver bridled at the fact that Parish with customary ruthless insouciance had employed "a confidential agent to . . . exclude us and every other person from Veracruz."[73] Like many regulation-wise U.S. merchants trading with the Caribbean, Oliver had dispatched ships to Spanish colonial ports without so advising Baltimore port officials. "[O]ur people," he observed in 1802, "are in the habit of clearing for ports without any intention to go there."[74] His intermittent, unauthorized operations were transformed when John Craig drew him into his operations with Spain's Caja de Consolidación and its director, Sixto Espinosa. Spain's policy was to announce publicly, for the benefit of the English public, the neutral merchant houses authorized to trade with its colonies in America, while covertly arranging with Ouvrard—and through him with Hope, Barings, and Craig—for the bulk of shipments to and from Spain's most important overseas port, Veracruz. It was part of Spain's crisis management to keep options open, to have a fallback position.

To cobble together another cover for shipping flour to Havana and Caracas to feed plantation slaves and for exporting those colonies' sugar and coffee and, above all, the silver of New Spain, Soler had allocated in peacetime a flour contract to an ex-viceroy of New Spain, the marqués de Branciforte, related by marriage to Godoy. In wartime this contract had to be reassigned. First, on 19 February 1805 Sixto Espinosa in a *convenio* assigned 167,180 *pesos* of *consolidación* funds to Francisco Caballero Sarmiento at Tenerife, in the Canaries, for the purchase of wine from a local merchant, Diego Barry, who in turn consigned the shipment to Caballero Sarmiento's brother-in-law, the Philadelphia merchant John Craig.[75] Craig was to invest the proceeds of the wine sales in "flours and other products," reads the *convenio*, "for Havana and Caracas." Second, two weeks later, on 1 March 1805, a royal order added Craig's firm to those already authorized as neutrals in the order of 24 December 1804; not publicized was that Branciforte's contract had been transferred to Craig.[76] As a nominally independent neutral operator, Craig was also given *permisos* "para hacer expediciones en buques neutrales a Veracruz, la Habana y Caracas"; the intent was to have Craig appear as the nominal proprietor of what were really Spanish government funds, to use "his name to cover these funds as neutral and insure them as such." And if his vessels were intercepted by English corsairs, the *convenio* with Craig stipulated, "Craig will claim them in and out of court as his own property without mentioning other names in view of the confidence in his firm."[77] To supervise the arrangement, Craig was directed to dispatch to the Venezuelan port of La Guayra as his representative *(apoderado)* Caballero Sarmiento, who was in fact the watchdog of the Caja de Consolidación.[78]

Soler and Espinosa's desperate tactics of expediency achieved their goal. Before Parish could distribute Ouvrard's *permisos,* Craig and Oliver early in 1805 had already activated theirs and set up agents at Havana (Pablo Serra) and Veracruz (Procopio J. Pollock); by late 1805 they had exported from Veracruz "almost or mostly all of the value of the shipment from America."[79] In October 1805, encouraged by reports that London was approving "licenses to neutral vessels to carry cargoes from England to the Spanish colonies," Oliver commented to his London agent Barings that "we have so little confidence in the Spaniards that we intend to carry on the trade in small fast sailing vessels from this country and never trust much in their power at one time." Distrust rather than pity characterizes the attitude of the self-confident toward those dangling in the wind. Three months later, on 7 January 1806, the potential value of Spain's *permisos* began to crowd out distrust, and Oliver confided to Alexander Baring that "we ascertained our real situation which we find to be far beyond our expectations and such as was never before granted to any person." Exploiting that "real situation" made Robert Oliver one of the richest citizens in the United States, if not *the* richest, by 1808.[80]

In March 1805 Parish's brashness and Oliver's (for Craig-Oliver) stubbornness had to be reconciled if both were to maximize their El Dorado. It took only two months to bring the would-be monopolists Parish and Oliver to agree on the advantages of shared monopoly over oligopolistic competition. At first Parish complained to Spain's minister at Philadelphia, the marqués de Casa Irujo, about Oliver and Craig's "proceedings," only to have Casa Irujo decide that Oliver's "Royal Order is as goods as his, that he [Casa Irujo] will not take any steps to interfere with us," and, most critical, that "our order is considered in full force." Gleefully Oliver predicted to his Veracruz agent, Pollock, that Parish's neutral cover would soon be blown, leading to English seizure of the "vessels carrying his passports . . . which will increase the insurance considerably and perhaps put an end to his operations." Once Parish's goods proved to be overpriced or subject to seizure at sea, "ours would be certain" and the "interest of the European government [Spain] as effectually promoted by our operations as by his." Later letters enjoined Pollock to "endeavor to defeat" Parish's aims and specified, "We hope you will not permit Parish's French agent [Villanueva] to defeat us."[81]

Yet over the following three weeks the level of interfirm warfare subsided. "Mr. Parish . . . has appealed to us to carry his views into effect," Oliver informed Sixto Espinosa on 29 March, and on 15 April their commercial hostilities ended. On that day Oliver confided to Pollock that his remarks about Parish's "illiberality" had been inaccurate, because Craig had been "deceived by an interested person as to Parish's views and intentions," a change of heart perhaps induced by the fear that Craig's licenses might not be renewed and that they had to "act under Mr. Parish's which can admit of no doubt." Pollock was now ordered to cooperate with Parish's Veracruz agent "Villanueva": "You will render account to him of business entrusted to you." To sugar this drastic turnabout, Pollock was assured that Parish had consented "to permit us to employ you," for "if anything happens to Villa-nueva, Parish will make you agent." On leaving Veracruz, Pollock was to "destroy all papers which can . . . expose our operations to that port."[82]

Oliver appended a curious postscript indicating an almost pathological preoccupation with destroying evidence of former hostility. He informed Pollock that "Parish requests you remove all unfavorable impressions . . . destroy all letters on the subject. . . . You will do so in presence of bearer, Mr. Wilson, who has an account of them," and then reiterated in the same paragraph "our wish to destroy even [*sic*] evidence of hostility to Mr. Parish with whom we are on the best of terms."[83] The changeover of agents was confirmed on 16 April, when Oliver sent his first communication to "Villa-nueva" as part of the agreement "to consign the whole of our shipments to Mr. J. G. Villanueva."[84] Henceforth "Villanueva" was not to honor any further permissions issued by Parish; as Oliver put it bluntly, "to put a stop to competition, for otherwise the business is not worth following."[85] Either Oliver could resort to hyperbole when obliged or Adam Smith was only too accurate when he commented that all merchants felt most comfortable with monopoly.

The licenses that made possible the now-shared monopoly were running out, and Oliver and Craig were anxious to continue a highly profitable commercial operation at Veracruz. In March 1806 Oliver was predicting that Parish's "operations to Veracruz will not last long," and four months later he found them "nearly exhausted" and said that Parish "is not likely to receive any more."[86] Oliver and Craig had banked on an extension of their *permisos,* a hope confirmed when Madrid granted Craig a renewal.[87] With satisfaction Oliver boasted on 7 August to Tomás Murphy, at Veracruz, that he and Craig now had "more extensive powers," that they could dispense with "passports or documents," and, Oliver added confidently, that "Mr. Espinosa has confided to Mr. Craig . . . the exclusive supply of Cuba . . . and Carracas with flour under the privilege granted to the Marquis of Branciforte."[88] Over about twelve months Oliver, through Craig, had managed to absorb Ouvrard's licenses, available by exclusive arrangement with David Parish, and after July 1806 he could contemplate what he and Craig hoped would be virtually exclusive entry to Veracruz—until they learned in late 1806 of Soler's arrangements with two London firms, Gordon & Murphy, and Reid, Irving & Company.

Although Oliver and Craig traded at Veracruz, Havana, and La Guayra from about mid-1805 to sometime in 1809, their peak operations spanned the months from spring 1806 to early 1807. Over approximately twenty-four

months Oliver exploited the arrangements initiated by Espinosa with Ouvrard and, through him, with Hope, Barings, and their agent Parish, with
Caballero Sarmiento and, through him, with Craig-Oliver, all the while
enjoying the toleration of English authorities for neutral firms and neutral
shipping of the United States serving New Spain's port of Veracruz. The
international conjuncture after 1804 had induced the governments of Spain,
France, and England to serve public and private ends by relying upon the
profit-motivated skills of neutral merchants and shippers of the Atlantic seaboard of the United States. In the long run England's placet for Oliver's
operations was a tactic against France and its submetropole, imperial Spain,
a technique of the diplomacy of economic warfare.

Like Hope's Labouchère, Oliver and Craig depended upon reliable agents
to manage long-distance commercial operations. At La Guayra, Caballero
Sarmiento proved no source of anxiety; nor, for that matter, was there any
reason to question the trustworthiness of their man at Havana, Pablo Serra.
In any event, the volume of Oliver's trade through these agents was negligible compared with the trading at Veracruz initially handled by Matías
Lorenzo Murphy, Tomás Murphy's brother, and by Procopio Pollock. By
the end of 1805, when Oliver was just activating Craig's licenses, he wrote
rather warmly to Matías Murphy to advise that "your friend Mr. John Craig
of Philadelphia" was forwarding "several articles as remembrance for your
kindness to his nephew," James Sarmiento. At the end of January 1806 Murphy and Pollock received instructions to sell the cargo of the schooner *Dash*
and forward proceeds in "Dollars, Cochineal, Sugars and hides . . . we
would prefer to have the principal part of the returns in Dollars."[89] In February the emphasis switched to proceeds in dollars and cochineal, and Oliver wanted to know "the article most likely to answer at Veracruz." Then in
early March Oliver learned of the extraordinary markup over a cargo's prime
cost that Parish's agent, "Villanueva," was arranging, and he wrote to Murphy and Pollock: "How is this to be reconciled with the cargoes in which I
was interested? . . . We hear you have been deceived by the broker. . . . We
beg you to explain."[90]

Such suspicions may have been a factor in seeking an accommodation
with Parish and obtaining the service of his Veracruz agent. In mid-April,
when Oliver showed growing impatience with Matías Murphy's tendency
to remit proceeds in cochineal and sugar rather than dollars, he pressed him
to "advance the probable value of our cargoes in Dollars" or instead to
freight the ships with "stone or sand ballast" if sugar prices were too high.[91]
Oliver's letterbook has no correspondence with Murphy or Pollock after
mid-April 1806, probably because his suspicions were confirmed by "anon-

ymous" informants at Veracruz, as well as by his new agent, "Villanueva." Capitalizing on Oliver's emphasis on selling his cargoes "with dispatch" ("dispatch is of more importance than any return cargo, except dollars"),[92] Murphy had, Oliver wrote "Villanueva," "cheated us out of a large sum of money and . . . a combination was formed to purchase our cargoes . . . which accounts for our losses and heavy deductions on the sales." Losses on the last ship consigned to Murphy and Pollock had totaled more than ten thousand dollars.[93] "Villanueva" was directed to "sell by the package which will prevent combination."[94] Pollock returned to Baltimore, later to sail as supercargo aboard a merchantman "for the purposes of smuggling near Lima," Oliver commented acidly. Pollock was, he said, "unquestionably a very ordinary fellow, and we regret exceedingly having anything to do with him."[95] However, Oliver maintained formal relations with Matías Murphy despite "Villanueva"'s report that "Murphy was the purchaser of your cargoes."[96]

Oliver's new, and Parish's old, agent was adequate but not without problems. The arrangement with the French Basque Lestapis, alias "Villanueva," lasted until Oliver began to wind down his Veracruz operation in early 1808. At first "Villanueva" received 5 percent commission on all consignments made to him (and presumably on silver and other commodities he exported), an arrangement quickly modified on the ground that English admiralty courts might judge this "an indirect interest" and question "the neutrality of our property." Instead, "Villanueva" accepted the promise of a "proportionate compensation" that ultimately came to a lump payment of twenty thousand dollars.[97] Business was seasoned with personal favors such as enrolling "Villanueva"'s nephew ("young Cruzat"), with Parish's approval, in one of the "best colleges in this country," frequented by U.S., French, English, and Spanish "boys" superintended by a "Society of French priests" whose director was "well known in the Spanish colonies."[98]

On the other hand, the arrangements had drawbacks. For one, "Villanueva" failed to furnish the detailed commercial information Oliver needed to choose items for the Veracruz market; for another, language seemed to be a barrier. As Oliver remarked to a Savannah merchant with Caribbean interests, "[I]t is disagreeable and inconvenient to carry on an extensive business with men who do not understand our language." He would have preferred to deal with Tomás Murphy, but his commissions were too high.[99] Underlying reservations about "Villanueva" was the suspicion that the French agent was not aggressively defending Oliver's shipments at the Veracruz customs house. Oliver found questionable the practice of Veracruz's customs officers to assign high valuations to non-Spanish ("foreign") articles. He had estimated an overall duty rate of 12.5 percent on his muslins and dimitys, but "Villanueva" reportedly had to pay 56 percent and 38 percent, respectively, which Oliver found all the more unacceptable because he believed, as he complained to "Villanueva," that "the same kind of goods in other vessels have paid considerably less."[100] Withal, "Villanueva" served two masters creditably over two years, shipping back high-value colonial staples and silver. When Parish's and Oliver-Craig's licenses ran out, he sailed away to Baltimore with his recent bride, picked up his "compensation," and retired to Béarn.[101] To tie up the loose ends of his consignment business and remit *pesos* to Amsterdam on the remainder of the French account, he left in charge the two leading Veracruz merchants who had helped dispose of his consignments, Pedro Miguel de Echeverría and Francisco Luís de Septién.[102]

Oliver's complaints about the management of his business at Veracruz by Pollock and Murphy should not imply that Oliver was a naïf operating without guile. Like other U.S. merchants of the Atlantic coast during the early days of the republic, Oliver shared the perception that war, not peace, nourished commercial speculation. In the months after Amiens, he complained to Francis Baring that "the commerce of this country continues unpromising. . . . We find it difficult to employ our funds with the least prospect of success." But once renewed warfare seemed imminent, he brightened, saying that "war will enable us to place some more profitable business in your hands," since "new channels will no doubt open."[103] Opening new channels left few grounds for scruples. Oliver knowingly shipped goods on the Spanish government's prohibited list (English and East Indian cottons) and was prepared to move them into New Spain by one means or another.[104] Since the military and civilian bureaucracy at the port of Veracruz could be "managed," Oliver forwarded "articles for your different friends and particularly for the military commander [García Dávila]" that might prove troublesome, since "the smallest article sometimes affords a pretext to the British to capture our vessels." On the other hand, concealment of articles omitted from bills of lading also created problems: "The package for Mr. Villanueva is too large for the private apartment in the Trunk where we generally conceal our private . . . [crossed out] papers."[105] Exasperated by the discrimination of Veracruz customs officials after almost two years of dealing with that port, Oliver could not suppress the observation that "the persons who value our goods are not governed by any fixed principle," followed by the suggestion that "Villanueva" might "find it for our Interest to give them a little money to enable those to judge more correctly in the future."[106] Later such "management," as Oliver put it, of officials in Spanish American ports assumed more drastic form. In 1809, when he received a supplementary license to ship to Veracruz, Oliver directed his supercargo aboard *Fly,* in the event Veracruz customs rejected the cargo authorized by the *permiso,* to "endeavor to sell it deliverable at sea or proceed to the Havanna and value on Mr. Pablo Serra."[107]

Oliver employed bribery and procurement of *permisos* and English *pasavantes* and also closely supervised successive Veracruz agents for the sole purpose of selling to New Spain when goods there were scarce because of the English blockade, permitting only a few neutrals to operate at that colony's main port. While Madrid's interest was primarily in the silver exports of Veracruz, neutral intermediaries such as Parish, Oliver, and later Gordon & Murphy were motivated by attractive commissions on silver transfers and, in Oliver's case, earnings on goods selected from domestic and foreign assortments at Baltimore. For Oliver, a newcomer to New Spain's consumer preferences, it was necessary, first, to select New Spain's exportables other than silver and, second, after sizing up the composition of local import demand, to draw upon an international supply network.

Before and after 1803, Oliver's operations to Demerara, Barbados, Kingston and later Havana and Veracruz included disposal of return cargoes of sugar exchanged for his shipments of provisions, mainly flours. When Caballero Sarmiento, Craig's brother-in-law, opened an office at La Guayra in Venezuela, he bought cocoa.[108] Of course, the principal commodity at Veracruz was silver, yet pressure to export the colony's sugar, hides, and what at least for Oliver was a new colonial staple, cochineal, promised both profits and problems. As Oliver eased into the Veracruz marketplace, he had to turn to his principal European correspondent, Francis Baring, to "beg your opinion" of the dyestuff and its "probable value in London" and to ask him to advise whether there were at Veracruz "any article . . . but cochineal which would sell to advantage in London."[109] Although of the "very first quality," seroons of Oaxaca's cochineal were an "article little known in Baltimore" in 1806, while New Spain's sugars and hides could not compete pricewise with those shipped from Havana and the Rio de la Plata.[110] In the spring of 1806 Oliver insisted that the agents Pollock, Matías Murphy, and "Villanueva" "advance the probable value of our Cargoes in Dollars," even limit returns to "money and ballast," since "[w]e find the articles generally exported from Veracruz will not answer in this country."[111] Like generations of merchants from Spain residing in New Spain, Oliver niched himself profitably into, and at the same time reinforced, the structures of Spain's transatlantic trade and its orientation. He grudgingly accepted colonial staples but chortled that "[o]ne of our vessels arrived . . . from Veracruz with 150,000 dollars on board."[112]

By trial and some error spread over months, along with persistent prodding of his agents, Oliver slowly gauged the appropriate assortment of goods to match profitably New Spain's consumption preferences. Properly chosen cargo shipped aboard small, fast vessels—one, his *Meteor,* he called proudly the "fastest ship in the world"[113]—facilitated short sailing time, quick turnaround time in port, rapid turnover on shore, low inventories, and large unit profits, which were all the more desirable because the Spanish licenses were finite and inevitably competitors would be drawn in and hostilities end unpredictably.

Over nine months, from January to September 1806, Oliver proved a quick learner. He began by asking a Hamburg trader for linens "suitable to the Veracruz market," covering his ignorance by floating the judgment that "fine Platillas and Brittanias are the best article," when his intended direction was that "you may add a little of any other goods that you know will answer equally well . . . of the very best quality."[114] Since the agents Matías Murphy and Procopio Pollock failed—or balked—at advising "the article most likely to answer at Veracruz," Oliver had to turn in May to Parish's father, at Hamburg, to order "for the market of Veracruz" thousands of pieces of the "very finest Platillas you can procure" and "fine Brittanias," along with "Bramantes, Florette and Crude" and "fine Diaper Table linen"— a logical bet on New Spain's wealthy consumers' preference for prestigious luxury goods.[115]

Unfortunately for Oliver, other neutral suppliers were also experimenting. When Oliver learned at the end of May that "German linens are plenty and low" at Veracruz, he opted for the more risky enterprise of shipping "chiefly prohibited goods."[116] Since Spain's prohibited list contained a wide variety of textiles not stocked at Baltimore—as he had to explain to "Villanueva," "the taste and fashions of America [are] very different from that of the People of Mexico"—Oliver had to rely upon accurate information from Veracruz before "importing goods which a peace or suspension of our powers might leave on our hands for years and finally sell at a great loss." Which suggests the reality of what at the time was called "speculation." So "Villanueva" was to send samples "as often as it is convenient," omitting velvets or calicoes ("we know what will answer"). Here Oliver's judgment failed him, for he learned shortly that New Spain's discriminating consumers preferred velvets, chintzes, and calicoes, which were "entirely out of use here," and he confessed to his Veracruz agent with exasperation that it was "impossible to procure in the United States articles exactly calculated for the Veracruz market."[117]

Oliver's commercial correspondence of 1806 illuminates the education of a Baltimore merchant-entrepreneur entering the Spanish American market without experience. Gradually he came to understand that English manufacturers of chintzes and calicoes, as well as English re-exporters of East Asian cottons, shipped products specific to the U.S. market, preparing very different assortments for Spanish American markets they had managed to test extensively in the eighteenth century. At one point Oliver despaired of finding at Boston, New York, or Philadelphia supplies of chintzes and calicoes "calculated for Veracruz"; they had to be ordered from England. Further, by late August 1806 he could see that the prices of cottons, unlike those of other fabrics, "would not be lowered by peace but on the contrary-wise."[118]

When Oliver finally had access to reliable commercial information about the composition of import demand at Veracruz, in late 1806, it came not from "Villanueva," Matías Murphy, or Pollock—their "lists of goods . . . all differed . . . none . . . gave us the necessary information as to assortment"—but from a "young man" returning to Baltimore with a "complete view of the subject."[119] Now Oliver could prepare two shopping lists of traditional, high-quality, high-priced goods "intended for the Veracruz market": one sent to Oliver's Trieste correspondent (Holland & Company) for thousands of pieces of *platillas, britannias, bramantes,* and *floretes,* along with "Milan steel," Castile soap, eighty-eight thousand windowglass panes, and pint-size tumblers; the other sent to Hamburg (John Parish & Company) for linens and woolens (creas, Hessians, caserillas, lawns, rouans, brown Flemish shirting). The "whole of these goods," he wrote to Holland & Company, "must be fine and of the very best quality."[120] Thereafter, however, one detects a shift by Oliver to large quantities of "very cheap" East India goods, since "cotton goods . . . we presume would sell to advantage in peace," as "Villanueva" had recommended.[121] Oliver's insistence upon conforming to consumers' preferences in New Spain produced quick results: the average value of cargo per ship at Veracruz was $76,969 before September 1806; thereafter it doubled to $157,246, the last two shipments averaging $170,820.[122]

At the end of 1806 Oliver wrote to a Norfolk, Virginia, correspondent that his "shipments consist chiefly of British manufactures" and that he was deeply concerned by the tightened English monitoring of Caribbean shipping.[123] He wrote to Baring Brothers reiterating that "the principal part of our shipments to Veracruz are British manufactures," and he ordered from London quantities of cottons such as velvets ("blue . . . white . . . handsome colors"), dimities, muslins, chintzes, and calicoes ("with handsome figures—no dark grounds"), English nankeens, Pullicat and white muslin neckerchiefs, cotton stockings, and thread, plus small quantities of wide cashmeres and silk stockings. The last of Oliver's cargoes to Veracruz suggest a balanced selection of German linens, Catalan wines, and an array of English manufactures or re-exports—chintzes, muslins, handkerchiefs, nankeens, and East India "goods" to the astonishingly high value of one hundred thousand dollars, astonishing since by his own admission his cargo values generally averaged only half that sum ("[small] sells much better than large cargoes").[124]

Persistent inquiry about the composition of New Spain's demand for imported textiles was a key factor making profitable the speculation of a merchant of the United States probing a colonial economy and culture differing markedly from the Anglo-American ambiance of Baltimore. *Speculation* is the most accurate word: Oliver's time frame had to be short, since it was conditioned primarily by wartime shortages, and peace could come without warning. Hence Oliver's emphasis upon cargoes with a ceiling of fifty thousand dollars, upon "dispatch," upon "early sale of . . . cargo," upon "early sale of every article belonging to us" at Veracruz, upon quick departures from that port whether or not there was a full cargo of exportables other than silver.[125] A second, critical factor behind Oliver's success was his preexisting connections to European agents ("friends") to supply his assortments or handle shipments. Baring Brothers of London was a principal correspondent supplemented in Germany (John Parish & Company of Hamburg), the Low Countries (Hope & Company of Amsterdam, David Parish & Company of Antwerp), Austria (Holland and Company of Trieste), and Spain (Henry Dowell & Company at Cadiz, Grivignie & Company at Málaga, Larrard & Company at Barcelona), not to overlook his "confidential friend" at Madrid, the merchant-banking firm of Patrick Joyes & Company.[126]

This contrasts strikingly with the Cadiz commercial pattern reproduced overseas at Veracruz and Mexico City by the structural constraints of Spain's Atlantic system, which customarily left to European merchants at Cadiz the import of merchandise for re-export to America. And unlike Cadiz merchants, most of whom were financed by foreign residents, Oliver did not borrow to any appreciable extent to finance his "speculation" to Veracruz and other Caribbean ports. Such contrasts notwithstanding, Robert Oliver shared with the merchants of Cadiz and Barcelona, Veracruz and Mexico

City, the expectation of enjoying a monopolistic position or the next best position, shared monopoly. It is an expectation that commercial capitalism shares with subsequent stages of development under capitalism.

Aspiration for market dominance is a theme recurrent in Oliver's correspondence from December 1805 to February 1808, from his initial entry into the Veracruz marketplace to his withdrawal. It surfaced in a letter of December 1806 to Sixto Espinosa, in which he complained that a shipment to Havana had encountered a "bad market which will always be the case as long as the port remains open." Once he had merged operations with those of David Parish, he directed his agent "Villanueva" to "put a stop to competition for otherwise the business is not worth following."[127] By early January 1807 Oliver was fretting about stepped-up licensing of other shippers in the United States on the part of London, which led him to complain to Espinosa that Parish's *permisos,* combined with those of Gordon & Murphy at Veracruz, "will make the trade no object."[128] Sensing modifications in English policy that might enhance the Anglo-Spanish firm of Gordon & Murphy at Veracruz, Oliver proposed in February 1807 that Gordon & Murphy's London headquarters share commercial information about shipping and cargoes to Veracruz "for our government." His proposal was unambiguous: "If we knew that you were sending to Veracruz a quantity of any particular kind of goods, we would of course leave such goods out entirely and avoid as much as possible glutting the market with any particular articles." Oliver continued pointedly: "It is in your interest as well as ours to regulate your shipments so as to prevent abundant supplies."[129] Spain's centuries-old policy of managed or regulated transatlantic trade was based on the same thinking.

Although Gordon & Murphy did not reciprocate, Oliver's trade to Veracruz continued strong through 1807. Then his and Parish's *permisos* began to peter out; Oliver's colleague and relative by marriage, John Craig, died; and in February 1808 Oliver advised Espinosa that he intended to terminate his operations. As usual, he had a complaint: the Spanish government selected its diplomats poorly. "[M]any . . . act very contrary to our view of propriety," he said, probably a criticism of Casa Irujo at Philadelphia, and he predicted that "you will find yourself quickly disappointed by the operations of Gordon & Murphy of London." With unaccustomed circumspection he added, "we have no right to meddle in the business of others."[130]

The prospect of virtual monopoly sustained Oliver's interest in Veracruz for two years, and then he tapered off operations. He learned of a steep increase in traffic between Jamaica and Veracruz and that "immense" quantities of imports were filtering clandestinely into Veracruz from New

Orleans—as Iturrigaray and Ciriaco de Cevallos suspected. As he observed in a letter to Sixto Espinosa, "The means by which these goods are introduced at Veracruz are fraudulent in the extreme and the same game is now playing from the Havana under His Majesty's late order in favor of that Island."[131] Oliver's withdrawal was, of course, noticed by Mexico City's *almaceneros,* who were informed of business activity at Veracruz by their agents. Virtually at the same time that Oliver drafted a letter to Madrid, at Mexico City Gabriel Iturbe e Iraeta breathed a sigh of relief over the prospect that neutral traders would soon be reduced, if not eliminated, and that "consequently commerce has begun to breathe," since one could hope to return to a more managed market. Indeed, there was more than relief; there was satisfaction. When Iturbe, evidently following closely the operations of Oliver's agent at Veracruz, learned of "Villanueva"'s departure for Baltimore, he wrote jubilantly, "May God do well by Villanueva, who is leaving," adding, tongue in cheek, "and better that he never return with his *permisos.*"[132]

The Murphys of Veracruz and London: Madrid's English Option

It seems to be a paradox of finance that public penury usually correlates with private profit. The device that Soler and Sixto Espinosa had ideated to transfer New Spain' silver to Spain proved politically costly to the metropole because it helped to destabilize colonial authority at Mexico City, yet it was extraordinarily profitable to its neutral financial intermediaries— Oliver, Craig, Parish, the Hope-Baring consortium, Gordon & Murphy, and Reid, Irving & Company. Precisely how profitable remains to be seen.

Oliver's overture to Gordon & Murphy of London marks his skill at detecting in 1806 significant changes in London's tactics of economic warfare against France and its reluctant Spanish ally. Oliver's perception of the change first surfaced in his correspondence of 15 October, when he mentioned Gordon & Murphy's arrangement with the Spanish government "on a large scale for sending goods to Veracruz and extracting money," information supplied by a "confidential friend at Madrid," probably the banker Patrick Joyes. Later Joyes forwarded a copy of a license given to Gordon & Murphy.[133] More details about the Gordon & Murphy agreement followed, namely, that the London firm had assigned some licenses to cover three U.S. ships routed first to Cadiz for a consignment of quicksilver and other cargo "on account of government," then to Veracruz. News of the English licenses—"a wonderful change in the British system"—induced Oliver to ask Barings to "procure them for our vessels trading to Veracruz";

since Barings had obtained only two, Oliver had to work out his own agreement with Gordon & Murphy.[134] There was, however, more to the "wonderful change" than Oliver realized. To be sure, he noted that now English
authorities were licensing domestic firms to hire U.S.-registered shipping.
Yet he failed to integrate this with other information also available in late
1806 about England's new naval tactics, that "British cruisers in the West
Indies and on our coast intend to capture every vessel bound to or from
Veracruz." Like the French, the English would spare no pain to monitor
silver flows from the world's largest supplier. Did Oliver fail to realize that
London had resolved to exercise fully the maritime hegemony in the Atlantic that Trafalgar had confirmed the previous year by putting transfers of
silver from New Spain to Europe and Spain under closer surveillance in
cooperation with authorities at Madrid, who were now issuing licenses to
English commercial houses?[135]

Open to speculation is what motivated the new Whig ministry of William Grenville in 1806 to monitor more directly trade flows between New
Spain and Spain. After the battle of Austerlitz, the war against Napoleonic
France forced the English more than before to employ a mix of economic
and military weapons. London could use New Spain's silver *pesos* to solidify
the opposition of the Third Coalition to French expansionism under
Bonaparte, and the East India Company relied upon silver in its Asian
trades.[136] By distributing licenses to major English commercial houses and
permitting their neutral intermediaries to enter Cadiz en route to Veracruz,
London could benefit those in their traditional "Spanish Trades" who were
losing ground to Caribbean smugglers operating out of Kingston and
Providence to Veracruz and Havana. Further, English-licensed neutral shipping, when loading at Cadiz mercury of the Spanish government's monopoly, also received Spanish licenses authorizing off-loading of other goods
at Veracruz. Mercury was indispensable for efficiently processing New
Spain's silver ores into coin and bullion, in which both governments shared
a vital interest. To the Madrid government, which was precariously dependent upon transatlantic shipments of silver from the operations of New
Spain's *consolidación,* an informal, alternative arrangement with the English
government via the Anglo-Spanish firm of Gordon & Murphy promised a
degree of autonomy from the hegemony of France. Recall that Madrid,
London, and Paris had accurate figures on the extraordinary transfer of
Spanish-American silver, roughly 60 percent from Veracruz alone, arriving
at Cadiz and, to a lesser degree, at Galician ports from 1801 to 1804. In
midsummer 1804 England's consul at Cadiz, James Duff, forwarded to
Downing Street a "pretty accurate idea of the importation into this country

since the Peace in October 1801 . . . effective dollars 170,658,752," or the equivalent of 33.4 million pounds sterling, in specie and staples—a conservative understatement, Duff underscored.[137]

In point of fact, after Austerlitz authorities in Madrid decided to terminate the primary role of Ouvrard, and thereby of Hope and Barings too, in neutral trade to the American colonies, abandoning reliance on the French government and signaling their interest in direct licensing of English firms. Godoy's regime had to balance one hegemon against the other, and the tilt toward London was logical. With Madrid's approval, two large consortia at London requested that the Board of Trade authorize their proposed silver operations. The first to apply, in February 1806, was a group headed by the London branch of the Santander firm Fermín de Tastet & Company; through its agent, J. Taylor, the consortium promised, in behalf of London merchant-bankers and coparticipants at Hamburg and Lisbon, to purchase at Madrid silver drafts on the treasuries of Spain's colonies from the Banco de San Carlos, the Compañía de Filipinas, or private citizens. Gordon & Murphy, the second group to apply, offered to export up to 10 million *pesos* from Veracruz. Both consortia accepted London's prescription that all outgoing cargoes contain a high percentage by value of English manufactures.[138]

On purely ad hoc, pragmatic grounds, Madrid's decision was tenable, unavoidable following the English navy's spectacular victory at Trafalgar over joint Franco-Spanish navies. Now only English manufacturers and exporters could dispatch cargoes relatively risk free via Cadiz to Veracruz and Havana, promising markets when sales to the European continent were blocked. A further consideration was the possibility that this overture by the Spanish state might lead London to abandon plans for aggression against major Spanish colonial ports in the western Atlantic. An apparently unplanned device to secure the position of intermediary between two hegemons at war in 1806 seems to have foreshadowed Madrid's dual strategy for the survival of its empire that emerged in the critical spring of 1808, in the aftermath of the Escorial affair.

Coincidentally, the ministry headed by Grenville, who in 1795 had urged the Spanish government to abandon its ties with France in return for England's nonintervention in Spain's empire in America, now authorized Fermín de Tastet, Gordon & Murphy, and eight other "principal houses" over the months June–September 1806 to transfer silver via neutral shipping.[139] Grenville, presumably at the insistence of his fellow minister Auckland and the Board of Trade, stipulated that the neutral vessels must leave English ports with cargoes of English manufactures equal to the value of silver drafts to be obtained at Madrid and, more important, that English warships must be allowed to call at Veracruz even in wartime to load silver obtained through drafts on the colonial treasury at Mexico City.[140] Fermín de Tastet could purchase drafts of up to 1.2 million *pesos* on colonial treasuries at both Mexico City and Buenos Aires; however, Gordon & Murphy obtained the lion's share of the silver transfers, authorization for the purchase of 10 million *pesos* at Mexico City.[141] An appropriate number of permissions were distributed, ten to Gordon & Murphy alone.

The Spanish government's privileging Gordon & Murphy with the transfer of an impressive volume of silver reflects repeated contacts between Madrid and the Anglo-Spanish Murphy and Cotarro families of Málaga and their widening range of commercial operations. Juan Murphy y Eliot had developed business ties to an important section of Spain's Hacienda ministry, the Real Negociación del Giro, or Real Giro; maintained correspondence with Colonial Minister Gálvez; and opened a branch of the family business as Gordon, Murphy at London. Meanwhile Tomás, one of several sons, entered the Veracruz merchant community in the late 1780s or early 1790s, served as an officer of its *consulado,* and cemented links to the commercial elites of Veracruz and inland at the Guanajuato silver-mining center. About 1805 or 1806 there was solid ground for Soler's confidence in this Irish Catholic, Anglo-Spanish family, whose commercial and financial networks stretched from Málaga to Madrid and London and from Kingston and Havana to its base in the port of Veracruz.[142]

One may backtrack further. Juan Murphy opened contacts with the Real Giro, which, as normal practice, used government funds to buy colonial staples for sale in the metropole and Europe. Part of this working capital came from the government's sale of confiscated Jesuit properties *(temporalidades)*.[143] Consequently, in 1784 Juan Murphy, along with other *malagueños,* could offer cargo space aboard ships of their Compañía de Navieros de Málaga to carry to Veracruz products of the Spanish government's monopoly of playing cards, as well as cigarette and stamped paper.[144] In the 1790s Juan Murphy's brother Tomás entered the Veracruz trading community. He was one of only two in the merchant communities of Veracruz and Mexico City, it will be recalled, who supported Viceroy Revillagigedo's position on the benefits of *comercio libre* extended in 1789 to the colony of New Spain. Later, during *comercio neutro,* 1797–1799, Tomás Murphy's Havana agent, Francisco Santa Cruz, went off to Kingston to retrieve prizes taken by the English. At this time Tomás became related to Viceroy Azanza (now a *concuñado*), since they married the Alegría y Yöldi sisters of Veracruz.[145] It was Azanza who authorized the unloading of prize cargoes retrieved at Kingston that were consigned to his *concuñado* Murphy at Veracruz, not to mention shipments to Murphy aboard the U.S. ship *Nimble* of merchandise and official mail from Havana to Veracruz under the authorization of the intendant of Havana, Luís de Viguri.[146] Needless to say, a group of competitive merchants at Veracruz bitterly assailed Viceroy Azanza, who seemed to be privileging Anglophile commercial interests connected to Havana and New England counterparts.

Neither the Murphys' business culture nor their dynamism was welcome at Cadiz or Veracruz, a predictable reaction. Officers of the Cadiz *consulado* were suspicious of Juan Murphy ("brother of the one established at Veracruz"), and they noted in 1799 that Juan, his brother Tomás, and "other Havana influentials" were weaving networks linking merchants in New England, Havana, and Veracruz. For their part, Veracruz *consulado* officers urged Madrid to reject "the pretensions of some private individuals to send shipments from foreign ports under various pretexts," alluding to Tomás and his business associates Miguel de Lizardi and Pedro Miguel de Echeverría at Veracruz.[147] Repeatedly the Murphys cooperated with the Real Giro: Tomás Murphy advanced 430,000 *pesos* to buy sugar and cochineal on the Real Giro's account at Veracruz in 1799, while Juan, passing through Madrid on the way to London—"where I have established a merchant firm under the name of Gordon y Murphy," he advised Antonio Noriega y Bada, a *tesorero general* of the Hacienda who was head of the *Real Giro*—offered his services to the Real Giro, assuring Noriega of "the confidence you merit of the firm of my brothers Murphy y Cotarro at Veracruz."[148] In February and March 1803 Noriega, with Soler's approval, contracted with Juan Murphy to transfer to Cadiz one hundred thousand *pesos* annually over five years from Caracas's treasury. The contract omits the mode of transfer, except that Murphy's agents at Caracas would claim the funds, while Murphy's house at Cadiz would honor drafts *(letras)* within one month of presentation.[149]

There was, in addition, a late-developing sector of Tomás Murphy's trading operations that buttressed the credentials at London of his brother Juan's firm, Gordon & Murphy. Let us recall that following the bankruptcy in 1802 of the decades-old silver-transporting firm of Oteyza and Vertíz, which had sent ripples through New Spain's economy, two new *casas conductoras de plata* appeared: that of the Peredos (Diego Fernández Peredo and his cousin Juan Manuel Fernández Peredo), backed by Spanish immigrants of *montañés* origin; and Michaus y Uzcola, which grouped *vizcaíno* merchants and *criollo* mine owners. Tomás Murphy, along with the influential *criollo* mine owners of Guanajuato, Juan Bautista Fagoaga and the conde de Valenciana, figured as a prominent stockholder *(socio)* in the firm of Michaus y Uzcola; he was now well positioned to tap major silver producers in New Spain's mining center and, in fact, later became a stockholder in Guanajuato's "Mellado" mine.[150] There is, furthermore, a perhaps tenuous link between Gordon & Murphy and silver-mining Guanajuato: A "Paliar" was reported at Guanajuato during the 1790s; in 1806 a representative of Gordon & Murphy named Ignacio Palyart went ashore at Veracruz from the HMS *Resistance* to arrange for loading 3.1 million *pesos*.[151] Coincidence? In addition to Tomás Murphy's Basque/*criollo* connections in New Spain, he formed commercial contacts in the Caribbean basin at Havana (Pedro Juan de Erice), La Guayra (José Benito de Austria y Achútegui), and Kingston. Overall, in light of the years that Juan Murphy and his family participated in Spanish governmental enterprises in America, it is hardly surprising that when Godoy and Soler resolved to replicate an Ouvrard-like arrangement with English firms, enjoying London's cooperation, they sent their representative, Zaratea, to confer with Gordon & Murphy.[152]

The English government's preference for Gordon & Murphy is evident in its arrangement with the firm on 27 March 1806 to transfer 10 million *pesos fuertes* from Veracruz, months before it handed licenses to Tastet & Company. Preference aside, Soler and Sixto Espinosa probably had deduced that contracts covering large-scale commercial and financial transactions between government and private interests demanded careful drafting lest the errors of ambiguity in the Ouvrard agreements be repeated. This is obvious in the public contract of 18 May 1806 signed by Sixto Espinosa in his multiple capacity as member of the "Consejo . . . en el Supremo de Hacienda, Ministro de la Junta general de Comercio, Moneda y Minas, de la Comisión gubernativa de Consolidación de Vales Reales, Caxas de extinción y descuento y su Contador General" and by Juan Murphy for Gordon & Murphy ("his commercial firm at London"). This contract underscored the firm's intermediary role in the movement of Spanish government–owned goods of the Real Giro, with which the Murphys had had years of contact.[153] The London firm agreed to negotiate with the English government for ultimately thirty-five or more licenses *(pasavantes)* authorizing neutral ships to leave from Spanish, neutral European or American ports, from the Canaries or the Windward Islands of the Caribbean, and enter Spain's colonial ports at Veracruz, Cartagena, La Guayra, and other ports. Outbound cargo could include "all kinds of goods, fruits, wares, and merchandise"; inbound, the proceeds of sales in "money, fruits, and products of . . . America." All cargo was subject to normal customs duties in *pesos* levied at peninsular or colonial ports. Gordon & Murphy agreed to furnish

Sixto Espinosa with the specifics of each ship ("captain, flag, number of Spanish tons . . . port of departure and . . . destination in America") so that specific government orders, along with a certification of cargo ("number, weight or size, quality and value of all goods, fruits, and wares"), could be issued. Not only did the London firm accept the cost and risk of each expedition but nowhere was the participation of Spain's Hacienda or its Caja de Consolidación manifested. The firm could charter neutral vessels and arrange with neutral firms "of solid reputation" to claim ownership of cargo in order effectively "to neutralize its cargoes."[154]

These elaborate arrangements camouflaged the fact that part of the neutral vessels' cargo space was allocated to the Hacienda and the Caja de Consolidación. Outbound from Spain, 33 percent of cargo space would contain government-owned mercury (30,000 *quintales*), cigarette and stamped paper (150,000 reams), bulls of indulgence, and playing cards. Inbound to England or the European continent, 25 percent of cargo could consist of Soconusco cocoa, Havana tobacco, cochineal, indigo, sugar, or quinine purchased on government account. The freight charges on government cargo were deductible from duties payable; exports on government account from colonial ports had to appear consigned to Gordon & Murphy of London, which was responsible for the prompt sale and remittance of proceeds, less 4 percent commission. The firm's major source of earnings would come from goods shipped on its own account, along with those of Spain's Real Hacienda and Caja de Consolidación. In sum, the public contract gave the appearance of a particularly privileged private enterprise rather than a basically government one.[155]

Such, in essence, were the major provisions of the "public" Gordon & Murphy contract, which, examined alone, was a tactic to circumvent the English blockade of ports on the European continent and in the Spanish Caribbean, permitting the Spanish colonies to meet part of their import needs and to export coin and perishable staples. As a consequence, Spain's Hacienda would receive 4 percent of net profits of Gordon & Murphy's shipments plus export-import duties and the proceeds from sales of the government's shipments. Metropolitan authorities would be able to draw on these revenues "to pay the credits or letters of exchange drawn on Gordon y Murphy." Moreover, the Madrid government obligated the London firm to negotiate English licenses for neutral shipping involved, each license to allow exit from all ports "even when those ports may be blockaded by the squadrons of His British Majesty." Since neutral vessels could depart even from Spanish ports under blockade, English naval officers found themselves escorting ships from the closely blockaded port of Cadiz. As Admiral Collingwood (who commanded a naval division at Trafalgar) wrote to his wife in bemused wonderment, "What a curious war!" Last, Gordon & Murphy agreed to provide an essential service in wartime: two or more *barquitos* under Spanish or neutral registry to carry official mail monthly from Veracruz, Havana, and Cartagena to the company's agents at Kingston for rerouting to the firm's London headquarters, along with two neutral packet boats bearing government mail directly from Veracruz and Havana to Lisbon. The *barquitos,* which also required English *pasavantes,* could carry cargo. It is hard not to conclude that the *public* contract of 18 May simply expanded the role that the Murphy brothers had fulfilled earlier under *comercio neutro,* namely, the handling of common cargo in wartime.[156]

Buried in one article *(condición)* of the public contract, however, is the phrase alerting cognoscenti that Gordon & Murphy's intermediation involved more than handling European goods and colonial staples. For article 25 stipulated that the London firm maintain a "weekly and informative correspondence" with the Caja de Consolidación concerning the progress of its public contract as well as of "the contract . . . concerning the *peso* business," clearly a reference to the 27 March agreement between the firm and the English government for transferring 10 million *pesos fuertes* from Veracruz. This *contrata* was, in effect, a second, secret contract circulated among Sixto Espinosa, Gordon & Murphy, and Reid, Irving & Company that was no doubt known to English authorities and certainly was known to Spain's high colonial officials in America.[157]

Sixto Espinosa and Juan Murphy signed the public and secret contracts at Madrid on 18 May 1806. Within twenty-four hours Soler sent off a summary of both texts to Viceroy Iturrigaray at Mexico City under the "top secret" *(muy reservada)* classification.[158] According to Soler's summary, Juan Murphy had initiated the contracts jointly with Reid, Irving, an aspect kept from the public. More significantly, along with the summary went the full text of the secret contract, which detailed the compensation to the two London firms for their services to the Spanish government and stated that under their *permiso* they could export from Veracruz and Cartagena up to 10 million *pesos fuertes.*[159] The cooperation of New Spain's chief colonial officer, Iturrigaray, would be indispensable in carrying out a complex process of extraordinary importance, and he had to be so informed.

The *contrata de pesos* was anchored on London's willingness to honor its understanding with the two London firms by issuing necessary licenses for the departure of neutral shipping from friendly or enemy ports. Unwilling to risk misuse of the drafts *(libranzas)* or letters of credit *(letras)* that Soler and Sixto Espinosa had to deliver to their London intermediaries, the Spanish government's finance experts were meticulous about the security of their contract. For example, they insisted that Sixto Espinosa hold in deposit the original contract of 27 March, made with "los Mylores del Tesoro Real," and they dispatched to London a personal agent who was to deliver the first *libranzas* only when the London firms produced the English government's passports. Soler and Sixto Espinosa spelled out precisely the types of drafts issued *(libranzas* or *letras)* over the stipulated period of fourteen months; the funds on which the drafts were drawn, Hacienda or Caja de Consolidación; the vessels employed; and the frequency of reports of ship sailings. *Libranzas* or *letras* endorsed to the London firms would be presented to colonial officials by the accredited agents of Gordon & Murphy (at Veracruz they were Ignacio Palyart, José White, or Juan Murphy's brother Tomás); *libranzas* would be drawn on colonial treasuries, *letras* on Consolidación funds, both to be honored "punctually." Agents would remit *pesos* free of duty aboard Spanish or neutral ships, and when necessary, *pesos* could be transshipped at sea to English vessels.[160]

Utilizing the contracts permitted Madrid to draw immediately upon London for funds. To that end, the agents in colonial ports were ordered to write *letras* against the *pesos* collected and shipped, half on the account of Gordon & Murphy, half on that of Reid, Irving, at the exchange rate of £177 per one thousand *pesos,* the *letras* to be forwarded to Sixto Espinosa for presentation within five months of the date of issue. One can understand the emphasis on "weekly and informative correspondence," the monthly dispatch of ships to Kingston and packet boats to Lisbon with government mail ("especially concerning funds, the sale of ecclesiastical properties, of pious foundations, redemption of loans, and other sections of *consolidación de vales*"), and on forwarding to Sixto Espinosa in quadruplicate *letras* drawn upon Gordon & Murphy.[161] And to remove any reservations of Viceroy Iturrigaray about collaborating with the English in wartime, Soler closed his "muy reservada" letter with the pointed observation that "it is the sovereign will that Your Excellency make the most vigorous efforts to ensure that goals . . . are achieved with all necessary promptness and secrecy."[162] Within months, Iturrigaray seemed to critics a schizoid colonial administrator, maintaining a public posture of defense against English naval provocations at Veracruz, while privately executing Madrid's orders to the contrary. Once again, Madrid's desperate deals to tap New Spain's resources left a loyal, literal-minded colonial officer turning in the wind.

Iturrigaray received Soler's summary of the contracts seven months later, after they were known to the Baltimore merchants Robert and John Oliver and Juan Murphy's brother Tomás at Veracruz. On 12 December 1806 a

Málaga-based ship, the *Eliza y Ana,* delivered Soler's instructions, along with instructions to deposit with Gordon & Murphy's agent at Veracruz and with a Mexico City *almacenero,* Lorenzo Angulo Guardamino, a *comisionado* of the Casa de Consolidación, 3.1 million *pesos* drawn on Mexico City's Junta Superior de Consolidación. The *Eliza y Ana* was followed by a Gordon & Murphy *barquito* from Kingston carrying a government cargo consigned to Tomás Murphy.[163] As Iturrigaray readied the 3.1 million *pesos* for shipment aboard a neutral vessel, the intendant of Veracruz, Pedro Alonso, reported the unexpected arrival of an English warship seeking permission to anchor in the lee of Veracruz's major defense works, San Juan de Ulua, in order to load 3.1 million *pesos* under a contract between "La Corte de Madrid" and Gordon & Murphy and Reid, Irving & Company with the "consent of the British Government." The Spanish translation of the letter of Captain Adams, of the HMS *Resistance,* stated that he had orders from his government to take money aboard.[164] Iturrigaray concurred with the recommendation of the anxious intendant that Gordon & Murphy's agents aboard the *Resistance,* Ignacio Palyart and Juan Davidson, take possession of "the silver . . . outside the port" under his instructions "to transship the funds . . . at sea to any vessels, even if English." The waters of Veracruz having been successfully tested, in May 1807 a second English warship, the HMS *Thames,* with Palyart aboard and bearing another draft, this one for 2 million *pesos,* entered Veracruz.[165]

In all, as David Parish's agent at New Orleans reported, four frigates of England's royal navy "quietly appeared one after the other, in the roads of Veracruz, and without any interruption took on board about fourteen million *pesos* from Mexico City's Real Hacienda for shipment to England."[166] The English warships represented, however, only part of the Gordon & Murphy contracts; more important were the mail and packet boats, which the firm supplied with about thirty-eight English and Spanish licenses to sail to Veracruz from London via Cadiz, from Barcelona, Cartagena de Levante, and Lisbon, from U.S. Atlantic ports and New Orleans.[167] At Veracruz they unloaded government mercury, paper, playing cards, and every kind of merchandise, as well as Gordon & Murphy's "many millions of *pesos fuertes,* mostly in cotton goods,"[168] until the unexpected armistice between Spain and England in the spring of 1808 provided an embittered Cadiz *consulado* with an excuse to detain the departure of Gordon & Murphy's *Amalia* for Veracruz and provided the equally soured Veracruz *consulado* with its pretext for rejecting from Kingston two Gordon & Murphy vessels with cargoes having a combined worth of 1 million *pesos.*[169] Meanwhile, as late as March 1808 the Mexico City *almacenero* Gabriel Iturbe e Iraeta, when writing to Veracruz about heavy trading in English goods there, observed that "now we have arriving from Jamaica another mailboat belonging to [Tomás] Murphy, which will surely cause a sensation."[170]

The Contract Policy: An Assessment

Once the Spanish government had realigned itself with France after 1796, its policies showed increasing sensitivity to its insolvency, to the economic crosscurrents of strategic colonies such as Cuba, Venezuela, and New Spain, and to innovative tactics to maintain communications between metropole and colonies, between Cadiz and Veracruz (or more precisely, between Madrid and Mexico City), against superior English naval forces in the Spanish Atlantic. As an ally of France in its war with England from 1797 to 1801, Madrid had to innovate in economic policy; the initial tactic was Saavedra's sponsorship of *comercio neutro* instead of the traditional *gracias*. Two factors in the short term improved the metropole's finances. First was the extraordinary postwar inflow of silver from Veracruz and La Plata in 1801–4, which buoyed the *vales reales,* excited speculators (a high percentage at Seville and Cadiz), and revived the confidence of Spanish merchants in their transatlantic trading structures. Nonetheless, planning—focused on the Hacienda and the Caja de Consolidación—continued for the contingency of renewed war at sea. The second factor, *consolidación,* supported the *vales reales* by satisfying interest and amortization payments.

Once hostilities reopened between Spain and England in 1804, the Hacienda secretary and his director of the Caja de Consolidación, Soler and Sixto Espinosa, knew that merchants at Cadiz and Barcelona, Veracruz and Mexico City, would reject a revived *comercio neutro,* so they moved on to another tactic to preserve communication by sea. They used contracts with French and then English firms to provide critical supplies of mercury and stamped paper and to withdraw government funds from the most productive colony, New Spain; to incentivate their merchant intermediaries, they dangled the potential profits from forwarding their own cargoes under the guise of neutral shippers and shipping. High officials at Madrid hardly had to be reminded by the bishop-elect of Michoacán, Manuel Abad y Queipo, that the colony of New Spain provided the metropole with "double the net returns of the other overseas possessions."[171] These considerations provide perspective for reviewing the outcomes of the Ouvrard-Hope-Parish contracts as well as those of Gordon & Murphy.

Eighteen months apart, the contracts of November 1804 and May 1806 covered shipments of critical government materials, transfers of silver and high-value staples, and the contracting firms' own cargoes. Compared with the detailed "English" contract of Gordon & Murphy, the first, or "French," contract with Ouvrard was loosely drafted. No government cargo was specified, a large number of blank licenses were issued, no specific transfers of silver mentioned; Ouvrard could even lay claim to a monopoly of trade between Spain and its American colonies, quite in the tradition of France's mercantilist *exclusif.* By contrast, the Gordon & Murphy and Reid, Irving contracts showed a keener appreciation of operating with London firms and, through them, with the English government to rein in its wide-ranging naval forces in the Atlantic basin. Here they spelled out the nature and quantities of government cargo outbound and inbound, commissions, even the disposition of the government's cargo in Europe. The total of government drafts and letters of credit was tallied, to be available only on condition of receipt of licenses from London and the funds remitted from the Spanish colonies. Careful drafting of the English contracts probably accounts for the larger returns to the Spanish government and to associated private interests.

The income flows generated through the operations of Gordon & Murphy and Parish-Oliver enterprises are a matter of conjecture. Proximate values are ascertainable with crude upper- and lower-bound estimates. As for imports at Veracruz, reworking the invoice value of Gordon & Murphy cargo aboard thirty-nine ships yields 2,728,740 *pesos* (69,986 *pesos* per vessel); a government estimate of 1810 claimed seven times that amount, or 18,620,864 *pesos* (477,458 per vessel).[172] Perhaps invoice values of the first estimate were grossly undervalued to reduce customs and other duties, and perhaps those of the second estimate were overvalued in order to magnify the Spanish government's claims on Gordon & Murphy.[173] Possibly the second estimate incorporates the value of government goods, for example, exports of 20,457 *quintales* of mercury and 105,057 of paper.

According to data in Stuart Bruchey's careful inspection of Robert Oliver's ledgers, the net proceeds at Veracruz of the thirty-seven vessels dispatched by Oliver and Oliver-Parish total 4,694,239 dollars or *pesos* (126,871 per ship), only 25 percent of the high estimate of Gordon & Murphy cargo per ship. However, the Oliver-Parish figures omit shipments sent by Parish's agent Vincent Nolte from New Orleans to Veracruz. Tentatively, then, both the "English" and "French" contracts supplied New Spain in seventy-six ships cargo valued at 7,422,979 or 23,315,103 *pesos* over roughly thirty months, a high proportion consisting of textiles—linens, woolens, and especially what middle- and high-income consumers in New Spain would buy, East Indian and English cotton goods.

More reliable are estimates of silver exports from Veracruz, since the contract holders preferred precious metals over colonial staples and there is a strong presumption that their bills of lading submitted for clearance to Veracruz port officials were undervalued. One Spanish government report puts Gordon & Murphy specie exports at 8.2 million *pesos;* another claims three times that amount, or 27,825,504; a derived estimate of Oliver-Parish silver exports is 19,620,000, which, with Gordon & Murphy's 8.2 million, totals 27,820,000. This approximates the official value of silver exports on private account from Veracruz to Havana and neutral ports, 29,969,590, over the period 1805–8.[174] Depending on the estimates for Gordon & Murphy's exports—8.2 million and 27,825,504—we obtain two estimates of silver exported on private account, 27,820,000 and an upper figure of 47,445,504. If we add the official value of silver exports drawn by Madrid on Mexico City's Real Hacienda over the period 1805–8, 12,950,272, we obtain two estimates of exports on private and royal account, 40,770,272 and 60,395,776 *pesos.*[175]

The plausibility of the upper figure is supported by total silver exports from Veracruz to Spain in peacetime, 1801–4, which came to 71,534,723 *pesos.* Whatever the estimates, the silver transfers from 1805 to 1808 were extraordinarily large. In one of the Spanish empire's most critical moments, during the seven months from August 1807 to March 1808 "Villanueva" and Tomás Murphy exported on government account, mainly aboard English warships coming to Veracruz, a minimum of 8,231,476 *pesos.*[176] There seems to be a positive correlation between large exports of New Spain's "hard dollars" and the upsurge in England's subsidies to the European continent, rising from £6.6 million to £12.4 over the two years 1808–10.[177]

As often happens when a financially strapped government must resort to the private sector, national or foreign—whether merchants, merchant-bankers, or plain speculators—the profits of the firms were disproportionately high. Ouvrard, despite his contretemps with Napoleon, received satisfactory returns on an operation he supervised nominally.[178] His first intermediary, Hope & Company, netted, conservatively, from $300,000 to $500,000;[179] the second, Baring Brothers, turned their participation into "their most extraordinary operation." David Parish earned between $721,000 and $1 million.[180] As for Robert Oliver, an Irish emigrant who arrived at Baltimore in 1783 rich only in hopes, he managed to retire from international trade in 1809 after a mere three years of Veracruz operations, from which he earned thirteen times the profits of the nine preceding years preceding the Veracruz operation, becoming one of the few millionaires in the United States of his day.[181]

The Murphy accounts have yet to turn up. We know that Murat considered Juan Murphy one of Spain's richest men in 1808. Gordon & Murphy promptly placed at the disposal of Spain's Junta Central in the early months of its troubled existence about 1 million *pesos* collected from New Spain's *consolidación,* along with the income on sales of government-owned Cuban tobaccos — cigars, snuff, and quinine.[182] As for Tomás Murphy, he went on to become one of New Spain's prominent merchants, with mining properties in Guanajuato.

How much specie exported from the colony of New Spain ultimately entered Spain's Hacienda and Caja de Consolidación remains conjectural. Probably most of the 9.7 million *pesos* collected by Mexico City's Junta de Consolidación passed through the hands of "Villanueva" and the Murphys.[183] In any event, the sheer magnitude of the *peso* drain from New Spain after 1802, driven by the contracts signed by Soler and Sixto Espinosa and fed in part by *consolidación,* were not unnoticed by the people of the colony of New Spain. When the revolutionary leader Miguel Hidalgo occupied Valladolid (Morelia) in October 1810, he promised that with independence from Spain "poverty will be uprooted . . . the export of money blocked."[184] Decapitalization by any other name is still decapitalization.

Epilogue: The Threat of *Comercio Neutro* Renewed

Madrid's recourse to the contracts with foreign firms that required neutral shipping bearing all categories of cargo and entrusted with carrying official correspondence between Kingston and Veracruz inevitably obliged the Spanish government to mollify the most influential merchant communities in its transatlantic system at Cadiz, Veracruz, Mexico City, and Havana. Whatever the intention, Madrid's directives governing routes and cargo of shipping, Spanish and non-Spanish, going to the colonies or sailing between Caribbean ports and Veracruz, appeared threatening rather than conciliatory to those *consulados,* Havana excepted of course.

In May 1804, foreshadowing the subsequent flow of European manufactures under the contracts of the previous November and December, Godoy's ministry lifted the requirement that at least 50 percent of the cargo of Spanish vessels bound for the colonies consist of national products. Then in August his ministry further authorized that cargo unsold in the colonial port of original destination could be re-exported to other Spanish colonial ports.[185] A pragmatic measure, to be sure; nonetheless, in view of the inadequacies of production in the metropole, the May order troubled Barcelona's textile manufacturers, sheltered behind protective tariffs. The effort to rectify this situation in 1805 at the insistence of Foreign Minister Pedro Cevallos is a measure of the influence of anxious exporters at Barcelona and Cadiz.[186] Meanwhile, the arrival of ships under neutral flag at Spanish ports in and around the Caribbean promised to complicate the calculations of colonial inventories by Cadiz exporters. Madrid deepened their anxiety by eliminating what Cadiz had always insisted on, that Spanish shipping clear from metropolitan ports for only one colonial port ("con un solo registro"). On 16 June came the unexpected and contradictory ruling that "at the request of the Consulado de Cadiz" Spanish ships bound for the colonies could now "enter ports other than their main destination," where they could sell all or part of their cargo and then choose to return to a port "more suitable." This order appeared when Soler was contracting with Gordon & Murphy, Fermín de Tastet, and other "English" commercial houses.[187]

These modifications still left intact Veracruz's longstanding control over the reexport of European goods to the Spanish Caribbean, to Cuba, Yucatan, and Puerto Rico. By mid-1806, however, as a large volume of cargo unloaded from neutral carriers backed up in warehouses at Havana and Campeche, the privileged position of Veracruz's merchants came under attack. Merchants at Campeche, sensing the opportunity to re-export to Veracruz licit mixed with smuggled items, railed against the "unfortunate remains of the old disastrous monopoly" enjoyed by Veracruz. As a consequence of "the power and influence of that wealthy market of New Spain," that port could now re-export to Campeche European imports introduced on packet boats from London and Kingston, "drawing on the exclusive privileges that the Company of Gordon y Murphy enjoys."[188]

At this point Cuban interests joined Campeche to insist on an equal right to re-export to Veracruz and Campeche. Cuba's intendant, Rafael Gómez Roubaud, backed by local merchants and planter interests, now reviewed Havana's balance of trade for 1805, finding that neutral carriers, overwhelmingly from U.S. ports, accounted for 94 percent of imports and 88 percent of Havana's exports and a deficit on the balance of trade of more than 6 million *pesos* ("an enormous and prejudicial amount"), presumably because U.S. sugar purchases were limited.[189] Cuba, Gómez Roubaud insisted, now needed a "path to other Spanish possessions"—an indirect reference to Veracruz and Campeche—"for excess foreign goods exchanged for agricultural products." In this fashion Havana merchants might also obtain needed specie, even if this meant "repealing former Royal orders prohibiting such trade."[190]

Perhaps convinced by Gómez Roubaud's argument or responding to the pressure of Havana's agents at Madrid, Godoy's ministry had to yield. In

December 1806 Campeche received authorization to re-export to Veracruz surplus imports received directly from metropolitan ports, followed in May 1807 by an order legalizing Havana's re-exports of national and foreign goods imported from Spain to Puerto Rico, Campeche, and, most important, Veracruz.[191] The members of Havana's *consulado* jumped to the conclusion that this legislation opened "wide a door hitherto closed to us" by establishing between the two ports "complete reciprocity."[192] The satisfaction of merchants at Havana and Campeche was matched by the bitterness of those at Veracruz and Cadiz. At Cadiz the legislation outraged Mariano Malancó, who had just invested more than fifty thousand *pesos* in the purchase of brandy intended for sale at Veracruz under a *gracia* granted by Madrid.[193] To Veracruz's *consulado,* watching Havana ("where ships from the United States constantly enter") turn into a "well-stocked warehouse" of legal and smuggled goods brought by neutrals, there was no question that Havana's overstocked merchants were under pressure to export both local rums and European imports to Veracruz and Campeche, all counter to the "spirit and tenor of colonial legislation and regulations, to the preferential rights of the motherland, national interests, and the general rights of commerce." Liberty may have been the "soul of mercantile enterprise," but it could not be "absoluta."[194] In the spring of the critical year of 1808, Arango y Parreño's earlier vision of Havana as the Caribbean's new "great warehouse of the American emporium" seemed to be materializing—and upsetting.

In fact, during the first eight months of 1808 a planter-merchant alliance within Havana's business community and *consulado* threatened to transform what had been *comercio neutro* into *comercio directo.* It was a profound shock to Spain's pseudomercantilist Atlantic system, and it undermined New Spain's dominant role in the trade of the Spanish Caribbean. Led by the sugar planter and publicist Arango, collaborating with the merchant-banker Pedro Juan de Erice, the Havana planter-merchant alliance was exploiting a fracture in the Spanish transatlantic system created by the stepped-up economic warfare between France and England, compounded in late 1807 by the U.S. Embargo Act. To Havana's joint planter and trading interests this translated into the imminent cutoff of neutral carriers from U.S. ports entering Havana with flour, other foodstuffs, and volumes of mainly English manufactures.[195]

Havana's port records comparing two three-year peacetime intervals, 1792–94 and 1802–4, substantiated what any well-run mercantile establishment might glean from its own accounts. The total value of imports, Spanish and foreign, from metropolitan ports in the latter period was down 20 percent from the previous period, despite price inflation; and Havana's principal supplier in the metropole, Cadiz, had sent 26 percent less of both Spanish and non-Spanish goods, almost 40 percent less of "Foreign" items, while the value per shipment had slipped by 32 percent. There were more ships from Cadiz, which introduced half of Havana's total imports in 1802–4 (which were 81 million *reales de vellón*), but the value of the goods they carried (40.4 million) was less.[196]

For Havana interests certain conclusions were ineluctable. Havana's economic situation was critical: inventories of perishable sugars were backing up (two-thirds of the last harvest was unsold); prospects for the profitable disposal of the next harvest were equally bleak, since unit costs were rising; and there was growing competition overseas at London and European sugar markets from the production of the English Caribbean islands and now resurgent Brazil.[197] Meanwhile, the metropole's manufacturing capacity, shipping facilities, and re-export fees had to be reappraised. Complicating matters was Havana's dependence upon trade with U.S. ports, whose shipping brought European goods and especially U.S. flours, which were one-third cheaper than New Spain's Puebla-grown product, which was exported from Veracruz in a volume inadequate to meet Cuban demand.[198] Moreover, since U.S. merchants preferred only small quantities of sugar as return cargo, Havana's traders insisted that they required silver specie to cover their trade deficit. When they tried to sell rums and sugars to New Spain for specie, however, Mexico City's officials slapped a 27 percent surcharge on these products.[199] True, according to Finance Minister Soler's order of 10 May 1807, Havana could re-export manufactures to Campeche and Veracruz, but the opposition of Veracruz and Mexico City *almaceneros* was not to be underestimated.

Iturrigaray's Dilemma

By July 1808 the recent coup d'état at Aranjuez, the French occupation of the peninsula, and the Anglo-Spanish armistice automatically forced the suspension of Soler's legislative patchwork of wartime economic-policy expedients. Contracts with neutrals were terminated on cessation of hostilities with England; now there had to be a return to Spain's transatlantic system of trade with its colonies: recourse to Spanish-registry vessels and to what Havana's aroused merchants encapsulated as the policy of "closing the port to all shipping that is neither national nor from allies."[200] While merchants at Barcelona, Cadiz, Veracruz, and Mexico City welcomed the rollback—at Cadiz and Veracruz, Gordon & Murphy's neutral ships were now rejected—Havana's interests resisted. A sharp cleavage was opening between New Spain's silver and Cuba's plantation interests, between what were now the twin pillars of the economy of Spain in colonial America.

Heading Havana's dissident, persuasive minority favoring an open-port policy were the publicist and planter Arango and the prominent merchants and merchant-bankers Pedro Juan de Erice, Bernabé Martínez de Pinillos, Antonio Malagamba, and Martín Madán, with reliable contacts at Veracruz and Cadiz. They proceeded to catalog the shortcomings of efforts to preserve the Spanish empire's "comercio nacional." They minced no words about the low output of peninsular manufacture, claimed that on occasion Havana itself had re-exported flour to Cadiz to cover the metropole's recent grain shortages, and complained about the lack of Spanish-registry shipping and its unusually high cargo rates and insurance premiums, as well as the metropole's high import and re-export duties.[201] In effect, they were attacking the rationale of Spain's whole regulated transatlantic commercial system, rejecting the myth that the metropolitan economy might soon "recover" to the point of fulfilling the colonial compact. "Let's have no illusions," they asserted flatly, "the Metropole cannot supply us now, probably not even for some time." The role of colony and metropole was now inverted; it was necessary "to open our eyes . . . the destiny of that Mother Country . . . is really dependent upon, or directly related to, the condition of our forces."[202] Equally unrestrained was criticism of "powerful Mexico" and those traders at Mexico City and Veracruz who hoped to preserve an economic hegemony over Havana. Protestations to the contrary, New Spain's flours shipped from Puebla could not satisfy Cuba's needs; they certainly could not match the volume and price of the U.S. product. Finally, it was, they felt, simply unrealistic for New Spain's merchants to block Havana's merchants from re-exporting New Spain's silver, since obviously no "fetters" could hold back "our hoarded and protected precious metals."[203]

Thus the issue of a permanent solution to Havana merchants' pursuit of an open-port policy was brought into the open by the events at Aranjuez in the spring of 1808 and the subsequent French invasion of the peninsula, dividing Havana's business community in the summer of 1808, when both Havana and Mexico City had to question the legitimacy of competing juntas in insurgent Spain and when the two *comisionados* of Seville's self-styled Junta Suprema, Juan Jabat and Manuel de Jáuregui, were passing through Havana on their way to Veracruz and Mexico City. From the Havana merchants Laiseca, Queralto, Serra, and Bustillo, Seville's agents no doubt learned that Arango y Parreño—*criollo* planter, officer of both the *ayuntamiento* and the *consulado* of Havana, networked to Cuba's *hacendados* and merchants—was insisting that Veracruz's port officials suspend surcharges on Cuba's sugars and rums and free Havaneros to export silver from Veracruz; that Cuba be authorized to export to allied or friendly countries and their colonies; and, most important, that Cuba be authorized to establish a "direct exchange" with the United States.[204] This was a vision that Arango, Erice, and their supporters pursued vigorously, and it would be vigorously countered by interlocked Cadiz, Veracruz, and Mexico City merchant interests over the next two years and more, and with surprising results.

Yet the effort of Havana merchants and planters to turn their port into a major entrepôt of Spain's Caribbean empire depended primarily upon their major suppliers of the moment, the United States and Jamaica. From the Atlantic ports of the United States came provisions, lumber, and European goods; a large volume of European manufactures that Havana's merchants intended for reexport to Veracruz and Campeche probably came from Kingston. In that critical period of economic warfare in Europe from 1806 to 1811, when England's exports to the European continent were falling dramatically, there occurred the export spurt to Spain and what English trade statistics listed ambiguously as "Foreign West Indies," which included New Spain and South America, the "two outlets [that] constituted the main source of new trade in those years." Jamaica's shipping records for 1810 listing arrivals and departures of "Spanish" vessels, a considerable number from Cuban ports, are one indicator of Kingston's importance to Havana's aggressive merchants.[205] U.S. merchants relied upon Kingston as an entrepôt; there they sold Cuban provisions for silver, which they took back to Havana to purchase sugars, or bought European goods from Kingston's traders, which they sent on to Veracruz, often without proper documentation.[206] Most irritating and potentially more threatening to many Veracruz traders was the direct link developing between Veracruz and Kingston under "trade permitted with neutral ships," those packet boats operated by Gordon & Murphy that introduced non-Spanish goods ("every category of wares recovered, or of English Manufacture"), as well as the export of unregistered *pesos* under cover of purchasing prize cargoes seized by the English navy or corsairs, sold at Kingston to merchants from Veracruz authorized to participate in such auctions.[207] Veracruz's traders did not look kindly upon cotton textiles re-exported from Campeche (that "English trading post") originating in India and East Asia.[208]

The corporative representative of Cadiz's merchants, their *consulado*, consistently opposed any move by Madrid to open its transatlantic trade to neutral carriers from 1797 on. After 1804, through agents, Cadiz heard of the surge of neutral ships and cargoes at Veracruz and "the development in that Kingdom of trade with neutral ships," and it vowed to register its official opposition to such policies in its capacity at "the head of this commerce." Unfailingly it held to the principle of equal access of Spaniards in the metropole to the economic preserve that the American colonies had constituted for centuries, condemning *gracias* and *permisos* as evidence of *privilegio*, while nursing a forceful rejection of contracts signed by Godoy, Soler and Sixto Espinosa with such firms as Gordon & Murphy.

Especially galling were the contractual arrangements of Gordon & Murphy because they were highly visible. By contrast, Parish's connection to Veracruz was masked by Lestapis, alias "Villanueva." Cadiz claimed to have no information about "the nature of the business of Gordon & Murphy with . . . the Real Caja," insisting that it had learned of them "only . . . through the usual news channels." Gordon & Murphy's contract was one of "those corrupt *gracias*" that had nothing to do with national economic policy; in the tradition of personalizing policy defects, the *consulado*'s officers considered them the consequence of "the overwhelming power of a disloyal favorite," Godoy, who had misled Charles IV "to realize personal aims" that contravened "the laws of Spain and the Indies to the ruination of national commerce and without benefiting the Treasury." For at issue was the "incontrovertible maxim of jurisprudence and economics that there must be no *gracias* nor privileges . . . directly contravening fundamental establishments."[209]

Overseas, supporters of Spain's traditional transatlantic trade system, notably those at Veracruz, were equally sensitive to resurgent privilege in the form of the publicized *permisos* of 24 December 1804 and the participation of neutrals on behalf of the Caja de Consolidación. Cargoes introduced by neutrals competed with those smuggled, and Veracruz's bitterness was compounded by repeated confrontation with the colony's chief officer, Viceroy Iturrigaray, over his and Ciriaco de Cevallo's antismuggling measures at Veracruz for monitoring coastal navigation and shifting the port's commerce temporarily inland to Jalapa. Veracruz had been upset in 1797 by *comercio neutro*, "in whose shadow foreigners became masters of our trade with America," and although formally revoked, it persisted in the shape of the "shocking introduction" of illegal wares. Then had come the double blow, the return to pre-1797 trade structures—in late 1804 *permisos* issued to neutrals in Europe and the United States, followed in 1806 by the "ruinosas consequencias" of Madrid's contracts with Gordon & Murphy for transferring the Caja's funds.[210]

Between late September 1805 and the end of the following January, Veracruz's merchants felt the effects of the rulings of November and December

1804. Five ships, two from New Orleans and three from Baltimore, including Oliver's *Matchless,* were reported anchored at Veracruz equipped with *permisos*—the results of the Ouvrard-Hope-Parish licenses—and all laden with textiles. A special meeting of *consulado* members, a *junta de gobierno,* agreed that shipping from the United States constituted the gravest threat to "esta preciosa colonia" and that there was an obvious contradiction between the abandonment of *gracias* and *privilegios* in June 1804 and the neutral *firmas agraciadas* of the following December. On 15 November the junta petitioned Soler at Madrid, directly bypassing Viceroy Iturrigaray—an explicit mode of disrespect—to refuse entry of "Anglo-American" shipping and revoke "every *gracia.*"[211]

Two months later the reaction of Veracruz to aggressive marketing by U.S. merchants, "whose rapid advances . . . our zealous loyalty cannot observe quietly," boiled up in an angry note to Iturrigaray. Craig and Oliver's *Matchless,* with Procopio Pollock on board, had entered Veracruz a second time since the previous November (Oliver had sought out Baltimore's fastest schooners, as he often boasted), bearing a cargo of government mercury and blasting powder but also prohibited wares such as English cottons and platillas royals, brittanias, and Morlaix-style creas, which undermined Spain's "industry and workshops, mainly in . . . Catalonia." Only the previous month, the junta had noted the commercial intelligence that U.S. shipmasters had obtained by calling at Veracruz, and the *Matchless*'s second voyage (it had arrived in February) proved this contention. For the *Matchless*'s first cargo had omitted from its manifest any prohibited goods because Oliver had believed his license did not permit them, but learning of demand for such goods, Oliver had included them on his vessel's second trip, stimulated by the chance to "bypass the . . . surveillance of our Higher Authorities." The junta pressed the viceroy to declare such cargo illegal and "subject to confiscation" or to order it held in deposit until Madrid resolved the issue.[212]

Irritated by the consistently critical stance of the Veracruz *consulado* and its bypassing him to contact Hacienda Minister Soler directly, Iturrigaray shot back his reply within three days. He cited the judgment of a colonial civil servant on the spot at Veracruz, Pedro Telmo Landero, to the effect that the order of 1 March 1805 adding John Craig's firm to the others listed in the order of 24 December 1804 was so broad that there could be no question about Craig's *permiso* to forward any type of cargo "without exception." On this ground, Iturrigaray affirmed emphatically, royal legislation was not subject to a *consulado*'s interpretation, and the *Matchless*'s cargo was to be offloaded and immediately delivered to its Veracruz consignee "without the least hindrance."[213] Although yet another special junta of the *consulado* repeated to Madrid directly its lingering questioning of Soler's intent—it questioned rhetorically how the government could "concede openly to foreigners what it denies . . . to its favorite vassals," a justifiable question under the circumstance—Madrid did not overrule New Spain's viceroy.[214]

Doubtless the reaction of Veracruz's *consulado* to the influx of vessels from U.S. ports, which led Oliver to boast that "the port of Veracruz is open to American vessels," forced Iturrigaray to direct English warships like the HMS *Resistance* to take aboard silver out of sight of Veracruz. This hardly mollified critical merchants at Veracruz and Mexico City, who were troubled by his handling of the ships sent by Nolte, Oliver-Craig, and Gordon & Murphy and legitimized by Soler's and Godoy's "privileges for the navigation and direct trade of foreigners in the Ports of the Indies."[215] In the hindsight of the officers of Mexico City's *consulado*, Gordon & Murphy had taken advantage of "abominable, treasonous, and criminal permits granted at moments of lunacy," just as their trading operations were "treasonous because approved by the English during a bloody War."[216]

Virtually in the same category, according to the Veracruz merchant community, was Iturrigaray's unquestioning compliance with directives from Madrid that sanctioned the unlimited export of New Spain's silver and its sequel, "the fatal consequences of transferring pious funds to the la Real Caja de Consolidación."[217] To the Mexico City *almaceneros* Chavarri, Ágreda, and García Noriega, who questioned Iturrigaray's unbending adherence to orders from Madrid, Godoy and Iturrigaray were identical. Godoy was a "villain," and as for high colonial administrators like Iturrigaray, who had executed Madrid's orders unhesitatingly, "there is nothing more detestable in the administration of the Americas than a weak authority that believes it is obeying the Sovereign by carrying out orders literally and blindly in cases prohibited by law."[218]

Part Four

Toward the Second

War of Succession

13. "Treasures in the New World"

 . . . .

The greatest commercial and political undertaking . . . using the treasures in the new world for the benefit of commerce in general, and in particular for that of Spain and France.

Gabriel-Julien Ouvrard

Unfortunately, the subsidy was Spanish silver, and that was in America.   Maurice Payard

[Contrast] the despotism of irrationality and disorder with the tyranny of reason and order.

Jacques Arna

Behind the intervention of French forces in Spain in early 1808 was a legacy of structures and attitudes persisting during the Revolution, the Directoire, the Consulat, and the Empire: pressure for access to Spanish and Spanish colonial staples and consumers and to inflows of American (now mainly Mexican) silver, along with the hope of tying, even subordinating, the Spanish metropolitan and colonial economies to French interest groups.

More specifically, persistent pressures behind France's occupation of the Iberian Peninsula are identifiable. American silver was important to the French economy in the eighteenth century, a prominence heightened in the 1780s. The revolutionary years in France and their aftermath only accentuated the need for silver from New Spain, as *assignats* depreciated rapidly and budgetary deficits resulting from military operations and infrastructural outlays demanded greater revenues. There is a clear nexus between the Franco-Spanish treaty of mutual defense of 1796, the agreement on a financial subsidy by Spain to France in 1804, and silver from Mexico City in the Paris banking crisis of 1805. Inexorably the Banque de France, the speculations of the war contractors *(munitionnaires)* Gabriel-Julien Ouvrard and Jacques-Ignace Vanlerberghe, and Mexican *pesos* became linked issues magnifying for Napoleon and French policymakers the economic potential of Spain's overseas possessions. Contributing to this emphasis on New Spain in the western Atlantic was the revolution in Saint-Domingue, resulting in the loss of its sugar, molasses, and coffee and the decision to sell Louisiana to the United States. Now France might import from Spain's Caribbean islands and circum-Caribbean colonies sugar, coffee, and, for France's textile industries, cotton, indigo, and cochineal. Thus, France's public and private sectors saw in Spain and its colonies a source for those commodities previously imported from Saint-Domingue whose re-export to continental Europe had been a major element contributing to the growth of France's foreign trade and its favorable trade balances in the eighteenth century, as well as to the expansion of its Atlantic ports at Bordeaux and Nantes. In short, behind France's Spanish policy not only before but also after 1789 lay the long-term perception of France's civil servants, diplomats, financiers, manufacturers, and merchants, that Spain's colonial world might function more efficiently under French direction.

In these specifics one locates both long-term and contingent factors shaping the diplomacy of the Directoire, the Consulat, and the Empire vis-à-vis metropolitan and colonial Spain. Industrial, financial, and strategic interests of France, fused in the crucible of competing English and French imperialisms, flowed into Napoleon's grand design to incorporate Spain and its Atlantic possessions under French hegemony and—an unintended consequence—the crisis of the Spanish imperial system. Like the first French intervention, in the War of the Spanish Succession, at the beginning of the eighteenth century, in which access to Spain's colonial possessions through trade in goods and African slaves had figured prominently, France's second intervention in the peninsula, under the Grand Empire, was motivated in no small measure by industrial and financial interests as well as by the more apparent military and strategic ones.

Even before 1789 the flow of silver from Spain's colonies into France had slackened as Spanish authorities tightened surveillance at the border. Spain's war against France in 1793–95 reduced the flow to a trickle. Then came the loss of access to Saint-Domingue's tropical staples—sugar, coffee and indigo—which curbed French re-exports to western Europe and brought trade deficits and a decline in revenues; over the decade after 1789, exports fell by 50 percent.[1] These factors were compounded by military outlays, disorganized tax collection, budgetary deficits, and inflation. In the inflationary episode, specie in circulation fell by about 85 percent, from 2 billion *livres tournois* to about 300 million. Thus, internal and international conflict left a legacy of public debt that the Directoire could not readily manage. By

1796 it had to abandon paper, returning to specie as an "essential condition given the circumstances, social consolidation, and economic recovery."[2] Silver inflows became indispensable.

Recovery began with deficit reduction in 1798 and 1799 and peace with England in 1801. Specie levels rose on renewal of foreign trade, particularly with Spain, and through sales of naval supplies to a Spanish fleet at Brest and grain exports to Spain, both paid for in silver.[3] But the respite was brief. With renewed hostilities in 1803, deficits recurred and the government turned to the "ressources extraordinaires" of occupied areas of Italy and, as we shall see, to claims on Spain's colonial revenues in specie, mainly those of New Spain.[4]

About 1803 France had in place financial structures replacing the expedients of the revolutionary era. Now there was an extended—perhaps overextended—system of military procurement by contractors, supplying provisions, pay, and equipment for the armed forces; the Trésor Public, drawing revenue in direct taxes through departmental collectors (receveurs généraux);[5] and—an innovation for a government and public viscerally devoted to hard money—the Banque de France, a semiprivate institution authorized to issue large-denominational banknotes redeemable in specie on sight. Since the Trésor Public's revenues, mainly from the land tax, were usually delayed and short of ever-growing outlays, Treasury Minister Barbé-Marbois adopted the expedient of discounting, through either private bankers or the Banque de France, the bonds secured on anticipated collections (obligations) deposited with the Trésor by the receveurs.[6] To be sure, contractors, receveurs, and the Trésor Public had existed before 1789 under different rubrics. Not so the Banque, that early, major creation of the Consulat headed by a military nationalist and hard money enthusiast, Napoleon Bonaparte. The Banque's goal, he once wrote, was to discount paper "of every merchant firm in France at 4 percent annually."[7]

The Banque symbolized financial independence to merchants and manufacturers, who had felt exploited in the eighteenth century by the dominant Genevan bankers, who maintained agents at Cadiz, the center of specie inflows across the Atlantic.[8] Equally symbolic were two of the Banque's first fifteen regents, Jean-Barthélemy LeCouteulx de Canteleu and Léon Basterrèche, both of whom were involved in Spanish finance. The LeCouteulx fortune stemmed originally from a merchant house maintained since 1722 at Cadiz; LeCouteulx was the Paris agent of Spain's Hacienda and the recently formed Banco Nacional de San Carlos. Basterrèche had accumulated wealth first in trade at Bayonne, then in a Parisian banking firm, where he managed the funds of the trading arm of Spain's finance ministry, its Real

Giro.[9] The Banque quickly became the major engine of short-term credit during the Consulat and the Empire, servicing the private sector of merchants, manufacturers, war contractors, and, of course, the Trésor Public. The ratio of its cash supply *(encaisse)* to sight notes in circulation, by statute fixed at 1:3, determined the level of public confidence in the franc, as became evident in 1805.[10]

There was nothing exceptional about the preoccupation of the French government and its financier-contractors with Spain's silver imports during the Consulat and the Empire. If anything, the mirage of New Spain's silver *pesos* was only magnified after 1796. In that year Paris, abandoning depreciated *assignats* for admittedly scarce specie, pressured Madrid to lift restrictions on specie outflows, since "only this operation can impart to circulation in France the maximum activity that it is capable of."[11] As the import of Saint-Domingue's loss sank in, French businessmen and civil servants looked enviously at Spain, which was drawing upon its American colonies "quinet, cochineal, vermilion, and especially bars of gold and silver, as well as *pesos,* which until the last [diplomatic] rupture had supplied our mint."[12]

The French Republic's finances remained precarious in 1798 and 1799, and the Directoire experimented with drastic budget slashing, shifting to specie despite a shortage aggravated by export levels 50 percent below those before the Revolution. Symptomatic of future expedients, the Directoire alleviated its financial squeeze in part by using windfalls shipped from Italy by a brilliant, unexpectedly successful army officer.[13] In no small measure, this commander's coup d'état in 1799 was rooted in the Directoire's incapacity to control inflation, in fiscal incompetence, and in generalized conditions of industrial and export stagnation, all undermining the confidence of the Parisian financial community. Hence the support of some bankers for the coup d'état masterminded by the brothers Napoleon and Lucien Bonaparte.[14] Their Consulat inherited a France in which "realistically government had no funds, the armies and civil service were unpaid."[15] Immediately, the "banquiers du 18 Brumaire"—Perregaux, Mallet, Germain, Davillier, and others—assigned high priority to founding first a commercial discount organization (the Caisse de Comptes Courants) and then the Banque de France.[16]

Looking beyond the Pyrenees to Madrid, the French found a government whose fiscal expedients perplexed them, whose revenues after 1795 consistently fell below expenditures, but one that could count ultimately on colonial silver *pesos* to arrive sooner or later.[17] Besides, it is comforting to dwell upon another government's fiscal incompetence. Madrid, France's agents reported in 1798, would be unable to disburse 12 million *pesos* unless "silver arrives from America," and they diligently reported the arrival at Santoña, on the Bay of Biscay, of 5 million *pesos* shipped from Veracruz.[18] They linked the immediate solvency of the Spanish government to the recent expropriation of ecclesiastical properties under *consolidación* and to its colonial revenues, none of which were as promising as those of the mining colony par excellence, New Spain, where a "prodigious advance" in mining output had been registered over the previous twenty-five years.[19] Permeating the French government and financial circles by 1800 was the notion of "Spanish wealth," the "established truth" of seemingly limitless production of precious metals—the "piastres du Mexique" and the "piastres du Pérou." Bonaparte too believed in the "wealth of the government of Madrid," a belief also shared by many among France's old and new *bourgeoisie d'affaires*.[20] Over the next five years the mirage of New Spain's silver contributed to the financial crisis at Paris and to Bonaparte's personal intervention in the operations of the *munitionnaires* Ouvrard and Vanlerberghe, the principal partners *(fournisseurs)* in the multiple operations of their Compagnie des Négociants Réunis.

In many respects 1803 marked a turning point in the French government's finances and closer ties between Mexico City's colonial treasury, Madrid's Hacienda under Soler, and France's Trésor Public under Barbé-Marbois, an ex-intendant of Saint-Domingue. The financial drain of the failed military recolonization of Saint-Domingue, the loss of hope in a revived French hegemony in the Caribbean, and the maritime consequences of an imminent renewal of conflict with England induced the French government—without giving prior notice to its ally, Spain—abruptly to sell Louisiana to the United States for 80 million *livres tournois* just three years after Spain had transferred that vast territory to France. The Amsterdam firm of Hope & Company handled this transaction.[21] The French government needed hard currency for projected military operations, and to the expected U.S. payments Napoleon added the specie now demanded from its neutral ally, Spain, a monthly subsidy of 4 million francs (roughly 800,000 *pesos fuertes*). Spain's subsidy, handled by Hacienda Minister Soler and his director of the Caja de Consolidación, Sixto Espinosa, was payable in drafts, or *traites,* in *pesos fuertes* on Mexico City's treasury. According to an anonymous, acute English observer in 1804, "France has people, but not 'money,' the other requisite for war [,which] can be supplied but scantily. . . . The resources of Spain have been constantly drained to support those armies." More precise at that moment was William Jacob, who apparently knew the colony of New Spain well: "The independence of Spanish America would deprive France of that channel which at present provides France with the ability to destroy the Peace of the World."[22] In 1804 Jacob predicted French intervention in Portugal and Spain and the likely English reaction.

By demanding a subsidy from a reluctant ally in 1803, the French government put the issue of its monthly subsidy front and center. To be sure, when the subsidy arrangement was signed in October 1803, Spain was still neutral and in principle could continue to receive at Cadiz those extraordinary sums in silver recorded meticulously by English and French agents there, silver principally from Guanajuato and Zacatecas via Veracruz. In light of large, foreseeable military expenditures, the French government desperately needed the Spanish subsidy; in fact, in late 1803 Bonaparte notified Martínez de Hervás, a banker and Spain's Hacienda agent at Paris, that he would station armed forces on the border near Bayonne until the subsidy was paid.[23] In the meantime, the Trésor Public's Barbé-Marbois had to turn to domestic contractors for short-term financing of France's armed forces.[24] The Compagnie des Négociants Réunis became his preferred instrument because its principals—Ouvrard, Vanlerberghe, Michel *aîné*—seemed to mix market expertise in subcontracting with imaginative credit manipulation. Of course, *munitionnaires* like Ouvrard inspired criticism of superprofiteering and a propensity toward correspondingly lavish personal consumption; some viewed their proclivities as scandalous, while others detected the essence of entrepreneurial risktaking. During France's revolutionary decade Vanlerberghe, for instance, avoided a brush with the guillotine by discreet emigration. But in the postrevolutionary regime *munitionnaires* set the tone.

The older of the two principal associates, Vanlerberghe, grew up at Douai, in northern France, and speculated in the grain trade. An émigré during the Terror, he was back in France in 1798 and removed from police surveillance the following year, when he offered the Directoire a loan of 4 million francs. In the subsistence crisis of 1801–2 the Consulat, failing to interest other Paris contractors, turned to Vanlerberghe to import grain.[25] His supply and credit networks led to a contract to provision Bonaparte's forces readying for the second Italian campaign.[26] Thereafter his government contracts multiplied; over seven years, 1800–1807, they totaled more than 300 million francs, putting him in contact with the Michel brothers, Armand Séguin, Médard Desprez, and, of course, Ouvrard.[27]

Ouvrard's background was in the "bourgeoisie aisée." Son of a paper manufacturer in western France, he clerked in a Nantes firm dealing in colonial staples before the Revolution, speculated in paper during the Revolution, and by 1799, when he was not yet thirty, had amassed an "enormous and . . . quickly acquired fortune." His debut in government finance came when he, like Vanlerberghe, loaned the Directoire money, in his case 10 million francs, and then contracted to provision the French navy.[28] This led to another contract also to provision the Spanish fleet at Brest, which netted him 4 million francs in silver drafts on Mexico City's treasury, as French authorities stipulated.[29] Talleyrand, with an aristocrat's acute sense of easy money, probably intervened with Spain's agents at Paris to award Ouvrard the contract. A Spanish diplomat was later shocked by the "scandalous speculation that greedy men, protected by powerful men, had made on provisioning the Spanish fleet . . . in the Port of Brest."[30] These contracts with the Spanish government pushed young Ouvrard, "just integrated into the world of the new, postrevolutionary finance," into the limelight.[31] Ouvrard and Vanlerberghe handled well their métier as intermediaries between a government usually behind in making payments and its importunate suppliers, as "real adventurers" whose risk- and profit-taking propensities reinvigorated "the directing classes and founded a solid bourgeoisie."[32]

An enterprising bourgeois could scarcely overlook the 33 percent spread between the rate at which New Spain's silver was obtained, 3.75 francs per *peso,* and the rate at which it was exchanged in Europe, 5 francs per *peso,* luring Ouvrard, Vanlerberghe, and their Compagnie des Négociants Réunis ever deeper into French and Spanish government finance over a twelve-month period beginning in December 1803. Within weeks of the signing of the Spanish subsidy agreement with France, Vanlerberghe, probably acting as Ouvrard's straw man, proposed to advance to the Trésor Public 32 million francs, the equivalent of eight months of the promised subsidy. The offer was predicated on a number of assumptions; for example, Spain's installments might be delayed, since Madrid could not honor on sight letters of exchange drawn on colonial revenues; or French insistence on prompt payment might conceivably induce Madrid to turn elsewhere, to offer London and other European financial centers silver *pesos* "payable in Mexico," affording them a profit of "several million in cash." His proposal, Vanlerberghe wrote Bonaparte, would ensure prompt payment of the Spanish subsidy, along with "every possible profit for circulation and the trade balance of France."[33]

Four months later, in April 1804, 32 million francs of the Spanish subsidy was repackaged into a 50 million franc deal between the Trésor Public and the Compagnie des Négociants Réunis, which employed as its intermediary with the Trésor Public a regent of the Banque de France, the exchange specialist Médard Desprez. In exchange for five monthly advances of 10 million francs each, the French government turned over to the Négociants Réunis Spanish drafts (bills of exchange) equivalent to the subsidy payments, exchangeable at the Trésor Public for *obligations* deposited by *receveurs généraux*. In practical fashion, Ouvrard and Vanlerberghe discounted the *obligations* for specie at the Banque de France. "The Trésor guaranteed in this fashion the credit it granted," or as Bonaparte later surmised, "We have paid a subsidy to Spain rather than drawing on the one she owed us."[34] Here was the basis of what became an escalating pyramid of financial operations, a type of revolving door of credits, linking the Trésor Public, the Négociants Réunis, and the Banque de France to Spain's finance ministry and, in the western Atlantic, to the treasury of the colony of New Spain, all founded on the shipment by sea of silver *pesos* exported from Veracruz to cover Spain's subsidy to France's Trésor Public. To the Trésor's Barbé-Marbois, consolidating short-term borrowing with one financial syndicate on the collateral security of future receipts, in large measure from Mexico City, while contracting with the same syndicate for military and naval supplies was attractive: there were interest savings, and it appeared that the Négociants Réunis could draw upon inexhaustible credit for its financial outreach.[35]

Pyramiding is perhaps no exaggeration. In mid-1804 Barbé-Marbois turned again to the Ouvrard group for further credits up to 120 million francs for general disbursements, the syndicate receiving in return partial payment in the form of drafts on the subsidy from Spain—more promissory notes in *pesos*. At the same time, the syndicate continued to provision France's armed forces so satisfactorily that in 1805 Bonaparte renewed their contract. In effect, Ouvrard and Vanlerberghe were participating in a form of "early financing of the war," Bonaparte's coming campaign against Austria and Russia.[36]

The operations of the Trésor Public with the Négociants Réunis in 1804 were already critically dependent upon silver *pesos* from New Spain embedded in the Spanish subsidy, to the extent that in the second half of 1804 "French finances could not survive without this money."[37] An increasingly anxious Barbé-Marbois, foreseeing a huge shortfall of 116 million francs in September, dispatched at Bonaparte's insistence a prominent principal of the Négociants Réunis, Ouvrard, to Madrid to accelerate *peso* transfers to France.[38] In October, however, the English government signaled that it would block American silver from reaching Spain for transfer to France, where it could finance military operations against the English-led Third Coalition. In fact, without a formal declaration of hostilities, an English squadron intercepted a Spanish convoy of four vessels from La Plata with silver inbound for Cadiz. Now access to American silver *pesos* became difficult and complex for both Spain and France. Silver hoarding occurred on a large scale in France, and the exchange value of rarified *pesos* soared.[39]

Barbé-Marbois had dispatched Ouvrard to Madrid to ensure coverage of Spain's delayed subsidy payments by obtaining Madrid's consent for Ouvrard to negotiate with Amsterdam's bankers for a loan secured on Mexico City's government silver.[40] Ouvrard, characteristically, gave this objective secondary consideration, for in late November he arranged to transfer Mexico City's receipts from *consolidación* operations through a complex of neutral covers. In addition, ever the *fournisseur* and *brasseur d'affaires,* he promised to deliver up to 2 million *quintales* of French grains to ease Spain's subsistence crisis, adding a contract to provision Spain's armed forces. The grain exports received prompt approval from the French government, which insisted, however, on an export duty of 4 francs per *quintal,* which Vanlerberghe charged to the growing Spanish account, leading Barbé-Marbois to gloat to Bonaparte: "I am hastening the arrival of *pesos* from Spain in a variety of ways. The *pesos* that are the price of grains shipped to Spain will quickly balance this important and useful operation."[41] Moreover, Madrid did authorize negotiations for a loan at Amsterdam, although they were stalled until July 1805 and were only completed the following November. Spain obtained 10 million guilders, secured on 8.5 million *pesos* in Mexico City's treasury.[42]

In late 1805, however, the pyramid of financial deals engineered by Ouvrard and the Négociants Réunis began to crumble. Vanlerberghe, having diverted the funds originally intended for financing the provisioning of France's armed forces to cover Ouvrard's contracts with Madrid and besieged by impatient creditors, demanded repeatedly from the Trésor Public short-term loans precisely when both the Trésor and the Banque de France had virtually no cash reserves, and Napoleon had to be informed that "we are waiting for the *pesos* from Spain . . . we must hope for specie from Spain."[43] In December 1805 the Négociants Réunis owed the Trésor Public more than 73 million francs, which was more than France had netted from the recent sale of Louisiana. "Mexican silver was the only solution to the shortage of funds."[44]

The crisis surfaced in the sudden illiquidity of the Banque de France, its temporary inability to redeem on sight banknotes *(billets)* payable in specie over a period of roughly eight months, from April to December 1805. Underneath, however, the crisis reflected the brittle confidence of segments of the Parisian *bourgeoisie d'affaires* of bankers, merchants, and speculators in the stability of the new imperial order's military expansion and its efforts to finance perennial deficits with *peso* drafts on distant Mexico City's treasury, issued by Madrid to cover the subsidy payments due the Trésor Public.[45]

The Banque de France had begun operations in 1800 on subscribed capital of 30 million francs in specie. Now, in the midst of the discount operations of the Trésor Public, by virtue of what the *receveurs généraux* deposited and the bills of merchant-bankers the Banque's earnings fluctuated with the level of its note issues and discount operations. After four years, in September 1804, when Napoleon ordered Barbé-Marbois to have Ouvrard meet with Finance Minister Soler at Madrid, the Banque's specie reserve (its *encaisse*) held 8.6 million francs, after plummeting from February's high of 27.2 million. It had surged back to 23 million by the following April, only to collapse over the next five months, bottoming out at 1.2 million in September 1805 as skittish noteholders cashed 43 million francs. Since in April there had been 86.9 million francs of its banknotes in circulation, and there were probably more in September, the Banque's liquidity ratio had fallen to dangerous lows.[46] Withdrawals from its *encaisse* were made, first, by the Trésor to pay military contractors, among the principal *fournisseurs* being, of course, the Négociants Réunis; and, second, by private bankers and businessmen, who preferred specie over banknotes, many transferring their funds for safekeeping to Amsterdam and London.

To be sure, withdrawals were motivated by fear of the depreciation of paper much like what had happened to the *assignats* or was happening to the *vales reales* of Spain's Banco Nacional de San Carlos, in which some French speculators were invested. There were, moreover, other factors behind the crisis. France's merchandise balance with Spain over the four years 1800–1804 was decidedly deficitary, more than 100 million francs (20 million *pesos fuertes*) incurred mainly in 1803 and again in 1804.[47] French textile exports were stagnating. This does not contradict the possibility that production centers had raised capacity but could not market output because consumers in France were affected by years of inflation.[48] Concurrently in 1806 and 1807 the linen manufacturers of Saint-Quentin, Mayenne, Finisterre, Ile-et-Vilaine, and Aude complained about the drop in exports to Spain destined for re-export to the American colonies and consequently rising unemployment.[49]

The illiquidity of the Banque de France and the Trésor Public in the closing months of 1805 was worsened by demands for short-term credits from large-scale military contractors like Ouvrard and Vanlerberghe's Négociants Réunis, who were responding to their subcontractors.[50] At issue was the growing volume of drafts on Mexico City, whose specie transfers were being rerouted circuitously to penetrate England's Atlantic blockade. Ouvrard had been discounting his drafts at the Banque, accumulated through multiple contracts with the Spanish government for provisioning its armed forces and supplying its navy with sailcloth and copper sheathing; he also speculated in imports of Spanish merino wool. In fact, Barbé-Marbois's correspondence with Bonaparte in 1804 and 1805 referred repeatedly to the Trésor's operations with the principals of the Négociants Réunis as he began to perceive how Ouvrard's operations inextricably mixed "the business of the *pesos* from Mexico . . . the supply of grain to Spain" with Ouvrard's contracts for the armed forces of France and his borrowing from the Banque and the Trésor.[51] He trusted that once Spanish authorities applied "all their attention and customary honesty in money matters to Ouvrard et Cie," then "all the difficulties surrounding today's business activity will be eased." Otherwise, Barbé-Marbois warned Madrid, in the fall of 1805 there could be a crisis that "our enemies have a great interest in worsening."[52]

Indeed, in late September that crisis peaked amid rumors that Bonaparte had drawn down the Banque's cash reserve to finance military operations and that the Négociants Réunis was insisting on further advances. Crowds lined up at the Banque insisting on exchanging banknotes for specie, the *encaisse* plummeted to 1.3 million francs, and "our hopes hung on the arrival" of 20 million francs from Spain, already bled by massive *peso* transfers to European financial centers.[53] As the Banque's reserve shrank, it bought up *pesos* on Paris exchanges, at commercial centers along the border at Bayonne and Perpignan, even in Spain itself. It sent special agents to collect 90 million francs from surrounding *départements* and coined more than 17 million francs from receipts of silver *pesos*.[54] Desprez, on behalf of the Négociants Réunis, promised to deliver 7 million *pesos* but, characteristically, delivered only 1.6 million. These measures, supplemented by rationing of the silver reserve and, above all, the revival of confidence in the business community on news of French victories at Ulm and Austerlitz helped replenish the Banque's cash reserve. From a low of 1.2 million francs in late September, the reserve inched upward to reach 12 million on 30 December and 14.3 million in early January 1806.[55]

The "inextricable confusion" of private and public interests in the operations of Ouvrard and the Compagnie des Négociants Réunis began to unravel in the second half of 1805 in the course of the liquidity crisis.[56] Commencing in May, Desprez, representing the Négociants Réunis as *fournisseur général* of the armed forces, requested extraordinarily large discounts of its credit instruments. By the end of September he was demanding 3 million francs plus daily sums of 1 million over several weeks; in early October his discounts at the Banque totaled 105 million, and in mid-November he returned for more.[57] "The service in behalf of Spain," Barbé-Marbois told Bonaparte, was bankrupting the Compagnie des Négociants Réunis.[58]

By initially accepting the intermediation of the Négociants Réunis to collect Spain's subsidy while simultaneously awarding it military contracts, Barbé-Marbois unwittingly transformed Ouvrard and Vanlerberghe into large debtors whose demands could not be easily rejected. In an inversion of roles, the French government had become dependent upon a large, importunate debtor. For its part, the Négociants Réunis became enmeshed in a web of its own making—as a financial intermediary between Madrid and Paris and between Madrid and Amsterdam and as general contractor for France's armed forces, not to mention its private deals in Spain and its American colonies.[59] In correspondence of September 1805 Barbé-Marbois impressed upon the Banque's regents the need to continue supporting the Compagnie in the mutual interest of "shareholders, bankers, and merchants and . . . the Trésor Public."[60] By early November he recognized reluctantly that the Compagnie, despite its many services, including commercial agreements with the Spanish government promising "specie imports," had to be liquidated to avoid "all kinds of trouble . . . at every commercial center and at Paris." The Compagnie's "immense transactions" with the Spanish government had simply undermined it, and in this sense Spain's inability to deliver New Spain's promised *pesos* caused the crash.[61] In January 1806 the Compagnie declared bankruptcy. As soon as Bonaparte returned to Paris at the end of the month, he terminated the government's relations with the Négociants Réunis.

More to the point, by early January the acute phase of the financial crisis had passed as the Banque's reserves climbed to a level where selective controls on note redemption could be discarded. To be sure, industrial stagnation and unemployment continued through 1806. In fact, emergency measures by the regents of the Banque literally to cart into Paris silver from the treasuries of surrounding *départements* and to buy up *pesos* anywhere in France and Spain, together with Bonaparte's military victories, effectively stemmed the run on the Banque. Why, then, did Bonaparte insist on personally settling accounts with Ouvrard?

Perspective is in order. Ouvrard and his close associate Vanlerberghe were only the more prominent financial speculators churned up by revolution and war in the overlapping phases of late commercial and early industrial capitalism. These *bourgeois*—their analogs were the *fermiers généraux* of pre-1789 times—flourished in the chaotic years after 1789 as the French state's fiscal structure came apart and expedients became the norm. Since the French armed forces had expanded rapidly, the state turned for multiple military services to financiers, to whom payment was often deferred at added interest charges. *Fournisseurs* were indispensable, although their profiteering and conspicuous consumption patterns did not generate universal respect. Bonaparte used them; he was suspicious of their plundering activities, but when he needed them, as in the fall of 1805, he approved Barbé-Marbois's decision to renew credits to the Négociants Réunis. In their case, demands upon the Banque de France were also the product of speculation in the *pesos* of distant colonial Mexico City.

Bonaparte and his circle sponsored the Banque de France because his Brumaire backers had urged it, partly because it serviced French businessmen, partly because in quickly discounting *obligations* of the general revenue collectors the Banque expanded the credit resources of the Trésor Public, which was plagued by revenue shortfalls and delayed receipts. Over eighteen months, from 1804 to 1805, these resources were put under pressure by the principals of the Négociants Réunis—by Ouvrard, Vanlerberghe, and Desprez. Beginning with the acceptance of *peso* drafts in April 1804, Ouvrard and the Compagnie acquired a large volume of them collectible at Mexico City's Real Hacienda. Ouvrard discounted the drafts at the Trésor Public and the Banque de France, and the French government assumed that the Négociants Réunis was fulfilling its contracts with the armed forces. Yet in late 1805, during the financial crisis at Paris—triggered by the English blockade that made it impossible for Spain to deliver silver *pesos*—Bonaparte and his associates wondered whether the Négociants Réunis was, in fact, servicing the French contracts or diverting credits received to fulfilling its Spanish contracts.[62] The *fournisseurs* were now considered "agents recognized by the government of Spain, as suppliers of foodstuffs and provisioners to the navy and assisting the same government, the Trésor Public, and France's army and naval forces." The Banque's commission of inquiry expressed an astonishment that was probably feigned: "Incompatible obligations, a frightening bundle of various businesses!"[63]

In the aftermath of the theatrical showdown that Bonaparte staged on 26 January 1806, when he told Ouvrard that he would like to erect a gallows "high enough to serve as an example to all France," he jibed at Barbé-Marbois that Ouvrard, Vanlerberghe, and Desprez had duped him with promises of the "trésors du Mexico," the Compagnie des Négociants Réunis was liquidated, its assets (including the warehoused Spanish merino wools) confiscated, and Barbé-Marbois dismissed and replaced by Mollien.[64]

A banking commission's examination of the Compagnie's accounts confirmed the critics' suspicions.[65] Over the short life of its operations with the Trésor Public, the Compagnie had received credits in *obligations* of the *récéveurs généraux* held by the Trésor to the tune of 140 million francs. As collateral security, the Compagnie had offered 86.5 million francs, of which 37.1 million (43%) represented the expected proceeds of the loan floated by Hope & Company (8.5 million francs) plus *peso* drafts on Mexico City's treasury (28.6 million).[66] The volume and scope of Ouvrard and Vanlerberghe's financial activities with Madrid also confirmed the suspicion that they had diverted French government funds to finance their highly profitable contracts with the Spanish government.[67]

Profits were nothing new; at issue was whose monies had been used. In about twelve months Ouvrard and Vanlerberghe had managed to advance to the Spanish government 80.6 million francs, fully 55.6 million (69%) in credits on Paris and other European financial centers.[68] Ominously, appended to the 28.6 million francs claimed on Mexico City and listed among the Compagnie's assets was the observation, "The influence of France to receive what it deserves guaranteed that if these acceptances were not paid, *they would be later*" (emphasis added). Asking rhetorically how "ordinary persons" could bundle a package of credits of 80 million francs offered in one year to the Spanish government, the banking commissioners answered: by drawing upon France's Trésor Public—"the only means they had"—to sustain their speculations and meet their Spanish contracts.[69]

Over the next three months, from February to May 1806, the Trésor Public, under Mollien's direction, confiscated the assets of the Compagnie Ouvrard-Vanlerberghe, then pressed on to collect what it considered Madrid's debt to the French government. Inevitably the burden of payment fell upon Spain's wealthiest American colony, New Spain. Initially, Spain's agent at Paris, Eugenio Izquierdo, "one of the men in Europe best informed about trade, especially Spain's," refused to honor drafts presented by the Banque de France on the ground that they had been made out to Ouvrard.[70] One suspects that French arm-twisting produced a settlement, "that goal . . . so important to our finances,"[71] in May. Spain's representative rejected responsibility for money and goods not supplied by Ouvrard, cutting French demands by 45 percent, from 106.5 million francs to 58.3 million; of this balance, 34.3 million, or 59 percent, was earmarked for collection at Mexico City.[72] This sum, equivalent to 9.6 million *pesos fuertes,* was withdrawn from 1806 to 1808 from Veracruz in English warships and distributed through stratagems devised by Hope of Amsterdam and Barings of London.[73] Barings's agent at New Orleans later calculated that eventually Veracruz exported 14 million *pesos,* which probably understates total withdrawals from Mexico City. One point was clear: no longer would Ouvrard and associates, as private intermediaries between the two governments, skim what Manuel Godoy labeled "the scandalous profits businessmen seek."[74] Others—the Hopes and Barings, Parish and Nolte, Oliver, Craig, and Gordon & Murphy—effortlessly, and profitably, replaced them.

The episode of the Compagnie des Négociants Réunis traces the diaspora of New Spain's silver through circuits integrating America and Europe, New Spain and France, Madrid's Hacienda and at Paris the Trésor Public and Banque de France. France's textile manufacturers envisioned outlets in New Spain, and the French government needed that colony's silver *pesos* to finance its armies under the Consulat and the Empire. In the international rivalry pitting English against French imperialists both before and after 1789, both sought access to New Spain's trade and silver. The irony of Ouvrard's contract with Sixto Espinosa in November 1804 was that it gave U.S. and English merchants a channel for transferring silver, from Veracruz across the Atlantic to Europe, to finance Spain's subsidy to France. Thereby the French government transferred Spain's American consumers "to English commercial firms."[75]

Bonaparte and his advisers Hauterive, Talleyrand, and Barbé-Marbois were aware of New Spain's resources, even magnified them. Alexander von Humboldt's four-volume *Essai politique sur le royaume de la Nouvelle Espagne*, which circulated in draft form in New Spain, Spain, and France from 1804 to 1808, probably strengthened that illusion. Bonaparte ridiculed Barbé-Marbois's faith in New Spain's wealth, yet he pursued tenaciously Madrid's promised but delayed payments. Twice in November 1806 he wrote Mollien about New Spain's silver, first to ask for an accounting of "my transactions with Spain and those *pesos*," then to complain that "the delay in payments from Spain is alarming," and in March 1807 he wrote that "for one year I have drawn almost nothing from our *peso* credits."[76] André Fugier has argued that the experience with Ouvrard, Vanlerberghe, and the Négociants Réunis sharpened Bonaparte's conviction that its American colonies made Spain the "richest power in Europe," damned by incompetent civil servants. Incompetence—failure to pay in Mexico City's *pesos* the installments stipulated under the terms of the subsidy and other Spanish contracts—had shaken "the whole economic life of France" in 1805.[77] This was hardly a new perception. Renovating Spain's administration in order better to exploit her colonial resources for the ultimate benefit of the French economy long had been the driving force behind France's diplomatic relations with Spain.

No sooner had French forces under Murat established their headquarters at Madrid in 1808 than a commission of Spanish government finance experts headed by Sixto Espinosa—"that great instrument of every operation relating to paper money, credit, and expedients"—was handed a detailed questionnaire. In turn the commission produced surveys of government income and expenditure and a comprehensive report on the operations of the famed, perhaps now defamed, Caja de Consolidación.[78] Asked for, among other things, more precise data on tax collections in the metropole and the colonies, the commissioners could supply no detailed report without further research.

No doubt Murat, Napoleon's representative at Madrid, was discouraged; he should hardly have been surprised.

14. "La tempestad que nos amenazaba"

. . . .

To understand the tempest that menaced us, it is enough to recall that with the elimination of the Bourbon Family Pact we lost any balance in the contest between the maritime powers for control of the seas.   Junta Económica, Consulado de la Habana, 17 October 1811

The plans conceived by the Committee of Public Safety that the Directoire had attempted to carry out . . . Napoleon pushed them to the limit: the downfall of the House of Bourbon and the total vassalage of Spain to France.   Albert Sorel

Anglomania is widespread among us, and those not so afflicted are categorized not as Good Spaniards but as French.   Bernardo Iriarte, 20 March 1806

In the last phase of commercial capitalism in the late eighteenth century, unequal economic growth and development in western Europe produced a hierarchy of national economies: England and France in the more developed category, Holland next, and far behind, among the less developed, Spain and Portugal, despite (or because of) their long-held overseas empires. Relations between Bourbon France and Bourbon Spain approximated those between an "advanced" and a "backward," or "less developed," economy, to employ current usage. The relationship was dynamic, as interest groups in both economies jockeyed to adjust the relationship to their own advantage. Those trusting in mutually advantageous adjustments formed a minority of civil servants and even a few men of business. Throughout the century a fundament of French policy toward Spain and its diplomatic implementation remained the production and export of finished goods benefiting from special Spanish tariff provisions, targeted at high-income consumers in Spain and its colonies, and balanced by return flows of silver *pesos* and raw materials from the mining colonies in the western Atlantic.

The relationship between "hegemonic" France and "dependent" Spain and Spanish America was strengthened by the gains of trade unequally shared but nonetheless available, by mutual interest in containing England's trading and commercial power, and, when French interests deemed necessary, by the reason of military force. The so-called family pact was always a marriage of much convenience.

During the final decades of prerevolutionary France, many French civil servants and businessmen found the Franco-Spanish alliance of 1761, the "Third Family Pact," eroded by English and German economic inroads and French diplomatic disinterest and incompetence. As the disaffected put it, "The people in charge of important diplomatic affairs simply lacked commercial expertise."[1] French exporters were irritated as well by the barely concealed mistrust—they took it to be Francophobia—of Madrid's civil servants along with port and customs personnel at Barcelona, Valencia, Santander, and especially Spain's major port, Cadiz. No doubt the post-1783 expanded trade between Spain and its colonies had backward linkages to France, fueling an upsurge in licit and illicit specie flows from Spain into France and its associated French illusion of the limitless wealth of Spain, really of its colonies. The expansion also reminded French businessmen that the Spanish government had over decades studiously sidetracked a commercial treaty promised in the 1761 pact, while adopting the device of tariff revision in 1781 to protect infant industry by curbing or prohibiting categories of France's principal exports, textiles.

Relations between the two governments soured rapidly between 1789 and 1795. To officials in Spain, French governments in the turbulent, immediate post-1789 years seemed to reject the Family Pact's guarantees of mutual territorial integrity—one French critic dismissed it as "that league against the people . . . the shield protecting the weakness of Spain"[2]—when Paris failed to support Madrid in rejecting an English foothold at Nootka Sound.[3] Nor were the Spanish reassured when the revolutionary regime in France committed regicide against the Spanish royal family's Bourbon relatives and revolutionary rhetoric produced the most massive slave insurrection in history on France's island colony of Saint-Domingue, close to Spain's major Caribbean colony, Cuba. That insurrection occasioned a quick reflex among manufacturers and merchants along France's Atlantic coast from Rouen to Le Havre, Nantes, La Rochelle, and Bordeaux and, in the Mediterranean, to Marseilles, underscoring the critical importance of those "splendid and wealthy overseas possessions that have created the good fortune and prosperity of the Empire."[4]

Worse followed for the French government when Bourbon Spain abandoned the alliance in 1793 for collaboration in England's effort to contain revolution in France. The traditional Franco-Spanish common front against England's commercial and naval expansion collapsed; "we lost any balance," to quote Cuban merchants, "in the contest between the maritime powers for control of the sea."[5] During warfare from 1793 to 1795 more was at stake than mutual defense arrangements. France's exports to Spain and its colonies dried up, aggravated by the cutoff of specie flowing across the Pyrenees and the ruthless expulsion of more than seventy-five hundred French nationals from Mexico City and Veracruz, from Cadiz, Seville, Alicante, Valencia, and Barcelona, causing "tremendous disruption . . . in commercial affairs." Expelled by Godoy's viceregal appointee to New Spain, the marqués de Branciforte, French merchants there were incensed by summary deportation to Cadiz, where "for two years we filled the prisons of Spain, where they only stopped short of crucifying us." They did recall gratefully that two members of the Mexico City Audiencia, *alcaldes de corte* Manuel de Urrutia and Manuel Antonio de la Bodega, had tried to protect them.[6]

French businessmen's fear that revolutionary legislation might upset their profitable "compact" with the French colonies, based on the *exclusif*, was confirmed by the uncontainable slave insurrection on Saint-Domingue. No wonder the defeat of Spanish forces in southwestern France, followed in 1794 by France's counterthrust into northern Spain and the prospect of dictating the terms of peace, revived hope of recouping the loss of overseas colonies by expanding trade with Spain and *its* colonies. A defeated Spain— "a colossus of gilded clay ready to collapse at the first shock"—might be pressured to yield at last major commercial concessions, including direct access of French exporters to Spain's American colonies.[7] Frustrated French businessmen, irritated by the "culpable negligence and secret maneuvers of our ministers, ambassadors, consuls, and other diplomats," by Madrid's welcoming ten thousand counterrevolutionary émigrés from France ("tarnished individuals in the general opinion, public vampires"), and by Madrid's decision to suspend specie outflows to France, causing a "deadly stagnation of credit in our principal commercial centers," now found in defeated Spain the "remedy for our most urgent problems."[8] A dictated peace might bring back Spanish-American dyestuffs, "which have become absolutely necessary in France and Europe," along with "bars of gold and silver," and might bring to French merchant shipping the opportunity to enter Spain's colonial ports. No wonder recently appointed Prime Minister Godoy received a letter in 1796 warning against any economic measures by the Spanish government that might irritate French merchants in Spain.[9]

Once Madrid initiated a suspension of hostilities and negotiation of a treaty of peace, signed in 1795, both governments found an opportunity to establish an economic framework for reaffirming the interrupted alliance. An economic consensus of sorts, at minimum a return to the basic structure of the Family Pact, was indispensable for renewing a common front against the dominant economy in Europe, England's. Appropriately, the two governments included among their negotiators the former chargé d'affaires at Madrid and author of a well-informed study of Spain, Jean-François Bourgoing, representing France; and for Spain two French-speaking finance experts and men of business, Francisco Cabarrús and Simón de Aragorri y Olavide (marqués de Iranda). Paris and Madrid sought advice in preparation for what would be a contest over critical technical points in which apparent equality masked real inequality for Spain's domestic and colonial interests. Spain's experience in commercial treaty making had invariably allowed more powerful states to treat it, as Bernardo Iriarte graphically phrased it, "with one foot on its neck."[10] Moreover, Iriarte added pointedly, England's trade expert, Charles Jenkinson, Lord Hawkesbury, was wary of the disutility to English interests of treaties of commerce in general. In addition, Madrid also relied on two veteran consular officials, Juan Bautista Virio, then opportunely on leave at Madrid after serving at Hamburg and then London, and its consul at St. Petersburg, Antonio Colombi, a prominent army officer shortly to serve with France's Army of the Rhine under General Jean Moreau.[11] As for Paris, the Comité du Salut Public and then its successor government, the Directoire, solicited reports and recommendations from exporters, manufacturers, and diplomats.

Both governments shared an interest in preserving France's hegemony in western Europe and the integrity of Spain's possessions in the western Atlantic. The forthcoming treaty, Iriarte wrote to his diplomat brother, Domingo, was "both logical and needed . . . indispensable for both nations."[12] In Spain's view, trade arrangements should crown decades of economic nationalism nurtured during the long reign of Charles III, in which "every kind of fetter"—unwelcome tariff concessions—had been gradually eliminated, and cabinet ministers had envisioned the industrialization of the metropole on the basis of cheap domestic labor, local and colonial raw materials, and middle- and high-income consumers in the colonies. From an analysis of the record of Spain's treaty making, Juan Bautista Virio drew the principle that the "security and tranquility" of Spain, France, and the rest of Europe required mutual friendship founded on "equal independence in negotiations." Virio hoped that France's negotiators would avoid advancing "false premises . . . with the desire of enslaving the world to its own interests and ambition." For French representatives to insist upon Spain's unquestioning confirmation of former trade concessions would reveal "a tyrannical nature, similar to that of ordinary outlaws or pirates." Subdued nationalism and sensitivity to European opinion were now irrepressible among many in Spain's political class. Virio expected close Franco-Spanish collaboration such that no other country might take advantage of the "other's inferiority, deadening elements of its existence."[13] For a diplomat with extensive trade experience as a consular officer in western Europe, Virio was uncommonly idealistic.

Madrid officials also received an apparently unsolicited memoir from Francisco Solano, an army officer then assigned to the Paris embassy. Franco-Spanish collaboration, he ventured to propose to Godoy, was indispensable if England's "plans for hegemony in Europe" were to be blocked, because England intended to destroy the trade of Europe's competing maritime nations. He predicted that England, capitalizing on its bases in India (and presumably its recently obtained foothold at Nootka Sound in North America), would attack Spain's colonies along the Pacific coast as a way to seize resources for the liquidation of its "enormous public debt." On the other hand, a timely alliance of Europe's threatened maritime powers, Spain, Holland, and France, could mount an attack upon England to preserve their colonial establishments and avoid the "total collapse of their trade." Sketching an alliance, Solano advanced as its guiding principle "the candidness and moderation in treaties and goals," alluding to predictable hard bargaining between victorious France and recently defeated Spain.

Solano's position was shared by military officers, who in the late 1790s and into the first decade of the next century felt that Spain's international policy required cooperation with France and French interests, whether the regime there was monarchical or republican, to assist in the defense of the American colonies against English naval and commercial penetration. Solano's family had a colonial background. Born at Caracas in 1768, son of that colony's governor, he was sent as an adolescent to the metropole, where he made his military career as an infantry officer and participated in the occupation of Pensacola. In the late 1790s he was an observer attached to the staff of French General Moreau, who successfully led the Army of the Rhine and who backed Bonaparte's coup d'état of 1799. Solano's association with Moreau and his presumed Francophile orientation would have disastrous consequences for him at Cadiz in 1808, when French forces were driving south into Andalusia.[14]

Were the nationalists Virio and Solano, diplomat and military officer, blind to the reality of France's unleashed, imperialist *bourgeoisie d'affaires*? Not Virio, at any rate. He warned Godoy that signs were evident of a "consuming commercial spirit among the French at Madrid, who are spread out as if Spain were a land of Hottentots."[15] Virio's analysis was not off the mark. In principle, there *was* a contradiction between aiding the economic development of an ally and French demands that undermined Spanish efforts to stimulate manufacture and trade. In the flush of a stunning victory over Europe's contra-revolutionary regimes, both government and business in France gave great weight to economic factors in foreign policy, to ensure for "national industry a dominant role in Europe."[16] First, the Comité du Salut Public instructed its negotiators on its priorities: "to engage Spain in a commercial treaty, which is more important than a treaty of alliance."[17] Next, in 1797 the Directoire's negotiator Jacques Vincent Delacroix, concluding that France's military power had done the impossible, argued that French "prepondérance" should extend to France's shipping, trade, and industry, part of what Fugier later interpreted as a design for "real industrial colonization" of less developed Europe. In Spain's case, this meant for French interests unrestricted access to fine Spanish merino wools and *pesos* from the American colonies, both "indispensable in monetary planning."[18]

The congruence of economic objectives in foreign policy with the interests of "merchants and the most skilled manufacturers of the Republic" is beyond question if one examines businessmen's outlook.[19] French merchants and manufacturers sensed that many among the Spanish elites believed, despite their reluctance to admit it publicly, that their country was ineluctably tied to the French economy by a "law of nature."[20] Spain's prosperity, as analyzed by French manufacturers and merchants, was linked to France's industrial and trade growth; at least in the aftermath of military victory, the French government should insist on favorable commercial concessions. At one level French exporters hoped to reestablish and even enlarge their intermediation in distributing to northern Europe both Spain's and its American colonies' raw materials and foodstuffs, such as Cuban sugars, for instance. The recent disruption of Saint-Domingue's economy by insurgent African slaves made this prospect immediately attractive in 1795.[21] Since Frenchmen put great stock in Spain's domestic and colonial resource endowments, they reasoned, as did some Spanish political economists, that economic logic dictated that Madrid's policies favor agriculture over industrial development; an industrial base in Spain was unnecessary, they believed, for "a nation possessing mines." Instead, the Spanish state should improve its supervision of the trade and mining sectors of its colonies.[22] Logical, but hardly disinterested.

Raw materials were one side of the diplomatic equation, foreign consumers of French products the other.[23] Since there was, some French businessmen conceded, greater current demand for their products in Spain and its colonies than in France, which had been impoverished by recent revolution and war—some even asserting that "consumption in Spain and its overseas possessions is stronger than in France"—Madrid had to reformulate its tariffs.[24] More moderate (or less aggressive) Frenchmen, some entertaining the notion of a proto–customs union, believed that Madrid should reduce duties on such major French export items as woolens and linens, remove prohibitions on imported cottons and silks, and—the real objective—permit unrestricted silver outflows.[25]

There was a hard core, however, whose members insisted that the Spanish government reaffirm the economic concessions imbedded in the Family Pact of 1761 (what nationalist Spaniards now rejected as "imaginary and useless reciprocity"), some even demanding reaffirmation of concessions Spain had been pressured into granting the Hanse ports in 1647 and of the *convenio de Eminente* and the *pie del fardo* to France in 1659 and 1690.[26] The triumphant postrevolutionary bourgeoisie in France looked back nostalgically, imagining the late seventeenth century under Colbert as the splendiferous era of Franco-Spanish collaboration. It was, moreover, consistent with long-term French policy that Spain preserve its Atlantic trade monopoly, which French analysts pragmatically never considered a true colonial compact: the infrastructure of the metropole's economy remained visibly underdeveloped. Hence, French interest groups would demand repeatedly "important concessions in their colonies," which included turning over territory (Peru), recovering territory (Louisiana), and admitting French shipping and goods in selected Spanish colonial ports, a concession urged by merchants of Nantes, France's main slaving port, and of its major woolen manufacturing center at Abbeville.[27]

The first order of business, of course, was to demand from Spain "first of all the largest possible sum in specie . . . to restore credit in our national paper," in other words, to insist upon the transfer from Spain of "millions de piastres."[28] The mines of Guanajuato and the Mexico City mint—the *odeur des piastres*—would figure prominently in France's relations with Spain in the years between peacemaking at Basel in 1795 and the abdication of the Spanish Bourbons to the Emperor of the French at Bayonne thirteen years later.

Pursuing a Commercial Treaty

Memoirs, dispatches, and observations drafted by French diplomats in Spain from 1795 to 1798 offer a measure of the congruence between French interest groups and foreign policy vis-à-vis Spain and America. In general these diplomatic materials temper the aggressive stance of French manufacturers and exporters toward Spain's domestic and colonial policies by virtue of historical perspective, sensitivity to traditional structures, and the willingness to shape them to French ends with "ménagement."

Paramount is an underlying theme redressing the decline in exports to a country that in the eighteenth century was considered a prime trading partner of France. It was clear, moreover, that the effective trading focus was the colonies in America, for which "Spain" was the surrogate; Spain's attraction to French interests was a function of its "dépendance de l'Amérique."[29] More specifically, the French understood that the silver mines of New Spain and Peru were still major sources of the metropole's and other European nations' income and wealth, since the Spanish transatlantic system forced "America to give up all its silver . . . the sole resource of European commerce." All Europe, therefore, had a stake in sustaining Spain's colonial system. Put another way, Europe's economies found a major outlet for their products in Spain's American colonies, which, in turn, furnished an indispensable instrument of Europe's expanding economy, silver *pesos*.

There were further reasons for helping Spain perpetuate its colonial trade monopoly. First, France, unlike England, lacked the maritime and naval resources to penetrate directly into Spain's transatlantic world on a sustained basis; by default it had to operate within Spain's overseas trade structures. Second, unless Spain maintained its sovereignty in America, consumers there would sooner rather than later reject monopoly pricing of imports for cheaper goods of comparable quality shipped from England and from East Asian and South Asian ports. Unwilling or unable to foresee fully the consequences of England's industrial growth, Frenchmen envisioned a competition limited to quality products from France's and Asia's artisanal workshops. It followed that only rank "amateurs of the human race" would contemplate disrupting Spain's metropole-colony nexus: liberation of its American colonies could have disastrous repercussions throughout Europe's economies. Without the silver of Spain's American colonies, Europe would regress to the status of "un peuple agricole."[30]

France's acceptance of Spain's transatlantic structures did not mean that its recent military victory over Spain should be downplayed in commercial treaty negotiations. It might, in fact, provide leverage to form a new web of relations linking France, Spain's American colonies, and their metropole. French military superiority might curb Spanish economic nationalism, limit England's market penetration, and reorient French diplomacy to satisfy those interests who were convinced that prerevolutionary diplomacy had neglected them. A legacy of victory on land over counterrevolutionary forces in 1795 was France's illusion of hegemony over Spain and its empire and, over the next two decades, the reality of frustration.

According to reports by French agents in Spain, at the core of the decline in France's exports to Spain and America was Spain's economic policy over the three decades of Charles III's reign, that "new regime," as one French agent called it. Under the first of Spain's Bourbon administrations—the age of Philip V, when "those wonderful times of our trade with Spain lasted but a moment"—French fashions and fabrics had stimulated sales of French products. This silvered age ended when Spanish civil servants, recognizing the possibilities in effective rather than nominal dominion of their "Indies," which supplied mainly precious metals, resolved sometime after 1759, under Charles III, to foster manufactures, that is, to "industrialize" the national economy. Spain would supply European goods to its American consumers, retaining silver *pesos* and transforming its economy into "the richest, the most powerful, and the leader of all nations."[31] Had this policy effectively supplied demand in Mexico and Peru, for example, and had the Spanish metropole become both "inventive and hardworking," Europe's manufacturers and merchants might have lost control forever over the sales areas developed after the discovery of America. To French observers, this policy failure was clearly consoling.

Yet, even though economic nationalism had produced little success, Spain's trade barriers—the bête noire of French businessmen and civil servants—remained. The French government, according to critics of its economic policy, had failed to react vigorously, preferring simply to cut back on exports and imports. Meanwhile, exporters in England profited from French passivity and from their collusion with Spain's customs officers, who manipulated regulations to favor English goods, turning France into "a nation proscribed in the eyes of the Spanish government," reduced to the operations of "peddlers selling only smuggled goods." In the eyes of French agents reviewing the interplay of Franco-Spanish economic interests, merchants and diplomatic agents of the prerevolutionary regime stood condemned. Prestigious French firms with long-term Cadiz branches, like the LeCouteulx of Rouen and the Magon of Saint-Malo, had diverted their resources to financial intermediation at Paris, which Spain's new Banco de San Carlos privileged, and preferred to withhold complaint in order to enjoy special treatment from Spanish authorities, who were really assisted by French diplomats maintaining "disgraceful silence." French exporters were weakened further when the Spanish government sided with England in the First Coalition against France, in 1793–95, thereby yielding to England "disgusting supremacy" and sanctioning "monopoly and odious privileges."[32] Tunnel vision may produce contradictions not wholly incompatible; England's technological innovations, as well as its credit and marketing networks, were consistently minimized.

Little unanimity surfaced on how to improve trade with "Spain." Some wanted to pressure Madrid to remove French cottons and silks from the prohibited list; others wanted lower duties or a maximum level of duties on French products well below those of competitor countries.[33] More important, French goods re-exported from Cadiz to the colonies in America (as most were) should be dutied, they insisted, at the same rate as Spanish products; and re-exports of French goods might be encouraged by modifying Spain's insistence on the proportion of one-third foreign to two-thirds domestic goods by value in all exports from the peninsula to the colonies. Of course, there was full agreement on the main objective of French economic policy toward Spain: to reduce England's economic hegemony while expanding specie flows from Spain into France. France's diplomatic agents endorsed the unlimited silver inflow from Spain, since "only this operation can impart to circulation in France the degree of activity it is capable of."[34]

Last of the major trade barriers, there was marked divergence in the recommendations of French diplomats for a commercial treaty or, failing that, a looser convention with Spain. On the one hand, there was the hawkish approach of a former chargé d'affaires at Madrid, the diplomat and author Bourgoing, who urged France's negotiators to operate from a position of domination, to which "our recent victories justify attention."[35] Bourgoing had in mind satisfying the French demands he repeatedly had to process: that French speciality goods, such as hats and silk stockings, along with ready-made clothing, be removed from the list of items prohibited for re-export to the colonies and that the embargo on silver transfers be lifted. Curious, and an example of Bourgoing's extraordinary insensitivity, in view of his awareness of the Spanish government's goal of eliminating unfavorable commercial concessions, was his recommendation to reinstate privileged treatment of French linens and other items covered by the *convenio de Eminente* and the *pie del fardo*—he was particularly intent on lowering the duties on Breton linens—those concessions extracted from Spanish authorities at the end of the seventeenth century and particularly irritating to Spanish economic nationalists in the second half of the eighteenth.

Balancing Bourgoing's views were those of diplomats like Dhermand and Truguet, posted by the Directoire to Madrid. Theirs was a different perspective on how to realize French objectives. Consul general at Madrid in 1796 and subsequently chief of commercial reporting at the Foreign

Office, Dhermand had no hope of pressuring the young, recently appointed and still insecure prime minister, Godoy ("hungering for brilliant innovations"), to abandon a nationalistic economic policy. Dhermand detected widespread Francophobia despite Spaniards' muted recognition that "the prosperity of Spanish commerce is basically tied to that of French commerce." It was thus unrealistic to try to persuade Spanish authorities "to abandon their ruinous mania . . . for supporting sterile manufactures" or to recommend instead a physiocratic focus on population growth and agricultural expansion. It was equally impractical to expect Spain to lower tariff schedules before the country had reestablished financial stability. To offer Spanish negotiators a commercial treaty based on the principle of "réciprocité parfaite" was futile, since they recognized the reality of the "disparity of its territorial and industrial resources" compared with those of France. For two years the English had tried and failed to extract a commercial treaty from Spain, Dhermand reminded the Directoire; it would be better to avoid fruitless negotiations and accept conditions specified in the Family Pact or in treaties of the earlier, seventeenth-century, "that epoch of great splendor."[36]

A similarly realistic approach characterized Truguet, who served for a short time as ambassador to Madrid. He was an odd amalgam of pre-1789 career naval officer, then convinced republican and supporter of the Revolution's ideals. Son of a naval officer, Truguet as a young officer had served in the Caribbean campaigns of 1779–83, during which he made the acquaintance of a Spanish colonial officer who subsequently became "Caracas"'s intendant, Francisco Saavedra. His favorable opinion of Saavedra was confirmed by subsequent contacts at Madrid, first when Saavedra was finance minister and then when he served as prime minister after Godoy resigned in 1798. Truguet went to Madrid convinced that he might, in his words, "carry the torch of philosophy and Reason," and he believed Saavedra to be a kindred spirit. During conversation with him, Truguet learned that Saavedra was "quite decided to realize all the plans for reform," even prepared to confront what always confounded French reformers, "fanatisme." Truguet concluded that this was the moment to cement ties with "notre alliée naturelle" in order to reap advantages that no country but Spain could provide.[37] Hence his optimism about resolving with Spanish counterparts "all outstanding commercial and colonial questions," including the return of Louisiana to France. The two nations, Truguet felt, shared a mutual interest in colonial trade; both had to defend their colonial possessions from "the ambition and . . . treachery of our natural Enemies, the English and the Americans."[38] France could recover from the effects of revolution by improving ties with neighbors like Spain, applying "moderation, fair consideration . . . loyalty" and respecting "religieusement" all treaties. This required posting to Spain committed representatives of France, "true enlightened republicans," rather than "anarchistes et royalistes" hitherto designated under the incoherent Directoire.[39] Truguet wanted Spanish collaborators rather than subalterns.

French Policy Defined: Hauterive

The contradictory opinions that hawkish bourgeois and more moderate diplomats filed with the Directoire and the necessity of having Spain as an ally in France's conflict with England in 1796 (the Second Coalition) explain the failure of the Directoire to obtain a commercial treaty with Spain. France's foreign policy was clarified, however, after Bonaparte's coup d'état of 18 Brumaire 1799 in a well-timed grand design elaborated by the comte d'Hauterive, a respected foreign-affairs expert influenced by former foreign minister Choiseul and an influential figure in the formulation of French policy toward Spain and its Americas. In 1800—five years after the Peace of Basel, four years after the Franco-Spanish defense alliance (San Ildefonso), and only months after the seizure of power by General Napoleon Bonaparte—Hauterive's *De l'état de la France à la fin de l'an VIII* presented to the European reading public what remained for the next decades the most comprehensive blueprint of French political and economic policy, a *direction d'intention,* toward England and western Europe. London immediately recognized its importance, for within a year an English translation appeared.[40]

De l'état de la France was a declaration of France's Spanish policy as well. For many years Hauterive had headed the Foreign Ministry's "Midi" section (covering Spain, Portugal, Genoa, and Turkey), processing correspondence from French representatives at Madrid, Cadiz (one of the French diplomatic service's key consular posts), and elsewhere in the peninsula. Like many upwardly mobile figures whose careers commenced under the Bourbons and continued under the Convention, the Directoire, the Consulat, and the Empire, Hauterive warmed to dynamic titled and nontitled personalities of the old and new regimes, to Colbert ("the true author of the humbling of the nobility") and to Bonaparte ("one who . . . has a great destiny to fulfill").[41] A dedicated *fonctionnaire* of "positive, clear, and practical ideas" and supporter of diplomatic tradition over innovation, Hauterive in social background, career, networks, and overall outlook typified structural continuities in the French civil service. As a contemporary put it deftly, his principles "will reappear henceforth in his reports, in his work in all areas."[42] Talleyrand was the public face of French foreign policy, Hauterive its guiding hand.

One of thirteen children in an upper-level peasant household, perhaps of the "noblesse pauvre de province" in southeastern France (Dauphiné), he was early boarded with a local curate, who later sent him off to an Oratorian *collège* at Grenoble. Teaching at the *collège* years later, he was drawn to and befriended by former foreign minister Choiseul, at whose estate (Chanteloup) he met Talleyrand. Later, while serving as consul at New York in 1793, Hauterive renewed contact there with the émigré Talleyrand.[43] Choiseul's kinship networks and career had made him the center of a faction in France that found in collaboration with Bourbon Spain the way to draw upon the resources of Spain's colonies in the struggle to contain England's imperialism. Through two cousins Choiseul was related to a Nantes slave-trading family, the Walshes. Antoine Walsh was a cofounder of the Compagnie des Indes. Another investor in that company was the grandfather of Choiseul's wife, Antoine Crozat, who in 1717 had planned to use Louisiana to carry on "un commerce reglé avec les Espagnols du Mexique."[44] To many in France's Foreign Ministry in 1797, the incompetence of Choiseul's successors "has brought us to our present state." One suspects that Hauterive's peasant background nourished his faith in agriculture rather than manufacture as the bedrock of the French economy, while his admiration of Choiseul's world-view influenced his broad perspective of the diplomatic relations of France, England, and Europe.

His point of departure was France's extraordinary recovery from the effects of revolution, political instability, and the "guerre de la révolution," a recovery now buttressed by France's military power and economic resilience. These conditions, he judged, made 1800 the moment to formulate what the settlements at Westphalia a century and a half earlier had initiated but England's subsequent growth had undone. Hauterive's *système*—despite his effort to extract universal principles from the historical record—was France-centered.[45] The Westphalian arrangements, he argued, had established for an unexpectedly brief time a "general equilibrium" in Europe founded upon sovereign, independent states and the absence of a superpower (he derided as pure exaggeration criticism of France as a hegemonic power in post-Westphalian Europe). Two related developments had undermined the Westphalian equilibrium: first, Europe's involvement in "spéculations coloniales" and its "système maritime et colonial," altering "the harmony of their political relations"; and second, expansion of the English economy, leading to "the enslavement of all other [nations]" (20–24).

The astonishing growth of England's overseas trade, merchant marine, and naval forces thoroughly upset the Westphalian equilibrium in the second half of the eighteenth century. England's pattern of economic warfare—"the notion of keeping their industry in a permanent state of contradiction and warfare with all other industries"—separating England from Continental interests, began under Cromwell, the "dark conjurer," and the Navigation Acts. Hauterive, a believer in linkage, or "combinaisons sociales," of trade, administration, and government, admired how the Navigation Acts interwove "the power of the state," "the commercial interest of the nation," and private commercial enterprise (27–28, 36). While the linkage was appropriate, Hauterive found that England's unilateral pursuit of national interest—England's hegemony—had upset the European state system, inducing a "partial equilibrium" rather than the more desirable "general equilibrium." England's fusion of trade and government now menaced, in Hauterive's prism, Europe's manufactures and trade by insisting upon its definition of neutrality and appropriate trade controls. Unchecked, England might achieve "une préponderance positive" and "une supériorité de privilège" leading to a Europe "commercialement subjugée" (30, 147). In some key respects, Hauterive was not far off the mark: England's flexible manipulation of its trade controls would endanger Cadiz's access to Veracruz.

By the eve of the French Revolution, England's hegemony had rendered the internal and external relations of the states of Europe "indecisive . . . discordant . . . unstable." The first counterrevolutionary European coalition, of 1793–95, finally shattered the enfeebled European state system. The war of containment against France, organized by England, was the result of Europe's misperceptions of national interest; it ended 150 years of "impolitic lack of foresight . . . blindness." Just as social disorder had produced the French Revolution, Hauterive advanced, so the absence of universally recognized principles and consequent political disorder in the European state system inspired the aggression against France. Here Hauterive singled out and branded Spain as the first monarchy to declare war upon France, although it was "its most indispensable ally" (5, 42, 48).

France's military success and then economic recovery, exaggerated by Hauterive, offered an opportunity to reshape Europe's shattered international order. It was now incumbent upon France "to play the most active, powerful part" in a new international order. Hauterive's proposed "système fédératif continental," designed to support "the independence of the weak" (i.e., "states unequal in power"), was constructed around a powerful core, France, which he insisted posed no threat to European security. It had resisted the First Coalition, only to secure peace and block England's project for an "equilibre partiel"; it had no territorial designs upon neighboring states, since within its own borders were the economic resources undergirding a stable economy (48, 52–54, 106). Unlike England's inherently unstable "industrie commerciale," France's fundamental "industrie agricole" would better withstand unexpected shocks of revolution or war. Further, to a hardmoney advocate like Hauterive, France's financial structure was more securely based upon precious metals, which "stand alone," than was England's, whose "floods of paper monies, treasury, marine, and bank notes" nourished "illusions favoring credit" (249, 269–70).

Of course, there was a political dimension to France's role in Hauterive's conception of the new Europe. By 1800 France had put behind it its phase of "exaltation révolutionnaire"; the bitter clash between "ignorance and enlightenment, passions and principles, institutions and customs" was now over. Recognizing, finally, that the civil service had to draw upon the talents of people of property, many of them among the newly minted *bourgeoisie d'affaires,* Hauterive envisioned the postrevolutionary (presumably Bonapartist) government in France recruiting cadres from "this class, men most capable of participating in the preservation of rights and the administration of the nation's interests." A chain of "social links" had been reforged, and political stability restored, by integrating business and government (334–37). He welcomed the era of rule by class rather than by estate, in which propertied interests of the old and new regimes could be effectively integrated, bringing together, one might venture to say, Hauterive and Talleyrand, LeCouteulx and Ouvrard. Hauterive and Napoleon, career civil servant and military officer, would be eminently complementary, epitomizing the new man forged by the French Revolution and shaping the Grand Empire.

Did the economy and armed forces of France immediately after the Revolution make it a superpower and, like England, a threat to Europe's desired "équilibre général"? Hardly, Hauterive insisted, not because its power was undeniable, but because of the ends to which France was now fully committed. It was in the process of fitting together elements of a new "système fédératif," employing its military superiority only to lay down the foundation for a new "équilibre politique" that would balance the rights and responsibilities of those "states of unequal strength." Capable of overwhelming Spain, invading Holland, and incorporating Genoa, French authorities had chosen instead alliance over conquest. As proof of France's self-imposed territorial restraint, Hauterive singled out its treatment of Switzerland and

Italy after occupation by French troops—visible evidence of the Republic's interest in a real "système fédératif" to ensure "justice . . . guarantee . . . lasting hope" (37, 88). An instance of national interest trumping reality?

The counterpoise to England's hegemony was, therefore, France, its "continentwide federal system" and at its core a "système maritime" uniting Europe's "maritime" states—France, Spain, Holland, and Genoa. Victory in Europe had obligated France, indeed given it the right, to forge a new international order adapted to Europe's current situation and the "existing connections between the parties." From his dissection of English policy Hauterive concluded that the new European order had to fuse "the interest of seaborne commerce with those of continental commerce, between general and national commerce, between national commerce and public power" (44–48, 90–91, 155). The new order's economic basis required a federative navigation act creating a kind of customs union. Shipping and merchandise of member states would profit by equal treatment in respective ports; even coastal shipping would be open to cooperating states. Import restrictions would be rescinded; in an obvious allusion to Spain's tariff policy, Hauterive declared that prohibitions had backfired but that some, however, might be retained as weapons of economic warfare against English competition. In a gesture to calm Spanish interests, he omitted from his customs union the "rule of reciprocity," which would allow the participation of foreign shipping between a metropole and its colonies; that is, he omitted it for the time being. Explicit affirmation of a Europe-wide free-trade zone was purposely left implicit lest it bestir those "interested in preventing the adoption of [these truths]." Obviously, these implicit interests were Spanish authorities, as were those unnamed who "live from day to day . . . seeking to forget in the pleasure or boredom of an inactive existence, the drawbacks of dependence, the vices of dependence, of poverty, and the perils of wickedness" (199–201).

Hauterive's Spanish audience could profit from his historical perspective and from his projected international political and economic order. Of course, no system builder occupying high visibility in the Foreign Office could afford to dilute universal principles with overly explicit references to the shortcomings of would-be member states. There were, however, references to Spain: to the "baleful influence that seeking distant treasures had exerted on Spain's prosperity" (25); to the misery and fiscal disorder following Spain's entry into the First Coalition, against "its most indispensable ally" (44); to past benefits of Franco-Spanish cooperation after the Treaty of the Pyrenees in 1659 (97).

To Spanish authorities seeking to preserve their transatlantic system, however, there were threats implicit in Hauterive's grand design. It required little perspicacity to conclude that Hauterive counterpoised to English imperialism a French variety preaching the unity and independence of weaker European states. Spain's political class could hardly be reassured of French foreign policy if they recalled the comments of a Spanish negotiator at Basel, the canny Francisco Cabarrús, referring candidly to the Directoire's financial record, legislation, and diplomacy as "a model of highway robbery" and to its treatment of occupied Switzerland as "a warning to all other peoples." Another Spaniard, the future viceroy of New Spain, Miguel Azanza, was convinced that the occupation of Switzerland and Italy had inspired French civil servants to contemplate comparable treatment for Spain, "whose conquest . . . and wealth, they said, was the only way to oppose the coalition and conquer all Europe."[46]

Hauterive could be explicit about the interrelationship of member states' economies in his Continental federation, which he defined as "an uninterrupted exchange of all goods." Similar was his striking definition of the territorial boundaries of his coprosperity sphere: "We may truly say that consumers belong less to the nation they live in than to the one whose production they consume . . . the population of any nation whose industry exports what it creates is composed, first of all, of those who consume their home products and, then, of those who consume [products] from elsewhere." To Spanish authorities rejecting reiterated French requests for direct access to ports in the Spanish colonies, this concept posed a real and ever-present menace, enhanced by its explicit intention to mobilize "subventions militaires" against those states refusing to cooperate in his "système fédératif continental" (91–92, 206–7).

Hauterive's design for a European coprosperity sphere, when examined in its colonial projection, was a new tactic for an old strategy to extract commercial concessions from the Spanish government. This was the French negotiators' main concern once hostilities between Bourbon Spain and the French Republic ended at Basel in July 1795, when it was agreed to return to prewar commercial relations, then to plan for a new commercial treaty and—this was implicit—renew the Franco-Spanish alliance.[47] This materialized one year later in the mutual-defense treaty signed at San Ildefonso in August 1796. The trajectory of rapprochement was forecast by England's envoy to Madrid, Bute: "The Treaty of Peace will be shortly followed by a Treaty of Alliance and a Treaty of Alliance by Hostilities."[48]

San Ildefonso was a compromise of French and Spanish shopping lists. French exporters aimed at a more open market in Spain, especially at the major port of Cadiz, where their goods were re-exported to the main colonial markets in America. They were prepared, therefore, to have their government guarantee the integrity of Spain's American colonies—the source of its "richessse et son crédit"—against English and North American pressures. The basis of France's policy toward "Spain" was unambiguous: "It's America who settles all the balances. It is in its entrails that we will be able to liquidate them all. It's a problem of . . . having Spain favor France and deliver to this country preferably what it receives from America."[49] To these desiderata the French government added Spain's naval cooperation as vital in confronting far superior English forces. Alone, France lacked a powerful, wide-ranging navy, which explains Hauterive's emphasis upon maritime and naval cooperation between Spain, Holland, and France. Spain's civil servants and merchants alike saw in French collaboration a major instrument for protecting the Spanish colonies from English aggression; they feared that England might demand New Spain as an "objet de compensation" for its recently lost North American colonies.[50] The mutual concern of Spanish and French authorities in 1795 and 1796 was England's commercial, maritime, and naval hegemony, which imperiled an area where Spain had a direct, and France an indirect, interest: New Spain and the Caribbean, Perú and the colonies in South America. Once England were contained, France's policymakers could pursue their colonial objective; meanwhile, "we must treat [Spain] like an old infant."[51]

San Ildefonso

In the months after Basel, high priority was given to mutual-defense arrangements combined—so the French planned—with efforts to insert into the treaty of defense what they knew Spain's negotiators would try to sidestep: "the germs of a trade treaty." The choice of French commercial experts, the draft of a treaty, instructions from the Directoire (Foreign Minister Delacroix in particular) to the French ambassador at Madrid (General Pérignon)—all were evidence of the French ministry's intention to inject into the defense treaty major economic clauses. "Our goal," Delacroix clarified for Pérignon, "is to ensure the continuation of the spirit of the old family pact in those clauses that favor the commerce of the two nations."[52]

One of the experts assigned to draft the treaty was Dhermand, who was experienced in Franco-Spanish trade negotiations. In what was probably Dhermand's draft, eight of twenty-one articles referred directly or indirectly to trade issues, an indication of their real importance compared with those committing Spain to join France in a war with England or specifying the nature of the defense collaboration to be made. The territorial integrity of the two countries, in Europe and overseas, would be guaranteed by diplomatic action and, if necessary, by military and naval contingents. The French hoped to press Spain to return Louisiana, in order to make it an effective buffer protecting Spain's most important colony, New Spain, from merchants and settlers infiltrating from the United States. Not only was Spain's colonial world to be defended but France would insist on renovating Spain's transatlantic trade system to stop England's "violations and depredations . . . introduced in the trade of its colonies." Those possessions would continue to absorb French manufactures; hence clauses were inserted in the draft that in effect would weaken Spain's tariff schedules by lifting prohibitions on certain French products, stipulating prior mutual agreement for the insertion of new prohibitions, publishing new customs regulations, and imposing a duty cap of 10 percent of the prime cost on all domestic products exchanged. The intention of the French draft was indicated by a revealing marginal note appended to the article eliminating certain prohibitions: "We sidestepped discussing the liberty of commerce so as not to disturb Spanish principles, but the wording of the article is equivalent."[53]

The Directoire's instructions to Ambassador Pérignon fleshed out the underlying argument of the draft treaty, highlighting the preoccupation of French interests with Spain's weakness as a colonial power in the face of England's overwhelming resources—its merchant marine (4,000), seamen (100,000), and 1.5 million tons of shipping, compared with 1,100 ships totaling 175,000 tons for the rest of the Atlantic world. Delacroix's instructions also reveal anxiety over the defense of Spain's wealthiest colony, New Spain.[54] Spain, he wrote Pérignon, had failed to administer Louisiana efficiently after 1763; instead of turning it into a "barrière pour le Mexique," Spain had instead left it in a "stagnant condition, in which that colony's population and crafts have remained," in sharp contrast to the dynamism and "insatiable avidité des Américains." Delacroix prophesied colonial instability. "If Spain's colonial system is indispensable for controlling its interior provinces, it is not applicable to a province that should be a barrier against a constantly advancing people." This, he concluded, justified the return of Louisiana to France, "especially destined to guarantee a balance in America," because in French hands it would be used to defend Spain's most vital colonial area, New Spain. The emphasis on recovering Louisiana points up the critical role the French government assigned that territory: to wall off New Spain from U.S. expansionists and to serve as a base for recovering French influence in the Caribbean, which had been gravely compromised by the Haitian rebellion. To put to rest Spanish fear of French imperialism in America, along with lingering doubts of "our capabilities and . . . our fidelity to our responsibilities," Pérignon was to inform Spain's negotiators that France would uphold Spain's system of "commerce colonial exclusif."[55] "Liberté de commerce" went unmentioned.

In fact, the Treaty of San Ildefonso produced far less than the French hoped for, given their evident military superiority, their careful preparation for negotiations, and their economic goals. They obtained agreement only on matters of defense, mainly because the threat from England was paramount: the first fourteen articles guaranteed the integrity of the allies' "States, territories, islands, and marketplaces" and specified types and quantities of military and naval assistance to be available on demand. Two articles would shortly have an unsuspected importance: one stipulating assistance even when one party had no direct involvement in the other's conflicts and one requiring its ally to pay full maintenance costs for military and/or naval units stationed in its ally's "territory or ports." Of the treaty's nineteen articles, only the fifteenth mentioned one of the core objectives of the French negotiators: a commercial treaty, "to be arranged soon," that would offer most-favored-nation status in agricultural and industrial products and provide protection for neutral shipping in wartime.[56]

Factors other than England's economic and naval resources explain the willingness of France's negotiators to postpone the all-important commercial treaty. There was the possibility that once Spain halted commercial contacts with England in wartime, French exporters might "take possession once again of Spain's principal markets." Second, persistent pressure from the French government for trade concessions might lead Spanish authorities to dam "that river of gold that French industry is beginning to channel from the heights of the Pyrenees into the south of our Republic." The less overt pressure, the better: "France has little to gain from tangling with Spain; and she has much to lose."[57] Disheartened at failing to sign simultaneously a mutual-defense accord and a treaty of commerce, Ambassador Pérignon recommended that the Directoire quickly call upon "three well-known merchants from Cadiz, Marseilles, and Bordeaux to come up with a plan."[58] The choice of ports suggests the nodules of French exchanges with Spain. This recommendation, however, was not pursued.

Thus, once again Spain's representatives succeeded in sidelining what they envisioned as an inevitable and by now traditional outcome, an unequal treaty of commerce. Yet, although avoiding commercial concessions, Madrid could not stop French merchants from "arranging to have *pesos* come from Spain."[59] The financial burden of the defense treaty—stationing Admiral Mazarredo's fleet at Brest in 1799 and, in 1803, the requirements of the agreed-upon subsidy—would lead to the involvement (or, more appropriately perhaps, entanglement) of France's Trésor Public with Ouvrard's Négociants Réunis in Spanish and Mexican finance.

Signed on 18 August 1796, the treaty of mutual defense or assistance went into effect when Spain entered the second Anglo-French conflict—in effect, the Second Coalition against France—this time to support the French Republic. Over the next seven years of warfare (1796–1801) and peace (1801–3), the common enemy drew together the Spanish monarchy and the French Republic, while unequal economic structures kept them apart. The prospect of a French-dominated coprosperity sphere could not win support from merchants at Cadiz and Barcelona, and certainly not from Catalan protoindustrialists insisting upon an unmodified Spanish transatlantic system. Promises of economic collaboration in the treaties of Basel—the return to pre-1793 economic relations—and San Ildefonso were not realized, nor did Spaniards dissipate what the French considered inveterate Francophobia, that counterpart of Anglomania. In hearing the complaints of France's agents at Cadiz and Madrid, Spanish civil servants maintained an anti-French stance, surreptitiously preferring English merchants and goods, harassing French merchants, shipping, and goods, and in general welcoming counterrevolutionary émigrés and pro-English sentiments. They found Spanish military and civil servants complacent with respect to the English: "There is hardly any governor, garrison commander, any civil or military official, any judge or employee, that the English have not won over."[60] The French government and businessmen wanted Spain and its American possessions to be subordinate rather than coequal; the Spanish government's policy of maneuvering between two major imperialist powers—the hallmark of Godoy's administration—was, the French thought, simply incomprehensible and, in point of fact, favored the presumed common enemy. So the Franco-Spanish alliance satisfied neither, and what the French considered most desirable—a commercial treaty and direct access to the consumers of those colonial possessions in America—was skillfully parried by Madrid.

French Expansionism

The coup d'état at Paris in late 1799, installing a remarkably competent military commander and astute politician as first consul in the regime superseding the Directoire, led inexorably to the reaffirmation of French economic nationalism and ultimately to economic aggression—to "overseas expansion," as Fugier put it, and to "the influence or the political domination of the continent."[61] In addition to the Parisian banking and merchant groups backing the coup (Bonaparte coveted the title of "restorer of commerce"), he courted, and was courted by, manufacturers and exporters who wished to exploit the economic and especially the financial position of Spain and its colonies overseas in the Western Hemisphere. After trade surpluses with Spain in some years after Basel, in 1801 France had a deficit, and exchanges with Spain and its colonies figured large in France's aggregate foreign trade.[62] Spain's colonies were ever more inviting and necessary as consumers of French textiles and luxury goods and as *the* source of silver, not to mention the tropical staples like sugars, molasses, coffee, and indigo that Saint-Domingue had supplied before 1792. That Caribbean colony had also been a major distribution point for smuggling French goods into Spain's Caribbean ports in exchange for silver, a function now virtually absorbed by Jamaica. The coterie around General Bonaparte, including personnel like Hauterive and Talleyrand, former residents in ex-colonial Philadelphia and exposed to former foreign minister Choiseul's colonialist vision, could remind him of Spain's possessions in the western Atlantic. Moreover, diplomatic reporting from Spain reinforced the French perception of a faction-ridden bureaucracy and political class there, incompetently administrating both the metropole and its empire; this perception was reinforced by reports from Madrid of a reactionary clergy and incompetent aristocracy, which Francisco Goya's etchings vividly portrayed. To French *fonctionnaires* and men of business, the neighbor beyond the Pyrenees lacked organization and administrative efficiency, and if Spain did not mend its ways, then "the results would be terrible for the Spanish monarchy," as Talleyrand remarked to General Bonaparte's brother Lucien, who was on his way to his Madrid ambassadorship.[63] Bonaparte's aggressive bent was, if anything, carefully stoked by French business interests.

Spain's domestic and colonial economies became a critical issue in 1802, when the peace signed at Amiens ended the French government's second major conflict with England and its coalitions since 1789. Despite Hauterive's proposal for extensive economic collaboration among Europe's "maritime" nations, Bonaparte's Consulat gave priority to France's economic recovery by stressing protectionism while decrying comparable Spanish measures. Madrid's trust in the realliance with France was not strengthened when French representatives at Amiens were willing to shift Spanish Trinidad to English sovereignty, while pressing Spain to return Louisiana to French control. Both positions indicated a low priority for the principle of territorial integrity spelled out in the San Ildefonso treaty of mutual assistance. Nor was Spanish anxiety lessened by French protests over Spanish protectionism: that Spain, in violation of San Ildefonso agreements, failed to lower tariffs on French products to pre-1793 levels; that Madrid in fact had raised barriers to French cotton textiles and discriminated against French shipping, resident merchants, and seamen in favor of English shipping, merchants, and goods.

The litany was hardly new except for the vigor with which French complaints were pressed, along with their timing. The sudden trade deficit of 1801, when Spain absorbed 70 percent of France's exports and provided 76 percent of its imports, becoming France's major trade partner, was attributed to longstanding Spanish tariff schedules and continued prohibitions.[64] Jean Chaptal, then interior minister under the Consulat, was ordered to draft a commercial treaty with Spain. Other collaborators, enthused by reports of the wealth of New Spain, its silver and its high consumption propensities, described by Ouvrard's brother after visiting Mexico City and the mining center of Guanajuato, reminded Bonaparte of Spain's "overriding importance." And there was General Bonaparte's new envoy to Madrid, General Beurnonville, a tepid convert to the Consulat, who preferred to be addressed as "M. le Comte," a career military officer and colonel under the Bourbon monarchy and marshal under the Republic in 1792 who had participated in Bonaparte's coup d'état.[65] To Bonaparte, partisan of economic expansionism, married to a woman raised in France's Caribbean plantation world of sugar and slavery, domination and luxury, it was convenient that Beurnonville had prepared a jeremiad against Spain's "système d'oppression et de récrimination" aimed at French interests, that "they skin French citizens with impunity," that "they render retroactive prohibitive regulations," causing customs warehouses in Spain's ports to fill up with "French goods withheld or confiscated." Beurnonville's critique ended with an appeal to Bonaparte: "Citoyen Premier Consul, commerce protests and expects from you the protection it merits." He begged Bonaparte "to apply to that country your regenerative influence" if the Spanish government failed to respond favorably to reasonable proposals.[66]

On the other hand, French protectionism, galling to Spanish interests, took concrete form in July 1802 in the form of increased rates on imports of colonial staples that discriminated between those arriving from French colonies and those arriving from Spain and other sources.[67] It exemplified what the Spanish economist José Canga Argüelles interpreted as the product of France's recent navigation act, tariffs, and prohibitive legislation, framed "to increase its power at the expense of its allies and by breaking the most solemn agreements."[68] Since Spain was a large re-exporter of colonial staples such as sugar, indigo, and hides, whose production had grown over the second half the eighteenth century, France's new tariff schedules seemed specifically to screen out Spain's re-exports in violation of reciprocity in the commercial clauses of the San Ildefonso treaty. Its new policy, according to Canga Argüelles, contradicted France's publicly professed desire to stimulate intra-European exchanges. Or was it an only indicative of impatience with Madrid's deft sidestepping a commercial treaty? It was, at any rate, a kind of trade war between two ostensible allies.

Madrid's trade experts, for their part, had been scanning changing European tariff schedules since 1801 and concluded that France's policy gave Spanish exporters "better reasons for complaint and annoyance" than did the policies of any other European nation. Relying on military omnipotence, France's policy toward allies was *"impose shackles . . . and impoverish them."*[69] At least so it seemed to Finance Minister Miguel Cayetano Soler and Canga Argüelles, who was a trade specialist in his ministry, both men emblematic of the economic nationalism widespread in their country since the first decade of the long reign of Charles III and currently evident in publications and manuscripts. Promulgation of the revised French tariff schedule galvanized Soler to ask Canga Argüelles to make a comparative analysis of French and Spanish customs schedules and trade regulations based upon hard data—"information and . . . documents." Canga Argüelles, drawing upon a database of France's *Code de commerce, Bibliothèque commercial, Encyclopédie diplomatique, Annales des arts et manufactures,* Peuchet's *Dictionnaire,* and the official *Moniteur,* produced an analysis that underscored France's discrimination against Spain and its benefits to French exporters and shipowners.[70]

At the outset Canga Argüelles tried to formulate the rationale behind France's recent tariff revisions: "Since French manufactures have felt the effects of a long and costly war, and the revolution has reduced the number of its colonies, . . . this explains why the French government has expedited exports of French goods . . . and insists on . . . exclusive sales."[71] These revisions, he claimed, undermined reciprocity in the international division of labor dear to Spanish economists of the late eighteenth century, who had banked on the long-neglected potential of export agriculture in the American colonies. If France shipped manufactures to "Spain," reciprocity dictated that it import Spain's wines, wools, cotton, olive oil, and soda ash, along with the riches coming from its colonies. He substantiated his analysis with statistical tables tracing changes in French tariffs on colonial staples from 1788 to 1801. These showed reductions over the period 1788 to 1792, when the Convention had passed its navigation act; in 1802, however, under the decidedly protectionist Consulat, headed by General Bonaparte, French duties on imports of Spanish and other foreign sugar, coffee, and cocoa had been 1,250–1,500 percent higher than on French colonial staples. Characteristically, the rates on raw materials needed in France's leading manufacture—cotton and indigo—had been only slightly higher. Clearly, Canga Argüelles noted, the French had had no interest in stimulating production of sugar in Cuba or cocoa in Venezuela, which contradicted their presumed interest in maintaining good relations with their neighbor and "guaranteeing the possession of its colonies."[72] In the same vein, he found that the French tariff discriminated against Spanish shipping in French ports. For example, a 150-ton French vessel in a Spanish port paid a tax per ton of 295 *reales de vellón,* while a Spanish ship of comparable size in a French port paid more than twelve times as much. In fact, pursuit of such protectionism by a self-styled ally would oblige Spain to disrupt its plans. An official representation by Madrid to Paris was explicit: Spaniards, Prime Minister Godoy wrote to the French foreign ministry, had found that "Spain's trade has barely been protected in France, where the French have repelled Spaniards and disregarded their requests."[73]

Exasperation and impotence are the bitter tea of the weak on the table of unequal exchange. Madrid's authorities had failed in their protests against the French tariff modifications. In the next phase, to prepare countermeasures Finance Minister Soler asked Canga Argüelles to provide specifics on the French revisions; once he had Canga Argüelles's report in hand, Soler had to take action. Rhetoric aside, reciprocity between a powerful state and a weak one forced the weaker to retaliate by subterfuge. "We lack power," Soler confessed candidly to Canga Argüelles, and they must therefore avoid antagonizing head-on the "enemy of our happiness," lest they irritate the "unfriendly powerful neighbor"—virtually the advice of a head of the Colonial Office three decades earlier, José de Gálvez. Soler then directed Canga Argüelles to consult others secretly in order to draft a stage-by-stage readjustment of Spanish rates. Under no circumstances was a new tariff schedule to be published; instead, Canga Argüelles would issue the revisions on his own authority. The Spanish labyrinth of unpublished customs regulations and duties and the seemingly idiosyncratic patterns of its customs officers— typical Spanish chicanery in the view of impatient French exporters—were in reality weapons of a weak state operating according to its own "methodical plan for innovations that ought to be achieved in the most convenient fashion."[74] This operational style had forestalled the commercial treaty promised in 1795 and still unrealized in 1802.

The Price of Neutrality: The *Subside Convenable*

Yet another approach remained whereby the French government might obtain New Spain's coveted silver, and it was essayed in May 1803, when France and England again went to war. Paris demanded immediately that Madrid honor a commitment in the San Ildefonso treaty of mutual assistance: a subsidy in lieu of troops. Superficially, this could be a quick fix for France's financial problems in wartime and for Spain's weak defense posture, and it highlighted the centrality of New Spain's silver in the Spanish economy and in French military operations in central Europe. It confirmed, moreover, the French government's illusion of Spain's colonial wealth, provided that its imperial system were efficiently administered, by France if necessary.

Again, a broad context may explain France's preference for a subsidy over army and naval contingents promised in the Franco-Spanish treaties. The mutual-assistance treaty of 1796 had drawn Spain into revolutionary France's second war with England, a conflict that had already drained Spain's financial resources. For the first time since 1782, Madrid's pipeline to a major source of its public and private wealth—its American colonies and especially New Spain—was seriously compromised. The impact upon Madrid's fiscal and commercial sectors has already been analyzed: the progressive secularization of specific church holdings and the recourse to *comercio neutro* despite the vigorous opposition of traders at Cadiz, Veracruz, and Mexico City. The pivotal factor in the viability of trade by neutrals, an independent variable, was the English government's toleration of neutral shipping from neutral ports in northern Europe and the United States, permitting limited contact between Spain and its main colonial ports of Veracruz, Havana, La Guayra, and Cartagena.

After the settlement at Amiens in 1802, government finance in Spain and France improved. Peace revived one of western Europe's busiest Atlantic ports, Cadiz, where shipping from the colonies in the western Atlantic brought cargoes of staples and unprecedented consignments of precious metals on government and private account, funds and raw materials retained abroad for safekeeping during the English blockade.[75] Here was substantiation, if it were needed, of the necessity of open maritime communications between the metropole in Spain and its Caribbean ports in wartime, the overriding necessity of neutral status and shipping when Europe's superpowers conflicted. "Neutrality," the secretary of the Cadiz *consulado* wrote a high civil servant and former merchant in New Spain at the close of 1803, could provide that "peace essential for Commerce."[76] A neutral Spain, moreover, could afford France's manufacturers and exporters indirect access to Spain's colonial markets through its transatlantic system, along with the possibility of fewer complaints about Spain's tariff schedules and customs regulations. Neutral status might also ensure the flow of silver from New Spain, whose mines and high consumption levels had dazzled the brother of financier–war contractor–speculator Ouvrard on his visits to Guanajuato and Mexico City. By improving its financial situation, the Consulat might better underwrite renewed military operations, which, despite the respite of Amiens, were assumed to be inevitable; and the estimated budgetary shortfall of 1802–3 might be lowered with the assistance of silver from America forwarded to Paris from Madrid. The personal financial rewards to Lucien Bonaparte during his brief stint as Napoleon's emissary to Madrid left few doubting Madrid's (and, for that matter, New Spain's) financial possibilities.[77]

On taking control in 1799, the Consulat lacked the funds to finance French naval operations in the South Atlantic off the Rio de la Plata. On request, Madrid—as it had done to subsidize France's support of the North American insurgents in the early 1780s—assigned funds to France, in this case 1.5 million *pesos,* through the Hacienda agent at Paris, Martínez de Hervás, a friend of fellow speculator and now France's foreign minister, Talleyrand. To pragmatic, highly placed French *fonctionnaires,* including the first consul, if the Spanish government now plead poverty when asked for financial support for its ally at war, this would demonstrate ill will toward the new France, or at best, proof of its "total incapacity to take advantage of its wealth."[78]

And a neutral Spain had more advantages for France. One of the strong points of the San Ildefonso treaty was the size of Spain's navy; the combined Franco-Spanish squadrons constituted a force roughly equivalent to one-third of England's—hardly overwhelming, yet not to be dismissed. On the other hand, French naval officers' assessment of Spain's naval establishment at bases at Cadiz and other peninsular ports was poor. Perhaps the most attractive spin-off of the Spanish fleet harbored at Brest was superprofits to *munitionnaires* like Ouvrard. As we have seen, the trail of New Spain's silver had brought Ouvrard from Brest to Paris and on to Madrid, and his brother to New Spain. Finally, were Spain to remain neutral, and London respectful of that status, there might be no English assault upon Spain's American colonies. England's capture of Trinidad in 1797 had led France to acquiesce to its formal transfer to English sovereignty, despite the Franco-Spanish agreement to maintain the integrity of Spain in America. Most important, if France accepted the neutrality of Spain, it might also tolerate the neutrality of England's dependent ally, Portugal. It was then widely held that French occupation of Portugal would surely trigger retaliation in the form of English occupation of Brazil's ports and, in the domino theorizing of that era, penetration into the Rio de la Plata and the flight of the Portuguese royal family to Brazil. Viewed in this broad context, the subsidy clauses in the Franco-Spanish treaty of 1803, much like Spain's expected contribution to Hauterive's coprosperity model, depended not upon Spain but upon its colonies, mainly New Spain.

Logically, then, upon renewing hostilities with England in May 1803, French officials preferred a financial contribution from their neutral ally rather than the military and naval support stipulated in the treaty of 1796 in order to cover present and foreseeable budgetary outlays. Since the thousands of men in the expeditionary corps sent to Saint-Domingue under Bonaparte's brother-in-law, Leclerc, had failed to suppress that insurgency, the French government concluded that there was no point in retaining Louisiana, which Spain had just returned reluctantly to France in 1800 on the premise (and promise) that it would be kept as a buffer between the silver mines of New Spain and expansionist elements in the United States. With what was by now characteristic arrogance, the Consulat promptly sold Louisiana to the United States in May 1803, netting roughly 50 million francs. A monthly subsidy from Madrid of 4–6 million francs over one year would alone deliver virtually the same amount. At the end of May, Talleyrand approached his friend Martínez de Hervás, diplomat, banker, and now father-in-law of General Bonaparte's army colleague General Duroc, to fix Spain's financial contribution as a neutral ally.[79]

Was it more than coincidence that in the same month, on learning of the imminent arrival at Cadiz of 79.5 million francs in silver (37.5 on government account) shipped from New Spain,[80] Paris requested the promised monthly subsidy of 6 million francs, 2 million to be retained by Spain to cover outstanding French claims. When Madrid's response was delayed, Bonaparte—encouraged by Talleyrand's assumption that Madrid could readily afford the *subside convenable*—demanded the subsidy, modifications of Spanish tariffs to facilitate the re-export of French cottons to the American colonies, and the long-postponed commercial treaty. The French government wanted to know, and quickly, "where we are with Spain."[81] No longer able to stall the French, Spanish officials had to decide on a course of action.

Spain's decision is known, but how it was engineered remains obscure. There was one proposal that Godoy asserted he laid on the table, and there was a counterproposal by other high officials. Since Godoy's version is available only in the memoirs he published decades later to justify his administrative and political role, the proposal is suspect. Fugier's otherwise meticulous coverage of this period makes no mention of Godoy's version. At any rate, Godoy claims that in fulfillment of his country's commitment to the alliance and to bypass overt financing of French military operations, he offered an "experiment in free trade" for the duration of hostilities. He sketched a kind of customs union whose tariffs would be low and that omitted mutual prohibitions on imports and/or re-exports. From this arrangement French exporters would receive two advantages: access to Spain's "colonial staples and goods" for distribution in France and continental Europe and opportunities to form mutually profitable Franco-Spanish business partnerships for overseas trade. On balance, Godoy had simply re-formulated the French practice of operating inside Spain's transatlantic trade system, just as his *comercio libre* connoted no more and no less than what had already been legislated.[82]

Godoy's proposal was carefully nuanced, reflecting a practical assessment of the Spanish economy. As he noted, some Spanish manufacture would be protected (he calculated the French might tolerate this); in the case of other manufactures, Godoy believed—as had Dupont de Nemours when defending the Anglo-French commercial treaty of 1786—that inefficient domestic monopolies needed exposure to competition or, in some instances, limited subsidies. Besides, he acknowledged realistically, Spain remained essentially an agricultural nation exporting domestic and colonial staples, whether fine new wools or "our very valuable colonial products." Franco-Spanish commercial enterprises could be an improvement, Godoy advanced, over the colonial trade monopoly, which was no longer sustainable without undermining colonial loyalties—"without displeasing them and alienating their hearts."[83] His seeming grasp of one of the most explosive issues in the American colonies just before their independence, the imperial trade monopoly belatedly masked as *comercio libre,* may reflect merely the sensitivity of hindsight that his memoires provided.

Godoy's startling concession of an "experiment in free trade" circulated among cabinet officers, since it covered "very serious matters . . . of economics and finance." Predictably, it was criticized by Foreign Minister Pedro Cevallos, Justice Minister Caballero, and other tradition-bound nationalists (in 1808, opponents of Godoy), who found it detrimental to domestic manufacture; they all warned that it would increase unemployment and possibly lead to urban riots. Charles IV, who had vivid memories of the violent Madrid *motín* of 1766 against Hacienda Minister Esquilache, turned down Godoy's proposal and accepted instead Cevallos's proposal for the financial subsidy. England, assured Cevallos who prided himself on his knowledge of European diplomacy and international law, would tolerate subsidy payments that a neutral Spain had promised its ally by treaty. During October and November 1803 a Franco-Spanish subsidy was negotiated, Spain agreeing to send monthly payments of 4 million francs (about 800,000 *pesos fuertes*) to France's Trésor Public. Within weeks the Consulat demanded immediate payment of the previous five months' subsidy, 20 million francs. Otherwise, an army corps stationed near the Spanish border at Bayonne would remain.[84]

Pivotal to the execution of this treaty—the independent variable—was the attitude of London. To be sure, during hostilities of the Second Coalition, from 1797 to 1801, the English government had respected neutral shipping crossing the Atlantic to Spain's colonial ports at Veracruz, Havana, Cartagena, and Montevideo, ensuring the brief success of the Spanish policy of *comercio neutro,* but there was no monthly subsidy transferable from Veracruz and other ports across the Atlantic to Cadiz and then on to France. The international scene had changed since Amiens: now not only was there an extraordinary volume of silver moving from the New World to the Spanish metropole and, if the terms of the subsidy were met, to France's Trésor Public but England confronted a government in France that was better organized than under the Directoire and aggressively pushing French economic interests in Europe and overseas. Initially lacking the treaty's details, London appeared to tolerate the concept of a "war subsidy." However, once it became clear that the flows of silver might move indefinitely from America to Spain and on to France, the English government resolved "to detain all ships laden with silver for Spain" and put the resolution immediately into effect in late 1804, prior to a formal declaration of hostilities with Spain.[85]

An English squadron's peacetime seizure of Spanish warships bearing millions of silver *pesos* from Montevideo brought public expressions of shock by officials at Madrid. In fact, it could hardly have been a surprise, given Spaniards' perceptions of the English government's recent policies and attitudes. For instance, in joint Anglo-Spanish naval operations against France in the First Coalition, 1793–95, Spanish officers had resented the English navy's high-handed treatment of Spain's cooperating warships at Toulon, the seizure of Spanish ships as prizes of war, and the activity of English smugglers near Spain's colonial ports, all of which worsened subsequently with English expansion in the Caribbean, notably the occupation of Trinidad in 1797. On the other hand, Spain's rapprochement with France under the Directoire, continued under the aggressive Consulat, did threaten

English interests in western Europe. It required little imagination to foresee English countermeasures against both the Consulat and its allies. Was Cevallos's faith—if indeed it was faith—in England's respect for neutrality provisions (embedded in treaties) justified? Once London concluded that silver subsidies to the French war machine might continue indefinitely, Spain's neutrality became a fragile commodity.

The veteran Anglophobe and now retired diplomat Bernardo Iriarte— brother of Spain's chief negotiator in peacemaking with France at Basel in 1795—jotted down in February 1804 his confused and bemused wonderment at news of the subsidy payments: "Daily one sees extraordinary things done by the government, incomprehensible and contradictory. Typical is the Real Subsidio," crafted to preserve Spain's neutrality. "However," he asked himself realistically, "is it possible that England will fail to consider it an indirect act of war by providing its foe with the means to do so?" His prediction followed: "Finally they will force us to enter the conflict, and *as a preliminary act they will seize some of our ships returning from our Indies with funds*" (emphasis added). Months later, on 12 November, his irrepressible "habit of reflection . . . and writing, which obliges me to make my voice heard by reaching for the nearest pen," led him to jot down, "My earlier prediction that ultimately we will have to go to war has proven correct."[86] It is not hard to imagine the disillusionment, bordering on despair and cynicism, of Iriarte, a nationalist wary of England's economic and naval power ever since his service in Spain's London embassy in the late 1750s, ever hopeful that governmental and private groups in France might respect Spain's aspirations for international status as a resurgent and economically viable ally.

The Decision to Intervene

In mid-1805 France's military strategy was focused on driving into central Europe, toward Austria and Prussia. Spain was left to arrange the movement of silver, now mainly from Veracruz under neutral "covers," and supplies of raw materials. The symbiosis of Spain's colonial economy with France's war economy was viable only as long as the English navy respected the international principle of the freedom of neutral shipping in wartime. We have already noted the indispensable role of Madrid's contracts with firms in neutral ports of Europe and the United States, even with firms at London, in preserving maritime communication between the colonies and their Spanish metropole. As the conflict intensified, Spain's colonial roots were at grave risk, particularly after 1805.

One measure of that risk was the policies of France and England toward Portugal. All understood that if French strategy eliminated Portugal's neutral status by military occupation, a strategy necessitating the movement of troops through northwestern Spain and sustained logistical support, London would retaliate. Mindful of the pivotal role of a neutral Portugal, Godoy hastened to remind Bonaparte in late 1806 of an informal understanding between Madrid and London that England, "as reward for our consideration of the court at Lisbon, . . . would respect our colonies in America."[87] The form of London's retaliation was predictable, given the size, mobility, and firepower of the English navy, just magnified by "a decisive and total victory" at Trafalgar, when a saddened and despairing Iriarte like most Spaniards had to absorb the reality that "our fleet has been totally destroyed, every bit of it."[88] There the myth of Spain as a naval power was dissipated, opening the most critical epoch after three hundred years of Spanish colonialism in America.

Confirmation of England's hegemony over Atlantic seaways meant a free hand at last to penetrate the Iberian colonial economies through uninterrupted direct contact for marketing products now blocked from European consumers by French economic controls and to access precious metals. Now English exporters could expand smuggling off the coasts of Spain's colonies in and around the Caribbean, in the South Atlantic, and along the Pacific coast; if necessary, English amphibious forces could assault major colonial ports. Few underestimated the mobility of England's naval forces. When it was rumored that an English fleet of one hundred ships escorting twenty thousand soldiers had put to sea in March 1805, it was assumed that the target was Havana, "and from there to send expeditionary forces wherever they choose." English joined by "Anglo-American" forces would then "become masters of our overseas colonies," wrote one of Iriarte's correspondents, adding, "What a dismaying thought."[89] For their part, French commercial groups, searching for joint status with Spanish merchants and shippers along the lines of the federative system publicized by Hauterive, could revive their strategy of operations within Spain's managed transatlantic trade. This pattern of economic cooperation was viscerally distrusted by Cadiz oligopolists.

Those commercial interests already prominent in French government policymaking before 1806 now brought into clear focus the unbounded opportunities in the Iberian Peninsula and, far more important, in Spain's colonies of New Spain and Cuba. This became clear between mid-1807 and mid-1808, that critical moment of Spanish imperialism in the western Atlantic, when the interests of business and government in France coalesced behind the military machine pushing into central Europe; it could also be directed into the Iberian states and, through them, to their colonies in America. Direct military intervention by France, supported by factions within Spain itself, might achieve what both the Franco-Spanish alliance and the ever-postponed treaty of commerce had failed to produce, namely, efficient administration in the peninsula and colonies, financial solvency, and, through judicious economic cooperation, at least postponement of insurgency in Spain overseas. This French utopia of a colonial coprosperity sphere, explicitly articulated in early 1808 as the French army crossed the Pyrenees, was not, however, widely shared in Spain by men of business and the political class. Theirs was a more pragmatic vision of the fate of Spain's colonial world if they yielded such major concessions. Long before, many had foreseen that, when necessary, England would mobilize resources either to occupy strategic areas or to sponsor insurgents in America. This prophetic vision no doubt fueled the anxiety of Spain's chief of state, Godoy, when, in November 1805, it was reported that "his anxiety about the Spanish colonies is stronger than ever."[90]

Godoy's anxiety was justified as Spain and its empire were ground between English and French millstones. On the one hand, French economic policy became overtly expansionist, seeking to displace English exporters wherever they were dominant,[91] while an increasingly insolvent government at Madrid was under pressure to make overdue payments on its subsidy. On the other hand, disaster at Trafalgar highlighted the tenuous maritime links between Spain and its major colonial ports at Veracruz and Havana, Montevideo and Buenos Aires, and the reality of suspended transfers of colonial silver. The reach of England's naval power, awesome before Trafalgar, was now confirmed by reports of English troops occupying Buenos Aires in September 1806. It was all predictable, to be sure, but nonetheless unnerving to policymakers in Spain. Informed, worried Spaniards immediately concluded that "this alone means that we may already have lost Chile, Lima, Potosí . . . now it will be impossible to trade with them."[92] French observers decided that the loss of Buenos Aires would ignite "the great coming revolution menacing the Spanish monarchy" unless there were broad improvements in the administrative apparatus.[93]

Long in doubt of the Spanish government's commitment to mutual defense and troubled by what they likened to fiscal incompetence and military and naval impotence, French officials felt even more unsure of Madrid's cooperation after they analyzed a vaguely worded, patriotic manifesto issued over Godoy's signature in October 1806, urging the Spanish peoples to prepare to counter an unspecified "enemy."[94] Coming only weeks after the unsettling news of the fall of Buenos Aires, the ambiguous proclamation expressed the dilemma facing a weakening metropolitan government that was incapable of maintaining contact with its overseas possessions: whether to support the alliance with France, which was insistent on major economic concessions in the colonies, or to turn to an equally aggressive England in order to avoid further colonial losses. Hesitant Spanish authorities could not resolve this dilemma; the decision was left to the more powerful neighbor north of the Pyrenees. Sometime in late 1806 French policy jelled: the solution for handling a reluctant Spanish ally whose military and naval potential was now minimal and whose economic cooperation was at best grudging was military occupation and a change of regime. The Spanish Bourbon monarchy, like the French, would have to go. Typically French was the rationalization of force: peninsular and colonial modernization would come through sound administration: "Just twenty years of perfect administration will be enough to restore [the Spanish empire] to the level of the greatest empires."[95]

Administration was a code word for the power to radically reorient Madrid's economic policies. Now the French contemplated a kind of satellization[96] to stimulate Spain's colonial economies, capture government revenues lost through fiscal mismanagement, and transform Spain into "the richest power in Europe" and a profitable partner for the French economy. Bonaparte, who was presumably the "acteur principal" in shaping France's international policy, was responding to the tide of economic nationalism in France. In a foretaste of the continental system, the Consulat in February 1806 prohibited imports of English and other goods into France and raised tariff barriers on goods from Spain to protect French manufacturers, their employees, and French artisans. Bonaparte was candid: "I spend government funds," he remarked of subsidies to domestic manufacturers, "only to prevent unemployment of workers." It was also felt that "Napoleon . . . strongly supported the interests of French industry."[97] Consistent with this protectionist policy, the French government refused to permit a Bordeaux sugar refiner to erect a plant at Cadiz, arguing that it was improper for a French manufacturer "to consider establishing in a foreign land any factory or facilitating" what might advance the out-migration of skilled workers.[98]

When this beggar-thy-neighbor approach brought countervailing measures from Spanish authorities, French businessmen objected. Carcassonne's chamber of commerce, claiming to represent woolen manufacturers at Louviers, Reims, and other textile centers, criticized what it considered a 450 percent rise in Spain's duties on French woolens, whose volume often reached 1 million *elles* annually, exported to Barcelona and Cadiz for further handling, constituting an export "of unlimited benefit to French industry." Retaliation by raising French duties on imports of indigo, cochineal, and raw wools from Spain would surely lead to large-scale smuggling into France, higher production costs, uncompetitive products, and the loss of the Spanish market where there was "impressive consumption, which alone compensated French mills for the lack of exports to the Levant, the coasts of Africa, China, India, etc." Consequently, orders went out to French ministries to overhaul commercial arrangements with Spain and Italy.[99] Meanwhile, French residents in Spain complained about the volume of merchandise that English merchants smuggled into Spain from Gibraltar under the complacent eyes of Spanish customs personnel, who, according to a French innkeeper located on the road between Barcelona and Sigüenza, systematically "hinder French tradesmen . . . don't doubt that before long it will be impossible for us to operate in that land, which puts our manufactories at risk and affects all France adversely. That country's trade has always been advantageous, considering only its domestic trade, without that of the Americas."[100]

The business and government sectors in France were even more articulate about the status and potential of "the colonies of Spain, which provide the most important outlet for our manufactures."[101] Driving the reinforced colonial interest was the loss of Saint-Domingue's slave trade and the sugar and coffee staples whose re-export from France's Atlantic ports had made it "the most powerful and rich" emporium of western Europe. Nor can we overlook Saint-Domingue's profitable smuggling of French "laces, blonde laces, batistes, cambrics, muslins, veils, tammy-cloths, gold braid" to Spain's Caribbean ports.[102] More coveted were the silver *pesos* of New Spain, which had once again become important during the 1805 financial crisis at Paris. Gabriel-Julien Ouvrard claimed to have passed along to Bonaparte his brother's vivid impressions of visiting Mexico City and the colony's mining centers, which had led to "precise information about the trade and resources" of New Spain, where he could observe "the means of Spain's prosperity and inexhaustible treasures to be obtained by well-thought-out exploitation." There Bonaparte would find, Ouvrard wrote, the "resources he has been seeking in the conquered peoples" in Europe.[103]

At the silver-mining center of Guanajuato Ouvrard's brother found demand for specific French products—"linen and thread of Brittany, hats, silk stockings, woolens, serges, tammies, silks of Lyon, panne of Amiens . . . every kind of mercery." The port of Veracruz also impressed him with "the extent, convenience, and magnificence of its commercial stores, which make this city literally the warehouse of Mexico"; apparently, *comercio libre*

426 • *Toward the Second War of Succession*

and *comercio neutro* had transformed the sleepy port that Antonio de Ulloa had visited in the late 1770s.[104] Another observer marveled at New Spain's resource endowments, rendering that colony "the center of the world's commerce," and still another warned of a movement for independence stoked by English interests seeking to monopolize the commerce of Spain's colonies in America.[105] It was still possible for a leader of Bonaparte's ability and stature, ran the tenor of such reports to French authorities, "to settle the fate of the wavering Americas" in exchange for guaranteeing Spain the integrity of its possessions in western Europe and America. With France's collaboration, Spain would be positioned to concentrate on reforms in sensitive colonies like New Spain, whose exports could easily be "tripled and quadrupled."[106] Of such delusions is El Dorado made.

Yet New Spain was only one chessman in France's overall strategy of expansion in Europe and the western Atlantic in 1806. The mirage of the West in France also fed upon the situation in the Caribbean, upon the "Antilles d'Amérique," the "Isles d'Amérique," and on the Caribbean's southern rim, the "Caracas."[107] Spain's colonial situation was viewed as critical, even explosive: "Spain is in a terrible crisis. . . . She is on the verge of ruin," a condition reflecting its incompetence as a colonial power.[108] The Spanish metropole had neither generated nor followed a grand design of colonial development, preferring to rely upon inflows of precious metals to meet its fiscal needs. Worse, French analysts claimed, modifications in its transatlantic trading system since 1778 had brought little improvement: its tariff schedules for the colonial trades, as well as tax policy there, had embittered the colonial peoples, whose import needs might be met by approving trade with neutral nations in wartime, as France had decreed for its Caribbean possessions in 1784, after the English colonies in North America had won their independence. Spain was ineffective as a colonial power, and its predicament was compounded by fiscal laxity and military and naval incompetence at home. Metropolitan Spain was failing to satisfy the compact with its colonies precisely when they were entering a phase of accelerated export growth. In the darkened lens of French policymakers, Spaniards "administer their colonies miserably . . . it is impossible for them to keep all the colonies under their control."[109] The combination of imminent explosion in the American colonies—the French, after all, could not forget their own bitter struggle to hold on to Saint-Domingue—and disintegration in the metropole was creating prime conditions for English merchant interests to penetrate Spain's colonial core, the Caribbean zone, with the support of the equally expansionist United States in a tacit "Anglo-American" alliance in economic warfare.

Central to French strategy remained Hauterive's analysis of the way England's trade and naval hegemony excluded competition and his conclusion that a counterhegemony was necessary. "England," observed Pons, drawing from his experience at "Caracas," "would like to monopolize the trade of the four quarters of the world."[110] Other *fonctionnaires* speculated on how the English might use their advantages to penetrate Spain's Caribbean world. In a wide-ranging, perceptive, anonymous "Mémoir secret" probably drafted in late 1806, a French strategist predicted that the English would move out from their island bases of Jamaica and recently acquired Trinidad toward Saint-Domingue, Puerto Rico, and rapidly developing Cuba.[111] From these points English naval units could dominate a vast area from the Mississippi Valley to the Orinoco, from New Spain to Venezuela. Their merchants could fan latent dissatisfaction in the restless zones of New Spain, Cuba, and Venezuela to fashion a commercial monopoly by indirect application of economic power or, the *ultima ratio,* by conquest.

Military success in western Europe after 1800 under General Bonaparte led, however, to the abandonment of a salient feature of Hauterive's grand design: the concept of a counterhegemonic force of the maritime economies of Europe fused in a federative system evaporated, and with it went the principle of the territorial integrity of the collaborating states. Instead, the French government under the Grand Empire contemplated direct intervention by taking control of Peru and Cuba and assuming major responsibility for preserving Spanish sovereignty in the western Atlantic, along with, of course, its "efficient" exploitation. Hegemony would replace collaboration. "France is the only power that can henceforth keep these colonies in line and protect them from England." Implicit was the assumption that the Spanish colonies had to choose between English and French hegemony to attain "the splendor that was once Saint-Domingue." French authorities persuaded themselves that many among Spain's colonial elites—such as General Santiago Liniers, viceroy and mastermind of the defeat of English troops at Buenos Aires in 1806, who had confided to Bonaparte his "sentiments of a true Frenchman"—would prefer the protection of a powerful France.[112]

Occupation of Cuba and Puerto Rico, for example, could bring real material benefits, favoring "France's trade, its preponderance in Europe, and the renovation of its navy" to the tune of predicted annual French exports of 80 million francs exchanged for 20 million in colonial staples, it being hoped that Spain's trade deficit would be covered by *peso* flows. In addition, processing of staples would ensure high rates of employment in France. In the prominence given Cuba's potential export performance and its linkages—to the African slave trade, to the expansion of plantations, to milling equipment and sugar exports, to the incorporation of "thousands" of refugees from Saint-Domingue[113]—one senses the hope that Cuba might compensate France for the loss of Saint-Domingue and revive "France's trade with Europe in new, extensive, and profitable branches." France's design for Cuba, ran one recommendation, should prepare "gradual means to take possession [of Cuba] at the proper time," since a smoothly executed takeover would "heavily influence the commercial, financial, and maritime future of the French empire." For the many colonialist-minded French in the years after Bonaparte's coup d'état of Brumaire, there was always the attractive "vision of a great French empire including the Gulf of Mexico and the Caribbean islands" once a Franco-Spanish treaty of commerce legitimated direct French participation in Spain's Atlantic system.[114]

In 1806, plans to thwart English designs on Spain's colonies still required a modicum of collaboration from Spanish authorities. So direct trade between France's Atlantic ports and Spain's colonial ones, first advanced and then abandoned in 1795, was not resurrected. A patina of collaboration with Spain, "by virtue of interest, position, the leading ally of France," obliged French exporters to continue for a time to use Cadiz as a colonial entrepôt.[115] However, in September and November 1807 economic warfare intensified, just when the judicial proceedings of the Escorial affair were exposing deep fault lines in the Spanish monarchy, revealing political instability at Madrid. At this juncture Paris finally signaled its radical change in relations with both Iberian states; the era of uneasy alliance with Madrid was fast fading, replaced by military intervention beyond the Pyrenees "to exploit fully and easily the Peninsula and America."[116] No longer was it a question of whether to occupy the Iberian Peninsula to seal off contacts with England. Although Madrid seemed willing to collaborate in the occupation of still-neutral Portugal, Spanish high officials had no illusions about its immediate consequences; they expected the English to retaliate by occupying a Brazilian port or—what some had long contemplated—transporting the Braganza royal family, along with high Portuguese civil servants, across the Atlantic to Portugal's main colony. In either case, English naval forces based in Brazilian ports could then threaten the Spanish empire in the Rio de la Plata.

In mid-July 1807 Bonaparte's inner circle already understood that the military occupation of Portugal was in an advanced stage of planning and that initially, at least, the collaboration of Madrid was unavoidable. Hauterive, at the Foreign Office's South Europe desk, now crafted a Franco-Spanish treaty in which this erstwhile proponent of a European "système féderatif" coolly recommended that imperial France "save the southern states of Europe."[117] In late October, when details of the Fontainebleau treaty were hammered out with Spain's representatives, the French hoped to improve the situation of their Trésor Public by accelerating payment of Spain's overdue subsidy, then calculated at 15.5 million francs, then dropped the issue when the Spaniards objected. They also abandoned a provision advanced by Hauterive that would have shifted to French sovereignty a zone of northern Spain including Irún, Fuenterrabía, and the port of Pasajes, an excellent site for shipyard construction.[118]

Spain, however, came away with a provision whose significance would not become apparent until later: the French government recognized an added title created by Madrid for Charles IV, "Emperor of the Two Americas." This directed the loyalty of the colonies ultimately to the legitimate monarch rather than to Castile and Leon. Far more important for Paris was what Bonaparte's principal negotiator and confidant at Madrid, General Duroc, obtained: permission for French army units to cross northwestern Spain en route to Portugal's capital at Lisbon and to set up military garrisons, rest camps, storage depots, field hospitals, and police posts; northwestern Spain would be firmly controlled by French forces established within a few days' march from Madrid. At last French troops could pass through the Pyrenees in peacetime and be within striking distance of the center of the Spanish empire.[119] The treaty of Fontainebleau, Albert Sorel noted a century ago, "was only the preface to the dark tragedy of Bayonne." On the day the treaty was initialed, almost prophetically the Théâtre-Français, in Paris, performed Les Chateaux en Espagne.[120]

Barde's Memo, 1807

It was hardly coincidental that days before completion of the treaty a Bordeaux merchant and former resident in a Spanish colony in America, R. Barde, sent Paris a long follow-up to his unsolicited memorandum on French trade, drafted in July 1807, when planning for an Iberian intervention crystallized and "France was on the eve of a large-scale phase of maritime activity."[121]

Barde's extended addendum focused on what since 1806 had become the French government's preoccupation with Spain's Caribbean and circum-Caribbean colonies, Mexico, Cuba, and Venezuela—mining and plantation America, whose trade potential had long attracted foreign merchants probing for "a way of entry." Spain's domestic output, claimed Barde, could satisfy at best only a fraction, 5–10 percent, of demand in its "immenses colonies." For decades English export interests had demanded, and received, from the Spanish government concessions in its colonial trades, including toleration of smuggling from the islands of Jamaica and Providence, an activity fostered by Spain's colonial civil service. Now it was the turn of France. Barde was convinced that French manufacturers and export merchants could satisfy the profitable demand for imports in Spain's colonies, which, in turn, would expand their exports to new, large-scale purchasers of colonial staples. For aid in terminating "dependence" upon English merchants, Spain should offer concessions to French businessmen, particularly since shared interests would create virtually "a single nation," which suggests how diffused Hauterive's concept of a proto–customs union was. Of course, political considerations were not paramount to Barde. His goal was an aspect of France's post–Saint-Domingue syndrome that stressed access overseas to "markets and . . . wealth" in colonies France "might never obtain," without government expenditures on expeditionary forces (like those under Le Clerc, which had been lost in the effort to recolonize Saint-Domingue), overseas bases, or subsidies. Barde's principal recommendation sketched what a triumphant bourgeoise had demanded in 1795, "the entry of the French into the Spanish colonies in America to compete in trade with Spaniards themselves," the nightmare of merchants, American- and Spanish-born, *criollo* and *peninsular,* in the colonies.[122]

In the exuberantly expansionist climate of France in 1807, as producers and exporters pressured the government to have Madrid open its empire in America, Barde's July memorandum triggered quick reaction. Through a friend, an *inspecteur général des études,* the Interior Ministry turned to him for suggestions about the possible composition of French exports to Spanish America. His response was an informed survey of French products categorized by dry goods (linens, woolens, mercery, fashions, hardware) and agricultural staples (wines and brandies, grains and flours, fruits and salt beef). He tied each item to its area of production to underline the nationwide stake of French enterprise in the Spanish colonies, for example, the textile manufacture producing linens (Béarn, Maine, Anjou, Brittany, Normandy, Picardy, Champagne, Perche, Auvergne, Marseille, Dauphiné); woolens (Elboeuf, Louviers, Les Andelys, Abbeville, Sédan, Verviers); and silks (Avignon, Nîmes, Lyon, Tours, Paris). Such export possibilities, Barde substantiated, "interest virtually all the manufactories of France . . . almost every *département* participates more or less in the immense increase in outlets that commerce will seek in the Spanish colonies."[123]

Barde went on to point out other benefits of expanded exchanges with Spanish America. He envisioned an entrepôt trade with Hamburg, Bremen, and Lübeck involving the exchange of French wines and brandies, oils, soaps, and fruit for Westphalian, Saxon, and Silesian linens (the *contra-hechos,* or imitations), which French merchants could then re-export to Spain's colonies, where they were rapidly displacing similar French products. In addition there were the profits to be made from French monopolization of the slave trade between Africa and those colonies (which Bonaparte had relegitimized), an operation Spaniards had abandoned to the enterprise of English merchants. In French hands, Barde confidently predicted, that trade would offer the commerce and industry of France "extremely important" advantages. And last, Barde reiterated his recommendation to press Madrid for the entry of French merchant shipping into Spain's colonial ports. To this he appended suggestions for lowering Spain's tariffs by 2–4 percent below those levied on Spanish goods exported to the colonies.

These demands, Barde insisted, had to be formalized in a commercial treaty. Spain's negotiators could not reject them if France's representatives knew how "to maximize France's influence, its immense preponderance, and all the rights acquired to guide Spain toward its true interests." This tactic—hardly a way to reason together—was the only way to strip the English of Spain's *faveurs* and "reduce their power and monopolies." This prospect, he had to confess, filled him with "feelings of enthusiasm and exaltation" as he imagined prospective gains for "the manufactures and maritime trade of France."[124]

Barde's approach was not unique and probably reinforced the projections of policymakers at Paris. Over the next six months, from October 1807 to the following April, Barde's radical recommendation that French ships go directly to Spain's colonial ports became a leitmotif of private preoccupation and governmental policy. In December a French agent stationed at Madrid, Chabannes, drafted a report advancing the hawkish proposition that the French government should "become the master of the government at Madrid" in order to obtain for French traders "a virtual trade monopoly in all Spanish possessions." Trade monopoly would be a way for Spain and its colonies to tender "a form of tribute to the industry of France in the name of an ally."[125]

Barde, Chabannes, and others in late 1807 and early 1808 obviously had the attention of Bonaparte (Pradt reported that Bonaparte waxed lyrical when thinking of the "grandeur of the thrones of Mexico and Peru") and his immediate associates, who viewed Spain as "an immensely wealthy country, thanks to its resources in America."[126] By February 1808, when French troops were moving into northern Spain, Cretêt, of the Interior

Ministry, an ex-governor of the Banque de France and no stranger to businessmen, summarized candidly the commercial concessions French exporters were insisting upon, none of which were novel by this time: publication of all Spain's tariff schedules and regulations to eliminate the "unintelligibility of Spanish tariffs," which gave customs officials "a large, baleful and arbitrary attitude," along with across-the-board duty reductions in order to fashion Spain into "an outlet for French products and manufactures." Last, Cretêt addressed what he termed "one of the most important questions" in negotiating with Madrid, "the right to introduce into the American colonies" goods not produced by Spanish manufacturers. To his thinking, these modifications in Spain's commercial policy would increase France's exports and compensate "a balance all too often unfavorable with other states" with silver *pesos*. As he delicately phrased a harsh reality, Spain's economic situation put its government under pressure "somehow . . . to open itself to French commerce." Two months later Cretêt had orders to flesh out plans for the development of France's overseas trade.[127]

In the months preceding the order to Cretêt, the government was flooded by other advice, much of it unsolicited, focused on Spain's colonies, since "the wealth and prosperity of the Spains . . . are the Indies."[128] Those colonies, repositories of "Spain's largest body of movable riches," currently retained funds transferable to Spain, and now was the time for France to tap into "the immense capital lying in the mints of the new world." A M. Auguste, who claimed two years' residence in New Spain and personal acquaintance with the bishop-elect of Michoacán, Abad y Queipo, hoped to return there as an official agent to win over "all the social classes."[129] An irrepressible Ouvrard wrote Bonaparte on 22 March 1808 that this was the hour "to concentrate in Your Majesty's hands all Spain's resources."[130] France's businessmen, its *hommes d'affaires,* backed their government's plan to intervene, by force if necessary, to open the Spanish Atlantic to their shipping and goods.

Hence French pressure on Spain to modify its tariff structures and managed transatlantic trading system. By the end of February 1808, the *odeur des piastres* was overpowering in France, and the Escorial affair had produced "apathy and paralysis" at Madrid, causing Iriarte to note apprehensively, "What will be the outcome! How fatal and transcendental the consequences!"[131] Bonaparte's associates Duroc and Talleyrand, who considered Spain "a land ripe for pillage, like another Italy," asked Madrid to recall Eugenio Izquierdo, its reliable agent at Paris, and give him fresh instructions on a long list of issues, three of prime economic importance and already much debated.[132]

Both Duroc and Talleyrand held Izquierdo in high esteem. He was a competent intermediary between Madrid and Paris, a progressive, Navarre-born Spaniard who knew France well. Educated in Aragon and then at Paris, he cultivated scientific interests, botany and chemistry. A nationalist, he hoped to correct the general European view of Spain as backward. In Paris in the 1790s he was considered a "republican," tolerant of the Revolution's impact. He had also displayed financial skills: he had been an agent of the Banco de San Carlos in 1804–5, knew Francisco Cabarrús, and had arranged a loan with Hope & Company of Amsterdam (1805) repayable with funds of the *consolidación*. Godoy had sent him to Paris to dissuade Bonaparte from occupying Portugal; there he had examined Spain's financial obligations to France under the subsidy arrangements negotiated with the Trésor Public's Barbé-Marbois. To Bonaparte he was enlightened, versed in trade as well as in financial issues. He was acquainted with Pierre-Nicolai Berryer, a lawyer for the wealthy Magon and LeCouteulx merchant-bankers of Paris; Berryer later noted that at one time Izquierdo "predicted the outcome of that war of 1808 waged by Bonaparte in Europe."[133]

The issues to be resolved concerned Spain's tariffs, which were damaging to French products in particular; completion of negotiations for a commercial treaty; and equal status for nationals of France and Spain in Europe and overseas in the colonies.[134] Demand for Spanish tariff revision came from specific sectors of French manufacture: from Lyon hatmakers, whose products found in Spain "their main outlet"; from linen manufacturers in Brittany and Normandy, who wanted duties lower than those on Silesian imports; from woolen manufacturers at Carcassonne, Elboeuf, Sedan, and Aix-la-Chapelle; and from voile manufacturers of Reims, Amien, Abbeville, and Le Mans.[135] Izquierdo, who saw signs of imminent French aggression everywhere, hurried back to Madrid, stopping at Bayonne, where he probably conversed with Spain's diplomat stationed there, Juan Bautista Virio, the political economist and former consular agent in Germany and England. At Madrid and Aranjuez Izquierdo spent a week in discussions with key government officials, including Finance Minister Soler and Prime Minister Godoy.[136] Godoy's recollection of his government's response to these French demands paints a firmer position than in fact was taken. He claims that Izquierdo was instructed to insist that there had been no particular discrimination against imports from France, that the complaints of French merchants backed by their consular officers were unfounded.[137] On returning to Paris, Izquierdo was again pressured for economic concessions by Duroc and Talleyrand, who rejected the Spanish government's position, repeated their demands for trade concessions, and noted pointedly that

French army units were already inside Spain. It was clear that the French aimed to provide what the Continental system was designed to block—imports from England or other countries—to ensure that Spain "receives from us everything that neither England nor any other country can supply."[138] Izquierdo had to yield, granting entry of French merchant vessels into Spain's colonial ports but denying the right of French nationals to reside there.[139]

On the other hand, Izquierdo—contrary to Godoy's version of his instructions—may have received much latitude in mollifying French authorities. Izquierdo warned Talleyrand that once Spain's commercial concessions to French interests were known to London, retaliation would take the form of severing all maritime contact between Spain and its American colonies and indefinite prolongation of the war. This opinion he voiced one evening as he accompanied Gabriel-Julien Ouvrard, who was certainly no stranger to France's persistent demands to share in Spain's managed transatlantic trade, to Berryer's home. "His dark presentiments," Berryer later recalled, "were all realized." Then, together Izquierdo and Ouvrard, Spanish civil servant and French speculator, left to attend Talleyrand's salon.[140]

In the early months of 1808 the French government and French businessmen were, however, in no mood for predictions of disaster. A massive buildup of military forces, coupled with recovery from the economic trough of the revolutionary years, promised French visionaries indefinite expansion on the European continent and overseas in the Spanish colonies, where Napoleon envisioned wonderful "results . . . for the world."[141] One publication advertised the "incalculable advantages" that granting French nationals direct access to Spain's colonial ports would bring to their respective merchants. France's Foreign Office even circularized Viceroy Iturrigaray in New Spain and officials elsewhere about the growth possibilities for the colonies that would flow from prospective Franco-Spanish collaboration: "The strongest bond that will unite France to Spain cannot help but bring advantages to the colonies in America, opening a wide field to its commerce." And characteristically, Bonaparte, on the road to Bayonne and what would be his historic meeting with the Spanish Bourbons, promised Bordeaux's merchants that they would find compensation for losses in the western Atlantic through their participation in *the commerce of the American colonies belonging to the friendly neighbors of France*."[142] When Juan Bautista Virio, a good friend and correspondent of Bernardo Iriarte's, reported Bonaparte's comments on 26 April 1808, the era of Godoy and Charles IV had been over for more than a month, and the Spanish Bourbons were pawns in a grand design to draw imperial France into the Spanish labyrinth.

Franco-Spanish relations in the thirteen critical years between 1795 and 1808, between Basel and Bayonne, should be placed within a long historical context, a chronological framework of more than a century between the accession of the first Bourbon in Spain in 1700 and the abdication of his grandson in 1808. In that century a primary interest of French manufacturers and exporters was expanding commercial exchanges with Spain's colonies in America. Direct, usually illegal access to those colonial ports could not be sustained from 1705 to 1722, because Madrid resisted hegemonic pressures, English and French, so London and Paris left intact the shell of Spain's system of managed transatlantic trade. French exporters had to probe that system indirectly, through Cadiz, where they used commercial concessions obtained in the seventeenth century, and through smuggling from ports on Saint-Domingue in the Caribbean. English exporters penetrated the Spanish colonies from *their* Caribbean ports via the "imperialism of smuggling," a foretaste of the nineteenth-century "imperialism of free trade."

In France an equilibrium was fashioned between manufacturing and exporting interests and between financiers and government, the former group insisting on trade concessions from nationalistic Spanish governments, the latter tolerating what it minimized as nominal Spanish nationalism, while enhancing merchant bankers' financial intermediation at Paris and stressing naval cooperation against England in wartime. Protecting domestic and colonial interests led Madrid to chip away at the seventeenth-century concessions constraining Spanish sovereignty and balk at new commercial treaties, "especially with any powerful nation." The results were mixed: Spanish policy gradually retrieved nominal sovereignty, but it failed to develop a manufacturing base, which was essential for fulfilling a colonial compact.

Thus, the decade of revolution in France gave space to those sectors of the French bourgeoisie that were dissatisfied with the by-now traditional arrangements with Spain, impatient with what they viewed as ineffective, ill-conceived, and therefore false nationalism, embittered by the cozy relationship among Bourbon France's diplomatic representatives, merchant-bankers, and their Spanish counterparts—an "aristocratic" internationalism. French bourgeois saw opportunities beckoning in the underdeveloped Spanish colonial world and concluded that Spain's management of its colonial economies relied basically on mining and the export of precious metals. Spain's domestic economy had not, could not, and—they were confident—would not alone furnish the goods and services its transatlantic empire required. The priorities of Spain's underdeveloped economy, ran the French diagnosis, were to enlarge its labor force and stimulate agriculture and raw materials exports, leaving to more developed France the task of meeting the colonies' import requirements. The international division of labor in the phase of late commercial capitalism was already markedly unequal.

The symbiotic relation between the Consulat and the Empire, on the one hand, and French exporters pressing to enter Spain's colonial markets on a larger scale, on the other, produced the anomaly of a government of revolutionary origin disposed to shore up the old order in the Spanish empire. This is not, of course, a unique example of a regime radical at home that proceeds to cultivate conservatism abroad. Hence we have French manufacturers, exporters, and civil servants seeking liberty to operate within Spain's imperial system in order to enforce the pre-1789 system of "commerce exclusif"; a product of a decade of revolution, the freewheeling speculator Ouvrard, planning with Madrid officials in 1804 a shared monopoly of colonial trade; and the France of revolutionary principles restoring the African slave trade, a mainstay of Bourbon France's Atlantic economy. Hauterive's "système féderatif" was rich in anomalies and in potential benefits to those at its core.

French leaders mistook Anglophobia for Francophilia, one of many misapprehensions that had tragic consequences. When riflemen at the orders of Bonaparte's representative at Madrid, his brother-in-law Joachim Murat, executed some urban rioters on 2 May 1808, in order to shock and awe any armed resistance, the old order in Spain entered a long-term crisis. The abdication of Charles IV and his heir, Fernando, to the emperor of the French at virtually the same time at Bayonne would undermine the main objective of France's strategy for Spain, preservation of the Spanish colonial system in the western Atlantic.

15. The National Drama, Act I: Conspiracy at the Escorial

   ·

The Escorial Affair was considered . . . the opening act of a national tragedy.

Martí Gilabert

Doesn't Your Most Serene Highness see what a complex of interests, relations, and consequences such an extraordinary event produces?

Simón de Viegas to Manuel Godoy, November 1807 (unsent)

Did Spain's diplomatic agents at Paris—Eugenio Izquierdo, for one—overlook the financial, commercial, and strategic pressures in France—that prompted Bonaparte to intervene aggressively in Spain and its empire after Trafalgar? Official reporting suggests otherwise.

Doubtless the movement of French and French-commanded troops into Spain in late 1807 and early 1808 was dictated by military strategy and the arrogance of power as the ideals of the Revolution became imperialist. One must keep in mind, moreover, the Frenchmen who banked on the collaboration of Spain's high civil servants, men of business, army officers, and aristocratic landlords, who might accept limited top-down reform and more order, dual goals of many eighteenth-century enlightened members of Spain's—and Europe's—intelligentsia in civil society. There were also among Bonaparte's inner circle people like General Duroc and the diplomats Talleyrand and Hauterive, who needed no convincing to pressure the clearly destabilizing government at Madrid once the Escorial affair, enmeshing Prime Minister Godoy, Charles IV, and the Prince of Asturias, began to unravel in the weeks and months after October 1807. For their part, Spanish officials were aware of underlying French ambivalence toward Spain at least since 1793 (when Spain had briefly abandoned France to join the First Coalition), increasingly so after Godoy's ambiguous warning to the nation in 1806 of an unnamed enemy. Bonaparte, a remarkable strategist, would not want on his southern frontier a dubious ally, one whose government might abruptly permit English forces to open a second front—what the subsequent "Peninsular" war was all about—when his military operations were concentrated in central Europe against Prussia and Austria.

Spain's Bourbon monarchs had relied upon competent prime ministers drawn from the gentry rather than the aristocracy, never more so than under Charles IV and María Luisa, both of whom were closely identified with Manuel Godoy after 1793. While we have yet to understand fully the decision-making process under Godoy, after about 1800 he was considered their faithful confidant and the ultimate shaper of domestic and international policies. London distrusted him for relations with Paris that supported French international policy; Paris distrusted him for his readiness to compromise with London, if only to prevent an English amphibious move against a major colonial port in that sensitive international cockpit, the Caribbean—Havana or Veracruz. This was the effect of his policy "to keep Spain independent, unsuccessful however, despite pressure from the French and the English."[1] In 1807 and 1808 the prize for the two most powerful states in Europe and the Atlantic was the Spanish empire in America, in particular New Spain's silver and consumers. This was the situation confronting Godoy, a "conjuncture in which experience was useless; when no norms of response that might be used effectively were available, given the novelty of what was going on."[2] By 1807 the issue for both Paris and London was how to mold Spanish policy, and under the circumstances this meant removing the Bourbons' confidant and adviser while leaving intact the structures of monarchy and consequently the allegiance of the overseas colonies. If it was impossible to isolate Godoy from Charles and María Luisa, or if somehow the three were removed, or fled, then who or what would replace them while maintaining nominal continuity—their son and heir, Fernando, the Prince of Asturias, and the *fernandistas* counseling him? The other option, imposing a new monarchy—there was the recent precedent of the French in Holland—might force colonial elites and administrators to question their allegiance to the metropole, with possibly awesome consequences.

In Spain the ruling coalition of high civil servants, military, aristocracy, and clergy had to plan to respond to reports that Bonaparte and his associates intended to intervene in the peninsula, beginning with the occupation of Portugal. They, along with the overt and covert agents of France and England at Madrid, were cognizant of the issues splitting civil servants, military, and, perhaps to a lesser extent, aristocrats into, broadly speaking, Francophiles and Anglophiles.[3] The aristocracy's major grievance was the longstanding policy of the Bourbon monarchy to assign important civil posts to gentry of proven competence, with few exceptions sidelining aristocrats. In the mid-1790s the conde de Teba had published what could have been an aristocrat's manifesto, detailing "reservations . . . held by traditionalists who were upset because legitimate and respectable traditions were unrecognized and ignored."[4] No doubt the aristocratic faction, with symptoms of seignorial reaction, had sympathizers among the high civil service, notably Cevallos and Caballero, who was uniquely positioned at the Ministry of Justice, where he remained "una fuerza política durante el reinado."[5] It should be recalled that a much decorated (perhaps politically ingenuous) naval officer like Alejandro Malaspina, disillusioned with Madrid's government, civil society, and the surprising replacement of Aranda by Manuel Godoy, on returning in 1795 searched for support among the aristocracy and from a high civil servant like Caballero ("reactionary intriguer"), who rejected Godoy and his entourage.[6] Equally critical were elements in the clerical establishment who held fast to "ultramontane prejudices," such as the radical fundamentalist-preacher Diego de Cadiz.[7]

The most difficult faction to analyze was the nationalists among the military and civil service, many with colonial exposure and troubled by the fissions they discerned in colonial society and, after 1796, by the divisive issue of the colonies' external trade in wartime. Perhaps they were the last *proyectistas,* still hoping to "renovate" the *ancien régime*'s structures and values in order to better resist external pressure on Spain's domestic and colonial policies and the threat to the "integrity" of the Spanish empire in America. Their faith in renovation under the *ancien régime* was now minimal, and some late *proyectistas,* ever seeking useful models abroad, admired with reservation the results of liberal renovation under authoritarian government in postrevolutionary France, Bonaparte's France. At last Spain too might have effective reform from the top down. Might the drama at the Escorial provide an opening to reform or the road to disaster?

The Event

The event raising the curtain on the national drama that would transform paralysis into action and crisis into insurgency occurred at the autumn residence of the court, at San Lorenzo del Escorial, on 27 October 1807. On that day the Treaty of Fontainebleau was signed, one week after French troops had begun to enter Spain en route to Lisbon. Also on that day, Fernando, Prince of Asturias, Charles IV's heir, was confined to his quarters after the discovery in his room of documents revealing a conspiracy directed against Godoy. The discovery was not serendipitous. Charles had found on his desk a cryptic note: "Prince Fernando is preparing a movement in the palace: Your Majesty's Crown is in danger." The anonymous source reported "what the Prince's servants told me."[8] The documents incriminated Fernando along with the duque del Infantado, Juan de Escoiquiz, and grandees, military officers, and members of Fernando's household.[9]

Among the sequestered documents, four were highly incriminating. First, a *representación* in Fernando's hand addressed to Charles accused Godoy of crimes "known to the whole nation and all Europe" and urged his dismissal, arrest, and trial in order to defend Spain and the reigning dynasty. Another document, a "sham letter," advised Fernando to persuade his mother to abandon Godoy and support the marriage of Fernando, recently widowed, to a relative of Bonaparte's in order to maintain the Bourbons in Spain. A third, anonymous item was a "Letter from Talavera," which directed Fernando to establish unofficial contact with France's ambassador, François de Beauharnais, using the anonymous author as a go-between.[10] The fourth was an item that Godoy later claimed he had spotted (and examined) among the sequestered papers, a letter that he alleged María Luisa had subsequently removed. In it, according to Godoy, Fernando had written that he had weighed "well-known operations" and would play the role of San Hermenegildo. However, Fernando had added, "lacking vocation of martyr," he wanted assurance that "everything was arranged and coordinated" if his *representación* to his father criticizing Godoy brought retaliation.[11]

Godoy appeared on the Spanish political scene to replace First Minister Aranda as a result of bitter division over foreign policy. This had been a recurrent problem in the eighteenth century, even when the French and Spanish Bourbons were joined in an alliance designed to protect Spain's New World colonies against English aggression and/or occupation. In 1793 the French Revolution was in its most radical phase, the French Bourbons had just been guillotined, the English had managed to cobble together the First Coalition to contain the Revolution, and Aranda, the nominal leader of the so-called *partido aragonés,* had reluctantly joined the coalition. A former ambassador to Paris, Aranda foresaw the repercussions of Spain's abandonment of the long alliance with France, forced at some future moment to confront a powerful England alone. Godoy's appointment was a political shock, intended to alert the Spanish governing class that Charles IV's regime might still innovate in policy and action. From 1793 to 1808, with a brief intermission, Godoy, the royal family's dedicated confidant and Spain's most prominent political figure, would emerge as prime minister and, in a sense, Charles and María Luisa's alter ego and, to some biographers, Spain's first modern dictator.[12] Godoy has emerged in recent historiography as a multifaceted leader, formerly much maligned, recently rehabilitated and, in some respects, seen as very much a product of the unpredictable years preceding the Escorial affair.[13]

Two facets of Godoy's administration stand out. Unlike his predecessors, Floridablanca, for instance, he quickly developed an exceptionally intimate relationship with the royal family, who showered him with privilege, honors, and, key to his role, trust. Since his social background was of the lesser gentry of Extremadura and he had come to Madrid as a young junior officer of the Guardias de Corps, the Royal Guards, during what has been called "the convulsed decade of the nineties,"[14] much of the court aristocracy and allied high clergy—the core of the integrated political and social elites— quickly concluded that he would not serve their interests and formed the basis of his opposition (the *partido reaccionario*). The aristocrats of this post-Aranda faction resented the established Bourbon policy of excluding them from prominent political posts; clerics distrusted the surviving progressive figures of Spain's late eighteenth-century *luces, renovadores* like Jovellanos, Meléndez Valdés, Goya, and Cabarrús, whom Godoy cultivated.[15] They also feared the anticlerical tendencies of the *renovadores,* their readiness to tap the impressive landed wealth and income of the Spanish church as the public debt mushroomed in wartime and to adapt to the imperative to adjust colonial trade policy. Typical of the opposition was their treatment of Gaspar de Jovellanos, distinguished civil servant and author of the recently published *Informe . . . en el expediente de ley agraria,* after his appointment under Godoy as minister of Gracia y Justicia. To quote Jovellanos: "The public shame caused me by its publication . . . no one will ever know nor imagine . . . how much calumny blackened my principles and intentions."[16] And calumny was what they poured on Godoy, who insisted that he belonged to no faction, after 1805.[17]

Under Godoy in 1795, at the end of the First Coalition, and despite the surviving revolutionary currents and ideology of the Directoire, the Franco-Spanish alliance was reaffirmed at San Ildefonso. Henceforth France, under Directoire, Consulat, and Empire, would be the counterweight to England's possible aggression against Spain's American colonies. In official publications, the protection of the colonies and especially of their trade with the metropole was a subordinate issue when it was not submerged, but the political class remained painfully aware of the colonial problem. Characteristic is María Luisa's comment to Godoy in a note of 1806 expressing her fear that Bonaparte "would like to strip us of the Floridas, and if he succeeds, we will lose Mexico; although Paris wants everything we have there."[18]

The second phase of Godoy's career came in the eight tumultuous years after 1800, when he received—some might argue, accumulated—unprecedentedly broad powers as Charles IV's chief executive after the renewal of hostilities against England in 1804 and the formation of the Third Coalition against Bonapartist France. Spain and especially its American empire were now threatened by aggressive English amphibious forces, and Spain had to maintain France as its ally. This position, however, was assaulted by the *partido aristocrático-católico,* a coalition whose influential members schemed to remove a seemingly omnipotent Godoy and replace him with someone who would permit them access to power, privilege, and honors—what an aristocracy presumably enjoyed—and change the direction of Spain's policy toward England. This faction nurtured the hope that the ousting of Godoy, followed by the abdication of Charles himself, might open the succession to the Prince of Asturias, the recently widowed Fernando. This ultimate objective, the crowning of Fernando, was implicit; their immediate objective was to get rid of Godoy.[19]

After 1806 Godoy's position became untenable. As part of the alliance with France, Spain, instead of supplying troops to support Bonaparte's campaigns in central Europe, paid a monthly subsidy. English naval forces blockaded the major peninsular port trading with the colonies, Cadiz, interrupting commercial exchanges in the Spanish Atlantic and encouraging the already widespread smuggling in the Caribbean. At home, the economic situation was deteriorating, trade with the colonies and the rest of Europe fell off, customs returns—a major source of revenue—slackened, and wartime expenditures soared. In an effort to distance Spain from Bonaparte's military operations before the victory at Jena in 1806, Godoy, with royal approval, issued his ill-timed, ambiguous proclamation implying the hope of forming a coalition of neutral nations. After Jena, however, Bonaparte seemed unstoppable; worse, his doubts that he could rely upon the support of Godoy, that is, of Spain, were reinforced. In Bonaparte's view, as in the view of Godoy's opposition, Godoy—apparent architect of policy and now vulnerable—had to go. Thus, from 1806 on, Bonaparte clearly was courted by the *partido reaccionario* of aristocracy, clergy, highly placed civil servants like Cevallos and Caballero,[20] and military disaffected by Godoy-inspired changes. Escoiquiz, former tutor and now mentor of Fernando, colluding with Godoy's opposition, planned to oust Godoy, and ultimately Charles IV and Luisa, by a palace coup.[21] Through Escoiquiz, Fernando was put in contact with the French ambassador, Beauharnais; turned to Bonaparte for a French wife; and then moved against his parents.

Since Godoy was ill and in Madrid at that moment, Charles, at the Escorial, had to handle quickly this grave threat to his government organized by elements of the aristocracy—Infantado, Ayerbe, Orgaz[22]—a kind of Spanish fronde. He called his secretary of Gracia y Justicia, Caballero, to join María Luisa in examining the documents. Charles could no doubt recall the aborted coup by disaffected Portuguese aristocrats against Pombal and the covert role of some Spanish aristocrats in the *motín* of Esquilache of 1766; Godoy never forgot Charles's abiding dread of "the slightest shadow of disturbance or riot," a "fear" that Caballero "cultivated frequently."[23] The materials in Fernando's quarters outlined a plan to change government policy by changing leadership, removing Godoy—the royal family's trusted instrument—and inviting French intervention to ensure the continuity of the Bourbon monarchy in Spain through the immediate accession of Fernando. The senior *fiscal* of the Consejo de Castilla, Simón de Viegas, was probably present when Charles, María Luisa, and Caballero examined the documents.

Apparently Charles and María Luisa had few reservations about Caballero, whom they considered "un hombre honrado,"[24] appointed in 1798 as ministei of Giacia y Justicia to replace the recently dismissed and exiled Jovellanos, who was not the only prominent victim of Inquisition pressure. Godoy was never the imperious autocrat critics liked to imagine; he always had to perform a high-wire political balancing act, seeking an equilibrium between restive traditionalist and ultramontane groups among aristocrats and clergy, on the one hand, and, on the other, the surviving representatives of Spain's Christian enlightenment, its *luces,* among them late *proyectistas.* Jovellanos was one such *proyectista.* Lawyer, physiocrat, civil servant, littérateur, friend of Meléndez Valdés, Goya, and Cabarrús, he was a very public intellectual, and already a despairing one. It was logical for Madrid's Real Sociedad Económica, at the request of the Floridablanca ministry, to pick Jovellanos to draft a moderate government response to the radical agrarian reform of early revolutionary France. Jovellanos wrestled with this charge to produce in 1795 his widely circulated proposal for agrarian reform, an antirevolutionary physiocratic manifesto. Although it was essentially a mild reformist tract, Spain's vested landed interests, secular and clerical, were nonetheless troubled by its understated criticism of undercultivated or poorly cultivated properties and exploited farm laborers (the impoverished *jornaleros* whom Portillo had described to Godoy), especially in Andalusia and Extremadura, and its recommendation that inefficiently farmed ecclesiastical properties be sold to middle and small cultivators.[25] Jovellanos's conservative replacement, Caballero, "open enemy of enlightenment,"[26] would hold the post of secretary of Gracia y Justicia over the next decade, a link to Spain's right-wing opposition in high government circles, a brake on surviving would-be *novadores* in Godoy's administration until the debacle at Aranjuez in March 1808.[27]

Caballero's credentials seemed respectable. A native of the province of Salamanca, he was a member of a gentry family with an uncle who became secretary of war, and a graduate of the University of Salamanca, a major channel of elite reproduction.[28] His first bureaucratic post was as *fiscal togado* in a bureau of the War Ministry at Seville, where he must have absorbed the influence of Andalusian landlords and their Cadiz merchant colleagues.[29] Caballero's influential uncle probably accounts for his next post: he became a member of the elite corps of civil servants directly under the Consejo de Castilla and generally slated for high posts, Madrid's Sala de Alcaldes de Casa y Corte. There he married a lady-in-waiting *(camarista)* of María Luisa's, frequented the royal household,[30] rubbed shoulders with Fernando's former tutor Escoiquiz, and perceived the unique trusting relationship between the royal couple and Manuel Godoy. Godoy and others, however, distrusted him,[31] but he remained in the government as a source of intelligence about, and a useful conduit to, disaffected aristocrats and clergymen. At Gracia y Justicia he reportedly criticized reform-minded army officers like the conde de O'Farrill; removed Jovellanos's friend, the progressive civil servant Meléndez Valdés, from his *fiscalía* in the Sala de Alcaldes de Casa y Corte; and was somehow involved in the abrupt recall of Miguel Azanza, viceroy of New Spain, who had insisted on enforcing *comercio neutro* despite complaints from the powerful *almaceneros* of Mexico City, Veracruz, and Cadiz.[32] Caballero was inducted into the Orden de Carlos III in 1797 and then the military Order of Santiago in 1807; that same year, he took his uncle's title, marqués de Caballero. His years as a cabinet member; his exchanges with Soler and Sixto Espinosa over fiscal and financial policies—*consolidación,* for one;[33] his response to complaints from restless aristocratic and clerical groups, ever distrustful and envious of Godoy and his empowerment by Charles; and his presence at royal residences may explain Charles's fateful decision to ask for Caballero's advice in handling the striking infidelity of the royal family's son and heir, Fernando.[34]

Relying on Caballero's judicial competence and oddly unsuspecting of his motivation, Charles immediately followed his advice: "Work in the open, prepare safeguards, speak to the nation, and select judges . . . to draw up charges, and let nature take it course; except that the king might later use his sovereign clemency with the Prince of Asturias"—in brief, that Charles publicize the facts of an in-house conspiracy, order a judicial investigation, and proceed to try all the accused.[35] The last part of Caballero's recommendation is significant: it contained an escape clause, the alternative of a royal (and paternal) pardon. Persuaded by both Caballero and Felix de Amat, the royal confessor, that any other procedure risked violent public reaction, Charles appointed an investigating committee made up of Antonio Árias Mon y Velarde, dean and acting *gobernador* of the Consejo de Castilla; the Consejo's senior *fiscal,* Simón de Viegas; and the secretaries of State, Hacienda, and Marine, Pedro Cevallos, Miguel Cayetano Soler, and Francisco Gil y Lemos, respectively.[36]

Two days later, on 29 October, they gathered at the Escorial in the early evening to interrogate Fernando about the documents found in his quarters. He refused to respond to his questioners, insisting that the papers were in the handwriting of his recently deceased wife, María Antonia, daughter of the bitterly Francophobic queen of Naples, a sister of Marie Antoinette's. Thereupon Charles ordered Fernando's house arrest to abort the aristocracy's plan. Father and son, king and heir, were on a collision course.

Exasperated and anxious, Charles took another decisive step, again relying on Caballero's advice.[37] He signed a personal note to Bonaparte avowing that his son was conspiring to dethrone and assassinate him and María Luisa. Confiding that he was considering disinheriting Fernando in favor of a younger son, he asked for Bonaparte's advice.[38] This extraordinary letter was followed by Charles's equally extraordinary decision to sign a decree—there was a draft written by Godoy—reviewed pro forma by Mon y Velarde as acting head of the Consejo, and precipitously published on 30 October in the *Gaceta de Madrid*. In the decree, Charles IV reported that there were documents revealing a "horrible and daring" plan hatched against him at the Escorial and including Fernando's disturbing confession that finding his father's existence "a heavy burden . . . he had confessed a plan to dethrone him." The decree reported that Fernando had been arrested and others detained; Charles vowed that the results of an investigation headed by the governor of the Consejo de Castilla and including other ministers would be duly published.[39]

Also on 30 October, in the first of private, unsolicited depositions to Secretary of Gracia y Justicia Caballero, Fernando confessed that his mentor, Escoiquiz—rather than Fernando's deceased wife, María Antonia—had authored the incriminating documents. More startling, he handed over two undisclosed documents that he had copied and signed at Escoiquiz's prompting, which clearly raised the Escorial affair far above the level of petty palace intrigues. The first, an undated decree to become effective on the death of Charles, ordered Godoy's arrest and trial and assigned military and political authority to a wealthy aristocrat, the very visible duque del Infantado.[40]

Far more incriminating was the second document, Fernando's personal letter to Bonaparte requesting protection against Godoy and marriage to a Bonaparte. Responding to Caballero's questioning, Fernando explained that in the spring of 1807, on learning that Ambassador Beauharnais wanted to consult him about an "important matter," he had sought Escoiquiz's advice. In his "Letter from Talavera" Escoiquiz, exploiting his role as intermediary between aristocratic dissidents and Fernando, whose mentality he recognized, replied that Bonaparte had probably instructed Beauharnais to sound out Fernando about a possible marriage alliance. After Escoiquiz opined that it would be dangerous to reject the proposal of "a man both frightening and powerful," who at the "slightest annoyance" could eliminate Spain's royal family, Fernando authorized him to negotiate unofficially through Beauharnais. Escoiquiz reported that when Bonaparte subsequently insisted upon a letter signed by Fernando soliciting the marriage, Fernando copied and signed one to Bonaparte, drafted by Escoiquiz, on 11 October. Fernando added that Escoiquiz had destroyed his original draft;[41] an investigating *fiscal* would have no clear fingerprints. Did Escoiquiz suggest to Beauharnais the proposal to marry a Bourbon to a Bonaparte?

Subsequently, in two undated letters to Charles and another to María Luisa, Fernando acknowledged his *delicuencia* and begged forgiveness.[42] On 3 November Charles pardoned him conditioned on Fernando's good behavior; and on 5 November a decree circulated containing Fernando's two letters of contrition and announcing the forthcoming trial of those implicated by Fernando. The grandees and others were arrested.[43] Also on 5 November, Charles wrote Bonaparte, vehemently protesting Beauharnais's meddling in Spain's domestic affairs but omitting mention of his pardon of Fernando. In a scathing reply, Bonaparte denied receiving letters from Fernando or intervening in Spain's domestic affairs. This he followed with a request that references to himself or Beauharnais be omitted from the upcoming trial.[44]

Furthermore, on the day of Fernando's pardon, Caballero announced what was probably his selection of Árias Mon y Velarde[45] and two *consejeros* of the Consejo de Castilla—Sebastián de Torres and Domingo Fernández Campomanes—to begin the judicial investigation of the accused. Following the Spanish criminal procedure Caballero had recommended, the members of the newly appointed court and assistants took depositions in preparation of a *sumaria* of the evidence, the basis of an indictment to be drawn up by the senior prosecutor *(fiscal)* of the Consejo Real.

Interrogations continued until the end of November, when the Consejo's *fiscal*, Simón de Viegas, proceeded to the Escorial to review the *sumaria*'s evidence and draft an indictment. On 28 December Viegas indicted Escoiquiz and Infantado on charges of conspiracy and treason, recommending capital punishment for them and lesser sentences for their accomplices. Two weeks later, the defense lawyers for Escoiquiz and Infantado presented a rebuttal of Viegas's charges, arguing that a lack of credible evidence confirmed their clients' innocence and loyalty. The trial ended in late January, when a panel expanded by eight additional *consejeros* gathered at the sickbed of a member receiving last rites, who cast a vote for exoneration.[46] Although a unanimous verdict ultimately cleared the defendants, Escoiquiz, Infantado, and others were placed in internal exile.

Such are the generally accepted "facts" of the Causa del Escorial, which bore earmarks of other palace or preemptive coups involving personal ambitions and political factions dividing the court. However, the profound internal disunity between crown and aristocracy now publicly revealed; the circulation of anonymous, bawdy pasquinades mocking Godoy and the royal family;[47] the unprecedented appeals to Bonaparte by Charles IV and his son precisely when French forces were occupying strategic points in northern Spain along the route to Lisbon; and above all the dramatic aftermath give the Escorial episode a significance inviting careful analysis of its complex dynamic. More specifically, did the documents in Fernando's possession reveal an aristocratic minicoup designed to maintain Spain's Bourbon monarchy through the succession of Fernando precisely when French intervention seemed imminent?

The Trial

At the beginning of the twenty-first century, when judicial investigation of those at the center of political power in Western culture has become common, it is hard to grasp the public's shock at Charles IV's announcement of his son's treason and intended regicide. Then came Charles's conditional pardon (an act of sovereign justice) after Fernando's confession, repentance, disclosure of his associates, and the dismaying prospect that his supporters' criminal trial might confirm their and his guilt. Persuaded that Godoy was behind Charles's accusation against his son and heir, "popular" opinion now directed its animosity toward Godoy and supported the "desired prince," soon to succeed his father. At this point public opinion became a critical factor in the process. At the same time, elite figures among the high civil service *(golillas)* foresaw the end of Godoy's influence once evidence introduced in the trial failed to confirm the guilt of the *fernandista* faction. This prospect became critical in the trial's dénouement.

The trial itself—Fernando's appeal to Bonaparte, along with the exchanges between Escoiquiz and Beauharnais, were deliberately excluded—revolved around four issues: first, Charles's decree of 30 October, which accused Fernando of high treason and promised to publicize the fate of his accomplices; second, Charles's conditional pardon bestowed upon Fernando after his confession; third, evidence in Fernando's room, along with the information produced by depositions that confirmed the conspirators' intent to undermine Godoy's authority as illegitimate and immoral; and fourth, *fiscal* Simón de Viegas's indictment, which justified Charles's October decree on the ground that to attack a king's personal adviser, Godoy, was to attack the king, and therefore also treasonable. *En bloc,* these issues, in the context of Godoy's plummeting authority and Fernando's enhanced popularity, determined the trial's outcome. Examined separately, each point offers clues to the underlying premeditated logic of the Escorial affair—why Meléndez Valdés could envision the political scenario that followed.

The government's case against Fernando and his coconspirators was badly flawed, defense lawyers argued. The 30 October decree merely declared the existence of a plot against Charles and a planned regicide, then ordered an investigation and punishment—all to be publicized. The decree's text was ambiguous: it asserted that while Fernando admitted to a plan to dethrone his father, he denied authorship (it did not have his signature, only the formulaic "I the King"). For Fernando to assert that his father's life was "a heavy burden" for him was not the equivalent of a planned assassination. Further, the defense insisted, Charles had ordered only an investigation *(indagación),* not a trial. These and other flaws aside, the fact remained that the king had unilaterally declared that treason had been committed, yet the judges were barred from qualifying the crime or even deciding whether one had actually been committed.

Furthermore, the preliminary depositions of the accused provided little basis to substantiate an indictment. Escoiquiz later claimed that he had immediately perceived that there was nothing to fear from his sympathetic interrogation by Domingo Fernández Campomanes and concluded that deliberate omission of all reference to Bonaparte, as well as to his exchanges with Ambassador Beauharnais, had removed the only tenable charge, that of lese majesty.[48]

The testimony of the principal defendants concurred on the origin of a plan that empowered the duque del Infantado and would confirm the role of Escoiquiz following Charles's death. As the army officer Tomás de Jáuregui testified, during conversations over the summer of 1806 Godoy's brother and Luís de Viguri, the ex-intendant of Havana, had sought his support for a plot to alter the succession to the throne of Spain in Godoy's favor, alleging Charles's precarious health and Fernando's "incapacity."[49] Shocked, Jauregui had shared this information with his brother, Manuel Francisco de Jáuregui, of the Guardias de Corps, who had reported it to his aristocratic friends the conde de Orgaz and the duque del Infantado, since "as grandees they could defend the good cause better than anyone else in case of necessity."[50] Later Infantado had assented when Escoiquiz, striving to forestall a move in Godoy's favor, drafted an undated decree instructing all civil and military leaders to accept Infantado's authority in the event of Charles's death. Copied and signed by Fernando, Escoiquiz's draft had been concealed by Infantado, who claimed to have destroyed it on learning of the events of 27 October.[51]

Other depositions add little to this basic story. The brief interrogation of Luis de Viguri and Godoy's brother Diego ended with their firm denial of statements attributed to them by Tomás de Jáuregui. The aristocrats Infantado, Orgaz, and Ayerbe in their short and evasive statements affirmed their loyalty to the Spanish Bourbons, whose rights they said they would defend against any "suspected interloper."[52] The testimony of the duque de San Carlos, Fernando's former *ayo* and Escoiquiz's "intimate friend," who was later questioned in Navarre (where he was by then the viceroy), contributed little new evidence.

Interrogation of Fernando's mathematics tutor, Pedro Giraldo, whom Fernando identified as a link to the French embassy (and in fact a spy for Godoy), failed to elicit a confession. Questioned about secret intelligence reports in his possession prepared for an unnamed official in the ministry of Estado (someone he thought was close to María Luisa), Giraldo refused to identify the *fernandista* grandees disguised with sobriquets; interrogators failed to press him further. Along with Manuel Villena, Fernando's equerry, also implicated by Fernando as an intermediary with the French, Giraldo was excluded from Viegas's indictment for "reasons of state."

There is an unexpected facet of the judicial interrogation. Interrogators devoted inordinate attention to verifying disaffection among the Guardias de Corps. Some in the "American" company had lost seniority as a result of Godoy's recent reorganization of the corps.[53] Confiscation of their correspondence and the duress to which some were subjected contrast with the deferential treatment given the principals accused. Although letters revealed the officers' usually frustrated efforts to gain their own and relatives' advancement through contacts made during assignment at court, no evidence surfaced of organized military involvement in the Escorial affair.[54]

The pivotal figure in the trial was, of course, Juan de Escoiquiz, tutor (recommended by Godoy) and then confidant of Fernando, associate of certain aristocrats at court; his letters found in Fernando's quarters had urged contacting the French ambassador, then requesting marriage to a relative of Bonaparte's. Escoiquiz began his testimony with the declaration that "far from thinking of hiding the truth . . . his every hope was to pour out his heart at the royal feet of his sovereigns." Deftly avoiding potential legal charges and adroitly exploiting his deposition to advance the *fernandista* project, he claimed that his vitriolic charges against Godoy in the papers in Fernando's possession required no substantiation; they merely repeated opinions widespread "among all classes, high, middle, and lowest."[55] Reiterating anxiety over Fernando's fate and over that of Charles, María Luisa, and of Spain as a whole, Escoiquiz emphasized that this preoccupation had prompted his draft of the decree empowering Infantado, as well as the draft of Fernando's marriage proposal. After Escoiquiz's interrogation, it was the turn of the senior *fiscal* of the Consejo de Castilla, Simón de Viegas.

Viegas was an archetypical high public servant, the product of a centuries-old state civil service, with its rooted structures and its unswerving loyalty to the political structures of the old regime and to those in power who represented it—crown, state secretaries, and, of course, the still prestigious Consejo de Castilla. As the case unfolded, Viegas had to choose between loyalty and self-survival. He was caught between the logic of criminal procedure and the logic of politics.

After reviewing evidence, drafting a *sumaria*, and overcoming unavoidable delays, Viegas handed up the preordained indictment on 28 December. He charged Escoiquiz and Infantado with conspiracy and treason, subject to the death penalty. Fernando's confidant, Escoiquiz, was charged with "the enormous offense of . . . dazzling a mind unprepared by the aid of experience, to make the Very Serene Prince of Asturias independent of his King and Father and even prevent the King himself from discussing matters with the Queen, stirring reciprocal sentiments of disunity and distrust in a marriage whose harmony cannot be endangered without scandal and the risk of universal upheaval."[56] A conspiracy to undermine the subordination of a royal heir to his father constituted treason, "since according to the Ley de Partida, this brings man to evil, under color of good." Further, in depicting Charles IV as an "inert machine, lacking judgment and rationality, leaving him no more than the physical movement of his hand to sign the decrees put before him," Escoiquiz had indeed violated, Viegas found, the very Leyes de Partida that punished conspiracy against the king or even an attempt "to have him lose while alive the honor of his dignity." By seeking to separate king from his queen, "who has played so large a role in his successes" (here Viegas was insightful), Escoiquiz had tricked Fernando into participating in a project of whose consequences he was naively unaware. Here Viegas was on solid ground.

Viegas found equally treasonous Escoiquiz's attack on Godoy, whom Viegas lauded as "public defender of the monarchy" and "Spanish hero," whose "wise and consummate policy and skill in affairs of state have, in the delicate and perilous situation of public affairs, permitted Spain to be a spectator at the stormy theater of Europe, while other powers go about destroying themselves." Godoy's preeminence and the extensive powers given him by Charles IV as *almirante generalísimo,* which was equivalent in status to that of *adelantado* in the Leyes de Partida, underscored Charles's trust in Godoy. It followed that an attack upon his life and honor constituted an attack upon the king and therefore merited similar punishment.

In addition to indicting Escoiquiz as ideator of the conspiracy, Viegas charged Infantado with complicity, since he had accepted the military and political power authorized in that undated decree in Escoiquiz's hand. This was a "serious crime" carrying "terrible consequences"; it too was a capital offense. Viegas left unstated that the political class understood that the campaign of anonymous pasquinades posted on Madrid's street corners was aimed at reempowering sidelined aristocrats. Viegas concluded by observing that the aristocratic conspirators had hoped that when Charles IV died they "would be masters of the government of the kingdom," a goal they had tried to disguise with "frivolous" statements.

As for efforts to justify conspiracy on the flimsy basis of random and ambiguous conversations Tomás de Jáuregui had with Diego de Godoy and Luís de Viguri, the *fiscal* Viegas dismissed them as incredible: "No sensible man in the world could give credence to such reports."[57]

The Indictment

Simón de Viegas's indictment proved decisive in the outcome of the Escorial trial. Analysis of its genesis reveals the complex inner dynamic of the case. *Fiscal* Viegas emerges as an important and contradictory figure largely because he later reexamined his own role. Viegas was denigrated by partisan contemporaries and later historians as opportunist and as Godoy's sycophant. Closer analysis highlights the personal dilemma of a high-ranking jurist unable to abandon a crucial role in the case. His rational, often self-deprecating analysis of the experience illuminates the convoluted workings of the old regime in this critical juncture of Spain's modern history, as the aristocracy planned to reoccupy positions of power.

Viegas was a career public servant of modest social origin who had earned a solid reputation as a jurist and cautious advocate of legal reform.[58] Referring to Viegas's treatise on logic, Jovellanos characterized him as reflective, pursuing consistently a few interests, and an intellectual of unusual insight.[59] Viegas once described himself as conciliatory in disposition: "It is not my character to see or do harm to others . . . I profess the pacific policy based upon love, not the noisy and bloodthirsty one, which I abhor." A lawyer at the top of his profession but without prestigious patrons, described as a "reforming spirit in the legal profession," he might be perceived as reserved and perhaps overly accommodating, as most successful civil servants of the time had to be. He did have a lighter side: he was a skilled guitarist.[60]

Present at the first high-level meeting at the Escorial on 29 October, Viegas immediately understood the explosive implications of the affair for the Bourbon dynasty and Spain, for Godoy, and for himself as the probable prosecutor in a trial to whose outcome Charles IV committed himself and the Consejo de Castilla. Sometime in November, probably after reviewing the key documents and before his formal assignment to the case on 30 November, Viegas decided to alert Godoy to their far-reaching consequences.

Since Viegas recognized that the last draft of Charles's 30 October decree accusing Fernando was in Godoy's handwriting—a critical fact that he would not overlook—Viegas composed a much reworked draft of a candid, analytical letter to Godoy.[61] He questioned circumspectly the foresight, perspicacity, and intent of those who had counseled him on how to handle the incident. "I have no intention of discrediting in your eyes the confidants or advisers you may have had—all must have spoken in good faith and said what they understood," he wrote,[62] "but I must say that they have understood little, since each step that . . . they have suggested to you or that they have permitted without calling it to your attention has brought you to the precipice." "Those papers"—presumably the documents found in Fernando's quarters—had been so alarming that he confessed he had not had a tranquil moment since. He continued, perhaps ironically, that although he did not wish to perturb "your manly and majestic calm [Godoy] . . . I would like you to take precautions against the risks that my reflection and love for you show me." Asking "your great talent" to concentrate on this grave matter, he proceeded to his analysis.[63]

At the outset Viegas advised Godoy that the matter "must not be pursued or determined by passing or momentary interests, because this matter absolutely and indispensably will pass to future centuries and will be noteworthy in the history of the Nation." At stake were Charles's and María Luisa's "honor, your life, and Spain's destiny," and he hoped Godoy would judge whether "a matter of this nature will demand of me little care and dedication." Then Viegas spelled out the multiple implications of Charles's actions: "The Prince of Asturias is denounced before Europe by his Father and King for the dreadful and sacrilegious attempted parricide and regicide. There is no worse sin."[64] Regardless of the veracity of rumors circulating with regard to Fernando's proposal for a marriage, any European ruler contemplating the marriage must first find Fernando cleared of the crime his father had imputed to him. On the other hand, those strongly attached to Fernando would hardly allow his name to be dishonored. However, the premature royal pardon, far from removing Fernando's guilt, confirmed it, even implicating high-ranking accomplices. His respect for Charles IV and the "decorum of his deliberations" aside, Viegas saw no solution to the dilemma that would not diminish respect for the state nor seriously weaken its authority. In the end, he concluded, "it seems that it can only end in a formal retraction," warning Godoy that at any time "We? You? must await a formal demand to clear him." The case should therefore be formally dismissed.[65]

Looking ahead, Viegas predicted that unless Fernando's dishonor were immediately removed, Fernando would one day remove it with blood, justifying his vengeance by invoking the "glorious cause of justice." Yet the royal pardon protecting Fernando from judicial action prevented exoneration by that very fact. Were Fernando not cleared of charges before becoming king, surely he would demand a declaration of his innocence, arguing that Godoy—who had provided the final draft of the 30 October decree—rather than Charles was really responsible for the decrees incriminating him.

In the meantime, how might Fernando react to the moral quandary of his father's pardon when his aristocratic collaborators, implicated in his confession, were imprisoned and brought to trial for a crime in which he was the main, legally responsible party? "Doesn't Your Serene Highness see what a complex of interests, relations, and consequences such an extraordinary event produces?" he asked Godoy. As loyal *fiscal* of the Consejo de Castilla and servant of the regime, Viegas added the dismal prospect that once Fernando's guilt was confirmed by the exoneration of his associates, the "nation" would be acclaiming as Charles's successor "the most sacrilegious criminal imaginable!" A king "with no reputation among his vassals" would be no king at all. In a scenario reminiscent of France twenty years earlier, Viegas predicted the outcome the regime had long opposed: a representative polity. "The Cortes would be convoked," followed by a "devastating fermentation."

Finally, Viegas pointedly reminded Godoy, the documents in Fernando's quarters were specifically targeted at Godoy, not Charles, and in this sense criminal charges against Fernando had no substance. "Señor Almirante, the Prince of Asturias is not his father's enemy; Your Serene Highness is; and we cannot categorize that as a crime worthy of punishment, rather as a wrong threatening many wrongs that must be avoided." And in the margin of his heavily reworked draft he repeated his critical recommendation: "Every effort must be made to disprove the offense." And he reiterated the menace, "This conspiracy is not against the K. but against A.: and this must not serve as accusation but as protection."

Then Viegas had second thoughts about sending this frank appraisal to Godoy. He drafted another letter, then began a third, "short and carefully phrased," in which he tried again to impress on Godoy the gravity of his situation. "The future is pregnant with the past; let's present it with a sound fetus, because he who conceived it is warning of the birth of a devouring monster." On further reflection, he decided not to send this draft either. However, "nonetheless," he recalled later, "I stopped thinking of the matter."[66] Did he fear personal consequences if his candid analysis were introduced in a trial of Godoy? Might he be judged partial to Godoy? How else might three drafts, none ever sent, be interpreted?

During the month of November, Viegas agonized over the legal dilemma and political pitfalls the case presented, as well as his future as *fiscal*. A man of rigorous logic and cautious disposition, he finally came up with a solution that might reconcile the interests of all parties: it would restore Fernando's honor, do the least damage to the authority of Charles IV, preserve Godoy's reputation, minimize the threat of French intervention in Spain's internal politics, even serve the aspiration of the Consejo de Castilla and disaffected aristocrats to recover the authority lost in recent years. His "plan de paz" proposed that Charles, on the basis of a simple finding of the Consejo rather than a formal trial, immediately declare Fernando innocent and that Fernando return to Madrid amid public acclaim, thenceforth participating in state affairs as his preparation for the responsibilities of subsequent kingship. Thereby the Consejo could refurbish its image as national symbol of law and justice, and acting governor Árias Mon y Velarde would be rewarded for carrying out his "plan" by appointment as *gobernador* of the Consejo de Castilla and a member of the Consejo de Estado. In return for procedural reforms, the Consejo de Castilla would reassume censorship of publications and the exercise of police power in Madrid.[67]

Viegas had gone to the Escorial as the Consejo's *fiscal* on 30 November to review evidence for an indictment. As he had foreseen in the multiple drafts of his letter to Godoy, nothing in the *sumaria* of the interrogations altered the view he had formed in November.[68] However, after Mon y Velarde reminded him twice that Charles was awaiting his report *(informe)*, Viegas, still hoping to avoid a trial—the worst-case scenario—entrusted his "plan de paz" (but not a *sumaria*) to Godoy for presentation to Charles IV on 14 December. His fear that his plan would be rejected was confirmed the next morning: Godoy reported that Viegas had deeply disappointed Charles ("he had lost the King's good opinion"), who had vetoed the plan. Viegas was now ordered to demand confessions, draw up the indictment, and proceed with the trial.[69] We may only conclude that Godoy, or Charles, or both had lost touch with reality or were convinced of an assassination plot, part of a palace coup d'état.

How Viegas was now alternately cajoled and intimidated by Godoy and, as we shall see, pressured both by Gracia y Justicia Secretary Caballero and Hacienda Secretary Soler to indict Escoiquiz and Infantado for conspiracy and treason with a recommendation of capital punishment remains obscure despite Viegas's efforts to shed responsibility, then and later. No doubt he foresaw the publicity and inevitable political polarization that the forthcoming trial and sentence of guilt or, more likely, innocence might produce, not to mention his personal risk as the *fiscal*. The risk was obvious: once Viegas learned that Godoy had destroyed Viegas's "plan de paz" and demanded any earlier drafts (presumably also to be destroyed), he realized that he must safeguard his notes and his person.[70] He decided to safeguard the notes, made before leaving Madrid for the Escorial, on the situation so "extraordinary" in which he found himself. On 16 December he entrusted secretly to the prior of the prestigious Monasterio de San Lorenzo del Escorial a sealed envelope *(pliego)* containing drafts of his critical (but undelivered) letter to Godoy, along with a decree pronouncing Crown Prince Fernando innocent. Also included was a memorandum he had prepared to explain his decision to proceed with the trial in response to a royal order transmitted orally by Godoy, despite Viegas's foreboding that those pushing for the trial would live to regret it.[71]

The prediction came true soon enough. Three months later Godoy would be arrested in the course of the coup at Aranjuez and Charles IV's abdication to Fernando. *Fiscal* Viegas, now the target of *fernandista*-inspired mob violence, wrote on 20 March to the prior of San Lorenzo to release the documents in the *pliego* to one of three individuals.[72] The prior immediately assured Viegas that he would personally deliver the sealed envelope entrusted to his safekeeping in December.[73] Viegas enclosed the prior's reply along with a new *memoria* addressed to the duque del Infantado (whom he had been pressured to declare guilty with a sentence of capital punishment); Fernando had already appointed Infantado president of the Consejo de Castilla. Viegas's *memoria* charged that Godoy had maneuvered to blame him for "those iniquitous measures"—the indictment; he begged Infantado to explain to Fernando that as *fiscal* he had been obliged to execute Charles's orders, communicated by Godoy, which now put him in a dangerously exposed position. He also told Infantado that he was preparing for the Consejo a full account of his role in the trial.[74]

Fiscal Viegas's Choice: The Price of Loyalty

After Fernando returned to Madrid as king after the March coup at Aranjuez, Viegas sent him on 30 March a *representación* detailing his dilemma as *fiscal,* the dangers he had foreseen in pursuing the trial under duress according to the "order or disorder planned," and his imminent prosecution by *fernandistas.*[75] "Ever since I was chosen as Fiscal in the Causa del Escorial," ran his representation, "the way of carrying out the commission was an enigma to me, since it was given as truth what was not, and moreover a monstrous anachronism was committed by substantiating a case after the sentencing." The reason: "It was given as truth what was not, because Your Majesty was supposed to be part of the conspiracy against the life of the King father, and there was the anachronism of substantiating a case already judged, because the case and my charge were understood to include Your Majesty's associates in the enterprise that the decree of 30 October . . . qualified as conspiracy against the King's life." The *asociados* had been revealed to Charles by Fernando's own declaration; they were included in the same royal decree identifying them as traitors *(infidentes),* hence the sentence. "If the conspiracy was true . . . the case had already been judged by no less a person than the King himself, who had ordered its substantiation, and it was unlawful to raise the question whether the enterprise had or had not been an act of disloyalty, much less when the assessment given by the oracle of justice had been executed by no less than the person of Your Majesty." Viegas went on to explain that he had used all his "political and philosophical reflection," as well as the most appropriate language he could muster, to win Godoy's approval for his "plan de paz." This would have declared at the outset Fernando's innocence on the basis ("como resultado") of the investigation promised by royal decree in October 1807. However, Godoy had informed him that Charles and María Luisa had rejected the "plan," insisting on a rigorous indictment of Fernando's supporters. Thus, his *representación* pointed out, if Fernando's innocence had been questioned, now Viegas suffered from public charges, at Madrid and elsewhere in Spain, of adulation, libel, and bureaucratic complaisance.

At this point a desperate Viegas raised the key issue: who was really responsible for the trial and its preordained outcome? Although he alone had served loyally, now he alone had to bear the brunt of public hostility for his prominent role in the trial he had tried to avoid. "In those very critical circumstances when terror and slander held sway over opinions, not excepting those of the royal Parents, who had the false idea that there was a conspiracy," he protested bitterly to Fernando, "the only voice in favor of Your Majesty was mine, and I am the sole sufferer." Ironically and pointedly he asked, "Did the ministers of Your Majesty speak up? Did the Consejo or any other tribunal of the Kingdom speak? Did the grandees?" "Ah, Señor!" he continued, "now everyone celebrates the triumph over the slanderer [Godoy]; but at that time everyone let him triumph! Everyone saw the bloody destruction done in honor of Your Majesty and kept silent." *Fiscal* Viegas was now abandoning caution for dangerous finger-pointing.

Viegas concluded his 30 March *representación* to Fernando with a plea for a public declaration that he had faithfully executed a royal mandate as a loyal public servant. However, should Fernando now deny his request for "the discretion followed in this matter," he wanted to be tried in Spain's highest court, the Consejo de Castilla. For the most convincing proof of his loyalty, he called on Charles IV and María Luisa to exonerate him. Last, if these pleas were rejected, he requested permission to publish his own defense, his *representación*.

Back in December 1807 fear of Charles IV's anger and of Godoy's retaliation had induced Viegas to comply with a procedure he believed was unsubstantiated and dangerous. Now, in the following March, that fear had been replaced by fear of imminent physical attack by *fernandista* mobs and by concern for his honor, career, and "posthumous reputation" under Fernando's regime. These preoccupations explain Viegas's decision following Fernando's accession to prepare repeated explanations of his actions; the internal consistency and circumstantial details of Viegas's declarations lend credibility to the *fiscal*'s situation. They also explain another, by far his lengthiest exposé of the overlooked, complex political chemistry of the Escorial trial: an "Exposición" addressed to the Consejo de Castilla and Infantado, now its president, drafted prior to Infantado's departure for Bayonne in the company of other grandees and associates of Fernando to meet Bonaparte, a prelude to the dramatic political transformation in the spring of 1808.[76]

Viegas's strange, self-deprecating *exposición* began abruptly with a confession of his "fright and cowardice" at the Escorial in December, and it ended equally abruptly on the note that he had not wished to be present when the sentence ending the trial was voted by the *consejo*. His new version of the Escorial affair carefully reconstructed and analyzed what had taken place at his meetings with Godoy from 15 to 17 December. For the first time, he referred specifically to the role of members of the cabinet, the ministers of Gracia y Justicia and Hacienda, Caballero and Soler, respectively. He offered no explanation why their activities had not been mentioned earlier.

Viegas's purpose was to present an insider's exposé of how Godoy had manipulated power and the king's authority to play on Viegas's fear of being called a traitor in order to persuade him to obtain the indictment from Soler and sign it.[77] His details provide insight into the nature of Godoy's power by suggesting how the *privado* used his *privanza* with Charles to play individuals and factions against one another and thus to manipulate Charles himself. Godoy used this tactic in the Escorial case, leading Viegas to recall other situations in which Godoy had played on Viegas's sense of responsibility to force him to follow his political line. The main aim of the *exposición* was to lay bare Godoy's "skill in having dislike of those iniquitous measure fall upon me" and the adroit tactics by which Godoy had systematically fortified personal power through a system of domineering clientelism exercised in the name of the king.

In his 30 March appeal to Fernando, Viegas had asserted that, like the public at large, he had become convinced that "sinister skills . . . bewitching the right reason of the King Father, were manipulating such dreadful events; that is, we understood that they were manipulating those skills, but none of us knew which they were." He now explained how a mysterious, Machiavellian-like operation had occurred through the "mastery that a depraved individual can acquire over the reason of a just one," alluding as much to himself as to Charles IV.[78]

Viegas returned to that decisive, "notable" meeting of 15 December, when Godoy had reported that he had read his "plan de paz" to Charles and María Luisa and that the king had rejected it, insisting that Viegas as *fiscal* proceed with the indictment and trial of Infantado, Escoiquiz, and the grandees involved.[79] Godoy, he recalled, had quoted an observation made by Charles at the time—"Didn't I tell you that Viegas belongs to Villafranca's faction?"—adding that he had assured Charles that Viegas was really "on the side of reason, nothing more." From this Viegas had to conclude that Charles had been persuaded that he was unreliable, allied with the exiled marqués de Villafranca and presumably with other dissenting aristocrats, and therefore dangerous and that only Godoy stood between him and Charles's disfavor. In return, Viegas, as a faithful client, was expected to forget his "plan" and execute Godoy's orders without criticism. As Viegas put it, "All with the idea that I would become afraid of the path [the *plan de paz*] that I had started on and that out of gratitude to him, and to disprove His Majesty's opinion, I would do whatever he proposed."[80]

In recalling Charles's reference to Villafranca as reported by Godoy, Viegas began to retrace how Godoy had used him for his own political ends, the indictment he had been obliged to sign being but the last and most damaging of these tactics.[81] He recalled that before 1806 he had frequented the marqueses de Villafranca, both intimates of Fernando and his Anglophile Neapolitan wife, Carolina, and publicly critical of Godoy.[82] However, shortly before their exile from the court, during a public reception Godoy, ostentatiously and in a pose of familiarity, had called Viegas aside to caution him against such visits. Fearing that he too might be exiled from Madrid, Viegas quickly and quietly complied, failing, however, to explain to the Villafrancas the reason for his absence: "Spies were everywhere, in all classes."[83] And there was more. Right after Villafranca and other grandees were exiled from the court, Godoy's mistress, Pepa Tudó, together with the condesa de Gálvez, had spread the rumor that Viegas had denounced them, a rumor Viegas had to vehemently deny. It was then that he perceived that Godoy intended to isolate him from the *grandeza* and possible protection from that quarter, making him entirely dependent on Godoy, a conclusion confirmed, Viegas wrote, by Godoy's studied comment during the memorable 15 December meeting that the king associated Viegas with the aristocratic faction against him, headed by Villafranca.[84]

Viegas interpreted the Villafranca incident as part of a strategy by which Godoy had led Charles to believe that Fernando was "stupid, bad, dangerous, in a word a traitor," that Godoy was "the only one faithful to King and Crown," and that by such reasoning "he categorized as treasonous everything that accused or attacked him in any way, as though everything aimed to strip the King of a dedicated supporter of his life and government." Skilled in drawing general principles from particular facts, the *fiscal* concluded ruefully that "the effects of the suggestion are composed of the cunning of the suggestor and the favorable disposition, confidence, and lack of perspicacity on the part of the suggested person," Viegas himself.[85] Gullibility, he now realized, also applied to Charles himself and others. "You need a talent with a sinister mind, a decided propensity for dishonesty, for machination," he wrote of Godoy, "to play constantly with so many loose ends, at the same time assuring all those whom he mesmerizes with a certain consistency, so that they see matters not as they are, . . . allowing them to see only that part of the truth that fits his ideas."[86]

Further details of that 15 December meeting, when he had consented reluctantly to draft the indictment, substantiated Viegas's conclusion that Godoy had trapped him. Following his private talk with Godoy, and after Godoy cajoled him into displaying his proficiency with the guitar,[87] the ministers of Gracia y Justicia and Hacienda, Caballero and Soler, appeared. After Godoy summarized Viegas's reservations about the proposed indictment, each minister addressed him as though he were a tyro ("impérito"), insisting that Fernando had indeed been a traitor to his father along with Infantado and Escoiquiz. Caballero mused that Charles might disinherit Fernando, while Soler offered to cite to the *fiscal* (a learned jurist) the appropriate legal text justifying capital punishment for Infantado and Escoiquiz. For his part, Viegas doubted that the two ministers really believed they could persuade him, "because both knew well that I could not entertain such absurd ideas, whether my own or suggested by them." However, they spoke "confident that they could flatter the Almirante and that the same fear that made them speak would make me keep silent."[88] Viegas could only conclude that Caballero and Soler were Godoy's willing, collaborating clients.

Without challenging the arguments of Caballero and Soler, Viegas then consented to present an indictment of treason, as he felt bound to, after Godoy reported that Charles had rejected his "plan de paz."[89] Now he recommended that Escoiquiz and Infantado "be declared traitors," but with his explicit, self-defending proviso that "this is no proof that I did so, but that the King had so declared them as cooperating with the Prince, declared a traitor." He had not communicated this proviso earlier to Godoy, who continued to try to persuade Viegas of Fernando's treason. Repeatedly referring to Soler as a legal authority who could provide the specific statute, Godoy insisted that Fernando had been a traitor "inasmuch as he had slandered him, hoping to estrange him from the King, and that treason committed against himself as Almirante corresponded with what the Ley described as committed against the Condestable (so he said, because he forgot that the Ley referred instead to the Adelantado)." King and *privado,*

Charles and Godoy, were inseparable in Viegas's view. He confessed that he had not ventured to question Godoy's legal reasoning, lest he say anything "that might impede the progress in the discoveries I was making at that meeting."[90]

The next day, 16 December, in another private meeting with Godoy, Viegas consented to "move ahead to an indictment requesting capital punishment." However, at the same time he again warned Godoy of the consequences of proceeding with the trial. One would clearly have been a wave of popular retaliation against Godoy, and against himself as author of the indictment.[91] Godoy reassured him, referring to the protection promised him by Bonaparte ("his own principality in Portugal") and implying that he, Godoy, would protect Viegas. For proof Godoy then took from his desk and read Viegas's *exposición* and "the whole original correspondence with the Court of France, so that I might see . . . the treaty of 27 October on the division of Portugal, thinking I would be happy, or at least assured by the idea of the intimacy and confidence he had with the Emperor and his Ministers."

Still unconvinced, and intent upon dispelling the perception that solely fear for his personal security had motivated his "plan de paz," Viegas reiterated his concern for "the common good of the Nation (embodied in the well-being of the Prince of Asturias)," as well as Godoy's fate. He reminded Godoy that a Portuguese principality could hardly protect him from the consequences already pointed out and insisted that it still would not be "unseemly" for Charles to reestablish Fernando's honor, since it would not contradict the decree of 30 October, which had merely promised an investigation. In fact, "it was more honest, easier, and of better consequences to excuse the hasty manner in which the first decree was framed than to ratify it with additional measures that over time would be mishandled." He declared that when Caballero and Soler had entered the meeting on the previous day, "he had found them so obliging and obsequious, facilitating everything, that there would come a day when they would say it was proper to undo everything, just as then they said it was proper to do; and as long as there was no threat to them, they maintained their decorum and that of the memory of the King."[92] Without reply, Godoy, according to Viegas's *exposición,* moved away to stir embers in the fireplace. Only when Viegas observed obliquely that "one needs to fear that Prince and that the life of the King is as fallible as ours" did Godoy reply, "I surely would be foolish if I expected," and then he muttered, "It may be that he will not reign."[93]

It is plausible that Viegas simply invented Godoy's comment. Regardless of his perception of Godoy's intentions and his own fears for himself and the "greater" interests of the "Nation," as a loyal public servant he agreed to draft the indictment proposed by his superior and apparently ideated by Soler.[94] Viegas was probably not surprised, therefore, that after reviewing a draft of the indictment, Godoy sent him to Soler. That minister, whom Viegas had to visit secretly the evening of 17 December, revealed that once Fernando's papers had been discovered on 27 October, Charles had asked him, as one trained in the law, to research the statutes covering the situation. Soler, after stating that he had done so, took a document (which he claimed Charles had praised) and read it to Viegas, adding that after writing it "in a single night," he had had it copied and then destroyed his original draft. More to the point, Soler confided that Fernando's "treason" had been induced by Carolina, his first wife. In fact, the design of dethroning Charles IV, Soler noted, was really the work of Carolina's mother, the queen of Naples, together with the czar of Russia and the English.[95]

Soler's legal brief, in which Viegas found amplified the verbose legal non sequiturs he had heard from Godoy, confirmed his worst fears: "Just as they fooled the King, presenting as mine what they had me say, so they presented to me as coming from the King what they said and did, the difference being that the King did not know of it, but I did; this did not matter to them, since they knew their secret was safe because I was afraid."[96] In fact, Viegas felt obligated to model his indictment on Soler's brief, even copying the additions Soler subsequently provided. The *fiscal* took pains, moreover, to explain in his *exposición* that at that time he was sure that neither Caballero nor Soler could have believed, any more than he, that Fernando was guilty of planning parricide nor that Escoiquiz and Infantado might be proven guilty on the basis of his indictment. Viegas assumed that Caballero and Soler had acted merely as "business agents" and that Soler had been assigned the task of framing the indictment.[97]

Viegas ended his *exposición* to the Consejo and Infantado with the assertion that "they had made the King believe everything." From the 30 October decree in which Carles IV claimed that his life had been endangered many times, the *fiscal* deduced that Charles had long been led to believe that his life was at risk, that his own children "sought to take his life," that only Godoy was loyal, and indeed that an attack on Godoy was ultimate proof of conspiracy against his own life.[98] Looking back, Viegas marveled at the internal consistency ("relaciones tan conformes") in the sequence of political events since Trafalgar and even before. All revealed to him the fissioning of Spain's civil society and Godoy's role. All, he felt, coincided "to find treason in the person who labels as traitors those who have not been."[99]

Viegas had to confess that he had participated in the risky scheme, torn between laughter at the farce that had trapped him and indignation at witnessing "the secrecy with which they pursued the case, where everything . . . was used to justify for the King how the Prince was handled, because they would say"—here one sees the prestige Viegas had earned as a learned jurist—"that when a Jurist of my reputation includes accomplices in the penalty for treason, then His Majesty could understand his son's offense." He spelled out the consequences, personal and national: "What a misfortune to have to live by such dangerous tricks! What disrespect for the King's inattention! How sacrilegious is the action of the mother against the honor of husband and son, to the ruin and dishonor of the whole Nation too!" These very persons, he noted, then hypocritically had implored Charles to commute the death sentence to exile and "a disgraceful mitigation in the sentencing for good behavior." In this fashion "el buen Señor" had been well "repaid for the mildness of his decrees; offended by the one he loved; content with the zeal of those who tricked him and exposed his conduct to the most indecorous censure of the Nation and all Europe."[100]

The ease with which the defense undermined the points of his indictment was no surprise to Viegas. The longest brief, by Juan Madrid Dávila for Escoiquiz (largely written by Escoiquiz himself), refuted the indictment, using the chance to project again the image of Fernando's innocence and Godoy's guilt. Infantado's lawyer, José de Salas, denied that the duke was guilty merely because he had accepted the undated decree giving him political and military authority on the death of Charles.

By mid-January, however, the situation had worsened: the Treaty of Fontainebleau was already a dead letter; French forces controlled Portugal and were rapidly extending their occupation of Spain. Viegas knew that the judges were gathering at the Escorial to decide the case and, far more important, that he as *fiscal,* together with the Consejo de Castilla, was fated to play a decisive role in Godoy's eclipse. And play his role he did. In his *informe* presented at the last hearing ("dia de la vista"), Viegas undertook "to destroy everything written in the indictment: an arduous, difficult, and ingenious task . . . for which I flatter myself. Justice and love guided me."[101] When the defense denied that any crime had been committed, Viegas had to concede that although the king "had said they were disloyal . . . I could not prove it."[102]

At this point abandoning Godoy's defense based on the assimilation of *rey* and *adelantado* in the laws of the Siete Partidas, he fell back to his original position: that the defendants were guilty because the crux of the matter was not whether a crime had been committed but that the king had so declared and the accused had confessed. Although his justification had been fallacious in citing the Leyes de Partida, the royal decree remained in its original legal force. Further, since the defendants had confessed their guilt, they were guilty. The royal dictum, Viegas insisted, was like that of God, whose reasons were inscrutable and whose wisdom was infinite.[103] Ever searching for legal consistency, ever loyal to the regime, to its monarch, and to the Consejo de Castilla, and perhaps acting, too, from personal and professional pride (what Soler later derided as "caprice"), Viegas refused to retract the charge against Fernando's supporters: guilty by virtue of the royal decree and their confessions.[104]

Late in January, in a final statement to the jury of eleven members of the Consejo de Castilla, Viegas seemed to exonerate Charles IV from responsibility for the consequences of his 30 October decree. In March, he incorporated his *informe,* as further proof of loyalty to Charles and Fernando, in a final *representación* to the Consejo de Castilla. Quoting the *informe* verbatim, Viegas praised Charles and eulogized the Consejo, writing that the king "could render justice himself . . . but entrusted [the issue] to a Junta that embodies the license of the law and the fidelity of the Sovereign . . . A Junta of Ministers selected from his high Consejo; from that Consejo of which Charles V said . . . it was the pillar of the State and carried the conscience of the King and the hopes of the Fatherland." In citing his *informe* he hoped to emphasize the "respect the Ministers should have for themselves and that their sentence was open to public censure out of respect for the general opinion, always favorable to the Prince." In support of what he hoped might be the impact of his *informe* on the jury of *consejeros,* he cited the comment of one of the defense lawyers: "It strikes me that Señor Viegas has prepared an *informe* designed to have the Junta do nothing about his request."[105] That lawyer had gotten Viegas's message, his plea for understanding and compassion.

The Process of the Indictment

Viegas's successive explanations of his role in the Causa del Escorial confirm that he drafted the indictment driven by understandable fear of Godoy's retaliation. Here, fear and cowardice were intertwined. But this conclusion fails to clarify the process by which the *fiscal* submitted the indictment— why he proposed to cover up the Escorial affair with his "plan de paz" and then drafted an indictment that he knew could not withstand legal scrutiny; why he stated subsequently that guilt had been proven solely because the sovereign had so ruled; and finally, why he exhorted the jury to use the prerogative granted by the sovereign.

Casuistic as Viegas's final resolution of his dilemma is, his reconstruction of the origin and outcome of the indictment illuminates the inner dynamic of the Escorial affair and the roles of those involved. First, it highlights the 30 October decree in determining the jury's finding of innocence and the responsibility of high civil servants collaborating with disaffected aristocrats in the palace coup to remove Godoy. Second, by granting Godoy an immunity equal to that of the king, it appears to confirm Escoiquiz's accusation that Godoy had indeed supplanted Charles's authority. Third, Viegas's claim that when Escoiquiz maligned María Luisa and Charles ("inert machine"), it confirmed Escoiquiz's warning of the political dangers in the peculiar personal relationship between Godoy and María Luisa and Charles IV. Viegas's indictment, as he had tried to enlighten—and alert—Godoy, determined that the trial would ultimately focus on Godoy, making him the victim of the trial.

Viegas's varying explanations match both his evolving comprehension of the case and its shifting political context. At first he interpreted "so extraordinary a situation" as the consequence of Godoy's ill-counseled drafting of the decree signed by Charles. Subsequent examination of the evidence and, above all, Godoy's insistence that Viegas formulate an indictment based on the Siete Partidas led Viegas to conclude that Godoy—seconded by Caballero and Soler—was the author of the attack on Fernando. In reviewing the rapid polarization of public opinion after Trafalgar and the mounting opposition to Godoy's understandably erratic domestic and foreign policies, he placed the Escorial case in the larger context of Spain's imperial crisis. The end of civil society that he saw in the atmosphere of intrigue and mutual incrimination between Francophiles and Francophobes, exemplified by Villafranca's exile and Godoy's remark, moved him to find Godoy responsible for the destruction of that society and to see his removal as desirable. In November Viegas had warned Godoy of the pitfalls awaiting him and the monarchy by incriminating Fernando, and then devised his "plan de paz" to stabilize the situation; later external and internal developments had led him to embrace the foretold outcome of the Escorial trial.

Viegas's reassessment clarifies another crucial element in the trial: the origin of the decision to use the Siete Partidas to serve Godoy's intentions. From Godoy's reliance first on Caballero and Soler to persuade Viegas to recommend capital punishment for Infantado and Escoiquiz and then on Soler's presentation of the legal basis for such a recommendation, the *fiscal* concluded that the two ministers had not been acting independently, but as *agentes de negocios;* presumably they too had been motivated by fear or by loyalty to Godoy. Had Caballero and Soler in fact been instruments of the *privado* in pressuring Viegas to prepare the Draconian indictment, although neither they nor Godoy really intended to implement it? Had they so convinced Godoy that he followed their advice and drafted the indictment of Fernando in the decree of 30 October, as Viegas noted? Fragmentary but more significant evidence suggests that they were not Godoy's instruments.

Just as Viegas's need to protect himself from mob violence and defend his "posthumous reputation" led to his explanations and reflections just analyzed, similarly Soler sought to clear himself once Fernando became king. In so doing he shed more light on the Escorial's peculiar mechanics. A week after the coup at Aranjuez in March, Soler, dismissed from his post as secretary of the Hacienda and his Madrid town house torched by *fernandista* mobs, wrote to Caballero on 28 March from the Escorial that the prior of the monastery there had just told him that he had handed to Infantado Viegas's sealed envelope containing the "plan de paz" that had displeased Charles, María Luisa, and Godoy. Included in the envelope was Viegas's memo on what he termed "all that occurred in preparing his *fiscal's* response in which he acted at the express order of the King to avoid greater harm that to the contrary threatened us and doubtless would have prevented the great benefit Spain now enjoys." Soler added that the prior had reported that "no one had spoken of me [Soler], at the same time that you [Caballero] promised me and must have done so with the Duque, Escoiquiz, and the principal judges that when Viegas's exposition was read the compulsory and necessary reason for my intervention in a task diametrically opposed to my way of thinking would be known, proven by [my] having obtained effectively along with you and Cevallos the pardon of the Prince of Asturias."

Soler reminded Caballero that both had threatened to resign if Fernando was not granted a pardon. He recalled that both had insisted that the trial be pursued in strict conformity with the law and that there be no fewer than eleven judges, ruling out "all those whom you and I thought capable of any wickedness, whose procedures could at least promote the success that was verified, denying and rendering useless the Fiscal response that had motivated force and the most ridiculous whim."[106] Soler was now turning on Viegas. He appealed to Caballero to fulfill his promise to clear him, since Caballero was "the only one who can restore my standing, unjustly lost after ten years of sacrifice, misfortunes, and ignominious slanders the evil one has made us endure."[107] Now Soler turned on Godoy. Although he was sure that an investigation would eventually exonerate him, he urged Caballero to intervene quickly to restore his reputation, "lost along with the unjustified burning of my belongings," and his social status in Spanish society, "which cannot be restored in any way at this time."[108]

Two days later Caballero forwarded Fernando's order that Soler testify that Godoy had written Charles's 30 October decree—precisely what Viegas had observed earlier. A week later Soler replied that on the morning of 30 October, "when the Queen Mother spoke to me about the sad event of the night before [Fernando's arrest], she told me that very soon there would appear a Decree about the matter, without explaining to me its context."[109] Upset—"this news disturbed me excessively"—Soler, finding Caballero alone in the royal palace's Sala de Batallas, had expressed anguish and apprehension caused by Charles's 30 October decree. Unexpectedly, Soler testified, Caballero had then taken from his pocket a draft of the decree and asked him to identify the handwriting, adding that the king had ordered him to copy and return it. Recognizing Godoy's script, Soler warned Caballero that "whatever might be the context of the Decree, he should take the most suitable precautions to state that he had only obeyed the order of the King, and you agreed to carry this out in the manner you later described to me."[110]

This exchange between two ministers the morning of 30 October 1807 is highly significant, given their subsequent complicity in mid-December in persuading Viegas to file the peculiar indictment of 30 October, which would shape the trial's outcome. It will be recalled that Viegas claimed that neither Caballero nor Soler had believed in the validity of their reasoning and that Soler, in handing Viegas the draft of what "the king wanted," had seemed to be acting as Godoy's "agente de negocios."[111] Moreover, Viegas concluded that by confusing *adelantado* with *condestable* in the Siete Partidas, Godoy had revealed that he was unfamiliar with law codes; Viegas also recalled that Soler had explained to him that Charles had asked him to find the statute covering the case. Had Soler researched the statute?

Viegas, recalling Soler's excuse for not handing him his original draft, deduced that someone else had ideated the reference to the Siete Partidas and presumably drafted the indictment copied by Godoy. Who, then, had been responsible for suggesting the fateful strategy to Godoy? Caballero, long Godoy's political antagonist, rival for the king's confidence, skilled in criminal law, and adept at court intrigue? Beyond doubt Caballero's participation in Godoy's downfall was crucial, as he claimed in 1814 in defending himself against critics. In March 1808 Caballero, who had "brought matters to the point they were"—to cite a French source—did not yet need to clear himself, unlike Viegas and Soler.[112] But six years later he felt impelled to introduce a missing clue to the murky origin of the 30 October decree that, with the indictment, became the crux of the Causa.

In 1814 Caballero tried to rebut Escoiquiz's claim that after the March coup at Aranjuez, Fernando VII's ministerial appointees had questioned his loyalty. He insisted that he had been the first to charge Godoy with libeling the then crown prince, Fernando. When Caballero examined the 30 October decree, whose final draft, he recalled, was in Godoy's handwriting, he had gathered his colleagues to show them the decree and denounce Godoy for falsely accusing Fernando of parricide "as the decree stated." For proof he cited another figure, Pedro Cevallos, who "in view of his honesty . . . is incapable of anything less than the truth."[113] Thus it would appear that Caballero was the first, in the company of Charles and María Luisa, to examine the document found in Fernando's quarters; the first to counsel Charles to inform the public and call for a trial; the first government official to receive and implement the 30 October decree ultimately drafted by Godoy; and the first to denounce Godoy to colleagues for the decree's false charges. He was probably responsible for creating the possibility of a trial in which Godoy, not Fernando, would be the ultimate victim. And it would appear that Caballero had major responsibility for shifting the thrust of the trial from Fernando's associates to what became Godoy's *escarmiento,* the classic object lesson of a public official.[114]

There is a near consensus on Caballero's role in the onset of Spain's political crisis in 1807 and early 1808, yet he remains an enigmatic figure. Did he in fact make the decisions attributed to him, and if so, was Charles so frightened by events that he accepted Caballero's advice without further consultation? Or was Caballero merely a point man for others involved, another *agente de negocios?* Unfortunately, the available record does not provide clear answers.

Godoy, for his part, never denied writing the decree nor promoting the 20 December indictment on which the trial and its outcome were based. According to his explanation, Charles IV had sent to him in Madrid, when he was ill and feverish, a confused note about finding incriminating papers in Fernando's possession.[115] He had written back immediately, recommending solely precautionary measures, careful inquiry followed by merely a warning to Fernando and the exile of his accomplices—all with minimal publicity; only if it was unavoidable should judicial proceedings be initiated. Along with other key documents, however, his response to Charles had also been destroyed, he claimed, by enemies. Late in the evening of 29 October Charles's second note, reporting Fernando's refusal to talk and his arrest, arrived, accompanied by the draft of the royal decree in which Godoy recognized Caballero's stern juridical mentality and unrelieved judicial legal style.[116] Still ill and ill-informed, Godoy managed to redraft the decree in language more appropriate to the benign image of Charles IV and yet retain the substance of the original draft.[117] Godoy was fingering Caballero.

How much Godoy gleaned of the situation from Charles's letters or other sources; what Caballero's original draft was, if indeed there was one; why Godoy failed to guard these documents; why Godoy returned the decree now drafted in his own handwriting—all may ultimately be ascribed to Godoy's loyalty to Charles IV, to illness, ignorance, fear, haste, the egotism of power, or that ineptitude often attributed to him.[118] Whatever the reasons for his week-long absence at this critical moment, once he reached the Escorial on 3 November, he was confronted with a *fait accompli*. Escoiquiz's skillfully contrived attack on Godoy was in Caballero's possession; Fernando and his entourage had been arrested; and Fernando had confessed his role in the preemptive empowerment of Infantado and the letter to Bonaparte. Meanwhile, Charles had dispatched his letter to Bonaparte accusing Fernando of regicide and threatening to disinherit him, and his decree publicizing the conspiracy and announcing an investigation by the Consejo de Castilla had been published. These could not be rescinded; the principal determinants of the Escorial trial were locked in place.

If neither Godoy nor Charles was aware of the trap for Godoy in the discovered documents, couched in terms clearly intended to outrage the king and his favorite, are there other explanations for Godoy's determined insouciance in November—his disregard of Viegas's warning that he was the real target of the discovered papers or his support of Charles's insistence that Viegas draft (or redraft) the indictment (probably the work of Caballero)? One explanation may be Caballero and Soler's apparent support for the indictment. Another, highly dubious explanation may be his misplaced confidence in his personal benefit from collaboration with the French in the occupation of Portugal, a principality that Bonaparte promised to carve out for him in Portugal at a moment when Godoy was anxious about his personal security at Madrid.

The connection between Godoy's sense of political isolation, his odd faith in Bonaparte, and the Escorial affair are highlighted in two letters of 1806 and 1807 seeking French support against his political opposition. The first, addressed to Bonaparte, claimed that the queen of Naples was plotting with her daughter, Fernando's wife, to assassinate Godoy, Charles, and María Luisa. "Their Majesties are daily threatened with poisoning, as I am also," he complained. "The King has written to the King of Naples, his brother, threatening him vengefully . . . but it is necessary, sire, that Your

Imperial and Royal Majesty end these dangers."[119] Despite reliable reports of French designs upon Spain and its empire in America, Godoy continued to seek salvation in Bonaparte as late as December 1807, during the Escorial trial, when he thanked Bonaparte for the promised Portuguese principality, offering in return "the sword and strong heart of the most respectful of your admirers."[120]

This letter to Bonaparte accompanied an even more revealing note to Joaquin Murat, who was then attached to Bonaparte's staff in Italy. After a paragraph of extraordinary adulation, Godoy referred to the Treaty of Fontainebleau and the peace of mind it had given him. Godoy felt that if Charles IV should die, "under the Emperor's protection" he would have nothing to fear from the aristocratic opposition. "I have no other friend in the world but Your Highness," he confided, adding that "I am persuaded that your power probably saved me grief." In late December Godoy was preoccupied with the progress of the case against "the criminal groups around the Prince of Asturias." Charles IV, he confided to Murat, "has resolved not to use his sovereign Authority, whereby he could judge them himself, and has given the Judges freedom to consult His Majesty about the sentence." Although the two most accused deserved capital punishment, María Luisa had intervened with Charles to grant them clemency, and he predicted that the sentence of capital punishment would be commuted to internal exile.[121]

Thus, as late as 24 December, only four days before Viegas presented his indictment, Godoy remained certain of the outcome of the trial, a conviction of guilt. Did he also believe that Fernando might be excluded from the succession on the basis of a conditional pardon but undenied guilt, as Charles's private letter to Bonaparte and Viegas's analysis of the situation suggested? Bonaparte, as we shall see, briefly entertained and even prepared for Fernando's possible exclusion early in 1808. The outcome of the Escorial affair and the breakdown of the Treaty of Fontainebleau would, however, shortly strip Godoy of power and prepare the Spanish scene for greater changes.

As the Escorial trial unfolded after the appearance of the October decree in the *Gaceta de Madrid,* the royal pardon granted to Fernando, and then the indictment presented to the Consejo, its outcome, so contrary to Godoy's expectation, was foreseeable. Key cabinet officers—Caballero, Cevallos, Soler, and Gil y Lemos—were ready to undermine the authority of Charles's *privado.*[122] In rejecting the "plan de paz," which Viegas considered the least destabilizing solution, Godoy had decided on a path of action that, if supported by highly placed civil servants, could have no result other than the loss of status that he feared he must share with Charles IV. Looking back years after the Escorial episode, Godoy justified his decision to move against Fernando: "I would have been a traitor if, on learning that the prince and heir was conspiring in this fashion . . . I had not roused the justice of his father and provoked an *escarmiento*."[123]

The Escorial Affair as *Escarmiento:* The *Golpistas*

Who initiated the conspiracy to remove a high-level executive enjoying royal favor by the classic Spanish formula, an *escarmiento*? For *escarmiento* was what the Escorial trial became once Charles's secretary of Gracia y Justicia, Caballero, showed the royal decree of 30 October to Soler, Cevallos, Gil y Lemos, and Arias Mon and accused Godoy of libeling the crown prince. One historian has concluded that the Escorial began as a conspiracy by Godoy against Fernando, who "provided the weapon," but it backfired. Did Escoiquiz provide that weapon—the purposefully provocative documents in Fernando's possession—expecting that Godoy's reaction (as Viegas foresaw) would lead him "to the precipice"? Was Godoy the target of an *escarmiento* from the beginning? Were Caballero, Charles's other ministers, and certain aristocrats Escoiquiz's abettors? Or was Caballero their point man, their master of ceremonies? These unresolved questions suggest the complexity of a recurrent phenomenon in Spain's old regime: the political *escarmiento*—a minicoup—against a highly empowered minister or confidant of the king, in which alienated interest groups collaborated.

A political *escarmiento* was a carefully choreographed object lesson in which an opposition faction without legitimate avenues of countering or removing a powerful minister sought "to trample on him and show him to the world as a traitor to State and King . . . as a great villain."[124] An *aparato de desgracia* might take a variety of forms, such as the secret sequestration of an unpopular minister at night, subsequently justified by a campaign of denigration, as was done in removing the popular marqués de la Ensenada in 1754. Or it might originate with a campaign to discredit a leading civil servant and end in riots triggered by an incident stemming from a measure considered unjust and a violation of recognized rights directly attributed to him. Such a scenario had brought Esquilache's removal in 1766.[125] A decade later the mere threat of similar violence induced Grimaldi's resignation; less than twenty years later the conde de Aranda, whose arrogance was proverbial to the point of predictability, was tricked into committing an act of disrespect *(desacato)* to Charles IV that triggered his removal. In other words, an *escarmiento* aggregated various elements of propaganda, fear, provocation, and force majeure.[126]

When aimed at the highest government level, an *escarmiento* was usually crafted by figures within the power structure united by the desire to remove one whose policies threatened many elite interests. Because the target's power stemmed directly from the monarch and could not be challenged overtly, opponents concealed themselves by contriving a situation in which he would make a move that outraged "public opinion," usually inflamed by anonymous lampoons, by arousing "popular" violence and bringing about his downfall. In the case of a minister who was dependent on subordinates to formalize, process, and execute his policies, this was not difficult, since the manner in which those policies were enacted and then enforced often provided the pretext for the attack. This happened to Godoy, as it had to Esquilache four decades earlier. In the Madrid riots that forced the departure of Esquilache, both methods were required to destroy the Italian minister to whom Charles III had given wide authority to realize a *regeneración* of Spain. However, Charles's initial refusal to abandon Esquilache resulted in a temporary loss of royal prestige and the authority of the state when the monarch and the royal family had to flee from Madrid to Aranjuez at night.[127]

In 1807, of course, the opposition to Godoy recognized the bond between Charles and his *privado*. The opposition was also aware of the political damage to state authority caused by Esquilache's removal forty-one years earlier. Perhaps memories of the French Revolution led one of Godoy's opponents in Valencia to advise friends in Madrid to avoid popular riots at all cost. An informant ("a very wise man") of the secret agent Pedro Giraldo warned that "in such cases it's good to prepare the coup without revealing the intention; distributing pamphlets brings on disorder and achieves nothing." Rather, the incisive Valencian argued, "we must win over the heart of the upper classes because relying upon the crowd runs the risk that it will follow the loudest voice."[128]

Key actors in *escarmientos* tended to remain anonymous. If the operation failed, they usually escaped punishment; if it succeeded, their role was judiciously overlooked. The strategy of an *escarmiento* was devised, one suspects, by idea men of modest status whose role as advisers to, and collaborators with, elite elements was readily concealed. They were the ideators *(inductores),* sponsored by the abettors *(fautores),* who in turn moved the *motores,* who were often elements of the populace.[129] The *fautores'* high status protected them, while *motores* were lost in an anonymous collectivity; if individually identified, they were executed or pardoned.[130] Under the old regime, the *escarmiento* furnished the political opposition with an effective tool of last resort.

Pedro Giraldo, an intelligence agent, tried to define and analyze groups coalescing in opposition to Godoy and to predict their pattern of action. The most visible *fautores* in the *fernandista* opposition, the *grandeza*, would, he foretold, "throw the stone" and then take cover. Merchants who anticipated the event were, however, wary of committing themselves until the outcome seemed assured and "profitable." The people would act "like a magnetic needle . . . drawn to the most powerful magnet." The real strategists—idea men—Giraldo located among lawyers. "What they can provide is the ideas and a plan; they . . . are fearsome . . . because they delude and distract with a discourse apparently substantiated; if they begin to cite rights, they twist them, but they are not the ones who lead the attack."[131] His analysis could fit Charles's cabinet secretaries Caballero and Soler.

In the Escorial affair, Escoiquiz would be the *inducto,* crafting the provocation that incited Godoy to move against Fernando and his associates. His carefully prepared text offered Godoy grounds on which to accuse the heir apparent and his followers of treason against Charles IV and against himself as intimate adviser. Godoy could do this by writing (or rewriting) the 30 October decree. The decree, however, could only be substantiated if the documents in Fernando's room were legally determined an attack on the honor of Charles through his counselor, Godoy. Enjoying Charles's apparently unbounded confidence, accustomed to acting in his name, Godoy quickly embraced the evidence, as constructed by Soler, as well as recourse to the Siete Partidas, which Soler pretended to have researched. Charles also interpreted Escoiquiz's outrageous attacks on his *privado* as an attack on himself; hence he signed the 30 October decree.

Caballero knew that the draft of the decree (which he probably initiated) in Godoy's handwriting was unsubstantiated by the evidence left by Escoiquiz, hence that Godoy might be proven guilty of libel and consequently eliminated. By sharing this perception with other ministers as well as with the governor of the Consejo de Castilla (who was responsible for the publication of the decree), Cevallos, Gil y Lemos, and even Viegas and Soler became perhaps willing accomplices in Godoy's ouster.

One may ask whether Escoiquiz and Caballero were responsible for the *escarmiento* of Godoy. While Escoiquiz played a central role in the Escorial affair, he later implicated others within Cevallos's ministry of foreign affairs, just as Caballero subsequently appealed to the "unquestioned veracity" of Cevallos to refute charges of his disloyalty to Fernando. Although Caballero, for years Godoy's bitter antagonist, was the point man in initiating the *escarmiento* of Charles's *privado,* other top-level civil servants had concluded that Godoy's ouster was key to any solution of the political and economic crisis in Spain and its empire in America, which had been escalating since Trafalgar, perhaps even a decade earlier.

That solution, Escoiquiz had clarified in documents found in Fernando's possession, meant avoiding at all costs a "disastrous war with France," which was now inevitable if Godoy remained in power. It was believed that the short-term threat could come by land, from the postrevolutionary, militarized colossus north of the Pyrenees dominated by a career army officer leagued with a *bourgeoisie triomphante,* the archetypical authoritarian and liberal state. The survival of Spain and its colonial empire, reasoned Escoiquiz, Caballero, and probably First Minister Cevallos, now depended on formulating an imaginative, canny "French" strategy—a "gran plan"—for survival. So Escoiquiz persuaded the widower Fernando that marriage to a "princess of the Emperor's family" could forestall such a calamity, and he drafted Fernando's letter of 11 October to Bonaparte precisely to solicit French occupation. Thus, though the French "connection" was excluded from the trial proceedings "for reasons of state," the Escorial affair included an agenda that directly addressed the external threat posed by the entry of French forces into Spain, begun only days before the dramatic political "theater" opened on 27 October at the royal residence at the Escorial.

There is a final aspect to the Escorial affair and its objective, removing Godoy: were he to remain as confidant of Charles and María Luisa, might he in desperation counsel following the example of the Braganzas of Portugal, flight to refuge in an American colony in the fall of 1807 to avoid seizure by French forces of occupation, then opening the ports of the American colonies to trade with all allied and neutral countries in the great war in the Atlantic? This issue would lie at the heart of the March 1808 coup at Aranjuez, in which Caballero's intervention once again, as at the Escorial in late 1807, would be decisive, opening the road to Bayonne.

By Way of Conclusion

The last decade of the "first" Spanish empire in America was its most critical. It was also a time when the English economy pioneered the transition from high commercial to industrial capitalism and when an irrepressible conflict between France and England for hegemony in the Atlantic rendered irrelevant what Madrid had cultivated since 1700, a tenuous neutrality aided by a flexible alliance with one hegemon, France, to protect Spain's American colonies and their maritime route to the metropole. Spain's empire builders in the sixteenth century had set in place a monopoly trade system to exclude *direct* foreign participation in their transatlantic system of armed convoys returning to the metropole invariably with silver. It was a system codified by José de Veitia Linage in 1672 and reaffirmed by Rafael Antúnez y Acevedo in 1797, both justifying that system's fundamental structures. The pursuit of neutrality in the eighteenth century had helped defend the Spanish seaborne empire's lifeline across the Atlantic, notably its trade with the valuable overseas colony New Spain. In 1797, however, once England's royal navy defeated a Spanish fleet at Cape Saint Vincent, off the coast of Portugal, the secular transatlantic lifeline and ultimately the structure of the empire in America were at serious risk.

Over the eighteenth century this trading structure maximized New Spain's mines and consumers and led Madrid's policymakers carefully to insulate that colony as much as possible from reforms. The occupation of Havana and Manila by English naval forces in the great war at midcentury, however, provided Madrid the opening to initiate two major colonial reforms, the intendancy system and *comercio libre*, which were hesitantly put in place with the primary aim of increasing Spain's transatlantic trade. Meanwhile, New Spain enhanced its function as a submetropole in the

Spanish Caribbean, re-exporting a growing volume of imports from, and colonial staples to, the metropole.

For centuries European powers, mainly Holland in the seventeenth century, followed by England in the eighteenth, probed Spain's "closed" transatlantic system because it was the world's main source of silver for intra-European trade and intercontinental trade with the Far East. London's effort to penetrate the system in the eighteenth century was two-pronged: through Spanish intermediaries at Cadiz and through smuggling in the Caribbean, However, by the last quarter of the century England's navy had become an omnipresent, well-financed, well-trained and well-officered instrument of commercial expansion; many naval commanders, such as Rodney, Jervis, Collingwood, and Nelson, once served in the Caribbean.

Protecting the transatlantic system upon which Spain had become inordinately dependent had to be a major factor in Madrid's domestic and international policies, whether protecting Cadiz's dominant role in Spain's colonial trades or warding off English aggression. A posture of neutrality in a century of continual international conflict necessitated mollifying English as well as French interests and was reflected in the contending factions in Spain's political classes, Anglophile or Francophile but always nationalistic, whose influence waxed and waned. It became a posture difficult to maintain after 1789, when regicide was committed under the French Convention, which led Spain temporarily to abandon its French ally to join the First Coalition. After 1795 Spain returned to its flexible alliance with France, participating in resisting England's Second and Third coalitions. Inevitably came disaster at sea and an indefensible transatlantic connection: defeat at the hands of the English navy in 1797 at Cape Saint Vincent and in 1805 at Trafalgar. In a very real sense, the defeat at Cape Saint Vincent was the ominous beginning of a tumultuous decade of war interrupted, in 1801–3, by uncertain peace. London patrolled the waters off the peninsula and, in the Caribbean, shipping to Veracruz and other colonial ports; England rather than Spain now controlled Spain's transatlantic lifeline to the silver *pesos* of New Spain. What Spain had managed to prevent over 250 years of colonial rule in the western Atlantic was foundering in the interaction between war and debt, the "fate of empires," to paraphrase John Gray.[1]

Under Godoy's leadership Madrid was pressed repeatedly to reformulate policies satisfactory to expansionist interests in Europe's two most developed economies in order to preserve Spain's colonial possessions, its monarchy, and its institutions and to curb factional conflict over domestic, colonial, and international policies. When we rethink the coming of insurgency in Spain and its sequel overseas, revolution in New Spain, by highlighting the colonial factor in Madrid's decision making, Godoy emerges as only a pragmatist. After 1804 his was an impossible task. As an empathetic Gonzalo Anes has framed Godoy's dilemma, "Godoy had to act at that conjunction when experience was inapplicable, for which there were no norms of behavior to follow with efficacy, given the novelty of all that was happening."[2]

As French military units under Junot marched toward Lisbon and Murat's troops neared Madrid, how might Godoy's government best preserve monarchy and empire? There were at least three options. One, it could follow the example of the Braganza royal family, which in late 1807 had boarded English warships in Lisbon's harbor to find refuge in the colony of Brazil, then opened Portugal's "closed" transatlantic system to the shipping of any allied or friendly nation. Two, it could flee to New Spain, a colonial frontier on the western fringe of the Atlantic system, which might provide the peaceable kingdom imagined. This was hardly a wise choice, since that colony was fissioning on many levels, markedly so after 1789, as colonial officers on the ground realized. From Revillagigedo and Azanza to Iturrigaray, viceroys struggled to execute colonial policies—a few well thought out, more mere ad hoc improvisations, most of them stymied—despite the resistance of local representatives of mercantile, mining, and agricultural power elites. Or, third, despite the odds, it could appeal for national resistance to French occupation. Spain and New Spain were at the edge of crisis.

Notes

. . . .

Abbreviations and Acronyms

AAEPar	Quai d'Orsay (Paris)
AE	Affaires étrangères
AESC	*Annales: Économies, Sociétés, Civilisations*
AGI	Archivo General de Indias (Seville)
AGN	Archivo General de la Nación (Mexico City)
AGSim	Archivo General (Simancas)
AHH	Archivo Histórico de Hacienda (Mexico City)
AHN	Archivo Histórico National (Madrid)
ANPar	Archives Nationales (Paris)
ARPal	Archivo del Real Palacio (Madrid)
BAE	*Biblioteca de Autores Españoles*
BMus	British Museum (London)
BNMad	Biblioteca National (Madrid)
BNMex	Biblioteca Nacional (Mexico City)
BNPar	Bibliothèque Nationale (Paris)
BRAHM	Biblioteca de la Real Academia de la Historia (Madrid)
CC	Correspondance Consulaire
CP	Correspondance Politique
DGR	Dirección General de Rentas
DMex	*Diario de Mexico*
EHR	*Economic History Review*
HMex	*Historia Mexicana*
HSA	Hispanic Society of America (New York)
M et D	Mémoires et Documents
MN	Museo Naval (Madrid)
RHCF	*Revue de l'Histoire des Colonies Françaises*

Preface

1. John Keane, *Tom Paine* (London, 1995), xviii.
2. C. McGrath, News of the Week, *New York Times,* 17 June 2007.

1. Continuity and Crisis, 1789–1797

EPIGRAPHS: Camponanes, "Apuntaciones sabre el comercio de las Indias," ARPal, Ayala, 2867; Gardoqui, "Estado de nuestro comercio activo y pasivo."

1. Floridablanca, "Memorial presentado al rey Carlos III," 336.
2. Portillo, "Memoria sobre los perjuicios del agro."
3. For biographical details, see Valdés y Bazán, *Exposición documentada;* and Valdés y Osores, *El baylío don Antonio Valdés.*
4. Valdés y Bazán, *Exposición documentada,* 6.
5. One of Valdés's initial *circulares* to the colonies was a request for reports to be forwarded secretly ("por la via reservada") on local issues, improper activities, and incompetent officials. Arzobispo de México to conde de Floridablanca, 26 June 1787, AHN, Estado, 2839.
6. Real Orden, 30 July 1787, BNMad, MS 3535, fol. 477r.
7. "Expediente promovido . . . sobre fixar la linea de agua en . . . los buques a Yndias," AGI, Ind. Gen., 2316; Real Orden, 11 Dec. 1787, cited in Manuel González Guiral to Antonio Valdés, 23 Jan. 1788, ibid., 2313^b.
8. AGI, Consulados, Correspondencia, 62, fol. 111v.
9. Valdés, letter of 28 Dec. 1795, AGI, Ind. Gen., 1623; Villalobos, *Comercio y contrabando,* 383–84.
10. The opposition of New Spain's mine owners and the merchants *(aviadores)* who financed them obliged Valdés to back down; responsibility for mercury assignments was returned to the viceroys. Humboldt, *Ensayo político,* 383–84.
11. The discussion of Malaspina's return and imprisonment is based primarily on the contributions of Emilio Soler, Antonio Menchaca, and Barry Gough in Palau Baquero and Orozco Acuaviva, *Malaspina, '92;* and Beerman, *El diario del proceso y encarcelamiento.*
12. Palau Baquero and Orozco Acuaviva, *Malaspina, '92,* 14.
13. Beerman, *El diario del proceso y encarcelamiento,* 51.
14. Palau Baquero and Orozco Acuaviva, *Malaspina, '92,* 11.
15. *Proyectismo* may be defined as the eighteenth-century analysis of current economic conditions and speculation on how to improve them.
16. Palau Baquero and Orozco Acuaviva, *Malaspina, '92,* 10, 27, 31.
17. Las Casas was part of a group close to the conde de Aranda that included Antonio Ricardos, O'Reilly, and the banker Simón de Aragorri (marqués de Iranda).
18. *Elogios fúnebres;* Calcagno, *Diccionario biográfico cubano,* 171; Ferrer del Rio, *Historia,* 4:246; Suárez de Tangil y de Angulo, *Nobiliario cubano,* 36; Urrutia y Montoya, *Teatro histórico,* 462–68.
19. Friedlander, *Historia económica de Cuba,* 123–26; Moreno Fraginals, *El ingenio,* 1:13, 35; Francisco Xavier de Elío, letter of 21 Mar. 1800, AHN, Estado, 574, no. 1.
20. Rúbio Mañé, "Síntesis histórica." For Revillagigedo's remarkable final report, see Revillagigedo, "Notable carta reservada."

21. *Spain: Exports, Domestic and Re-exports*
(*reales de vellón*)

1778	74,515,962
1783–85	343,347,441
1789–91	329,650,427

Source: Fisher, *Commercial Relations,* 46, table 6.

Distribution of Exports to American Colonies by Port (%)

	Cadiz	Barcelona (1)	Malaga (2)	Santander (3)	Total (1–3)
1778	67.4	11.6	5.3	6.4	23.3
1783–85	80.0	20.6	4.1	3.6	28.3
1789–91	77.2	10.5	4.0	2.8	17.3

Source: Ibid., 49, table 7.

22. Gardoqui, "Estado de nuestro comercio activo y pasivo."

23. Stein, "Reality in Microcosm," 117–18. The last flota to New Spain under Antonio de Ulloa, in 1778, carried a cargo with an estimated value of 40 million *pesos,* 70% in foreign merchandise. "Observaciones sobre el sistema presente de navegación," 1778, AHN, Estado, 3188³, no. 420.

24. Consejo de Estado, "Actas," May 1794, AHN, Estado, libro 8d.

25. Guiral to Valdés, 23 Jan. 1788, AGI, Ind. Gen., 2313ᵇ. Cf. the comment of Bernabé Portillo, Cadiz, 1794: "[E]s menester conocer con exactitud las relaciones de los géneros, esto es, volumen, valor y necesidad." "Suplemento," n. 3.

26. Miguel Antonio Soler to Manuel Godoy, 26 Nov. 1801, AGI, Ind. Gen., 2319.

27. To the contrary, Matilla Tascón finds that under Philip IV in 1623 orders were issued to form a trade balance; the results are not known. *Balanza del comercio exterior de España,* iii.

28. Bosher, *French Finances,* 8–9.

29. "Exposición," Gardoqui to Consejo de Estado, 16 May 1794, AHN, Estado, 924.

30. Muro, "Revillagigedo y el comercio libre," 299 n. 2, 300–303; Stein, "Reality in Microcosm," 112 n. 3; Guiral (Cadiz) to Valdés, 23 Jan. 1788, AGI, Ind. Gen., 2326ᵇ.

31. Guiral (Cadiz) to Valdés, 23 Jan. 1788, AGI, Ind. Gen., 2326ᵇ; Consulado de Cadiz (Juan Phelipe de Oyarzával, Francisco de Valle, Juan Francisco de Veamurguía) to Guiral, 11 Jan. 1788, AGI, Consulados, Correspondencia, 47.

32. Larruga, *Memorias políticas y económicas,* 4:295.

33. Directores generales de rentas (Josef de Ibarra, Manuel Sixto Espinosa, Joseph Diaz Robles) to Francisco Saavedra, 21 Aug. 1798, AGSim, Secretaría y Superintendencia de Hacienda, 967.

34. Reprinted in Matilla Tascón, *Balanza del comercio exterior de España,* 175–215.

35. Real Orden, 20 Mar. 1800, AHN, Hacienda, 8052, fol. 236r; Real Orden, 19 May 1802, cited in Austria, "Memoria, 1804," "Exposicion," n. 4.

36. Enciso Recio, *Prensa económica del siglo XVIII,* 51–55. For the prospectus and the editor's checklist, see ibid., 89–91.

37. Junta de Comercio y Moneda, 10 Nov. 1791, AGSim, Secretaría y Superintendencia de Hacienda, 967.

38. Enciso Recio, *Prensa económica del siglo XVIII*, 28 n. 6; communications to Larruga and Gallardo from the *consulados* of La Coruña, Bilbao, Burgos, Santander, Barcelona, Seville, and Cadiz, AGSim, Secretaría y Superintendencia de Hacienda, 967.

39. Diego María Gallard, letter of 5 Aug. 1794, AGSim, Secretaría y Superintendencia de Hacienda, 967; Enciso Recio, *Prensa económica del siglo XVIII*, 85–86.

40. Consulado de Santander to Gardoqui, AGSim, Secretaría y Superintendencia de Hacienda, 967.

41. The junta consisted of José Ramos, José Antonio Gutiérrez de la Huerta, Joaquin de Areyzaga, Miguel de Iribarren, Tomás Izquierdo, Pedro Martínez de Murguía, Gerónimo de Quintanilla Pérez, Antonio ODuyer, Leonardo de Noguera, Francisco de Xado y Costillo, Francisco Bustamante y Guerra and Pedro Antonio Ocruly. AGSim, Secretaría y Superintendencia de Hacienda, 967.

42. Gutiérrez de la Huerta and Iribarren, "Papel del Consulado de Cadiz," 24 Nov. 1792, ibid.

43. Gutiérrez de la Huerta and Iribarren, "Papel del Consulado de Cadiz," and Consulado de Cadiz to Gardoqui, 17 May 1793, ibid.

44. "Nota," 27 May 1793, ibid.

45. Enciso Recio, *Prensa económico del siglo XVIII*, 27 n. 1, 27–38, 83.

46. Members of the Junta de Comercio (Ibarra, Sixto Espinosa, Robles) were incensed by "la incoherencia y aún de la diversidad monstruosa con que proceden las Aduanas . . . la falta de reunión y aún de conocimieto de los datos esenciales." "Informe," 21 Aug. 1798, AGSim, Secretaría y Superintendencia de Hacienda, 967.

47. "Reflexiones sobre el comercio," probably authored by Larruga and Gallard, in Enciso Recio, *Prensa económico del siglo XVIII*, 96–97.

48. *Correo Mercantil de España y sus Indias*, 10 Jan. 1803, quoted in Enciso Recio, *Prensa económico del siglo XVIII*, 48 n. 45.

49. Enciso Recio, *Prensa económico del siglo XVIII*, 52 n. 56.

50. This material is conveniently listed in Enciso Recio, *Prensa económica del siglo XVIII*, 106–11.

51. Ibid., 84–86.

52. See Fontana i Lázaro, *La Hacienda en la historia de España*.

53. Ventura Caro to Floridablanca, 4 Feb. 1792, AHN, Estado, 2839²; Tomás Antonio Marien y Arróspide to Godoy, 31 Jan. 1792, AHN, Estado, 3211.

54. *El Conciso* (Cadiz), 26 Feb. 1813.

55. Consejo de Estado, "Actas," 16 May 1794, AHN, Estado, libro 8d.

56. Reglamento para el gobierno de los Directores de Real Hacienda y Comercio de Indias, BRAHM, Mata Linares, 79.

57. Ibid.; Consulado de Cadiz, "Informe" to Gardoqui, 11 Nov. 1794, AHN, Estado, 4570².

58. Joaquin de Fonsdeviela to Consulado de Cadiz, Sept. 1791, summarizing Reales Ordenes of 30 Apr. and 9 Aug. 1791, in Servicio Histórico Militar, Fraile, 863:32; Francisco Machado to Presidente Juez de Arribadas, Pedro de Prado . . . Juan Rafael de Ozta, 29 Aug. 1791.

59. J. B. Dops Peróchegui to José de Gálvez, 1786, AGI, Ind. Gen., 2312.

60. "Informe jurídico," ibid., 2316.

61. Antúnez y Acevedo, *Memorias históricas,* 81.

62. Fiscal, 22 Oct. 1790, AGI, Ind. Gen., 2318. Four years later conditions at Cadiz had not improved: "Quando se simplificará el método complicadísimo que aora se obserba en el despacho, particularmente en Cádiz, donde se han sugetado a las mismas vejaciones, y formalidades, nuestros frutos, y los géneros de nuestras fábricas, que los que vienen de fuera en Buques extrangeros?" Portillo, "Suplemento," n. 3.

63. Foreign shipping was "en posesión del cabotage o navegación mercante (en que emplean unos 30 mil marineros." In freight, insurance, and commissions this represented an annual outflow of 11 million *pesos.* "Observaciones sobre el sistema presente de navegación."

64. Ferret, "Exposición histórica," fols. 231r–232r, 279r.

65. Ibid., fols. 233r, 250r; Consulado de Cadiz, 22 June 1804, AGSim, Secretaría y Superintendencia de Hacienda, 281–84. Given Cadiz's dominant position in Spain's overseas trade, it is not surprising that "[l]a emigración a el Extrangero y a nuestras colonias de Indias de los marineros" was common among seamen who signed on at Cadiz. More significant, from 1779 to 1788 the number of seamen per ship rose by 25%, the number of ships by only 16%. Uriortua, "Informe sobre la libertad del comercio."

66. Ferret, "Exposición histórica," fol. 278v. "La ganancia [de los fletes en la Navegación de Ultramar] seduxo a los labradores y artesanos, y varios individuos de estas y otras clases quisieron ser porcionistas y se interesaron en un negocio que no exigía gastos de escritorio ni nociones de comercio" (ibid., fol. 279r).

67. Dops Perochégui to Gálvez, 1/86.

68. Consulado de Cadiz to Cirujano Mayor Domingo Vidal, 26 Oct. 1796, AGI, Consulados, Correspondencia, 50, fol. 197r.

69. Ferret, "Exposición histórica," fols. 278r–279r. Cf. "[L]a infidelidad con que han rendido sus cuentas muchos sobrecargos y patrones del comercio y carrera de America." Ibid.

70. Ibid., fol. 280r.

71. Ibid., fols. 281v–282r.

72. Ibid., fol. 294v; Portillo, "Discurso político," par. 18.

73. Uriortua, "Informe sobre la libertad del comercio"; PRO, Customs 17/14, fol. 14r.

74. Junta de Estado to Juez de Arribadas, 1 Mar. 1791, AGI, Ind. Gen., 2316.

75. AGI, Ind. Gen., 2318.

76. Los dueños de navíos, "Memorial," Cadiz, 16 Apr. 1791, ibid., 2316.

77. Consejo de Estado, "Actas," 14 Feb. 1791, AHN, Estado, libro 4d.

78. Eugenio Llaguno, for the Junta de Estado, to Juez de Arribadas, 1 Mar. 1791, AGI, Ind. Gen., 2316; Gardoqui to Consulado de Veracruz, 27 May 1796, AGN, Consulado, 2, exp. 5; Real Orden, 21 Jan. 1792, Servicio Histórico Militar, Fraile, 863:34.

79. Consulado de Cadiz, "Informe," 11 Nov. 1794, punto 2, AHN, Estado, 4570²; Consulado de Cadiz, Junta General, 18 Apr. 1792, AGI, Ind. Gen., 2317.

80. Larruga, *Memorias políticas y económicas,* 3:271.

81. *Semanario Erudito de Valladares* 27 (1798): 230–31; AHN, Estado, 3188.

82. Francisco Cabarrús to Floridablanca, [1780s], AHN, Estado, 2944.

83. Larruga, *Memorias políticas y económicas*, 4:289–90; Vicente Basadre, "Memoria . . . sobre gusanos de seda," 1802, par. 9, AGI, Mexico, 2996. Larruga found that issues of trade and navigation were widely dispersed among the Consejo de Castilla and its Sala de Alcaldes, the Consejo de Indias, the Ministerio de Marina, the Superintendencia y Dirección de Rentas, the Superintendentes Particulares, and the Jueces Privativos de Fábricas.

84. Josef Francisco Vila, Aranjuez, 23 May 1793, AHN, Estado, 4570². As early as 1784 Malaga merchants petitioned for a ruling that would permit them to exclude ships from other peninsular ports (and, of course, foreign vessels) in handling Malaga's exports, thereby privileging local ship *patrones*. A special junta then recommended a national commercial code and a court to oversee "el fomento y prosperidad de nuestro comercio y navegación." Consulado de Malaga, Junta, 20 Sept. 1784, MN, MS 444.

85. Vila to Godoy, 12 May 1797, AHN, Estado, 4570², exp. 49. Vila's self-description presents the making of a nationalist bourgeois in commerce: "nacido y educado en una de los puertos y plazas de comercio . . . desde sus tiernos años, he podido conocer muy de cerca nuestro atraso y quanto nos adelantan los extrangeros en . . . industria, administración y economía política." Vila to Godoy, 23 May 1793, ibid.

86. Consulado de Cadiz (Juan Tomás de Micheo, José Ramos, Manuel Ruiz), "Informe," to Manuel Ximénez Breton, 11 Nov. 1794; Consulado de Barcelona (Joaquín Roca y Battle, Francisco Puget y Clorina, Felix Prat, Josef Erogues), 22 Apr. 1795; and Consulado de Valencia (Francisco Pastor y Fernández, Vicente Famart y Genovés), 27 Feb. 1796, all in AHN, Estado, 4570².

87. Real Decreto, 7 Oct. 1794, ibid.

88. Consulado de Cadiz, "Informe," to Manuel Ximénez Breton, 11 Nov. 1794, AHN, Estado, 4570².

89. Cf. the comment of a French observer at Valencia in 1793: "Le consulat . . . presque entièrement composé de gens peu instruits dont la plupart ont été simples ouvriers . . . absolument incapables de juger les grandes affaires de commerce." Ibid.

90. "Consulta . . . por el Gobernador del Consejo Conde de Campomanes y el Fiscal del Consejo de Hacienda Josef Ibarra," AHN, Estado, 4570².

91. Burkholder and Chandler, *From Impotence to Authority*, 176, 201, 212, 214, 221.

92. Vila to Godoy, 12 May 1797, AHN, Estado, 4570², exp. 49.

93. Breton to Mariano Luís Urquijo, Madrid, 16 May 1799, AHN, Estado, 4570², exp. 49.

94. Juan Batista Virio to Bernardo Iriarte, Bayonne, 2 Apr. 1808, AHN, Estado, 2817. The Consulado de Cadiz did draft its version of a commercial code in 1781, but by 1794 no action had yet occurred. Consulado de Cadiz, "Informe," 11 Nov. 1794, AHN, Estado, 4570².

2. War and the Colonies

EPIGRAPHS: Consejo de Estado, 24 Aug. 1792, AHN, Estado, 2863, no. 20; Bernardo Iriarte to Domingo Iriarte, "Apuntamientos y borradores."

1. *Spain: Budgetary Deficits, 1793–1795*
   (*reales de vellón*)

Year	Income	Expenditure	(+/−)
1793	602,602,171	708,807,327	−106,205,156
1794	584,161,180	946,481,585	−468,525,061
1795	607,279,693	1,029,709,136	−422,429,443
Total			−997,159,660

Source: Pedro Varela, "Memoria de Hacienda, 1796," in Lafuente, *Historia general,* 15:228 n. 2.

2. Godoy depicted Floridablanca's administrative style as follows: "[S]e encerró en sus principios . . . evitó las discussiones . . . concentró en sus manos todos los resortes de la administración." *Memorias,* 1:44.

3. Corona Baratech, *Revolución y reacción,* 202–3.

4. Prince of Asturias to Aranda, 15 Mar. 1781, AHN, Estado, 2863, no. 4.

5. Corona Baratech, *Revolución y reacción,* 201, 203, 207.

6. Cf. Iriarte, "Apuntamientos sobre el odio": "El Conde de Floridablanca, motor principal de este odio [against France], arraigado en nuestra Nación durante la dominación de la casa de Austria."

7. Corona Baratech, *Revolución y reacción,* 240–42.

8. Iriarte, "Apuntamientos sobre el odio."

9. Prince of Asturias to Aranda, 19 June 1781, AHN, Estado, 2863, no. 4, carta 1.

10. Defourneaux, *Pablo de Olavide,* 309–95.

11. Condorcet to Aranda, Paris, 11 Mar. 1792, AHN, Estado, 2863, no. 16.

12. Aranda to Prince of Asturias, 22 Apr. 1781, ibid., no. 3.

13. Aranda to Floridablanca, 21 July 1785, in Spell, "Illustrious Spaniard in Philadelphia," 138.

14. Corona Baratech, *Revolución y reacción,* 224. One may speculate that Aranda was current in 1792 with the changing colonial situation based on reports from his former protégés Luis de Las Casas, conde de O'Reilly, and Miguel José Azanza, not to mention Francisco Saavedra.

15. Bourgoing, *Tableau de l'Espagne moderne,* 1:107.

16. In 1792 Bourgoing was probably the best-informed Spanish "expert" in the French foreign ministry at the time. Secretary of the Madrid embassy from 1777 to 1785, a good friend of the influential Madrid banker Aragorri (marqués de Iranda), he prepared for the ministry a detailed analysis of the Spain he knew, "Mémoire sur l'état actuel de l'Espagne," probably the basis of his *Tableau.* Apparently there was considerable correspondence between him and Alexander von Humboldt. AAEPar, M et D, Espagne, 146, fols. 15r–150r; Barthélemy, "Report," ANPar, AF III, 61, doc. 249, plaque 2; ANPar, AF II, 64, doc. 470, no. 22; Humboldt, *Essai politique,* 2:72; Defourneaux, "Le problème de la terre," 57 n. l; Lafuente, *Historia general,* 15:188.

17. Bourgoing is reported to have brought with him to Madrid a "facción jacobina." Corona Baratech, *Revolución y reacción,* 248.

18. Consejo de Estado, "Registro de las actas y reales disposiciones," May 1792, AHN, Estado, libro 5d.

19. As Bourgoing put it, "écarter de sa patrie le fléau de la guerre." *Tableau de l'Espagne moderne,* 1:188.

20. Consejo de Estado, 30 Apr., 24 Aug. 1792, AHN, Estado, 2863, no. 20.

21. Gardoqui's full title was Secretario de Estado, Despacho Universal de Hacienda y Superintendencia general de ella, la de su cobre, y distribucion, la Presidencia de la Junta General de Comercio, Moneda y Minas, y la Superintendencia General de Fábricas y Casas de Moneda.

22. Franco, *Diego de Gardoqui,* 144–48; Guerra y Sánchez et al., *Historia de Cuba,* 2:130; Antón de Olmet, *El cuerpo diplomático español,* 3:331–33; AHN, Estado, 2839², 2863; AHN, Junta de Estado, 31 Mar. 1797, libro 11d, fol. 31r.

23. Consejo de Estado, "Actas," 14 May 1792, AHN, Estado, libro 5d.

24. Ibid., 28 May, 22 June 1792.

25. Yet to be investigated is the impact of reports from Saint-Domingue, where some merchants and planters, hamstrung by French protectionism, now demanded autonomy, even independence, the better to trade with U.S. merchants at Baltimore, Philadelphia, and New York.

26. Consejo de Estado, "Actas," 12 Oct. 1792, AHN, Estado, libro 5d.

27. Bourgoing, *Tableau de l'Espagne moderne,* 1:187; Consejo de Estado, "Actas," 24 Aug. 1792, AHN, Estado, libro 5d.

28. Bernardo Iriarte to Domingo Iriarte, "Apuntamientos y borradores."

29. Consejo de Estado, "Actas," 25 June 1792, AHN, Estado, libro 5d.

30. Consejo de Estado, "Actas," 12 June 1795, ibid., libro 10d.

31. A manuscript copy of the "Memoria" is in BNMad, MS 13,228; a printed version is in BNMex, Lafragua, 315 (originally in the possession of the conde de la Cortina). See also Whitaker, "Pseudo-Aranda Memorial of 1783."

32. Consejo de Estado, "Actas," 24 Aug. 1792, AHN, Estado, libro 5d.

33. Bernardo Iriarte to Domingo Iriarte, "Apuntamientos y borradores"; Bourgoing, "Exposé succinct de la position politique actuelle de la France vis-à-vis de l'Espagne," Madrid, 6 June 1792, AAEPar, CP, Espagne, supplément 17, fol. 275r.

34. Consejo de Estado, "Actas," 24 Aug. 1792, AHN, Estado, libro 5d.

35. See "Proceso formado al conde de Aranda."

36. Consejo de Estado, "Actas," 16 Nov. 1792, AHN, Estado, libro 5d; Lafuente, *Historia general,* 15:199; Hellman, *Jovellanos y Goya,* 152.

37. As Corona Baratech has synthesized Godoy's dilemma, in foreign policy he tried "salvaguardar le independencia nacional y la libertad de decisión frente a la presión inglesa para apartarla de Francia, y a la de Napoleón para combatir a la secular enemiga, Inglaterra." *Revolución y reacción,* 282.

38. For a long-delayed revisionist view of Godoy, see Rúspoli, *Godoy,* esp. the prologue by Gonzalo Anes Álvarez.

39. Corona Baratech, *Revolución y reacción,* 269–71, 274–75; Godoy, *Memorias,* 1:234–35.

40. Seco Serrano, "Estudio preliminar," in Godoy, *Memorias,* 1:liv–lv and n. 121.

41. Herr, *Eighteenth-Century Revolution in Spain,* 368, 348–75. See also Martínez de Villela, *A la nación española,* 6.

42. Consejo de Estado, "Actas," 14 Jan. 1793, AHN, Estado, libro 5d. Aranda continued to argue that the Spanish government should maintain a form of armed neutrality. Lafuente, *Historia general,* 15:204.

43. Puyabry, letter of 25 Feb. 1793, AAEPar, Espagne, t. 32, fol. 13r; Godoy, *Memorias,* 1:66.

44. Seco Serrano, "Estudio preliminar," lxvi–lxviii; Corona Baratech, *Revolución y reacción,* 262–64.

45. Consejo de Estado, "Actas," 13 Dec. 1793 and 9 May 1794, AHN, Estado, libros 6d and 7d.

46. Seco Serrano, "Estudio preliminar," xxiii; Muriel, *Historia de Carlos IV,* 2:199.

47. Godoy, *Memorias,* 1:66.

48. Muriel, *Historia de Carlos IV,* 2:199; Consejo de Estado, "Actas," 12 June 1795, AHN, Estado, libro 10d.

49. Muriel, *Historia de Carlos IV,* 2:200. Cf. Lafuente, *Historia general,* vol. 15. Muriel suggests that Godoy and Anduaga, secretary of the Consejo, planned the confrontation. *Historia de Carlos IV,* 2:199.

50. Muriel, *Historia de Carlos IV,* 2:203.

51. Godoy, *Memorias,* 1:67–70, printed in Muriel, *Historia de Carlos IV,* 2:199–203. Godoy summarized what appears to be the full text.

52. Consejo de Estado, "Actas," 12 June 1795, AHN, Estado, libro 10d.

53. Muriel, *Historia de Carlos IV,* 2:204.

54. Prince of Asturias to Aranda, Madrid, 19 Mar. 1781, AHN, Estado, 2863, no. 4, carta 1; Godoy, *Memorias,* 1:80; Consejo de Estado, "Actas," July 1794, AHN, Estado, libro 8d.

55. This is the leitmotif of the historical reconstruction in Rúspoli's *Godoy.*

56. Fugier, *Napoléon et l'Espagne,* 1:8–9.

57. Consejo de Estado, "Registro de las actas y reales disposiciones," July 1794, AHN, Estado, libro 8d, fol. 19v.

58. Consejo de Estado, "Actas," 17 Apr. 1795, ibid., libro 10d.

59. Alejandro Malaspina, letter of 8 Sept. 1795, BRAHM.

60. Fugier, *Napoléon et l'Espagne,* 1:19–26.

61. Ibid., 26–27, 30.

62. "Dépouillement de renseignements sur les moyens de faire prospérer le commerce et l'industrie . . . dans ses relations avec l'Espagne . . . puiser à de bonnes sources dans les villes de fabriques et de commerce," An 3 [1795], ANPar, AE, B III, 345; AAEPar, CP, Espagne, supplément 18, fols. 205r–209r.

63. Godoy, *Memorias,* 1:125–26, 128–30, 133–34, 137, 140, 149–50.

64. Ibid., 436–38.

65. Consejo de Estado, "Actas," 14 May 1795, AHN, Estado, libro 10d.

66. In 1793 the *consulado* and the Tribunal de Minería loaned the metropolitan Hacienda 2 million *pesos* (at 5%); from 1792 to 1796 fully 30% of the metropole's revenues came from the American colonies, the largest contributor being New Spain. Marichal, *La bancarrota del virreinato,* 100, 123.

67. The changing times were captured by Gaspar de Jovellanos in the despairing lines of one of his "Sátiras": "Así mísera Iberia, así retratas a Roma su barbarie, así desmientes el siglo de las luces, y eternizas el padrón horroroso de tu infamia." Helman, *Jovellanos y Goya,* 73.

68. Consejo de Estado, "Actas," 27 Nov. 1795, AHN, Estado, libro 10d. Jovellanos's diary entry for 19 June 1796 notes receipt of a letter from Valdés reporting that he was in good health and "contento de su tranquilidad." Jovellanos, *Obras,* 376.

69. Corona Baratech, *Revolución y reacción,* 289.

70. Actually Varela was proposing to revive Olivares's policy of utilizing Portuguese Jewish merchant-bankers at Amsterdam to finance Spain's military operations in Europe. See Studnicki-Gisbert, "Visiting 1640."

71. Consejo de Estado, "Actas," 31 Mar. 1797, AHN, Estado, libro 11d.

3. The Late *Proyectistas*

EPIGRAPHS: Menchaca, in Palau Baquero and Orozco Acuaviva, *Malaspina, '92,* 12; Bernardo Iriarte, 20 Mar. 1806, BMus, Egerton MS 571, fols. 199r–203r.

1. Cf. Cabarrús, *Cartas sobre los obstáculos,* 106: "Diez milliones dependen para su subsistencia y sus comodidades de medio millon."

2. Elorza, *La ideología liberal en la ilustración española.*

3. Cabarrús, *Cartas sobre los obstáculos,* 120.

4. Consejo de Estado, "Registro de las actas y reales disposiciones," 14 May 1792, AHN, Estado, libro 5d.

5. "Papel de apuntamientos," 1790, AHN, Estado, 2848, app. 9, doc. 8.

6. Consejo de Estado, "Registro de las actas y reales dispociones," 16 May 1794, AHN, Estado, libros 7d, 8d; Monconill, letter, 1792, AHN, Estado 2839[2].

7. "Observaciones sobre el estado actual de las Américas, y medios que parecen más convenientes para su defensa" (paper prepared by, but not read by, Antonio Valdés), Consejo de Estado, "Actas," 28 May 1792, AHN, Estado, libro 5d.

8. Consejo de Estado, "Actas," 14 May 1792, ibid.

9. Antonio Valdés, "Apuntamientos," Consejo de Estado, "Actas," 14 Apr. 1788, ibid., libro 2d.

10. Gardoqui, "Dictamen," 12 Oct. 1792, AHN, Estado, 2863, no. 15.

11. Gardoqui, draft of a Real Cédula, 7 Nov. 1792, ibid., letra "B."

12. Consejo de Estado, 16, 17 Nov. 1792, AHN, Estado, 2863.

13. Real Cédula countersigned by Gardoqui, 9 June 1793, AHN, Hacienda, Ordenes Generales, 1793.

14. Cf. Portillo, "Proyecto del Discurso Político . . . y Reflexiones": "El crítico actual Estado Político de la Europa; los inmensos gastos que ocasiona la presente guerra [con Francia]." "Discurso Político . . . y Reflexiones."

15. Consejo de Estado, "Registro de las actas y reales disposiciones," 9 May 1794, AHN, Estado, libro 7d.

16. The following paragraphs are based upon Gardoqui, "Estado de Nuestro comercio activo y pasivo."

17. In 1790–94 the colonies supplied on average 32% of aggregate *ingresos ordinarios* of Spain's Tesoreria General. Marichal, *La bancarrota del virreinato,* 304.

18. AHN, Estado, libro 8d.

19. "Extracto del Discurso político sobre la agricultura, la industria y el comercio . . . y del Suplemento que a él acompaña; y Reflexiones sobre la ejecución del establecimiento que se propone," AHN, Estado, 3208, no. 344-10.

20. Portillo, "Discurso político," par. 7; idem, "Suplemento," n. 7.

21. Portillo cited no publication of well-informed Simón Nicolas Henri Linguet.

22. Fundamental to the thinking of Spain's neo-*proyectistas* in state service were, on the one hand, preoccupation with a mushrooming public debt and, on the other, recognition of the inefficient management of church-owned farmland and the presence of impoverished "clérigos incongruos." Disentailment of ecclesiastical real estate at this juncture had nothing to do with anticlericalism; the state and the clergy simply needed more income.

23. For Arroyal's courageous critique of Spain's vested interests, see his *Cartas económico-políticas al conde de Lerena* and the observations in Elorza, *La ideología liberal en la ilustración española*, 236–37 and esp. 240–41.

24. Portillo to Godoy, Cadiz, 11 Apr. 1794, AHN, Estado, 3208, no. 344-4; Portillo, "Suplemento," n. 5.

25. Portillo, "Discurso político."

26. Portillo was probably quoting from Linguet's *Esprit de l'histoire générale de l'Europe depuis l'an 476 jusqu'a la paix de Westphalie* (London, 1783).

27. Portillo, "Discurso político," pars. 7–8.

28. Ibid., pars. 10–11, 14. Portillo was probably alluding to Campomanes's *Tratado de la regalía de amortización*.

29. Portillo, "Discurso político," pars. 15–17, 20.

30. Ibid., par. 34; Portillo, "Suplemento," n. 7. Along with other bureaucrat-intellectuals, Portillo thought that the solution to Spain's agrarian problem was the sale of ecclesiastical properties, beginning with those of the *hermandades* (brotherhoods) and *obras pías* (pious works); returns on sales would then be invested in government funds offering 3% and secured on specific government taxes. Obviously, this foreshadowed the fiscal policy behind the process of *consolidación,* first in the metropole and then in the American colonies. Cf. Portillo, "Memoria sobre la elección," sent to Gardoqui.

31. Portillo, "Discurso político," pars. 32, 34; idem, "Memoria sobre la elección."

32. Portillo, "Suplemento," n. 7. Olavide's settlements were also designed to protect the movement from Cadiz to Madrid of mule teams freighting silver *pesos* from the colonies.

33. Portillo, "Establecimiento de lugares nuevos convirtiendo en proprietarios muchos jornaleros," AHN, Estado, 3208, no. 344-10.

34. Portillo, "Discurso político," pars. 31–32, 34; idem, "Suplemento," n. 7. Portillo's proposed agrarian reform would allow renters to become co-proprietors by payment of an annual *canon*. Ibid.

35. Portillo, "Discurso político," par. 14; idem, "Suplemento," n. 5.

36. Real Orden, 1 June 1797, AHN, Hacienda, libro 8049, no. 594, fol. 179r; Toreno, *Historia,* 1:240. In 1796 Portillo was warmly supported, and predictably so, by Francisco Saavedra for appointment as a *supernumerario* in the Hacienda. AHN, Estado, 3212, no. 13.

37. Virio was hardworking and prolific. In 1808 he submitted to the Hacienda's head official, Miguel Cayetano Soler, a detailed paper *(informe)* on the course of reform in Austria-Hungary under María Teresa and Joseph II and on economic societies, the single tax, public education, and customs systems. In a letter from

Bayonne in April 1808 he complained to both Azanza and Iriarte that Soler had not replied. AHN, Estado, 2817.

38. Virio to Bernardo Iriarte, 1792. The letter was dictated to "joven Gardoqui," accompanying Virio. Iriarte Papers, BMus, Egerton MS 369, fols. 149r–152v.

39. Cotarelo y Mori, *Iriarte y su época;* Fugier, *Napoléon et l'Espagne*, 1:8. Curiously, France's representative at Basel, François Barthélemy, wrote of Domingo Iriarte that "[l]es détails de commerce lui étaient absolument étrangères." Barthélemy to Comité de Salut Public, An 4, ANPar, AF III, 61, dossier 245, plaque l.

40. Boislecomte, "Étude," AAEPar, M et D, Espagne, 97, fol. 93r–v; AHN, Estado, 2817.

41. Virio, "Reflexiones," followed by "Apuntamiento." Colombi's contribution is missing from this legajo.

42. Virio, "Reflexiones."

43. *Diario de Madrid*, 1 Feb. 1808, in Cotarelo y Mori, *Iriarte y su época*, 425. Significantly, the *Profecia* was reprinted along with additional materials in the last days of Charles IV's reign. Iriarte to Francisco de Angulo, 9 Feb. 1808, ibid.

44. Virio, "Apuntamiento," fol. 13r; hereafter cited in the text.

45. Years later, at the critical hour of imminent intervention in Spain (really, occupation) by French forces under Joachim Murat, Virio still contemplated reform from the top down along the lines of enlightened rulers like María Teresa and Joseph II as the road ahead for Spain. Virio (at Bayonne) to Iriarte, 26 Apr. 1808, AHN, Estado, 2817.

46. Another paper by Virio, one on trade with England, submitted to Godoy for publication, was rejected. "Copia de carta de un español domiciliado en Londres," BMus, Egerton MS 368, fol. 18r.

47. Bernardo Iriarte to Domingo Iriarte, "Apuntamientos y borradores." In a letter to the conde de Miranda of 2 Aug. 1797 Bernardo defined himself, probably accurately, as "semi-golilla." AHN, Estado, 2817.

48. Cotarelo y Mori, *Iriarte y su época*, 7.

49. Bourguet, *Choiseul*, 90. Vicente Palacio Atard finds him "el más decidido partidario de la alianza francesa." *El tercer pacto de familia*, 117.

50. Cotarelo y Mori, *Iriarte y su época*, 425. Virio claimed that Iriarte and José Nicolás de Azara had translated Gerónimo de Uztáriz's *Theorica* from its French edition. AHN, Estado, 2848, apartado 14. Iriarte's critical view of England's commercial policy apparently began to develop when he was in the London embassy, drafting protests about illegal English prizes when Spain was still neutral in the Seven Years' War and about illegal cutting of logwood on the coast of Honduras. Iriarte, "Copia de memorias," London, AHN, Estado, 2848. On these themes, see also BMus, Egerton MS 368, fols. 164ff.

51. Cf. Iriarte's "Primer conversación mía con del Conde de Floridablanca quando vino de Roma al Ministerio de Estado," along with his "Apuntamiento sobre el odio," AHN, Estado, 2817.

52. AHN, Estado, 2817; Jean Sarrailh, *La España ilustrada de la segunda mitad del siglo xviii* (Mexico City, 1957), 364.

53. Anes Álvarez, *El antiguo régimen*, 216; AHN, Estado, 2817.

54. Minute of a letter from Iriarte, in Madrid, to Floridablanca, 21 June 1782, BMus, Egerton MS 378, fols. 1r–7r; AHN, Estado, 2817.

55. AHN, Estado, 2817.

56. Bernardo Iriarte to Antonio Ximénez Navarro, 20 Mar. 1806, BMus, Egerton MS 571, fols. 199r–203r.

57. In his papers Iriarte recorded "el odio personal del Conde de Floridablanca a los Franceses y como suscitó entre ellos y los Españoles el antiguo odio Austríaco." AHN, Estado, 2817.

58. AHN, Estado, 2848.

59. AHN, Estado, 2817.

60. AHN, Estado, 2848. Apropos his position with respect to the Nootka settlement, Iriarte insisted that "mi voto fué enteramente opuesto a lo que se hizo y ajustó en la Convencion." AHN, Estado, 2817.

61. AHN, Estado, 2817; Vitale, *Intepretación marxista,* 1:174.

62. AHN, Estado, 2817.

63. Ibid., Iriarte's emphasis.

64. Ibid.

65. Ibid. This was one of Bonaparte's later objectives for French exporters.

66. Bernardo Iriarte to Domingo Iriarte, "Apuntamientos y borradores."

67. AHN, Estado, 2817.

68. Ibid.

69. BMus, Egerton MS 282, fol. 28r; ibid., Egerton MS 383, cited in Kossok, *Historia de la Santa Alianza,* 142 n. 56. In 1808 Iriarte drafted a report entitled "Sobre el riesgo de que perdamos las Américas." Vitale, *Interpretación marxista,* 1:174.

70. Murat proceeded to appoint Gonzalo O'Farrill and Iriarte to the Suprema Junta de Gobierno in May 1808. García, *Documentos históricos mexicanos,* 2:8–9. See also La Forest, *Correspondance,* 2:231.

71. See Cabarrús, "A la especie de perfección que necesita el comercio," which was forwarded to Floridablanca, on 30 Mar. 1783. AHN, Estado, 2944.

72. See Foronda, "Sobre lo honrosa que es la profesión del comercio," in his *Miscelánea.* See also Elorza, *La ideología liberal en la ilustración española,* 124–25.

73. Basadre, "Memoria sobre los beneficios."

74. Basadre, autobiographical sketch, 1 Mar. 1797, AGI, Mexico, 2508; Fonseca and Urrutia, *Historia general,* 1:374, 380–81; Francisco Saavedra, 13 Dec. 1794, AGI, Mexico, 2506; Lucena Salmoral, "La memoria de Basadre de 1818."

75. Basadre's concept of the relationship between social harmony, interdependence, and trade is highly reminiscent of Foronda, *Miscelánea,* 20, discussed in Elorza, *La ideología liberal en la ilustración española,* 125.

76. Basadre, "Memoria sobre los beneficios," fols. 1v–2v.

77. Ibid., fols. 3v, 4v–5r.

78. Ibid., fol. 2r.

79. Ibid., fols. 8v–9r.

80. *Sátira segunda, Carta de un vecino de Fuencarral a un abogado de Madrid, sobre el libre comercio de los huevos,* printed in *BAE* 59:277–79.

81. García-Baquero González, "Estudio preliminar," x–xviii.

82. Ibid., xii.

83. Francisco Viana to Gardoqui, 10 Apr. 1795, in Whitaker, "Documents," 380–81.

84. Antúnez y Acevedo, *Memorias históricas,* iii.

85. Whitaker, "Documents," 379–80, 382.

86. Tomás González Carbajal had suggested this. Ibid., 385–86.

87. Antúnez y Acevedo, *Memorias históricas,* vi.

88. Ibid., 10–25.

89. Ibid., 112.

90. This was a correction pointed out by Campomanes in a letter to Pedro Varela of 19 Apr. 1797. Whitaker, "Documents," 388–89.

91. Antúnez y Acevedo (Madrid) to Gardoqui, 18 June 1794, ibid., 379–80.

92. Viana to Gardoqui, 10 Apr. 1795, ibid., 380–82.

93. Antúnez y Acevedo (Cadiz) to Gardoqui, 4 Aug. 1795, ibid., 382.

94. Tomás Josef González Carvajal to Gardoqui, 18 Feb. 1796, ibid., 383–86. Viana's influence on the decision to proceed with *comercio libre* in 1789 has been overlooked.

95. Antúnez y Acevedo to Gardoqui, 25 June 1796, ibid., 386.

96. Pedro Rodríguez de Campomanes to Varela, 19 Apr. 1797, ibid., 388–89.

97. Whitaker, "Documents," 379.

4. Reorganizing New Spain's External Trade

EPIGRAPHS: Manuel García Herreros, "Informe," in "Sobre averiguar," fol. 47v; Tomás Murphy, "Informe," ibid., fol. 240r; II conde de Revillagigedo, in Rúbio Mañé, "Anuario histórico," 486.

1. In fact, in October 1779 Madrid asked New Spain's viceroy for data on widely consumed "frutos y mercaderías" and for a reasonable estimate of respective quantities. Luis Muro considered this a forerunner of a subsequent formal inquiry, which materialized in an order of 30 October 1787. Muro, "Revillagigedo y el comercio libre," 299 n. 2, 300. Muro's treatment of this theme is by far the most reliable and comprehensive.

2. For his delaying tactic, Gálvez received annual payments of four thousand *pesos* in "gratitud." Matías Alqueza, "Memoria patriotica liberal de Nueva España," Colección Hijar, Madrid, 8, no. 4.

3. Muro, "Revillagigedo y el comercio libre," 300, 302. Viceroy Flores was ordered to request data from the Consulado de México and report annually on the colony's commercial growth.

4. The funds were considerable, for Revillagigedo owned properties inherited from his father's estate in Andalusia (his mother was an *andaluza*). Rúbio Mañé, "Anuario histórico," 459, 488. Argus-eyed and often cynical, Francisco Carrasco, high up in the Hacienda for decades, knew of the spoils available to high colonial officials: "Virreyes hemos visto con medio millón, con millón y con dos millones de pesos, que en el curso de sus virreinatos han pedido y alcanzaado aumento de sueldos." AHN, Estado, 3211, parte 2, fols. 13r–14v.

5. That *tertulias* were a major source of Revillagigedo's reflections is corroborated by his "vivo retirado de las conversaciones del gran mundo y el estudio de las cosas de Estado no se hace tanto con libros como en las conferencias." Rúbio Mañé, "Anuario histórico," 460. Somewhat contradictory?

6. Cf. ibid., 479: "Hay cierto cuerpo de comercio en España de pocos individuos que se ha hecho formidable, que en lugar de fomentar y reedificar el comercio general y las fabricas todo lo destruye."

7. Ibid., 490.

8. Ibid., 470–71. Cf. 488: "Que las Indias rindan más utilidad a la Corona debe ser sin duda el mayor cuidado de nuestro gabinete."

9. He found Spain subject to "subordinación y dependencia" by France, a "dependencia [que] se conoce demasiado en la monarquía española." Ibid., 474.

10. Ibid., 473, 483, 482.

11. Rúbio Mañé, "Anuario histórico." This article is framed on what Rúbio Mañé called a "copiosa correspondencia . . . acerca de los problemas" of Spain in a letter of 1774 (459).

12. Palau Baquero and Orozco Aquaviva, *Malaspina, '92,* 14.

13. Muro, "Revillagigedo y el comercio libre," 306–7. Revillagigedo's announcement declares his conviction: "Siendo mui repetidas . . . las diferentes providencias . . . deveria haver resultado el maior aumento del tráfico mercantil." "Sobre averiguar," fol. 1r.

14. The respondents were Diego de Ágreda, Antonio Basoco, Manuel García Herreros, Ramon de Goicochea, Lorenzo Angulo Guardamino, Francisco Ignacio de Yraeta, Isidro Antonio de Icaza, Juan Fernando de Meoqui, Ángel Puyade, Gaspar Martín Vicario, Francisco Vidal, and Juan Antonio Yermo.

15. On the confabulations of 115 merchants to present a solid opposition that quietly organized "acuerdos, y consultas," see "Ensayo apologético," BNMex, MS 1334, fol. 248v.

16. Muro, "Revillagigedo y el comercio libre," 307, 316. Later Revillagigedo made of point of explaining that he had had to wait three years to obtain data from Mexico City and Veracruz customs officers, who had furnished prices, not volume. Torre Villar, *Instrucciones y memorias,* 2:1109.

17. "Ensayo apologético," fols. 247r–287r.

18. Murphy, "Informe," 20 July 1793, fols. 234r–249r.

19. Marichal, *La bancarrota del virreinato,* 115; Martínez López-Cano and Valle Pavón, *El crédito en Nueva España,* 139–40.

20. García Herreros, "Informe," fols. 40r–46v; Antonio Basoco, "Informe," in "Sobre averiguar," fol. 74r; Ángel Puyade, "Informe," ibid., fols. 188r–197r; Isidro Antonio de Icaza, "Informe," ibid.

21. García Herreros, "Informe," fol. 44r.

22. Ibid., fols. 41v–42r.

23. Ibid., fol. 62v.

24. Basoco moved into the "arbitrio de imponer el caudal a réditos . . . y recogiendo lo que está en España." "Informe," fol. 74r. A *vizcaíno* from Gordejuela, he was called to New Spain by his prominent *almacenero* uncle, the marqués de Castañiza, whose daughter Maria Teresa he married. A member of the Consulado de México as of 1767, he amassed an immense fortune in trade, then in mining (Zacatecas) and agriculture (Chalco). AGN, AHH, 502-4; Tutino, "Hacienda Social Relations in Mexico," 502; Howe, *Mining Guild,* 92; Brading, *Miners and Merchants,* 124–28.

25. García Herreros, "Informe," fol. 42r.

26. Puyade, "Informe," fol. 190r.

27. See García Herreros, "Informe," fol. 44r: "Los géneros ordinarios que se labran en España son de poco consumo en este reyno, cuyo temperamento en lo general no sufre ropa pesada, y por la poca curiosidad con que los benefician y empacan."

28. Ibid. As for the "otras clases de gentes ínfimas por el mixto, que siempre aspiran a representar y parecer más de lo que son, gastando quanto adquiesen, resulta que es muy raro que logra medianas comodidades." Ibid.

29. Gaspar Martín Vicario, "Informe," ibid.; García Herreros, ibid. The comparison of trade with the human body is repeated in "Representación del Consulado al Virrey Revillagigedo, apoyando la petición de los comerciantes, 2 enero 1792," in Florescano and Castillo, *Controversia*, 1:257.

30. García Herreros, "Informe," fol. 40v.

31. Cf. BNMex, MS 1334, fol. 225v: "La comunicación con el otro Reyno [Peru] por la mar del Sur sería gran auxilio para purgarse este de los sobrantes, que inutiliza la moda." See also, in the same vein, Icaza, "Informe," fol. 82r.

32. García Herreros, "Informe," fol. 45v.

33. Puyade, "Informe," fol. 90r.

34. "Representación de los 115 comerciantes al Consulado, 2 diciembre 1791," in Florescano and Castillo, *Controversia*, 1:245–51. Among the signers were respondents to Revillagigedo's questionnaire: Isidro Antonio de Icaza, Juan Fernando de Meoqui, and Gaspar Martín Vicario. Notably absent were Basoco (but not his relative Domingo de Castañiza), Ágreda, and Iraeta.

35. "Representación del Consulado al Virrey Revillagigedo," 1:252–58.

36. See Marichal, *La bancarrota del virreinato*, 111–21, where merchants' lending to the government is detailed.

37. "Representación del Consulado al Virrey Revillagigedo," 1:253–55, 257.

38. Ibid., 254–55.

39. Ibid., 255–58.

40. In June 1791 Posada had declined to opine "por imposibilidad absoluta, y carencia de innumerables datos, sin los quales mi resolución . . . estaría sugeta a error." AGN, Consulado, 123, fol. 4v. By January 1792 he had had a change of heart, and he presented a *dictamen* decidedly critical of the 115 Mexico City merchant magnates. Ibid., fols. 290r–301r, reprinted in Florescano and Castillo, *Controversia*, 1:259–69.

41. Miguel Páez de la Cadena, "Dictamen del superintendente de la Real Aduana, 1792," in Florescano and Castillo, *Controversia*, 1:270–99. There is a manuscript version of this dictamen, perhaps the original, in AGN, Consulado, 123, fols. 302r–332.

42. AGN, Alcabalas, 276; Linda Salvucci, "Costumbres viejos, 'hombres nuevos,'" 253 n. 61; AGN, Consulado, 123, fol. 312r; Brading, *Miners and Merchants*, 52, 62; Calderón Quijano, *Los virreyes de la Nueva España en el reinado de Carlos III*, 2:52. At his death, after forty-two years as a civil servant, Páez left an estate of 135,000 *pesos* plus urban and rural properties in southern Andalusia.

43. According to Antonio Menchaca, he was "estudiar la situación de las Indias, como objetivo primordial expedicionario." Palau Baquero and Orozco Aquaviva, *Malaspina, '92*, 14. When Malaspina sent Páez de la Cadena "un interrogatorio amis-

toso que me havía prometido contextación, pero ésta fué vaga, nada expresiva, y chocante." Malaspina replied in the same vein. Malaspina to Arcadio de Pineda, 26 Oct. 1791, MN, MS 316, fol. 134r.

44. "Reflexiones de la Secretaria, 1797," AGI, Mexico, 2515; "Ensayo apologético," in Florescano and Castillo, *Controversia,* 1:332–33.

45. Páez de la Cadena, "Dictamen del superintendente de la Real Aduana," in ibid., 288–89.

46. Ibid., 293.

47. Ibid., 276.

48. Ibid., 285–87. Cf. ibid., 286: "Haber en la última Guerra aprontado en el breve espacio de *cuatro* días *dos millones y medio de pesos;* el un millón buscado a réditos de que aún satisface el de quinientos mil (que no ha reintegrado la Real Hacienda) y lo restante con préstamos *voluntarios* de Comerciantes que se privaron de su giro y premio."

49. Ibid., 286. The criticism of very prosperous Guanajuato mine owners indicated the ever-present tension between independent proprietors and their creditors.

50. Ibid., 290.

51. Ibid., 276–77.

52. On Yraeta, see Yuste, "Francisco Ignacio de Yraeta y el comercio transpacifico"; idem, "Comercio y crédito de géneros asiáticos en el mercado novo-hispano: Francisco Ygnacio y Yraeta, 1767–1797," in Martínez López-Cano and Valle Pavón, *El crédito en Nueva España,* 106–30; Torales Pacheco, García Díaz, and Yuste, *La compañia de comercio Francisco Ignacio de Yraeta;* and Stein, "Francisco Ignacio de Yraeta y Azcárate."

53. Diego de Ágreda, "Informe," in "Sobre averiguar," fols. 57r–65r.

54. Little is known of Tomás Murphy's career before 1790. He had at least three brothers, Matías Lorenzo (who joined him at Veracruz), Juan, and perhaps Diego Murphy y Porro. His father had emigrated from Waterford, Ireland, to Málaga in 1755 and married Barbara Porro at Gibraltar in 1757. Over the next half-century Murphys were found at Cadiz (Juan, a merchant naturalized in 1786), Madrid (Juan, now a banker), London (the firm of Gordon & Murphy), Charleston, South Carolina (Diego, a consul of Spain), and Saint Thomas and Jamaica in the Caribbean. The Murphys created an "Atlantic" family network that ranged from wine merchandising to shipping, trade, banking, and, under Tomás, mining in New Spain (the "Mellado" and "Moran" mines). This family saga deserves an author. Sources are scattered: Fugier, *Napoléon et l'Espagne,* 2:183–84; Jiménez Codinach, *La Gran Bretaña,* 223–24; Bustamante, *Suplemento,* 256; AGI, Mexico, 2513, 2997, 2319; AGI, Consulados, Correspondencia, 51 and 61, fol. 8r; AHN, Consejos, 20,728, quad. 2; ANPar, AF IV, 1614, plaque 2, no. 172; Archivo del Sagrario, Mexico City, Libro de Testamentos 11, fol. 33r; Museo del Instituto Nacional de Antropología e Historia (Mexico City), Antigua, 432, Epistolario de Don T. Murphy (1810–13).

55. A facsimile edition of the *Recopilación* was published in 1981–87. On Beleña, see Biblioteca de Real Palacio (Madrid), MSS Ayala, 2819, fol. 52r–v; Calderón Quijano, *Los virreyes de la Nueva España en el reinado de Carlos III,* 1:262; Howe, *Mining Guild,* 194–95; and Priestley, *Gálvez,* 215, 244 n. 14.

56. On Posada, see also Burkholder and Chandler, *From Impotence to Authority,* 177, 200, 206, 207, 216.

57. Rodríguez García, *El fiscal de Real Hacienda;* Hamnett, *Politics and Trade,* 58–59; AGI, Mexico, 1515, n. 162.

58. Ágreda, "Informe," fols. 57r–65r; Yraeta, "Informe," fols. 87r–89v.

59. Ágreda, "Informe," fols. 58r, 63v; Yraeta, "Informe," fol. 86v.

60. Yraeta, "Informe," fol. 86v.

61. Ibid., fol. 89r–v; Ágreda, "Informe," fols. 59v–60r. Ágreda offered details on how he managed to earn only 5.5% on one sale at Veracruz of imports worth 35,956 *pesos* "con aumento de 21 por ciento al principal de los efectos, tercera parte a tres meses, la otra a seis, y el resto a un año de plazo." Ibid., 59v.

62. Yraeta, "Informe," fol. 89r.

63. Ágreda, "Informe," fols. 58r–59r.

64. Ibid., fols. 62r, 64r.

65. Murphy, "Informe," fol. 241r.

66. Ibid., fols. 238v, 235v–236r, 234r, 236r–238r.

67. Cf. ibid., fol. 242r: "Pues mirando a la América baxo el concepto de quanto pueda dar consumo a aquellos frutos y mercancías, es destructiva la subsistencia de estas fábricas. Quanto mayor sería el consumo de los Paños, bayetas, sombreros, Cintería, y pintados de España, si no se huvivesen protegido las fábricas de estos mismos efectos en este Reyno?" Clearly, Murphy had digested the position of the Consulado de Barcelona in its 1787 "Informe sobre el comercio de América," published in Madrid's *Espíritu de los Mejores Diarios Literarios,* 30 Mar. 1789. Murphy, "Informe," fol. 245r.

68. Murphy, "Informe," fol. 242v.

69. Cf. Posada, "Dictamen," fol. 297v: "Ahorra . . . el Mercader de fuera un 30 o 36 por ciento en bajar a Veracruz."

70. Murphy, "Informe," fols. 247r–248r.

71. Ibid., fols. 238r, 248r–249v.

72. Hernández de Alba, "Informe," BNMex, MS 1334, fol. 231v; Burkholder and Chandler, *From Impotence to Authority,* 178, 216, 217, 227.

73. Hernández de Alba, "Informe," fol. 232r.

74. Ibid. See also ibid., fol. 233r: "Atracados por ellos los Principales renglones de las Flotas, en la Feria de Xalapa, los conducían a esta capital, donde formavan como un depósito o Almacen general, adonde por fuerza havían de acudir a surtirse todos los comerciantes del Reyno." Note that Posada had no illusions about the tradition-bound merchant, who "todavía se cree que las flotas vuelvan y las convenciones secretas resuciten!" Ibid., fol. 295v.

75. Posada, "Dictamen," fols. 291r, 295r, 299v. Posada's support of *comercio libre* was of a piece with his progressive views, shared with his Cienfuegos relative Gaspar de Jovellanos, another Asturian from the Oviedo area. Jovellanos, *Diarios, BAE* 50:193; for Posada's vigorous criticism of *repartimiento,* see AGI, Lima, 1119.

76. Posada, "Dictamen," fols. 295v–296r.

77. Hernández de Alba made no bones about being "partidario de las pocas personas que . . . el comercio en América se ha aumentado y vigorizado. se ha ramificado en más número de indibiduos comerciantes." "Informe," fol. 232r–v.

78. Ibid., fols. 234r–237r.

79. Beleña, "Informe reservado"; "Ensayo apologético," AGN, Consulado, 123. The title of the "Ensayo" continues, "Reflexiones imparciales sobre las pretensiones de negociantes de esta Nueva España," obviously signaling the author's approach. The *estados* frequently cited by Revillagigedo in a final report were presumably attached to the "Ensayo." See "Colección de estados de valores de Real Hacienda que manifiestan . . . para apoyo del ensayo Apologético sobre Comercio libre," BNMex, MS 1334. There were 18 tables attached.

80. "Ensayo apologético," in Florescano and Castillo, *Controversia,* 1:305.

81. Revillagigedo's characterization was accurate. Priestley, *Gálvez,* 215, 244 n. 14; Beleña, "Informe reservado"; Biblioteca de Real Palacio (Madrid), MSS Ayala, 2859, fol. 52r–v; Calderón Quijano, *Los virreyes de Nueva España en el reinado de Carlos III,* 1:262.

82. Beleña was an accomplished legal scholar. See his *Recopilación.*

83. Beleña, "Informe reservado," 205.

84. Ibid., 208.

85. Ibid., 214.

86. "Ensayo apologético," in Florescano and Castillo, *Controversia,* 1:304.

87. Ibid., 302–3.

88. Ibid., 303–5.

89. Ibid., 321. Article 4 of the Real Cédula of 21 January 1735 prohibited "los Limeños, y Mexicanos, remitiesen caudales a España para empleos de pura negociación, por que notandose que cargavan el tercio o la quarta parte de las flotas en géneros escogidos y del principal consumo, perjudicavan en la misma cantidad a los cargadores espanoles." The prohibition was removed in 1738.

90. Ibid., 320, summarizing arguments in pars. 58–67.

91. Ibid., 320–21, 325, 344, 322.

92. Ibid., 361.

93. Ibid., 364–65.

94. Luis Muro synthesized admirably the antecedents of Madrid's inquiry apropos *comercio libre* in "Revillagigedo y el comercio libre," 300–303, 305–9. Its justification for data from Mexico City's *consulado* was explicit: the *flota* system had generated "ganancias exorbitantes a una sola clase en perjuicio de las demas" (300).

95. Ibid., 307.

96. Revillagigedo wrote that "[p]ara ello he formado los Estados de extracción de caudales y efectos, introducción de éstos, productos de Diezmos de los principales Obispados," plus data from customs at Veracruz and Mexico City, the Tribunal de Cuentas, and the Mexico City mint. "El virrey de Nueva España," 13–14; hereafter, with one exception, cited in the text.

97. Revillagigedo, like other observers of New Spain's silver-mining industry, was concerned about its presumed technological drawbacks.

98. Juárez Nieto found that after 1778 a number of leading provincial merchants of Michoacan—Lejarza, Olarte, Quevedo, and Goyzueta—were bypassing Mexico City to purchase directly at Veracruz imported silks, cocoa, ironware, velvets, linens, Bordeaux wines, and glassware. *Oligarquía,* 50.

99. These bottlenecks had been a major theme of his 1774 letter. See Rúbio Mañé, "Anuario histórico," 477–88.

100. This was precisely his position in 1774. Rúbio Mañé, "Anuario histórico," 486.

101. As Revillagigedo put it, "Su manutención cuesta crecida suma de pesos por los sueldos de que disfrutan el Prior y los Cónsulaes, Asesores y demás dependientes y los agentes que mantienen en la Corte." "El virrey de Nueva España," 34. During his decades of residence at Court, must have frequently noted the presence of those "agentes."

102. John Brewer, in *Times Literary Supplement*, 22 Oct. 2004, 4.

103. In the customary advice to his viceregal successor Revillagigedo, discussing the *comercio libre* issue, referred *only* to colonial civil servants—"ministros, intendente, Tribunal de Cuentas, the *fiscal de Real Hacienda*—as supporters of his position. Torre Villar, *Instrucciones y memorias,* 2:1105–6.

5. A Hegemony Threatened

EPIGRAPHS: Tomás Murphy, "Representación a los señores presidentes y vocales de la Junta de Govierno, Veracruz, 6 Dec. 1802," AGI, Mexico, 2510; Pedro Pablo Vélez to Consulado de Veracruz, 15 June 1808, AGI, Mexico, 2516; AGN, Consulado, 222, exp. 1.

1. Deans-Smith, *Bureaucrats, Planters, and Workers,* 61.

2. On provenances, see the lists in Souto Mantecón, *Mar abierto,* 91–96.

3. In 1807 the floating population of the port included numbered more than seven thousand.

Estimated Population, Veracruz, Selected Years

1789	6,000
1799	8,109
1804	16,000
1807	20,000

Source: Souto Mantecón, *Mar abierto,* 102.

4. As the merchant Tomás Murphy expressed it years later, "En efecto el reglamento de 12 de octubre de 1778 puede mirarse por los Veracruzanos como la cédula de erección de su Pueblo." "Representación."

5. Uztáriz and Miranda issued formal invitations to convene at Cos's home. Pedro Zavala, *recaudador* of the Consulado de México's *avería* at Veracruz, 14 Feb. 1781, AGN, AHH, 677-1. The most enlightening and comprehensive study of the Consulado de Veracruz is Souto Mantecón, *Mar abierto.* See also Ortiz de la Tabla Ducasse, *Comercio exterior de Veracruz;* and Booker, *Veracruz Merchants.*

6. AGI, Mexico, 2506. Their petition bore the title "El comercio español de Vera-Cruz propone a V.M. el establecimiento de un consulado independiente del de Megico." Appended is a list of petitioners, many of whom subsequently became prominent, including Antonio Sáenz de Santa María and Gaspar Sáenz Rico.

7. AGN, Consulado, 222, exp. 1.

8. AGI, Mexico, 2506. The choice of two is curious: the Consejo de Indias's list of eligibles for office in the proposed *consulado* has 47 names, 14 (perhaps more) identifiable and only 8 *criollo.* Souto Mantecón, *Mar abierto,* 93–94.

9. Pedro Zavala, the Consulado de México's agent at Veracruz, informed the *consulado* of the junta's formation. Zavala to Consulado de México, 14 Feb. 1781, AGN, AHH, 677-1; Marichal, *La bancarrota del virreinato*, 116.

10. "Nota," 10 Feb. 1794, AGI, Mexico, 2506. The Cadiz *consulado*'s opposition to the Veracruz proposal is not clear. In a letter to Madrid on 21 October 1783 Cadiz hoped to make Jalapa rather than Veracruz the major entry point *(almacén general)* for New Spain's imports, on the ground that epidemics had made Veracruz "el Panteón de los Españoles" and residence there was "terrible y peligroso . . . a todo Español, y aún más a los Mercaderes de aquel Reyno"—no doubt a reference to the recurrence of yellow fever. AGI, Consulados, Correspondencia, 46.

11. The phrase is "no ha podido encontrarse por exactas diligencias que se han hecho." Andrés Gil de la Torre and Miguel Ignacio de Miranda, 24 Sept. 1789, AGI, Mexico, 2506.

12. Ibid. The official bureaucratese followed this interpretation. In 1794 it was asserted that the formation of the Consulado de Veracruz had been approved but that "a tiempo de . . . executarla, se traspapeló el expediente, y nunca más volvió a parecer." "Nota," 10 Feb. 1794, AGI, Mexico, 2506.

13. Campomanes, "Adición particular," AHN, Estado, 3208[1].

14. No friend of those desiring a Veracruz *consulado,* Viceroy Branciforte later observed that Corbalán's *informe* was the "principal apoyo de la representación que hicieron los comerciantes de Veracruz y de las ordenanzas que ellos mismos formaron." Branciforete to Ministro de Hacienda, 17 Oct. 1796, AGN, Correspondencia de virreyes, 2nd ser., 33, no. 857. Gil de la Torre and Miranda forwarded to incoming Viceroy Revillagigedo their 1781 draft of the ordinances, unchanged, on 24 Sept. 1789. AGI, Mexico, 2506. In 1791 Guadalajara's merchants also petitioned for a *consulado;* they were supported by the intendant Jacobo Ugarte y Loyola, who had been one of the very few intendants in New Spain to recommend abolition of *repartimiento.* See BNMad, MS 19710.

15. Revillagigedo to Valdés, 11 Nov. 1789, AGN, Correspondencia de virreyes, 2nd ser., 30, fols. 8v–9v.

16. González Carbajal, one of the last of the Spanish developmentalist civil servants, was credited by the knowledgeable bureaucrat Pedro Aparici with "la principal parte en el establecimiento de este [Veracruz] y los demás consulados de América, y está instruido intimamente en todo lo concerniente a ellos." AGI, Mexico, 2508.

17. Consulado de Cadiz to Francisco Antonio de la Torre, its representative at Veracruz, AGI, Consulados, Correspondencia, 98, fol. 270r.

18. Florescano and Castillo, *Controversia,* 1:248–49, 253, 273, 280ff.

19. AGI, Mexico, 2515; BNMad, MS 19710.

20. Consejo de Estado, 1 Feb. 1792, AGI, Mexico, 2506. Also present were Antonio Valdés, Campo Alange, Gardoqui, Godoy (duque de Alcudia), Acuña, and the secretary, Eugenio Llaguno.

21. "De la erección del Consulado de Veracruz: Sobre señalamiento de su territorio y nombramiento de los primeros empleos, 1794." BRAHM, Mata Linares, 68, fol. 2r–v.

22. Consulado de México (marqués de Santa Cruz, Tomás Domingo de Acha, Francisco Santa María) to Gardoqui, 28 Apr. 1794, AGI, Mexico, 2506.

23. *Allocations of Select Consulado Funds*
   (*pesos*/per year)

Recipients	Allocation
Juzgado de la Acordada	9,000
Regimiento urbana del comercio de Mexico	5,000
Academia d San Carlos	3,000
Consejo de Indias	2,000
Hospital de San Lázaro	500
Total	19,500

Source: Consulado de Mexico (marqués de Santa Cruz, Thomás Domingo de Acha, Francisco Santa María) to Gardoqui, 28 Apr. 1794, AGI, Mexico, 2506.

Note: The 19,500 *pesos* disbursed constituted about one-third of total receipts of the *avería* administered by the Consulado de Mexico.

24. Fernando José Mangino to Gardoqui, "Instancia," AGI, Mexico, 2506. The following paragraphs are based upon his *instancia*.

25. Mangino used this approach even though he was advised that "el Rey tiene resuelto erigir en Veracruz un consulado." Gardoqui to Mangino, 8 Jan. 1794, AGI, Mexico, 2506. Mangino's *instancia* is summarized in ibid. and in BRAHM, Mata Linares, 68.

26. Mangino, "Resumen de la erección del Consulado de Veracruz," 27 Jan. 1794, AGI, Mexico, 2506.

27. Cf. Consulado de México to Gardoqui, 28 Apr. 1794, AGI, Mexico, 2506: "[S]e digne mandar se suspendan las Erecciones de los dos Consulados . . . hasta oir a este."

28. It was rumored that Mangino received 1,500 *pesos fuertes* annually from the Consulado de México and that his assistant received another 500. In the Madrid of the 1790s, 30,000 *reales de vellón* went a long way. Mangino, "Resumen de la erección del Consulado de Veracruz."

29. BRAHM, Mata Linares, 68. The anonymous bureaucrat's statement was dated 10 Feb. 1794.

30. Mangino to Gardoqui, 21 Feb. 1794, AGI, Mexico, 2506. Mangino wrote: "[C]onozco personalmente a muchos de los sugetos del comercio de Veracruz."

31. Consulado de México to Gardoqui, 28 Apr. 1784, AGI, Mexico, 2506.

32. Madrid followed Mangino's recommendation in selecting Andrés Gil de la Torre as prior, but in selecting Miranda and Remigio Fernandes as consuls it did not. Of nine *consiliarios* appointed by Madrid, only three were drawn from the original petitioners for a local *consulado*. AGI, Mexico, 2506.

33. Note Basadre's interpretation: "En la Havana se concedió a su consulado por jurisdicción toda la Ysla de Cuba. En Goatemala la comprehensión de la Capitanía General, y lo mismo se verificó en Caracas, Buenos Ayres, Chile y Guadalajara; pero Veracruz quedó precisamente sugeto a lo correspondiente al Govierno, y solo se le concedió de la Yntendencia la Villa de Xalapa." Basadre, "Memoria . . . sobre gusanos de seda," 1802, AGI, Mexico, 2996.

34. Vélez to Consulado de Veracruz, 15 June 1808, AGI, Mexico, 2516.

35. Mangino to Gardoqui, 21 Feb. 1794, AGI, Mexico, 2506.

36. AGI, Mexico, 2992.

37. José María Quirós, "Memoria de instituto, 1819," par. 39, AGI, Mexico, 2519; Prinsep, *Carta al Exmo. Señor Duque de Frías,* 22; Branciforte to Consejo de Indias, Mexico City, 27 Oct. 1796, AGI, Mexico, 2507; BNMex, Reales Ordenes, 27, 1396; Basadre, "Memoria," AGI, Ind. Gen., 2439, par. 33.

38. Note the following critiques of Veracruz traditionalists: "por que algunos comerciantes de Veracruz vendan a más precio las existencias que tienen y saquen exorvitantes ganancias" ("Testimonio . . . Nueva Gaditana," AGI, Mexico, 2514); "han preferido la estagnación de sus especulaciones y el anonadamiento de sus fortunas, a las considerables ventajas que les hubiera producido el comercio directo con los extrangeros" (Prior y Consules del Consulado de Veracruz [Sierra, Guerra y Ágreda, Yzaguirre], 25 June 1816, AGI, Mexico, 2994).

39. Consulado de Veracruz to Ministro de Hacienda, AGI, Mexico, 2994.

40. AGI, Ind. Gen., 2466.

41. "Llegará el caso de que [la Metrópoli] deba renunciar para siempre el giro de las Yndias, y recivir en este ramo la ley que quieran imponer los Consulados, y Comerciantes americanos." Consulado de Cadiz (Manuel Ruiz, Pedro Martínez de Murguía), 8 May 1797, AGI, Ind. Gen., 2466. *Americanos* here included, of course, *peninsulares* in the colonies and *criollos.*

42. Cadiz merchants feared that re-exports from Havana might "despertar los deseos y apetito de los Mexicanos que hasta aora han sabido carecer de los objectos de luxo, o pagarlos sin repugnancia a los precios altos que les han dado los tiempos presentes." Consulado de Cadiz to SM, 5 Mar. 1799, AGI, Consulados, Correspondencia, 51.

43. This argument was clearly ideated by the officers of the Consulado de México (Francisco de Chavarri, Diego de Ágreda, Lorenzo García Noriega), writing on 1 June 1811: "La Nueva España nada ganaría relativamente al comercio en depender de Cuba, y no de la Peninsula, antes bien empeoraba con el desvanecimiento de sus corresponsales, y negocios radicados en los diversos puertos de la Matriz, y empeoraba tambien con el monopolio de los Ysleños." AGN, AHH, 216-11.

44. Austria, "Memoria, 1804," par. 53.

45. Cf. a series of remarks apropos Jalapa merchants in the late 1780s, many of whom later shifted their operations to Veracruz: "No . . . son de la matrícula de España; pero desde el sixtema del libre comercio estendieron sus giro a negociaciones de su cuenta o la agena directamente con la Matriz . . . y mecanizan al mismo tiempo en sus tiendas antiguas o modernas, creyéndose sin embargo autorizados de los mismos fueros y privilegios que los lexítimos comerciantes de España." "Sobre alcabalas" (1786), BNMex, Reales Ordenes, 27, 1396. Years later Austria explained similarly the viewpoint of Veracruz independents when he claimed that *comercio libre* opened the colonial trades to "los intereses de todos los Españoles de Europa, o América, aunque no están incluidos en la matrícula de los consulados de España ni aún los de América, y sin ser por consequencia de los listados como cargadores a Indias." Austria, "Segundo escrito," AGI, Mexico, 2510.

46. "[L]os que podían rescatar nuestros buques y efectos nacionales, lograban por efecto de la misma hacerse de fondos en las Islas Inglesas; ya se dexa conocer el uso que algunos de nuestros comerciantes harían de esta sencilla operación." *Jornal Económico y Mercantil de Veracruz,* no. 148 (26 July 1806).

47. Cf. Austria, "Noticias y reflexiones . . . 1799": "Sirviendo la Habana [in

1797–99] en mucha parte de linea de comunicación; siendo los comerciantes de aquella Plaza y los de Veracruz, los que principalmente la tenían en acción; y los Anglo-Americanos Agentes intermediarios de dicho comercio, todo conforme con la mayor facilidad que de este modo se presentava para realizar las especulaciones."

48. AGI, Mexico, 2507, fols. 8v–9r.

49. In 1796 Tomás Murphy was a partner *(socio)* in the London merchant house of William Duff Gordon. Jiménez Codinach, *La Gran Bretaña,* cited in Souto Mantecón, *Mar abierto,* 104 and n. 19.

50. The quotation is from a manuscript of the *Correo's* first number, 1 Oct. 1792, AGSim, Secretaría and Superintendencia de Hacienda 22, 967, no. 520.

51. Javier Ortiz de la Tabla Ducasse published the sixteen *memorias de instituto* of the *consulados'* secretaries—four drafted by Basadre, three by Austria, and nine by Quirós—in *Memorias políticas y económicas* with a long introduction. The following paragraphs summarize the approaches of Basadre and Quirós.

52. AGI, Mexico, 2507, fols. 8v–9r.

53. Basadre, "Memoria, 1796," AGI, Mexico, 2507, in Ortiz de la Tabla Ducasse, *Memorias políticas y económicas,* 3.

54. Basadre's travel expenses were paid by the Mexico City treasury. Basadre, letter of 1 Mar. 1797, AGI, Mexico, 2508. His plan was titled: "Proyecto . . . a beneficio del Estado, Real hacienda y causa pública en el interesante ramo de peletería de la costa occidental de California."

55. Hacienda Secretary Gardoqui found Basadre to be an "hombre de talento y dispuesto al trabajo" as well as "uno de los hombres más hábiles y de más conocimiento en el comercio y en las cosas de América que yo he tratado." Souto Mantecón provides biographical details in *Mar abierto,* 118–20.

56. For biographical details, see Fonseca and Urrutia, *Historia general,* 1:374, 380–82; BRAHM, Mata Linares, 68, fol. 524v; AGI, Mexico, 2506, 2508, 2510, 2513; AHN, Consejos, 21,082; and MN, MS 317, fols. 1r–8v. Basadre's four *memorias* are available in Ortiz de la Tabla Ducasse, *Memorias políticas y económicas,* 11–74.

57. Basadre categorized Austria's work as "de contínua asistencia." AGI, Mexico, 2510.

58. Remigio Fernandes, a supporter of Basadre's and an ex-prior, wrote the Hacienda secretary that Basadre "varias veces ha trahido a las Juntas papeles y reflexiones de comercio importantes con los estudios de la balanza, y se los han despreciado." Remigio Fernandes to Soler, 8 Apr. 1802, AGI, Mexico, 2510.

59. Letter signed by Basadre and Austria to Soler, 6 Dec. 1800, and Consejo de Indias, "Nota," 11 Mar. 1801, both in AGI, Mexico, 2510.

60. Remigio Fernandes to Soler, 8 Apr. 1802, AGI, Mexico, 2510.

61. *Gazeta de México,* 21 July 1802. Echeverría's *consiliarios* were Alberto Herrero, Pedro Antonio de Garay y Llano, and Rafael Canalías y Alvareda. Echeverría's extended (Navarrese) family had roots in Veracruz. Juan José de Echeverría was a merchant there in 1781; Francisco Xavier de Echeverría was the son-in-law of José Mariano de Almanza, born at Veracruz; Almanza and Pedro Miguel de Echeverría were *fiadores* of a shipment unloaded at Veracruz under *comercio neutro* and consigned to Tomás Murphy. Pedro Miguel was a *consulado* officer in 1795; sometime after 1799 he established commercial ties with Havana's leading merchant, Pedro Juan de Erice, as well as with Baltimore's Robert Oliver. Pedro Miguel was the pro-

prietor of what was considered "one of the wealthiest and most respectable firms of Veracruz," one of two firms used by Oliver's agent at Veracruz in 1806–8. Nolte, *Fifty Years in both hemispheres,* 98.

62. Basadre, "Extracto de lo principal que contiene un papel presentado al . . . Príncipe Generalísimo Almirante [Godoy] en . . . 1807. Madrid," MN, MS 317, fols. 1r–8v. Here Basadre, now in Madrid, advised Godoy on the extent and value of smuggling at Veracruz. Souto Mantecón, *Mar abierto,* 220 n. 11.

63. AHN, Consejos, 21,081, ramo 3, fol. 23r. Basadre confirmed a document forwarded by Viceroy Iturrigaray to the Junta Suprema after the Bourbons resigned to Napoleon at Bayonne. Real Alcazar de Sevilla, 21 Nov. 1808.

64. Austria's early support for *comercio neutro* distanced him immediately from Veracruz's traditionalists, who also distrusted the close relationship between his brother, José Benito, and Tomás Murphy. On the other hand, José Donato de Austria criticized the trade proposals of Valentín de Foronda, consul at Philadelphia, for failing to recognize that Spain's Atlantic trade still needed some government management lest it be overwhelmed by English merchants. There is a limited bibliography: AGI, Mexico, 2509, 2510, 2511, 2996; AHN, Hacienda, 3871; and "Informe económico sobre el comercio de América en 1800," in *Revista de Historia* (Caracas) 21 (1864), which may be his "Noticias y reflexiones . . . 1799."

65. In 1802 Murphy y Cotarro reported that Josef Benito de Austria was their agent for cacao purchases at La Guayra, Venezuela. AHN, Hacienda, 3871.

66. Austria's support is not surprising; he had served under Francisco de Saavedra, the first intendant of Venezuela, a proponent of *comercio neutro.* For his Venezuelan years, see Souto Mantecón, *Mar abierto,* 123–24.

67. Austria to Soler, 8 Apr. 1802, AGI, Mexico, 2996; Consulado de Veracruz to Soler, 7 Jan. 1804, AGI, Mexico, 2511.

68. Quirós had come to Veracruz from his birthplace in Andalusia and engaged in trade with the peninsula, where his Cadiz agent was Carlos Malagamba. His expertise in trading with the metropole led to his *Guía de negociantes: Compendio de la legislación mercantil,* which was carefully edited by Pedro Pérez Herrero in 1986. Aware of the persistent role of peninsular Spaniards as straw men for foreign merchants, in 1816 he proposed the adoption of a kind of navigation act to prevent the entry of English merchants. An example of the peninsular immigrant integrated into the Veracruz commercial world who was also an effective *consulado* employee, in the postcolonial Mexico of 1822 he was a member of Veracruz's *diputación provincial.* See esp. Souto Mantecón, *Mar abierto,* 123–25; Smith, "José María Quirós"; BRAHM, Mata Linares, 73; AGN, AHH, 629-1, fol. 11r; and AGI, Mexico, 2516, 2511, 2994.

69. Cancelada, now retired to Cadiz, reprinted Quirós's "Carta . . . leída en primera junta de gobierno del Consulado de Veracruz," 10 Jan. 1812, in his periodical financed by Cadiz merchants, the *Telégrafo Americano,* on 6 Feb. 1812.

70. Prinsep, *Carta al Exmo. Señor Duque de Frías,* 22–23.

71. Ortiz de la Tabla, *Memorias políticas y económicas,* ix–x.

72. In Basadre's view, smallholders formed a nursery from which *colonos* might ultimately move up, passing, he noted, from the status of *hortelanos* to a "clase suprema de hacendados." Basadre, "Memoria de instituto, 1801," AGI, Mexico, 2509.

73. Basadre had in mind an import-substitution industry to replace what the Flemish had managed to eliminate "en España el tiempo que reynó en ella la Casa

de Austria, de que se originó entre otros males, el atraso, decadencia y abandono de los artefactos nacionales y por consequencia dieron entrada en la peninsula a varios artículos extrangeros, no solo para su respectivo consumo sino tambien para proveer las colonias de ultramar." Basadre, "Memoria . . . sobre gusanos de seda," 1802, AGI, Mexico, 2996. His facts are indisputable.

74. Such a central planning body would presumably collect and publish data on producers and production in a "registro fiel" of agricultural, ranching, and commercial entrepreneurs. Basadre, "Memoria, 1804," AGI, Mexico, 2996.

75. Quirós, "Memoria, 1807," AGI, Mexico, 2997.

76. Quirós was obviously aware of Madrid's colonization project in the Sierra Morena (Andalusia) entrusted to Pablo de Olavide in the 1770s. Quirós recommended comparable immigrant settlements in the vicinity of Veracruz and, following the government's policy for the Sierra Morena, that municipal and government taxes on their output be suspended. Ibid.

77. Ibid., citing Real Orden, 22 Nov. 1792.

78. Quirós utilized, for example, a trade balance for Veracruz prepared since the founding of the *consulado* in 1796 in order to compare the volume of textile imports of the *flota* of 1772 (commanded by Luís de Córdoba) with the imports of 1802–4. For precious metals exports he cited Solórzano Pereira, a report by the second conde de Revillagigedo, and Alexander von Humboldt's *Tablas geográficas*. "Memoria . . . comercio libre, 1808." AGI, Mexico, 2997.

79. Ibid.

80. Underutilization of land, Quirós felt, was ultimately the origin of holdings "eriales y valdíos" and of cities "recargadas de gente ociosa y vagamunda." He probably had in mind the colony of New Spain.

81. "Memoria . . . comercio libre, 1808." AGI, Mexico, 2997.

82. Normally the religious establishment allocated four-ninths of tithe income to such ends.

6. Mining and Its Fissures

EPIGRAPHS: Pérez Rosales, *Familia, poder, riqueza*, 253; Humboldt, *Ensayo político*, 353; Castro Gutiérrez, *Nueva ley y nuevo Rey*, dedication; Mentz, "Coyuntura minera," 44.

1. Cf. Branciforte, "Relación," 1296: "En los Reales Tribunales del Consulado de México y la Minería, dos firmes columnas que sostienen admirablemente los dos importantes ramos de su gobierno y responsabilidades . . . que . . . tienen los vireyes para auxiliar con caudales las urgencias de la Corona." More recently, Josep María Fradera has put New Spain in a wider context: "El esfuerzo militar de la monarquía debería descansar sobre la capacidad del gran Virreinato del que dependía aquellas posesiones [Cuba, Puerto Rico and the Philippines]." Fradera, *Colonias*, 32.

2. Humboldt, *Ensayo político*, 458. Humboldt credited much of his data to a mining survey prepared by Fausto de Elhuyar. *Essai politique*, 3:335.

3. "Noticias de Nueva España," New York Public Library, Rich Collection, fol. 6v; Ward, *Mexico*, 1:397; A. Martin, "État des mines du Mexique," 6 July 1827, AAEPar, Commerce, Mexique, 1, fols. 212r–216r. The number of mineworkers in 1805 was estimated by Austria, "Memoria, 1805," AGN, AHH, 1864-4. Astonished

by the importance of mining in New Spain, Viceroy Revillagigedo compared the local fixation on silver to the emphasis in the U.S. "confederation" on agriculture. BNMex, Reales Ordenes, 27. A Cadiz merchant calculated that in the 1780s New Spain produced annually three times the output of Peru's mines. Gutiérrez de la Huerta, Sept. 1789, Archivo de las Cortes, Expedientes, legajo 5, no. 88.

4. The colony of New Spain absorbed an estimated 34% of all Spain's exports to its American colonies in 1808. M. Peuchet, *État des colonies,* 1:280.

5. Howe, *Mining Guild,* 30. Elhuyar, Beleña's contemporary in the colony, noted the positive correlation between rising silver-mining output and the colonial government's income, markedly so between 1764 (6 million *pesos*) and 1792 (19 million), substantiating "que en lo principal todo ha dependido en estos países en el siglo pasado, como en los anteriores, del cultivo de sus minas." Elhuyar, *Memoria sobre el influjo,* 55.

6. *Silver Coinage, New Spain, 1537–1821*

    (*pesos*)

	Total	Annual Average
1537–1771	441,629,211	1,900,000
1772–1821	869,216,943	17,400,000

Source: Howe, *Mining Guild,* app. A.

7. *Silver and Gold Coinage, Mexico City Mint, 1789–1810*

    (*pesos*)

1789	21,129,911	1800	18,685,674
1790	18,063,688	1801	16,568,442
1791	21,121,713	1802	18,798,599
1792	24,195,041	1803	23,166,906
1793	24,312,942	1804	27,090,001
1794	22,011,031	1805	27,165,888
1795	24,593,481	1806	24,736,020
1796	25,644,627	1807	22,014,699
1797	25,080,038	1808	1,886,500
1798	24,004,589	1809	26,172,982
1799	22,053,125	1810	19,046,188

Source: "Demostración de la plata y oro acuñados en la casa de moneda de Mexico," *Águila Mexicano,* 16 Aug. 1823, reprinted with minor changes in Ward, *Mexico,* 1:386, tables 1–2.

8. [Donato de Austria or Quirós], "Balanza, 1805," AGN, AHH, 1869-4; Lerdo de Tejada, *Apuntes,* 386 n. 8. The 1805 data are from *Águila Mexicano,* reprinted in Romano, *Moneda,* table 1.1.

9. England's Board of Trade, preoccupied with New Spain's silver output, calculated an average annual production of 21,734,126 *pesos* over 1796–1810. PRO, BT 6/54.

10. Ward, *Mexico,* 1:412. For example, a rise in maize prices drove up mining costs; Guanajuato's mining operations employed 14,000 horses and mules daily.

11. Brading, *Miners and Merchants,* 133–40; Humboldt, *Essai politique,* 3:335. The Consulado de México traced the spurt in output to population growth, the "luces" brought by *comercio libre* (1778), a drop in the price of mercury, and "La Valenciana."

"Noticias publicadas de Nueva España en 1805." Humboldt listed similar factors. *Essai politique,* 4:96.

12. Garner, "Zacatecas," 207–13.

13. Suárez Argüello, "Los bancos de rescate de platas," 100–101.

14. Humboldt, *Essai politique,* 4:148.

15. As a Spanish commission of inquiry reported nostalgically to the Cortes in 1821, "[L]a Valenciana producía anualmente tanto como el Perú entero." *Dictamen de la comisión especial . . . ramo de minería* (Madrid, 1821), 4, repeating Humboldt's similar comparison. Humboldt, *Essai politique,* 4:148, places New Spain's precious-metals production in perspective: about 1808 New Spain produced about 69% (23 million *pesos*) of world production (39 million). M. Peuchet, *État des colonies,* 1:280.

16. Brading, *Miners and Merchants,* 250.

17. Such concentrated ownership had its critics. Cf. "Sobre venta de bienes," Nov. 1805, BNMad, MS 19709, no. 34: "El [ramo] de minería compuesto de 10 a 12 hombres ricos, y el resto de pobres habilitados."

18. Brading, *Miners and Merchants,* 206, 285; Langue, *Mines, terre et société,* 148.

19. Garner, "Zacatecas," 185, 191, 213, 216, 326. One of Zacatecas's most productive mines, "Quebradilla," registered 60% of this *minería*'s output in 1809–10.

20. Ibid., 195; Howe, *Mining Guild,* 151.

21. Humboldt, *Ensayo político,* 353–54, 473–80, 607, 609; Ward, *Mexico,* 1:463.

22. Humboldt, *Ensayo político,* 353–54; Brading, *Miners and Merchants,* 132; Alamán, *Historia de Méjico,* vol. 1, app. 6. France's agents at Madrid carefully reported at this time on the situation of New Spain's key mines, noting the restiveness of mine owners confronting rising operating costs. "Mémoire secret: Coup d'oeil politique et secret."

23. Brading, *Miners and Merchants,* 285; Humboldt, *Ensayo político,* 353. Garner hypothesizes that it was Madrid's policy to avoid oversupplying mercury. "Zacatecas," 229.

24. The patio process is described in Elhuyar, "Reflections," 483–85; Bakewell, *Silver Mining and Society,* 136–45; and Brading, *Miners and Merchants,* 137–39.

25. Ward, *Mexico,* 2:335.

26. Iturrigaray to Soler, 27 Oct. 1803, AGI, Mexico, 2247. Ten months earlier Iturrigaray had emphasized that "la minería es el único medio de que se restaablezca (y todos los ramos del Erario, la industria y el comercio)." Iturrigaray to Soler, 29 Jan. 1803, AGN, Correspondencia de virreyes, 2nd ser., 213.

27. Foncerrada, *Foncerrada michoacanense,* 9.

28. *Mercury Imports, New Spain, 1761–1782*
   (*quintales*)

	Annual Average
1761	5,000–6,000
1762–66	7,150
1767–71	10,600
1772–77	10,600
1778–82[a]	11,800

Sources: Gamboa, *Comentarios,* 28; Humboldt, *Ensayo político,* 384.

[a]In 1782 at least 26,500 *quintales* arrived at Veracruz. Howe, *Mining Guild,* 258.

29. Humboldt, *Ensayo político,* 481 n. 1a. Iturrigaray claimed that he had distributed a total of roughly 80,000 *quintales.* García Sala, *El exmo. Sr. D. José de Iturrigaray,* 26.

30. Levene, *Documentos para la historia argentina,* 442; Albuerne, *Orígen,* 80. In 1798–1801 many mine owners, unable to have their ores processed for lack of mercury, had to borrow from churches' *obras pías.* Tribunal de Minería to Iturrigaray, 1805, BNMex, 1667.

31. "Nota de las cantidades de pesos que . . . Minería ha desembolsado en donativos graciosos: México, 10 Feb. 1798," AGI, Mexico, 2246.

32. Iturrigaray to Soler, 27 Dec. 1803 and 20 June 1806, AGN, Correspondencia de virreyes, 2nd ser., 214 and 229.

Mercury Imports, New Spain, 1802–1804
  (quintales)

1802	34,000
1803	50,000
1804	20,000

Source: AGN, AHH, 1869-7.

33. For example, Matías Murphy, Tomás Murphy's brother, was investing in the "Mellado" mine.

34. Soler to Cevallos, 15 Feb. 1808, AHN, Estado, 5618. At the same time, Madrid contracted for the purchase of 33,000 flasks to ship mercury to New Spain, the cost to be billed to the colonial treasury at Mexico City. The London firm of Gordon & Murphy was commissioned to send vessels to San Sebastian to pick up the flasks. Iturrigaray to Soler, 13 Feb. 1808, AGN, Correspondencia de virreyes, 2nd ser., 236.

35. Rayas to Miguel Bataller, 21 Oct. 1808, in García Sala, *El exmo. Sr. D. José de Iturrigaray,* app. 7; Humboldt, *Essai politique,* 4:915; Joaquina Aranguren, AHN, Consejos, 21081, ramo 1, fol. 113r. The conde de Valenciana (Obregón) was the first mine owner to proposition Iturrigaray. Lizarza, *Discurso,* 32. Mine owners' payments to Viceroy Iturrigaray in return for mercury allocations were justified thus: "[E]n parte los mismos mineros eran los que habían introducido esta viciosa y injusta pención a causa del ahinco con que procuran y porfiaban llebar más porción de azogues que otros." Mine proprietors bribing Joaquina Aranguren, a servant and *chihuahua* (confidant) of the viceroy's wife, included Antonio Uzcola, Fermín de Apecechea, Miguel Angel Michaus, José María Fagoaga, Antonio Basoco, Francisco Cortina González, Francisco Alonso Terán, and José Martínez Barenque. Castillejos, 21 Feb. 1809, in García, *Documentos históricos mexicanos,* 1:121.

36. García Sala, *El exmo. Sr. D. José de Iturrigaray,* 32.

37. Iturrigaray to Contador General de Azogues, 21 Oct. 1807, AGN, AHH, 449-7. The monopsony of mercury provided about 50% of aggregate revenues from all the colonial government's monopolies. Pérez Rosales, *Familia, poder, riqueza,* 66.

38. Iturrigaray to Soler, 27 July 1808, AGN, Correspondencia de virreyes, 2nd ser., 214; Pablo Frayle y Santa María to J. Avila, 28 July 1802, AGN, Consulado, 25, exp. 2, fols. 2r–3r. The cost of transporting mercury from Veracruz to Mexico City and beyond was covered by mine owners. Pérez Rosales, *Familia, poder, riqueza,* 68–69.

39. AHN, Consejos, 21,082, quad. 3.1. When Valladolid investors formed a company to operate a local mine, they contacted the *montañés* merchant Francisco Alonso de Terán, in Mexico City, to petition for a mercury allotment. Juárez Nieto, *Oligarquía*, 116–17.

40. Fonseca and Urrutia, *Historia general*, 1:345; Azanza to Saavedra, 21 July 1798, AGI, Mexico, 1587. Revillagigedo grasped the details of mercury distribution: "[C]ada seis meses se destinan y remiten de esta capital a las Cajas Reales del Reino, las partidas necesarias de aquel ingrediente, repartiendose por tercias partes . . . los mineros lo reciben bajo de fianzas, por el término de seis meses, satisfacen en plata pasta quintada, y pagan en el acto de sacar los azogues el importe de sus fletes de conducción." "Dictamen . . . intendencias," in Chávez Orozco, *Documentos*, 4:63. For the handling of mercury until the mid-eighteenth century, see Heredia Herrera, *La renta del azogue*.

41. Ward, *Mexico*, 1:396; Joseph Palacio de Romaña to Ignacio Olascuaga (*reservado* [confidential]), AGN, AHH, 25, exp. 1a; Humboldt, *Essai politique*, 4:90–91. Cf. Iturrigaray to Soler, 27 Oct. 1803, AGI, Mexico, 2242: "Persuadido de VE de que el medio más propio de restablecer y aún de aumentar la felicidad de estos dominios y de toda la Monarquía es el de las quantiosas remesas de azogue a este Reyno. . . . En sola la famosa Mina nombrada Valenciana . . . podrían emplearse anualmente 5,6 quintales." He said that an ample mercury supply *"es el más fecundo, el mejor y único medio de que se progresasen todos los ramos del Erario . . . sin necesidad de otros arbitrios se pudiese acudir a las cargas de la Real Hacienda en estos dominios y a las preferentes atenciones de esa metrópoli"* (emphasis added by the Consejo de Indias). When Colonial Secretary Valdés requested data on mercury consumption in order to have Madrid control its distribution, he got no cooperation, and "la distribution du mercure resta comme auparavant, abandonnée au vice-roi de la Nouvelle Espagne." Humboldt, *Essai politique*, 4:91. In 1787 the Consejo de Indias lacked data on mercury shipments to New Spain. Consejo de Indias, "Dictamen," 3 Oct. 1787, AGI, Mexico, 2505.

42. Brading, *Miners and Merchants*, 279–81; Azanza to Hacienda de Indias, 22 June 1795, AGN, Mexico, 1587.

43. The marqués de Rayas, of Guanajuato, added that "no me faltan fundamentos para creer que los domésticos, interlocutores en semejantes solicitudes, y no SE, eran los aprovechados en qualquier exceso." One of those domestics, was Joaquina Aranguren (*chihuahua* of Iturrigaray's wife). Rayas to Miguel Bataller, AHN, Consejos, 21,081, ramo 1, fol. 113r.

44. Iturrigaray's *apoderado* for his *residencia* (appropriately enough, Rayas) defended the ex-viceroy's mercury allotments: "[H]ay ciertas minas ricas y de la mayor extensión en sus labores que pueden sacar tantos metales como azogues se proporcionen por lo que con tanto afán procuran lograr la mayor cantidad de dicho ingrediente pues no son como los aventureros que van a ver si hallan o no veta . . . por consiguiente los tales mineros de negociaciones conocidos son los que multiplican la plata y la amonedación, siendo de esta clase los sugetos a quienes repartió [Iturrigaray] extraordinariamente los azogues, y de aqui procedió que si bien Iturrigaray le importó (sean 10,000 onzas [de plata] o algo más) a trueque de ellas, los mineros sacaron un cúmulo de plata." Rayas, AHN, Consejos, 21,081, cargo 16, quad. 19. Iturrigaray did admit to "motivos muy particulares de estrechez" with the estab-

lished mine owner Romero de Terreros. García Sala, *El exmo. Sr. D. José de Iturriga-ray*, 26–27.

45. Brading, *Miners and Merchants*, 171–72; Pérez Rosales, *Familia, poder, riqueza*, 40, 44, 47–48; Vargas-Lobsinger, *Formación y decadencia de una fortuna*, 37–41; Langue, *Mines, terre et société*, 133–34.

46. Pérez Rosales, *Familia, poder, riqueza*, 149.

47. Cf. Pérez Rosales, *Familia, poder, riqueza*, 150 n. 104: "[L]a presencia del grupo vasco novohispano en los negocios comerciales y minas," referring to promi-nent figures such as Fagoaga, Arozqueta and Aldaco; or Castro Gutiérrez, *Nueva ley y nuevo rey*, 228: "[Basques] tenían . . . una aguda conciencia, un sentido de superi-oridad que los llevaba a apoyarse mutuamente." And María Teresa Huerta, "Co-merciantes en tierra adentro," in Valle Pavón, *Mercaderes*, 24–25, apropos Luis Sáenz de Tagle: "mostró una predisposición a relacionarse con miembros de la comunidad montañesa, de los que había un buen número."

48. Brading, *Miners and Merchants*, 330.

49. Ibid., 332–35.

50. Ibid., 299, 339.

51. Ibid., 333–34. Revillagigedo held a negative view of mine owners in general: "Seducidos con el atractivo de la minería . . . repugnan abrazar otras profeciones que podrían serles y al Estado de una felicidad más sólida, o menos contingente; pero las preocupaciones son incurables." Revillagigedo, "Dictamen . . . sobre com-ercio libre de este reino," fol. 292r.

52. Brading, *Miners and Merchants*, 336–37.

53. Ibid., 201. Brading later notes the role of "a group of independent refiners, mainly Basque in origin" (203).

54. Marichal, *La bancarrota del virreinato*, 109–21.

55. Howe, *Mining Guild*, 128–31, esp. 128–29, 144.

56. Brading, *Miners and Merchants*, 164; Howe, *Mining Guild*, 165.

57. Brading, *Miners and Merchants*, 178, 180; Howe, *Mining Guild*, 191.

58. Elhuyar, *Memoria sobre el influjo*, 53. The purpose of article 152 was "precaver la ocultación y fraudulentas estracciones del oro y plata en pasta, que los mineros necesitados vendían a los mercaderes y rescatadores de estos metales, en manifiesta contravención de las leyes que prohiben la adquisición y comercio de ellos antes de estar quitados." Small-scale miners, not to mention the workers keeping their *partido*, would bargain with *rescatadores* for the best price. AGN, AHH, 635-2, fol. 15r.

59. Howe, *Mining Guild*, 200.

60. Brading, *Miners and Merchants*, 44, 201–2, 204, 206–7; Couturier, *Silver King*, 178.

61. Brading, *Miners and Merchants*, 337–38. Lucas Alamán noted the ethnic ori-gins of the confrontation between *europeos* and *americanos*. *Historia de Méjico*, 1:15–17, 45–46.

62. Behind the success of the "empresa Veta Grande" were *criollos* of Basque origin. Torales Pacheco, *Ilustrados en la Nueva España*, 222–23; for some succinct biographies, see those on Goya (173–74 and n. 65) and Basoco (168–70).

63. Brading, *Miners and Merchants*, 338. Brading also described the divisions as follows: "whereas the chief miners of Zacatecas appear to have been peninsular, in Guanajuato they were . . . nearly all creoles" (169). On the other hand, Frédérique

Langue has argued that "Zacatecas ne présente pas d'opposition ethnique tranchée, entre peninsulaires et *criollos*. Les uns et les autres forment un group d'intérêt . . . de pression entrêmement solide." *Mines, terre et société*, 367–68.

64. Langue, *Mines, terre et société*, 140, 143, 201; Pérez Rosales, *Familia, poder, riqueza*, 77, 80, 86.

65. Langue, *Mines, terre et société*, 137–39, 146; Brading, *Miners and Merchants*, 202, 205–7. We have converted Brading's table 18 at the rate of 8.5 *pesos* per mark.

66. Langue, *Mines, terre et société*, 138.

67. Brading, *Miners and Merchants*, 203–4; Langue, *Mines, terre et société*, 144; Garner, "Zacatecas," 326.

68. Brading, *Miners and Merchants*, 203, 339. Pérez Rosales, *Familia, poder, riqueza*, 171–74, treats the Zacatecas situation in detail.

69. Iturrigaray to Soler, 27 Aug. 1804 and 26 Feb. 1807, AGN, Correspondencia de virreyes, 2nd ser., 219 and 233; Lizarza, *Discurso*, in Hernández y Dávalos, *Colección de documentos*, 1:725ff.

70. These proprietors were labeled *gachupines*, godless money worshippers, in the early months of 1810, just before the outbreak of rebellion. Garner, "Zacatecas," 329 n. 22, citing Hamill, *Hidalgo Revolt*, 30.

71. Among Guanajuato mine owners approving Iturrigaray's removal were José de Septien, José María Chico, Francisco Iriarte, and Martín de la Riva. AHN, Consejos, 21,082, quad. 19.

72. Garner, "Zacatecas," 236.

73. Among Iturrigaray's former supporters later figured *criollo* mine owners donating fifteen thousand *pesos* to support Viceroy Venegas in his effort to suppress Hidalgo's revolt—Fagoaga, Anza, the marqués de Rayas, the conde de Valenciana, Olloqui. Pérez Rosales, *Familia, poder, riqueza*, 212.

74. Consulado de Veracruz (Remigio Fernández, Felipe Quintana, José Gil de Partearroyo) to Soler, 1 Dec. 1802, AGI, Mexico, 2511; "Balanza del Comercio de Veracruz . . . 1802," AGI, Consulados, Correspondencia con América, 217. "Durante años (hasta 1802) la casa tenía el monopolio de las cargas reales entre Veracruz y México, es decir, fué la única casa conductora de plata." Its bankruptcy was announced as a "considerable descuvierto de pesos que se ha advertido en la casa del difunto D. Pedro de Vertiz, en el que igualmente se manda se proceda al embargo de los bienes de D. Juan José Oteiza." Concurso de Pedro Vertiz y Juan José de Oteiza, quad. 4B, libro 1, Archivo Judicial de los Tribunales de México. Richard Salvucci graciously called this material to our attention.

75. Consulado de México, 23 Dec. 1803, AGI, Mexico, 2511.

76. Consulado de Veracruz (Remigio Fernández, José Gil de Partearroyo) to Soler, 1 Dec. 1802, AGI, Mexico, 2511. Such was the confidence in the Casa de Vértiz y Oteyza that "no solo consignaba en ella los caudales que eran de conducta a Veracruz, sino muchas otras gruesas sumas que depositaban ciegamente para hir disponiendo según las ocurrencias." Consequently, the firm's abrupt collapse shocked the colony's business community—"el trastorno, confusión y laberinto entre los tenedores de conocimientos, sus endosantes remitentes en la gruesa cantidad de más de 1,000,000 de pesos que giraba en Papal dentro de esta Plaza." Ibid.

77. On this point, see AGN, AHH, 635-2, fol. 19r.

78. Brading, *Miners and Merchants*, 174; Concurso de Pedro Vertiz y Juan José

de Oteiza, quad. 4B, libro 1, Archivo Judicial de los Tribunales de México. The firm also owned near the capital a flour mill (Tacubaya), an *obraje* (Coyoacán), and two *haciendas* in the vicinity of Chalco. One of the Durango *haciendas,* "San Diego del Ojo," was valued at 260,000 *pesos,* and a *tienda* there—hundreds of miles from Mexico City—was stocked with high-quality European textiles: "Bretañas anchas lexítimas superfinas, Bretañas anchas superfinas, finas, Puntiví or platillas, Ruan de Silecia, Durais, Pañuelos de Bayajan finos de varios colores, muselina estampada, plata de azogue." Ibid.

79. Brading, *Miners and Merchants,* 192–93, 205. Juan Fernández Peredo lost some 55,000 *pesos* in the 1790s in Zacatecas's "Quebradilla" mine. Langue, *Mines, terre et société,* 146.

80. Concurso de Pedro Vertiz y Juan José de Oteiza, quad. 3C, fol. 53v. Almost two decades later, a defense of the firm's operations claimed that in 1802 it had suffered only a short-term liquidity crisis, but "un poderoso partido que, empeñado en su ruina y exterminio, trataba aún de hacer odioso su nombre," downplaying the firm's "bondad y general beneficencia." No details of the *partido*'s membership were given. *Sucincta relación del estado.*

81. "Manifiesto al Público por la Compañía establecida en esta Capital para la Conducción de los Caudales del Rey y de los Particulares a los Puertos de Veracruz y Acapulco." *Gazeta de México,* 28 Jan. 1804; "Compañía de plata Michaus y Uscola: escritura, fianzas," AGN, Consulado, 17, exp. 13.

82. Diego Fernández Peredo, who had formed his commercial firm in 1776, declared he had just "celebrado Compañía por el término de 6 años, para la conducta de Caudales particulares, com mi Primo D. Juan Manuel Fernández Peredo; mediante la qual nos hemos constituido ambos a dicha conducción, con general hipoteca de todos nuestros bienes." In addition, the "Manifiesto," published on 24 January 1804, assured "todo individuo así de esta ciudad como los de fuera podrá poner o remitir en derechura sus intereses, ya efectivos, o ya en Libranzas, para so cobre y embío a donde los destinaren." AGN, Consulado, 17, exp. 12.

83. The *montañés* Heras Soto became a critic of Tomás Murphy's trade with Jamaica after 1805.

84. Well before 1790, ethnic friction had flared over the election of electors to choose the then powerful *diputados* of the local *diputación.* A factor in the friction was the disproportionate share of mercury assigned in 1781 to two *criollo* members of the junta of electors, the proprietors of "Valenciana," Obregón and Otero. In the 1783 election of electores, *montañeses* led by José Hernández Chico, joined by Francisco Septien y Arce, replaced Obregón and Otero as electors and chose as *diputados* Hernández Chico and Septien y Arce. Brading, *Miners and Merchants,* 330–31.

85. Ibid., 335–36; Howe, *Mining Guild,* 164–65, 197–209, esp. 209.

86. Howe, *Mining Guild,* 211 n. 79, 222–23.

87. Friction among *almaceneros, vizcaínos* versus *montañeses,* had been the source of bitter electioneering in the Consulado de México in 1742, forcing viceregal intervention and the subsequent alternation of high offices between the two ethnic interest groups.

88. Cf. "[F]rente a los sometidos, actuaban [*vizaínos, montañeses*] de manera unida y coherente, dejando a un lado sus divergencias." Castro Gutiérrez, *Nueva ley y nuevo rey,* 228; Couturier, *Silver King,* 84–90 (Pachuca).

89. Austria, "Memoria, 1805," AGN, AHH, 1869-4; Navarro y Noriega, *Memoria,* 29 n. 16. Aggregating family members by a factor of 4–5 yields a mining population of 120,000–150,000, omitting the thousands employed on nearby cattle and agricultural estates. Among them were many mulattoes. Arrangoiz y Berzábal, *Méjico desde 1808 hasta 1867,* 1:13.

90. Zacatecas's "La Quebradilla" employed 2,550 workers—1,415 underground and 1,135 at the surface (1,135). Langue, *Mines, terre et société,* 144. As for *peones* bearing heavy ore bags, "l'on peut considérer comme les bêtes de somme des mines du Mexique. . . . On rencontre dans les mines des files de 50 a 60 de ces portefaix, parmi lesquels il y a des vieillards sexagénaires et des enfants de 10 a 12 ans." Humboldt, *Essai politique,* 4:36–37. Cf. the earlier comment of Humboldt's major informant on mining, Elhuyar: "[T]he ore or water is raised or lowered . . . on the shoulders of hundreds of workers and boys." "Reflections," 481.

91. Cf. the jeremiad of Bishop San José Muro: "[E]n los 30,000 barrenadores, faeneros, tenateros y barreteros, etc., empleados, se tendría el dolor de saberse que la quinta parte o 6,000 perecian anualmente para la propagación por pasar al sepulcro o quedar cadavéricos, dignos objetos de la compasión y del estado, que los mantiene. . . . El plan de la Valenciana dista de la voca mina 615 varas perpendiculares. Y a quien no estremece los gritos de la humanidad al ver metidos en esos abismos sin respiración, oprimidos del frío o calor, ocuparse los ombres toda la semana en travajos mortíferos; para gastar lo que ganaron en pocas horas, los Domingos, en embriaguéz y juegos, en las rameras que los esperan; de que resultan muertos, heridos y blásfemas." Muro to Alejandro Ramírez, 9 Sept. 1805, AGI, Ind. Gen., 2319. For an elite criollo's defense of mine owners' labor policies, see Foncerrada, *Foncerrada michoacanense,* 11.

92. Titulo 12, artículo 9: "Que a los indios de repartimiento, como concluida la tanda han de regresar a sus pueblos." Valladolid's intendant Juan Antonio Riaño reported to Viceroy Iturrigaray that he had suppressed *repartimiento de indios* as contrary to "la felicidad pública." Juárez Nieto, *Oligarquía,* 81.

93. Mentz, "Coyuntura minera," 24, 32, 44; Humboldt, *Essai politique,* 4:45. More recently, David Brading concluded that "Mexican mine-workers, far from being the oppressed peons of legend, constituted a free, well-paid, geographically mobile labour force which in many areas acted as the virtual partners of the owners." *Miners and Merchants,* 146, 149. On the other hand, in 1805 Bishop San José Muro vehemently contradicted Humboldt's contention, stating: "Distante las justicias de impedir esas concurrencias, autoriza la ordenanza al propietario de la Mina, falto de gentes, para que la recoja a lazo, como si fueran toros cimarrones del monte. El célebre Cardenal Richelieu bien nos satirizaba esa practica, quando exortaba a sus franceses, a que meneasen la Lanzadera para atraer la plata que los españoles adquieren con tanto trabajo." Muro to Alejandro Ramírez, 9 Sept. 1805, AGI, Ind. Gen., 2319. Earlier, Abbé Raynal had criticized mineworkers conditions: "On voyoit aux mineurs les rides, la faiblesse, le tremblement, la caducité, à l'age de la santé vigoureuse." *Histoire philosophique et politique,* 4:198. Cf. Navarrete Gómez, "Crisis y supervivencia," 115: "[N]unca se dejó de solicitar el envío de indios de repartimiento, petición que siempre encontró una férrea resistencia de parte de los pueblos afectados."

94. Langue, *Mines, terre et société,* 321; Garner, "Zacatecas," 324–26; Castro

Gutiérrez, *Nueva ley y nuevo rey,* 83; Mentz, "Coyuntura minera," 44. The insurgent Padre José María Cos, recalling prerevolutionary Zacatecas, noted the "seething hatred" toward Apecechea (a large investor in "Quebradilla") and his group, who were scorned as "foreign thieves who come here to plunder what is ours." Hamnett, *Roots of Insurgency,* 126.

95. Mentz, "Coyuntura minera," 42. Viceroy Cruillas reported to José de Gálvez in 1766 on the constant underlying tension: "[H]ay una masa agitada y extendida en todo el reino que con leve chispa puede abrazarlo todo." Castro Gutiérrez, 113. See also Bustamante, *Suplemento,* 279.

96. Iturrigaray to Suprema Junta de Sevilla, 3 Sept. 1808, in García Sala, *El exmo. Sr. D. José de Iturrigaray,* app. 18. Elsewhere in this defense of Iturrigaray's performance is the reference to "espíritus revoltosos e insubordinados . . . en fin por la rivalidad de los partidos que la ignorancia ha fundado en nuestras posesiones americanas" (36).

97. For Madrid's investigation of the presumed criminal activity of the *mercaderes de plata* Valdivielso, Fagoaga, and Isidro de la Madrid in the operations of the Mexico City Casa de Moneda in the 1720s, see *Memorial ajustado.*

98. On the Fagoaga dynasty, there is the outstanding study by Laura Pérez Rosales, *Familia, poder, riqueza y subversión:* "Es interesante observar la presencia del grupo vasco novohispano en los negocios comerciales y mineros. Los vascos son un ejemplo destacable para apreciar la importancia de las redes étnicas como forma de asociación" (150 n. 104). At Zacatecas after about 1780, well-established Basques had to confront competition from fresh Basque immigrants.

The Fagoaga were involved in mining operations in central and northern regions of the colony, at Sombrerete, Sultepec, Temascaltepec, Michoacán, Guanajuato, Huautla, and Taxco. At Taxco, for example, they were linked to the newly immigrant mine owners Apezechea, Bernardo Iriarte, the Pemartíns, and Manual de Rétegui. Brading, *Miners and Merchants,* 201–3. And at Zacatecas, Apezechea collaborated with Rétegui and Anza and had the support of other recent immigrants. Langue, *Mines, terre et société,* 323.

99. María Teresa Huerta notes that Sáenz de Tagle "mostró una predisposición a relacionarse con miembros de la comunidad montañesa." "Comerciantes de tierra adentro," 24–25.

100. Guillermina del Valle Pavón, "Apertura comercial del imperio y reconstitución de facciones en el Consulado de México," and Souto Mantecón, "Las prácticas políticas en el antiguo régimen," in Valle Pavón, *Mercaderes,* 262–63 and 299, respectively. See also Hausberger, "Las elecciones."

101. At San Luis Potosí the *alcalde mayor* announced in 1784 the formation of a junta of "vecinos bien intencionados" to invest in a "Compañía de Sujetos" to expand the operations of the Cerro de San Pedro mine. This was duly reported in the *Gazeta de México,* 14 Jan. 1784, to draw the attention of "todo el Reyno" and "quienes quiera hacerse Accionistas." Coincidentally, one of Mexico City's wealthiest *almaceneros,* Basoco, joined two partners to invest an impressive sum of 600,000 *pesos* in Bolaños's mines. Brading, *Miners and Merchants,* 127.

102. AGN, AHH, 25-1.

103. Elhuyar, "Reflections," 473.

104. Brading, *Miners and Merchants,* 169. Brading finds that at the end of the

colonial era "Guanajuato's elite was almost entirely composed of recent arrivals, new rich, gachupin merchants and creole miners" and a "peculiar predominance of Montañeses within Guanajuato's immigrant and mercantile community" (318, 324).

105. Iturrigaray to Soler, 26 June 1806, AGN, Correspondencia de virreyes, 2nd ser., 229.

106. Howe, *Mining Guild,* 392–93.

107. Ibid., 392.

108. García Sala, *El exmo. Sr. D. José de Iturrigaray,* 56.

7. Export Agriculture

EPIGRAPHS: *Correo Mercantil de España y sus Indias,* 9 July 1795, 447; Patch, *Maya and Spaniard in Yucatan,* 167; Baskes, *Indians, Merchants, and Markets,* 61.

1. On materials prepared for Revillagigedo, see BNMex, MS 1334. Abad y Queipo estimated growth in agricultural output from 1788 to 1808 at more than 33%. "Representación." And Humboldt valued agricultural output at 29 million *pesos. Essai politique,* 3:285–86. See also Rosensweig Hernández, "La economía novo-hispana," 465–71.

2. Officers of the Consulado de México boasted in 1796 that their guild "se componía de sugetos de caudales más opulentos . . . poseyendo haciendas y crías de ganado aún en las partes más distantes." AGI, Mexico, 1144, fol. 198r. In Spain the growth of the American colonies' agricultural producción was publicized enthusiastically in the government-sponsored trade publication *Correo Mercantil de España y sus Indias,* 9 July 1795, 447: "[e]fectivamente el aspecto de la agricultura y tráfico de nuestras colonias de dia en dia va mejorando en beneficio recíproco de las colonias y su metropoli."

3. Lerner, "Consideraciones," 337, 342; Fernando Navarro y Noriega, "Estado de la población . . . en . . . 1810," in Navarro y Noriega, *Memoria.*

4. Moreno Fraginals, *El ingenio,* vol. 1; Le Riverend, *Historia económica de Cuba,* 151–54; Deerr, *History of Sugar,* 1:129–30.

5. The effect of Saint-Domingue's slave insurrection on New Spain's sugar planters was noted by Páez de la Cadena in 1792. "Dictamen del superintendente de la Real Aduana," in Florescano and Castillo, *Controversia,* 1:276–78. See also the detailed, enlightening study of Sánchez Santiró, *Azúcar y poder;* and on the wide impact of the Haitian revolution, Geggus, *Impact of the Haitian Revolution.*

6. The secretary of the Veracruz *consulado* recalled nostalgically: "Cuando la Habana, Campeche, Tabasco y la Costa Firme se proveían desde este Reyno de los víveres que demandaban sus consumos . . . el maíz, las semillas y carnes." "Memoria, 1818," fol. 6r, AGN, AHH, 216-7-1.

7. Florescano, *Precios del maíz,* 150–53 and esp. 176–79, 190. Basadre, the Veracruz *consulado*'s secretary, was vexed by "propietarios de España y América . . . posehidos del egoismo" and the "poderoso que posee en la jurisdicción de este puerto un mayorazgo de considerable extension." "Memoria sobre la introducción de colonos," Jan. 1801, AGI, Mexico, 2509.

8. Ayuntamiento de México, BNMex, MS 1667-7, fol. 16r–v.

9. Abad y Queipo, "Representaciones . . . Valladolid," BNMex, MS 1667-8, fols. 13v–14r.

10. Cf. "Muchos comerciantes ricos hayan comprado haciendas, porque sus almacenes ya no tienen proporción para ser haviadores de las tiendas de varreo aqui y de fuera." AGN, AHH, 635-2.

11. Hamnett, *Politics and Trade*, 5–6, 95–120; Baskes, *Indians, Merchants, and Markets*, esp. 62–109.

12. Cf. Pastor, "El repartimiento de mercancías," 201.

13. *Repartimiento* is succinctly summarized in Patch and Cáceres Menéndez, "Towards a Reinterpretation of Spanish Colonialism and the *Repartimiento.*"

14. "Yndize comprehensibo de todos los gobiernos, corregimientos y alcaldías mayores que tiene la gobernación del virreynato de Mexico," New York Public Library. Cf. "Ydea general del comercio de Yndias, Tolosa de Guipúzcoa, 1 marzo 1776," in Florescano and Castillo, *Controversia*, 1:23–68.

15. On *repartimiento*, see, among others, the classic study by Hamnett, *Politics and Trade in Southern Mexico*, 14, 19–23, 43–44, 47; Pastor, "El repartimiento de mercancías," 201–36; Patch, *Maya and Spaniard in Yucatan;* idem, "Imperial Politics and Local Economy"; and Baskes, *Indians, Merchants, and Markets*, 20–38. There is, in addition, the now classic study by Alfredo Moreno Cebrián, *El corregidor de indios y la economía peruana del siglo XVIII*. The informative footnotes in Patch and Cáceres Menéndez, "Towards a Reinterpretation of Spanish Colonialism and the *Repartimiento*," also provide the most relevant bibliography.

16. As one Oaxaca-based merchant reported apropos the lure of *grana* profits: "[E]l aprecio de las Alcaldías mayores de esta provincia; el empeño en solicitarlas en la corte de España, y el que los nombrados para ellas encontrasen immediatamente fianzas para tributos y habilitaciones quantiosas de ciento, de doscientos, y de trescientos mil pesos anuales para cada una de las jurisdicciones de este suelo." Manuel Antonio Saravia to Intendente de Provincia Joseph María Lasso, AGN, Industria y Comercio, 20, fol. 188r.

17. Diputados del Comercio de Oaxaca (Francisco Antonio Goytia, Juan Francisco de la Vega, Josef Castañeda, Juan Berberana), 10 Sept. 1810, AGN, Industria y Comercio, 20, fol. 201r.

18. Patch and Cáceres Menéndez, "Towards a Reinterpretation of Spanish Colonialism and the *Repartimiento*," 23.

19. Taylor, *Landlord and Peasant*, 160–61; Humboldt, *Essai politique*, 3:259.

20. Deans-Smith, *Bureaucrats, Planters, and Workers*, esp. ch. 4.

21. García Navarro, *Intendencias en Indias*, 128–31; Stein, "Bureaucracy and Business," 24. In 1810, just weeks before the outbreak of revolution in the colony, Oaxaca's *peninsular* merchants still insisted on the necessity of *repartimiento*. Ibid., 63 n. 2.

22. Patch, *Maya and Spaniard in Yucatan*, 81, 165. Cf. Baskes, *Indians, Merchants, and Markets*, 6, describing *repartimiento* as "arguably the most important institution of Spanish-Amerindian economic exchange."

23. Cf. Pastor, "El repartimiento de mercancías," 201, 235: "[E]l comercio de 'repartimiento' se convirtió en la principal forma de hacer una fortuna usufructuando los cargos de gobierno" and "una . . . abrumadora mayoría de indígenas cuya resistencia al mercado había exigido el surgimiento del repartimiento forzoso."

24. Humboldt found that most of the cochineal traded at Veracruz came from small *nopaleries* farmed by "extremement pauvres" Native Americans. *Essai politique*, 3:259.

25. Baskes, *Indians, Merchants, and Markets,* esp. 110–27, outlines this aspect of *repartimiento.*

26. Ibid., 50–53, 75–76; Pastor, "El repartimiento de mercancías," 231.

27. Valladolid's intendant Juan Antonio Riaño wanted to terminate "un comercio que estaba en manos de un reducido y monopolista grupo de individuos confabulados con justicias corruptos." Franco Cáceres, *La intendencia de Valladolid de Michoacán,* 77.

28. Cf. Perelman, *Invention of Capitalism,* 2: "Alongside their work on pure economic theory, the classical political economists engaged in a parallel project: to promote the forcible reconstruction of society into a purely market-oriented system."

29. Baskes, *Indians, Merchants, and Markets,* 179–81; Pastor, "El repartimiento de mercancías," 235.

30. Pastor, "El repartimiento de mercancías," 231, 235–36.

31. Patch, *Maya and Spaniard in Yucatan,* 141; Deans-Smith, *Bureaucrats, Planters, and Workers,* 117–18.

32. Hamnett, *Politics and Trade,* 104–5, 109, 177, 180. The secretary of Veracruz's *consulado* was aware that Mexico City *almaceneros* used earnings in silver to speculate in *grana* exports, earning in one year at least 50% on their investment. Quirós, "Memoria . . . 1814," AGI, Ind. Gen., 2467. In 1799 many of these newcomers opposed *comercio neutro,* favoring instead trade from Havana to Veracruz to supply scarce items. AGI, Ind. Gen., 2466, fol. 52r. Noteworthy is the presence of Muñóz, Echeverria, and Puerto Vicario among the 115 Veracruz merchants supporting Spain's managed colonial trade. Souto Mantecón, *Mar abierto,* 237, anexo 1.

33. Hamnett, *Politics and Trade,* 104–5.

34. Baskes, *Indians, Merchants, and Markets,* 32, esp. 180–83.

35. Murphy y Cotarro to Antonio Noriega, 28 Oct. 1802, AHN, Hacienda, 3871. These *socios* added that "no presentando en este Reyno obgetos que merezcan atención, excepto grana y el azucar."

36. The contract was signed at Veracruz on 26 Nov. 1803. AGN, Consulado, 14, exp. 1, fol. 8r.

37. Exports of 1802 were detailed by Austria in his *memoria* of that year: "La cantidad de grana fina extraída equivale . . . a dos cosechas." Austria, "Observaciones," no. 8, in "Memoria, 1802," AGI, Mexico, 2510.

Grana *Exports, Veracruz, 1796–1808*

	(arrobas)	(pesos)		(arrobas)	(pesos)
1796	6,112	439,609	1802	43,277	3,303,470
1797	838	54,471	1803	27,251	2,191,399
1798	12,220	804,903	1804	11,737	1,220,193
1799	40,602	2,703,471	1805	n.d.	n.d.
1800	5,150	379,256	1806	4,254	425,400
1801	3,848	298,258	1807	2,823	282,300
			1808	7,374	737,400

Source: Hamnett, *Politics and Trade,* 175 app. 6.

38. Hamnett, *Politics and Trade,* 103.

39. Francisco Antonio Goytia, Antonio Sánchez, et al., "Expediente formado

sobre la solicitud delos Diputados del Comercio de Oaxaca . . . sobre el estanco de la grana," 11 May 1811, AGN, AHH, 502–5.

40. AGN, Industria y Comercio, 20.

41. A recent estimate of sugar production's percentage of New Spain's "national income" over the decade 1800–1810 is only 6.6%. Romero S. and Jauregui F., "Comentarios," 128.

42. *Composition of Exports, Veracruz, 1796–1803*
    (*pesos*)

	Total Value	Sugar	Cochineal
1796	9,313,387	1,347,231	439,609
1797	1,423,079	159,834	54,471
1798	3,371,328	212,691	804,903
1799	8,715,956	479,062	2,703,471
1800	6,058,470	287,277	379,256
1801	1,970,573	25,157	298,258
1802	38,447,367	1,454,240	3,303,470
1803	14,482,918	1,495,056	2,191,399

Sources: Lerdo de Tejada, *Comercio exterior de México*, doc. 14; "Balanza general del comercio . . . Veracruz, 1796 . . . 1807," AGI, Mexico, 2994.

43. In 1792 Spain imported 1,320,674 *arrobas* from the colonies, 296,850 of those from Veracruz. *Balanza del comercio de España*, 210–11.

44. *Sugar Exports, Veracruz and Havana, 1796–1808*
    (*arrobas*)

	Veracruz	Havana		Veracruz	Havana
1796	346,361	1,926,000	1803	483,944	n.a[a]
1797	60,835	1,889,052	1804	381,509	n.a.
1798	79,568	2,157,964	1805	n.a	n.a.
1799	150,881	2,649,632	1806	41,020	2,509,160
1800	87,570	2,273,592	1807	23,203	2,900,352
1801	9,148	2,557,456	1808	n.a.	2,005,968
1802	431,867	2,676,924			

Sources: For Veracruz exports, "Balanza general del comercio . . . Veracruz . . . , 1796 . . . 1807," AGI, Mexico, 2994. For Havana exports, AGI, Mexico, 2997, and AGI, Santo Domingo, 2195; Lerdo de Tejada, *Comercio exterior de México*, docs. 15–23.

[a]Humboldt estimated sugar exports (1803) from all Cuban ports to be about six times those from Veracruz. *Essai politique*, 3:184

45. Barrett, *Sugar Hacienda*, 4; Humboldt, *Ensayo político*, 286–87. In 1793 Tomás Murphy predicted that New Spain's sugar export boom would be brief, cut short by a fall in prices and high local transport costs. AGN, Consulado, 123, exps. 1–3, fol. 243v.

46. Hernández Palomo, *El aguardiente de caña*, 51, 53, 106; Yermo, "Sobre todo género de agricultura," fol. 10r–v.

47. In the 1780s it was considered a "trama normal" to send water-filled barrels

from Veracruz to Jalapa, where they were emptied, filled with *aguardiente de caña* mixed with small quantities of *aguardiente de Castilla,* and sold as imported brandy. Hernández Palomo, *El aguardiente de caña,* 95. Revillagigedo estimated New Spain's annual consumption of brandy at 200,000 barrels, 50,000 imported. Zamora y Coronado, *Biblioteca de legislación ultramarine,* 1:142.

48. Yermo, "Sobre todo género de agricultura," fol. 10r–v; Hernández Palomo, *El aguardiente de caña,* 104.

49. Sánchez Santiró, *Azúcar y poder,* 65.

50. *Sugar Exports, Veracruz, 1800–1810*
    (metric tons)

1800	1,007	1808	681
1801	105	1809	2,771
1802	4,966	1810	1,377
1803	5,565		

Source: Sánchez Santiró, *Azúcar y poder,* 204 table 2, 204–5.

51. Sánchez Santiró, *Azúcar y poder,* 57–59. Christiana Borchart de Moreno—unlike Priestley, Brading, Arcila Farías, and Florescano—found that an overwhelming proportion of these sugar properties were acquired by merchants *before* 1779. *Los mercaderes y el capitalismo,* 135 (table), 136.

52. Sánchez Santiró, *Azúcar y poder,* 285–86, 292. Sugar plantations in the Cuernavaca-Cuautla region, where many *consulado* members were proprietors, expanded their output by 50% from 1791–94 to 1804, responding in large measure to the rising international price level. Ibid., 205–6.

53. Hernández Palomo, *El aguardiente de caña,* 108; Humboldt, *Ensayo político,* 286; AGN, AHH, 442-25.

54. Quirós, "Memoria de instituto, 1808," AGI, Mexico, 2997; Barrett, *Sugar Hacienda,* 135.

55. "De venta de azúcares," fols. 4v–21r; Martín Rafael de Michelena to Administrador General de la Real Aduana, 17 Aug. 1812, Archivo de San Ignacio (Las Vizcaynas), no. 5.

56. Austria, "Reflexiones acerca del comercio de Veracruz en . . . 1797," AGI, Mexico, 2995; Murphy y Porro, 13 Aug. 1798, AGI, Ind. Gen., 3218. This may explain the petition of Murphy y Porro in 1798 requesting "permiso para introducir por el Puerto de Cádiz libre de todos derechos 8,000 quintales de azucar de la Habana o Veracruz." Madrid's reply: "No hay lugar." Murphy y Porro, 13 Aug. 1798, AGI, Ind. Gen., 2318.

57. Arango y Parreño, "Informe del síndico," 106.

58. Azanza, 28 Feb. 1799, AGI, Ind. Gen., 2320.

59. Consulado de la Habana to Soler, Feb. 1808, AGI, Mexico, 2514; Iturrigaray to Soler, 16 July 1807, AGI, Ind. Gen., 2320. Arango y Parreño noted that Veracruz customs authorities put a 27% duty on the Cuban product (47 *reales* per *pipa*), the equivalent of "154 por ciento del costo que tenía aqui el caldo." "Informe del síndico," 93–94.

60. One government analysis calculated that of the total outflow of New Spain's silver on government account, 44.6 million *pesos* went to Spain, while 115.1 million

went to the Caribbean possessions and the Philippines. Consejo de Indias, "Nota," Mar. 1796, AGI, Mexico, 2507.

61. Quirós, "Memoria de Instituto, 1814," AGI, Ind. Gen., 2463.

62. Campechanos were vociferous critics of the monopolistic pricing of flours shipped from Veracruz. Regil, *Memoria*.

63. Ramón de Posada, "Sobre libertad y aumento del comercio de la Nueva España con la isla de Cuba," AGN, Industria y comercio, 14, exp. 5. The link between financial subsidies (*situados*) from the colony of New Spain and its exports to the Caribbean was obvious. On purely pragmatic grounds, Madrid granted *permisos* to U.S. grain exporters in the 1780s to provision Havana's garrison. Consulado de Veracruz, 22 July 1806, AGN, Consulado, 49.

64. Calderón Quijano, *Los virreyes de Nueva España en el reinado de Carlos III*, 2:121. Viceroy Mayorga ordered an increase in flour exports to Havana at inflated prices set by the *provedor de viveres* at Puebla, who bought up large quantities; he may have shipped 200,000 *tercios* (200 *libras* per *tercio*). Ramón de Posada was highly critical of the *provedor*, Joaquín Cosío, brother of the Veracruz *almacenero* Pedro de Cosío. Consejo de Indias, "Nota," 9 Nov. 1796, AGI, Mexico, 2318.

65. Quirós, "Memoria de instituto, 1809," fol. 3r, AGI, Mexico, 2997; Páez de la Cadena to Revillagigedo, "Dictamen," AGN, Consulado, 123, exps. 1–3, fol. 309r. Humboldt came up with an average yield ratio of New Spain's wheat productivity of 1:22–25, somewhat lower than that of Abad y Queipo ("une personne respectable et éclairée qui habite les colonies espagnoles depuis 30 ans"). *Essai politique*, 3:81 n. 2, citing Abad y Queipo's "Sobre la fertilidad de las tierras de Nueva España." Because of differential transport costs, Philadelphia flour at Havana was sold for 11 *pesos*, ½ *real*, Puebla's for 16 *pesos*, ¼ *real*. Arango y Parreño, "Informe de síndico," 21–22.

66. *Flour Exports, Veracruz to Spanish Colonies, 1789–1794, 1802–1810*
(*tercios*)

1789	6,316	1804	26,371
1790	8,431	1805	2,968
1791	10,180	1806	2,669
1792	2,020	1807	5,574
1793	13,244	1808	21,073
1794	6,001	1809	26,724
1802	22,858	1810	16,033
1803	19,496		

Sources: For 1789–94, Arango y Parreño, "Informe del síndico"; for 1802–10, Lerdo de Tejada, *Comercio exterior de México*, docs. 15–23.

67. Veracruz could supply on average about 10% of Havana's total flour imports (80,000 *tercios*). Arango y Parreño, "Informe del síndico," 95.

68. Consulado de Veracruz, 22 July 1806, AGN, Consulado, 49.

69. Basadre, 5 Mar. 1795, AGI, Mexico, 2922.

70. Austria, "Reflexiones acerca del comercio de Veracruz en . . . 1797," AGI, Mexico, 2995.

71. Basadre, 28 Feb. 1797, AGI, Mexico, 2922; Ayuntamiento de Puebla to Azanza, 3 Sept. 1798, AGN, Industria y comercio, 20, exp. 5, fol. 152r.

72. Bando, 3 Aug. 1802, in *Gazeta de México,* 18 Aug. 1802; Palacios to Olascuaga, 11 Aug. 1802, AGN, AHH, 25-1.

73. Flon to Iturrigaray, 13 Jan. 1804, AGN, AHH, 917-3; Consulado de Veracruz to Pedro Garibay, 26 July 1809, AGI, Ind. Gen., 2462.

74. Arango y Parreño, "Informe del síndico," 93–94.

75. Ibid., 93, 95–96.

76. José Mariano Beristain, "Instrucción que . . . Puebla remitia al diputado general del Reyno de la Nueva España . . . en Cortes," AGN, BN, 1749-3.

8. *Comercio Neutro / Comercio Directo*

EPIGRAPHS: Arango y Parreño, "Informe del síndico," 45–46; Consulado de Cadiz, "Representación . . . contra lo mandado en RO de 18 de noviembre," 3 Dec. 1797, BRAHM, Mata Linares, 12; Amicus Plato, sed magis Amigo Veritas [Valentín de Foronda or Carlos Martínez de Irujo?], "Reflexiones sobre el comercio en tiempo de guerra, 1800," fol. 375r.

1. In what Canga Argüelles considered an average year of prosperous Anglo-Spanish trade (probably in the early 1790s) he found imports from England of 200 million *reales de vellón,* of which more than half (118 million) consisted of textiles, most of which were re-exported to the American colonies. *Diccionario de hacienda,* 1:561–62. Spain's trade deficits were covered by 95 million *reales de vellón* in specie.

2. Baring, *Inquiry,* 32.

3. Tarrade, *Le commerce colonial de la France,* vol. 1, ch. 8; *Jornal Económico Mercantil de Veracruz,* no. 146 (24 July 1806); Amicus Plato, sed magis Amigo Veritas, "Reflexiones," fol. 387v.

4. Over the years 1757–91, according to a statistical survey ordered by Viceroy Revillagigedo, exports of New Spain's silver *pesos* on government account to the destination categorized as "America" (in fact, mainly Cuba) totaled 266,489,441 *pesos,* almost four times the sum (60,009,195) transferred to "Spain." This led to the obvious conclusion: "Puede decirse que el producto líquido de las rentas de Nueva Espana más que VM la disfrutan las Yslas, o por delito de ellas, los Extrangeros." BNMex, MS 1398. There is a comparable estimate in AGI, Mexico, 2507.

5. Arango y Parreño, "Informe del síndico."

6. Hussey, *Caracas Company,* 288–89; AGI, Ind. Gen., 2311.

7. AGI, Ind. Gen., 2319.

8. AGI, Ind. Gen., 2318, 2466; AGN, Civil, 1666, exp. 2; AHN, Estado, 3208[2]; Archivo de las Cortes, Expedientes, Legajo 71, no. 53; AGN, Correspondencia de virreyes, 2nd ser., 33, fols. 426r–427r; Arango y Parreño, *Obras,* 1:283.

9. Moreno Fraginals, *El ingenio,* 1:51.

10. Ibid., vol. 1.

11. Consulado de la Habana to Gardoqui, 26 Nov. 1796, AGI, Ind. Gen., 2466.

12. Gabriel Raimundo de Azcárate to Consulado de Cadiz, 2 Mar. 1797, ibid.

13. Arango y Parreño, "Informe del síndico," 45–46 and note d; Consulado de la Habana to Varela, 23 May 1797, AGI, Ind. Gen., 2466.

14. Consulado de Cadiz, "Representacción . . . contra lo mandado en RO de 18 de noviembre."

15. Consulado de Cadiz, "Testimonio del expediente formado a instancia del Consulado de la Habana," 8 May 1797, AGI, Ind. Gen., 2466.

16. López Cantos, *Don Francisco de Saavedra;* Gómez Imaz, *Sevilla en 1808;* Saavedra, *Diario de don Francisco de Saavedra.* Saavedra's correspondence and memorials are deposited with the Jesuit order at Seville.

17. Saavedra to Varela, 9 Apr. 1797, AGI, Ind. Gen., 2466.

18. Ibid.

19. Marichal, *La bancarrota del virreinato,* 99–138.

20. Abad y Queipo in Hernández y Dávalos, *Documentos,* 2:855; Iturrigaray to Soler, 27 Aug. 1804, AGN, Correspondencia de virreyes, 2nd ser., 219, no. 586; BNMad, MS 13978.

21. Consulado de Veracruz, 22 July 1806, AGN, Consulado, 49, exp. 3.

22. Tedde de Lorca, *El banco de San Carlos,* 43–47; Vilar, *Oro y moneda,* 346–47.

23. Using *vales* emissions as surrogate for the public debt yields 451,764,704 *reales de vellón* in 1780–82 and 963,763,198 in 1794–95, for a total of 1,415,527,902. AAEPar, M et D, Espagne, 152, fol. 47r.

24. In 1797 Juan Bautista Virio managed the Dirección del Fomento General, a mark of appreciation of his previous economic reporting as consul at Hamburg. AHN, Estado, 4570; Canga Argüelles, *Diccionario de hacienda,* 1:77–78.

25. Canga Argüelles, *Diccionario de hacienda,* 1:77–78.

26. AHN, Estado, 229/24.

27. Canga Argüelles, *Diccionario de hacienda,* 1:79.

28. *Veracruz to Spain: Precious Metals Shipments, 1796–1806*
(*pesos fuertes*)

1796	5,453,843	1802	25,564,574
1797	9,604	1803	7,498,759
1798	1,104,177	1804	14,275,420
1799	2,774,647	1805	77,599
1800	4,197,946	1806	19,287,710
1801	274,882		

Source: Canga Argüelles, *Diccionario de hacienda,* 2:294, based on Austria's "Memoria, 1808."

29. Barbier and Klein, "Revolutionary Wars and Public Finances," 328.

30. *Receipts of the Madrid Treasury, 1795–1797 (selected items)*
(*reales de vellón*)

	Total	Cadiz	Indies
1795	1,047,446,000	105,756,000	26,761,000
1796	653,162,000	157,007,000	10,772,000
1797	651,845,000	44,420,000	12,653,000

Source: Barbier and Klein, "Revolutionary Wars and Public Finances," 329, 338.

31. Canga Argüelles, *Diccionario de hacienda,* 1:48.

32. Saavedra's experience as "Caracas"'s first intendant had given him a solid grasp of the situation of Caribbean ports like Havana and the importance of flexibility: "Si sus retornos son mas breves, sus ganancias seguras y multiplicadas, da salida

a una multitud de producciones que no sufren viages largos; se hace con cortos capitales, admite buques mui pequeños y en varias partes de América es poco más que un cabotage . . . siempre debe mirarse como un recurso extremo para los casos de necesidad urgente e irremediable." Saavedra to Varela, 2 Apr. 1797, AGI, Ind. Gen., 2466.

33. Cabarrús, "Representación de una junta celebrada en casa del marqués de Yranda . . . 1798," BMus, Egerton MS 369, fol. 200v.

34. Real Orden, 17 Nov. 1797, *Gazeta de México*, 18 Aug. 1798.

35. Esteban Fernández de León, "Equivocaciones . . . Castillo Negrete," 16 May 1812, AGI, Ind. Gen., 2464; Consulado de Cadiz to Soler, 4 June 1799, AGI, Consulados, Correspondencia, 51.

36. Consulado de Cadiz, "Representación . . . contra lo mandado en RO de 18 de Noviembre."

37. Saavedra to Consulado de Cadiz, 22 Dec. 1797, AGI, Ind. Gen., 2466; Consulado de Cadiz to Saavedra, 30 Jan. 1798, AGI, Consulados, Correspondencia, 51.

38. On the general situation at Veracruz, see Consulado de Cadiz, "Testimonio del expediente formado a instancia del Consulado de la Habana."

39. Note the sharp drop in precious metals exports, Veracruz to Spain, and consequently the retention of *pesos,* from a high of 5.453,843 *pesos* (1796) to 9,604 (1797). Canga Argüelles, *Diccionario de hacienda,* 2:294.

40. *Balanza de comercio de España,* 179–80, 181–83, 184–87. Josep María Fontana i Lázaro emphasized the role of re-exports from Spain to its colonies in "Colapso y transformación." See also the corrective comments in Prados de la Escosura, "Comercio exterior y cambio económico."

41. Austria, "Reflexiones acerca del comercio de Veracruz en . . . 1797."

42. Consulado de Cadiz, 8 May 1797, AGI, Ind. Gen., 2466.

43. Azanza to Soler, 28 Feb. 1799, AGI, Mexico, 2510.

44. For Erice's multiple activities, see Guerra y Sánchez et al., *Historia de la nación cubana,* 3:251; and Moreno Fraginals, *El ingenio,* 1:71, 100, 108.

45. "Testimonio del expediente . . . la fragata *Halcyon,*" AGI, Mexico, 2508; Erice, letter of 12 Aug. 1798, AGI, Mexico, 2509.

46. Pedro María Ramírez to Felix de Aguirre, 5 Jan. 1799; "Testimonio del expediente . . . de Felix de Aguirre," AGI, Mexico, 2510.

47. Consulado de Cadiz, 5 Mar. 1799, AGI, Consulados, Correspondencia, 51.

48. "Testimonio del expediente . . . Amalia. Veracruz, 18 June 1799," AGI, Mexico, 2510.

49. Consulado de Cadiz, "Testimonio del expediente formado a instancia del Consulado de la Habana."

50. Azanza to Soler, 31 Oct. 1799, AGI, Mexico, 2510; Consulado de la Habana, 28 July 1798, AGN, AHH, Mexico, 215–19.

51. Consulado de Cadiz, "Testimonio del expediente formado a instancia del Consulado de la Habana," fols. 4v–9r.

52. The *Gazeta de México* of 14 Apr. 1801 alerted New Spain's merchants to a forthcoming Havana publication, *Aurora, o Correo Político-Económico,* which promised news from Europe and America on trade, agriculture and shipping.

53. For biographical details, see Arango y Parreño, *Obras,* vol. 1. See also Tomich, "Wealth of Empire."

54. Consulado de la Habana to Gardoqui, 5 Jan. 1796, AGI, Ind. Gen., 2466. On the basis of style and content, this letter is probably the work of Arango.

55. Arango y Parreño to Intendente, 18 July 1798, AGI, Ind. Gen., 2466, fols. 4v–9r.

56. On Azanza's background, see Caro Baroja, *La hora Navarra del XVIII,* 386–89 and n. 81; Calderón Quijano, *Los virreyes de Nueva España en el reinado de Carlos IV,* 2:3–35; and Humboldt, *Ensayo político,* 549. For Azanza's view of New Spain, see Torre Villar, *Instrucción reservada.*

57. For biographical details on Azanza, see Bustamante, *Suplemento,* 228.

58. Azanza to Soler, 29 Apr. 1799, AGI, Ind. Gen., 2466.

59. Francisco Guillén to Azanza, AGI, Ind. Gen., 2467.

60. Andrés Gil de la Torre and Juan Antonio Reyes, 23 Oct. 1798, in Consulado de Cadiz, "Testimonio del expediente formado a instancia del Consulado de la Habana," fols. 43r–45v; Juan Felipe Laurnaga and Basadre, 23 Oct. 1798, AGI, Mexico, 2508, no. 1.

61. Consulado de Veracruz to Soler, 28 Feb. 1799, AGI, Mexico, 2508.

62. Francisco Antonio de la Torre to Azanza, 17 Oct. 1798, AGI, Ind. Gen., 2466, fols. 29v–30r.

63. Lorenzo Hernández de Alba, 23 Sept. 1798, AGN, AHH, 215–19.

64. Miranda, AGI, Ind. Gen., 2466.

65. Austria, "Noticias y reflexiones político-mercantiles acerca del comercio de 1798," AGI, Mexico, 2508.

66. Austria, "Noticias y reflexiones . . . 1799."

67. Austria to Soler, 25 Feb. 1800, AGI, Mexico, 2509.

68. Burkholder and Chandler, *From Impotence to Authority,* 180.

69. Azanza to Soler, 12 Aug. 1799, AGI, Ind. Gen., 2467; Azanza to Saavedra, 26 Nov. 1798, AGI, Mexico, 1588, no. 187. As the table below indicates, U.S. Atlantic ports provided roughly 71% by value of all neutral shipments received at Veracruz from May 1798 to April 1800. Hamburg, however, furnished the most valuable cargo per vessel. Apropos of U.S. merchants at Kingston, Matthew Atkinson & Company "connected with the House of Messrs. Baring & Co., of London . . . now have upwards of 100,000 dollars which they wish to send to Philadelphia and in the course of this month . . . will be able to collect double that sum . . . people here . . . have occasion to transmit specie to America." William Savage, U.S. Consul, to T. Pickering, 15 Oct. 1799. From January to April 1801, thirty U.S. ships collected "the enormous sum of 716,000 dollars." Savage to Pickering, 11 Apr. 1801.

Neutral Ports Supplying Veracruz, May 1798–April 1800
(*pesos fuertes*)

Port	Total Cargo Value	No. of Ships	Value per Ship
Baltimore	499,107	12	41,592
New York	353,233	8	44,154
Philadelphia	108,696	3	36,232
Charleston	118,358	4	29,590
Salem/Beverly	20,780	3	6,927
Saint Thomas	81,855	3	27,285
Hamburg	361,525	7	51,646

Source: AHN, Consejos, 20,729, pieza 13.

70. "Extracto," AHN, Consejos, 20,729.

71. Manuel de la Bodega to Azanza, AGI, Ind. Gen., 2466, fols. 54r–55r.

72. Soler to Azanza, 20 Apr. 1799, AGN, Marina, 3, exp. 20. The rationalization was based on fact. Cf. Merchants of Kingston interested in the trade to the Spanish colonies under the Free Port Act, "Memorial," Nov. 1807, PRO, CO 137/119: During wartime, 1796–1801, British merchants "did engage in a trade to the Spanish colonies whereby large quantities of British manufactures and other goods were exported, and returns in specie and the valuable productions of the said colonies were derived . . . credits to a considerable extent were given to the Spanish traders to this market, whereby large sums became due and are still owing to British merchants." Merchants from the Spanish colonies "claimed they had licenses and were authorized by Spanish governments to do so; they are now known to have been fraudulent." According to Rafael Morant, reflecting years later, the British "se constituyeron protectores de los Españoles empleados en el mismo tráfico illicito, dandoles escolta hasta poner en nuestras costas las mercaderías que extraigan de Jamaica." 30 June 1814, AGI, Estado, 86. In 1798–99 the most active Kingston merchants were Alexander Shaw, J. Barnes, and Moses Bravo. PRO, BT 6 6/235.

73. This was clearly the interpretation of Amicus Plato, sed magis Amica Veritas, "Reflexiones."

74. Consulado de Cadiz to Casa Rábago, 29 Apr. 1799, AGI, Consulados, Correspondencia, 51, fols. 505r–506r.

75. Francisco Viana to Cristóval de Góngora, 22 July 1814, AGI, Ind. Gen., 2463.

76. Azanza to Soler, 22 June, 27 July, 20 October 1798, AGI, Ind. Gen., 1587.

77. Soler, "Estado de la Real Hacienda . . . 1798," BRAHM, Sempere y Guarinos, 10, fol. 210r.

78. Rafael Morant, 30 June 1814, AGI, Estado, 86.

79. Cadiz, along with Barcelona and Santander, epitomizes a bourgeoisie rooted in Spain's coastal cities, with limited networks to the peninsula's agricultural heartland, and dominated by aristocratic and clerical estate owners, a bourgeoisie best defined as "periférico." On this point, see Gonzalo Anes Álvarez, *Economía e "ilustración";* and Elorza, *La ideología liberal en la ilustración española.*

80. Amicus Plato, sed magis Amica Veritas, "Reflexiones sobre el comercio." On learning of the revocation of *comercio neutro,* Foronda (or, improbably, Carlos Martínez de Irujo) drafted these "Reflexiones" in four days, impelled to remove the "velo con que el error ha sabido cubrirse durante siglos enteros" (fol. 378r). This manuscript lacks the statistical material contained in Tatham, *Communications.* Tatham's edition includes a table of the impressive coinage of Mexico City's Casa de Moneda in 1795. Colón, *Impresos españoles en Filadelfia,* does not include the "Reflexiones." Note that the folio citations to this work by Foronda/Amicus Plato in the following paragraphs refer to the BRAHM manuscript. The "Reflexiones" should be compared with Foronda's *Carta sobre lo que debe hacer un príncipe.*

81. In the prologue, the author highlighted the salience of agriculture, quoting Adam Smith: "It is the mass of surpluses occasioned by the whole of the cultivators that forms the revenue of every other class in society." "Reflexiones," fol. 378r. Elsewhere he labeled agriculture "the richest mine in America." Tatham, *Communications,* 13.

82. Foronda's mother was a González de Echávarri; his maternal grandfather, Domingo González de Echávarri, a *consejero de S.M.* and a *secretario del Consejo.* An Antonio González de Echávarri is listed as *escribano y notario público de Indios* in New Spain, *oidor jubilado* of the Audiencia de Mexico (1769), *consejero togado* of the Consejo de Indias (1770), and *prefecto* of Madrid's influential *vizcaína* Congregación de San Ignacio (1772).

83. "Reflexiones," fol. 380r. This was an idea elaborated in earlier essays (1787) on "Lo honroso que es la profesión del comercio," the Banco Nacional de San Carlos, and the Compañía de Filipinas. Despite evident respect for the merchant's métier, Foronda had reservations about the "monopolistas de Cádiz": "Había en España [under the "antiguo sistema"] una opinión, por desgracia muy acreditada, que hacía mirar al comercio, y al comerciante, como dos cosas idénticas."

84. The spectrum of Foronda's interests is suggested by essays published in his 1787 *Miscelánea,* viz., "Utilidad de la Compañía de Filipinas" and "Banco de San Carlos." The quotation is from "Lo honroso que es la profesión del comercio," in *Miscelánea,* 30; Marcelino Menéndez y Pelayo linked him to Cabarrús. For a brief biography, see Antón del Olmet, *El cuerpo diplomático español,* 3:339–45; see also Barrenechea, *Valentín de Foronda.*

85. Foronda, *Miscelánea,* 17 (on the Compañía de Filipinas), 8, 14 (on the Banco de San Carlos). On Foronda's "liberalism," see Antonio Elorza, "La difusión de la ideología ilustrada: El 'Espíritu de los Mejores Diarios' y Valentín de Foronda," in *La ideología liberal en la ilustración española,* ch. 6. On his Philadelphia writings, see Onís, "Don Valentín de Foronda." Barrenechea notes Foronda's "relaciones y amistad con los personajes ilustrados . . . participación en las instituciones y sociedades progresistas de la época . . . colaboración en los periódicos mas avanzados." *Valentín de Foronda,* 283.

86. It is possible that Foronda's preocupation with plantation agriculture in the Caribbean was sparked by works of a former colonial officer in Saint-Domingue, Pierre-Paul Le Mercier de la Rivière, esp. *L'intérêt général de l'état.*

87. Austria, secretary of the Veracruz *consulado* and critical of the "Reflexiones," recognized the circulation of trade news among Caribbean merchants. See Austria, "Así se transmiten las ideas," 159.

88. "Reflexiones," fol. 386v. Cf. fol. 381r–v and 386v: "Rotas las cadenas, y franca y libre la carrera [de Indias], el particular sabe y sabrá siempre mejor que el Gobierno, el empleo más productivo, que puede dar, o a su capital, o a su trabajo"; "El interés particular . . . el resorte principal del corazón humano."

89. Appointed consul at Venice, Foronda was sent instead to Philadelphia (1801), where he served eight years as chargé d'affaires, reentering Spain at Seville in January 1810. His replacement, Luís de Onís, probably offended by his liberalism and parsimony, had no kind words for his predecessor: "El Gobierno no responde a sus Oficios; los españoles no lo acatan como Representante de la Nación; no trata a nadie, haciendo una vida obscura . . . no tiene coche como debía, ni hace el honor correspondiente al sueldo que disfruta." Antón de Olmet, *El cuerpo diplomático español,* vol. 3.

90. Foronda, *Apuntes ligeros.*

91. Foronda hoped that his readers would not interpret his "Reflexiones" as a

knee-jerk reaction to *comercio neutro*'s unexpected revocation, "si mi situación no me hubiera permitido tener informes muy correctos y por canales desinteresados, sobre el modo con que se ha llevado a efecto el dicho decreto." "Reflexiones," fol. 5r. Years earlier, Foronda had had reservations about the metropole's emphasis on colonial silver mining: "De qué le sirve a España tan dilatados Países y Minas tan copiosas, si con todas estas ventajas es más pobre que otros países que carecen de semejantes socorros?" Foronda, *Miscelánea*, 31.

92. Amicus Plato, sed magis Amica Veritas, "Reflexiones," fol. 386r.

93. Ibid., fols. 375v, 393r. Foronda castigated those self-serving "dos docenas de particulares . . . por el monopolio" (fol. 406r).

94. Insurrection in the British colonies in North America, reacting to England's imperial restrictions, was earlier discussed in Ugartiria, "Carta segunda," 997. Elorza believes that Foronda drafted but never published a letter advocating "la disolución del imperio colonial español" in his early years as consul general at Philadelphia. *La ideología liberal en la ilustración española*, 121. Elorza probably had in mind Aranda's 1782 memoir suggesting disaggregation of the empire.

95. Amicus Plato, sed magis Amica Veritas, "Reflexiones," fols. 387v–388r.

96. Ibid., fols. 391v–392r, 395r, 398r–v.

97. Tatham, *Communications*, 41; Amicus Plato, sed magis Amica Veritas, "Reflexiones," fols. 398v, 411r–v.

98. Edwards, *History, Civil and Comercial*.

99. Amicus Plato, sed magis Amica Veritas, fol. 413r–v. Foronda was impressed by England's mills at Birmingham and Sheffield, by their products—"quincallería, fundiciones, planchas de hierro, clavos" (fol. 383v).

100. Cerdán complained that rumor had it that copies of the "Reflexiones" had been addressed to high colonial officers of Guatemala, its "presidente, gobernador y capitán-general." "Apuntamientos en defensa de la Real Orden de 20 de Abril de 1799, combatida en un papel dado a luz por un español en Filadelfia por el regente de la Audiencia de Guatemala. 1800," AGN, Historia, 400. I am indebted to the late Luis Chávez Orozco for the opportunity to consult this item in his private collection.

101. Burkholder and Chandler, *From Impotence to Authority*, 178, 196, 199, 204, 206.

102. Cerdán, "Apuntamientos," 1–4, 6, 11.

103. Cf. ibid., 3–4: "Don Carlos de Irujo, a quien hago la justicia de creer, incapaz de incurrir en tan horrible desacato aún por su solo ministerio." There seems to have been a clear intellectual "fit" between Martínez de Irujo and Foronda: they were political economists who regretted what Foronda once described as the wrong paths taken by the Spanish government in the distant past ("por nuestra desgracia"), and both admired Adam Smith; in fact, Irujo published a translation of *The Wealth of Nations*. Elorza, *La ideología liberal en la ilustración española*, 192.

104. Cerdán, "Apuntamientos," 3–4, 6, 9, 11.

105. Ibid., 13–15, 20.

106. Ibid., 14, 21–22, 24.

107. Ibid., 16–17. He had to add candidly that "estas sagradas leyes son por desgracia despreciadas . . . por todas las naciones mismas."

108. Ibid., 8, 10, 16, 20, 35–36, 38.

109. Ibid., 6, 10–11, 17.

110. *Boletín del Archivo Nacional de Cuba* 43 (1946): 155.

111. ANPar, AF III, dossier 248, no. 43.

112. Miguel López's firm received a *gracia* to ship goods from a neutral port in a neutral vessel to Havana, and from Havana to Veracruz. AGI, Mexico, 2510.

113. Menéndez, Conde y Compañía, Petición, 8 Sept. 1798, AGI, Ind. Gen., 2318.

114. Consulado de Cadiz to Madrid, 9 Oct. 1798, AGI, Consulados, Correspondencia, 51, fols. 347r–348r. Somewhat later the *consulado*—secular supporter of *its* port monopoly of colonial trade—explained that "todos [los privilegios] son diametralmente opuestos a la actividad y libertad del comercio en general." AGI, Consulados, Libro de Juntas, n. 67-2, fol. 42v.

115. AGI, Mexico, 2509. In a note to Viceroy Azanza, Francisco Antonio de la Torre recommended prohibiting all imports "a menos de que procedan directamente de Europa de Puertos neutrales, o de España." Ibid.

116. AGI, Mexico, 2510. Unless otherwise stated, the sources for the following paragraphs are from this source.

117. Marginal note to "Petición del conde de Casa Flores," 18 May 1798. Saavedra ordered Viceroy Azanza to be sure that "la gracia de la extracción de frutos por Veracruz a Payses estrangeros *se disimula para evitar iguales solicitudes.*" 22 May 1798.

118. Azanza to Soler, 26 Apr. 1799.

119. The rejection reads: "SM no ha venido en acceder a estas solicitudes." 19 June 1799.

120. Casa Flores to S.M., 11 June 1799.

121. Casa Flores to Soler, 23 Aug., 17, 26 Sept. 1799.

122. Casa Flores to Soler, 15 Jan. 1803.

123. In petitioning María Luisa, Casa Flores felt impelled to explain the use of his agent, Bustamante y Guerra, who "por casualidad se hallaba en Aranjuez . . . Este ha hecho cabeza en el particular y ha practicado quantas diligencias han sido precisas, haviendo gastado en ellas casi un año de tiempo." Casa Flores to Señora, 2 July 1799.

124. Tomás Murphy's lawyer at Veracruz insisted that any Spanish merchant, wherever his residence, could ship his goods from the neutral port of Hamburg. He pointed out that Brentano, Barbero y Urbieta was a Spanish firm. "Testimonio del expediente . . . Amalia," fols. 3v–6r.

125. Among the textiles loaded at Hamburg were *platillas reales, ruanes, estopillas lisas* and *rayadas, clarines, arabias,* and *floretes.* Ralph Davis found that under neutral trading tolerated by London briefly after 1798, exports of British cotton goods to the neutral ports of Hamburg and Bremen, presumably for re-export, skyrocketed. *Industrial Revolution,* 16.

126. Thomas Boyle, master of the *Amalia,* declared that the cargo was the property of Erice. 15 Dec. 1798, AGI, Mexico, 2508. In March 1798 a vigilant Consulado de Cadiz recorded, apropos of Madrid's *gracias particulares* under *comercio neutro,* that "Juan Morfi," "hermano del ya insinuado establecido en Veracruz," was travel-

ing from Málaga to Madrid, Lisbon, and then aboard an "embarcación Anglo-Americana" to Boston. There he would set up "un grueso giro" between Boston, Havana, and his brother Tomás at Veracruz in association with "otros poderosos de la Habana." 5 Mar. 1799, AGI, Consulados, Correspondencia, 51.

127. "Testimonio del expediente . . . Amalia," 4 Mar. 1799, fols. 2r–v, 4v–5r.

128. Alba, 30 June 1799.

129. Alba, 18 July 1799, followed by Benito de Austria, "Segundo escrito"; "Testimonio del expediente . . . Amalia" (18 July 1799) and Guillén (28 Aug. 1799), fols. 19r–25v.

130. Azanza to Soler, 31 Oct. 1799, AGI, Mexico, 2510. In Castillo y Negrete's opinion, the *Amalia* had entered Veracruz "con entero arreglo a la Real Orden de 18 de Noviembre de 97."

131. AGI, Mexico, 2509. The Consulado de Cadiz decided not to overtly thank Brancifore "por sus buenos oficios contra la solicitud del Consulado de la Habana y subsistencia de la RO de 18 de Noviembre de 1797." The reason: "Que podía tenerse por oficiosidad inoportuna, no habiendo precedida correspondencia anterior con SE [Saavedra]sobre el asunto, y que tal vez podría causar algun resentimiento al Sr. Ministro de Estado cuyo fabor hemos procurado para la faborable resolución," namely, recall of *comercio neutro* in 1799. AGI, Consulados, Correspondencia, 51, fols. 96r–97r.

132. Santa Cruz used letters of credit granted by Urbieta y Compañía, of Hamburg. Santa Cruz to Murphy, 24 Sept. 1798, AGI, Ind. Gen., 2468.

133. AGI, Mexico, 2509. Intelligence would cover "los designios de los Yngleses contra nuestras posesions, sus fuerzas marítimas y terrestres, sus despachos de comboyes a Europa."

134. Ibid.

9. "Informal" *Comercio Neutro,* 1804–1808

EPIGRAPHS: Stephen, *War in Disguise,* 8; Conde de Casa Alta to Floridablanca, 25 Nov. 1808, AHN, Consejos, 21,081, ramo 3 de la sumaria; Baring, *Inquiry,* 32.

1. Real Orden, 24 Mar. 1798, to intendants at Havana and Caracas, virrey de Buenos Aires, gobernador de Veracruz, AGI, Ind. Gen., 2318. The Cadiz *consulado*'s Madrid agent, Casa Rávago, transmitted this request to cover the *donativo* (1 million *pesos*) to support the war against France (1792) and the *préstamo* (2 million *pesos*) for the war against England (1798).

2. Cerdán de Landa Simón Pontero, *Disertación preliminar,* 37.

3. Consulado de Veracruz to Soler, 6 Feb. 1800, in "Indice . . . representaciones," AGN, AHH, 1869–6; Consulado de Veracruz to Secretario de Indias, 15 Mar. 1815, AGI, Ind. Gen., 2464; Zamora y Coronado, *Biblioteca de legislación ultramarina,* 3:263ff.; Fernández de León, "Equivocaciones . . . Castillo Negrete." AGI Ind. Gen., 2464; Virrey Marquina, "Bando," 11 Sept. 1801, Indiana University, L. Harper Collection, cat. 14, no. 720.

4. Davis, *Industrial Revolution,* 15, 19 (table 6). One should not overemphasize England as Spain's trading partner at this time; the total value of England's exchanges with Spain were only slightly greater than those of France. Prados de la Escosura, "Comercio exterior y cambio económico," 189 (table 7).

5. *Justice and Policy,* 18; Consulado de Veracruz to Iturrigaray, 13 Feb. 1806, AGI, Mexico, 2516; Consulado de Veracruz to Rey, 24 Feb. 1806, AGI, Mexico, 2997.

6. According to the Real Orden of 21 June 1804, "[N]o se admita en lo succesivo instancia alguna solicitando gracias y privilegios de qualquiera clase o naturaleza relativos al comercio de España con sus Américas." Consulado de Veracruz to Soler, 15 Nov. 1805, AGI, Mexico, 2512. And according to the Real Orden of 1 Aug. 1804, "[P]ermitió la restracción de unos a otros puertos de América de los efectos europeos introducidos en ellos, y que no hayan tenido despacho." Francisco Xavier Borbón, AGN, Historia, 537–7, fol. 10r.

7. AGI, Mexico, 2516.

8. The contradiction in the two royal orders was explicit in the complaint of Veracruz signed by the *consulado* officers Tomás Murphy, Juan Bautista Lobo, and Domingo Lagoa de Miranda concerning the presence of *buques neutrales* in the port of Veracruz. Consulado de Veracruz to Soler, 15 Nov. 1805, AGI, Mexico, 2512.

9. This Real Orden directed to New Spain was signed at the Escorial; the manuscript is in AGI, Mexico, 2516.

10. On 1 March Soler directed the chargé d'affaires at Philadelphia, Casa Irujo, to inform Iturrigaray to add the Philadelphia firm of John Craig, who had assumed the *permiso* originally assigned to the ex-viceroy of New Spain, marqués de Branciforte. The contract covered the sale of flour to Cuba and Caracas. Casa Irujo to Iturrigaray, Philadelphia, 22 Sept. 1805, AGI, Mexico, 2516. In fact, the Craig contract also granted shipments to Montevideo in the Rio de La Plata.

11. A follow-up Real Orden dated 24 Dec. 1804, stated that the indicated firms established in the neutral ports of Europe and America were obligated to have their ships returning to Europe allocate one-third of cargo space to "frutos y efectos de ese pays que SM quiera hacer venir por su cuenta." The products "se han de entregar anticipadamente a los correspondientes de dichas casas"; if the products were not available, the balance of the assigned cargo space would be filled on the account of the contracted firms with cacao of Soconosco, cochineal, and indigo. AGN, Reales Cedulas, 191, fol. 285r–v.

12. Duties included *rentas generales* according to *aranceles de mirada* available in colonial customs houses; *internación* (33% of *rentas generales*); *consolidación* (also 33% of *rentas generales*); *consulado;* and, last, re-export duties based on those of *comercio libre* of 1778 and subsequent modifications.

13. Ruiz y Pablo, *Historia de la Real Junta Particular,* 275–76.

14. AGI, Mexico, 2997; Consulado de Veracruz to Iturrigaray, 13 Feb. 1806, AGI, Mexico, 2516.

15. Crouzet, *L'économie britannique,* 1:179–80; Quirós, "Memoria de instituto, 1819."

16. Stephen, *War in Disguise,* 8.

17. AGN, Consulado, 21.

18. Francisco Xavier Borbón, *fiscal de Real Hacienda,* referred cryptically to the previous order authorizing "la estracción de uno a otros puertos de . . . efectos . . . que no hayan tenido despacho." Borbón to Iturrigaray, 18 Feb. 1808, AGN, Historia, 537, exp. 7, fol. 10r.

19. *Cuba's Balance of Trade with the United States, 1805*
    (*pesos*)

	Total	U.S.	U.S. as % of Total
Imports	11,265,007	10,541,138	93.5
Exports	5,072,981	4,452,472	87.7
Balance	–6,192,026	–6,088,666	98.3

Source: AGI, Mexico, 2513.

20. Consulado de la Habana (conde de O'Reilly, Juan Joseph de Iguarán, Bonificio González Larriñaga), 22 Feb. 1808, AGI, Mexico, 2513; *Extracto instructivo de un expediente sobre la escandalosa infracción . . . de un permiso* (Cadiz, 1811).

21. Consulado de la Habana, 22 Feb. 1808, AGI, Mexico, 2513.

22. Cuba's planters claimed that four hundred *ingenios* produced about sixty thousand *bocoyes de miel* annually. Distilled into rum, much had formerly been bought by merchants from the United States, whose operations had been affected by the U.S. Embargo Act of late 1807.

23. Consulado de Cadiz to Supremo Consejo de Regencia, 24 Sept. 1811, AGI, Consulados, Correspondencia con España, 53.

24. Consulado de Veracruz to Iturrigaray, 13 Feb. 1806, AGI, Mexico, 2516. The largest quantities consisted of *bretañas* (3,000 *piezas*) plus *piezas coletas de China* (1,800 *piezas*).

25. Ibid. Iturrigaray's brusque, pointed reply rankled; it is mentioned in a Consulado de Veracruz complaint of 1 March 1809 — months after the viceroy's ouster. AGI, Mexico, 2997.

26. Consulado de Veracruz to Soler, 24 Feb. 1806, AGI, Mexico, 2516. Godoy's contradictory policies were evident in his order as *almirante* (20 Mar. 1807) directing the confiscation of any English property consigned to Spanish nationals aboard any incoming vessels. A perplexed Iturrigaray brought to Soler's attention that this order in effect canceled that of May 1806 permitting trade with Jamaica under special circumstances. Iturrigary to Soler (*reservado*), 17 June 1807, AGN, Correspondencia de virreyes, 2nd ser., 233, no. 1253, fol. 233r.

27. Quirós, "Memoria de instituto, 1813," AGI, Mexico, 2516.

28. Cf. the comments of a defender of Iturrigaray's execution of Madrid's policy: "[L]o que daba márgen al disgusto de muchos comerciantes de Veracruz, y no pocos de México, fue las serias y eficazes Providencias que [Iturrigaray] tomó para evitar el contrabando que tanto nos ha destruido en otras guerras con la misma Potencia [England]." Casa Alta to Floridablanca, deposition in Iturrigaray's behalf, 25 Nov. 1808, AHN, Consejos, Residencias, Iturrigaray, 21,081, ramo 3 de la sumaria.

29. Iturrigaray to Godoy, 5 May 1805, AGI, Mexico, 2513. When Iturrigaray ordered a naval officer at Veracruz, Bernardo Ortíz, to choose personnel for coast guard duty, Ortíz replied that many would prove unreliable, since "cumpliendo sólo en la apariencia las ordenes de VE no huviera correspondido a la substancia de ellas." Ortíz to Iturrigaray, 20 Apr. 1805, ibid.

30. The *instrucción* is mentioned in Ciriaco de Cevallos to D. Grandallana, 5 Sept. 1804, MN (Viso del Marqués), MS 1208. The problems of controlling smug-

gling are exemplified in "Plan de resguardos unidos de Mexico," BNMex, MS 1389, fols. 266r–284r.

31. The intendant at Veracruz, Pedro Telmo Landero, reported learning of "clandestinas introducciones de efectos prohibidos, venidos por lo que se presume del Puerto de Campeche." Landero to Iturrigaray, 6 July 1805, AGI, Mexico, 2513.

32. Earlier, Austria had recommended convoyed shipping and the removal of silver bullion and valuable exports such as cochineal and indigo to Jalapa in the event of an English invasion. Austria, "Reflexiones, 1798," AGI, Mexico, 2508. Subsequently, in 1803, a *fiscal* of the Audiencia de Mexico, Ambrosio Sagarzurieta, seconded by Colonel Pedro Garibay, also proposed withdrawing to Jalapa. AGI, Mexico, 2511. For the fears of the Veracruz merchant community, see Consulado de Veracruz to Soler, 30 Nov. 1803, AGI, Consulados, Correspondencia con America, 218.

33. AHN, Consejos, 21,082, quad. 4; Iturrigaray to Consulado de Veracruz, 2 Sept. 1806, and Iturrigaray to Godoy, 17 Sept. 1806, AGI, Mexico, 2997.

34. Ciriaco de Cevallos to D. Grandallana, 25 Jan. 1805, MN (Viso), MS 1294.

35. Quirós, "Balanza, 1805," in Lerdo de Tejada, *Apuntes,* 3:385 n. 2.

36. Promotor fiscal de Real Hacienda, 13 Mar. 1805, AGN, Comisos; Ciriaco de Cevallos to Iturrigaray *(reservado),* 9 Sept. 1806, AGI, Mexico, 2513. Iturrigaray took drastic steps, "quedando prohivido por ahora y hasta nueva providencia que pueda celebrarse en esa ciudad venta alguna mercantil." Iturrigaray to Consulado de Veracruz, 14 Mar. 1805, AGI, Mexico, 2516.

37. Iturrigaray to Bernardo de Ortíz, 20 Mar. 1805, AGI, Mexico, 2513. Veracruz's intendant advised Iturrigaray to pay special attention to the "gefes del resguardo" and their underlings ("una de las puertas por donde conducen los defraudadores") and that future conflict with England would demand "medios extraordinarios y mucho más fuertes" than before. The *resguardo* concentrated on "el contrabando, y no a los contrabandistas." Promotor fiscal de Real Hacienda, 13 Mar. 1805, AGN, Comisos.

38. Iturrigaray's incentive was aimed at anyone "civil, militar, político o de Real Hacienda, sin excepción por consecuencia del Soldado, del Matriculado, del Paisano, del Administrador o Mayordomo de Hacienda o Rancho, de los que están sobre las costas y los caminos para internarse en el Reyno, y todos sus sirvientes tenga facultad para aprehender por sí estos contrabandos." "Resolución," 6 May 1805, AGI, Mexico, 2513. The Bethlehemite monk San José Muro praised Iturrigaray cryptically, since his directive "dividió diestramente los intereses de los dos partidos." 31 June 1805, AGN, Civil, 2133.

39. The preamble to Iturrigaray's directive explained his motivation: "En las guerras pasadas . . . se ha visto en precisión de sostener contra la Ynglaterra, han sido siempre sensibles los resultados de los contrabandos hechos por Veracruz y sus costas laterales," markedly so in 1797–1801. "Resolución," 6 May 1805, AGI, Mexico, 2513.

40. Iturrigaray to Godoy, 5 May 1805, ibid.

41. Iturrigaray to Godoy, 15 July 1805, ibid. The subtle patriotism of reward ("premio de . . . fiel acción") charmed the intendant of Veracruz, Pedro Telmo Landero, who committed himself patriotically to the "exterminio del escandaloso contrabando que se hace en este puerto y sus costas . . . lo miro y detesto con horror

porque él es una de las causas principales de la decadencia del Real Erario, de nuestra industria nacional, y de las fatales consequencias que tenemos a la vista." Landero to Iturrigaray, Veracruz, 18 May 1805, ibid.

42. Godoy to Soler, 30 Oct. 1805, ibid.

43. Ciriaco de Cevallos to Iturrigaray, 9 Sept. 1806, ibid.

44. Consulado de Veracruz to Soler, 28 Oct. 1806, ibid.

45. Iturrigaray insisted to Godoy that his drastic measures were designed "cortar el contrabando." Letter of 21 Feb. 1806, AGI, Mexico, 2997. Ciriaco de Cevallos, *comandante de Marina de Apostadero* at Veracruz, probably supplied Iturrigaray with data on "la introducción de contrabandos por los Barcos costaneros [los cuales] a pretexto de temporales o de persecución de enemigos, entran de arribada adonde les acomode, aun dexando atrás los Puertos de sus destinos como ha sucedido con algunos que han navegado sueltos con permisos de los governadores de Yucatán y de la Laguna de Términos." Iturrigaray to Soler, 25 Oct. 1806, AGI, Mexico, 2513.

46. Consulado de Veracruz to Iturrigaray, 25 Sept. 1806, AGI, Mexico, 2992.

47. Iturrigaray to Soler, 25 Oct. 1806, AGI, Mexico, 2513.

48. *Veracruz's External Trade, 1804–1805*

    (*pesos*)

	Imports	Exports	Total
1804	16,525,742	21,457,882	37,983,624
1805	3,352,343	902,794	4,255,137

Source: Lerdo de Tejada, *Apuntes,* 3:380–85.

49. *Veracruz Shipping, 1804–1805*

	From Spain	To Spain	Total
1804	107	78	230
1805	27	3	79

Source: Ibid.

50. Consulado de Veracruz to Iturrigaray, 12 Mar. 1806, AGI, Mexico, 2997.

51. In the Real Orden of 17 Sept. 1805, "previno el Señor Príncipe [Godoy] . . . que a las [reales ordenes] de 8 y 23 de Noviembre de 1804 sobre cerrar los puertos, se les había dado una extensión que no tenían."

52. The *consulado* officers Manuel Viya y Gibaja and Pedro de Echeverría admitted that the *consulado* and *ayuntamiento* of Veracruz had employed their Madrid *apoderado,* Pedro de Mantilla, to represent their interests. AGI, Mexico, 2997. In the papers of the Consejo de Indias there is a dossier with the covering remark "El Ayto y Consulado de Veracruz por medio de sus apoderados." AGI, Mexico, 2513. The most direct reference to cash transfers to agents is in a report from Mexico that Veracruz and Mexico City *almaceneros* financed representations with "gruesas sumas de dinero." Casa Alta to Floridablanca, 26 Nov. 1808, in Lizarza, *Discurso,* 34. This was confirmed by the *almacenero* Francisco Alonso Terán, who revealed that funds had been routed to Madrid via Bayonne to influence Godoy to reopen "el comercio de la costa." 31 Oct. 1808, AHN, Consejos, 21,081, ramo 3, fols. 103r–104r.

53. Consulado de Veracruz to Soler, 22 Feb. 1806, AGI, Mexico, 2997.

54. There was no evidence, claimed the Veracruz *consulado,* that "se hayan ingerido ni implicado en el criminal contrabando los Barcos de este tráfico." Smug-

glers, it insisted to the viceroy, simply took advantage "de los tiempos, de las derrotas inusitadas, de las recaladas más seguras, y de las embarcaciones más céleres." Consulado de Veracruz to Iturrigaray, 12 and 22 Feb. 1806, ibid.

55. Consulado de Veracruz to SM, 22 Feb. 1806, ibid.

56. The *consulado* cited, for example, the fact that the price of a *fanega* of Yucatecan salt had jumped from 18–20 *reales* to 48. Consulado de Veracruz to Iturrigaray, 12 Mar. 1806, ibid.

57. Consulado de Veracruz (signed by Tomás Murphy and Pedro de Echeverría) to SM, 20 Apr. 1806, ibid.

58. Contador General de Indias, Estevan Fernández de León, summarizing for the Consejo de Indias the exchanges between Iturrigaray and the Consulado de Veracruz. 4 Jan. 1810, AGI, Mexico, 2988.

59. Ciriaco de Cevallos to Iturrigaray, 9 Sept. 1806, AGI, Mexico, 2513. Although the Veracruz *consulado* claimed that it could not finance the purchase and arming of six *lanchas* to keep enemy ships from coastal waters, Iturrigaray insisted on pursuing his system of armed escorts. Iturrigaray to Consulado de Veracruz, 21 Oct. 1806, AGI, Mexico, 2997. He rejected the *consulado*'s counterproposal to station one soldier aboard every departing coastal vessel to control "el contrabando y la comunicación con el enemigo." Consulado de Veracruz to Ciriaco de Cevallos, 13 Oct. 1806, ibid. That certain sectors of Madrid's bureaucracy supported neither Iturrigaray nor his superior, Godoy, is evident in a notation of 4 June 1806 on the Real Orden directing Iturrigaray to soften his position on Veracruz's commercial activity: "Prevenguele que el Consulado ha ofrecido zelar el contrabando y costear los gastos de un resguardo extraordinario." AGI, Mexico, 2997. The anti-Iturrigaray bias is evident in the "Extracto," presumably by the Mesa de Marina, praising the "justicia y solidez con que los dos cuerpos [*consulado* and *ayuntamiento*] han reclamado las providencias de aquel Gefe." Ibid.

60. Consulado de Veracruz (Joaquín de Castillo y Bustamante, Manuel Antonio del Valle, Juan Thomás de Miguelena), 1 Mar. 1809, AGI, Mexico, 2997.

61. Iturrigaray to Bernardo de Orta (naval officer stationed at Veracruz), 20 Mar. 1805, and Iturrigaray to Godoy, 5 Mar. 1805, AGI, Mexico, 2513.

62. Iturrigaray to Consulado de Veracruz, 25 Jan. 1806, AGI, Mexico, 2516, and 20 Feb. 1806, AGI, Mexico, 2513; Iturrigaray to Godoy, 21 Feb. 1806, AGI, Mexico, 2997.

63. Iturrigaray to Godoy, 21 Feb. 1806, AGI, Mexico, 2997.

64. Iturrigaray to Consulado de Veracruz, 16 Mar. 1806, ibid.

65. Iturrigaray to Consulado de Veracruz and Ayuntamiento, 2 Sept. 1806, AGI, Mexico, 2997.

66. "Extracto," AGI, Mexico, 2997.

67. Iturrigaray to Consulado de Veracruz, 1 Aug. 1807, AGI, Mexico, 2513.

68. Consulado de Veracruz, 1 Mar. 1809, AGI, Mexico, 2997.

10. *Consolidación:* Spain

EPIGRAPHS: Soler, "Memoria . . . al de Estado, 1801," BMus, Egerton MS 369; "Résumé historique des opérations de la caisse royale de Consolidacion," AAEPar, M et D, Espagne, 152, fols 54v–55r.

1. Herr, "Hacia el derrumbe," 87.

2. On Spain, see Herr, "Hacia el derrumbe"; idem, *Rural Change and Royal Finances;* Anes Álvarez, *Las crisis agrarias en la España moderna;* and Tomás y Valiente, *El marco político.* On New Spain, see Lafuente Ferrari, *El virrey Iturrigaray;* Bernstein, *Modern and Contemporary Latin America;* Chávez Orozco, *Historia económica y social de México;* Flores Romero, "La consolidación de vales reales"; Hamnett, "Appropriation of Mexican Church Wealth"; Lavrín, "Execution of the Law of *Consolidación*"; Sugawara, *La deuda pública;* Hamnett, *Roots of Insurgency;* Chowning, *Wealth and Power in Provincial Mexico;* and Wobeser, *Dominación colonial.*

3. Herr, "Hacia el derrumbe," 87.

4. The Cadiz merchant community viewed the situation as "la aglomeración de fondos en las Américas . . . los plazos onerosos." Consulado de Cadiz to SM, 26 Sept. 1783, AGI, Consulados, Correspondencia con España, 90, fols. 4r–5r.

5. Gausa's recommendation: "buscar . . . cinco o seis casas de comercio de los mas acreditados de Madrid y Cádiz, y aún los mismos Gremios." Ferrer del Rio, *Historia,* 4:126.

6. Floridablanca, "Memorial," 334. The Cinco Gremios attracted only 50 million *reales.* Bourgoing, *Tableau de l'Espagne moderne,* 2:31–32.

7. Múzquiz to Francisco Montes, 19 Aug. 1782, AGI, Ind. Gen., 2311. Cadiz remained grateful to Montes for "la particular atención con que VS ha mirado siempre los intereses de todo el Cuerpo." AGI, Consulados, Correspondencia, 62, fol. 131r–v.

8. To quote Montes, an inveterate traditionalist in matters of Spain's transatlantic trade: "[R]establezcanse las reglas del año de 1720 . . . póngase justo término a la libertad [del comercio] immoderada, y me prometo hallar medios que sostengan las cargas del estado." BRAHM, Mata Linares, 6, fol. 188v.

9. Cabarrús later claimed a profit of 15 million *reales* on this deal; the Spanish government, 47.3 million. The proposal and subsequent comments are in AHN, Estado, 2839². Calderón Quijano, *El banco de San Carlos,* 43.

10. Boyetet to De Castries, 12 Mar. 1781, ANPar, AE, B I, 795, fol. 166r; Buist, *At spes non fracta,* 280–81.

11. The veteran merchant Eugenio de Santiago Palomares remarked in 1786 apropos of Madrid's banking establishment: "Así el oficio de Banqueros, como lo que rigurosamente se deve appellido comercio de por mayor, ha sido mirado con poca atención de los naturales." AHN, Estado, 3188².

12. Dickson, *Financial Revolution,* 11.

13. Calderón Quijano, *El banco de San Carlos,* 12–13.

14. Vilar, *Oro y moneda,* 335–37.

15. Floridablanca, "Memorial," 335.

16. *Gazeta de México,* 28 Jan. 1804, 15–16; Canga Argüelles, *Diccionario de hacienda,* 1:243; "Dictamen" prepared by Floridablanca for the Junta General del Banco Nacional, 23 June 1788, AHN, Estado, libro 2d, fol. 59v. On the origins and early decades of the bank's development, see Tedde de Lorca's comprehensive monograph *El banco de San Carlos,* 31–78.

17. For the charter, see Hamilton, "Monetary Problems in America"; idem, *War and Prices in Spain;* and Calderón Quijano, *El banco de San Carlos.* As for overseas

civil servants' share purchases, Francisco Viana (conde de Tepa) transferred from New Spain 500,000 *reales* for such purchases. Ibid., 17–18, 38.

18. Calderón Quijano, *El banco de San Carlos,* ch. 3; AGN, Correspondencia de virreyes, 2nd ser., 214, 27 Oct. 1803.

19. The charge of favoritism by the Banco de San Carlos's directors was specific, pinpointing "varias casas Francesas de Cadiz," such as Verduc, Jolif, Seré y Compañía. AHN, Hacienda, 3781[b], no. 3. Similarly mentioned was the manager of the bank's Málaga branch, Pedro Tisón.

20. Mirabeau, *Lettre,* 20, 24–26, 32, 39.

21. "Algunas cartas de Manuel Francisco de la Torre," Cadiz, 4 Jan. 1788, AHN, 2151[2], exp. 122.

22. For example, at Bayonne silver transfers were declining because "la Banque de Saint-Charles s'empare de tout." Dermigny, "Circuits de l'argent," 266 n. 5. Silver transfers from Cadiz to Lisbon and on to Bordeaux were traced to "les juifs portugais . . . en liaison avec les Magon de Saint-Malo," formerly of Cadiz. Crouzet, "Le commerce de Bordeaux," 230–31. For the case against Cabarrús, see AHN, Hacienda, 3731[b], no. 6. Antonio Flores commented: "El Banco cumple perfectamente bien con sus ofertas; en lugar de destruir el contrabando, la fomenta." "Observaciones," 5 May 1788, AGI, Consulados.

23. The debt rose from 132.5 million to 178 million pounds sterling. *Gaceta de Madrid,* 28 Jan. 1780.

24. "Sobre vales," BRAHM, Sempere y Guarinos, 26, fols. 244v–245r.

25. Montes wrote Hacienda Minister Múzquiz about "49,333 vales de la creación de 1 de Julio [1782] que se havían de reducir por la Casa de Cabarrús & Lalanne a dinero efectivo." "Expediente sobre la comisión dada al Tesorero General d. Francisco Montes" *(reservado),* AGI, Ind. Gen., 2311; conde de Gauza [Múzquiz] to conde de Lerena, 11 May 1784, AGSim, Secretaría y Superintendencia de Hacienda, 386.

26. Portillo, "Memoria sobre los perjuicios del agro."

27. Soler, "Estado de la Real Hacienda . . . 1798," fol. 207r.

28. *Demostración de los distinguidos servicios,* 10–11.

29. "Sobre vales," AGSim, Secretaría y Superintendencia de Hacienda, 10, fols. 247v–248r.

30. Ibid., fol. 249r.

31. Vale *Issues in Spain, 1780–1799*

	No. of *Vales*	Amount *(reales)*
1780	16,500	149,082,352
1781	17,667	79,813,270
1782	49,333	222,869,082
1793	53,333	240,939,670
1794	90,000	271,056,823
1795	155,000	451,764,705
1799	132,774	799,763,576

Source: AAEPar, M et D, Espagne, 152, fol. 47r.

32. Because it was amortized in four annual redemptions beginning in May 1799, the loan of 400 million *reales* was taken up quickly, Madrid absorbing 25% "dentro de pocos días." Soler, "Estado de la Real Hacienda . . . 1798," fol. 219v.

33. *Spain: Government Borrowing, 1795–1798*
     (*reales de vellón*)

	Shares	Denominations	Value	Type of Security
1795	24,000	(10,000)	240,000,000	Cadiz customs
1797	40,000	(4,000)	160,000,000	Stamped paper
1798	160,000	(2,500)	400,000,000	Colonial tobacco tax

Source: Soler, "Estado de la Real Hacienda . . . 1798," fols. 250v–251r.

34. At this time Godoy welcomed and received many suggestions for solving the government's financial predicament. AHN, Estado, 3211.

35. For biographical details, see Franco, "Diego de Gardoqui," 144–48.

36. "Consulta del Sr. Gardoqui en 1794," 6 Feb. 1794, BRAHM, Sempere y Guarinos, 10, fol. 189r. The fourteen statistical tables that accompanied his report are missing.

37. Quirós, "Memoria de instituto, 1813"; Marcos Ramón to Paulino Lalanne, 9 Aug. 1789, AHN, Hacienda, 3781 B, no. 5. Ramón ended his letter with the following: "Pero, eso es mejor para olvidado que no para discurrir sobre ello."

38. *Spain: Average Annual Customs Revenue, 1787–1798*
     (*reales vellón*)

1787–92	115,413,525
1793–95	108,117,575
1796–98	85,701,944

Source: Soler, "Memoria que el ministerio de hacienda pasa al de Estado . . . para ajuste del tratado definitivo de Paz con la Gran Bretaña, 28 Nov. 1801," BMus., Egerton MS369, fols. 213r–256r. Soler estimated that customs revenue averaged 15% of general revenue in peacetime, 25% in wartime.

39. *Spain: Budgetary Estimates, 1793 and 1797*
     (millions of *reales de vellón*)

	Income	Expenditure	Deficit
1793	584.1	708.8	124.7
1797	478.1	1,422.6	944.5

Source: BRAHM, Sempere y Guarinos, 10, fols. 202, 211–12.

40. *Spain: Discount Rates of Vales, 1795–1798*

	%		%
1795	10.4	1798*	18.3
1796	10.7	1798	18.6
1797	15.7		

Source: AAEPar, M et D, Espagne, 152, fols. 59r–60r.
* = January to May

41. Toreno, *Historia*, 1:22; León y Pizarro, *Memorias*, 1:61; Consul Roquesante, 13 Ventose An 7, AAEPar, CC, Cadiz, 92, fol. 57v.

42. Dalrymple to Viscount Castlereagh, 18 June 1808, PRO, FO 72/53; La Forest,

Correspondance, 1:251. For Saavedra's biography, see López Cantos, *Don Francisco de Saavedra;* and Saavedra, *Diario de Don Francisco de Saavedra,* 11–39. The Jesuit residence in Seville holds Saavedra's catalogued papers. Gómez Imaz, *Sevilla en 1808,* 52, 256.

43. It was believed that Aragorri had made his fortune by speculating "en gran escala," as an agent of the Compagnie des Indes and as an investor in the LeCouteulx trading firm at Cadiz. He was, predictably, a member of the so-called Francophile group in Madrid, which included the conde de O'Reilly. BNMad, MS 19711²; Fugier, *Napoléon et l'Espagne,* 1:23. For a critical assessment, see the comments of José Antonio de Armona in AHN, Consejos, 3211, parte 2, fol. 134r.

44. Francisco Carrasco, "Memorias," AHN, Consejos, 3211, parte 2, fol. 134r–v. For Aragorri's directorship of the Madrid *pósito,* see AGSim, Tribunal Mayor de Cuentas, *Guia,* 236; AHN, Estado, 2314; Hale, *Franklin in France,* 75; Iranda, "Correspondencia del . . . banquero español en Madrid," BNMad, MS 19971; and Ferrer del Rio, *Historia,* 4:248n. On his views of the Compañía de Filipinas, see BMus, Egerton MS 571, fols. 54ff.; and Girón Amarillas, *Recuerdos,* 123–24.

45. Antón de Olmet, *El cuerpo diplomático español,* 3:361; Floridablanca, "Testamento," cited in Rumeu de Armas, *Testamento político.*

46. Godoy, *Memorias,* 2:89, 249. Two of Soler's *memorias* are in Canga Argüelles, *Diccionario de hacienda,* 2:166–78; manuscript copies are in BRAHM, Sempere y Guarinos, 10, fols. 201r–241r. Soler's "Memoria . . . 18 Nov. 1801" is also in BMus, Egerton MS 369, fols. 213r 256r.

47. Soler, "Memoria sobre el estado actual de la real hacienda," in Canga Argüelles, *Diccionario de hacienda,* 2:167.

48. Ibid.

49. Plans for selling such religious property had been drafted in the Hacienda by Juan Sempere y Guarinos and Severo de Aguirre, then forwarded for approval to Gracia y Justicia. Ibid., 168.

50. Cabarrús, "Representación de una junta celebrada en casa del marqués de Yranda." This document was probably so titled by Bernardo Iriarte, another *juntero,* whose collection of Spanish materials is in the British Museum.

51. Ibid., fol. 201r. One would expect such sentiments from the author of a publication extolling the profession of merchant. Cf. his "A la perfección que necesita el comercio. 30 March 1783." AHN, Estado, 2944, fols. 7r–10r.

52. AHN, Estado, 2944, fols. 200r, 203v.

53. Ibid., fol. 200r–v.

54. Ibid., fols. 201v–202r.

55. Ibid., fol. 198r.

56. Soler, "Consulta . . . 1799," BRAHM, Sempere y Guarinos, 10, fols. 213v–214r. Canga Argüelles published this under the rubric "Exposición que hace al rey." The manuscript version in the BRAHM is the basis of the subsequent citations.

57. Buist, *At spes non fracta,* 281.

58. Soler, "Consulta . . . 1799," fols. 214v–215r.

59. Ibid., fols. 215r–216v. The average annual government expenditure for 1796–97, 898 million *reales,* represented an increase of 26.6% over the earlier period, 1793–95. Ibid., fol. 202r.

60. Ibid., fols. 205v, 216v.

61. Campomanes, *Tratado de la regalía de amortización;* Jovellanos, *Informe de la Sociedad Económica;* Olavide, "Informe . . . sobre la ley agraria"; Portillo, "Suplemento." n. 7.

62. Soler, "Consulta . . . 1799," fols. 205r–206v, 208r.

63. Ibid., fols. 205r–206r, 208r–209r, 239r.

64. Ibid., fols. 207r–208r, 210r.

65. See Herr, "Hacia el derrumbe," 47–48; and esp. idem, *Rural Change and Royal Finances,* 95–136. Further indication of Madrid's cautious approach is the order of properties to be sold: first, those of *obras pías* and *cofradías,* and only then properties of *hospitales, hospicios, casas de misericordia, de reclusión y de expósitos.* Ibid., 87. For contemporary comments on the effect of this policy, see the periodical *Conversaciones de Perico y Marica* (Madrid), 1788.66. The average monthly rate oscillated between 66% and 70%. "Résumé historique," fol. 60r.

67. Herr, "Hacia el derrumbe," 49–50.

68. *Spain: Silver Imports on Government Account, 1793–1797*
    (*reales de vellón*)

1793	141,727,551	1796	236,895,376
1794	195,717,966	1797	12,360,128
1795	138,764,376		

Source: Canga Argüelles, *Diccionario de hacienda,* 1:181, citing "las cuentas de tesorería general."

69. *Spain: Sales of Entailed Properties (religious and lay)*
    (millions of *reales*)

1798–99	42,823[a]	1805	106,918[c]
1800	68,340[a]	1806	135,951[c]
(1801–3)	111,373[b]	1807	208,042[c]
1800	48,521[c]		
1801	164,112[c]	Total	1,107,643
1802	144,796[c]		
1803	84,114[c]		
1804	122,653[c]		

Source: Herr, "Hacia el derrumbe," 88 n. 137.

Note: In Herr's text there are additional sums covering May 1807 to early 1808. A sharp fall in deposits in 1803, due perhaps to purchasers' reluctance to buy properties whose rents could not be changed, may have induced the government to lift the freeze on leases set in 1785. Ibid., 53.

[a]Sales under Caja de Amortización
[b]Supplementary sales under Caja de Amortización
[c]Sales under Caja de Consolidación

70. Herr, "Hacia el derrumbe," 69 (table 1).

71. "Branche d'Extinction: Résumé Général des sommes versées . . . dans la Caisse," in "Résumé historique," fol. 62r.

Spain: Receipts and Redemption of Vales, 1798–1808

	Receipts	*Vales* Redeemed	% Receipts
Caja de Amortización (1798–1800)	340,751,333	121,255,905	35.6
Caja de Consolidación (1800–1808)	1,292,091,913		
Cash	(442,498,139)	300,001,129	23.2
Vales	(849,593,774)		
Total	1,653,376,402	421,257,034	25.5

Sources: Francisco Gallardo, Manuel Sixto Espinosa, Antonio Noriega to Duque de Berg, June 1808, "Résumé historique," fols. 47r, 62r. For the reliability of these data, see Herr, "Hacia el derrumbe," 59, 65; and Hamilton, "War and Inflation in Spain."
Note: For the period 1780–95 only 5.8% of *vales* were redeemed; in 1800–1808 redemption equaled 13.7%. Over twenty-eight years the redemption rate was 18.2%.

72. Herr, "Hacia el derrumbe," 82.

73. Consul James Duff, 29 Aug. 1804, "Resumen General "and "Suplemento" to a "Nota de los caudales de Cadiz," PRO, FO 72/53.

74. The Caja would be reimbursed, to be sure, from specific tax revenues such as a 2% tax on all communal properties ("biens communaux"). "Résumé historique," fols. 54v–55r.

75. Portillo, "Suplemento.".

76. AAEPar, M et D, Espagne, 152, fols. 54v–55r.

77. The annual average of such receipts, 1803–1807, was 552.2 million *reales*.

78. Bernardo Iriarte to Domingo Iriarte, "Apuntamientos y borradores," Feb. 1804.

79. Ibid., 12 Nov. 1804.

80. Castro, *Historia de Cádiz*, 555–56; "Résumé historique," fol. 55r–v.

81. The average receipts for 1803–4 (103.4 million *reales*) were well under those of 1801–2 (154.5 million). "Résumé historique," fols. 55v, 88r.

82. Ibid., fols. 55v–56r. Their estimate of 75 million *reales* is significantly below Herr's figure of annual receipts (103 million) from alienated properties in 1798–1806. See ibid., fol. 56r; and Herr, "Hacia el derrumbe," 88.

83. Herr, "Hacia el derrumbe," 45 (table 2). In the Seville-Cadiz area the rate was 23%, second only to that of Madrid (25%).

84. "Résumé historique," fol. 64v; Real Orden, 27 Apr. 1801, AHN, Hacienda, libro 6012.

85. *Justice and Policy*, 13; "Résumé historique," fol. 56r.

86. "Résumé historique," fol. 56r.

Spain: Mean Annual Discount Rate on Vales, 1800–1808

	%		%
1800	55.46	1805	45.83
1801	53.56	1806	45.75
1802	18.62	1807	46.56
1803	34.83	1808	56.05
1804	37.43		

Source: "Résumé historique," fol. 60r.

87. Soler, "Memoria . . . 28 Nov. 1801," fols. 213r–256r, hereafter, with two exceptions, cited in the text. English negotiators soon discovered that their Spanish counterparts would offer no new commercial concessions. See also "Convention between the British and Spanish governments . . . by Mr. [Anthony] Merry and M. [Bernardo] de Lizaur," 1 May 1801, BMus, Egerton MS 369.

88. *Spain: Domestic and Foreign Debt, 1801*
(*reales*)

Total	4,108,052,771
Juros	762,041,680
Tobacco tax	242,021,544
Vales outstanding	200,000,000
Banco de San Carlos	164,000,000
Cinco Gremios	65,185,904
Loans	
In Spain	537,604,996
Fondo Vitalicio	123,405,900
Dutch loans	125,240,000

Source: Soler, "Memoria," fol. 219v, no. 1.

Note: Loans from colonial sources, current drafts on the Tesorería General, and obligations of the Caja de Consolidación are omitted.

89. The omission is all the more notable since Soler specifically presented statistics on the proportion of foreign to domestic products in exports to the American colonies. See Soler, "Memoria," fol. 219.

90. Hauterive, *De l'état de la France.*

91. Ibid., 187.

92. Ibid.

93. Consulado de Veracruz, "Representación," 22 July 1806, AGN, Consulado, 49.

11. *Consolidación:* New Spain

EPIGRAPHS: "Representación de la Tribunal de Minería," BNMex, 1667, exp. 19; Humboldt, *Essai politique,* 3:287; Malaspina, in Palau Baquero and Orozco Aquaviva, *Malaspina, '92,* 10.

1. Gisela von Wobeser, by contrast, holds that "los funcionarios españoles conocían muy bien la realidad de los reinos americanos," including the possibility that *consolidación* overseas might undermine the "integridad del Imperio español." Wobeser, *Dominación colonial,* 99. On this issue, see also Abad y Queipo, "Escrito presentado a Don Manuel Sixto Espinosa."

2. New Spain's ecclesiastical corporations held an estimated 40% of all *bienes eclesiasticas* in the American colonies. Wobeser, *Dominación colonial,* 230.

3. *Libranzas* (bills of exchange) totaling 32 million *pesos* drawn on colonial treasuries were prepared before the *decreto* (28 Nov. 1804) and its *instrucción* (26 Dec.). The decree reached Mexico City in April 1805. Ibid., 28, 47, 51.

4. Costeloe, *Church Wealth in Mexico,* 108; Farriss, *Crown and Clergy,* 251. "[C]

apellanías were not completely clerical benefices, but rather trust funds which the founders had established for the benefit of members of their family, and hence in terms of almost every one, preference in the order of recipients was given to close relatives." Costeloe, *Church Wealth in Mexico*, 60. The general range of endowments allocated to chantries appears to have been from 4,000 to 5,000 *pesos*. See AGN, BN, 1667.

5. Arrangoiz y Berazábal, *Méjico desde 1808 hasta 1867*, 1:35. Mexico City's Convento de la Concepción's income from outstanding mortgage loans totaled more than 400,000 *pesos* over the years 1763–1812. Lavrín, "Role of Nunneries," 380.

6. Lavrín, "Role of Nunneries," 375–76.

7. Taylor, *Lord and Peasant*, 141.

8. Antonio Porcel, in *Diario de las Cortes*, 20 Mar. 1813.

9. Tribunal de Minería to Iturrigaray, 1805, BNMex, 1667.

10. Villarroel, *México por dentro y fuera*, cited in Costeloe, *Church Wealth in Mexico*, 103 n. 1. The wealthy *criollo* José Miguel Guridi y Alcocer noted that *peninsulares* were usually the *mayordomos* of the wealthiest nunneries. *Contestación*, 20.

11. Revillagigedo, "Informe . . . sobre averiguar si hay decadencia en el comercio," *Boletín del Archivo General de la Nación* 1 (1930): 206.

12. Pérez y Comoto, *Representación*, 6; Hernández y Dávalos, *Documentos*, 1:759. On the day following his orchestration of the *golpe* (coup) against Viceroy Iturrigaray, Yermo asked Madrid to suspend execution of the *consolidación* and a duty on *aguardiente*. Sánchez Santiró, *Azúcar y poder*, 306.

13. Bakewell, *Silver Mining and Society*, 91, 212–14, 234; Brading, *Miners and Merchants*, 160–67, 170–79.

14. "Sobre la venta," BNMad, MS 19709, no. 34, fols. 4r–5r.

15. Tribunal de Minería, "Representación," in Sugawara, *La deuda pública*, 42.

16. To quote Enrique Florescano, "[E]n una sociedad de estructura agrícola dominante . . . la inversión más segura era la que tenía el respaldo de la propriedad territorial." Florescano, *Estructuras y problemas agrarios*, 169.

17. *New Spain: Gross Tithe Collections, 1771–1780 and 1781–1790* (*pesos fuertes*)

	1771–80	1781–90	%
Mexico	4,132,630	7,082,879	71.4
Puebla	2,965,601	3,508,884	18.3
Valladolid	2,710,200	3,239,400	19.5
Oaxaca	715,974	863,237	20.6
Guadalajara	1,889,724	2,579,108	36.5
Durango	943,028	1,080,313	14.6
Total	13,357,157	18,353,821	37.4*

Source: "Colección de estados de valores," BNMex, MS 1334, tables 3–9.
*Mean % change

18. Mora, *Obras sueltas*.

19. Flon to Iturrigaray, 28 Apr. 1803, AGI, Mexico, 2996.

20. Brading, *Haciendas and Ranchos*, 38.

21. Marichal, *La bancarrota del virreinato*, 161–210, provides a lucid account of the *consolidación* process.

22. Wobeser, *Dominación colonial*, 243, 255.

23. Lavrín, "Execution of the Law of *Consolidación*," 36–37.

24. The *hacendado* and merchant Gabriel de Yermo, mastermind of the coup that removed Viceroy Iturrigaray in 1808, managed to arrange a *composición* providing for "exhibición gradual" of the 400,000 *pesos* borrowed from *obras pías*. Alamán, *Historia de Méjico*, 1:227. For the slight impact of *consolidación* on heavily mortgaged *haciendas* owned by mining magnates such as the marqués de San Miguel de Aguayo, the conde de Regla (Romero de Terreros), José María and José Mariano Fagoaga, Ignacio Obregón, and the merchant-banker Miguel Ángel Michaus, see Vargas-Lobsinger, *Formación y decadencia de una fortuna*, 167–68; and Gutiérrez López, *Economía y política de la agrominería*, 143.

25. Lavrín, "Execution of the Law of *Consolidación*," 34–36; idem, "Problems and Policies," 62, 64–65.

26. Lavrín, "Execution of the Law of *Consolidación*," 34–36; Flores Caballero, *La contrarrevolución en la independencia*, 48 n. 79.

27. In 1811 Cadiz's *ayuntamiento* claimed that its residents held about 33% of outstanding *vales* bought after 1780; ultimately they held "la mayor parte de todos los vales reales." *Demostración de los distinguidos servicios*, 10–11.

28. Iturrigaray to Soler, 23 Dec. 1805, in Sugawara, *La deuda pública*, 46. Perhaps the cooperative stance of the members of the Consulado de México with *consolidación* stemmed from their hope that Madrid would maintain Spain's transatlantic system of managed trade. Martínez López-Cano and Valle Pavón, *El crédito en Nueva España*, 132.

29. Navarro y Noriega, *Memoria*.

New Spain: Distribution of Ranchos *in Selected* Intendancias, *1810*

Intendencia	No. of Ranchos
Mexico	871
Puebla	911
Valladolid	708
Guadalajara	511
Total	3,001
All *intendancias*	5,092

Source: Navarro y Noriega, *Memoria*, app.
Note: The 3,001 *ranchos* listed here represented 59% of the *ranchos* on all *intendencias*.

30. Cervantes Bello, "Consolidación," 215 (table 1), 216–17.

31. Rosensweig Hernández, "La economía novo-hispana," 491.

32. Antonio de San José Muro, letter no. 1, 1805, AGI, Mexico, 2319; Abad y Queipo, "Escrito presentado a Don Manuel Sixto Espinosa," 231; Junta, "Representaciones," AGN, AHH, 728-1.

33. Lavrín, "Execution of the Law of *Consolidación*," 37; Flores Caballero, *La contrarrevolución en la independencia*, 47.

34. Melchor Talamantes, quoted in Alamán, *Historia de Méjico*, 1:500 n. 18; Bustamante, *Campañas del General Calleja*, 109–10; Brading, "La situación económica."

35. Brading found that of ninety-nine property transfers in the Bajío from 1710 to 1810, only four occurred after *consolidación* was applied. *Haciendas and Ranchos,* 16–17; cf. Chowning, *Wealth and Power in Provincial Mexico.* The funds of religious corporations remained so considerable that Viceroy Venegas on arrival opened a "patriotic loan" addressed first to ecclesiastical bodies and then to secular ones. Venegas, *Proclama,* 24 Sept. 1810, Bancroft Library, University of California, Berkeley, microfilm roll 1203.05, 2:4, 15.

36. *New Spain:* Consolidación *Receipts, 1805–1809*
     (*pesos fuertes*)

Diocese	Receipts	% of Total Receipts	Liens/Loans	Property Sales
Mexico	5,253,219	51.3	4,631,950	621,269
Puebla	2,158,927	21.1	1,601,622	557,305
Valladolid	964,777	9.4	903,685	61,082
Guadalajara	891,560	8.7	841,927	
Oaxaca	547,613	5.3	547,613	
Merida	179,807	1.8	179,807	
Durango	135,281	1.3	135,281	
Monterrey	62,529	0.6	62,529	
Arizpe	43,042	0.4	43,042	
Subtotal	10,236,755	100.0	8,947,456	1,289,289 (12.6%)
Provincial				
Cajas	75,000			
Other*	774,000			
Total	11,085,755			

Source: Adapted from Lavrín, "Execution of the Law of *Consolidación,*" 35 (table 1), 44 n. 72, 45 (table 2).
   *Ecclesiastical collections

37. To Abad y Queipo's "valor de los bienes raíces de . . . piadosos destinos" (2.5–3 million *pesos*) have been added his "capitales de capellanías y obras pías" (44.5 million *pesos*), hence a minimum of 47 million *pesos.* On the other hand, Arnold Bauer claims that Abad y Queipo included the "capital value of *capellanías* and pious foundations"; by this calculation, "careful archival investigation would sharply reduce the volume of church lending in the colonial period." However, Abad y Queipo clearly referred to liquid assets available for loans, specified as "capital . . . de habilitación." Bauer, "Church and Spanish American Agrarian Structure," 93; Abad y Queipo, Manuel. "Escrito presentado a Don Manuel Sixto Espinosa," in Mora, *Obras sueltas,* 231–33.

38. Cervantes Bello, "Consolidación," 211.

39. *Spain and New Spain:* Consolidación *Receipts*
     (*reales de vellón*)

	Total Receipts	Years	Population	Year	Per Capita
Spain	1,505,101,000	9.3	10,541,221	1797	15.4
New Spain	221,715,100	3.0	6,122,354	1810	12.1

Sources: For Spain, Herr, "Hacia el derrumbe," 69 (table 1); for New Spain, Lavrín, "Execution of the Law of *Consolidación,*" 35 (table 1), 44 n. 72, 45 (table 2).

40. *Spain and New Spain: Distribution of* Consolidación *Receipts*

	Liens/Loans	%	Property Sales	%	Total
Spain	112,323,500	7.5	1,392,777,500	92.5	1,505,101,000
New Spain	178,949,320	87.4	25,805,720	12.6	204,755,040

Sources: Ibid.

41. *Spain:* Consolidación *Receipts from*
Fundaciones Eclesiásticas, *1798–1807*
   (thousands of *reales de vellón*)

		%
Madrid	215,937.1	14.0
Sevilla	157,044.9	10.4
Cadiz	145,318.9	9.6
All Spain	1,505,101.0	100.0

Source: Herr, "Hacia el derrumbe," 69 table 1.

42. Herr, "Hacia el derrumbe," 75 (table 3).

43. The phrase "expropriación del ahorro nacional" is Richard Salvucci's interpretation of Enrique Cárdenas's argument in *Cuando se originó el atraso económico de México,* reviewed in *HMex* 58 (2005): 78.

New Spain: Silver Exports, Veracruz to Spain, 1801–1804
   (*pesos fuertes*)

Government account	31,476,354
Nondiscriminated	3,500,000
Total	34,968,354

Source: PRO, FO 72/53.

44. Of total *consolidación* collections in the American colonies, 15.6 million *pesos,* New Spain supplied 10.5 million, or 67%. Wobeser, *Dominación colonial,* 50.

Spain and New Spain: Silver Receipts of the Caja de Consolidación
   (*reales de vellón*)

Spain (1798–1807)	338,692,602	60.4%
New Spain (1805–8)	221,715,100	39.6%
Total	560,407,702	100.0%

Sources: "Résumé historique," fol. 62; Lavrín, "Execution of the Law of *Consolidación,*" 45.

45. "Cedulario y papeles varios," fol. 109r, Bancroft Library, University of California, Berkeley.

12. Strange Saga

EPIGRAPHS: José Luyando, "Informe . . . acerca del estado de Nueva España," 6 Dec. 1810, Archivo de las Cortes, Expedientes, Comisión Ultramarina 22, no. 18; A. Raffalovich, "John Parish," *Journal des économistes,* 6th ser., 7 (1905): 208; Gabriel de Yermo to Junta Suprema de Sevilla, 1808, AHN, Consejos, 21,081, ramo 3, fol. 90r.

1. Pitkin, *Statistical View,* 36.
2. AGN, AHH, fol. 19r.
3. Spain's receipts of silver on government account supported the redemption of *vales nacionales* and interest on *obras pías* expropriated. Godoy, *Memorias,* 1:401.
4. Dermigny, "Circuits de l'argent," 264–66, 278.
5. "[S]e han agraciado diferentes casas extrangeras de Europa y América . . . por cuenta de Consolidación de vales reales de Madrid." Consulado de Veracruz al Virrey Iturrigaray, 15 Nov. 1805, AGI, Mexico, 2797. The non-Spanish merchant houses would trade with, and remove silver from, the ports of Veracruz, Havana, Caracas, and Montevideo. Souto Mantecón, *Mar abierto,* 190–91.
6. In 1798, during *comercio neutro,* Barings of London proposed to employ U.S.-registry ships to export silver from Veracruz. The proposal was sent to Felipe Sánchez, in Philadelphia, who communicated it to his uncle at Veracruz, José Ignacio de la Torre. In fact, Barings also wrote directly to Torre. Souto Mantecón, *Mar abierto,* 185.
7. *Estimates of Precious Metals Exports, Veracruz to Spain, 1802–1804*
   (*pesos fuertes*)

Destination	1802	1803	1804	1802–4
Spain *(a)*	16,384,955	14,734,279	12,516,013	43,635,247
Havana	7,954,266	1,358,402	767,121	10,079,789
Total				53,715,036
Spain *(b)*	25,564,574	7,498,759	14,275,420	47,338,753
America	3,749,988	1,855,876	2,654,182	8,260,046
Total				55,598,799
Spain *(c)*	25,976,929	13,116,759	25,733,109	64,826,209
Spain *(d)*	37,528,741	15,454,634	18,551,348	71,534,723

Sources: (a) AAE.Par, CP, Espagne, 96, fol. 141r; *(b)* "Balanza general," AGI, Mexico, 2997; *(c)* AGN, AHH, 395-7; *(d)* PRO, FO 72/53.

Note: Omitted are payments for imported slaves, Havana's flour imports, goods purchased at Jamaica and Trinidad, and smuggled wares that "en conjunto forman un objeto considerable." Viceroy Iturrigaray advised the Hacienda's Miguel Cayetano Soler at Madrid, "En pastas y moneda, excede notablemente a la que *aparecen* de los registros" (emphasis added).

8. *Precious Metals Exports, Spanish American Colonies to Spain,*
   October 1801–August 1804
   (*pesos fuertes*)

	Private Account	Government Account	No Category	Total
Veracruz	36,558,369 (57%)	31,476,354 (77.6%)	3,500,000	71,534,723 (63.3%)
Buenos Aires	13,558,369 (?)	2,315,295		16,534,723
Lima	10,402,665	5,206,080		15,608,475
Cartagena	3,245,760	1,530,356		4,776,116
Other			5,000,000	5,000,000
Total	63,993,663	40,528,356	8,500,000	113,001,748

Source: PRO, FO 72/53.

9. Iturrigaray to Soler, 27 Oct. 1803, 26 June, 27 July 1804, AGN, Correspondencia de virreyes, 2nd ser., 214, nos. 291, 514, 554.

10. Rafael Morant, 30 June 1814, AHN, Estado, 86. Cf. Villalobos, *Comercio y contrabando,* 211: "Para conseguir un permiso . . . era preciso siquiera 20 talegas, no promesas."

11. "[S]e continuaba con plena libertad la escandalosa introducción de todos géneros y efectos de comercio extrangero." José María Quirós, "Memoria de instituto, 1814."

12. Zaragoza to Presidente Juez de Arribadas, 26 Aug. 1802, AGI, Ind. Gen., 2319; Gibbs, *History,* 140–44.

13. For Osuna's license to buy grain for "pueblos de mis estados situados en (Extremadura and Andalusia)," see AHN, Estado, 5458 bis; Morant, 30 June 1814, AHN, Estado, 86.

14. *Correo Mercantil de España y sus Indias,* 23 July 1804; Mar. 1811, AGI, Consulados, Correspondencia, 57; Morant, 30 June 1814, AHN, Estado, 86.

15. "Reglamentos e instrucciones del Real Giro," AGSim, DGTesoro, inventario 23, legajo 93.

16. Morant, 30 June 1814, AHN, Estado, 86.

17. Davis, *Industrial Revolution,* 16.

18. Bernardo de Lizaur's career, like those of the merchants LeCouteulx (of Saint-Malo, Rouen, and Paris) and Juan and Tomás Murphy (of Málaga, Veracruz, Madrid, and London), reveals commercial networks created in the Spanish Atlantic. Lizaur went to "Caracas" in the late eighteenth century (Maracaibo, then La Guayra) as a factor of the Caracas Company; in 1800 he represented the Compañía de Filipinas at Cadiz, where he was probably related to the merchant firm of Vea Murguía y Lizaur. (Saavedra forwarded him funds for investment in "comercio de Indias.") It is not far-fetched to see in Lizaur's mission to London and his discussions there with Anthony Merry outlines of the subsequent pattern of silver transfers from Veracruz to England under Soler's *contratas* after 1805. Iturbe e Iraeta Papers, Princeton University Library, box 2a, 26 Nov. 1794; AGI, Ind. Gen., 2317; 8 Mar. 1801, PRO, FO 72/46.

19. S. Thornton to George Hammond, 20 Oct. 1800, and Anthony Merry to Hammond, 24 Jan. and 8 Mar. 1801, PRO, FO 72/46.

20. Soler to Intendente, Caracas, 9 Aug. 1805, dispatch seized aboard the Spanish *goleta Santa Cecilia,* U.S. Consular Dispatches, Kingston.

21. Ibid. See also Iturrigaray to Soler, 27 Aug. 1804, AGN, Correspondencia de virreyes, 2nd ser., 219, no. 584; and BMus, Add. MSS 13978.

22. License to Malancó, 15 Feb. 1807, AGI, Mexico, 2513; Iturrigaray to Soler, 16 July 1807, AGN, Correspondencia de virreyes, 2nd ser., 233, no. 1274.

23. Iturrigaray to Soler, 16 July 1807, AGN, Correspondencia de virreyes, 2nd ser., 233, no. 1274.

24. Consulado de Veracruz to Soler, 15 Nov. 1805, AGI, Mexico, 2512.

25. Consulado de Veracruz, 1 Mar. 1809, AGI, Mexico, 2997.

26. AHN, Estado, 5458 bis.

27. Armytage, *Free Port System in the British West Indies,* 110.

28. Council Office, Whitehall, extract, 17 June 1805, PRO, FO 72/56. William Pitt knew that David Parish, as the agent of the merchant-bankers Hope (Amsterdam) and Baring (London), had passed through London on his way to the United States to arrange for the shipment of 12 million *pesos fuertes* from Havana via the United

States to Paris. Chancellor of the Exchequer William Huskisson kept Pitt informed of the operations of the two merchant-banking firms. Jiménez Codinach, *La Gran Bretaña,* 211.

29. Armytage, *Free Port System in the British West Indies,* 110; Crouzet, *L'économie britannique,* 1:179–84; Lynch, "British Policy and Spanish America," 26–27.

30. Mexico City's *consulado* reported that the colony of New Spain had sent 66% of all colonial silver remissions received by the metropole. AGN, Consulado, 49, exp. 2.

31. Contrata, art. 9, AGI, Ind. Gen., 2472. The classic treatment of English involvement in New Spain's silver transfers is Jiménez Codinach, *La Gran Bretaña,* esp. 191–263.

32. Robert Oliver to José Gabriel Villanueva, 26 Dec. 1806, and Oliver to Conway & Whittle, 26 Dec. 1806, Oliver Papers, Letter Books, box 13, Maryland Historical Society, Baltimore.

33. Godoy, *Memorias,* 1:389.

34. Ibid., 389.

35. Ibid., 389–90.

36. Ibid., 390, 391, and esp. the revealing footnote on 378.

37. As a *munitionnaire* (1795–99) Ouvrard amassed 60 million francs. Jiménez Codinach, *La Gran Bretaña,* 211.

38. On Ouvrard, see Ouvrard, *Mémoires;* C. F. Lévy, *Un grand profiteur;* Payard, *Ouvrard;* Wolf, *Ouvrard;* and details in Buist, *At spes non fracta,* and in Jiménez Codinach's carefully researched *La Gran Bretaña,* 211.

39. Under Charles III and in the 1790s the LeCouteulx bank was one of three great banks in Paris, handling the payments abroad of Spain's Hacienda. The family was involved in the Spanish *asiento,* supplying slaves to the Spanish colonies in the 1690s and later to Havana (1781–86). LeCouteulx de Canteleu survived the Revolution and the Directoire, supported Bonaparte's coup d'état in 1799, and was subsequently a founder and regent of the Banque de France. Commercial operations with the colonies from Cadiz over the eighteenth century were the financial basis of this French family's fortune. Tornero Tinajero, *Crecimiento,* 41; Fugier, *Napoléon et l'Espagne,* 1:95 n. 1; Ramon, *Banque de France,* 17; Cavignac, *Jean Pellet,* 132; Dardel, "Crises et faillites," 394; Fontana i Lázaro, *Comercio y colonias,* 3:292 n. 21; AAEPar, CP, Espagne, supplément 19, no. 128.

40. Payard, *Ouvrard,* 106.

41. Ouvrard, *Mémoires,* 1:66.

42. Buist, *At spes non fracta,* 285.

43. Fugier, *Napoléon et l'Espagne,* 1:95 n. 1.

44. Ouvrard, *Mémoires,* 1:87.

45. Ibid., 66; Nolte, *Fifty Years in both hemispheres,* 67.

46. Ouvrard, *Mémoires,* 1:67.

47. Buist, *At spes non fracta,* 284–85.

48. Ibid., 302.

49. Ouvrard, *Mémoires,* 1:87.

50. Buist, *At spes non fracta,* 289.

51. In July 1806 Madrid authorities gave David Parish letters (*giros*) of credit for

1.25 million *pesos* on Mexico City's treasury, representing the government's participation in the operation of François Ouvrard & Cie. Ibid., 327.

52. Ibid., 289, 313 n. 1; Ouvrard, *Mémoires,* 1:96; Izquierdo to [Godoy], 16 Feb. 1806, ANPar, AF 1680.

53. Ouvrard, *Mémoires,* 2:135–42, 338–42.

54. "Dictamenes del fiscal," AHN, Estado, 2839.

55. Buist, *At spes non fracta,* 290.

56. Ibid.; Seco Serrano, *Historia de España,* 33:653.

57. Buist, *At spes non fracta,* 290.

58. Ibid.

59. Soler and Sixto Espinosa also contacted other bankers, offering letters of credit on the colonial treasury at Mexico City to Martínez de Hervás y Bastide (Paris), Croeze (Amsterdam), and David & Huyningen (Hamburg). Ibid., 303.

60. Ibid., 291–92.

61. Bruchey, *Robert Oliver,* 274; Buist, *At spes non fracta,* 293.

62. The contact with Francis Baring promised to facilitate the collaboration of the English government. Alexander Baring advised Robert Oliver to establish a "friendly exchange" with Hope & Company, informing Oliver that his brother-in-law was the director of Hope & Company. Oliver to Francis Baring, 1 Dec. 1803, Oliver Papers, box 11.

63. Hidy, *House of Baring,* 35.

64. Buist, *At spes non fracta,* 294–98.

65. Bruchey, *Robert Oliver,* 333 n. 379.

66. Buist, *At spes non fracta,* 306–7.

67. Iturrigaray to Azanza, 4 July 1808, AGN, Correspondencia de virreyes, 2nd ser., 236, no. 1586.

68. Buist, *At spes non fracta,* 296, 311. On "Villanueva," see Nolte, *Fifty Years in both hemispheres,* 98, 170. Villanueva operated at Veracruz through Echeverría, who had traded with non-Spaniards under *comercio neutro.* Echeverría handled Villanueva's incoming cargo—its off-loading, flow through customs, warehousing, and sale, as well as the preparation of outgoing cargo—and as the Veracruz agent of *consolidación* he also oversaw the export of outflows of silver drawn on *consolidación* by Villanueva and others. Viceroy Iturrigaray directed the intendant at the port to facilitate Echeverría's operations. Souto Mantecón, *Mar abierto,* 193–94 and n. 45.

69. Humphreys, *Tradition and Revolt,* 116 n. 1.

70. Parish arrived at New York bearing letters of introduction from Hope and Barings. An inveterate speculator, he bought properties in New York City and joined John Jacob Astor and Stephen Girard in lending to the U.S. government in 1813. Barings corresponded with him through the firm of Archibald Gracie. Jiménez Codinach, *La Gran Bretaña,* 211–12.

71. Bruchey, *Robert Oliver,* 276; Oliver to P. J. Pollock, 5 Mar. 1806, Oliver Papers, box 11. The firm of Clark & Company of New Orleans, which had a license to trade with Veracruz, boasted that it hoped to enjoy profits of at least 100%. Oliver to Villanueva, 16 Apr. 1806, ibid.

72. For Oliver's background, see Bruchey, *Robert Oliver,* 23.

73. Oliver to Pollock, 5 Mar. 1806, Oliver Papers, box 11.

74. Bruchey, *Robert Oliver,* 104 n. 28. As early as 1803 Oliver sent ships to buy

silver at Kingston and Demerara. Oliver to Francis Baring, 31 Dec. 1803, Oliver Papers, box 11.

75. Bruchey, *Robert Oliver,* 265–66; Oliver to Francisco Caballero Sarmiento, 12 Feb. 1806, Oliver to Pedro de Echeverría, 30 June 1806, and Oliver to Villanueva, 31 July 1806, all in Oliver Papers, box 11.

76. Ignacio Agudo y Andrade, 31 May 1829, AGI, Ind. Gen., 2473.

77. The contract is in AGI, Ind. Gen., 2473. Oliver employed the Madrid merchant-banking firm of Patrick Joyes & Company as intermediary in writing Sixto Espinosa. Oliver to Joyes & Company, 8 Dec. 1805, Oliver Papers, box 11.

78. The Regency, at Cadiz, later ordered Colonel Francisco Caballero Sarmiento to collect from U.S. merchants who had shipped to Veracruz and other Spanish colonial ports those duties normally paid on goods exported from peninsular ports to the colonies. In 1811 the total presumably owed was 2.5 million *pesos.* One estimate, assuming an average duty of 10%, topped 25 million. Cortes de Cádiz, "Actas secretas," *Diario de la Cortes,* 11 June 1811.

79. Oliver to Pablo Serra, 13 Dec. 1805, and Oliver to Matthew Murphy, 12 Feb. 1806, Oliver Papers, box 11; Consulado de Veracruz to Iturrigaray, 12 Mar. 1806, AGI, Mexico, 2997.

80. Oliver to Baring Brothers, 22 Oct. 1805, 7 Jan. 1806, Oliver Papers, box 11; Bruchey, *Robert Oliver,* 362.

81. Oliver to Pollock, 5 Mar. 1806, Oliver Papers, box 11.

82. Oliver also sent Villanueva a letter from "our mutual friend Mr. Parish, which will explain the nature of our arrangement with him." Oliver to Villanueva, 16 Apr. 1806, ibid.

83. Oliver to Pollock, 15 Apr. 1806, ibid.

84. Oliver to Villanueva, 16 Apr. 1806, ibid.

85. Oliver to Villanueva, 3 May 1806, ibid.

86. Oliver to Pollock, 6 Mar. 1806, and Oliver to Tomás Murphy, 31 July 1806, ibid.

87. Oliver to Tomás Murphy, 8 July 1806, ibid., box 13.

88. Oliver to Tomás Murphy, 7 Aug. 1806, ibid.

89. Oliver to Mateo Murphy, 1 Nov. 1805, and Oliver to Mateo Murphy and Pollock, 29 Jan. 1806, ibid., box 11.

90. Oliver to Mateo Murphy and Pollock, 12 Feb., 5 Mar. 1806, ibid.

91. Oliver to Mateo Murphy and Pollock, 15, 16 Apr. 1806, ibid.

92. Oliver to Mateo Murphy and Pollock, 16 Apr. 1806, ibid.

93. Oliver to Villanueva, 30, 31 May 1806, ibid.

94. Oliver to Villanueva, 3 May 1806, ibid.

95. Oliver to Mateo Murphy, 15 Oct. 1806, ibid., box 13.

96. Oliver to Villanueva, 31 May 1806, ibid.

97. Oliver to Villanueva, 31 July, 7 Aug. 1806, ibid.

98. Oliver to Villanueva, 7 July 1806, ibid.

99. Oliver to William Courtenay, 31 Jan. 1807, ibid.

100. Oliver to Villanueva, 8 July 1807, ibid.

101. Oliver to David Parish, 10 Sept. 1806, and Oliver to Villanueva, 1 Oct. 1806, ibid.

102. Nolte, *Fifty Years in both hemispheres,* 70. Nonetheless, on 24 June 1808 a

schooner from the United States entered Veracruz to collect from Villanueva letters of credit totaling about 2 million *pesos*. The *libranzas* were signed by Soler and endorsed by Sixto Espinosa and Arias Mon for Hope & Company, of Amsterdam. Iturrigaray to Azanza, 4 July 1808, AGN, Correspondencia de virreyes, 2nd ser., 236, no. 1586.

103. Oliver to Francis Baring, 1 Apr., 1 Sept., and 1 Dec. 1803, Oliver Papers, box 11.

104. In 1806 Oliver dispatched to Veracruz "mainly prohibited articles recommended in letters to Parish." Oliver to Villanueva, October 1806, ibid., box 13.

105. Oliver to Villanueva, 6 Sept., 24 Nov. 1806, ibid., ibid.

106. Oliver to Villanueva, 8 July 1807, ibid.

107. Oliver to Courtenay, 18 Apr. 1809, ibid.

108. Oliver to Pollock, 12 Feb. 1806, ibid., box 11.

109. Oliver to Francis Baring, 22 Oct. 1805, ibid.

110. Oliver to Francis Baring, 7 Jan. 1806, ibid.

111. Oliver to Mateo Murphy and Pollock, and Oliver to Villanueva, both 16 Apr. 1806, ibid.

112. Oliver to Hope & Company, 28 June 1806, ibid.

113. Oliver to Pollock, 6 Mar. 1806, ibid. Six months earlier Oliver had decided to use small and fast ships. Oliver to Baring Brothers, 22 Oct. 1805, ibid.

114. Oliver to Matthiesen & Gilliam, 7 Jan. 1806, ibid.

115. Oliver to Parish, 7 May 1806, ibid.

116. Oliver to Villanueva, 31 May 1806, ibid.

117. Oliver to Villanueva, 7, 27, 7 Aug., 15 Oct. 1806, ibid., box 13.

118. Oliver to Villanueva, 27 Aug., 15 Oct. 1806, ibid.

119. Oliver to Parish, 1 Sept. 1806, ibid.

120. Oliver to Holland & Company, 25 Sept. 1806, ibid.

121. Oliver to Villanueva, 15 Oct. 1806, ibid.

122. *Net Profits on Oliver's Shipments to Veracruz, 1805–1807*
    ($ US)

	Net Profit	Ships	Profit per Ship
5 Oct. 1805–15 Aug. 1806	1,077,570	14	76,969
16 Oct.–14 Nov. 1807	3,275,030	21	155,953
Dec. 1807	341,639	2	170,820
Total	4,694,239	37	

Source: Bruchey, *Robert Oliver,* 268, 329, and nn., 360, 332.

123. Oliver to Conway & Whittle, 26 Dec. 1806, Oliver Papers, box 13.

124. Oliver to Baring Brothers, 1 Jan. 1806, and "Memorandum of Articles Dispatched by Baring Brothers & Co. of London," ibid., box 11.

125. Oliver to Pollock and Mateo Murphy, 16 Apr. 1806, and Oliver to Pedro de Echeverría, 20 June 1806, ibid.; Oliver to Villanueva, 27 Aug. 1806, ibid., box 13.

126. These were Oliver's "friends" in Europe. Oliver to Villanueva, 23 Sept., 1 Oct. 1806, ibid., box 13.

127. Oliver to Sixto Espinosa, 8 Dec. 1805, and Oliver to Villanueva, 3 May 1806, ibid., box 11.

128. Oliver to Campbell & Whittle, 12 Jan. 1807, and Oliver to Sixto Espinosa, 4 Feb. 1807, ibid., box 13.

129. Oliver to Gordon & Murphy, 13 Mar. 1807, ibid.

130. Oliver to Sixto Espinosa, 9 Feb. 1808, ibid.

131. Ibid.

132. Gabriel de Iturbe e Iraeta to Juan Manuel Revuelta, 17 Feb., 25 May 1806, Iturbe e Iraeta Papers, Princeton University Library.

133. Oliver to Villanueva, 15 Oct. 1806, and Oliver to Baring Brothers, 11 Jan. 1807, Oliver Papers, box 13.

134. Oliver to Villanueva, 2 Jan., 5 Feb. 1808, Oliver to Baring Brothers, 10 Jan. 1807, and Oliver to Campbell & Whittle, 12 Jan. 1807, ibid.

135. Oliver to Villanueva, and Oliver to Conway & Whittle, both 26 Dec. 1806, ibid.

136. Jiménez Codinach, *La Gran Bretaña,* 210–11. Barings was also invested in the Asian trades; in addition, the firm was an early shareholder in the Spanish Compañia de Filipinas. Incidentally, Pitt authorized four royal navy frigates to carry 14 million *pesos* to England, presumably from Veracruz.

137. Duff to Hammond, 29 Aug. 1804, PRO, FO 72/53.

138. Armytage, *Free Port System in the British West Indies,* 110; Crouzet, *L'économie britannique,* 1:180–81; Lynch, "British Policy and Spanish America," 26–27.

139. Grenville authorized the arrangement that included Ouvrard, Hopes, and Barings. Lynch, "British Policy and Spanish America," 27 and n. 5.

140. Crouzet, *L'économie britannique,* 1:180; Bruchey, *Robert Oliver,* 295.

141. Crouzet, *L'économie britannique,* 1:181. Gordon & Murphy's agents at Veracruz—José White, Ignacio Palyart, and Tomás Murphy—could present *libranzas* signed by Soler for payment by either Mexico City's treasury or the Caja de Consolidación. Souto Mantecón, *Mar abierto,* 207.

142. Murphy y Eliot exported Malagan wines to England. A son, Juan, at Madrid, handled the flow of Hacienda funds to France's Trésor Public. In 1799 the Cadiz *consulado* noted that Juan was on his way to Madrid, then Lisbon, to take ship for New England to establish a "grueso giro . . . con la Havana y Veracruz." Fugier, *Napoléon et l'Espagne,* 2:183–84; AAEPar, CP, Espagne, 674, fol. 92r; AGI, Consulados, Correspondencia, 31; AHN, Estado, 4198².

143. In 1803 the Spanish warship *El Miño* carried government silver from Veracruz to Cadiz, including 100,000 *pesos fuertes* of "Temporalidades y Real Negociación del Giro." Felipe San Román to Antonio Noriega, 15 July 1803, AHN, Hacienda, 3871.

144. Bejarano Robles, *Historia,* 98–99.

145. Juan López Cancelada believed erroneously that Murphy had married a cousin of Azanza's. *Ruina de la Nueva España,* 10.

146. Azanza to Soler, 26 Mar. 1800, AGI, Mexico, 2510.

147. AGI, Consulados, Correspondencia con America, 51; Iturrigaray to Soler, 27 Dec. 1806, AGN, Correspondencia de virreyes, 2nd ser., 229, no. 1142.

148. Juan Murphy to Noriega, 9 Apr. 1803, AHN, Hacienda, 3871.

149. Noriega to Rafael de Ozta, 20 Mar. 1803, ibid.

150. Museo del Instituto Nacional de Antropología e Historia (Mexico City),

Antigua, 432, Epistolario de Don T. Murphy (1810–13). Jorge Flores called this correspondence to our attention.

151. Captain Adams, HMS *Resistance,* to Governor of Veracruz, 20 Dec. 1806, AGI, Mexico, 2513.

152. Buist, *At spes non fracta,* 324, 327, 328; AHN, Consejos, 20,729, fols. 21r–22r, 29r–30r.

153. AGI, Ind. Gen., 2472.

154. Crouzet, *L'économie britannique,* 1:181 and n. 50.

155. AGI, Ind. Gen., 2472.

156. Crouzet, *L'économie britannique,* 1:181 n. 51; AGI, Mexico, 2513.

157. AGI, Mexico, 2513.

158. Soler to Iturrigaray, 19 May 1806, AGI, Mexico, 2513; BNMex, Reales Cedulas, 1409, fols. 99r–103r.

159. BNMex, Reales Cedulas, 1409, fols. 104r–108v.

160. Letters of accreditation were issued to Palyart and White. Ibid., fol. 103r.

161. Ibid., fol. 120v.

162. Ibid., fol. 103r; Soler to Iturrigaray, 19 May 1806, AGI, Mexico, 2513.

163. Iturrigaray to Soler, 29 Dec. 1806, AGI, Mexico, 2513.

164. Captain Adams to Governor of Veracruz, 20 Dec. 1806, ibid.

165. Pedro de Alonso to Iturrigaray, 21 Dec. 1806, and Iturrigaray to Alonso, 23 Dec. 1806, ibid.; Iturrigaray to Soler, 23 May 1807, AGN, Correspondencia de virreyes, 2nd ser., 233, no. 1231.

166. Nolte, *Fifty Years in both hemispheres,* 78.

167. AGN, Reales Cedulas, 1409, fols. 198r–200r.

168. Quirós, "Memoria de instituto, 1819."

169. Francisco Antonio de la Torre to Consulado de Cadiz, 21 Apr. 1807, AGI, Consulados, Correspondencia con America, 218.

170. Iturbe e Iraeta, letter of 23 Mar. 1808, Iturbe e Iraeta Papers, Princeton University Library.

171. Hernández y Dávalos, *Documentos,* 2:855; Consulado de México, 22 July 1806, AGN, Consulado, 49, exp. 3.

172. AGI, Ind. Gen., 2472; AGI, Mexico, 2516.

173. Souto Mantecón, on the basis of an observation of Oliver's, stated that the official import figure was undervalued by 50%, hence a more accurate import estimate would be about 37 million. *Mar abierto,* 208.

174. Lerdo de Tejada, *Comercio exterior de México,* doc. 14.

175. *Veracruz: Estimates of Silver Exports on Private and Government Account*
  (pesos fuertes)

	Estimates	
Gordon & Murphy	8,200,000	27,825,504
Oliver/Oliver-Parish	19,620,000	19,620,000
Total on Private Account	27,820,000	47,445,504
Total on Government Account	12,950,272	12,950,272
Total on Private and Government Account	40,770,272	60,395,776

Sources: For Gordon & Murphy: AGI, Ind. Gen., 2516, 2472. For Oliver-Parish: Bruchey, *Robert Oliver,* 333; and Lavrín, "Execution of the Law of *Consolidación,*" n. 170.

176. *Veracruz: Silver Exports on Government Account,*
29 August 1807–21 March 1808
(*pesos*)

Shipped to:	
Baring Brothers	3,679,835
Gordon & Murphy and Reid, Irving	4,551,641
Total	8,231,476
Shipped by:	
Warships	4,477,759
Merchant vessels	3,753,171
Total	8,230,930

Source: "Noticias de las partidas embarcadas . . . por Villanueva y Tomás Murphy en plata y frutos," AGN, Consulado, 113, exp. 7.

177. Vilar, *Oro y moneda,* 379. The specie reserves of the Bank of England were reestablished in 1807 by silver imports from "Hispanic America." In the second half of 1808 the expenditure of the English government in money and silver bars, solely to support the resistance in Spain, was £3 million, and it was much higher in the following two years. Crouzet, *L'économie britannique,* 2:526, 534.

178. Parish to Labouchère, 18 May 1816, New York Historical Society, Parish Letterbook, VI, fols. 332r–338r.

179. Buist, *At spes non fracta,* 314–16.

180. Ibid., 316; Bruchey, *Robert Oliver,* 334.

181. Bruchey, *Robert Oliver,* 351.

182. AGI, Ind. Gen., 2472.

183. Lavrín, "Execution of the Law of *Consolidación,*" 35, 45. From October 1806 to September 1807 Lorenzo Angulo Guardamino, agent of New Spain's Junta de Consolidación, honored 5.5 million *pesos'* worth of letters of exchange; presumably the funds were exported. Ibid., 30–31 and n. 14.

184. Hernández y Dávalos, *Documentos,* 1:120.

185. Consulado de Veracruz to Gobierno Interino, 22 Dec. 1809, AGI, Mexico, 2997. Oddly, the May order stimulated shipments of English wares to the American colonies, and Godoy's manifesto of 20 December 1804 reacting to English aggression led the Veracruz *consulado* to gloat that by shutting down "nuestros puertos a la industria Ynglesa, será completa nuestra venganza; que veremos humillado el insoportable orgullo de estas infractores del derecho de gente; y que se perecerán rabiendo sobre montones de fardos y de efectos repelidos de todas partes." Consulado de Veracruz to Madrid, 24 Feb. 1806, ibid.

186. Ruiz y Pablo, *Historia de la Real Junta Particular,* 215–16.

187. Real Orden, 16 June 1806, AGN, Consulado, 2.

188. Regil, *Memoria,* 9. Iturrigaray acknowledged receipt of this order on 20 Jan. 1807. Iturrigaray to Soler, AGN, Correspondencia de virreyes, 2nd ser., 233, no. 1197.

189. *Havana: Foreign Trade, 1805*
   (*pesos fuertes*)

	Total	U.S. shipping	%
Imports	11,265,007	10,541,138	93.5
Exports	5,072,981	4,452,981	87.7

Source: Rafael Gómez Roubaud to Godoy, 6 Aug. 1806, AGI, Mexico, 2514.

190. Rafael Gómez Roubaud to Godoy, 6 Aug. 1806, AGI, Mexico, 2514.

191. Consulado de Veracruz to Gobierno Interino, 22 Dec. 1809, AGI, Mexico, 2997; Regil, *Memoria*, 9.

192. Real Orden, 10 May 1807, in *Gazeta de México*, 19 Aug. 1807; Consulado de la Habana (conde de O'Reilly, Juan Joseph de Iguarán, Bonifacio Gónzalez Larriñaga) to Madrid, 22 Feb. 1808, AGI, Mexico, 2513. A junta of Havana merchants made up of Iguarán and Erice later credited the order of 10 May 1807 to the insistence of Gómez Roubaud. Consulado de la Habana, Junta, 31 Oct. 1810, AGI, Mexico, 2514.

193. Malancó brought suit against the government for the loss of his *permiso*, attacking Gómez Roubaud, Havana's merchants ("Los Habaneros, fecundos en parafrasear a su arbitrio y animosidad"), and the order itself ("apócrifa o atribuido siniestramente al Rei . . . ilegal, subversiva, incongruente, intempestiva y espontánea, viciosa, nula y sin forma alguna leal"). *Extracto instructivo*, 6–7, 43.

194. Consulado de Veracruz (Joachín de Castillo y Bustamante, Manuel Antonio del Valle, Juan Thomás Miguelena) to Francisco Saavedra, 1 Mar. 1809, AGI, Mexico, 2997, fols. 11r–12r.

195. Acuerdo del Cabildo Secular, 5 Aug. 1808, fols. 5r–6r, in Consulado de la Habana, *Expediente instruido*.

196. *Havana: Three-Year Averages, Imports from Cadiz,*
   1792–1794 and 1802–1804
      (*reales de vellón*)

Imports	1792–94	1802–4	% change
Spanish			
Per year	18,118,405	13,460,876	
Per ship	654,882[a]	443,765[b]	
Total	54,355,215	40,382,630	–26
Non-Spanish			
Per year	13,445,406	8,271,089	
Per ship	485,976[a]	272,673[b]	
Total	40,336,220	24,813,267	–39

Source: "Estados . . . introducciones hechas desde la Metrópoli . . . a la Habana," Consulado de la Habana, *Expediente instruido*, apps. 2, 6–8.

[a]83 ships
[b]91 ships

197. Arango y Parreño, "Informe del síndico," 49, 53, 55–57.

198. Ibid., 21–22, and 94–96, apps. 7–8.

199. Ibid., 93–94.

200. "Acuerdo del Consulado, 11 Aug. 1808," in Consulado de la Habana, *Expediente instruido,* 8.

201. Consulado de la Habana, *Expediente instruido,* 20, 29–30; Arango y Parreño, "Informe del síndico," 53–57.

202. Consulado de la Habana, *Expediente instruido,* 30; Arango y Parreño, "Informe del síndico," 44.

203. Arango y Parreño, "Informe del síndico," 93–94.

204. Ibid., 104.

205. Gayer, Ross, and Schwartz, *Growth and Fluctuation of the British Economy,* 1:90.

"Spanish" Shipping, Kingston, 1810

	From	To
Cuba	54	68
Campeche	7	11
Puerto Rico	14	23
Other	124	417
Total	199	519

Source: PRO, CO 142/66.
Note: These data are very proximate. A major port, Veracruz, is omitted, and Spanish shipping was probably entered under other origins.

206. In July 1808, for example, Robert Oliver drew on Barings of London to buy cargo at Kingston for shipment to Veracruz. Bruchey, *Robert Oliver,* 342. In the same month, Iturrigaray reported to Miguel Azanza, at Madrid, the arrival of a U.S.-registry vessel, the *Columbia,* at Veracruz without a Spanish passport or consular certification. Iturrigaray to Azanza, AGN, Correspondencia de virreyes, 2nd ser., 276, no. 1586.

207. Francisco Antonio de la Torre, to Consulado de Cadiz, 21 Apr. 1807, AGI, Consulados, Correspondencia con América, 218. Cf. the following *reservado* report from Iturrigaray to Soler: "[4] buques españoles procedentes de Jamaica . . . han llegado sucesivamente . . . con las correspondencias de oficio . . . se han despachado . . . despues de verificada la venta de los efectos que han traydo." 21 Apr. 1807, AGN, Correspondencia de virreyes, 2nd ser., 239.

208. Consulado de Cadiz to Francisco de la Torre, 31 Aug. 1807, AGI, Consulados, Correspondencia con América, 65, fols. 73r–74r; *Grito de Campeche* (1814), 42.

209. Consulado de Cadiz (Salazar, Faxardo, Urrutia) to Consejo de Regencia, 4 Mar. 1812, AGI, Consulados, Correspondencia, 58, fols. 325r–328r.

210. Consulado de Veracruz (Francisco Antonio de la Sierra, Josef Xavier de Olazaabal, Francisco Guerra y Ágreda), "Representación," 18 Mar. 1815, AGI, Ind. Gen., 2463.

211. Consulado de Veracruz (Viya y Givaxa, García Puertas, Juan Bautista Lobo) to Soler, 15 Nov. 1805, AGI, Mexico, 2997.

212. Consulado de Veracruz to Iturrigaray, 13 Feb. 1806, ibid.

213. Iturrigaray to Consulado de Veracruz, 16 Feb. 1806, ibid; also in AGI, Mexico, 2516.

214. Consulado de Veracruz to Soler, 24 Feb. 1806, AGI, Mexico, 2997.

215. Lizarza, *Discurso*, 15; Consulado de México (Francisco de Chavarri, Diego de Ágreda, Lorenzao García Noriega), 1 June 1811, AGN, AHH, 216-11, fol. 115r.

216. "Representación del Consulado de México al Virrey [Venegas]," 14 Sept. 1811, AGN, AHH, 215-9, fol. 149r.

217. Consulado de Veracruz (Joachín de Castillo y Bustamante, Manuel Antonio del Valle, Juan Thomás de Miguelena) to SM, 1 Mar. 1809, AGI, Mexico, 2997.

218. Consulado de México (Francisco de Chavarri, Diego de Ágreda, Lorenzo García Noriega), 1 June 1811, AGN, AHH, 216-11, fol. 122r.

13. "Treasures in the New World"

EPIGRAPHS: Ouvrard, *Mémoires*, 1:135; Payard, *Ouvrard*, 161; Arnna, *Napoléon et son temps*, 9.
1. Industrial production fell by about 40%. Bergeron, "Problèmes économiques," 495.
2. Braudel and Labrousse, *Histoire économique et sociale*, 3, pt. 1: 6; Chabert, *Essai*, 354–58. France's ambassador at Madrid, General Dominique-Cathérine de Pérignon, was rumored to be involved in "contrebande de l'argent" in the form of 300,000 *livres tournois* of silver on a wagon headed for Bayonne. ANPar, AF III, 63, dossier 255, doc. 5 (21 Apr. 1797).
3. Cf. Labène to Paris, 13 July 1797, AAEPar, CP, Espagne, supplément 18, fol. 160r: "[Ce] fleuve d'or que l'industrie Française commence à faire couler du haut des Pyrénées dans le sein de notre République."
4. Braudel and Labrousse, *Histoire économique et sociale*, 3, pt. 1: 72.
5. Cf. Furet and Richet, *La Révolution française*, 256: "Le 'fournisseur' de la République simplement a remplacé le 'fermier du roi.'"
6. Under the Consulat, finance was reorganized. In each *département* a *receveur général* was responsible for collecting direct contributions, of which the most important was the monthly land tax; each *receveur général* had to deposit with the Caisse d'Amortissement a security *(cautionnement)*, 5% of the annual value of the land tax. Moreover, each year a *receveur* deposited with the Trésor Public *obligations* equal to expected annual collections—*obligations* redeemable every two to four months. Arnna, *Napoléon et son temps*, 12–13; Payard, *Ouvrard*, 100; Marion, *Histoire financière*, 4:180–81; Buist, *At spes non fracta*, 285.
7. Napoleon to Mollien, 15 May 1810, in Bonaparte, *Napoléon Ier*, 172. The empire's "rigorous metalism" may have constrained economic growth. Bergeron, "Problèmes économiques," 475 n. 5.
8. Cf. C. F. Lévy, "Supplément."
9. AHN, Hacienda, 3871.
10. Bergeron, "Problèmes économiques," 472.
11. "Observations sur les bases d'un traité de commerce entre la France et l'Espagne," AAEPar, M et D, Espagne, 209. Through Spanish contacts of the Parisian banker LeCouteulx, the government probably tapped various merchants to ship silver *pesos* out of Spain in 1792: 75,000 were seized by Spanish authorities and returned to Madrid. ANPar, AF III, 62, dossier 246, plaque 1.

12. Gautier, "Extrait d'un mémoire secret," Marseille, 4 Frimaire An 4, AAEPar, CP, Espagne, supplément 17, fol. 327r.

13. Marion, *Ce qu'il faut connaître des crises financières,* 94.

14. A war contractor for Napoleon's first Italian campaign, Jeanne-Pierre Collot, participated in financing the coup d'état of Brumaire 1799. Furet and Richet, *La Révolution française,* 256.

15. Gaudin, *Observations,* 1:154, quoted in Duchêne, *Guerre et finances,* 20. "L'anarchie financière comme l'anarchie politique et administrative, était a son comble." Marion, *Histoire financière,* 4:169.

16. The "banquiers de Brumaire" joined immediately with Récamier and Sevene to provide a loan to the Consulat; among the early members of the Banque de France's first *conseil de régence* were Perregaux, LeCouteulx, Mallet, Germain, Recamier and Sevene. Arnna, *Napoléon et son temps,* 34; Marion, *Histoire financière,* 4:174, 208.

17. French agents reported a deficit of 377 million *reales de vellón* (about 75.4 million francs) in the Spanish budget of 1796. In 1798 reports from Madrid claimed that government financial experts were worried about covering expenditures "depuis le retard qu'éprouvent ses gallions," anxiety repeated in 1799. ANPar, AF III, 62, dossier 247, plaque 2, and dossier 248, no. 1.

18. AAEPar, CP, Espagne, supplément 26, fol. 267r; ANPar, AF III, 62, dossier 249, plaque 2, no. 142.

19. Bourgoing, *Tableau de l'Espagne moderne,* 2:214, 215n, 216.

20. Fugier, *Napoléon et l'Espagne,* 1:92–93.

21. Buist, *At spes non fracta,* 57, 286.

22. *Justice and Policy,* 10; Harlow, *Founding of the Second British Empire,* 2:658.

23. Fugier, *Napoléon et l'Espagne,* 1:262–63. Fugier claimed that the overdue Spanish subsidy payments represented about 7% of planned French expenditures for the year from September 1803 to September 1804. Hervás, an affluent financier, owned a Parisian *palais,* which he later sold to Talleyrand; his daughter married General Duroc, a close collaborator of Bonaparte's. Seco Serrano, *Historia de España,* 33:653.

24. Ramon, *Banque de France,* 64–65.

25. Chabert, *Essai,* 359–60; Braudel and Labrousse, *Histoire économique et sociale,* 3, pt. 1: 89.

26. Buist, *At spes non fracta,* 286.

27. Payard, *Ouvrard,* 87–89, 93–96.

28. Arnna, *Napoléon et son temps,* 33. The naval contract and questions it raised are detailed in Payard, *Ouvrard,* 5–24ff. Regarding the prominent role of financiers like Ouvrard and Vanlerberghe in the Directoire, it has been commented that the links then established between private interest and politics began the "grand bal moderne de la finance et de la politique." Furet and Richet, *La Révolution française,* 245.

29. Ouvrard, *Mémoires,* 1:56; AAEPar, CP, supplément 18, fols. 338r–341r. As late as 1797 the French government still claimed that it had failed to receive more than 30 million *livres tournois* for naval stores supplied to Spain's navy during the wartime years 1779–81. ANPar, AF III, 63, dossier 254.

30. Letter to Múzquiz, 14 Dec. 1799, ANPar, AF 1679, fol. 339r; Fugier, *Napoléon*

et l'Espagne, 1:95 n. 1. The quotation is probably from a translation of a presumably encoded letter intercepted by the French police.

31. Bergeron, "Problèmes économiques," 155. Marcel Marion thought Ouvrard had been prominent well before Brumaire as one of the more visible of the "turbe de faiseurs d'affaires" flowering under the Directoire. Marion, *Histoire financière,* 4:175.

32. Braudel and Labrousse, *Histoire économique et sociale,* 3, pt. 1: 59. Far less critical of Ouvrard was Ramon, who admired him, describing him as "[t]ype du spéculateur né, chercheur d'occasions, amateur de risques, toujours prêt à embrasser l'univers dans ses combinaisons . . . successivement négociant en denrées coloniales, spéculateur sur le papier, banquier privé et banquier du Gouvernement, fournisseur des armées." Ramon, *Banque de France,* 65.

33. Payard, *Ouvrard,* 107–8. Preceding the Vanlerberghe-Ouvrard proposal was an offer by Robert Livingston and Daniel Parker, supported by Talleyrand. This was rejected. Buist, *At spes non fracta,* 290; Fugier, *Napoléon et l'Espagne,* 265. The proposal is in AAEPar, CP, Espagne, supplément 19, no. 123, fols. 314ff.

34. Payard, *Ouvrard,* 101–3; Buist, *At spes non fracta,* 284–85, 301–2; Arnna, *Napoléon et son temps;* Bonaparte, *Napoléon Ier,* 35; Fugier, *Napoléon et l'Espagne,* 2:17, 285. This would corroborate Eugenio Izquierdo's claim that Ouvrard executed his Spanish contracts "avec l'argent du Trésor de France." ANPar, AF 1680. Ouvrard retained control over the *obligations* until he received silver *pesos* from Spain, a delaying tactic that angered Napoleon. Fugier, *Napoléon et l'Espagne,* 2:9.

35. Payard, *Ouvrard,* 104–5.

36. Ibid., 102–4; Buist, *At spes non fracta,* 285; Bouvier, "Apropos de la crise," 507.

37. Fugier, *Napoléon et l'Espagne,* 1:262. According to Ramon, the Compagnie was "bâtissant sur les richesses inaccessibles du Mexique." *Banque de France,* 651.

38. Fugier, *Napoléon et l'Espagne,* 2:19.

39. Payard, *Ouvrard,* 108.

40. Ibid., 110.

41. Fugier, *Napoléon et l'Espagne,* 2:10, 18; Duchêne, *Guerre et finances,* 119.

42. Buist, *At spes non fracta,* 297–300. At this juncture, Beurnonville at Madrid, an admirer of Ouvrard's, wrote Barbé-Marbois that Ouvrard's operations at Madrid had one goal: "faire entrer tout le numéraire de l'Empire en France." Payard, *Ouvrard,* 130.

43. Payard, *Ouvrard,* 118–20; Fugier, *Napoléon et l'Espagne,* 2:18–19. Other financial firms were in similar straits, for example, the Banque Hervás, whose ties with the Spanish government were well known. Duchêne, *Guerre et finances,* 121–23.

44. Payard, *Ouvrard,* 127; Buist, *At spes non fracta,* 289.

45. Marion, Payard, and Ramon analyzed the crisis primarily as a banking phenomenon. Recently, some historians have observed the confluence of hitherto obscured factors: deficits in France's trade and current accounts, coupled with stagnation in manufactures. See Marion, *Histoire financière,* vol. 4; Payard, *Ouvrard;* Ramon, *Banque de France;* Chabert, *Essai,* 362–65; and esp. Bergeron, "Problèmes économiques," and Bouvier, "Apropos de la crise," 506–13. Soboul has summarized the recent views in Braudel and Labrousse, *Histoire économique et sociale,* 3, pt. 1: 88–91. Buist's analysis of the "Franco-Spanish crisis" emphasizes the interruption of

peso flows between Spain and France—between Spain's Hacienda and the Banque de France. *At spes non fracta,* 301–3.

46. Ramon, *Banque de France,* 63–64.

47. Jean Bouvier noted deficits in France's trade balance with Spain and the Low Countries just before 1805 and proposes a "hemorrhage" of invisibles accounting for balance-of-payments deficits. "Apropos de la crise," 509.

48. In 1795 observers noted the drop in levels of consumption in France and concluded that only "débouchées chez l'Étranger" could help manufacturers. "Observations sur de nouvelles liaisons de commerce entre la France et l'Espagne," forwarded to Comité de Salut Public, Thermidor, An 3, ANPar, AF III, 61, dossier 2245, plaque 4, fol. 6r.

49. Chabert, *Essai,* 363–65 and n. 85. Cf. ibid., 363: "La défaut de l'exportation de produits empêche les commandes et laisse les ouvriers sans travail." Fear of the social consequences of prolonged unemployment led the comte de Chaptal to urge direct loans to manufacturers, and he was seconded by Jean-Baptiste Champagny. Arnna, *Napoléon et son temps,* 76. Note that the prohibition of English products was issued in February 1806. Braudel and Labrousse, *Histoire économique et sociale,* 3, pt. 1: 90–91.

50. Payard, *Ouvrard,* 122–27.

51. Barbé-Marbois to Beurnonville, in Marion, *Histoire financière,* 4:278.

52. Ibid., 279. Bouvier has remarked that French businessmen were wary of the expansionist policy of the French Empire: "De larges milieux de la bourgeoisie d'affaires n'ont jamais adhéré ni longuement, ni totalment, a la politique de l'empereur de la bourgeoisie." "Apropos de la crise," 507.

53. Marion, *Histoire financière,* 4:28; Fugier, *Napoléon et l'Espagne,* 2:163. According to Odette Viennet, news of the formation of the Third Coalition against France undermined confidence in the banknotes of the Banque de France. Meanwhile, the Banque's cash reserves were already committed to supporting the Compagnie des Négociants Réunis. *Napoléon et l'industrie française,* 30 n. 1.

54. Perregaux, "Observations historiques sur la crise," 386, 388; Fugier, *Napoléon et l'Espagne,* 2:15–16; Ramon, *Banque de France,* 67. In April 1805 the Banque's cash reserves were 23 million francs; in September they plummeted to 1.2 million, and by December they had recovered to 12 million. By 1807 the average reserve topped 28 million. Ibid., 63–64, 80; Payard, *Ouvrard,* 114–15.

When the Banque entered the open market to buy *pesos,* several of its regents bought them for resale to the Banque two hours later "avec un gros bénéfice." Pelet de la Lozère, *Opinion de Napoléon,* quoted in Payard, *Ouvrard,* 139. The flow of *pesos* into Paris, especially from nearby *départments,* led Mollien to observe sardonically that silver was lacking everywhere but on the highways of France. Fugier, *Napoléon et l'Espagne,* 2:280.

55. Ramon, *Banque de France,* 70, 72.

56. Marion, *Histoire financière,* 4:278.

57. Ramon, *Banque de France,* 65–67.

58. Payard, *Ouvrard,* 123. Apparently, delayed payment of the Compagnie's drafts on Spain was the critical factor in its bankruptcy; the drafts represented 43% of its total assets. Marion, *Histoire financière,* 4:284 n. 1; Viennet, *Napoléon et l'industrie française,* 30 n. 1.

59. Arnna, *Napoléon et son temps,* annexe 1, 393.

60. Ramon, *Banque de France,* 70.

61. Payard, *Ouvrard,* 126–27; Buist, *At spes non fracta,* 302.

62. Bouvier, "Apropos de la crise," 508.

63. Arnna, *Napoléon et son temps,* annexe 2, 393.

64. Payard, *Ouvrard,* 135; Marion, *Histoire financière,* 4:284; Fugier, *Napoléon et l'Espagne,* 2:21. The involvement of the Banque de France to support the Compagnie led Napoleon to conclude that "la France manque d'hommes qui sachent ce que c'est qu'une banque." Ramon, *Banque de France,* 77.

65. In its investigation of the "énorme affaire" the commission gathered ninety-six documents, which constituted "une des curiosités de nos archives de finances." Oddly, in 1809 these *pièces justificatives* were mislaid, only to be recovered in 1814. Most of the correspondence disappeared. Payard, *Ouvrard,* 138–39.

66. Conseil Administratif des Finances, "Procès verbal," 17 Feb. 1806, in Arnna, *Napoléon et son temps,* annexe 2, 391.

67. A defender of the Compagnie des Négociants Réunis, Maurice Payard none-theless so concluded. *Ouvrard,* 140.

68. Arnna, *Napoléon et son temps,* 393.

69. Ibid., 391–93.

70. Lacépède to Napoleon, 28 Feb. 1806, ANPar, AF 1680.

71. AAEPar, CP, Espagne, 67, fol. 3r.

72. Payard, *Ouvrard,* 198; Buist, *At spes non fracta,* 306–8; Fugier, *Napoléon et l'Espagne,* 2:21–22.

Franco-Spanish Financial Agreement, 1806
  (francs)

	French Claims	Final Settlement
Espinosa's drafts on Madrid	32,582,351	24,000,000
Collectible in Spain [?]	34,375,163	34,375,163
Collectible in colonies	37,500,000	
Total	104,457,514	58,375,163
(or in *pesos* of 3.5 francs per *peso*)	28,421,960	16,678,618
Collectible in colonies (*pesos*)	20,535,761	9,821,475

Sources: Adapted from Payard, *Ouvrard,* 149; and "Convention, 10 Mai 1806," AAEPar, CP, Espagne, supplément 20, fols. 28r–30r.

73. Payard, *Ouvrard,* 150.

74. Godoy to Izquierdo, 16 Feb. 1806, ANPar, AF 1680.

75. Pichon, "Observations," AAEPar, M et D, Angleterre, 11, fol. 39v. In 1795, for example, deputies of Lyon had noted that as a result of the war ending that year, much of the market in Spain and its colonies for *étoffes, passementerie,* and *broderie* had been taken over by English merchants "en les remplaçant dans le gout des es-pagnols par les produits de leurs propres manufactures et de leurs établissements dans l'Inde." Députés extraordinaires de la Commune de Lyon to Comité de Salut Public, 19 Thermidor An 3, ANPar, AF II, 64, dossier 470, no. 22.

76. Arnna, *Napoléon et son temps,* 63, 67, 71.

77. Fugier, *Napoléon et l'Espagne,* 2:21–22.

78. AAEPar, M et D, Espagne, 152; ANPar, AF IV, 1608[b], plaque 2[1].

14. "La tempestad que nos amenazaba"

EPIGRAPHS: Junta Económica, Consulado de la Habana, 17 Oct. 1811; Sorel, "La diplomatie française," 277–278; Bernardo Iriarte, 20 Mar. 1806, BMus, Egerton MS 571, fols. 199r–203r.

1. Bureau de commerce près le Comité de Salut Public, "Rapport," 29 Thermidor An 3, ANPar, AF II, 64, dossier 470, no. 31.

2. "Aperçu sur une expédition en Espagne," ANPar, AF II, 64, dossier 471, no. 27.

3. *Official Papers relating to the Dispute between . . . Great Britain and Spain . . . Nootka Sound* (London, 1790); Pethick, *Nootka Connection.*

4. Chambre de Commerce de la cy-devant Normandie, "Addresse à l'Assemblée Nationale par les Sindics," 22 Mar. 1791, and "Trouble de St. Domingue," ANPar, D[xxv] 79, dossier 746, no. 46.

5. Junta Económica, Consulado de la Habana, 17 Oct. 1811, signed by conde de Santa Maria de Loreto, Francisco Laiseca, and Pedro Juan de Erice.

6. ANPar, AE, B III, 373; "Députés extraordinaires de la Commune de Lyon" to Comité de Salut Public, 19 Thermidor An 3. Bernardo Iriarte estimated that 7,664 men, women, and children were expelled from Spain, about 59% of the French resident there in 1791. However, about 10,000 émigrés, including nonjuring clergy, entered Spain. Iriarte Papers, AHN, Estado, 2817; ANPar, AF III, 62, dossier 250, plaque 1, nos. 46, 48 (30 Aug., 9 Sept. 1796).

7. "Aperçu sur une expédition en Espagne."

8. "Mémoire instructif" to the Assemblée Nationale, 23 Sept. 1792, AAEPar, M et D, Espagne, 209, fol. 233v; "Base d'un nouveau traité de commerce avec l'Espagne," ANPar, AE, B III, 335; "Aperçu sur une expédition en Espagne."

9. "Mémoire secret: Pièces sur les avantages d'un traité de commerce entre la république française et l'Espagne," Nov. 1795, AAEPar, M et D, Espagne, 210, no. 22; letter to Godoy, 2 Mar. 1796, AHN, Estado, 3208[2].

10. Bernardo Iriarte to Domingo Iriarte, AHN, Estado, 2817.

11. Cf. Louis Peche, negociant à Bayonne, "Extrait d'un mémoire par le citoyen," 10 Dec. 1796, ANPar, AF III, 63, dossier 254, doc. 3: "Le Prince de la Paix avait chargé secrètement deux personnes . . . en qui il mit la plus grande confiance d'un travail relatif à un nouveau pacte commercial avec la France."

12. Bernardo Iriarte to Domingo Iriarte, "Apuntamientos y borradores."

13. Virio, "Reflexiones." Virio was responding to Godoy's request for an "[a] juste de un tratado de comercio con la república francesa." As Virio's friend Bernardo Iriarte put it, France should help Spain to develop its "industria, opulencia, comercio y navegación mercantil . . . si quiere tener en ella una Aliada poderosa." AHN, Estado, 2817.

14. Castro, *Historia de Cádiz,* 551–603; Fugier, *Napoléon et l'Espagne,* 2:146; Bourgoing, *Tableau de l'Espagne moderne,* 3:164; Grandmaison, *L'ambassade française,* 308–9; AGI, Consulados, Correspondencia, 238, fol. 112v; Lohmann Villena, *Los americanos,* 2:451–52.

15. Francisco Solano, "Mémoire en espagnol et en français," Paris, 24 Feb. 1796, ANPar, AF III, 57, dossier 224, plaque 1, no. 14, probably an intercepted, then decoded document.

16. Fugier, *Napoléon et l'Espagne,* 1:109.

17. Sorel, "La diplomatie française," 246.

18. Delacroix to the French embassy at Madrid, AAEPar, CP, Espagne, supplément 18, fols. 19v–20v; Fugier, *Napoléon et l'Espagne,* 1:109.

19. Dhermand, consul general, to Paris, 5 Fructidor An 4, AAEPar, CC, 32, fols. 93v–94r; Bureau du commerce près du Comité de Salut Public, 8 Fructidor An 3, ANPar, AF III, 62, dossier 250, plaque l, doc. 6.

20. Louis Peche, "Extrait . . . de mémoire . . . traités de commerce avec l'Espagne," 10 Dec. 1796, ANPar, AF III, 63, dossier 254, doc. 4; Bernardo Iriarte to Domingo Iriarte, AHN, Estado, 2517.

21. Bernardo Iriarte to Domingo Iriarte, AHN, Estado, 2517. Cf. "Observations sur de nouvelles liaisons de commerce," ANPar, AF III, 61, dossier 245, plaque 4, fol. 1r: "Le seul moyen de suplir á un certain point au vide immense que la ruine des colonies à sucre fera éprouver à notre commerce."

22. "Observations sur de nouvelles liaisons de commerce," fol. 1r.

23. The members of Lyon's commercial association expected the French government "tourner toute son industrie vers la culture de son sol, renoncer a devenir manufacturière, telles doivent être les vues et la conduite de l'Espagne." Bureau consultatif du Commerce à Lyon to Relations Extérieures, "Extrait d'un mémoire sur le projet de traité de commerce avec l'Espagne," 25 Floréal An 5, ANPar, AF III, 62, dossier 250, plaque 1, doc. 49.

24. Ministre de l'Intérieur, "Observations générales sur un traité de commerce avec l'Espagne," ibid.

25. "Observations sur de nouvelles liaisons de commerce." On a proto–customs union, see "[que] tous nos ports d'Europe et des deux Indes soient réciproquement ouverts à tous nos navigateurs des deux nations."

26. Bernardo Iriarte, AHN, Estado, 2817; "Bases d'un nouveau traité de commerce avec l'Espagne," ANPar, AF III, 63, dossier 252, doc. 26.

27. "On [Abbeville] demande la liberté du commerce direct avec les possessions espagnoles aux Indes." "Dépouillement de renseignements sur les moyens." ANPar, AE B III, 345.

28. "Observations sur de nouvelles liaisons de commerce."

29. "Observations sur les bases d'un traité," fol. 267v. AAEPar, Met D, Espagne, 209.

30. Ibid.

31. "D'un traité de commerce avec l'Espagne: Des causes de la décadence du commerce français en Espagne et les moyens de la rétablir," ANPar, AE, B III, 335.

32. Ibid.

33. Technical improvements, their diffusion in France's cotton textile manufacture, and growth in output after 1799 may account for the recommendation that "[l]'objet sur lequel le Gouvernement français doit insister particulièrement, c'est sur la libre entrée des étoffes de coton de ses manufactures." These exports were calculated at 40 million francs per annum. "Observations sur les bases d'un traité," fol. 270r. On silk exports, see Consul Roquesante to Paris, 23 Frimaire An 5, ANPar, AF III, 63, dossier 254, doc. 2.

34. "Observations sur les bases d'un traité," fol. 270r.

35. Bourgoing, "Bases d'un nouveau traité de commerce avec l'Espagne," ANPar, AF III, 62, dossier 250, plaque 1, doc. 6.

36. Dhermand, to Paris, 5 Fructidor An 4, AAEPar, fols. 92r–94r. On departing Paris for his post at Madrid, Dhermand was instructed specifically to make "commerce de la France avec l'Espagne un des objets les plus essentiels de ses méditations et ses réflexiones." "Supplément aux instructions du citoyen Dhermand," 11 Vendémiaire An 4, AnPar, AF III, 64, dossier 469, doc. 66.

37. Truguet to Directoire, 4 Ventose, 2, 10, 14 Germinal An 6 (1798), ANPar, AF III, 63, dossier 256, doc. 32.

38. Truguet to Directoire, 23 Brumaire An 6 (1797), ibid., doc. 14.

39. Truguet to Merlin, 4 Ventose An 6, ibid., doc. 28.

40. Hauterive, *State of the French Republic at the End of the Year VIII.* See also idem, *Résultat de la politique de l'Angleterre.*

41. Hauterive, *De l'état de la France,* 104, 310. Hauterive and Fernand de Cussy coedited *Recueil des traités de commerce et de navigation de la France, avec les puissances Étrangères.*

42. Monfor, *Histoire de la vie.*

43. Baillou, *Les affaires étrangères et le corps diplomatique français,* 1:299, 328, 381, 391.

44. Thomas, *Cuba,* 56; Arthur Lévy, *Capitalistes,* 2:121, 450.

45. Hauterive, *De l'état de la France,* 58, 109; hereafter cited in the text.

46. Théremen to Directoire, 19 Mar. 1798, ANPar, AF III, 63, dossier 256, doc. 22; Azanza to Godoy, Paris, 26 Nov. 1799, BRAHM, Sempere y Guarinos, 13, fols. 376r–378r.

47. Canga Argüelles, *Diccionario de hacienda,* 1:122; Clercq, *Recueil des traités,* 1:247.

48. Fugier, *Napoléon et l'Espagne,* 1:9.

49. "Observations sur les bases d'un traité," fol. 268v.

50. Boislecomte, "Etude," fol. 93r–v.

51. Labène to Directoire?, 19 Jan. 1797, ANPar, AF III, 63, dossier 254, doc. 53.

52. Directoire to Pérignon, 9 June 1796, AAEPar, CP, Espagne, supplément 18, fols. 28r–30r.

53. "Traité d'alliance offensive et défensive entre la République française et Sa Majesté Catholique le Roi d'Espagne," ibid., fols. 4r–11v.

54. The threat of an English attack on New Spain was behind Madrid's haste to arrange a treaty of defense with France. Cf. Boislecomte, "Étude," fol. 93r–v.

55. Ministre des Relations Extérieures au Général Perignon, ambassadeur de la République à Madrid, 3 Floréal An 4, AAEPar, CP, Espagne, supplément 18, fols. 16r–21v.

56. Clercq, *Recueil des traités,* 1:287–89. Secret clauses obligated Spain to pressure Portugal to close its ports to English shipping in a war between England and the two allies and authorized French citizens to cut logwood in Yucatán.

57. Instructions to Pérignon, 1793, AAEPar, CP, Espagne, supplément 18, fols. 205r–209r; Labène to Directoire, 13 July 1797, ibid., fol. 160r.

58. Pérignon to Delacroix, 9 Aug. 1796, ibid., fol. 59r.

59. ANPar, AF III, 62, dossier 242, plaque 1.

60. Labène to Directoire, 29 Feb. 1797, ANPar, AF III, 63, dossier 254.

61. Fugier, *Napoléon et l'Espagne*, 1:163.

62. *France: Balance of Trade with Spain, 1795–1797 and 1801*
    (*reales de vellón*)

	To Spain	From Spain	Balance (+/−)
1795	175,000,000	84,500,000	+90,500,000
1796	184,821,154	33,790,841	+121,030,307
1797	144,278,661	31,479,512	+112,799,149
1801	217,465,200	289,690,000	−72,224,800

Source: Canga Argüelles, *Diccionario de hacienda*, 1:129.
Note: Chaptal claimed that the 1801 data reflected France's heavy imports of Spanish wools, soda ash, oils, and other raw materials.

63. AAEPar, CP, Espagne, supplément 18, fol. 333.

64. *Trade with Spain as % of Total Trade of France, 1801*

	To Spain			From Spain	
All Exports	*reales de vellón*	%	All Imports	*reales de vellón*	%
312.207,000	217,465,200	69.6	378,862,000	289,690,000	76.4

Source: Canga Argüelles, *Diccionario de hacienda*, 1:127.

65. Fugier, *Napoléon et l'Espagne*, 1:210–11 and n. 1.
66. ANPar, AF III, 1679, 18 Pluviose An 11.
67. Canga Argüelles, *Diccionario de hacienda*, 1:122.
68. Ibid., 135.
69. Ibid., 124. Bernardo Iriarte observed that at Amiens, for the first time in more than a century, Spain's negotiators had not renewed commercial concessions conceded in seventeenth-century treaties with England and France. Iriarte to Antonio Ximénez Navarro, 20 May 1806, BMus, Egerton MS 571, fol. 203r.
70. Canga Argüelles, *Diccionario de hacienda*, 1:126–28.
71. Ibid., 135.

French Import Duties on Selected Colonial Staples, 1788 and 1801
    (*reales de vellón* per *quintal*)

	1788		1801	
	French Colonies	Spanish Colonies	French Colonies	Spanish Colonies
Cotton	n.d.	12	4	6
Indigo	9	20	20	30
Sugar, raw	28	28	6	90
Sugar, refined	160	160	200	200
Cocoa	4	8	12	150
Hide (per)	2	2	100	160
Coffee	400	n.d.	200	150

Source: Canga Argüelles, *Diccionario de hacienda*, 1:123, 136.

72. Canga Argüelles, *Diccionario de hacienda*, 1:122–23, 136.
73. Godoy to Talleyrand, 30 Mar. 1803, AAEPar, CP, Espagne, 19 (supplément), no. 72, fol. 203r.
74. Canga Argüelles, *Diccionario de hacienda*, 1:126. Cf. R. Barde to Ministre de

l'Intérieure, 27 Oct. 1807, AAEPar, CP, Espagne, 672: "Toutes les sortes de vexa-
tions, de chicanes et de difficultés qui pourrait leur susciter par la suite de la jalousie,
la morosité et la malveillance de ces divers agens."

75. Fugier, *Napoléon et l'Espagne*, 1:189–90, summarizes Cadiz's post-1801 commercial revival and its effects.

76. José Fernando de Cossío to Toribio Montes, 17 Nov. 1803, AGI, Consulados, Correspondencia, 238, fol. 161r–v.

77. Lucien Bonaparte returned to Paris from his ambassadorship at Madrid
with, in his words, "indépendence de fortune." This included twenty paintings from
the Real Palacio del Retiro, other bargain-priced paintings, and at least 100 *écus* in
diamonds, some of which were later sold at Amsterdam. Fugier, *Napoléon et l'Espagne*,
1:175–76 and n. 1.

78. Napoleon believed, according to Fugier, that Spain's "renom de richesse"
was justified by the "fortune que des negociateurs avisés pouvaient acquérir chez
elle." Ibid., 183.

79. Ibid., 194–96, 205–6. Hervás bought the Parisian town house of Spain's
duque del Infantado to install his merchant bank; the *palais* was subsequently sold
to Talleyrand. Ibid., 261.

80. Grandmaison, *L'ambassade française*, 252–53.

81. Fugier, *Napoléon et l'Espagne*, 1:205, 217, 219, 221, 223, 240.

82. Godoy, *Memorias*, 1:389–90.

83. Ibid., 390.

84. Ibid., 391; Fugier, *Napoléon et l'Espagne*, 1:242–43, 263–64; Clercq, *Recueil des
traités*, 2:82–84.

85. *Papers Relative to the Discussion*, 45.

86. Bernardo Iriarte, Feb., 12 Nov. 1804, "Apuntamientos," AHN, Estado, 2817.

87. Godoy to Bonaparte, 21 Dec. 1806, ANPar, AF IV, 1680, dossier 7, doc. 23,
fols. 332r–333r.

88. Bernardo Iriarte, 25 Oct. 1805, Iriarte Papers, BMus, Egerton MS 282, fol.
28r.

89. Letter, Madrid, to Iriarte, 15 Mar. 1805, "Apuntamientos," AHN, Estado,
2817.

90. Fugier, *Napoléon et l'Espagne*, 2:128.

91. Morazé, *Les bourgeois conquérants*, 1:131.

92. Letter to Iriarte, 30 Sept. 1806, Iriarte Papers, BMus, Egerton MS 383.

93. Vandeul to Talleyrand, 6 Oct. 1806, AAEPar, CP, Espagne, 670, fols.
352r–354r.

94. Fugier, *Napoléon et l'Espagne*, 2:130. Fugier concluded that Godoy now
sought a rapprochement with England in order to get Spain out of the war. Ibid.,
121.

95. Chabannes, "Aperçu des moyens faciles par lesquels le gouvernement français peu se rendre maître du cabinet de Madrid et procurer à la France le commerce
presqu'exclusif de toutes les Possessions Espagnoles," 6 Dec. 1807, AAEPar, CP,
Espagne, 672, fol. 379v. Bonaparte's collaborators convinced him that Spain was
capable of a significant contribution to his conflict with England if it were governed
"à la française." Baillou, *Les affaires étrangères et le corps diplomatique français*, 1:492.
Similarly, Alexandre Laborde believed that Bonaparte wished to form his "nouvel

ordre social" outside France "par un administration habile" rather than by radical social change, which "il ne lui convenait pas d'accorder." *Aperçu*, 10.

96. The term *satellization* was purportedly Talleyrand's. Baillou, *Les affaires étrangères et le corps diplomatique français*, 1:459.

97. Chabert, *Essai*, 303, 367–68 and n. 107.

98. Bruno Lafite to Le Roy, French consul at Cadiz, 25 Nov. 1805, and [Lafite?] to Le Roy, An 14, AAEPar, CC, 96, fols. 406r–407r, and CC, 97 n. 1.

99. Chambre de Commerce de Carcassonne, "Mémoire: Tableau de comparaison des droits perçus jusqu'en avril de 1806 sur les draps ordinaires de Carcassonne à leur introduction en Espagne," and Ministre de l'Intérieure Champagne to Talleyrand, 25 June 1806, AAEPar, CP, Espagne, 670, fols. 59r–60r.

100. AAEPar, CP, Espagne, 670, fol. 305r.

101. Cadiz, 27 Thermidor An 8, AAEPar, CC, 93, fol. 238r.

102. Antoine Crisp, "Réflexions," 3 Mar. 1806, ANPar, F^{12} 506, no. 7.

103. Ouvrard, *Mémoires,* 1:67, 87.

104. Ouvrard le jeune, "Notes sur le Mexique (1802)," ANPar, AF IV, 1211.

105. Anon., ibid., nos. 24, 26.

106. "Mémoire sur les possessions espagnoles de l'Amérique méridionale," 1 Feb. 1806, to Murat, AAEPar, M et D, Amérique, 33, fols. 217r–218v. Bonaparte's decisiveness fascinated the elites in the Spanish colonies, François-Joseph de Pons reported. "Le nom de l'empereur a fait une si profonde impression dans le continent de l'Amérique." Letter of 4 June 1806, ANPar, AF IV, 1211, nos. 20–23.

107. Materials in ANPar, AF IV, 12ll, reveal the imperialist views of French interest groups on the Caribbean and circum-Caribbean areas and on India, Madagascar, Cochin China, and the Philippines.

108. Pons, "Mémoire sur la cession de la capitainerie générale de Caracas à la France," 1806, ANPar, AF IV, 1211.

109. "Memoire secret: Coup d'oeil politique et secret."

110. Pons, "Mémoire sur la cession de la capitainerie générale de Caracas à la France." For Pons's major analysis, see idem, *Voyage à la partie orientale de la Terre-Ferme.*

111. "Mémoire secret: Coup d'oeil politique et secret."

112. Fugier, *Napoléon et l'Espagne,* 2:386. On Liniers, see Groussac, *Santiago de Liniers;* and Lozier Almazán, *Liniers y su tiempo.*

113. The number estimated was as high as twenty thousand. Champagny to Beauharnais, 19 Oct. 1807, AAEPar, CP, Espagne, 672, fol. 170r.

114. "Mémoire secret: Coup d'oeil politique et secret," fols. 29r, 33r–34r, 39v, 41r, 45r–47r; Fugier, *Napoléon et l'Espagne,* 1:195.

115. Cf. "Mémoire secret: Précis sur les avantages d'un traité de commerce": "Le but essentiel . . . seroit de tâcher de pouvoir autoriser nos batiments marchands à mettre pied dans les établissements espagnols"; and "Dépouillement de renseignements sur les moyens"; Talleyrand to Beauharnais, 8 Aug. 1807, AAEPar, CP, Espagne, 671, no. 418: "La liberté du commerce direct avec les possessions espagnoles aux Indes."

116. Fugier, *Napoléon et l'Espagne,* 2:307.

117. Ibid., 258.

118. Ibid., 254–56, 259.

119. Ibid., 262.

120. Sorel, "La diplomatie française," 277; Fugier, *Napoléon et l'Espagne*, 2:262.

121. Fugier, *Napoléon et l'Espagne*, 2:259.

122. Barde to Napoleon, 6 July 1807, ANPar, K, 907.

123. Barde to Ministre de l'Intérieure, 27 Oct. 1807, AAEPar, CP, Espagne, 672, fols. 211r–216v. Abbé de Pradt at this moment pointed out that a major source of income in central and southwestern France was the "relations commerciales avec l'Espagne." Pradt, *Mémoires historiques*, 239.

124. Barde to Ministre de l'Intérieure, Bordeaux, 27 Oct. 1807, fols. 211r–216v.

125. Chabannes, "Aperçu des moyens faciles," AAEPar, CP, Espagne, 672, fols. 379r–382v.

126. Pradt, *Mémoires historiques*, 131, quoted in Fugier, *Napoléon et l'Espagne*, 2:307, 386 n. 4.

127. Cretêt, "Commerce de la France avec l'Espagne," 4 Feb. 1808, ANPar, AF IV, 174; Fugier, *Napoléon et l'Espagne*, 2:16 n. 1, 386 n. 2. Predictably, the main French manufacturing interests complaining to Cretêt were the linen producers of Rheims, Amiens, Abbeville, and Le Mans and woolen groups of Carcassonne, Elboeuf, Sedan, and Aix-la-Chapelle.

128. Champagny to Bonaparte, 1808, AAEPar, CP, Espagne, 673, fols. 138r–141r.

129. M. Auguste, "Extrait de mémoire sur les colonies espagnoles en Amérique, en février et mars 1808," ibid., fols. 479ff. Abad y Queipo, who had spent some time in France, understood French merchants' desire to expand their sales to the Spanish colonies. "Representación," Mar. 1809, in Mora, *Obras sueltas*, 242.

130. Ouvrard to Bonaparte, 22 Mar. 1808, AAEPar, CP, Espagne, 673, fol. 397r.

131. Fugier, *Napoléon et l'Espagne*, 2:307; Iriarte, "Apuntamientos y anuncios fatales," AHN, Estado, 2817.

132. Fugier, *Napoléon et l'Espagne*, 2:307.

133. Ibid., 1:60–61, 73, 208–9, 313, 434, 2:47; AHN, Estado, 2855^2, no. 40; ANPar, AF 1680 (28 Feb. 1806); AAEPar, M et D, Espagne, 152, fol. 58r; La Forest, *Correspondence*, 1:332; Elorza, *La ideología en la ilustración española*, 141; Berryer, *Souvenirs*, 1:328–30; Lafuente, *Historia general*, 16:172; Godoy, *Memorias*, 2:79, 282–83; Townsend, *Journey*, 2:270–72.

134. Godoy refers to the shopping list of French demands as "especies y cuestiones proponibles." *Memorias*, 2:270–77. See also Fugier, *Napoléon et l'Espagne*, 2:414, 435.

135. "Copie du rapport sur les relations commerciales de la France presenté a SM par le ministre de l'intérieure," 4 Feb 1808, AAEPar, CP, Espagne, 673.

136. Fugier, *Napoléon et l'Espagne*, 2:436.

137. Godoy, *Memorias*, 2:274.

138. Ibid., 512; AAEPar, CP, Espagne, 673, fol. 204r. Duroc and Talleyrand's demands (24 Mar. 1808) are in AAEPar, CP, Espagne, 673; Godoy, *Memorias*, 2:512–15; and Pérez Guzmán, 1:209 n. 2.

139. Fugier, *Napoléon et l'Espagne*, 2:437. Godoy omits any reference to granting French shippers permission to enter Spain's colonial ports. *Memorias*, 2:282.

140. "Réflections impartielles sur l'état actuel de l'Espagne (Victoria, 1808)," AAEPar, M et D, Espagne, 152, fol. 116r; Champagny, circular to the Spanish colo-

nies, 17 May 1808 (received at Veracruz 10 Aug. 1808), Servicio Histórico Militar, Fraile, 61:201v; Berryer, *Souvenirs,* 2:329–30.

141. Fugier, *Napoléon et l'Espagne,* 2:386 n. 4.

142. Virio to Bernardo Iriarte, 26 Apr. 1808, AHN, Estado, 2817, Virio's emphasis.

15. The National Drama, Act I

EPIGRAPHS: Martí Gilabert, *El proceso de El Escorial,* 37; Simón de Viegas to Godoy (unsent), Nov. 1807, ARPal, Papeles reservados de Fernando VII, vol. 2, fol. 625r.

1. Corona Baratech, *Las ideas políticas,* 39.

2. Anes Àlvarez, prologue to Rúspoli, *Godoy,* 12.

3. Palacio Atard once classified the factions as "críticos prudentes, revolucionarios ilusos, timeratos pusilánimes." *Agotamiento y decadencia en la España del siglo XVII,* quoted in Corona Baratech, *Las ideas políticas,* 10–11.

4. Domínguez Ortiz, *Sociedad y estado,* 498, quoted in Enciso Recio, "Presentación," 21.

5. Enciso Recio, "Presentación," 42.

6. Corona Baratech places Caballero in the "artido reaccionanario, conservador y enemigo de las reformas." *Las ideas políticas,* 41.

7. Caballero, "Réflexiones," May 1808, ANPar, AF IV, 1608^b, plaque 2^{iii}. The presence of the aristocratic-clerical opposition was, of course, recognized by Charles, María Luisa, and Godoy by 1805, if not earlier. Anonymous, often scurrilous, verses posted in Madrid were a clear indication. The high clerical establishment, critical of the late *proyectistas,* "desplegaba un celo especial contra aquellos ilustrados que urgían la reforma de las estructuras económicas fiscales." Juan Rico Giménez, "Godoy y Sempere y Guarinos," in Melón Jiménez, La Parra López, and Perez González, *Godoy y su tiempo,* 2:266.

8. Henao y Muñóz, *Los borbones,* 2:365.

9. Charles IV and María Luisa had wind of Fernando's involvement with the informal, aristocratic political opposition. Using the occasion of Fernando's formal weekly meetings with his parents, they searched his apartments for materials of possible conspiratorial activity and found them.

Basic sources of the Causa del Escorial are Archivo Secreto de Fernando VII (hereafter ARPal, AS, F VII); Escoiquiz, *Memorias, BAE* 97:1–152; and Godoy, *Memorias.* French sources consulted include AAEPar, CP, Espagne, 671–72; and ANPar, AF IV. Major secondary works include Fugier, *Napoléon et l'Espagne;* Izquierdo Hernández, *Antecedentes;* and Martí Gilabert, *El proceso de El Escorial,* clearly the most succinct reference to the Causa. For the recent revisionist views of a much maligned Godoy, see ibid.; Rúspoli, *Godoy;* and La Parra López, *Manuel Godoy.*

10. ARPal, AS, F VII, vol. 1, fols. 125r–147r. These documents are reproduced wholly or partly in Escoiquiz, *Memorias, BAE* 97:79–96.

11. Godoy, *Memorias,* 2:193–95; Izquierdo Hernández, *Antecedentes,* 232–33. Escoiquiz often referred Fernando to the story of San Hermenegildo, son of a Gothic king of Seville, who appealed to Justinian to halt the persecution of his stepmother, Gumersinda, and Hermenegildo's chief minister, Sisberto. Escoiquiz used these figures in alluding to Godoy, María Luisa, and Napoleon in his secret correspondence with Fernando. Fernando remained devoted to San Hermenegildo,

who was the subject of a dramatic parable celebrating his enthronement four months later. In 1814, on his return from exile in France, Fernando established the Orden de San Hermenegildo.

12. The royal family's unquestioning trust in Godoy comes through in a comment to him by María Luisa: "Dice el rey que tú hagas cuanto haya que hacer, que es lo que quiere, y que todo lo aprueba y lo sostendrá todo." Rúspoli, *Godoy,* 51.

13. For strikingly revisionist views of Godoy and his role, see La Parra López, *Manuel Godoy;* and Rúspoli, *Godoy.* For a synthesis of the earlier, mainly anti-Godoy literature, see ibid., 27; and La Parra López, *Manuel Godoy,* 27–30.

14. José Pablo Carrasco, "Godoy y la estadística española del Antiguo Régimen," in Melón Jiménez, La Parra López, and Perez González, *Godoy y su tiempo,* 1:211.

15. Cf. Alberola Romá, "La política económica en tiempos de Godoy," 409: "[Godoy] propició el despliegue de una política claramente avanzada para la España de su tiempo, apoyando y apoyándose en los grupos ilustrados del país y haciendo frente a la constante ofensiva política del partido aristocrático."

16. Helman, *Jovellanos y Goya,* 34.

17. Anes Álvarez, prologue to Rúspoli, *Godoy,* 17.

18. María Luisa to Godoy, 19 Oct. 1806, in Rúspoli, *Godoy,* 51. The colonial problem was behind one of Godoy's "proyectos políticos innovadores, como que en lugar de virreyes fuesen los infantes a América con el título de príncipes regentes," a revival of Aranda's suggestion to Charles in 1781. Ibid., 28.

19. Corona Baratech claims that the younger nobility always admired Aranda, "su oráculo, la cual no podían disimular la amargura que sufria con la caída y proscripción del conde de Aranda." Their bitterness never waned. *Revolución y reacción,* 275.

20. Caballero has received a generally derogatory press. At one point he urged Godoy not to resign, since "no hay nadie que no tema una gran ruina se me alejo de mi asiento." Years later, to be sure, Escoiquiz accused him of maintaining a "secreta inteligencia con el gobierno francés." Rúspoli, *Godoy,* 88–89; Escoiquiz, *Idea sencilla,* 15.

21. Small wonder that Godoy, at his last public ceremony, remarked to two clerics: "Yo estoy en el caso de desear vestirme . . . un saco, e ir a encerrarme a un desierto." Rúspoli, *Godoy,* 90.

22. Perhaps these were the aristocratic dissidents María Luisa had in mind when she reportedly excused Fernando's participation in the plot with "él no tiene culpa . . . sino dos o tres pícaros ambiciosos que le rodean." Pérez Galdós, quoted in Izquierdo Hernández, *Antecedentes,* 239 and n. 3.

23. Godoy, *Memorias,* 2:308. Cf. "Sus consejos, de que los reyes hacían tan grande caso en los negocios internos de su cargo." Ibid., 89.

24. Ibid., 1:258–59.

25. Jovellanos reported to Francisco Saavedra in 1797 that a special junta of Juan Bautista Virio, Juan Sempere y Guarinos, and Severo de Aguirre had been formed to design a project, one that foreshadowed the Caja de Amortización. The junta's report concluded that the government had the power to appropriate certain types of ecclesiastical properties, such as "hospitales, hospicios, patronatos, cofradías, capellanías laicales," many rarely averaging even 3% annually. They should not be sold to *manos muertas* or to *mayorazgos.* Jovellanos, *Diarios,* 2:458–65.

26. Corona Baratech, *Las ideas políticas,* 41. Critics claim that Caballero quietly supported the Inquisition in Jovellanos's removal from Gracia y Justicia. Godoy, *Memorias,* 1:192 n. 183; Helman, *Jovellanos y Goya,* 58.

27. Lafuente, *Historia general,* 15:199. As early as 1795 Caballero was linked to the "reacción tradicionalista y religiosa." Palau Baquero and Orozco Acuaviva, *Malaspina, '92,* 25.

28. At Salamanca Caballero had many friends among the generally traditionalist faculty. Lafuente, *Historia general,* 16:137.

29. Many of Caballero's maternal grandmother's family (Herrera) were in colonial service at Caracas, Havana, and New Spain in the 1790s. AHN, Orden de Carlos III, exp. 1016, no. 366.

30. In the royal household he knew how "aprovecharse de toda la chismografía de los pasillos de palacio." Helman, *Jovellanos y Goya,* 129.

31. See the extended, three-paragraph footnote on Caballero in Izquierdo Hernández, *Antecedentes,* 237.

32. AGI, Mexico, 1315.

33. Caballero may have been a quiet agent of ecclesiastical authorities blocking the work of the Caja de Amortización. Cf. "[O]n vit plusières foi les Prélats s'opposer par des menées secrètes . . . a la vente des fondations pieuses véritablement laiques." AAEPar, M et D, Espagne, 152.

34. There still remains the question why Charles IV and his wife trusted Caballero, whose ties to the clerical opposition they must have been aware of. Some contemporaries developed a strong antipathy toward Caballero, describing him as "gótico, sombrío y atravesado"; Godoy viewed him as an incarnation of Satan. Helman, *Jovellanos y Goya,* 58.

35. Godoy, *Memorias,* 2:195. Godoy's advice to Charles was far more cautious: "disímulo, prudencia y que no se llegase a los procedimiento judiciales" unless absolutely necessary. Izquierdo Hernández, *Antecedentes,* 236.

36. Martí Gilabert, *El proceso de El Escorial,* 235–39.

37. It seems odd that Caballero, in contact with the *partido aristocrático,* was unaware that the major objective of this faction was to secure Bonaparte's support for Godoy's planned ouster.

38. The text of this extraordinary letter (Escoiquiz, *Memorias, BAE* 97:137–38), the draft of which Godoy later claimed to have seen, was not part of the evidence in the subsequent trial; the original does not exist in French archives. It was first published in Paris in the *Moniteur* of 5 February 1810. A Spanish translation was published in Paris in 1814. Llorente, *Memorias,* 2:14; Godoy, *Memorias,* 2:203 n. 201; Izquierdo Hernández, *Antecedentes,* 250–53; Martí Gilabert, *El proceso de El Escorial,* 240–43.

39. Real Decreto, 30 Oct. 1807, Llorente, *Memorias,* 2:16; Godoy, *Memorias,* 2:201–2; Martí, *El proceso de El Escorial,* 240–44; Izquierdo Hernández, *Antecedentes,* 250–51. Caballero's advice to Charles and María Luisa was critical of the whole Causa del Escorial, as Izquierdo Hernández has highlighted. For instance, Caballero called for Árias Mon and other judges to assemble quickly at the Escorial; he recommended trying the Prince de Asturias as a common criminal, and he countersigned and had published the first step of the "proceso del Escorial." Izquierdo Hernández, *Antecedentes,* 235–39. Later Izquierdo Hernández stated his case against Caballero:

"[P]rimer acusador del Príncipe . . . responsable casi absoluto de la formación del Proceso y de la publicidad dada al malhadado asunto. . . . Juez instructor único hasta la constitución del Tribunal por él mismo nombrado y mentor despótico de los magistrados . . . influye en los Jueces hasta conseguir una sentencia más que absolutoria apologética para los acusados." Ibid., 278. Cf. Godoy's view: "[E]l verdadero promotor de aquel proceso, él que sabía todas las cosas, él que les dió más fuego." *Memorias,* 2:190, 343.

40. Escoiquiz, *Memorias, BAE* 97:23. Infantado claimed that he had destroyed the decree on learning of the seizure of Fernando's papers, but Escoiquiz later reconstructed it from memory, producing—probably with the assistance of his lawyer, Madrid Dávila—a document in convincing legal jargon that was entered into the evidence of the subsequent trial.

41. Ibid., app. 3. Like Charles's letter to Bonaparte of 29 October, Fernando's to Napoleon was not made public by the French until February 1810. Llorente published a Spanish translation in Paris in 1814. Llorente, *Memorias,* 2:1.

42. "Papa mío," runs one letter from the twenty-three-year-old prince. "He delincuado, he faltado a V.M. como rey y como padre, pero me arrepiento, y ofrezco a V.M. la obediencia más humilde. Nada debía hacer sin noticia de V.M.; pero fuí sorprendido. He delatado a los culpables, y pido a V.M. me perdone por haberle metido la otra noche, permitiendo besar sus reales pies su reconocido hijo—Fernando." ARPal, AS, F VII, vol. 1, fols. 157r–158r; Martí Gilabert, *El proceso de El Escorial,* 253; Izquierdo Hernández, *Antecedentes,* 260.

43. *Gaceta de Madrid,* 6 Nov. 1807. Escoiquiz, the duque del Infantado, the conde de Orgaz, el marqués de Ayerbe, el conde de Bornos, and others of Fernando's entourage were confined in the Escorial.

44. Precisely when Charles's letters reached Napoleon remains unclear. Couriers usually took seven days between Madrid and Paris. Napoleon may have received Charles's angry complaint against Beauharnais, dated 3 November, on 11 November and news of the pardon on 15 November. Far less clear are the dates when Fernando's letter of 11 October was actually dispatched and received. The letter did not leave Madrid before 20 or 22 October, perhaps later. Escoiquiz claims that Bonaparte received it after he received Charles's letter accusing Beauharnais of intervening in Spanish affairs. *Memorias, BAE* 97:32. As already noted, no texts or drafts of these letters exist.

45. Beerman has noted that Mon y Velarde supported Charles IV's decision to turn against France after the death of Marie Antoinette, as well as the charges against Malaspina. Palau Baquero and Orozco Acuaviva, *Malaspina, '92,* 46 and n. 49.

46. Hieronymite monks associated with members of the aristocracy are reported to have leaked the verdict to the public. Escoiquiz, *BAE* 97:54.

47. Perhaps the intimate off-color details about the royal family were supplied by Escoiquiz?

48. As Escoiquiz noted in self-congratulatory prose, "Apenas les ví cuando leí en sus semblantes la fortuna que tenía de haber caído en sus manos. Hombres generosos que, penetrados . . . de la inocencia de los pretendidos conspiradores y de que eran otras tantas víctimas de su lealtad y de su amor a la Patria. . . . Sean inmortales vuestros nombres en los fastos de la nobilísima nación española!" *Memorias, BAE* 97:40. Campomanes entered the Order of Carlos III in 1814, and the other inter-

rogator, Benito Arias de Posada (*alcalde de Casa y Corte* as of 1806), was promoted to the Consejo de Castilla after Fernando became king.

49. Briefly ill in 1806, Charles quickly recovered.

50. ARPal, AS, F VII, vol. 1, fols. 990r–996r. Tomás and Manuel Francisco de Jáuregui y Aróstegui were well connected members of the military. Sons of the ex-viceroy of Peru, Martín de Jáuregui, they were both cousins and brothers-in-law of the current viceroy of New Spain, José de Iturrigaray. Their mother, daughter of the ex-director of the Real Compañía de la Habana, was a prominent figure in Madrid society, holding a *tertulia* in her town house. Manuel Francisco's wife, daughter of the Cadiz merchant Casa Iglesias, later was prominent in the *fernandista* movement in Madrid, Cadiz, and New Spain.

51. Testimony of Orgaz and Infantado, ibid., fols. 969r–973r; Martí Gilabert, *El proceso de El Escorial,* 156–64; Izquierdo Hernández, *Antecedentes,* 266.

52. Infantado and Orgaz volunteered that Escoiquiz had once requested 300,000 *reales* "para agasajar a la familia del embajador de Francia" and that they had given him 50,000 and 40,000 *reales,* respectively, in the hope that a marriage between Fernando and a Bonaparte relative might avert Napoleonic designs on Spain. Ibid., fols. 968r–973r, 990r, 993r–995r; Martí Gilabert, *El proceso de El Escorial,* 156–65, 279–83; Izquierdo Hernández, *Antecedentes,* 268–70.

53. Beauharnais to Talleyrand, 27 Aug. 1807, AAEPar, CP, 671, fol. 467r.

54. See esp. the testimony of José Santos Vidaure, a *limeño,* and Angel Sotoca, from Buenos Aires, ARPal, Papales reservados de Fernando VII, vol. 1, fols. 288r, 323r.

55. ARPal, Papales reservados de Fernando VII, vol. 1, fols. 911r–976r; Escoiquiz, "Declaración," 14 Nov. l807, ibid., fol. 944r–v.

56. With the phrase "trastorno universal," did Viegas imply that he grasped the conspirators' objective, to undermine the royal couple in order to open the way for the accession of Fernando? Did he err in exaggerating Escoiquiz's role?

57. Viegas, "Acusación fiscal."

58. Information on Viegas is scant. He had been one of three jurists assigned to review a project to reform higher education proposed by Juan Picornel y Gomila in 1789. He served on the Sala de Alcaldes de Casa y Corte in 1801, and he was subsequently appointed a *fiscal* of the Consejo de Castilla, reflecting recognition of his expertise and responsibility.

59. Jovellanos described Viegas as "de los que leen mucho, ni muchas cosas, pero medita mucho, y esto vale más en un genio original como el suyo y para una ciencia hija de la meditación." Jovellanos, "Carta a Rafael Floranes," 20 Feb. 1807, *BAE* 86:232.

60. ARPal, Papales reservados de Fernando VII, vol. 2, fols. 619r, 648v; Pérez Sánchez and Sayre, *Goya,* lxviii.

61. Viegas, "Papel sin fecha."

62. "By confidants" surely he meant Caballero, Soler, and Gil y Lemos.

63. Perhaps there is a note of deprecation, if not irony, in Viegas's initial reaction to the Causa and to what he perceived as Godoy's insouciance in handling it. Clearly Viegas had little regard for Godoy's perspicacity, political or legal.

64. Note this extreme construction of factual and circumstantial evidence.

65. This was, on the face of it, a criticism of Caballero's advice.

66. Viegas, "Papel sin fecha." These documents, bearing signs of authenticity, were among the papers that Viegas entrusted to the prior of the monastery of the Escorial in mid-December 1807 and handed over to the Consejo de Castilla on 10 April 1808, the day after Fernando left for Bayonne. ARPal, Papales reservados de Fernando VII, vol. 2, fols. 624r–631r, 648r.

67. The "plan de paz" is detailed in Viegas's notes made at Madrid in November 1807 and in his explanatory declaration of 16 December, which he entrusted for safekeeping to the prior of the monastery at El Escorial. ArPal, Papeles reservados de Fernando VII, vol. 2, fols. 617v–619v. A summary is in Viegas's "Representación" presented to Fernando on 30 Mar. 1808. Ibid., vol. 1, fols. 1248r–1249v.

68. Ibid., vol. 2, fol. 648r.

69. Ibid., fol. 619v.

70. Viegas claimed that after reporting Charles IV's dissatisfaction, Godoy had demanded that Viegas surrender any drafts, with the obvious purpose of destroying all evidence. This raises the troublesome question whether Godoy in fact showed Viegas's "plan de paz" to Charles?

71. "Papel . . . escrito y firmado por Viegos en San Lorenzo, 16 Dic. 1807," ibid., fols. 615r–621r; "Papel que se dice . . . borrador de un decreto declarando la inocencia del Rey Nuestro Señor," ibid.; fols. 611r–614r. Both documents were among those given to the prior in mid-December and to the Consejo de Castilla five months later, on 10 April. Ibid., fols. 632r–634r.

72. "Considere VE mi tribulación y mi vergüenza," reads Viegas's appeal to the president of the Consejo de Castilla, "he tenido que hacerme fugitivo, y faltar ayer al Consejo, para librarme del furor del Pueblo." Ibid., fol. 636v. Days later he wrote that "se me acaba de avisar que inflamadaos con la Gazeta Extraordinaria los anímos se conspiras contra mi vida." Ibid., fol. 644r.

73. "Carta ecrita por el Prior de San Lorenzo a Viegas en 21 de marzo en contextación a otra suya que trata de haberle entregado un pliego en el mes de Diciemre." Ibid., fols. 632r–634r. The prior delivered the *pliego* to Infantado on 26 March.

74. "Memorial dirigido al Sr. Presidente del Consejo, 22 de marzo de 1808," ibid., fols. 635r–637r.

75. This *representación* replaced a briefer but substantially similar one of the previous day. ARPal, Papeles reservados de Fernando VII, vol. 1, fols. 1248r–1251v.

76. Ibid., vol. 2, fols. 645r–667r. Possibly this undated *exposición,* apparently completed between 1 and 10 April, was the memorandum Viegas had promised in his 22 March *memorial* to the Consejo de Castilla, which internal evidence indicates he was preparing on March 13. If so, an initial section may have been deleted, since it opens abruptly with a reference to the removal of Godoy and a statement that now that Viegas no longer feared seizure of his papers, he could write more freely about Godoy's role in the Escorial affair. The account of the trial in the *Gaceta de Madrid* of 30 Mar. may have been a factor in Viegas's final explanation, his "Exposición."

77. Ibid., fols. 648v, 652v.

78. Ibid., vol. 1, fol. 1248v.

79. Viegas, however, concluded that Godoy had only read it to María Luisa, since the king's letter, which Godoy showed him, stated that Charles had examined his plan and, while acknowledging its good intention, found it a "montón de desa-

ciertos," especially in the proposal to enhance the power of the Consejo de Castilla. Ibid, vol. 2, fols. 646v–647r.

80. Ibid., fol. 652v.

81. Viegas recalled that he had initially antagonized Godoy when, in a session of the Consejo de Castilla, he opposed Godoy's proposal to offer special privileges to the Basque port of Abando, which would be renamed Puerto de la Paz in Godoy's honor. Ibid.

82. Villafranca was the duque de Medina Sidonia, a wealthy Andalusian grandee; his wife, María Tomasa de Palafox y Portocorrero, was the daughter of the condesa de Montijo, then in internal exile; her brother, Eugenio Eulalio de Palafox, conde de Teba, was a confirmed *fernandista* who, as conde de Montijo in early 1808, was prominent in the *fernandista* insurgency.

83. Viegas does not elaborate on the circumstances of an earlier exile.

84. Ibid., fols. 652v–656v.

85. Viegas added that he perceived this only when writing it, since "las irregularidades sobre que hay que calcular son tantas y de una naturaleza tan extravagante y desconocida, la admiración se lo lleva todo, sin dar casi lugar al cálculo del orden que tiene entre sí, y dependencias de unas y otras." Ibid., fol. 652r–v.

86. Ibid., fols. 656v–657r.

87. On this probably premeditated occasion, Godoy brought out a poor guitar, which Viegas proceeded to play for Godoy, Padre Estela, and others present.

88. Ibid., fol. 657r–v.

89. Viegas wrote that even had he not yet resolved to accuse Infantado and Escoiquiz of treason—Charles's decree and the principals' confessions left no legal alternative—he would have done so, since "la situación de las cosas era para mí una amenaza muy terrible . . . de muerte." Ibid., fol. 650r–v.

90. Ibid., fol. 649r.

91. Earlier Viegas had described his dilemma as between incurring the displeasure of Charles IV if he refused to frame the indictment and incurring the anger of the *pueblo* if he did.

92. Ibid., fols. 658r–659r.

93. Ibid., fol. 659r–v.

94. Fanciful recollections of this nature abound in the record of the Causa del Escorial and its aftermath. For instance, Godoy reconstructed what was clearly a fancied scene of repentance and reconciliation preceding Charles's pardon of his son, which Godoy claimed he had recommended but others insisted he had opposed. Godoy claimed that he had supported the condition in the pardon, which might have precluded Fernando's accession to the throne. Godoy, *Memorias*.

95. ARPal, Papeles reservados de Fernando VII, vol. 2, fol. 662v.

96. Ibid.

97. Ibid., fols. 657r–v, 664r. It seems odd that Caballero had not been told to draw up the indictment.

98. Ibid., fol. 663r.

99. "Ahora que estoy escribiendo esto (13 de marzo de 1808) me asombra . . . las relaciones tan conformes que hay en los *sucesos políticos desde los combates navales,* y aún antes." Viegas was highlighting the realization that, after Trafalgar, maritime links to

the American colonies were severed, making peace with England an ineluctable priority for a growing segment of Spain's elites. Ibid., fol. 663v, Viegas's emphasis.

100. Ibid., fol. 660r–v.

101. Ibid., fol. 664v.

102. The defense in effect challenged the assumptions and legal reasoning of the prosecution based on the absence of incriminating documents, the hypothetical nature of the alleged crimes, and the laudable motives of the defendants.

103. According to Viegas, "Las impugnaciones de los defensores han recaído sobre las justificaciones que yo pretendí dar a la calificación dada por SM., siendo así que los oráculos deben acceptarse y seguirse suponiendolos justificados. Nunca han incurrido los Theólogos en mayores desaciertos que quando se han propuesto dar razón de la conducta y designios de Dios, cuya sabiduría es infinita y sus designios inescrutables." Ibid., fols. 664v–666r. See also Viegas's *representación* of 30 March to Fernando VII. Ibid., fol. 590r.

104. Infuriated by Viegas's failure to prove his case and the only one "que la sabía y no estaba ligado con la ley del secreto," Godoy began "publicar y condenar como injusta mi acusación para hacer recaer sobre mí el odio de una traición que yo confesé que no podía probar, y que como declarado en los Decretos, era todo la obra de su iniquidad." Ibid., fol. 666r.

105. Ibid., fols. 665r–666v. The original document is in ibid., vol. 1, fols. 1245r–1247r.

106. Perhaps *capricho* alludes to Viegas's insistence on returning to his original argument, namely, that the prosecution's case must rest on Charles IV's initial judgment of treason against Fernando and his principal supporters.

107. Soler may have been referring to Godoy's repeated interventions in matters of his jurisdiction as finance minister to obtain funds for extraneous ends.

108. "Carta del Sr. dn. Miguel Cayetano Soler, San Lorenzo," 28 Mar. 1807, ARPal, Papeles reservados de Fernando VII, vol. 1, fols. 1261r–1262v. On the same day, Soler wrote to Ventura Palacios, *oficial mayor* of Gracia y Justicia, to ask him to inform the minister of justice, Caballero, of the delivery of Viegas's *pliego* to Infantado, urging him to make sure that the Consejo de Castilla understood that "mi intervención fué forzada en virtud de formal precepto del Rey, y para evitar otros daños irreparables que quizá hubieran impedido el bien que ahora se disfruta." Otherwise Soler would suffer serious consequences "que me ofreció evitar." He added that he had joined Caballero, Cevallos, and Viegas to obtain Fernando's pardon — opposed by Godoy. Both letters were forwarded to the Consejo de Castilla on 3 April, 1808. Ibid., vol. 2, fols. 588r–589v.

109. Soler's recollection underscores María Luisa's and Charles IV's understanding of political issues.

110. Ibid., vol. 1, fols. 1260r–1268r. Apparently Soler concluded that Godoy intended to attack Fernando and his supporters under the name of the justice minister, Caballero. The two ministers must have agreed to support each other in testifying that Godoy had authored the decree and that Caballero had had to obey Charles IV's order to copy it. Apparently Cabalalero had removed the document when he was examining the materials found in Fernando's quarters.

111. Soler to Caballero, 28 Mar. 1808, ibid., vol. 2, fols. 587r–588v.

112. The French concluded that Caballero was responsible for pursuing the whole affair.

113. Cavallero to Escoiquiz, 4 Sept 1814, AAEPar, M et D, Espagne, 146, fols. 13ff.; Escoiquiz, *Idea sencilla*, in *BAE* 97:192. The appeal to Cevallos's probity is curious, since it was Cevallos who first published the report that Caballero was suspected of disloyalty and complicity with the French.

114. Carlos Seco Serrano has noted that in Godoy's post-1800 cabinet, Caballero "daría el matiz reaccionario . . . desde la penumbra proclivo a la intriga y al doble juego." *Historia de España*, 33:618.

115. Godoy, *Memorias*, 2:189.

116. Godoy, on arriving at the Escorial days later, found the same harsh approach in Charles's letter to Bonaparte.

117. Ibid., 196, 201–2.

118. Despite Godoy's admission that he had redrafted the 30 October decree, his explanation remains problematical given factors of time, distance, and his severe illness, so dramatically described in his memoirs. Additional doubts are raised by the absence of the original texts of any relevant communications, the questionable authorship of the decree (which resulted in the less than reliable testimony of Caballero and his subordinates in the justice ministry), not to mention allegations that Soler and four doctors attended the ill Godoy.

119. Martí Gilabert, *El proceso de El Escorial*, 131. Shortly afterward, Bonaparte removed Carolina and her husband from Naples and then installed his brother, Joseph, as king of Naples. The rationale: the couple's Anglophile policies.

120. Godoy, *Memorias*, 2:118.

121. Godoy to Gran Duque de Berg, 24 Dec. 1807, ANPar, AF IV, dossier 8, quoted in Pérez Villanueva, *Planteamiento*, 37–38.

122. Assuming that the subsequent defenses of Viegas, Soler, and Caballero were self-serving and false (as most historians have concluded), the outcome of the Escorial trial was assured. Whether Soler had acted as *agente de negocios* for Godoy, Caballero, or another party in pressing Viegas for an indictment was immaterial to the outcome of the trial. Equally irrelevant to the outcome was whether Viegas had pursued the indictment from fear of, or loyalty to, Godoy (as is generally believed) or because he saw the exoneration of the *fernandistas* as an inevitable, even politically desirable outcome. Whether Caballero aimed to discredit Charles IV and Fernando along with Godoy, possibly so conniving with the French, was also irrelevant to the outcome.

123. Godoy, *Memorias*, 2:188.

124. An *escarmiento* was basically designed to serve as a lesson to others. It could be innocuous and literary, as in the case of a seventeenth-century guide for newcomers to Madrid that proposed to regale and warn readers with stories of what awaited them: "Enseñar y escarmentravisar y entretener . . . esto es buen escarmentar." *Guía y avisos a los forasteros que vienen a la corte . . . lo que acontecció a unos recientes venidos* (Madrid, 1620). *Mal escarmentar* was actual violence meted out to the member of a group by other members to maintain obedience and discipline, a mafia-like technique of exemplary violence.

125. Rodríguez Villa, *Ensenada*, 268–69.

126. Under Philip V in the 1720s, after the Inquisition led to Melchor Macanaz's

escarmiento, the political *escarmiento* usually involved a charge of usurpation of royal authority or violation of personal rights rather than questioning orthodoxy. On Macanaz's removal, see Martín Gaite, *Macanaz.*

127. Once the initial coup failed to lead to Esquilache's dismissal, Charles III and his family fled to Aranjuez. The mob threatened to follow and even made new demands. The apparent collaboration of the Consejo de Castilla in the movement reduced the authority of the king, who then had to dismiss Esquilache. The subsequent expulsion of the Jesuits when the conde de Aranda was prime minister helped reestablish royal authority at home and abroad.

128. Giraldo quoted a Montfort, "hombre . . . muy sagaz." ARPal, Papeles reservados de Fernando VII, vol. 1, fol. 31. Escoiquiz later recorded that he, along with Infantado and others, had rejected the offer of the conde de Montijo to organize Madrid against Godoy because a coup of this nature might "abrir la puerta . . . a la guerra civil, y . . . dar justo motivo a su padre para desheredarle." The moment had not arrived, he added, to "poner en lugar debido al príncipe." Escoiquiz, *BAE* 97:27–28. That moment came six months later at Aranjuez, where a palace servant and the Guardias de Corps were reliable instruments of force majeure.

129. Navarro Latorre, *Hace doscientos años,* 43, 45, 48.

130. Spokesmen for the *pueblo* were often lay preachers who played on the rituals of religious fervor and penitence to demobilize the crowd in the aftermath of violence.

131. Pedro Giraldo, ARPal, Papeles reservados de Fernando VII, vol. 1, fols. 450r–460r.

By Way of Conclusion

1. Gray, "Utopia Falls," 16.
2. Anes Álvarez, prologue to Rúspoli, *Godoy,* 12.

Bibliography

Select Documents

Amicus Plato, sed magis Amica Veritas [Valentín de Foronda or Carlos Martínez de Irujo?]. "Reflexiones sobre el comercio en tiempo de guerra, 1800." BRAHM, Mata Linares, 168, fols. 375–420.

Austria, José Donato de. "Memoria, 1803." AGN, AHH, 1869-2.

———. "Memoria, 1804." AGN, AHH, 1869 3.

———. "Noticias y reflexiones político-mercantiles acerca del comercio, 1799." AGI, Mexico, 2509.

Basadre, Vicente. "Memoria sobre los beneficios que resultan al estado de la onrrosa profesión del comercio: Leyda en Junta de Gobierno que celebró el Real Consulado . . . 1796." AGI, Mexico, 2507.

Belena, Eusebio Ventura. "Informe reservado sobre el actual estado del comercio." AGN, Consulado, 123. Reprinted as "Informe reservado del oidor de la Audiencia de México . . . al . . . Virrey de Nueva España, conde de Revillagigedo, sobre el actual estado del comercio del mismo Reino (1791)" in Florescano and Castillo, *Controversia*, 1:183–234.

Bourgoing, Jean-François. "Exposé succinct de la position politique actuelle de la France vis-à-vis de l'Espagne: Madrid, 6 June 1796." AAEPar, CP, Espagne, Supplément 17.

"Causa de El Escorial." ARPal, Papeles Reservados de Fernando VII. 2 vols.

Cerdán de Landa y Simón Pontero, Ambrosio. "Apuntamientos en defensa de la Real Orden de 20 de Abril de 1799 combatida en un papel dado a luz por un español de Filadelfia por el regente de la Audiencia de Guatemala. 1800." AGN, Historia, 400.

Consejo de Estado. "Registro de las actas y reales disposiciones." AHN, Estado, libros 5d, 7d, 8d.

Consulado de Cadiz. "Representación . . . contra lo mandado en R de 18 de noviembre. 3 Dec. 1797." BRAHM, Mata Linares, 12.

"El comercio español de Veracruz propone a V.M. el establecimiento de un consulado independiente del de México." AGI, Mexico, 2506. Copy in AGN, Consulado, 222, exp. 1.

"Ensayo apologético por el comercio libre, con reflexiones imparciales sobre las pretensione de negocicantes." BNMex, MS 1334, fols. 247–87. Also printed in Florescano and Castillo, *Controversia,* 1:300–380.

Ferret, Zeferino. "Exposición histórica de las causas que más han influido en la decadencia de la marina española . . . 1813." MN, MS 444.

Gardoqui, Diego de. "Estado de nuestro comercio activo y pasivo, y medios de promover el primero en beneficio de la España, acomodándolos al sistema de sus rentas reales." Consejo de Estado, 16 May 1794. AHN, Estado, libro 8d.

Güemes-Pacheco de Padilla y Horcasitas, Juan Vicente, II conde de Revillagigedo. "Dictamen . . . sobre comercio libre de este reino." BNMex, Reales Ordenes, 27, no. 1396.

Iriarte, Bernardo. "Apuntamientos sobre el odio que se ha ido suscitando contra la nación francesa y sus malas consequencias sucesivas." AHN, Estado, 2817.

———. "Apuntamientos y borradores de mis cartas." AHN, Estado, 2817.

"Mémoire secret: Coup d'oeil politique et secret sur les vues des Anglais . . . le moyen de les empêcher de parvenir a leur but." ANPar, AF IV, 1211, no. 28.

Páez de la Cadena, Miguel. "Dictamen del superintendente de la Real Aduana, 1792." AGN, Consulado, 123, fols. 302r–332r.

Portillo, Bernabé. "Discurso político sobre la Agricultura, la Industria y el Comercio." Cadiz, 18 Mar. 1794. AHN, Estado, 3208, no. 344-4.

———. "Memoria sobre la elección de los recursos menos gravosos para las urgencias de la Guerra, y sobre proporcionar los fondos necesarios para hacerla con rigor." AHN, Estado, 3212, caja 2, no. 13.

———. "Memoria sobre los perjuicios del agro o quebranto de los vales reales: Cadiz, 20 Oct. 1796." AHN, Estado, 3212², caja 2, no. 13.

———. "Proyecto del Discurso Político . . . y Reflexiones." AHN, Estado, 3208, no. 344-10.

———. "Suplemento por notas al Discurso Político sobre la agricultura, la industria y el comercio." AHN, Estado, 3208, no. 344-4.

Posada, Ramón de. "Dictamen." AGN, Consulado, 123.

"Proceso formado al conde de Aranda por un parecer suyo acerca de la Guerra que fué leído en el Consejo de Estado presidido por el rey." In Muriel, *Historia de Carlos IV,* 1:196–204.

"Resumé historique des opérations de la caisse royale de Consolidación." AAEPar, M et D, Espagne, 152, fol. 62.

Revillagigedo, conde de. *See* Güemes-Pacheco de Padilla y Horcasitas.

"Sobre averiguar si ha o no decadencia en el comercio, hallar el remedio de ella en caso de haberla, y proporcionar los auxilios más convenientes para fomento del tráfico mercantil en este Reyno." AGN, Consulado, 123, exps. 1–3.

Viegas, Simón de. "Acusación fiscal." ARPal, Papeles Reservados de Fernando VII, vol. 1, fols. 117r–122v.

———. "Papel sin fecha que es un bordador de cierta exposición hecha por Viegas a Dn. Manuel Godoy, después de empezados a ver los papeles de la causa del Escorial. Consta de hojas escritas, y en gran parte rayadas." ARPal, Papeles Reservados de Fernando VII, vol. 2, fols. 624–28.

Virio, Juan Bautista. "Apuntamiento . . . para evitar los errores y contraprincipios que constituyen todos los tratados de comercio anteriormente hechos con la Francia y señaladamente con la Inglaterra." AHN, Estado, 2848, apartado 14.

———. "Reflexiones que exigen una atención seria antes de entrar en ajustes de tratados de comercio." AHN, Estado, 2848, apartado 14.

Yermo, Juan Antonio. "Sobre todo género de agricultura en la Nueva España, 22 Abril 1788." BNMex, MS 1304, fols. 82r–132r.

Published Sources

Abad y Queipo, Manuel. "Escrito presentado a Don Manuel Sixto Espinosa . . . a fin de que se suspendiese . . . la Real Cédula de 26 de Diciembre de 1804." In Sugawara, *La deuda pública*, 122–28; also in Mora, *Obras sueltas*, 231–41.

——— "Representación a nombre de los labradores y comerciantes de Valladolid de Michoacán . . . sobre enajenación de bienes raíces . . . para la consolidación de vales." In Sugawara, *La deuda pública*, 59–75.

Alamán, Lucas. *Historia de Méjico desde los primeros movimientos que prepararon su independencia en el año de 1808*. 5 vols. 1849–52. Mexico City, 1942.

Alberola Romá, Armando. "La política económica en tiempos de Godoy." In Melón Jiménez, La Parra López, and Pérez González, *Godoy y su tiempo*, 1:405–27.

Albuerne, Manuel de. *Orígen y estado de la causa formada sobre la Real Orden de 17 de mayo de 1810, que trata del comercio de América*. Cadiz, 1811.

Anes Álvarez, Gonzalo. *Economía e "ilustración" en la España del siglo xviii*. Barcelona, 1969.

———. *El antiguo régimen: Los Borbones*. Madrid, 1975.

———. *Las crisis agrarias en la España moderna*. Madrid, 1970.

———. Prologue to Rúspoli, *Goya*.

Antón de Olmet, Fernando de. *El cuerpo diplomático español en la guerra de independencia: Proceso de los orígenes de la decadencia española*. 6 vols. Madrid, 1912–14.

Antúnez y Acevedo, Rafael. *Memorias históricas sobre la legislación y gobierno del comercio de los españoles con sus colonias en las Indias occidentales*. 1797. Madrid, 1981.

Arango y Parreño, Francisco. "Informe del síndico." In Consulado de la Habana, *Expediente instruído*, app. 6.

———. *Obras*. 2 vols. Havana, 1952.

Armytage, Frances. *The Free Port System in the British West Indies: A Study in Commercial Policy, 1766–1822*. London, 1953.

Arnna, Jacques, ed. *Napoléon et son temps: Catalogue . . . de la collection de M. Émile Browet*. Paris, 1934.

Arrangoiz y Berzábal, Francisco. *Méjico desde 1808 hasta 1867*. 4 vols. Madrid, 1871–72.

Arroyal, León de. *Cartas económico-políticas al conde de Lerena*. Edited by J. Caso Gonzalez. Oviedo, 1971.

Austria, José Donato de. "Así se transmiten las ideas y así es que Cádiz, Barcelona, y Málaga saben más del comercio de Nueva España que Madrid." *Boletín del Archivo Nacional de Cuba* 43 (1946), 154–86.

Baillou, Jean. *Les affaires étrangères et le corps diplomatique français*. Vol. 1. *De l'ancien régime au second empire*. Paris, 1984.

Bakewell, Peter J. "Mining in Colonial Spanish America." In Bethell, *Cambridge History of Latin America*, 2:110–52.

———. *Silver Mining and Society in Colonial Mexico: Zacatecas, 1546–1700*. Cambridge, 1971.

Balanza del comercio de España con los dominios de . . . America en . . . 1792. In Matilla Tascón, *Balanza del comercio exterior*.

Barbier, J., and Herbert S. Klein. "Revolutionary Wars and Public Finances: The Madrid Treasury, 1784–1804." *Journal of Economic History* 41 (June 1981): 315–39.

Baring, Alexander. *An Inquiry into the Causes and Consequences of the Orders in Council*. London, 1808.

Barrenechea, José Manuel. *Valentín de Foronda: Reformador y economista ilustrado*. Vitoria, 1984.

Barrett, Ward J. *The Sugar Hacienda of the Marqueses del Valle*. Minneapolis, 1970.

Baskes, Jeremy. *Indians, Merchants, and Markets*. Stanford, CA, 2000.

Bauer, Arnold. "The Church and Spanish American Agrarian Structure, 1765–1865." *Americas* 28 (1971): 78–98.

Beerman, Eric. *El diario del proceso y encarcelamiento de Alejandro Malaspina, 1794–1803*. Madrid, 1992.

Bejarano Robles, Francisco. *Historia del Consulado y de la Junta de Comercio de Málaga, 1785–1859*. Madrid, 1947.

Beleña, Eusebio Buenaventura, ed. *Recopilación sumaria de todos los autos acordados de la Real Audiencia y Sala del Crimen de esta Nueva España*. 1787. Facsimile ed. Mexico City, 1981.

Bergeron, L. "Problèmes économiques de la France napoléonienne." *Revue d'Histoire Moderne et Contemporaine* 17 (1970): 469–505.

Bernstein, Harry. *Modern and Contemporary Latin America*. Philadelphia, 1952.

Berryer, Pierre-Nicolas. *Souvenirs de M. Berryer, doyen des avocats de Paris, de 1774 à 1838*. 2 vols. Paris, 1839.

Bethell, Leslie, ed. *The Cambridge History of Latin America*. 11 vols. Cambridge, 1984–.

Bonaparte, Napoléon. *Napoléon Ier: Lettres au comte Mollien, ministre du Trésor Public*. Edited by Jacques Arnna. Rochecorbon, 1959.

Booker, Jackie R. *Veracruz Merchants, 1770–1829: A Mercantile Elite in Late Bourbon and Early Independent Mexico*. Boulder, CO, 1993.

Borah, Woodrow, ed. *El gobierno provincial en la Nueva España, 1570–1787*. Mexico City, 1985.

Borchart de Moreno, Christiana Renate. *Los mercaderes y el capitalismo en la ciudad de México, 1759–1778*. Mexico City, 1984.

Bosher, J. F. *French Finances, 1770–1795: From Business to Bureaucracy*. Cambridge, 1970.

Bourgoing, Jean-François. *Tableau de l'Espagne moderne*. 4th ed. 3 vols. Paris, 1807.

Bourguet, Alfred. *Le duc de Choiseul et l'alliance espagnole*. Paris, 1906.

Bouvier, Jean. "Apropos la crise dite de 1805: Les crises économiques sous l'Empire." *Revue d'Histoire Moderne et Contemporaine* 17 (1970): 506–39.

Brading, David. *Haciendas and Ranchos in the Mexican Bajío: León, 1700–1860*. Cambridge, 1978.

———. "La situación económica de los hermanos don Manuel y don Miguel Hidalgo y Costilla, 1807." *Boletín del Archivo General de la Nación*, 2nd ser., 11 (1970): 23–82.

——. *Miners and Merchants in Bourbon Mexico, 1763–1810*. Cambridge, 1971.

Branciforte, marqués de. "Relación." In Torre Villar, *Instrucciones y memorias*, 2:1277–1308.

Braudel, Fernand, and Ernest Labrousse, eds. *Histoire économique et sociale de la France*. 4 vols. Paris, 1977–82.

Bruchey, Stuart Weems. *Robert Oliver, Merchant of Baltimore, 1783–1819*. Baltimore, 1956.

Buist, Marten G. *At spes non fracta: Hope & Co., 1770–1815*. The Hague, 1974.

Burkholder, Mark, and D. S. Chandler. *From Impotence to Authority: The Spanish Crown and the American Audiencias, 1687–1808*. Columbia, MO, 1977.

Bustamante, Carlos María de. *Campañas del General Calleja*. Mexico City, 1828.

——. *Suplemento a la historia de Los tres siglos de México*. México City, 1852.

Bustos Rodríguez, Manuel. *Época moderna: De la monarquía hispánica a la crisis del antiguo régimen*. Madrid, 2007.

Cabarrús, Francisco. *Cartas sobre los obstáculos que la naturaleza, la opinión y las leyes oponen a la felicidad pública*. 1795. Madrid, 1808.

Calcagno, Francisco. *Diccionario biográfico cubano*. 1878. Miami, 1996.

Calderón Quijano, José Antonio. *El banco de San Carlos y las comunidades de indios de la Nueva España*. Seville, 1963.

——, ed. *Los virreyes de Nueva España en el reinado de Carlos III (1759–1787)*. 2 vols. Seville, 1967.

——, ed. *Los virreyes de Nueva España en el reinado de Carlos IV (1787–1808)*. 2 vols. Seville, 1972.

Campomanes, Pedro Rodríguez de. *Tratado de la regalía de amortización en el qual se demuestra . . . el uso constante de la autoridad civil*. Madrid, 1765.

Canga Argüelles, José. *Diccionario de hacienda, con aplicación a España*. 2 vols. Madrid, 1833–34.

Caro Baroja, Julio. *La hora Navarra del XVIII (personas, familias, negocios, e ideas)*. Pamplona, 1969.

Castro, Adolfo de. *Historia de Cádiz y su provincia . . . hasta 1814*. Cadiz, 1858.

Castro Gutiérrez, Felipe. *Nueva ley y nuevo rey: Reformas borbónicas y rebelión popular en Nueva España*. Zamora, Michoacán, 1996.

Cavignac, Jean. *Jean Pellet, commerçant de gros, 1694–1772: Contribution à l'étude du négoce bordelais du XVIIIe siècle*. Paris, 1967.

Cerdán de Landa Simón Pontero, Ambrosio. *Disertación preliminar a los apuntamientos históricos . . . de los Señores . . . vireyes del Perú*. Lima, 1794.

Cervantes Bello, Francisco Javier. "La consolidación de los vales reales en Puebla y la crisis del crédito eclesiástico." In Martínez López-Cano and Valle Pavón, *El crédito en Nueva España*, 203–28.

Cevallos, Pedro. *Exposición de los hechos y maquinaciones que han preparado la usurpación de la corona de España, y los medios que el emperador de los franceses ha puesto en obra para realizarla*. Madrid, 1808.

——. *Manifesto imparcial y exacto de lo más importante ocurrido en Aranjuez, Madrid y Bayona. . . .* Cadiz, 1808.

Chabert, Alexandre. *Essai sur les mouvements des revenus et de l'activité économique en France de 1798 à 1820.* Paris, 1949.

Chávez Orozco, Luis. *Documentos para la historia económica de México.* 10 vols. Mexico City, 1933–35.

———. *Historia económica y social de México: Ensayo de interpretación.* Mexico City, 1938.

Chowning, Margaret. *Wealth and Power in Provincial Mexico: Michoacán from the Late Colony to the Revolution.* Stanford, CA, 1999.

Clercq, Alexandre J. H. de, ed. *Recueil des traités de la France.* 2 vols. Paris, 1864.

Coclanis, Peter A., ed. *The Atlantic Economy during the Seventeenth and Eighteenth Centuries: Organization, Operation, Practice, and Personnel.* Columbia, SC, 2005.

Colón, María. *Impresos españoles en Filadelfia durante los años 1800 a 1805.* Washington, DC, 1951.

Comisión organizadora del homenaje a Emeterio S. Santovenia. *Libro jubilar de Emeterio S. Santovenia en su cincuentario de escritor.* Havana, 1957.

Consulado de la Habana. *Expediente instruído por el Consulado de la Habana sobre los medios . . . para sacar la agricultura y comercio de esta Ysla del apuro en que se hallan.* Havana, 1808.

Corona Baratech, Carlos E. *Las ideas políticas en el reinado de Carlos IV.* Madrid, 1954.

———. *Revolución y reacción en el reinado de Carlos IV.* Madrid, 1957.

Costeloe, Michael F. *Church Wealth in Mexico: A Study of the "Juzgado de Capellanías" in the Archbishopric of Mexico, 1800–1856.* Cambridge, 1967.

Cotarelo y Mori, Emilio. *Iriarte y su época.* Madrid, 1897.

Couturier, Edith Boorstein. *The Silver King: The Remarkable Life of the Count of Regla in Colonial Mexico.* Albuquerque, 2003.

Crouzet, François. "La conjoncture bordelaise." In *Bordeaux au XVIIIe siècle,* edited by François-Georges Pareset, 288–324. Bordeaux, 1968.

———. "La croissance économique." In *Bordeaux au XVIIIe siècle,* edited by François-Georges Pareset, 191–220. Bordeaux, 1968.

———. "Le commerce de Bordeaux." In *Bordeaux au XVIIIe siècle,* edited by François-Georges Pareset, 221–86. Bordeaux, 1968.

———. *L'économie britannique et le blocus continental, 1806–1813.* 2 vols. Paris, 1958.

Dardel, Pierre. "Crises et faillites à Rouen et dans la Haute Normandie de 1740 à l'an V." *Revue d'Histoire Économique et Sociale* 27 (1948), 53–71.

Davis, Ralph. *The Industrial Revolution and British Overseas Trade.* Atlantic Highlands, NJ, 1979.

———. *The Rise of the Atlantic Economies.* Ithaca, NY, 1978.

Deans-Smith, Susan. *Bureaucrats, Planters, and Workers: The Making of the Tobacco Monopoly in Bourbon Mexico.* Austin, 1992.

Deerr, Noel. *The History of Sugar.* 3 vols. London, 1949–50.

Defourneaux, Marcellin. "Le problème de la terre en Andalousie au XVIIIe siècle et les projets de réforme agraire." *Revue Historique* 81 (1957): 42–57.

———. *Pablo de Olavide, ou l'afrancesado (1725–1803).* Paris, 1959.

Demostración de los distinguidos servicios . . . de Cadiz . . . por la sagrada causa de nuestra independencia. Cadiz, 1811.

Dermigny, L. "Circuits de l'argent et milieux d'affaires au XVIIIe siècle." *Revue Historique* 78 (1954): 239–78.

Dickson, Peter G. M. *The Financial Revolution in England: A study in the Development of public credit, 1688–1756.* New York, 1967.

Duchêne, Albert-Paul-André. *Guerre et finances: Une crise du trésor sous le premier empire.* Paris, 1940.

Edwards, Bryan. *The History, Civil and Commercial, of the British Colonies in the West Indies.* 3rd ed. 3 vols. London, 1801.

Elhuyar, Fausto de. *Memoria sobre el influjo de la minería en la agricultura, industria, población y civilización de la Nueva España en sus diferentes épocas: Con varias disertaciones relativas a puntos de economía pública con el propio ramo.* Madrid, 1825. Facsimile ed., Mexico, 1964.

———. "Reflections on the Working of the Mines and Refining Operations in the Real de Guanaxato, 1789." In Howe, *Mining Guild,* 472–89.

Elogios fúnebres del . . . Luis de las Casas y Aragorri. Havana, 1802.

Elorza, Antonio. *La ideología liberal en la ilustración española.* Madrid, 1970.

Enciso Recio, Luis Miguel. *Prensa económica del siglo XVIII: El Correo mercantil de España y sus Indias.* Valladolid, 1958.

———. "Presentación." In Morales Moya, *1802.*

"Ensayo apologético por el comercio libre, con reflexiones imparciales sobre las pretensiones de negociantes de esta Nueva España, refutadas por el . . . Fiscal de Real Hacienda y sostenidas en un papel póstumo." In Florescano and Castillo, *Controversia,* 1:300–380.

Escoiquiz, Juan. *Idea sencilla de las razones que motivaron el viage del rey D. Fernando VII a Bayona en el mes de abril de 1808, dada al público de España y de Europa.* Madrid, 1814. Also in *BAE* 97:189–226.

———. *Memorias de tiempos de Fernando VII. BAE* 97, 98. Madrid, 1957.

Extracto instructivo de un expediente sobre la escandalosa infracción . . . de un permiso. Cadiz, 1811.

Farriss, Nancy M. *Crown and Clergy in Colonial Mexico, 1759–1821: The Crisis of Ecclesiastical Privilege.* London, 1968.

Ferrer del Rio, Antonio. *Historia del reinado de Carlos III en España.* 4 vols. Madrid, 1856.

Finley, Ronald, and Kevin H. O'Rourke. *Power and Plenty: Trade, War, and the World Economy in the Second Millennium.* Princeton, NJ, 2008.

Fisher, John Robert. *Commercial Relations between Spain and Spanish America in the Era of Free Trade, 1778–1796.* Liverpool, 1985.

Flores Caballero, Romeo R. *La contrarrevolución en la independencia: Los españoles en la vida política, social y económica de México (1804–1838).* Mexico City, 1969.

Florescano, Enrique. *Estructuras y problemas agrarios de México (1500–1821).* Mexico City, 1971.

———. *Precios del maíz y crisis agrícola en México (1708–1810): Ensayo sobre el movimiento de los precios y sus consecuencias económicas y sociales.* Mexico City, 1969.

Florescano, Enrique, and Fernando Castillo, eds. *Controversia sobre la libertad de comercio en Nueva España, 1776–1818.* 2 vols. Mexico City, 1975.

Flores Romero, Romeo. "La consolidación de vales reales en la economía, la sociedad y la política novohispana." *HMex* 18 (1969): 334–78.

Floridablanca, conde de. "Memorial presentada al rey Carlos III." *BAE* 59:306–50.

Foncerrada, Melchor de. *Foncerrada michoacanense, oidor de México, habla a sus conpatriotos por la felicidad publica.* Mexico City, 1810.

Fonseca, Fabián, and Carlos de Urrutia. *Historia general de Real Hacienda.* 6 vols. Mexico City, 1845–53.

Fontana i Lázaro, Josep María. "Colapso y transformación del comercio exterior español entre 1792 y 1827." *Moneda y crédito,* no. 115 (1970): 3–23.

——, ed. *Comercio y colonias.* Banco de España, *La economía española al Final del Antiguo Régimen.* III. Madrid, 1982.

——. *La crisis del antíguo régimen, 1808–1833.* 2nd ed. Barcelona, 1983.

——. *La Hacienda en la historia de España, 1700–1931.* Madrid, 1980.

Foronda, Valentín de. *Apuntes ligeros sobre la nueva constitución proyectada por la Magestad de la Junta Suprema Española y reformas que intenta hacer en las leyes.* Philadelphia, 1809.

——. *Carta sobre lo que debe hacer un príncipe que tenga colonias a gran distancia.* Philadelphia, 1803.

——. *Miscelánea; ó, Colección de varios discursos.* Madrid, 1787.

——. See also *Reflexiones sobre el comercio.*

Fortea, José Ignacio, and Juan E. Gilabert, eds. *La ciudad portuaria atlántica en la historia, siglos XVI–XIX.* Santander, 2006.

Fradera, Josep María. *Colonias para después de un imperio.* Barcelona, 2005.

Franco, José Luciano. *Diego de Gardoqui y las negociaciones entre España y Norteamérica (1777–1790).* Havana, 1957.

Franco Cáceres, Ivan. *La intendencia de Valladolid de Michoacán, 1786–1809: Reforma administrative y exacción fiscal en una region de la Nueva España.* Mexico City, 2001.

Friedlander, H. *Historia económica de Cuba.* Havana, 1944.

Fugier, André. *Napoléon et l'Espagne, 1799–1808.* 2 vols. Paris, 1930.

Furet, François, and Denis Richet. *La Révolution française.* Paris, 1973.

Gamboa, Francisco. *Comentarios a las ordenanzas de minas.* Madrid, 1761.

García, Genaro, ed. *Documentos históricos mexicanos.* 7 vols. 1910–12. Mexico City, 1985.

García-Baquero González, Antonio, ed. "Estudio preliminar." In Antúnez y Acevedo, *Memorias históricas,* v–xxxv.

García de León, Antonio. "Sobre los origenes comerciales del Consulado de Veracruz: Comercio libre y mercado interno a fines del siglo XVIII, 1778–1795." In Hausberger and Ibarra, *Comercio y poder en América colonial,* 131–43.

García Navarro, Luis. *Intendencias en Indias.* Seville, 1959.

García Sala, Manuel de Santurio. *El exmo. Sr. D. José de Iturrigaray . . . vindicado en forma legal contra las falsas imputaciones de infidencia . . . por Juan López Cancelada.* Cadiz, 1812.

Garner, Richard L. "Zacatecas, 1750–1821: A Study of a Late Colonial Mexican City." PhD diss., University of Michigan, 1970.

Garner, Richard L., and Spiro E. Stefanou. *Economic Growth and Change in Bourbon Mexico.* Gainesville, FL, 1993.

Gayer, Arthur D., W. W. Rostow, and Anne Jacobson Schwartz. *The Growth and Fluctuation of the British Economy, 1790–1850.* 2 vols. Oxford, 1953.

Geggus, David P., ed. *The Impact of the Haitian Revolution in the Atlantic World.* Columbia, SC, 2001.

Gibbs, J. A. *The History of Anthony and Dorothea Gibbs.* London, 1922.

Girón Amarillas, Pedro. *Recuerdos (1778–1837).* Pamplona, 1978.

Godoy, Manuel. *Memorias del Príncipe de la Paz.* 2 vols. *BAE* 88, 89. Madrid, 1956.

Gómez Imaz, Manuel. *Sevilla en 1808: Servicios patrióticos de la Suprema Junta en 1808.* Seville, 1908.

Grafenstein, Johanna von. *Nueva España en el Circuncaribe, 1779–1808: Revolución, competencia imperial y vínculos intercoloniales.* Mexico City, 1997.

Grandmaison, Geoffroy de. *L'ambassade française en Espagne pendant la révolution (1789–1804).* Paris, 1892.

Gray, John. "Utopia Falls." *Harper's,* Dec. 2008.

Grito de Centralismo. Campeche, 1829.

Groussac, Paul. *Santiago de Liniers, conde de Buenos Aires, 1753–1810.* Buenos Aires, 1998.

Guerra y Sánchez, Ramiro, et al., eds. *Historia de la nación cubana.* 10 vols. Havana, 1952.

Guridi y Alcocer, José Miguel. *Representación de la diputación americana a las Cortes de España, en 1. de agosto de 1811.* London, 1812.

Gutiérrez López, Edgar Omar. *Económia y política de la agrominería en México: De la colonia a la nación independiente.* Mexico City, 2000.

Hale, Edwin Everett. *Franklin in France.* Boston, 1887–88.

Hamill, Hugh M. *The Hidalgo Revolt: Prelude to Mexican Independence.* Gainesville, FL, 1966.

Hamilton, Earl J. "Monetary Problems in America, 1751–1800." *Journal of Economic History* 4 (May 1944): 21–48.

———. "War and Inflation in Spain, 1780–1808." *Quarterly Journal of Economics* 59 (Nov. 1944): 36–77.

———. *War and Prices in Spain, 1651–1800.* Cambridge, MA, 1947.

Hamnett, Brian R. "The Appropriation of Mexican Church Wealth by the Spanish Bourbon Government: The 'Consolidación' of Vales Reales, 1805–1809." *Journal of Latin American Studies* 1, no. 2 (1989): 85–113.

———. *Politics and Trade in Southern Mexico, 1780–1821.* Cambridge, 1971.

———. *Roots of Insurgency: Mexican Regions, 1750–1824.* New York, 1986.

Harlow, Vincent T. *The Founding of the Second British Empire, 1763–93.* 2 vols. London, 1952–64.

Hausberger, Bernd. "Las elecciones . . . en el Consulado de México . . . en la formación de los partidos de los montañeses y los vizcaínos." In Hausberger and Ibarra, *Comercio y poder en América colonial,* 73–102.

Hausberger, Bernd, and Antonio Ibarra, eds. *Comercio y poder en América colonial: Los consulados de comerciantes, siglos XVII–XIX.* Madrid, 2003.

Hauterive, Alexandre Maurice Blanc de Lanautte, comte d'. *De l'état de la France à la fin de l'an VIII.* Paris, 1800.

———. *Resultat de la politique de l'Angleterre dans ces dernières années.* Paris, 1803.

———. *State of the French Republic at the End of the Year VIII.* London, 1801.

Hauterive, Alexandre Maurice Blanc de Lanautte, comte d', and Fernand de Cussy, eds. *Recueil des traités de commerce et de navigation de la France avec les puissances etrangères.* 8 vols. Paris, 1834–37.

Helman, Edith. *Jovellanos y Goya.* Madrid, 1970.

Henao y Munóz, Manuel. *Los borbones ante la revolución.* 2 vols. Madrid, 1869–70.

Heredia Herrero, Antonia. *La renta del azogue en Nueva España (1709–1751)*. Seville, 1978.

Hernández Palomo, José Jesús. *El aguardiente de caña en México, 1724–1810*. Seville, 1974.

Hernández y Dávalos, J. E., ed. *Colección de documentos para la historia de la guerra de independencia de México de 1808 a 1821*. 6 vols. 1877–82. Mexico City, 1985.

Herr, Richard. *The Eighteenth-Century Revolution in Spain*. Princeton, NJ, 1958.

———. "Hacia el derrumbe del antiguo regimen: Crisis fiscal y desamortización bajo Carlos IV." *Moneda y crédito*, no. 118 (1971): 37–100.

———. *Rural Change and Royal Finances in Spain at the End of the Old Regime*. Berkeley and Los Angeles, 1989.

Herrera Canales, Inés, ed. *La minería mexicana: De la colonia al siglo xx*. Mexico City, 1998.

Hidy, Ralph W. *The House of Baring in American Trade and Finance: English Merchant Bankers at Work, 1763–1861*. Cambridge, MA, 1949.

Howe, Walter. *The Mining Guild of New Spain and Its Tribunal General, 1770–1821*. Cambridge, MA, 1949.

Humboldt, Alexander von. *Ensayo político sobre el reino de la Nueva España*. 2nd ed. Mexico City, 1973.

———. *Essai politique sur le royaume de la Nouvelle Espagne*. 5 vols. Paris, 1811.

Humphreys, Robin A. *Tradition and Revolt in Latin America, and Other Essays*. London, 1969.

Hussey, Roland D. *The Caracas Company, 1728–1784: A Study in the History of Spanish Monopolistic Trade*. Cambridge, MA, 1934.

Izquierdo Hernández, Manuel. *Antecedentes y comienzos del reinado de Fernando VII*. Madrid, 1963.

Jiménez Codinach, Guadalupe. *La Gran Bretaña y la independencia de México, 1808–1821*. Mexico City, 1991.

Jovellanos, Gaspar de. *Diarios*. 3 vols. Oviedo, 1953–56.

———. *Informe de la Sociedad Económica de esta Corte al Real y Supremo Consejo de Castilla en el expediente de ley agraria*. Madrid, 1795.

———. *Obras publicadas e inéditas*. BAE 57 (1959).

Juárez Nieto, Carlos. *La oligarquía y el poder político en Valladolid de Michoacán, 1785–1810*. Morelia, 1994.

The Justice and Policy of a War with Spain Demonstrated. London, 1804.

Kossok, Manfred. *Historia de la Santa Alianza y la emancipación de América Latina*. Buenos Aires, 1968.

Laborde, Alexandre Louis Joseph, comte de. *Aperçu de la situation financière de l'Espagne*. Paris, 1823.

La Forest, Antoine R. C. H, comte de. *Correspondance du . . . ambassadeur de France en Espagne, 1808–1813*. 7 vols. Paris, 1905–13.

Lafuente, Modesto, ed. *Historia general de España desde los tiempos primitivos hasta la muerte de Fernando VII*. 25 vols. Barcelona, 1887–91.

Lafuente Ferrari, Enrique. *El virrey Iturrigaray y los orígenes de la independencia de México*. Madrid, 1941.

Langue, Frédérique. *Mines, terre et société à Zacatecas: De la fin du XVIIe siècle á l'independence*. Paris, 1992.

La Parra López, Emilio. *La alianza de Godoy con los revolucionaeios (España y Francia a fines del siglo XVIII)*. Madrid, 1992.

———. *Manuel Godoy: La aventura del poder.* Barcelona, 2002.

Larruga, Eugenio. *Memorias políticas y económicas sobre los frutos, comercio, fabricas y minas de España: Con inclusion de los reales decretos, órdenes, cédulas, aranceles y ordenanzas expedidas para su gobierno y fomento.* 45 vols. Madrid, 1787–1800.

Lavrín, Asunción. "The Execution of the Law of *Consolidación* in New Spain: Economic Aims and Results." *Hispanic American Historical Review* 53 (1973): 27–49.

———. "Problems and Policies in the Administration of Nunneries in Mexico, 1800–1830." *Americas* 28 (1971): 57–77.

———. "The Role of Nunneries in the Economy of New Spain in the Eighteenth Century." *Hispanic American Historical Review* 46 (1966): 371–93.

Le Mercier de la Rivière, Pierre-Paul. *L'intérêt général de l'État, ou, La liberté du commerce des blés.* Amsterdam, 1770.

León y Pizarro, José García de. *Memorias de la vida del . . . señor D. José García de León y Pizarro.* 3 vols. Madrid, 1894–97.

Lerdo de Tejada, Miguel. *Apuntes históricos de la heróica ciudad de Veracruz.* 3 vols. Mexico City, 1850–58.

———. *Comercio exterior de México, desde la conquista hasta hoy.* Mexico City, 1853.

Le Riverend, Julio. *Historia económica de Cuba.* Havana, 1967.

Lerner, Victoria. "Consideraciones sobre la población de la Nueva España (1793–1810) según Humboldt y Navarro y Noriega." *HMex* 17 (1968): 327–48.

Levene, Ricardo, ed. *Documentos para la historia argentina.* Vol. 6. *Comercio de Indias: Comercio libre (1778–1791).* Buenos Aires, 1915.

Lévy, Arthur. *Capitalistes et pouvoir au siècle des lumières.* 3 vols. Paris, 1969–80.

Lévy, C. F. "Supplément." *Bulletin d'histoire moderne,* 14th ser., 26 n. 13, in *Revue d'Histoire Moderne et Contemporaine* 17 (1970).

———. *Un grand profiteur de guerre sous la révolution, l'empire et la restauration, G.-J. Ouvrard.* Paris, 1929.

Lizarza, Facundo de. *Discurso que públia Don Facundo de Lizarza vindicando al . . . Señor Don José Iturrigaray de las falsas imputaciones de un quaderno titulado, por ironía, Verdad sabida, y buena fé guardada.* Cadiz, 1811.

Llorente, Juan Antonio. *Memorias para la historia de la revolución española, con documentos justificativos.* 3 vols. Paris, 1814–16.

Lohmann Villena, Guillermo. *Los americanos en las órdenes nobiliarias (1529–1900).* 2 vols. Madrid, 1947.

López Cancelada, Juan. *Conducta del excelentísimo señor don José Iturrigaray durante su gobierno en Nueva-España: Se contesta a la vindicación que publicó don Facundo Lizarza, cuaderno tercero y segundo en la material.* Cadiz, 1812.

———. *La verdad sabida y buena fé guardada: Orígen de la espantosa revolución de Nueva España comenzada en 15 de setiembre de 1810, defensa de su fidelidad; quaderno primero.* Cadiz, 1811.

———. *Ruina de la Nueva España si se declara el comercio libre con los extrangeros: Exprésanse los motivos.* Cadiz, 1811.

López Cantos, Ángel. *Don Francisco de Saavedra, segundo intendente de Caracas.* Seville, 1973.

Lozier Almazán, Bernard P. *Liniers y su tiempo.* Buenos Aires, 1990.

Lucena Salmoral, Manuel. "La memoria de Basadre de 1818 sobre comercio y contrabando en el Caribe." *Jahrbuch für Geschichte von Staat, Wirtschaft und Geselschaft Lateinamerika* 19 (1982): 223–37.

Lynch, John. "British Policy and Spanish America, 1783–1808," *Journal of Latin American Studies* 1 (May 1969): 1–30.

Marichal, Carlos. *La bancarrota del virreinato: Nueva España y las finanzas del imperio español, 1780–1810.* Mexico City, 1999.

Marion, Marcel. *Ce qu'il faut connaître des crises financières de notre histoire.* Paris, 1956.

——. *Histoire financière de la France depuis 1715–1818.* 5 vols. Paris, 1914–31.

Martí Gilabert, Francisco. *El motín de Aranjuez.* Pamplona, 1972.

——. *El proceso de El Escorial.* Pamplona, 1965.

Martínez de Villela, Ignacio. *A la nación española.* Cadiz, 1812.

Martínez López-Cano, María del Pilar, and Guillermina del Valle Pavón, eds. *El crédito en Nueva España.* Mexico City, 1998.

Martín Gaite, Cármen. *Macanaz, otro paciente de la Inquisición.* Madrid, 1975.

Matilla Tascón, Antonio, ed. *Balanza del comercio exterior de España en el año de 1795.* Madrid, 1964.

Melón Jiménez, Miguel Ángel, Emilio La Parra López, and Fernando Tomás Pérez González, eds. *Godoy y su tiempo.* 2 vols. Merida, 2003.

Memorial ajustado . . . contra Isidro de la Madrid . . . merceder de plata y Francisco Valdivielso mercader de plata y Francisco Fagoaga, mercader de plata . . . individuos de la Real Casa de Moneda . . . sobre el defecto de ley y peso de la moneda de plata labrada en ella. Madrid, 1734.

Menéndez Pidal, Ramon, ed. *Historia de España.* 42 vols. Madrid, 1935–2007.

Mentz, Brígida von. "Conjuntura minera y protesta campesina en el centro de Nueva España, Siglo xviii." In Herrera Canales, *La minería mexicana,* 23–45.

Mercier de la Rivière, Pierre-Paul. *L'intérêt general de l'état, ou la liberté du Commerce des blés.* Amsterdam, 1770.

Mirabeau, Honoré-Gabriel de Requeti, comte de. *De la banque d'Espagne dite de Saint Charles.* Paris, 1785.

——. *Lettre du comte de Mirabeau a M. Le Couteulx de la Noraye, sur la Banque de Saint-Charles & sur la Caisse-d'escompte.* Brussels, 1785.

Monfor, Artaud de. *Histoire de la vie et des travaux politiques du comte d'Hauterive.* Paris, 1839.

Mora, José María Luis. *Mexico y sus revoluciones.* 3 vols. Mexico City, 1950.

——. *Obras completas.* 8 vols. Mexico City, 1986–88.

——. *Obras sueltas.* 2nd ed. Mexico City, 1963.

Morales Moya, Antonio. *1802: España entre dos siglos.* II. *Ciencia y economía.* Madrid, 2003.

Morazé, Charles. *Les bourgeois conquérants.* 2 vols. Brussels, 1985.

Moreno Cebrián, Alfredo. *El corregidor de indios y la economía peruana del siglo XVIII: Los repartos forzosos de mercancías.* Madrid, 1977.

Moreno Fraginals, Manuel. *El ingenio: Complejo económico social cubano del azúcar.* 3 vols. Havana, 1978.

Muriel, Andrés. *Historia de Carlos IV.* Edited by Carlos Seco Serrano. 2 vols. *BAE* 114, 115.

Muro, Luis. "Revillagigedo y el comercio libre (1791–1792)." In *Extremos de América:*

Homenaje a don Daniel Cosío Villegas, by El Colegio de México, Centro de Estudios Históricos, 299–344. Mexico City, 1971.

Navarrete Gómez, David. "Crisis y supervivencia de una empresa minera a fines de la colonia: La Vizcaína (Real del Monte)." In Herrera Canales, *La minería mexicana,* 95–118.

Navarro Latorre, José. *Hace doscientos años: Estado actual de los problemas historícos del "Motín de Esquilache."* Madrid, 1966.

Navarro y Noriega, Fernando. *Memoria sobre la población del reino de Nueva España, escrita en el año de 1814.* 1820. Mexico City, 1954.

Nolte, Vincent. *Fifty Years in both hemispheres: or, Reminiscences of the life of a former merchant.* New York, 1854.

"Noticias publicadas de Nueva España en 1805 por el Tribunal del Consulado." *Boletín de la Sociedad Mexicana de Geographía y Estadística* 2 (1864): 44.

Olavide, Pablo de. "Informe . . . sobre la ley agraria." *Boletín de la Real Academia de la Historia* 139 (1956): 357–462.

Onís, José de. "Don Valentin de Foronda en los Estados Unidos." *Cuadernos Hispánoamericanos,* no. 207 (Mar. 1967): 448–64.

Ortiz de la Tabla Ducasse, Javier. *Comercio exterior de Veracruz, 1778–1821: Crisis de dependencia.* Seville, 1978.

———, ed. *Memorias políticas y económicas del consulado de Veracruz, 1796–1822.* Seville, 1985.

Ouvrard, Gabriel-Julien. *Mémoires de G.-J. Ouvrard: Sur sa vie et ses diverses opérations financières.* 3 vols. Paris, 1827.

Palacio Atard, Vicente. *El tercer pacto de familia.* Madrid, 1945.

Palau Baquero, Mercedes, and Antonio Orozco Aquaviva, eds. *Malaspina, '92: I jornadas internacionales; Madrid–Cádiz–La Coruna.* Cadiz, 1994.

Papers Relative to the Discussion in 1803, and 1804. London, 1805.

Pariset, Français-George, ed. *Bordeaux au XVIIIe siècle.* Bordeaux, 1968.

Pastor, Roberto. "El repartimiento de mercancías y los alcaldes mayores novohispanos: Un sistema de explotación de sus orígenes a la crisis de 1810." In Borah, *El gobierno provincial,* 201–37.

Patch, Robert. "Imperial Politics and Local Economy in Colonial Central America, 1670–1770." *Past and Present,* no. 143 (1994): 77–107.

———. *Maya and Spaniard in Yucatan, 1648–1812.* Stanford, CA, 1993.

Patch, Robert, and Beatriz Cáceres Menéndez. "Towards a Reinterpretation of Spanish Colonialism and the Repartimiento: Comments on Jeremy Baskes' 'Coerced or Voluntary.'" Photocopy.

Payard, Maurice. *Le financier G.-J. Ouvrard (1770–1846).* Reims, 1958.

Perelman, Michael. *The Invention of Capitalism: Classical Political Economy and the Secret History of Primitive Accumulation.* Durham, NC, 2000.

Pérez Rosales, Laura. *Familia, poder, riqueza y subversión: Los Fagoaga novohispanos, 1730–1830.* Mexico City, 2003.

Pérez Sánchez, Alfonso E., and Elizabeth Sayre, eds. *Goya and the Spirit of Enlightenment.* Boston, 1989.

Pérez Villanueva, Joaquín. *Planteamiento ideológico inicial de la guerra de independencia.* Valladolid, 1960.

Pérez y Comoto, Florencio. *Representación que a favor del libre comercio dirigieron al excelentísimo señor don Juan Ruiz de Apodaca.* Havana, 1818.

Perregaux, Jacques. "Observations historiques sur la crisis." In Arnna, *Napoléon et son temps.*

Pethick, Derek. *The Nootka Connection: Europe and the Northwest Coast, 1790–1795.* Vancouver, 1980.

Peuchet, J. *Dictionnaire universel de la géographie commerçante.* 5 vols. Paris, 1799–1800.

Peuchet, M. *État des colonies et du commerce des Européens dans les deux Indes, depuis 1783 jusqu'en 1821.* 2 vols. Paris, 1821.

Pietschmann, H., et al. *La revolución de independencia.* Mexico, 1995.

Pitkin, Timothy. *Statistical View of the Commerce of the United States of America . . . accompanied with Tables.* Hartford, CT, 1816.

Pons, François-Joseph de. *Voyage à la partie orientale de la Terre-Ferme, dans l'Amérique Méridionale, fait pendant les années 1801, 1802, 1803 et 1804: Contenant la description de la capitainerie générale de Carácas, composée des provinces de Vénézuéla, Maracaibo, Varinas, la Guiane Espagnole, Cumana, et de l'île de la Marguerite.* Paris, 1806.

Prados de la Escosura, Leandro. "Comercio exterior y cambio económico en España, 1792–1849." In *La economía española al final del antiguo regimen,* vol. 3, *Comercio y colonias,* ed. Josep María Fontana i Lázaro, 171–249. Madrid, 1982.

Pradt, Dominique Georges Frédéric de. *Mémoires historiques sur la révolution d'Espagne.* Paris, 1816.

Priestley, Herbert I. *José de Gálvez, Visitor-General of New Spain (1761–1771).* Philadelphia, 1980.

Prinsep, G. A. *Carta al Exmo. Señor Duque de Frías, sobre el comercio de Nueva España.* London, 1821.

Quirós, José María. *Guía de negociantes: Compendio de la legislación mercantil de España e Indias.* Edited by Pedro Pérez Herrero. Mexico City, 1986.

Ramon, Gabriel G. *Histoire de la Banque de France d'après les sources originales.* Paris, 1929.

Raynal, Abbé [Guillaume-Thomas-François]. *Histoire philosophique et politique des établissemens et du commerce des Européens dans les deux Indes.* 7 vols. Amsterdam, 1774.

Reflexiones sobre el comercio de España con sus colonias en América en tiempo de guerra por un Español en Philadelphia. Philadelphia, 1799; BRAHM Mata Linarés, 68, fols. 375–420.

Regil, Pedro Manuel. *Memoria instructiva sobre el comercio general de la provincial de Yucatán: y particularmente del puerto de Campeche.* Madrid, 1814.

Revillagigedo, conde de. "El virrey de Nueva España . . . informa." In Florescano and Castillo, *Controversia,* 2:13–58.

———. "Informe . . . sobre si hay decadencia en el comercio . . . en caso de haberla haller las causas . . . y sus remedios y proporcionar los auxilios más a propósito para dar mayor extencíon al tráfico mercantil." *Boletín del Archivo General de la Nación* 2, nos. 1 (1931): 190–211, 2 (1931): 196–211.

Riley, James C. *International Government Finance and the Amsterdam Capital Market, 1740–1815.* Cambridge, 1980.

Ringrose, David A. *Spain, Europe, and the "Spanish Miracle," 1700–1900.* Cambridge, 1996.

Rodríguez García, Vicente. *El fiscal de Real Hacienda en Nueva España: Don Ramón de Posada y Soto, 1781–1793.* Madrid, 1986.

Rodríguez Villa, Antonio. *Don Cenon de Somodevila, marqués de la Ensenada: Ensayo biográfico.* Madrid, 1878.

Romano, Ruggiero. *Moneda, seudomonedas y circulación monetaria en las economías de México.* Mexico City, 1998.

Romero S., María Eugenia, and Luis Antonio Jaúregui F. "Comentarios sobre el cálculo de renta nacional en la economía novohispana." *Investigación Económica,* no. 177 (1986): 105–40.

Rosensweig Hernández, Fernando. "La economía novo-hispana al comenzar el siglo XIX." *Ciencias Políticas y Sociales* 9 (1963): 455–94.

Rúbio Mañé, José Ignacio. "Anuario histórico de la vida del II conde de Revilla Gigedo, virrey de Nueva España." *Anuario de Estudios Americanos* 6 (1949): 453–96.

———. "Síntesis histórica de la vida del II conde de Revillagigedo." *Anuario de Estudios Americanos* 6 (1941): 453–96.

Ruiz y Pablo, Ángel. *Historia de la Real Junta Particular de Comercio de Barcelona, 1758 a 1847.* Barcelona, 1994.

Rumeu de Armas, Antonio. *El testamento político del conde de Floridablanca.* Madrid, 1962.

Rúspoli, Enrique. *Godoy: La lealtad de un gobernante ilustrado.* Madrid, 2004.

Saavedra, Francisco de. *Diario de don Francisco de Saavedra.* Edited by Francisco Morales Padrón. Seville, 2004.

Salvucci, Linda K. "'Costumbres viejos, 'hombres nuevos': José de Gálvez y la burocracia fiscal novohispana (1754–1800)." *HMex* 33 (1988): 224–64.

Sánchez Santiró, Ernest. *Azúcar y poder: Estructura socioeconómica de las alcaldías mayores de Cuernavaca y Cuautla de Amilpas, 1730–1821.* Mexico City, 2001.

———. "Comerciantes, mineros y hacendados: La integración de los mercaderes del Consulado de la ciudad de México en la propriedad minera y azucarera de Cuernavaca y Cuautla de Amilpas (1750–1821)." In Valle Pavón, *Mercaderes,* 159–90.

Seco Serrano, Carlos. "La política exterior de Carlos IV." In Menéndez Pidal, *Historia de España,* 31.2: 451–732.

Smith, Adam. *Compendio de la obra inglesa Riqueza de las naciones hecha por el marqués de Condorcet.* Edited and translated by Carlos Martínez de Irujo. Madrid, 1803.

Smith, Robert G. "José María Quirós: Balanza del comercio . . . e ideas económicas." *Trimestre económico* 13 (1947): 380–411.

Soler Pascual, Emilio. *La conspiración Malaspina (1795–1796).* Alicante, 1990.

Sorel, Albert. "La diplomatie française de 1792 a 1797: III. Le traité de Bâle . . . IV; Le traité entre la République et l'Espagne." *Revue Historique* 13 (1880): 241–78.

Souto Mantecón, Matilde. *El comercio exterior de México, 1713–1850: Entre la quiebra del sistema imperial y el surgimiento de una nación.* Mexico City, 2000.

———. *Mar abierto: La política y el comercio del consulado de Veracruz en el ocaso del sistema imperial.* Mexico City, 2001.

Spell, Jefferson R. "An Illustrious Spaniard in Philadelphia: Valentín de Foronda." *Hispanic Review* 4 (1936): 136–40.

Stein, Stanley J. "Bureaucracy and Business in the Spanish Empire, 1759–1804: Failure of a Bourbon Reform in Mexico." *Hispanic American Historical Review* 61 (1981): 2–28.

———. "Fransisco Ignacio de Yraeta y Azcárate, almacenero de la ciudad de Mexico, 1732–1797: Un ensayo de microhistoria." *HMex* 50 (2001): 459–512.

———. "Reality in Microcosm: The Debate over Trade with America, 1785–1789." *Historia Ibérica* 1 (1972): 111–19.

Stephen, James. *War in Disguise, or the Frauds of the Neutral Flags.* London, 1806.

Studnicki-Gisbert, D. "Visiting 1640: How the Party of Commercial Expansion Lost to the Party of Political Conservatism in Spain's Atlantic Empire, 1620–1650." In Coclanis, *Atlantic Economy,* 152–85.

Suárez Argüello, Clara Elena. "El parecer de la elite de comerciantes del Consulado de la ciudad de México ante la operación del libre comercio (1791–1793." In Hausberger and Ibarra, *Comercio y poder en América colonial,* 103–29.

———. "Los bancos de rescate de platas: Una opción alternativa para el financiamento de la minería? El caso de Zacatecas, 1791–1810." In Valle Pavón, *Mercaderes,* 98–132.

Suárez de Tangil y de Angulo, Fernando, Conde de Vallellano. *Nobiliaro cubano; o, Las grandes familias isleñas, por el conde de Vallellano . . . prólogo póstumo del excmo. sr. marqués de Laurencín.* Madrid, 1929.

Sucincta relation del estado en que se hallaban las casas de Vertiz y Oteiza al tiempo en que infundadamente se las hizo declarar fallidas. Mexico City, 1821.

Sugawara, H. Masae. *La deuda pública de España y la economía novohispana, 1804–1809.* Mexico City, 1976.

Tarrade, Jean. *Le commerce colonial de la France à la fin de l'ancien régime: L'évolution du régime de l'Exclusif de 1763 à 1789.* 2 vols. Paris, 1972.

Tatham, William [Valentín de Foronda or Carlos Martínez de Irujo?], ed. *Communications concerning the Agriculture and Commerce of America: containing Observations on the Commerce of Spain with her American Colonies in time of War; Written by a Spanish Gentleman in Philadelphia.* London, 1800.

Taylor, William B. *Landlord and Peasant in Colonial Oaxaca.* Stanford, CA, 1972.

Tedde de Lorca, Pedro. *El banco de San Carlos (1782–1829).* Madrid, 1988.

Tena Ramírez, Felipe, ed. *Leyes fundamentales de México, 1808–1964.* 2nd ed. Mexico City, 1964.

Thomas, Hugh. *Cuba, or The Pursuit of Freedom.* New York, 1998.

Tomás y Valiente, Francisco. *El marco político de la desamortización en España.* Esplugues de Llobregat, Catalonia, 1989.

Tomich, Dale. "The Wealth of Empire: Francisco Arango y Parreño, Political Economy and the Second Slavery in Cuba." *Comparative Studies in Society and History* 45 (2003): 4–28.

Torales Pacheco, María Cristina. *Ilustrados en la Nueva España: Los socios de la Real Sociedad Bascongada de Amigos del País.* Mexico City, 2001.

Torales Pacheco, María Cristina, Tarcisio García Díaz, and Carmen Yuste, eds. *La compañía de comercio de Francisco Ignacio de Yraeta (1767–1797).* 2 vols. Mexico City, 1985.

Toreno, José Maria Queipo de Llano Ruiz de Saravia, conde de. *Historia del levantamiento, guerra y revolución de España, por el conde de Toreno.* 3 vols. Paris, 1838.

Tornero Tinajero, Pablo. *Crecimiento económico y transformaciones sociales: Esclavos, hacendados y comerciantes en la Cuba colonial (1760–1840)*. Madrid, 1996.

Torre Villar, Ernesto de la, ed. *Instrucción reservada que dió . . . a su successor don Félix Berenguer de Marquina*. Mexico City, 1960.

———, ed. *Instrucciones y memorias de los virreyes novohispanos*. 2 vols. Mexico City, 1991.

Townsend, Joseph. *A Journey through Spain in 1786 and 1787*. 3rd ed. 2 vols. Dublin, 1792.

Tutino, John. "Hacienda Social Relations in Mexico: The Chalco Region in the Era of Independence." *Hispanic American Historical Review* 55 (1975): 496–528.

Ugartiria, J. "Carta segunda . . . acerca del comercio a Indias." *Espíritu de los Mejores Diarios Literarios*, no. 172 (16 Mar. 1789): 987–98.

Uriortua, F. X. "Informe sobre la libertad del comercio." *Espíritu de los Mejores Diarios Literarios*, no. 148 (29 Sept. 1788): 104–12.

Urrutia y Montoya, Ignacio José de. *Teatro histórico, jurídico y politico militar de Cuba y principalmente de su capital, La Habana*. Havana, 1962.

Valdés y Bazán, Antonio. *Exposición documentada que ha hecho . . . Valdés y Bazán*. Cadiz, 1813.

Valdés y Ozores, Micaela. *El baylío don Antonio Valdés: Un gobierno eficaz del siglo XVIII*. Madrid, 2004.

Valle Pavón, Guillermina del. "Antagonismo entre el Consulado de México y el Virrey Revillagigedo por la apertura commercial de Nueva España, 1789–1794." *Estudios de Historia Novohispana* 24 (2001): 111–37.

———, ed. *Mercaderes, comercio y consulados de Nueva España en el siglo XVIII*. Mexico City, 2003.

Vargas-Lobsinger, María. *Formación y decadencia de una fortuna: Los mayorazgos de San Miguel de Aguayo y de San Pedro del Alamo, 1583–1823*. Mexico City, 1992.

Viennet, Odette. *Napoléon et l'industrie française: La crise de 1810–1811*. Paris, 1948.

Vilar, Pierre. *Oro y moneda en la historia (1450–1920)*. Barcelona, 1969.

Villalobos, Sergio. *Comercio y contrabando en el Río de la Plata y Chile, 1700–1811*. Buenos Aires, 1965.

Villarroel, Hipólyto. *México por dentro y fuera bajo el gobierno de los vireyes, o sea enfermedades políticas que padece la capital de la N. España*. 1831. Mexico City, 1979.

Vitale, Luis. *Interpretación marxista de la historia de Chile*. 5 vols. Santiago de Chile, 1967.

Ward, Henry George. *Mexico*. 2nd ed. 2 vols. London, 1829.

Whitaker, Arthur P. "Documents Relating to Publication of the 'Memorias históricas' of Rafael Antúnez y Acevedo." *Hispanic American Historical Review* 10 (1930): 375–91.

———. *The Huancavelica Mercury Mine: A Contribution to the History of the Bourbon Renaissance in the Spanish Empire*. Cambridge, MA, 1941.

———. "The Pseudo-Aranda Memorial of 1783." *Hispanic American Historical Review* 17 (1937): 287–313.

———. *The United States and the Independence of Latin America, 1800–1830*. New York, 1964.

Wobeser, Gisela von. *Dominación colonial: La consolidación de vales reales en Nueva España, 1804–1812*. Mexico City, 2003.

——. "Gestación y contenido del Real Decreto de Consolidación de vales reales para América." *HMex* 51 (2002): 787–827.

Wolff, Otto. *Ouvrard, Speculator of Genius, 1770–1846.* New York, 1963.

"Ydea general de comercio de Indias. Tolosa de Guipúzcoa, 1 marzo 1776." In Florescano and Castillo, *Controversia,* 1:23–68.

Yun-Casalilla, Bartolomé. "Redes urbanas atlánticas en la formación de Europa: A favor y en contra de una interpretación *whig* de la historia europea." In Fortea and Gilabert, *La ciudad portuaria atlántica,* 357–77.

Yuste, Carmen. "Francisco Ignacio de Yraeta y el comercio transpacifico." *Estudios de Historia Novohispano* 9 (1987): 189–217.

Zamora y Coronado, José María. *Biblioteca de legislación ultramarina en forma de diccionario alfabético.* 7 vols. Madrid, 1844–49.

Index